CAPITALIZING *on* CHANGE

THE LUTHER H. HODGES JR. AND LUTHER H. HODGES SR.
SERIES ON BUSINESS, SOCIETY, AND THE STATE

William H. Becker, *editor*

A SOCIAL HISTORY *of*
AMERICAN BUSINESS

Capitalizing *on*
Change

STANLEY BUDER

THE UNIVERSITY OF
NORTH CAROLINA PRESS
CHAPEL HILL

© 2009 The University of North Carolina Press
All rights reserved

Designed by Courtney Leigh Baker
Set in Scala with Scala Sans display
by Keystone Typesetting, Inc.
Manufactured in the United States of America

The University of North Carolina Press has been
a member of the Green Press Initiative since 2003.

Library of Congress Cataloging-in-Publication Data
Buder, Stanley.
Capitalizing on change : a social history of American
business / Stanley Buder.
p. cm. — (The Luther H. Hodges Jr. and Luther H. Hodges
Sr. series on business, society, and the state)
Includes bibliographical references and index.
ISBN 978-0-8078-3231-8 (cloth : alk. paper)
1. Capitalism—United States—History. 2. Industries—
Social aspects—United States—History. I. Title.
HC110.C3B774 2009
338.0973—dc22   2008031784

13 12 11 10 09 5 4 3 2 1

TO OUR GRANDCHILDREN

Natalie and Nicole Weinrauch

Alex and Kara Buder

Contents

A section of illustrations appears after page 262.

Preface

In designing a government for "the People of the United States," the Founding Fathers had as their concern the prosperity of an economy resting on land, labor, and commerce. Nevertheless, they included a clause with far-reaching and ongoing consequences: "To promote the Progress of Science and Useful Arts, by securing for limited Times to Authors and Inventors the exclusive Rights to their respective Writings and Discoveries." An enduring connection had been struck in the new nation between inventiveness and profit, intellectual curiosity and individual gain. As the economist Joseph Schumpeter predicted, "Without innovation, no entrepreneurs, without entrepreneurial achievement, no capitalist returns and no capitalist propulsion."

Largely due to this "propulsion," we enter the twenty-first century with an information technology revolution under way whose implications for business activity are impossible to foresee, as those in its vanguard explore artificial intelligence, machines capable of human-like thought. Biotech developments and the human genome project promise to alter our very sense of disease and life expectancy, not to speak of the food we eat.

Capitalizing on change is America's genius. New types of business and new ways of doing business are springing up, offering an explosion of opportunities in these and other novel fields. Scholars describe a postindustrial society in which services and information have supplanted industry and goods as the basis of the American economy and speculate on whether new forms of flexible and transitory business organization may become the dominant business model. Technology, however, has also created immediate problems related to outsourcing, global warming, and the need to find ways of assuring energy independence, as well as problems of a more abstract nature such as the ethical issues involved in genetic engineering.

In tandem, business and technology pose the transformative power that we identify with progress and modernity. Social scientists suggest that the very rapidity and incessant restlessness of change—often accompanied by unexpected consequences—has resulted in "future shock," an element of uncertainty and apprehension that occurs as we contemplate societies in continuous flux. Yet it is necessary to bear in mind that innovation and technology neither originate nor perform in a vacuum. There is always a context that operates as either a facilitator or a brake.

Changing values influence the pace of innovation, and vice versa. Economic development, cultural change, and even political change interact in ways that in hindsight are reasonably ascertainable. A history of American business cannot, of course, tell us where in the long run we are going. It will, however, offer insight into how we have arrived at the present. Such a perspective hopefully will offer guidance, albeit imperfectly, on contemporary trends and how to anticipate and respond to future change. It should also underscore the too-often-neglected roles of political leadership, legal institutions, and social values in shaping business activity and their critical importance in navigating the currents of change. The unifying theme of this study is the interactive roles of business and government in advancing and occasionally blocking change. Change should not be simplistically identified with progress. It almost always exacts a price that requires examination. The question then becomes whether the price is worth paying and indeed who in the nation is paying the price.

Acknowledgments

Along the way, the following individuals in one manner or another extended helping hands that I greatly appreciate and wish to acknowledge: Ervand Abrahamian, Rena and David Appel, Robert Belknap, Micah Buder, Terry Buder, David Bushler, Ian Gordon, John Goulet, Bert Hansen, Robert Heller, Paul Koren, Deborah Lindrud, Nancy Rowan, Iris and Jay Sabot, Jennifer and Gary Sabot, Betsy Schwartz, Karen Warhol, Rebecca and James Weinrauch, Cynthia Whittaker, and Marlene and Richard Wortman.

I would also like to thank Chuck Grench and Paul Betz of the University of North Carolina Press; Dorothea Anderson, who copyedited the manuscript; and William Becker, the editor of the series in which this book appears.

For many reasons, my greatest debt is to my wife of forty-five years, Rachel Buder.

CAPITALIZING *on* CHANGE

Introduction

I perceive clearly that the extreme business energy, and
this almost maniacal Appetite for wealth prevalent in the
United States, are parts of amelioration and progress.
—WALT WHITMAN, Democratic Vistas *(1871)*

Sensible people everywhere acknowledge the overriding importance of economics in human development. Americans, however, go further. History has
forged a strikingly transparent association between the nation's economic
system and its institutions and values. To many Americans, democracy and
capitalism have symbiotically matured as transcendent themes of the nation's history. They regard their way of doing business as embodying a provi-
dential "American Way of Life" founded on free enterprise.[1]

   The nation's values have not particularly dwelled on the notion of the
ideal citizen and civic virtue but instead have celebrated the go-getter and
ambition. This may be because Americans wanted to face the future with
confidence. For the most part, they assumed the nation's onward progress
and, accordingly, and in good conscience, have single-mindedly pursued
personal profit and success. As early as the 1830s the French visitor Tocqueville found that Americans relied on "personal interest and [gave] free scope
to the unguided strength and common sense of individuals" in comparison
to other countries. Faith in their economic system as a positive force has
usually, though certainly not always, offered Americans comfort in confronting market-driven forces that might otherwise have seemed irrational and
even destructive, which has fostered the confidence needed to take risks and
welcome change.[2]

Language conveys a society's culture and value system. It is therefore not surprising that "brand new" and "new and improved" are Americanisms with positive connotations, or that "no problem" is one of the first phrases non-English speakers around the world learn. America's can-do optimism about change shapes individual and collective attitudes toward risk, reward, and opportunity. The readiness to "capitalize on change" largely explains the nation's entrepreneurial ethos. It lies at the heart of American capitalism, with its emphasis on personal freedom. Most probably Americans are no more enamored of money than other peoples, but their very national identity expresses material aspirations: the perennial reach for advancement and the American Dream.

Americans want to believe that persistence pays off—that if you work hard and smart good things will happen. These attitudes and core beliefs create a compelling national vision, stimulating action and an eagerness to embrace innovations that promise to enhance the economy's performance. It is not necessary to endorse these values—or even indeed to accept that they ever truly reflected America's reality—to recognize their pervasiveness and importance.

The study of national economic development suggests that culture, defined broadly, may well be the most important determining factor of economic progress. American culture optimistically, perhaps naively, identifies market-driven change with progress. The French newspaper *Le Monde* has remarked that Americans prefer "profitability and efficiency to history and tradition," which, although a stereotype, is nevertheless largely true. Indeed, Americans rarely compare themselves to other nations but instead measure progress by how far they have distanced themselves from their own past. They expect to do better than their parents and to have their children do better in turn. This is the tacit social contract between generations.

At a time when market capitalism stands triumphant worldwide, an effort to understand America's particular version is in order. This is especially critical because the United States has long perceived its global mission as spreading its own concept of democracy and free enterprise. To many of the world's people, American business is shorthand for what is at the same time desirable and disturbing about modern life. Compared to the business ethos of other nations, American capitalism is commonly viewed as incessantly restless, individualistic, and ruthlessly competitive—a system that deals harshly with those who fall by the wayside. Certainly there is much to criticize in the nation's past and present. Critics, however, too often ignore a historic continuous dialectic between the bottom-line materialism of the capitalist system and the civic and ethical values of the United States, between the economic forces propelling change and the national vision of social justice and the good life. Many of America's most important social values, including millennia-old religious traditions, stress the importance of noneconomic goals or rely on a concept of natural or universal rights derived from the social theorists of Western civilization. These emphasize the need for a broad distribution of income and education and opportunities for all Americans to have gainful employment that allows for self-respect and dignity.

A tension between the acquisitiveness of capitalism's "rational economic man" and the spiritual or nonmaterialistic side of human nature is inevitable and desirable. We strive both as individuals and as a nation for a balance between the two. Modern capitalist society must constantly confront the issue of how individuals may best uphold their ties to community while legitimately pursuing personal goals. It must also concern itself with the danger of powerful economic interests harming the national welfare by betraying the public trust.[3]

If, as the economist Joseph Schumpeter has proposed, an entrepreneurial ethos represents the most dynamic form of capitalism, America has come as close to this as any major modern nation. Its economy has long relied on the freedom offered entrepreneurial novelty as the agent of profit-driven change. Just about any good ideas—and plenty of bad ones—easily attract sufficient support for a trial.

Americans view the economy as a work in progress, as highly sensitive to market factors. It is the transformative interaction of business and American history—the relative ease and remarkable mutability in which mercantile capitalism evolved into industrial, then financial, and now global capitalism —that truly fascinates.

A history of American business must acknowledge two central themes: the change in business organization from the relatively simple to the complex and the loosely parallel growth of the use of the power of government to modify or control market forces when they have harmful consequences. In less than two centuries, the scale of business has been transformed from the hands-on activity of merchants relying on informal local networks of their fellows to the globally linked, joint venture activities of multinational corporations drawing on world capital markets.

Modern technology continually reworks our sense of time and space, and even our critical and emotional sensibilities, as the range of possibilities open to human enterprise expands at a mind-numbing pace. Economic choices reveal a people's view of the world: their sense of making, of getting, and of spending. Business history must not neglect the "demand side" in narrating the rise of the modern economy, because that is, perhaps even more than the workplace, where we live.

There are good reasons why American English is now the international language of business. As early as the 1920s many in the United States and elsewhere predicted an engulfing global consumer culture, the Americanization of everything. American brand names are household words all over the world, and even in backward nations the American way of life is at the same time deeply alien and strangely familiar.

American history has experienced repeatedly the triumphs of those demanding unimpeded development over those preferring restraints and continuity. This has been true alike for frontier and factory, consumer and community, technology and natural environment. Openness to the relentless competitive forces of innovation has been both America's strength and its weakness. It has encouraged hope for a better tomorrow based on increased efficiency and economic growth, even while challenging cherished values and sometimes threatening social cohesion. No other nation has expressed more consistently a preference for unrestrained individualism and diversity over order and stability. To Americans, market-driven changes are necessary to free choice and variety, even when they create new sets of discontents and psychic anxiety.

American reform movements, however, have long understood that markets lack an ethical compass. They indifferently allow bad things to happen as well as good, and when a market failure can be identified governmental intervention is often justified. Put simply, an unrestrained marketplace cannot be regarded as the singular ultimate goal of a society. Nor can business be excused from responsibility for the social consequences of its behavior. American business has always interacted with our values and institutions. It is the wellspring of the idea of growing an economy open to talent and industry that is at the core of America's secular theology. Accordingly, business history is best served by being placed in a broad context that considers social as well as economic developments, and yet this has rarely been the case. Business efficiency should be measured and balanced against social goals. The business of American business is rightfully, of course, business, but the ultimate goal of the nation must be a good society. This requires a moral authority greater than market imperatives.

American business history, as a distinct field of study, began only in the 1920s. Its practitioners shared with economists an interest in the causes of change in the market and in business organization and strategy; but they usually explained developments in terms of interpretive detail rather than impersonal market forces, placing the businessman and his profit motive front and center. An early school among business historians stressed the entrepreneur's innovative role in business practices. In operating more effectively than their competitors, entrepreneurs forced them to change or fail. The entrepreneurial interpretation relied heavily on the biographies of business titans, the Carnegies and the Rockefellers, while acknowledging that America's "special circumstances" promoted values conducive to their entrepreneurial genius. Entrepreneurship was seen less as a response to business imperatives than as something close to an American art form.

A very different view gained favor in the 1960s. The influential work of business historian Alfred Chandler (1918–2007) developed what is called the "managerial" or "institutional" approach. From this institutional perspective, the evolution of business change is seen as resulting mainly from impersonal forces—new technologies of production or distribution, the creation of new markets—which require innovative strategies. The managerial school thus places less importance on distinctive cultural and historical circumstances to explain American business history—for example, the technology and market of a petrochemical firm, not its nationality, determine its best strategy. From an institutional or "structural-functional" approach, business leaders and their organizations do or do not respond effectively to the challenges of change, and happenstance of personalities, political climate, or cultural values tend to be seen as of lesser significance than the effectiveness of business strategy and organization.

Perhaps the most important truth is that nothing regarding firm strategy, structure, or size is static or forever. One formula does not fit all. Firms in certain industries, as a result of the nature of their technology and activity, will find an advantage in bigness at a given point in time, and firms in another will find this advantage in smallness. Both integration and disintegration will continue to occur.

Even in a global economy, American business relies largely on America for its capital, laws, customers, and infrastructure, and, at the same time, the nation must depend on business for its goods, services, employment, social mobility, and standard of living—as well as its general sense of well-being. The problems of one must be the problems of the other, for business is the environment we all inhabit—the world of work, consumption, and competition for status, money, and power. Nevertheless, we live in a society, not a marketplace, and such values as individual dignity and equal opportunity, as well as general prosperity and a sense of social solidarity, must provide the bedrock for a viable American democracy. We are what we are largely by reason of our anchorage in community with others. Liberty and freedom, entrepreneurial or otherwise, must be generously defined but must also be compatible with socially desirable goals.[4] At the beginning of the twenty-first century, the United States is at a crossroads as critical as the one faced a century ago with the sudden rise of an industrial economy. A new order is arising, with the enormous capacity of globalization, immigration, and information technology to transform our economy and society. Changes already under way in technology and trade will require vast and unsettling adjustments in how Americans will work and live. In the recent past we have experienced the rise, fall, and resurrection of American business, each stage posing distinctive threats and promises and demanding the reconsideration of values and institutions. The tacit and ever-changing social contract of business with the American polity is also part of business history.

This book is divided into three parts. Part I, "Foundations of a Modern Economy," contains the first seven chapters, which treat the period from the seventeenth century through the end of the nineteenth century. Part II, "From Theodore Roosevelt to Reagan," carries the history to 1989. Part III, "The Turn of the Millennium," consists of three chronological chapters that end in the year 2008 and three thematic chapters. Of the latter, Chapter Sixteen examines the rise of a global economy since World War II and Chapter Seventeen describes the growing importance of small business and the changing nature of big business. A final chapter reflects on present trends and likely future problems of American business and society. This book's unifying theme is a concern with the way American free-market capitalism has interacted with social and political factors to accelerate the pace of social change and to help shape the modern world. Insight into this business system is fundamental to understanding the velocity of historical change, the very nature of modernity, and many of the critical social and economic issues confronting the United States at the start of the twenty-first century.

PART ONE

Foundations of a Modern Economy

CHAPTER ONE

Early Capitalism and the Rise of a Market Economy

[Capitalism is] the endless disturbance of all social conditions.
It is everlasting uncertainty. Everything fixed and frozen is
swept away, and all that is solid melts into air.—KARL MARX
AND FRIEDRICH ENGELS, Communist Manifesto *(1848)*

Edmund Burke, reflecting in 1790 on the French Revolution, blamed the *bourgeois gentilhomme* and the *nouveau riche*, the men of commerce and finance, for what he saw as a catastrophe threatening civilization. In the view of this eminent conservative, they had undermined the established order of king and Church. "The money interest," Burke wrote, "is in its nature more ready for any adventure, and its possessors more disposed to new enterprises of any kind. Being of a recent acquisition, it falls in more naturally with any novelties. It is therefore the kind of wealth which will be resorted to by all who wish for change."[1]

The history of capitalism properly begins at the point where the profit motive imbues the commercial classes of the society in question with a transformative energy—a relentless quest for wealth as capital—capable of a sustained challenge to traditional values and institutions. More than scholars, scientists, or even statesmen, risk-taking entrepreneurs have shaped the modern world by greatly expanding the realms of choice in human vocations and goods. They have done this—generally without intending to and often heedless of the consequences—through the competitive and unrelenting pursuit of profitable uses of material resources and human energy. Yet the businessperson's role as the critical catalyst of broad change is a relatively recent historical occurrence that is only about five centuries old.[2]

CAPITALISM AS A CATALYST OF CHANGE

Adam Smith, in The *Wealth of Nations* (1776), confidently assumed "a certain propensity in human nature . . . to truck, barter, and exchange one thing for another . . . [that] is common to all men."[3] Even if one does not accept Smith's belief in an immutable and universal human nature—a capitalist instinct built into our DNA—one must concede that men and women have long sought to profit from commercial activities. Archaeological findings from all continents offer evidence of prehistoric markets based on far-flung trading networks and specialization of crafts, while excavated Sumerian cities of the third millennium B.C. reveal gold coins from the Indus Valley, silver from southeast Turkey, and copper from the shores of the Arabian Sea. The market is an invention of very early civilization. Yet commercial activity alone is not sufficient to invite escalating social change. It is obvious that the principal systemic reason for this in the modern world has been the rise of what is called capitalism.

"Capitalism" as a term and concept to describe a particular type of economy is of relatively recent origin. Its origins as an intellectual construct can be traced to the ideological conflicts of the nineteenth century and the writings, among others, of Karl Marx, who, however, never employed the term. Indeed, it was the work of two German sociologists in the first decade of the twentieth century, Max Weber and Werner Sombart, that initiated its general usage. Considerable controversy over what constitutes a capitalist system exists, but there is a consensus that it rests on individuals relatively free to pursue self-interest in a market-oriented economy that offers protection to private property and contract and allows for unequal distribution of wealth. It is useful to regard capitalism as not only an economic system but also as a complex of legal, social, and cultural values and institutions. These begin to emerge in fifteenth-century Europe and then over time evolve toward what has been noted above as the features of a capitalist society.

A major way capitalism differs from other economic systems is in bringing about changes of great breadth and magnitude. Economic life for most of history changed at a shuffling gait, the tools and techniques of production remaining the same from generation to generation. The ways of the merchant and the marketplace were never as absolutely essential, or central, to the economies of precapitalist societies as they have been since. In a society with a circumscribed mental universe that neither needs nor desires change, individuals interested in or able to generate innovation rarely occur.

Indeed, only within the last several centuries has the pace of economic change developed exponentially, accompanied inevitably by other changes. Those associated with economic growth in finance, commerce, and manufacturing increasingly pursued political dominance. Their activities required the development of laws and practices supportive of a market economy, which often conflicted with traditional values and practices. New attitudes emerged with the triumph of materialistic self-interest over spiritual and conventional restraints. Individuals increasingly adopted novel ways of thinking and acting related to the increasing reach of a market economy.

Much of modern history can be interpreted as a struggle between the material values associated with capitalism and other and often antithetical cultural and religious values for precedence in human life. Developments of such historic importance necessarily emerge from a propitious confluence of events. Capitalism, with its attitudes, advantages, and risks, promoted flexibility and rationality from its earliest beginnings. The onset of capitalism signified the shifting of history into a gear of accelerating change.

THE RISE OF CAPITALISM

Midway through the fifteenth century, population growth in Western Europe combined with increasing economic activity to stimulate new types of trade. The fall of Constantinople to the Ottoman Turks in 1453 threatened to close off a major trade route between Europe and Asia. Europe, looking for ways to break out of its geographic isolation, searched for alternative sea routes to the East, sharpening an appetite for adventure and exploration. In 1498, Vasco da Gama, sailing under the flag of Portugal, rounded Africa's Cape of Good Hope to reach India, completing the first direct sea voyage from Europe to Asia. Commercial activity increased both within Europe and between Europe and Asia, to surpass in importance the older traditional Orient trade in such luxuries as silks. To support this expansion, Europe's commercial classes would develop new forms of commercial credit and far-flung trading networks. Within a century and a half of Vasco da Gama's voyage, the European centers of power and commerce had shifted from Venice and Genoa to areas along the Atlantic Ocean, the Baltic Sea, and the North Sea. The ports of Portugal and Spain and then the Lowlands, France, and England became bustling commercial centers. Their maritime activity took them across formerly impenetrable oceans and seas to establish the first great corporations and trading posts or colonies in the Americas and along the rims of Africa and Asia.[4]

Economic developments joined with religious, political, and intellectual changes—the collapse of feudalism, the intellectual flowering known as the Renaissance, the Protestant Reformation, and the rise of the central state—to usher in that phase of history often referred to as the early modern period, an age of European expansion. The sixteenth and seventeenth centuries marked not only a decisive turn in Europe's economy but also one of the great creative outbursts of human history. The seventeenth century has long been accepted as an age of revolution, one in which the foundations of modern science and philosophy were well and truly laid. Never before had Western civilization appeared more materialistic and work-driven. Its economic activity—increasingly preoccupied with the mechanisms of exchange, of loans, of commerce, and of extending markets—lubricated sweeping changes.

From roughly 1500 and the imperial colonizations ushered in by the voyages of Columbus, we can indeed think of world history for the next five centuries in terms of a gradually growing European presence and influence, for better or worse, throughout the globe. Having discovered the value of sea routes, England, France, Holland, Spain, and Portugal vied with one another to control them and to establish trade routes with Africa, Asia, and the Americas. After a millennium of slow change, an initial explosion of activity ushered in a chain reaction of technological and social change in the Western world, a reaction still accelerating. England and some other parts of Europe now managed a small but persistently positive rate of growth that nurtured probusiness values. By the eighteenth century, Western Europe had escaped what economists call the "Malthusian trap," in which rising populations periodically offset temporary gains in living standards.[5]

It is from the outset of this Age of Exploration that economic historians trace the origins of modern capitalism. Merchants, in their restlessly anxious competition, had generated this unstoppable, wealth-creating, driving force of history. But the essential features of capitalism emerged slowly over time. These include an orientation that increasingly made economic activity and its control, rather than religious devotion or military means, the central concern of society and the individual. Wealth was being produced in great quantities. As they accumulated wealth, those who possessed it as a rule strove to acquire more, just as those without increasingly desired it.

Capitalism as an economic system promotes the production and exchange of goods by market factors of cost, price, and demand in which the resulting profit is largely reinvested; capitalism encourages the view that the individual should act in terms of self-interested choice. Its tendency is toward an emphasis on individual expediency, what political theorist C. B. Macpherson has called "possessive individualism."[6] Behavior, as well as material objects, are assigned a monetary value, and economic restlessness is welcomed, becoming a powerful force for change. The drive toward innovation is strongly expressed in the creation of new markets and in the lowering of product costs.[7]

Boundless eagerness to amass wealth for the purpose of creating even more wealth is the great engine of capitalism, and this force promotes economic and social change as new wants are created. In this view of capitalism, both the archconservative Burke and the two German revolutionaries, Marx and Engels, agreed; British Marxist historian Eric Hobsbawm has made this thesis more explicit in commenting that "it is often assumed that an economy of private enterprise has an automatic bias toward innovation, but this is not so. It has a bias only toward profit."[8] Acquisitiveness alone, however, is not sufficient to create capitalism. Money is eagerly sought not merely for immediate gratification (or the pleasure of hoarding) but to earn more money. Large sums of money are mobilized as capital to be used for long-term investments. Capitalism's proponents have long praised the social utility of this profit motive and its ability to generate market-driven growth with concomitant social and political changes.

Wherever the capitalist spirit takes root, it acquires national characteristics that provide it with a legal and cultural context. There is no single, standard capitalist model; indeed, capitalism is compatible with a multitude of social and political arrangements. Yet it is often claimed that its purest form is an unrestrained market and a laissez-faire state. Capitalism's diversity does not exclude the strong probability of strife among a society's values, often resting on precapitalist assumptions. This tension helps explains why capitalism in its putative ideal form—of laissez-faire state and completely free market—has never existed and doubtless never can exist.

The utilitarian view that there is a *Homo oeconomicus*, motivated solely by the desire to achieve material goals and acting rationally to that end, is clearly a caricature: people do not always behave selfishly or, as economists would phrase it, according to "utility-maximizing norms." Cultural expectations profoundly influence behavior, as do biology and personality. Karl Polanyi has indeed suggested that it is actually the desire to be competent and influential that drives our actions: "Man's economy as a rule is submerged to his social relationships. He does not act so as to safeguard his individual interest in the possession of material goods; he acts so as to safeguard his social standing, his social claims, and his social assets. He values material goods only so far as they serve this end."[9]

Yet the demands of competitive markets oblige capitalists to act in particular ways if they are to survive in business. Without a dialectic between social values constituting a moral order and the self-seeking economic drive, the result of the capitalist impulse must be a Hobbesian war of all against all. It is true that economic self-interest and market imperatives often combine to produce highly immoral and destructive relationships, as evidenced by the history of New World slavery and the early factory system. Nevertheless, the twenty-first-century Western world, despite, or perhaps because of, its individualistic ethos, has created the ideal of a moral universalism never before so fully expressed. Responsible and compassionate concerns about the evils of the world, such as environmental pollution and abuse of human rights, coexist with selfishness and egoism in advanced capitalist nations. Idealism and capitalism are not incompatible; rather one challenges the other.

A struggle between forces resisting sweeping change, such as community norms and religious values, and the economic self-interest seeking the free expression of acquisitive individualism appears to exist in capitalist economies regardless of their cultural core. Societies have an innate need for social equilibrium and tend to seek to modify or redirect the unbridled greed that otherwise must lead to amoral behavior. Almost everyone recognizes that on some level narrow economic self-interest must give way on occasion to a more general good. This general good is moreover often regarded as inseparable from the individual's own sense of identity and well-being and thus represents a broader self-interest, based on a goodwill that prescribes altruistic, cooperative, and often self-sacrificing behavior.[10]

Yet over time capitalism pushes toward the concept of acquisitive or "possessive individualism." This may even be rationalized by the belief, as it indeed was by Adam Smith, that an individual freely—even selfishly—engaged in maximizing his own profit also meets societal needs through market mechanisms that ensure society's economic efficiency. In practice, the materialistic and individualistic ethos of capitalism, or in the economist Joseph

Schumpeter's phrase, "the cost-price calculus," requires taming by means of extensive concessions to older values. Societies deeply imbued with collectivist or communitarian concepts of social solidarity, for example, modern Japan and other Asian nations, still resist the thrust of capitalism's individualistic ethos. However, even such a highly individualistic capitalistic culture as the United States encourages altruistic behaviors in which individuals are encouraged to sacrifice economic self-interest for the greater good.

Some scholars and others have hypothesized that political democracy cannot exist without capitalism. Woodrow Wilson, for example, observed in his 1912 acceptance speech for the Democratic nomination for the presidency that without "freedom of enterprise there can be no freedom whatsoever."[11] But certainly capitalism can, and often does, persist without political democracy. Despite the claims of Marxists, there is as yet no systematic way to correlate economic development with comprehensive social or political change. Yet it does appear safe to assert that capitalism, to be effective, requires at a minimum a stable government of known and enforced laws.[12]

CAPITALISM AND THE RISE OF MARKETS

Historians have provided useful insights into the origins of that process of economic and other changes we call capitalism. The history of civilization can be largely written in terms of the appearance and disappearance of trading routes and the related experience of encountering and learning from strangers that often proved at least as important as acquiring their goods or diseases. As commerce expands, ignorance and isolation rooted in a parochial economy and limited trade yields to a broader outlook.

In the sixteenth and seventeenth centuries, however, it was less the development of new routes that led to profound change than the quantitative transformation of trade. Trade expanded from a limited business in high-cost, low-bulk luxury items (such as spices, silks, and fine textiles purchased by Italian merchants from Muslim traders) to a commerce between northwestern and northeastern Europe in relatively cheap goods for common consumption. Furs, salted fish, grain, timber, salt, woolen cloth, iron and iron products, wine, timber, and naval stores—articles with low-value-to-weight ratios—became staples of European trade. Seemingly small advances in technology acquired from the Muslims and then from European craftsmen and experimenters spawned ever-greater technical improvements, notably in seacraft, which in turn encouraged increased trade.

A European economy largely (and necessarily) oriented to self-sufficiency and the limited commerce of market fairs was greatly extended in scale and scope. This new trade in staples involved ordinary individuals for the first time in the goods of far-reaching markets. As more people moved into cities, the population became increasingly urban-minded and dependent on an ongoing process of commercialization. The merchant and artisan, not the noble knight, had become the central figures of the social and political organization of the cities. Historian M. M. Postan has observed: "In order to be professional and to conduct trade all year around merchants and artisans had to be exempt from the ties and liabilities which restricted the liberty of movement and freedom of contract of the lower orders of feudal society."[13]

In turn, the growing volume of trade required large-scale investments by the merchants of Antwerp, Amsterdam, London, and lesser cities, who sank their money into ships, warehouses, piers, barrels, carts, and finished goods. Greater commercial activity also required sophisticated banking techniques for doing business and capital and credit for operating costs. Northern European merchants sent their sons to Italian merchant houses to study the *arte della mercadenta*, including commercial arithmetic and double-entry bookkeeping.

Some of these practices were employed in the earlier trade of Venetian merchants with Asia through the Muslim East. But this market always remained relatively static and its potential limited. The extremely high cost of transportation—particularly overland freighting—determined that articles of trade be light and of low bulk relative to their value. As the Europeans lacked equivalent exchangeable commodities, they purchased desired luxuries with gold and silver. Their ships and caravans often carried full cargoes only in one direction—homeward. In contrast, Western Europe's growing trade with Eastern Europe in the late fifteenth century involved bulk staples as well as luxuries, and it moved in both directions.[14]

Constant change was the rule for this newer market in staples. Pepper, for example, a luxury at the beginning of the sixteenth century, was by the century's end a staple item of trade. This occurred because the Portuguese broke the Arab-Venetian monopoly over pepper by trading directly with India, slashing the price fivefold within a decade. Nutmeg trees, once growing only on the small Banda archipelago in the modern nation of Indonesia, were successfully transplanted to the Seychelles, Reunion, and Zanzibar by Europeans eager to expand the crop and its market.

The market's continuous expansion provided abundant opportunities for risk taking in pursuit of profit. This was especially true with the discovery of the New World. The sudden and large infusion after 1530 of the gold and silver mined and looted from Mexico and Peru into a Spain that largely relied on Dutch and Flemish merchants for commercial activity resulted in a rapid dispersal of the precious metals throughout Western Europe. Gold and silver in circulation throughout Europe possibly doubled in amount between 1500 and 1600, contributing to price inflation. Prices rose fourfold in the course of the sixteenth century, undermining the established economic order.[15]

Historians disagree over the details and significance of this development. But they do agree that the principal beneficiaries were the commercial classes, who used their new wealth to expand their activities and to respond quickly to changes in consumer demand. A shift of economic activity away from Iberia and Italy northward to Holland and then to England set the stage for the coming of the Industrial Revolution. The infusion of the gold and silver of the New World enabled Europe to live above its means. An emerging middle class now had a greatly increased ability to buy off and otherwise challenge the ruling landowning powers. Men of money sought to protect and enhance their positions and property by extending their political influence. But the great hereditary noble families remained at the ruling center of English political and social life well into the nineteenth century, and successful merchants often imitated their social superiors by acquiring country estates and purchasing titles.

In the long run, however, it was not the importation of the gold and silver from the New World (which had in any case ebbed greatly by the early seventeenth century) but the advent of large-scale trade in such new products as indigo, cocoa, sugar, slaves, and tobacco that most profoundly affected the rise of European capitalism, as did the transplanting of potatoes from America, which promoted an eighteenth-century population explosion in Europe. After the fifteenth century, commerce replaced agriculture as the most dynamic sector of the European economy. The need for specialized services to facilitate commercial activities and urban manufacture led to the swift rise of large cities centrally located on trading routes, further disrupting an older order already in decline.

The crown, embodying the growing sense of a national state, sought control over an unruly nobility and discovered an important ally in the commercial middle classes. Power in feudalism had largely rested on suzerainty over people, through control of land and the number of armed retainers one could summon to battle. But by the sixteenth century, money or other economic control of resources determined power. Growing greatly in population, towns, the natural centers of business and markets, gained in influence over the countryside. London tripled its population in the fifteenth century; Amsterdam increased from 10,000 residents at the start of the sixteenth century to over 100,000 at its end. The commercial classes of the towns positioned themselves to challenge the declining power and position of the feudal nobility. "City air," it was said, "made one free." Urban merchants used their resources to bring change. Capitalists commercialized agriculture, incorporated huge trading companies, backed the mercantilist policies of monarchs, and began applying their fortunes to manufacturing activities. As autonomous centers protected by civil law and commercial privileges, cities acted, in effect, as the "incubators of capitalism." Urban attitudes and urban styles of buying and selling increasingly had an impact on the countryside.

The expansion of markets made money loom ever larger in importance. As the accepted medium of exchange, it facilitated the buying and selling of goods and services. Since money is fungible, it is not necessary to trade one specific commodity desired by the seller for another desired by the buyer. The increased minting of standard coins by governments and banks allowed for the increasingly everyday use of money, while merchants and their banks developed ever-more-complex instruments of credit to minimize confusion over metal content and rates of exchange. Banks shifted funds from one account to another on written order and even allowed overdraft privileges to trusted clients. The use of money not only served to make payments but also to store up savings or capital. John Locke in the 1690s viewed money as a medium of exchange as less important than money as capital. For Locke, as summarized by C. B. Macpherson, "the purpose of agriculture, industry, and commerce was the accumulation of capital. And the purpose of capital was not to provide a consumable income for its owners, but to beget further capital by profitable investment."[16]

Money allowed entrepreneurs to move easily into new activities that required an investment, and sheer possession of money conveyed influence and status and provided a convenient mechanism for transferring capital to heirs. The rise of an economic system based on money would in time depersonalize values, make property legalistic and individualistic, and create a rational law of trade and possessions. *Pecunia alter sanguis*—money is another kind of blood—was a maxim of fifteenth-century Hanseatic merchants, who knew fully its critical importance to the growth of a market economy.

CAPITALISM, RELIGION, AND SOCIETY

As the universal measure of material value, money—along with the urge to acquire it—tacitly challenged feudal and religious codes antithetical to profit and commerce. Middle-class commercial values slowly replaced aristocratic or sacred values as the essential ethical perspective of civil society. Thomas Aquinas spoke for medieval theologians when he declared that "it is impossible for happiness, which is the last end of man, to consist in wealth," for true happiness consisted of a "vision of the divine essence."[17] The Church, teaching the European of the twelfth century the frailty of human life, often depicted a devout Christian as an otherworldly, pious mendicant and a truly noble leader as a powerful warrior. But in much of Europe by the seventeenth century the astute businessman as head of his prosperous family had replaced the mendicant as an ideal, while the merchant's values of economic imagination and practicality challenged the martial and courtly traditions of the aristocracy.

To secure the victory of merchants over warriors, the pursuit of profit had to be legitimated and then over time given precedence over aristocratic honor. (Nevertheless, the French term *nouveau riche*, conveying contempt for people who join the upper class through their own economic success, endures to this day.) Feudal Europe devoted a great part of its limited surplus wealth to erecting impressive cathedrals and maintaining great noble households. Such conspicuous ecclesiastic consumption eventually yielded to an interest among the commercial classes in amassing capital. The modest nature of household expenditures by thrifty Dutch burghers is easily discernible in the paintings of the seventeenth-century Dutch masters. Yet the presence in these paintings of books, musical instruments, and works of art portrays an educated class keenly aware of the power of human intelligence and imagination.

Sensible European monarchs of the early modern period recognized that the commercial classes largely controlled the crown's access to money and the power that flowed from it. Merchants ideally created a favorable balance of trade for a nation, attracting to it gold and silver. Their usefulness to the crown meant that the men of money were no longer defenseless before the men of armor. Although taxing them heavily might temporarily fill the national coffers to bursting, it would only prove counterproductive in the long run, and thus the needs and wants of the commercial class had to be considered. A shift in power necessarily followed, but only slowly, unevenly, and with a pace varying from place to place. The connection between economic activity and a country's military power was readily apparent. Warfare by now required paid standing professional armies equipped with expensive weaponry, including cannon and the specialists to man them. Hard pressed for money, governments promoted industry and trade.[18]

Tired of seeing the English share of the profit for the nation's wool fall to Flemish middlemen, the late Tudor kings actively assisted the development of an English finished wool industry. This was so successful that by the early seventeenth century London merchants controlled 95 percent of the European cloth trade. The humble status of the merchant in feudal Europe (as indeed in almost all precapitalist societies) had to be reconsidered, as did the prevailing religious-philosophical systems, with their restrictive views of trade, usury, and moneymaking in general. Above all, the state wanted to secure the revenue that provided its security and power. The purpose of a nation's trade was seen as amassing money that could be used to express and expand the power of the state.

The sixteenth and seventeenth centuries experienced acute tension between the new economic environment and traditional religious and social values. Increasingly, the scholars and lawyers of that time learned to couch their thinking in terms of expediency rather than abstruse philosophical issues of absolute right and wrong. Jurists became more concerned with legalistic details and less concerned with universal issues of morality, a quandary that Shakespeare toyed with to good effect in *The Merchant of Venice*. This does not mean that the tension between the utilitarian and the theological in the operations of the law or the economy was resolved, or indeed could be. Religious passions and assumptions would continue to motivate and shape the thrust toward commerce and colonies, but they became increasingly intertwined and compatible with worldly goals. The here and now increasingly replaced the hereafter as the priority of Western peoples.[19]

Similarly, the individual's desire for secure and free use of his property challenged traditional communal obligations and restraints on behavior and the use of property. When property rights became more formalized, they could be more easily and safely exchanged in the market. Land, labor, and capital also became increasingly viewed as separate market entities, and this encouraged the transfer of resources to their highest valued use, promoting and energizing a market economy in the process. Over time, laws regulating individual and social behavior would be substituted for hierarchical networks of rights and duties derived from the historic feudal past as the cement holding society together.[20]

Anthropologists regard a culture as a fund of social resources—a constellation of beliefs, practices, and organizations that confirm or reject existing arrangements of status, power, and identity. Cultures can therefore be either oppositional or accommodative, challenging the status quo or validating it. Oppositional trends, based on the protean rise of a commercial culture and its values, are discernible in the larger cities of Western Europe in the sixteenth and seventeenth centuries. Merchants with commercial know-how and liquid capital did not blindly adhere to hoary ways; spurred by the stick of competition or the carrot of new markets, they sought innovation to lower costs and to gain an advantage over rivals.[21]

Social bonds based on customary subordination to a superior loosened as increasingly formalized property rights challenged and sundered feudal practices. The modern connotation of the word "individual," according to Oxford historian Christopher Hill, "dates only from the late sixteenth or early seventeenth centuries."[22] By this, Hill means only a new, sharper sense of selfhood or the modern ego: the individual as an autonomous unit apart from the collective of family, community, and social order. This changed perception arose from the sense of inviolable personal borders conveyed to him (and only much later her) by a new sense of "natural rights" and increasingly formalized personal and property rights. The older idea of a hierarchic society was challenged in the commercial nations of England and the Netherlands by a new conception of individuals as each pursuing his own good under laws agreed upon with a sovereign power. Already in the writing of Hobbes and Locke, the human being is envisioned as conscious of his own worth and moral autonomy.[23]

The subtle and complex intellectual transformation of late seventeenth- and eighteenth-century Europe has come under intense scrutiny. J. G. A. Pocock has been a leader in challenging the view that the Enlightenment was a monolithic movement of radical dissent against feudal monarchy and ecclesiastic domination. He proposes instead several different Enlightenments. Each, he believed, influenced the interpretive strategies in which social thinkers grappled with the relationship of the individual to God and nature, king and country. Not all these themes emphasized individual self-interest.

Among the themes previously ignored, he suggests, is the strong sense of a need for social involvement based on communitarian values. And an anonymous seventeenth-century English pamphlet entitled "Civic Republicanism," presently the term used for this theme, emphasized that the individual's happiness is dependent on public happiness and that therefore public needs must receive priority. "The surest way to promote his personal happiness," Scottish moralist Francis Hutcheson wrote in the eighteenth century, is for a man "to do publicly useful actions."[24] Pocock's approach is in contrast to the former emphasis by historians on the "acquisitive individualism" that John Locke tacitly advanced with his views on property rights. But there is no need to take an either-or position. The significance of Civic Republicanism is that it suggests an "oppositional theme" in the Western world, a countercurrent of dissent challenging the tendency of capitalism to exalt the private over the public.[25]

Social values shape a behavior that is also rooted in something we call, without being able to define it adequately, human nature. It is probable that certain basic and immutable biological and psychological needs are behind the miscellany of cultural diversity and personality types we find in history. Even in a relatively pious age, as the Bible suggests, grasping, acquisitive individuals defied conventions and God's laws for the sake of money and material possessions, and the pursuits of status and power have been present throughout recorded history. Although human behavior and aspirations may be, at their root, more or less constants, their social contexts change. In a warrior society, merchants may rank low in the social order, as in seventeenth-century Japan, while enjoying elevated status in the contemporaneous commercial society of Amsterdam. What constitutes success in any society is culturally determined: every society has its own set of valuations—its hierarchy of values that determine the prestige of personal characteristics as well as activities and accomplishments.[26]

Certainly social values influence the degree and frequency of types of human behavior. Yet outspoken people exist in societies that encourage reticence, and vice versa. We view ourselves and define our values in terms of our own specific cultural context and its value system. No cultural value is freestanding; it instead assumes meaning as part of a cluster of related values that can be arranged in various ways at different times to take on new emphasis and changed meanings. People are also capable of believing conflicting ideas simultaneously, especially when self-interest acts to stimulate moral inconsistency and rationalization. As R. H. Tawney has aptly observed, "The heart of man holds mysteries of contradiction which live together in vigorous incompatibility."[27]

Ideas and interests take on lives of their own to become powerful forces. Thomas Hobbes wrote, in *Human Nature* in 1650, "Everyman, for his own part, calleth that which pleaseth and is delightful to himself, good; and that evil which displeaseth him." With the collapse of an older order, the psychological and social barriers to overtly thinking in terms of self-interest or acting as *Homo oeconomicus*, rational economic man, as defined by economists, began slowly to peel away. Jesus Christ held up poverty as a holy ideal, but in her study, *The Merchant of Prato: Francesco Di Marco Matini, 1335–1410*, Iris Origo brilliantly depicts a late fourteenth-century merchant who constantly violated the Church's restriction on usury, even though he was sufficiently devout to be uneasy and guilty about his wealth (but not enough to change his ways). Protestantism, with its emphasis on the material worldliness of the Old Testament—the virtues of diligence and the efficient mastery of the details of life—often reflected a keen understanding of the value of wealth "properly used." However, "properly used" may be viewed in different ways. It might be in terms of Pocock's Civic Republicanism, with its priority of the public over the private, or then again it could be interpreted to mean investment toward the goal of amassing ever-greater worldly treasure.

WEBER THESIS

In *The Protestant Ethic and the Spirit of Capitalism* (1904), German sociologist Max Weber attributed the outburst of economic and intellectual energy in the Netherlands and England in the early modern period to the advent of Protestantism. According to Weber, Protestant reformers, especially French theologian John Calvin, sought to revitalize a Christianity they believed wayward in its stress on church sacraments by sanctifying worldly work as a religious duty. Calvin placed highest priority on a self-disciplined approach to work in subduing sinful impulses, and thus his sense of secular "calling" as a way of serving God elevated merchant above priest. To Weber, Calvinism led to a highly individualistic religiosity. It created a psychological pressure that internalized values of thrift, honesty, persistence, and disciplined behavior, with worldly wealth regarded as evidence of grace. These were exactly the traits and values conducive to commercial success. People would live to work, believing that by so doing they served God and testified to their spiritual worthiness.[28]

Most scholars regard Weber's famous thesis of the "Protestant ethic" as exaggerated at best and reject as simplistic his claim of a direct causal relationship between Calvinism and capitalism. This does not necessarily rule out the possibility that the "unintended consequence" of internalizing such Calvinist values as the stress on education and self-discipline provided a cultural base favorable to capitalism. But Weber's critics believe he also erred in overemphasizing the importance of worldly success to Calvinist theologians. They argue that for Calvinists the glory of God and the good of the community remained paramount. Accordingly, magistrates and ministers outranked businessmen in the community's esteem.

William Perkins, one of the most influential early Calvinists in England, did think men were "honored for their riches." However, Perkins then continued: "I mean not riches simple but the uses of riches; namely as they are made instruments to uphold and maintain virtue."[29] Most scholars do agree with Weber that a strong cultural commitment to material improvement and work took hold in a rapidly commercializing northern Europe early in the seventeenth century. "If the Protestants, especially the Puritan element in Protestantism," wrote Louis B. Wright, "did not invent the gospel of work, they adopted it with such enthusiasm that it became a cardinal point in their social doctrine." What counted was work, as a calling, and people who lived to work represented an elite.[30]

But Calvinism must be regarded as much more than nascent capitalism. With its emphasis on the congregation, Calvinism combined a questioning attitude toward existing secular authority with a paradoxically strong commitment to moral communities based on shared precepts and values. Calvinism also represented a dialectic between capitalist and noncapitalist values. To quote once again from Perkins: "A vocation or calling is a certain kind of life, ordained and imposed on man by God for the common good: that is, for the benefit and good estate of mankind . . . and that common saying,

'Every man for himself and God for us all,' is wicked and is directed against every calling or honest kind of life."[31]

Contrary to Weber's view of Calvinism, the Puritans put God before man, authority before wealth, and community before the individual. In this regard, it fed the stream of Civic Republicanism. Yet Calvinist covenant theology, with its emphasis on voluntary binding arrangements between God and man, man and congregation, and congregation and government, strongly reinforced the notion of formal agreements or contracts as more important than a tacitly accepted customary practice. At least two values critical to American capitalism are implicit in these beliefs: public accountability and acceptance of impersonal norms.[32]

FROM STATUS TO SOCIAL CONTRACT

The merchant's respect for law and order and the importance of contract and private property radiated out from the urban marketplaces. When English judges at the end of the sixteenth century declared that "every contract executory is an actionable in itself" and that "a promise against a promise will maintain an action upon the case," the concept of a contract as a binding mutual commitment "for buying, selling, exchanging, borrowing, letting and taking to hire" had been firmly established. Here, too, Calvinist doctrines of covenant theology and individual accountability appear to have reinforced attitudes fostering commerce and trade. It added to the momentum leading to an economic system based on voluntary exchange by self-interested individuals. In the writings of Hobbes, we already discern the early glimmerings of recognition that a market economy encouraged an equality before the law in promoting the effective use of binding contractual agreements, and even that a market society, as Macpherson notes, "was visibly replacing hierarchical order by the objective order of the market, which did not require unequal rights for different ranks."[33]

As the vestiges of feudalism dropped away, the commercial classes of the towns identified their self-interest with the impulse toward a stronger central government and the safety and stability it represented. However, within a generation or two they had tempered their support of government, making it conditional. Merchants and their spokesmen came to argue that government found its authority not in religious sanction of the divine right of the monarchy but in a social contract: the "king in parliament." It was also asserted that government originated in the need to protect the safety and property of individuals. John Locke wrote in 1692 in the *Second Treatise of Civil Government* that "the great chief end of men uniting into commonwealth and putting themselves under government is the preservation of their property," and for this reason they entered into a social contract, the parties of which are assumed to be "free, equal, and independent."[34] Only half understanding the implications, the commercial classes reshaped their cultural setting and their religious and political values to buttress their economic interests against any potential threat from the state. The state in turn moved toward awareness of its need to command the allegiance and confidence of those who had money to lend—and to be taxed.[35]

In England and the Netherlands, the commercial classes of the seventeenth century sought increased influence over national policy, perceiving this as critical to their own interests and compatible with government's responsibility that, according to mercantilist theories, it must manage foreign trade exclusively in its own interests. "Mercantilism" is loosely defined as a body of economic policies and theories, roughly in favor between 1600 and 1800, designed to enhance the power of the monarch by providing him with funds to finance armies, navies, and the apparatus of government. Mercantilist theories and policies guided the relationship between a mother country and her colonies, envisioning a favorable balance of trade for the former, with the colonies providing needed raw material and markets for finished goods. Essentially a policy of empire building, mercantilism also reflected the excitement experienced by Europeans as they assessed the economic opportunities opened up by the discovery of the New World. Mercantilism reflected the belief that profit and trade gained by one nation invariably came at another nation's expense, so that enriching oneself also weakened one's rivals and potential foes. Between nations, as within nations, the distribution of property was recognized as determining political power. In a classic exposition of the premises of mercantilism, Locke wrote in 1674: "The chief end of trade is Riches & Power which beget each other. Riches consist in plenty and movables, that will yield a price to a foraigner, & are not likely to be consumed at home, but especially in plenty of gold and silver. Power consists in numbers of men, & ability to maintain them. Trade conduces to both these by increasing y [our] stock & y [our] people. & they to each other."[36]

It is clear that the dicta Locke prescribes for states he also assumes to hold true for individuals. Above and beyond the need to sustain life, the acquisition of wealth and power is the goal of individual effort. Following from this are several seminal conclusions. Some individuals are entitled to more wealth than others because they have labored more effectively, and the purpose of acquiring more than they need or intend to use is justified by their desire to turn wealth into capital.

In emphasizing the importance of Locke, it is not necessary to suggest, as Louis Hartz did in *The Liberal Tradition in America*, that he "dominates American political thought, as no thinker anywhere dominates the thought of a nation." It is sufficient that his writings and those of several of his contemporaries are revealing in their emphasis on money and property as the source of power and their protection as the reason for creating government. In contrast, a century and a half earlier, Machiavelli, in *The Prince* (1515), concentrated on politics as an autonomous exercise in princely power having little connection with the economy or the individual. A profound philosophical and theological grappling with the nature and problems of a market-oriented society is evident in seventeenth-century England, a time and place of extraordinary political and economic transition. A society once based firmly on custom and status is giving way to a society where market factors already shaped and permeated most social and political relationships. It is in this context of social and intellectual flux that Englishmen first ventured across the Atlantic to their colonies in North America.[37]

"English America" was born into a world where the changes in attitudes, laws, and activities identified with capitalism had already established a foothold and enjoyed rising momentum. Most of the first arrivals in English North America would come from the very country that had recently emerged as Europe's leading nation in advancing industry, commerce, and foreign trade. Within a century and a half, it would introduce the Industrial Revolution. Americans would be fortunate in their inheritance from the mother country, but they would also find the circumstances of their "New World" even freer of encumbrances to change than their old.

North America's Colonial Economy

Every Christian should have a calling . . . some settled business
wherein . . . he may glorify God by doing good for others and
getting of good for himself.—COTTON MATHER, Magnalia
Christi Americana *(1702)*

Europeans approached the New World as an extractive resource, viewing its
land in terms of the commodities and wealth it promised to yield. The
Spaniards and the Portuguese based the economic life of their American
Indies possessions on the *estancia*, or plantation, under which the crown
awarded titles and land to *conquistadores* and court favorites who coerced
tribute and labor from the Indians in cultivating such cash crops as sugar,
cacao, and tobacco. This form of feudal order established in Central and
South America, relying on servile labor (soon supplemented by the arrival of
African slaves), combined with strict regulation of trade and heavy exactions
imposed by Madrid on all economic activity to discourage the rise of a commercial middle class. Long after the end of colonial rule in the nineteenth
century, a legacy of these exploitative policies persisted in hindering Latin
American economic development. The experience of the English in North
America would be different almost from the start.[1]

SEVENTEENTH-CENTURY COLONIAL ECONOMY

Both the Dutch and the English sought profit from their New World colonies
by allowing trading companies to provide for their governance and development. These private initiatives were supported strongly by government. In

return for service to the crown, corporate charters bestowed upon the companies special privileges and even monopolies over certain trades. But only after a long war with Spain ended in 1604 did the English give serious consideration to planting colonies in the New World. Until then they remained satisfied to profit handsomely from buccaneering forays against bullion-laden Spanish galleons. London merchants, who had waxed rich and powerful through the growth of the cloth trade with the Netherlands, emerged at war's end as a leading force in establishing English colonies in North America and the Caribbean. Living in a city superbly situated for European commerce, Londoners now eagerly sought to exploit the growing transatlantic trade. This preponderant role played by private traders in staking out many of the areas to be colonized appears peculiar to the English, even when compared to the Dutch. A largely private colonizing impulse reflected the dynamic commercial economy of England and doubtless contributed greatly to the relative weakness of early colonial governments in North America.

Some fifty years earlier, in the mid-sixteenth century, English merchants had already learned that handsome profits could be made in foreign trade through the use of joint-stock companies. Though without limited liability, the corporations did offer the advantage of reduced competition and shared risk. They also possessed the potential for large-scale activity by combining the capital of many under the management of a few chosen by the stockholders. Their charters contained the crown's grant of a monopoly in a specified area of the world. The Muscovy Company (1555) in Russia and the Levant Company (1581) in the Near East, the first of these overseas trading corporations, had profited handsomely, with stockholders drawing dividends from operations while their initial investment represented equity in the form of capital formation. In 1606 the Virginia Company employed a variation on this scheme to undertake a colonizing venture in North America.[2]

The company's charter specifically required it to serve national goals, most importantly the securing of territory, in addition to striving for profit. The colonists and their children were not shareholders. As "servants" of the company, however, they received guarantees of the full "liberties, franchises, and immunities" enjoyed by Englishmen at home. This paradox would no doubt have caused trouble if the scheme had worked as anticipated, but it did not. Until 1619, the Virginia colony, founded in 1607, resembled more a labor camp than an English community, with most of the farming done by work gangs. In that year, the company, frustrated by failure at every turn, began to extend self-rule to the colonists, while adopting policies to promote individual landholdings. Two other factors hastened the transformation of the colony. The successful cultivation after 1612 of a distinctive New World crop, tobacco, brightened Virginia's economic prospects greatly, and a passing Dutch vessel in 1619 carried a small party of captive Africans, whom the colonists purchased.

Virginia now attracted settlers and prospered—but as a crown colony rather than as a company business. Individual pursuit of economic self-interest—what we would recognize as a type of free-enterprise economy—generally prevailed. The Virginia Company dissolved itself in 1624. There were, of course, important exceptions to free economic behavior—most notably, indentured servants, who, in payment for their passage to America, contracted their labor for a period of service and purchased Africans. As for the original inhabitants of the continent, the American Indians, they were evicted, slaughtered, killed off by disease, or brutally pushed aside.

Upon completing their term of service of four to seven years, white indentured servants assimilated into the general populace. This initially may even have been the case with some of the blacks, as English law did not recognize permanent servitude except for penal punishment. But tobacco's emergence as an important money crop created demand for a cheap and reliable form of labor, and the masters' economic self-interest led by the end of the seventeenth-century to slavery, a legal system of hereditary lifetime servitude based on race. With no legal rights, the slave was regarded as dehumanized property. In 1740, for example, South Carolina declared slaves to be chattel that could be purchased, sold, inherited, or seized to pay their master's debts. Slavery became the foundation for the rise of a plantation system as the primary economic and social organization of the southern colonies. The buying and selling of slaves, the infamous slave trade, remained throughout the colonial period, and indeed until the Civil War, as a highly important, lucrative business. Most of the original slaves in North America were imported from the West Indies and only a minority directly from Africa. But the great growth in the slave population occurred primarily as a result of natural increase. The importance of the slave trade to the American economy cannot be overemphasized. It constituted a highly profitable business and the hinge on which much of the transatlantic trade relied.[3]

Set apart by race and slavery, which had become intertwined, by 1776, blacks constituted approximately one-fifth of the population of the thirteen

British colonies on the American mainland. The large planters cemented their political dominance of the South by persuading its small white farmers that planters and farmers alike were equal in not being slaves. White workers soon saw their status as free and independent in contrast to slaves.

Economic historians Robert Fogel and Stanley Engerman have argued, in *Time on the Cross*, that slavery, which allowed almost unrestrained use of force to coerce labor, represented a highly profitable system for the planter class, explaining its rapid adoption. With the growth of slavery, blacks were subject to widespread exploitation and degradation, even when occasionally freed. European visitors to the southern colonies soon wrote of the slaves as a "nation within a nation."[4]

The failure of the Virginia Company underscored the weakness of efforts at a centralized command economy in a colony of Englishmen conscious of their rights—especially a colony that possessed such an abundance of land. Market forces, not the directors of joint-stock companies, determined the development of the colonial economy in such areas as crops grown, patterns of settlement, and inland population movement. Important economic differences among the several colonies are discernible as early as 1650, and their diverse economies, reflecting differences in geography and climate, separated the colonies into regional groupings. This led in time to conflicting sectional needs and interests, profoundly troubling to those who sought to forge a single nation. But diversity also encouraged the decentralization of decision making, which became a positive characteristic of the colonial, and later national, economy.

COLONIES IN THE EIGHTEENTH CENTURY

The colonial period of American history lasted a century and a half, during which time the familiar habits and beliefs of the old country struggled to come to terms with the new circumstances of America. The result is that well before the end of the colonial period the colonist differed from the Englishman, just as the Georgian differed from the New Yorker. Regional specialization based on climate, rainfall, soil type, suitability for crop production, and other natural factors explain colonial economic development and land use, a fact with far-reaching social and political consequences. Because sectional cultures became distinct early in the colonial period, there was no single "American" pattern of family and community organization.[5]

Regional specialization set off the northern colonies from the southern ones. It also, though much less dramatically, differentiated the New England colonies from the middle colonies, and even the older and upper southern colonies from the lower and newer colonies of Georgia and South Carolina. "The past is a foreign country; they do things differently there," the novelist L. P. Hartley has written. And certainly, in our age of space stations, ssTs, faxing, Internet, and inexpensive cell phones and global telephone networks, it is difficult to conceive of the uncertainties, time, money, and risks required for colonial travel and communication. Few colonists lived further than twenty-five miles from navigable water, and even domestic trade was usually accomplished by ship. Distance in the colonial period resulted in an intense local parochialism, setting near neighbors apart in dialect of speech, in loyalties, and in other ways. To travel between Philadelphia and New York, only ninety-five miles apart, by stagecoach in 1750 required a bone-wearying sixteen-hours-a-day journey of three days. Due to the expense involved, no bulky goods went between the two cities by land.

After 1620, tobacco became the staple crop of most of Virginia, Carolina, and Maryland. During the colonial era, the median size of tobacco plantations in the Chesapeake Bay area remained below twenty slaves. Rice growing became important in the 1680s in South Carolina and then later in Georgia. For the middle colonies, extending northward from Delaware to New York, wheat and flour emerged as the economic mainstays, and New England's craggy and infertile soil fostered a dependence on harvesting the sea and the forest.[6]

A network of colonial cities and towns organized trade by disseminating goods and communications. The important cities required access by water to the Atlantic since, initially, their principal function was to act as transfer points for resources and goods going to and coming from the British Isles and the West Indies. Colonial cities also acted as depots for immigrants and as administrative centers of government. Boston and Newport emerged as the leading New England cities, with Philadelphia and New York their counterparts in the middle colonies. Charleston, the only southern city of stature, did not compare to the other four in population or wealth. In 1690, its population stood at 1,100, in contrast to Boston's 7,000; New York and Philadelphia both hovered at around 4,000, and Newport numbered 2,600 inhabitants. The South's lag in urban development is not hard to explain given the region's limited commercial development, but other factors also played a role.

Tobacco and rice cultivation relied on large, relatively self-sufficient plantations worked by gangs of slaves. At first, the plantations were located in tidelands indented with numerous inlets, permitting this staple crop to be loaded from a local pier onto a tender and then onto a vessel bound for England. Thus there was no need for urban intermediaries and transshipment. The limited population of southern colonial cities also acted to inhibit the development of a commercial class in that region. This is not to deny that the planter elite eagerly exploited opportunities for land speculation and even on occasion for trade.

The market for colonial products was largely overseas, since in the seventeenth century domestic demand remained too small and too widely dispersed to challenge the foreign market. Most of the population was spread thin, functioning as relatively self-sufficient family units; the little exchange that occurred was local. With limited intercolonial trade, each major colonial port, along with its tributary back country, for the most part constituted a separate market removed from its neighbors. A temperate and salubrious climate, fertile soil, a long coastline, and many navigable rivers suggested, however, that sparse density and straitened trade need not be long-term problems. By 1700, there were some 250,000 settlers in the British North American colonies, a figure that rose to 1 million in 1750 and to over 2 million in 1770.

This dramatic increase—a doubling of population every twenty years—generated ever-greater demands for small-scale colonial manufacturing. It fostered an internal trade, which relied on coastal shipping and post roads, as well as the new roads and bridges that accompanied westward expansion. By the 1770s, on the eve of independence, the colonists had largely freed themselves from their former near-total dependence on Europe. This development offered a new measure of stability to the sharp seventeenth-century market fluctuations caused by European wars and variations in the overseas demand for American goods. Population growth fueled the process by which mercantile activities extended the sway of a market system and connected local economies into networks of well-established trading routes. Colonial ports cultivated their hinterlands, as their merchants and tradesmen looked to the interior with its country traders and shopkeepers to buy and sell locally produced and imported goods. But domestic markets remained thin and unpredictable, with a low level of available credit and easily saturated. Supply ships from England remained essential for populating and stocking the colonies, as they slowly gained the rudiments of self-sufficiency.

The economic well-being of the colonies always remained firmly bound to the overseas market. Changes in output were closely related to a rising or falling market for Virginia tobacco and Carolina rice in England—and the consequent adding or withdrawing of land from cultivation. Modern factors of productivity, such as increased labor specialization or improvements in productive technology, proved unimportant in agriculture and negligible in handicraft. What manufacturing did occur was generally a type of cottage industry or "putting-out," which some historians have called "proto-industrialization." In putting-out, rural families supplemented agricultural labor with forms of piecework manufacturing, such as shoemaking, on behalf of middlemen.

Colonial exports went to four principal overseas markets: the British Isles, the European mainland, the West Indies, and the Wine Islands of Madeira and the Canaries. By far the most important trade was conducted with the British Isles and was dominated by London merchants. The southern staples of tobacco and rice constituted the overwhelming bulk of American exports to England; other items of trade included wheat and flour, livestock, salted meat, indigo, furs and skins (especially beaver, which was used in hats), naval stores, and iron bars and pig iron. Since the British did not need the agricultural exports of the middle and New England colonies, the trade of these colonies with England mattered little compared to that shipped by the southern colonies. The North American tobacco trade was easily eclipsed in turn by the sugar trade of Jamaica and other Caribbean islands, England's most valuable colonies.

In theory, the colonial economy was conducted according to the Acts of Trade and Navigation imposed by England after 1651. These laws sought to regulate an already-flourishing trade that had been initiated by private traders with little official encouragement. In various ways, these laws tried to protect the colonial market for the mother country's goods by restricting local production. Additional rules restricted freedom of commerce and required the use of English or colonial crews and ships. Americans had to buy tea, spices, and drugs from English merchants, and certain colonial products, "enumerated items," could only be sold to England. In return for these restrictions on their economic freedom, the colonies relied on the mother country for government and defense. All of those concerned initially accepted this relationship as both natural and mutually useful.

British mercantilist policies reflected the prevailing European view that colonies existed to benefit the mother country. Merchants had to work within a pattern of trade that could generate revenue to sustain state expenditures on the navy and colonial defense. The colonists needed protection from hostile Spaniards, Frenchmen, and Indian tribes and had little reason or will to challenge the crown's efforts to build its strength in North America. The colonials also welcomed the security provided American merchant shipping by the British navy. The influence of commercial interests in Parliament eager for low taxes gave Britain a considerably smaller governmental bureaucracy and military than usual for a European power. Primarily concerned with affairs in England, the king's ministers left the colonies largely to their own devices. Moreover, the laxly administered Acts of Trade and Navigation could easily be evaded through smuggling.

Mercantilist policies proved acceptable to the colonists because they conformed to the natural pattern of the colonies' own early economic development. Primary products were exported and manufactured goods imported to the mother country, as would have happened in any case, and the colonists drew on Great Britain for immigrants and credit. Imperial practice and the conditions of trade thus enjoyed reasonable harmony for much of the colonial period. But there was one important exception to this generalization— London's policy of not allowing the colonies to coin money. This limited the transatlantic flow of British coin but did cause hardships. Of necessity, the colonists relied on foreign coins, notably the Spanish dollar obtained through trade with the Spanish West Indies—though the once generally accepted view of a bullion drain from the colonies to England due to a chronic balance of payment deficit has been challenged.[7]

With almost all of the colonial population living in rural areas, agricultural and other resource-intensive natural activities had to be the dominant form of economic activity. Apart from a few exceptions (notably indigo and naval stores), nothing in the Acts of Trade and Navigation significantly affected what the colonists grew or bought, nor can the low levels of colonial manufacturing be blamed on British policies. There are other explanations for this. The high cost of colonial wages due to the abundance of land and scarcity of labor, always remarked upon by awed travelers, discouraged domestic production. In contrast, English manufacturers produced on a scale that allowed for specialization. Over a fourth of all British exports were to its North American colonies. Neither in quality nor price could the colonials compete. The Acts of Trade and Navigation did become an issue after 1763, but by then there were other reasons to reconsider the colonial relationship.

In addition to the British Isles, Americans also traded with Southern Europe, Africa, and, most important, the West Indies. Trade with England was of a direct port-to-port type, but historians long believed that the other trading routes required more complex patterns: the famous triangles of trade. The most celebrated of these involved shipping rum and trinkets from New England to Africa in exchange for slaves, who were then taken aboard for the infamous "middle passage" to the West Indies; many slaves inevitably died on the journey as the result of horrendous overcrowding and cruel treatment. In the Caribbean islands, the slavers sold their human cargo and purchased sugar and molasses to be brought home to New England and distilled into rum. Some scholars suggest, however, that "triangular trades" were not as important as previously thought. They have even proposed that the term be replaced with the less misleading "Atlantic system." Revisionist historians have also challenged the belief that New England sailing vessels frequently switched routes while in passage, altering destinations in an opportunistic search for lucrative cargoes. Most sea captains, they argue, lacked such discretionary authority.[8]

American merchant ships, the new scholarship suggests, relied on route specialization and used a "shuttlecock" pattern, sailing from a home port to a destination and then directly returning. This route specialization reflected the merchant's need to develop reliable trading agents and a network of intermediaries that could only be sustained through regular use. Simple and repetitive operations worked best in a time of primitive communications. The continuing need to deal with each other in the future discouraged one party from taking advantage of the other and facilitated a system of accounting that was often dependent on extending book credit. Corresponding with each other, distant merchants pursued new customers, commissioned each other to sell goods, acquired commercial intelligence, and, if fortunate, learned of new opportunities. All aspects of their businesses were affected by the dynamic, competitive world of Atlantic commerce. As much as possible, merchants relied on family members to act as their agents. In the case of some merchants, notably Jews and Quakers, trading networks relied on coreligionists. The importance of personal relationships and loyalties cannot be overemphasized.[9]

Even if they kept operations simple, colonial merchants had much to engage them. Dressed in a cocked hat and ruffled shirt and adorning his head with a powdered periwig, the successful colonial merchant was a respected pillar of the community. Deferred to as a gentlemen, at a time when this appellation conveyed significant status, those of the first rank acted as importers and exporters and carried on both retail and wholesale operations. They sometimes loaned money for interest and bought and sold securities, mortgages, and debts. Often the larger merchants built and owned ships, as well as warehouses, piers, distilleries, ropeworks, and slaughterhouses—all while playing an important role in town affairs and sometimes dabbling in real estate and insurance. More modest operators limited their activities, constrained by their available financial resources. In the absence of specialized freight companies, merchants had to handle all aspects of transportation, while ship captains or sometimes supercargoes (agents with delegated powers) attended to details. Bernard Bailyn has written of the Boston merchant's need "to be ready to accept payment in all sorts of unexpected commodities and currencies, always to be seeking new markets in which to sell new kinds of goods and new kinds of goods to satisfy new markets. Versatility was one of the keys of success."[10]

The limits on the ability of merchants to react quickly to changing market conditions and to communicate with each other are underscored by the four months required to exchange correspondence between Boston and London as late as the 1750s. Networks to facilitate long-distance trade were established by merchants in the port cities. As already noted, they tended to be based on family ties or among coreligionists to maximize trust and loyalty.

The pace of business life was in keeping with this slowness of communication and the leisurely coming and going of sailing ships, which lacked fixed schedules. Merchants spent considerable time in coffeehouses to transact business and to socialize. This, however, was not an idle exercise, because it represented a potential source of information and new customers and contacts. Though the stimulating brew itself had been introduced to Europeans only at the end of the seventeenth century, coffeehouses soon served in port cities as centers for the brokering and underwriting of maritime insurance.

Merchants were wealthier and more politically important than any other group in the northern colonies. To open a commercial house in the 1770s required an estimated 2,000 pounds, a very handsome sum, in start-up capital.

A merchant's all-important flow of credit depended on personal ties and reputation and connections with an established London or Liverpool export house prepared to extend long-term credit to an American commercial establishment. Access to credit made the difference between success and failure. Bound by common ties of experience and self-interest, and very often religion and marriage as well, merchant elites required high levels of trust. Merchants understandably worked hard to establish themselves as trustworthy.

"In order to secure my Credit and Character," Benjamin Franklin commented of his early years in his *Autobiography*, "I took care not only to be in *Reality* Industrious and Frugal, but to avoid all *Appearances* of the Contrary." Terms of opprobrium such as "knave," "rogue," and "rascal" greeted merchants who failed to meet their obligations, with calamitous consequences. Making up 2 to 3 percent of the workforce, it was the colonial merchants who held the business system of the colonies together and who indeed often acted as a catalyst of change as they pursued their interests.[11]

But in the southern colonies pride of place on the social scale fell to the planter class. Although the circumstances of American life—widespread rural land ownership and population growth offering economic opportunities—provided a considerable degree of social mobility as compared to England, colonial society developed its own distinctions of wealth and status. The existence of slavery and a racial hierarchy has already been noted, but studies by historians demonstrate a highly skewed distribution of wealth even among whites. By the time of the American Revolution, the richest 10 percent of the free population held more than half of the colonies' wealth. Men of means believed that rank and status needed to be carefully observed if society was to remain ordered and secure. Certainly, wealth, education, and genteel bearing commanded power and demanded deference. Yet, compared to any European kingdom, North America lacked blatant social extremes among its white population. Benjamin Franklin could plausibly claim in 1782, in "From Information to Those Who Would Remove to America," that although there were "few People so miserable as the Poor of Europe, there are also very few that in Europe would be called rich; it is rather a general happy Mediocrity that prevails."[12]

FREEBORN COLONIALS

Freeborn colonials, unlike their counterparts in Europe, expected to better themselves socially. English children were educated—or more likely trained

—to assume their parents' "station in life," but this was not generally the case in the colonies. America's availability of land meant that raising an individual's expectations "to better himself" did not necessarily lead to personal disappointments and aggravate class tensions or inspire accusations of presumption. The Puritan theologian Cotton Mather could note in his *Essay to Do Good* (1710) that "obscure mechanics and husbandmen have risen to estates of which they had not the most distant expectations."[13]

Labor, being scarce, commanded higher wages than across the Atlantic, and limitless virgin soil beckoned the colonist westward to be his own master. Aside from slavery, Americans by the middle of the eighteenth century had little experience with the inherited inequalities of Europe that fed the social conflicts so pervasive prior to the French Revolution. In many ways, the American outlook began to differ from the European, and foreign visitors to the colonies remarked on an American optimism that acted as a powerful incentive to a strong work ethic. To Americans, hard work assured a material stake in life, the respect of others, and some influence in civil society. Most important, perhaps, personal independence—being one's own man—was identified with ownership of property.[14]

This is not surprising. What is startling is that American society promoted values and habits that have stood the test of time, easily adapting to and facilitating change. In the American emerging in the colonial period, an individual less inclined to defer to superiors or to rely on past habits and practices, we can discern in embryo a pragmatic modern man or woman striving to rationally pursue his or her self-interest. Over the centuries, the rest of the developed world has become more like Americans, while twentieth-century Americans still bear family likeness to their early forebears.

BENJAMIN FRANKLIN AND SELF-HELP

When Max Weber selected an individual to epitomize the Protestant ethic, he picked the American autodidact and polymath Benjamin Franklin. Franklin (1706–90), self-taught and self-made, was indeed an early exemplar of the rags to riches story that has spurred on generations of Americans. One of seventeen children of a Boston soap and candle maker, he had received barely two years of schooling before being apprenticed to his brother, a Boston printer. In 1723 Franklin ran away to Philadelphia. Here, by dint of hard work and steady application, he eventually started his own printing and publishing business. Its success allowed him to virtually retire at age forty-two, devoting himself thereafter to intellectual endeavors and a distinguished career of public service.

Franklin made a science of the conduct of his life and shared his insights with his countrymen in *Poor Richard's Almanac* and other writings. For the price of his almanac, a wide readership throughout the colonies often received Franklin's advice on how to get rich. Indeed, in 1736 he published *Necessary Hints to Those That Would Be Rich* as a how-to guide for the ambitious. Franklin was the first American to discover that others would pay handsomely for financial advice on how to gain wealth. Knowing a good thing, he quickly produced a string of books in a similar vein.

The adages and proverbs varied somewhat, but Franklin's message always remained the same: in America one could choose any career and then earn distinction and wealth through talent, hard work, and common sense. "The sleeping Fox catches no poultry," Franklin admonished, ominously adding that "there will be sleeping enough in the Grave." Franklin's gospel of success would have proven highly disruptive to Europe's social order but apparently made sense in an American context. Of course, Franklin was not selling his advice to women, slaves, indentured servants, or the many white males who lacked the functional literacy to read him.

It is easy to dismiss Franklin as a vulgar materialist and an early instance of the proverbial American braggart. But in truth he was neither. A fallen-away Puritan who had become a deist, he was a supple thinker who sought to encourage an American type that would be virtuous but not priggish, simple but not ignorant, optimistic and self-confident but not foolish. From his Puritan background he retained a sense of the importance of the commonwealth and public service; his American experience taught him flexibility, perseverance, and ambition. His colleague John Adams found in him a "Passion for Reputation and Fame, as hard as you can imagine, and his Time and Thoughts are chiefly employed to obtain it." For Franklin, these attributes provided the bedrock of character required for success.[15]

To these he added the insight offered by the Age of Reason, that critical reasoning and scientifically determined facts provided a knowledge capable of transforming humanity and its circumstances. In a 1780 letter to fellow scientist Joseph Priestley, Franklin regretted that he had been born too soon, for it was "impossible to imagine the height to which may be carried . . . the power of man over matter." He predicted that "agriculture may diminish its labour and double its produce; all disease may . . . be prevented and cured," and then went on to anticipate the airplane.[16] From an optimism and practicality rooted in American circumstances, Franklin extended his message to encompass the whole world. Franklin's thinking is testimony in part to American distinctiveness, but it also demonstrates the assumption that America's experience has a universal significance: the perennial conviction of being a nation on the threshold of a brilliant future opened by American leadership to the entire world.

Despite his posturing, Franklin was certainly not an ordinary American. When living in Europe, he often wore a rustic garb of homespun and a beaver cap, which may have amused and charmed but could not fool anyone with a modicum of discernment. The real Franklin was a cosmopolitan sophisticate at a time when over 90 percent of Americans lived on and worked the land, and his advice to them of "early to bed and early to rise" was superfluous. The arduous circumstances of their lives and the preciousness of homemade candles largely dictated this in any case.

THE FARM HOUSEHOLD
AS AN ECONOMIC AND SOCIAL WORLD

Any overview of the colonial economy must stress that the farm household remained the chief vehicle of colonial production and consumption, and continued so well into the industrial era. Most colonial Americans, an estimated 90 percent, engaged in largely subsistence farming and mostly made everything possible at home. This is not to suggest that they were self-sufficient. To acquire necessities they could not provide for themselves—glassware, nails, muskets, lead for bullets, and gunpowder—or things that were simply desired as "conveniences" or "superfluities"—such as linen or Wedgwood dishes—farmers swapped goods and services with each other and with country peddlers and local shopkeepers.

The larger market economy did not as yet define their existence. For a back-country farmer, an occasional visit from an itinerant peddler or a transaction with a local flour mill might constitute his principal commercial encounters. His primary concern was eking out a crude livelihood. T. H. Breen, however, has argued that in the years 1747 to 1771 colonial farmers, along with Americans of all social classes, were involved in buying consumer goods to a much greater extent than formerly thought.[17]

Mary Beth Norton has demonstrated, in *Founding Mothers and Fathers*, that the colonists in the early settlements embraced a profoundly patriarchal and hierarchical worldview. The father's authority was regarded as essential for the effective functioning of both the family and the civil society. He controlled the family's wealth and its allocations. The subordination of women—first to their fathers and then later to their husbands—rested firmly on law and custom. The critical importance of women's economic contributions did not translate into formal or legal power, and with the exception of widows, women had little independent legal status; they could not sue, draft wills, or enter into a contract. Yet, compared to Europe, American women had a greater role in the economy and more control over the fruits of their labor. Upper-class women sometimes achieved wide influence in church and community affairs, and widows often continued the business of their late husbands, whether shop or tavern. The often unsettled conditions of this New World undermined and weakened hierarchies of all sorts, even, to an extent, the patriarchal model of civil society, with its subordinated sphere for women.[18]

Chores were organized along lines of age and gender, and most of the ordinary family's clothing, foodstuffs, furniture, and utensils were produced within the household. Men tended the fields, chopped wood for fuel and fencing, slaughtered animals, hunted, fished, and built and repaired buildings; women cleaned and ordered the home, made and mended garments, and cooked and preserved food. Food preparation often involved keeping a garden, salting and smoking meat, pressing or boiling apples into cider or preserves, milking cows, and churning butter. Cleaning required soap to be made from fats, lye, and ashes and then used with water fetched in buckets from a stream or perhaps a well. Making a garment might start with spinning or weaving homespun cloth. When store-bought cloth was used, its cutting, fitting, and sewing was done by hand. (The word "distaff," a long spindle for holding wool, entered the language as a collective term for women, women's work, and the female line of descent.) Colonial women typically married between the ages of twenty and twenty-three, two years younger than the average age in Britain, and bore more children. The average colonial family raised seven children.[19]

The family needed some way to acquire necessities and luxuries it could not provide for itself—chiefly by having a surplus crop to sell. Men sometimes took on additional work as carpenters or blacksmiths; women raised chickens to sell the eggs for money. Large families were the rule, at a time when children from an early age represented pairs of helping hands rather than hands outstretched to receive sustenance until well past puberty. In a celebrated essay from 1751, "Causes and Consequences of Population Growth," Benjamin Franklin explained that Americans married earlier than the English and had more children because "land being thus plenty in America and so cheap, a [man] can in a short Time save Money enough to purchase a Piece of a new land . . . whereon he may subsist a family; such are not afraid to marry."[20]

The range of demands made on the colonial household merely to produce what it consumed makes one understand why the word "economy" is originally the Greek word for household management. It also challenges the romantic view of a simpler America as a nation of self-reliant yeoman farmers. Self-sufficiency never truly characterized most colonial life, for bartering and purchasing were everywhere present from the start. A shift from self-reliance to increasing dependence on the market made life easier but required goods and services available at prices within reach of a dispersed but rapidly growing market. This would not prove to be simple to accomplish. It would require a revolution in transportation and manufacturing, and these had changed little in the colonial period. Prior to 1790, roads were of little use for shipping bulky goods, and the business practices of merchants remained virtually identical, except for scale, to those of the first settlers.

PARTING OF THE WAYS

By the end of the colonial period, there was general agreement that Americans differed significantly from Europeans. Foreign visitors frequently commented that the colonists tended to be strongly individualistic, enjoying a degree of freedom and opportunity unique in the world and showing little deference to authority. A culture reflects a people's experiences with life. In the preindustrial era, climate and geography profoundly influenced what was possible and what was not; along with the seasons, they imposed a pattern and rhythm on life. The initial American experiences centered on survival—overcoming a wilderness and planting a civilization. To do all this, Americans had to improvise by adjusting old ways to new circumstances and learning from each other.

The colonies had come of age by the mid-1700s. Their coastal towns had developed into small but cosmopolitan centers of maritime commerce and craft production that rivaled such British ports as Hull, Bristol, and Glasgow. With a population of 25,000 in the 1760s, Philadelphia boasted the presence of London tailors, French periwig makers, and German metalworkers. In ground-floor workshops in their homes, colonial trained craftsmen made leather breeches and Windsor chairs that were highly valued throughout the North American colonies and the West Indies. A language and system of governance, as well as practical skills (such as European building techniques) brought by the first settlers, had been adapted to new circumstances of climate and topography. For example, lumber, expensive and used sparingly in England but abundant and cheap in the colonies, was extensively employed as a building material. The shortage of skilled labor meant that England's traditional seven-year apprenticeship had to be cut to three or four years in America. "Canoe," "maize," "moccasin," "squash," "succotash," and numerous other Indian words entered into the colonials' speech. Agricultural techniques, like most colonial ways, combined European practices and adaptations to special American circumstances.

Along with trade ties, Americans maintained close intellectual links to England and Europe. The well-to-do often went back and forth across the Atlantic. Family as well as commercial ties remained remarkably resilient over time and distance. English values lingered on to influence the hierarchy of the colonial social structure. The research of David Cressy and others warns us against the overemphasis on "American exceptionalism" committed by the generation of American historians writing after World War II in the context of the Cold War. Yet it is clear that the American colonies became more independent, with economic and demographic growth, even as England's wars and commercial ties reminded them of their roots.[21]

As the colonists acclimated to a new continent and flourished, they might still have regarded themselves as Englishmen, while recognizing their own virtues, rather than thinking themselves provincials in a backwater eddy. The mixture of Africans, several European nationalities, and Native Americans opened up new possibilities as alternatives to English practices. As their self-effacement departed, so did their awe of England as the metropolis. They in time came to believe themselves more virile and freer than Europeans.

In 1776, Adam Smith noted that cheap land gave the American the option of striking out on his own and acquiring acreage, while J. Hector St. John de Crèvecoeur conveyed the psychological implications of land ownership in promoting individualism and self-reliance, in *Letters from an American Farmer* (1782). Having by the 1750s pushed the frontier westward to the Appalachians, the Americans now concerned themselves with the next stage of development: not mere survival but individual and collective material improvement. An avaricious pursuit of land molded a set of attitudes that nurtured American restlessness and expansionism.[22]

With internal development came an increasing self-confidence and a loosening of dependence on English precedent and custom. Benjamin Franklin, writing in 1743 to propose the founding of the American Philosophical Society, noted that the colonies had progressed beyond the initial stage of settlement, during which concern for necessities had to absorb all energies, and now could afford the leisure to cultivate the arts and sciences. The colonial economy had progressed to where it had become considerably less reliant on England.[23]

A regard for the practical and useful soon became the hallmark of the colonial approach to business and the law. The colonists even claimed a God-given right to the "new continent," demonstrated by their ability to make the wilderness yield to settlement—with results providing justification. Enterprise and initiative received encouragement. Economic gains often resulted from trial and error, while learning was by doing and adapting. To the legal scholar J. Willard Hurst, Americans and their jurists preferred risk taking and development over a cautious and static use of property. Such a view promoted the release of individual creative energy. Debt and the debtor thus encountered a more sympathetic hearing in colonial courts than in English courts. Peter Hoffer has argued that there was an emergence of an "American way of law, a style of keeping order and resolving disputes" that was more open and informal than that practiced in English courts and cites Robert Beverly and Charles Campbell's proud claim in 1705 that Virginia courts "came to the merit of the case with all the Tricking and Foppery of the law happily avoided."[24]

Americans wanted to buy and sell land freely, and the colonial application of common law soon favored the doer and the developer against those inclined to the status quo. The substance of a law was deemed more important than its form, and the American deed and record system simplified property transfers. Traditional English restraints on property use or sale that reflected a desire to keep landholdings intact through the generations initially had been observed by the settlers but evolved over time toward a new conception of freely negotiable fee-simple property. The colonial period thus established precedent for the future United States in which legislators and courts adopted an instrumental conception of the law to redefine property arrangements and encourage new enterprise.[25]

Americans welcomed change and physical movement, identifying them with progress and civilization's inland advance. Inhabiting the thin edge of a vast continent, the colonists could afford to take risks and be mobile, for failure in one place only meant trying again elsewhere. The lesson that emerged from the American experience was to persevere. In England to go bankrupt meant loss of good name and ruination for life. Americans, however, were expected to pull themselves up by their bootstraps and start over—a virgin continent's expanse offered ample room for fresh efforts. The colonial period was an age in which merchants, planters, and some farmers had many interests and often started afresh in business and location several times in a lifetime. The effort in several colonies to transplant a patronage-dominated world crumbled over time. All of these factors promoted a practical-minded, businesslike society.

Outside of the South, a landed aristocracy did not lord it over the remainder of the population and expect forelock-tugging deference. There was no stigma attached to moneymaking in any legal occupation or in being restless and eager for change. A realistic optimism often paid off.

As early as the 1750s, some Americans, including Benjamin Franklin, gave thought to a union among the thirteen colonies to deal with such issues as collective defense, westward expansion, and Indian relations. But the idea failed to gain much support. American national consciousness was embryonic, and the various colonies had reason to suspect each other, particularly in their disputes over rival claims to western lands. Moreover, England disapproved of the proposed colonial union, and it was England that controlled the colonies' access to the world's foremost commercial empire.

Mercantilist limitations on commercial freedom rested lightly on colonial shoulders because, as previously noted, the London government's policies were largely ineffectual. All would change suddenly in 1763 when an English government, victorious over France in a protracted war, found itself desperate for funds. London now determined to force the colonists to directly pay the administrative and military costs of the North American empire. Parliament sought to strictly enforce the neglected Acts of Trade and Navigation. It also imposed new taxes, and London also moved to block great planters, like George Washington, from buying western lands.

POLITICAL DISCOURSE AND CIVIC DISOBEDIENCE

In uniting against the new imperial policies from 1763 to 1776, the colonials experienced a shared sense of outrage and a common pride in resistance. This would provide the basis for a developing sense of national unity. Merchants and lawyers from many cities met together in Boston, New York, and Philadelphia to plan resistance. English rule, no longer an asset, seemed a costly encumbrance, and concepts of self-interest were quickly joined to abstract disputations over natural rights and government. Arguments developed by Britons concerned with establishing the prerogatives of Parliament against the crown now would be employed by Americans to uphold colonial rights against both Parliament and crown. A sense of being "freeborn Englishmen" flourished in both England and America and eventually provided much of the justification for colonial revolt when perceived rights were violated.

But Americans ventured beyond English Whig thinkers in arguing the supremacy of individual rights over claims of government. Although retaining the idea of society as based on a contract for mutual advantage, the Americans placed greater emphasis on liberty and choice and far less importance on security than was customary among Englishmen. They extended their claims, often based largely on law and precedence, to rely more fully on the language of natural rights and of universal liberty. Bernard Bailyn, a Harvard historian of the colonial period, regarded the essence of the American Revolution as a process of radicalization, while another historian, Gordon S. Wood, has argued similarly that the American Revolution must be deemed profoundly radical. The full novelty of the concept of liberty as based on the abstract natural rights of all men, the historic rights of English subjects, would in time challenge a deferential and hierarchical social order.[26]

Lessons learned by Americans in the colonial period had long-reaching implications, which led them down the path to independence. Arguing from such specifics as "no taxation without representation" and the injustice of government grants of trade monopolies to private companies, Americans jumped to the sweeping generalization that a just government guaranteed individuals their security and then largely left them alone. Employing an English dissenting tradition that reached back to the civil war of the seventeenth century and its challenge to the authority of the crown, the colonials pushed this line of reasoning to a radical individualism. A commonplace conception of freedom saw it as the absence of constraints imposed by others —and if some constraint by government was necessary, government powers were also potentially dangerous. Thomas Paine expressed this profound sense of distrust toward government in his seminal 1776 pamphlet *Common Sense*: "Government, even in its best state, is but a necessary evil: in its worst state, an intolerable one."

The colonials metaphorically drew a line on the ground. Calling it natural rights, they warned the English government (and implicitly any government) not to step across. A merchant's regard for a contract as covenant—the basis of commerce and hence of progressive civilization—now underlay a remarkable view of government as necessarily limited by a social contract, and radical positions originally advanced to justify independence acquired lasting significance when Americans created their own government. A revolutionary tradition of political dissent and resistance to authority would be instrumental in shaping the United States, with its many constitutional restraints on governmental powers.

A view of political organization as emanating from voluntary exchanges made by individuals acting in their rational self-interest paralleled a similar view of economic transactions. This formulation does not, however, deny that collectivist themes reflecting Civic Republicanism also found expression in the whirligig of polemics spawned by the colonies' resistance to parliamentary policies.

The former colonials moved, albeit unevenly, to discard political and legal distinctions based on class. In the process of defining themselves as Americans, they advanced values that expressed a sense of equality based on a belief in natural law—universal norms applicable to all humanity. Distinctions of rank should not count in a court of law, because all emerged from the womb equal with inalienable rights. For the white American male at the time of the Revolution, self-respect required him to own property and be able to provide for his own family, to select his own religion and politics, and to not be beholden to others. (The anomaly of subjecting one race to slavery while expecting another to be independent and to call no one master was expediently downplayed.)

As legal scholars have long noted, contractual arrangements provided an alternative to traditional rights and obligations as both the philosophical and the legal cement binding society. Freedom was conceived primarily as the absence of constraints imposed by others and the right to engage in voluntary contractual exchanges; self-imposed constraints as stipulated in a contract, however, were legitimate.

By the revolutionary period, Americans had developed a passion for equality before the law. In due time, contract law, a relatively minor branch of English law until the eighteenth century, provided both mechanism and rationale for an economic system based on freely chosen and highly impersonal exchanges.

Contracts allowed individuals to pursue their interests in their own ways; they entered voluntarily into binding arrangements that specified obligations and prerogatives. The colonial and revolutionary experience weakened the neofeudal relationships with the help of a patriarchic household in which the master's role and responsibilities toward retainers was nearly indistinguishable from a father's toward his children. As late as 1770, a Pennsylvania statute required apprentices to dwell with the master to facilitate moral and religious instruction—but the law's very passage demonstrated that that formerly customary practice now needed legal buttressing. Even the wageworker of the revolutionary period was said to have "hired" or "contracted out" his labor. Merchants and landowners, buyers and sellers, formalized transactions through contracts, and the courts of the new nation carried this revolutionary momentum forward after 1790 to whittle away common law restraints on the "rights of contract." A market view of society, which equated economics with contractual relations and contractual relations with freedom, had come forward.[27]

Forces advancing individual freedom pressed against those emphasizing social control. The prevailing English view of society as connecting the highest order to the lowest order by a sanctified hierarchy that was not to be disturbed was being challenged. The traditional standards based on blood and family, valued by hereditary aristocrats from time immemorial, found few places to flourish. Ideally, the collapse of a repressive social order clears ground for a more progressive synthesis to emerge. But less desirable developments may occur that free the strong to exploit the weak. The American Revolution provides an early instance of the energizing tension between these conflicting tendencies in the nation's history.

As Gordon Wood has commented: "By every measure there was a sudden bursting forth, an explosion—not only of geographic movement but of entrepreneurial energy . . . and of pecuniary desires."[28] Colonial Americans pursued wealth avidly because few postfeudal institutions and attitudes restricted them, and even those few had been shaken by revolutionary fervor.

The antiauthoritarian bent of the revolutionary period combined with the individualism encouraged by American circumstances of relative plenty to threaten the social order. The need to strengthen social stability explained an American reliance on what sociologists refer to as "intermediate institutions"—family, community, church, and school—to define common values and goals. These provided largely voluntary arrangements to nurture social cohesiveness. Physical mobility and the increasing emphasis on individualism present after 1760 encouraged Americans to regard "intermediate institutions" as utilitarian—and indeed often transitory—institutions, to be evaluated in terms of worth and performance.

Some recent scholarship stresses that an ideology and rhetoric of Civic Republicanism emerged from the revolutionary era to influence strongly the early national period. This regarded the highest value as a "civic humanism," with independent citizens voluntarily subordinating their individual interests to the common good. Perhaps—but it was not the dominant theme.[29]

The justification for government's legitimacy in the revolutionary period was first and foremost the protection of individual rights. Accordingly, a government acting contrary to natural rights forfeited legitimacy. As James Otis wrote as early as 1764, in "The Rights of the British Colony Asserted and Proved," a parliamentary act in violation of natural law "would be contrary to eternal truth, equity, and justice, and consequently void." The values that predominated in the revolutionary era were primarily individualistic: a set of attitudes and values that emphasized the individual's sovereignty over his private world and his consensual entering into associations. Most certainly they have exerted a permanent and profound influence on the future nation's legal and economic development.[30]

AMERICAN EXCEPTIONALISM

It is dangerous to stress the exceptionalism of a people, because of the temptation to exaggerate. This is especially true for Americans, who too often have viewed themselves as a beacon on a hill lighting the way for all humanity. Yet it must be said that America from the start offered the seeds of capitalism a uniquely fertile soil. In 1782 Benjamin Franklin wrote a pamphlet of advice "From Information to Those Who Would Remove to America." America, he said, was a place where "People do not enquire concerning Stranger, What is he? But What can he do?"[31]

The inhibiting hand of the past, as represented by precapitalistic social forms, groups, and interests, was noticeably weak, with, of course, one striking exception: slavery. A conservative force in traditional societies, land in America acted as a revolutionary force. Its availability permitted the widespread property ownership that Americans regarded as the foundation for individual freedom.[32]

The American Revolution was not only against something; it was for something. Americans were drawn to the notion of communities as social inventions with manmade rules based on practical considerations and group consent. The colonial experience after 1763 emphasized the need to protect natural rights through an agreed-upon written constitution even before the establishment of government.

The newness of this society, its abundance of resources, the high cost of labor, and the restlessness and mobility of its population all promoted the free play of individual self-interest and fostered attitudes that emphasized acquisitive individualism. In 1776, Adam Smith discerned in his *Wealth of Nations*: "There are no colonies of which the progress has been more rapid than that of the English in North America. Plenty of good land and liberty to manage their affairs their own way seem to be the two great causes of the prosperity."[33]

People moved about freely, with obvious exceptions, for opportunity. The promise of success led them to prefer risk to security and stability. Rewards came often enough to encourage such behavior. Unlike Europe, with its vast hordes of underemployed poor, the colonies exhibited the remarkable phenomenon of rapid population growth accompanied by a rising standard of living. Population growth simply led to western movement rather than increasing pressure on limited resources. An optimism born of American circumstances suggested that poverty and gross economic inequalities need not reflect the eternal human condition but could be altered and reformed. In contrast to European societies, America evidenced a much more even distribution of wealth among its free population. A significance of this, as Joyce Appleby discerned, was that "there existed in America no large, menacing body of dispossessed men to remind the propertied classes that they had to stick together."[34]

If these aspirations constitute the core of the American Dream, as most Americans believe, then the American Dream preceded the nation, providing the bedrock ideology of its foundation. David Potter declared, in his astute study of the American character, *People of Plenty*: "European radical thought is prone to demand that the man of property be stripped of his carriage and his fine clothes. But American radical thought is likely to insist, instead, that the ordinary man is entitled to mass-produced copies, indistinguishable from the originals."[35] Even in the colonial period, foreign visitors commented with amazement on a similarity of dress across class lines and the casual manners of subordinates to superiors. Early on, as the word "master" acquired an association with slavery, first New Yorkers and then other colonists began to use the Dutch word "boss" as a substitute.

Bernard Bailyn has summed up the credo of supporters of independence as they transformed themselves into Americans: "Faith ran high that a better world than any that had ever been known could be built when authority was distrusted and held in constant scrutiny."[36] Underlying such sentiments was confidence in an inexhaustible continent of plenty combined with the germ of a remarkable idea of progress as "leveling up" the many rather than redistributing the wealth of the rich few. If the United States is a society initially organized around an ideology whose basic text can be summed up in a few words—liberty, individualism, and suspicion of strong government— then its roots must go back to the colonial period. The premise that it was possible for a nobody to become a somebody, to make something out of nothing, to acquire property and safely enjoy it had become a salient feature of American society even before the nation's birth.

The view of the colonial experience and its legacy presented in this chapter has accepted (while acknowledging an effort to cling to inherited English values and elite social structure) a growing American "exceptionalism" that encouraged individualism and ambition. This shaped a protocapitalist "ideology" of entrepreneurship and individualism that would come to fruition in the early national period, with its rapturous celebration of enterprising individuals. Many historians, beginning in the late 1960s, have tried to establish contrary and sometimes competing ideologies (under the loose rubric of "Civic Republicanism") that place priority on social goals of cooperation, civic duty, and, in general, the individual's obligations to community. These values were present in early American society and were certainly important. But they were not the determining force in laying the foundation of the American economic and business system. They did, however, contribute greatly to the creation of an American reform tradition, and this has helped shape the American business environment. What remains without cavil is that in 1776 Americans began the process of replacing a government over them with one under them.

Furthermore, government in the abstract was very largely stripped of its mystery. No longer ordained from on high or regarded as more important than the citizen, it was to be designed by the people to serve the functional purpose of promoting the safety and prosperity of free citizens laboring in their own interest. The two explicit limitations on the creators of this new type of government were that they required the consent of the governed and that they not violate the natural rights of the citizens. First, the colonists needed to create their new state governments; then they had to ponder the nature of the relationship of the states with each other before designing a national government with the right mix of powers and safeguards.

CHAPTER THREE

The Early National Economy, 1776–1820

The private interests of every individual must be a sentinel over the public rights.—JAMES MADISON, The Federalist Papers *No. 51 (1788)*

The great chief end of men uniting into commonwealth and putting themselves under government is the preservation of their property.—JOHN LOCKE, Two Treatises on Government *(1689)*

In 1787 Alexander Hamilton wrote in *The Federalist Papers* No. 1, "It seems to have been reserved to the people of this country, by their conduct and example, to decide the important question, whether societies of men are really capable or not of establishing good government from reflection and choice." The first half century after the Declaration of Independence marked a time of nation building. Public bodies and laws had to be designed and constructed, a sense of nationality inculcated.[1]

In the task of designing institutions, a consensus on certain fundamental values acted as guideposts. Government must show no favoritism, administer laws equally, and protect property and life while respecting civil rights. Beyond this was the tacit acceptance that the doors of opportunity had to be open to talent and virtue, at least for white males. Human nature, however, dictates that abstract ideals are always tempered by self-interest. So it was with the early republic. Nevertheless, profound antagonisms based on regional and class differences erupted, to be expressed in the emergence of political parties and sectional tensions.

THE ULTIMATE CHALLENGE

Farsighted contemporaries regarded the armed struggle against England as only the beginning of the American Revolution. To John Adams, "the revolution was in the minds of the people," who would press on to forge a radically new form of society.[2] A complex older way of life was being pulled apart; Americans in consequence had to create a new one. A social order originally based on hierarchy and patronage slowly gave ground to competition, openness, and freedom. Within a half century, Americans had constructed, with a written constitution providing the vital core, the political and legal framework they still rely on.

The primary concern was to protect the individual from a powerful and arbitrary state, while providing a government adequate to protect life and property and to advance commerce. The audacity required to sunder ties with England would be sustained in designing a nation. In the process, Americans established a strong sense of a distinctive national identity. The free laborer, in possession of the means of his livelihood and therefore not subservient to others, represented the backbone of the new republic and to many the essence of being an American.

The making of the United States was a remarkable adventure. The ultimate challenge rested, as indicated in the epigraph from *The Federalist*, in laying the political foundations of a consensual society. This required government to enjoy the voluntary consent of citizens who believed they benefited from a rule of law. The American Revolution introduced an experiment in weighing competing claims. The most critical of these was, How can the rights of the individual be balanced against the needs of society? New freedoms had to take form—and accept limitations.

GOVERNMENT BY THE CONSENT OF THE GOVERNED

The identification of political legitimacy with the protection of individual rights had to be balanced against the need to fashion effective government. The initial device used to reconcile the two was state constitutional conventions to draw up covenants between the people and their state governments. In 1787, this procedure would be extended to the formation of a central government. The idea of a fixed constitution signified the belief in universal natural rights as being antecedent to lawmakers and their laws, with government representing a social contract entered into for mutual advantage.

Standing as signposts on the way to the modern world are two documents that appeared in 1776 and that together establish a radically new vision of things to come. Both were fundamental expressions of the movement toward individual liberty and against the demands of government. One was written in a two-week period in June by a thirty-three-year-old southern planter and lawyer, the owner of several thousand acres and several hundred slaves. The other, more than 1,000 pages in two quarto volumes, represented the culmination of a life's inquiry by a Scotsman, a onetime professor of moral philosophy at the University of Glasgow. Each has cast a long shadow on how we have thought ever since, and each contributed greatly to the sentiment that government's role had to be radically curtailed.

Revised, abridged, and then adopted by the Continental Congress, Thomas Jefferson's Declaration of Independence remains, as he intended, "an expression of the American mind." Relying on the thinking of John Locke and other English constitutional theorists, Jefferson detailed the abuses by George III that justified the separation of the colonies from England. But it is the underlying premises of his argument, not the details of the charges, that continue to fascinate. Jefferson forcefully asserted that submission to government is voluntary and therefore may be justifiably withdrawn under certain circumstances. This was because "all men are created equal" and are in the very nature of things "endowed by their Creator with certain unalienable rights." Just as governments exist to secure these rights, violating them abrogates a government's legitimacy and then "it is the right of the people to alter or abolish it."

The Declaration of Independence brilliantly summarizes the views of those colonials who, seeking to break from England, had started to transform themselves into Americans. It makes clear their rejection of Europe's monarchies and hereditary privileges and distinctions. More important, it is a universal statement for all people and times that retains a strikingly fresh radicalism. Government, implies the Declaration of Independence, is only a human contrivance, albeit necessary, to be designed as a convenience. Natural rights, on the other hand, are inherent and transcendent, universal and inalienable. Thus Jefferson can confidently claim that government serves the individual, and not the other way around. Few Americans, past or present, have challenged this belief, which is at the very core of our national orthodoxy. Americans are summoned to war to fight to defend their rights and freedoms (though the reasoning has been sometimes very tortured), but never out of a demand for blind obedience to the callings of the state. The American ideal has always been, however, far nobler than the American reality. For most of the nation's history, there has been a wide gap between egalitarian ideals and discriminatory practices.

Nevertheless, the ideal remains all-important, acting as a catalyst for necessary reform at critical times. The Declaration established the ideological basis of the political process as a continuing call for renewal. As the creation of the people, government must continuously justify itself. The Declaration of Independence still stands as a powerful statement of one of the great achievements of modern times: the humanistic conception of essential and universal rights and the assertion that the power of reason can honor and guarantee these rights.[3]

SELF-INTEREST AS PUBLIC VIRTUE

Adam Smith explicitly addressed economic concerns and political issues only as they related to how self-interest and competition can operate to promote individual well-being and national prosperity. He complemented Jefferson's credo of natural rights with the argument that government advanced its own interests by allowing individuals freedom to pursue economic gain—or, simply put, that a harmony of interests necessarily exists between government and its citizens when the latter are free to serve their own economic bent. To Smith, the mercantilist belief that the individual and his property must be subordinated to and controlled by the political order is contrary to the society's true interests. The state's proper role is to sustain the legal conditions essential to a market economy, not to impose preconceived notions of what is good for the state; this is because when individuals and their enterprises are left alone to compete they serve the nation's material interests. It is best that "every man, *as long as he does not violate the laws of justice* [my italics], is left perfectly free to pursue his own interest his own way, and to bring both his industry and capital into competition with those of any other order of men."[4]

Adam Smith was a moral philosopher who, in wrestling with ethical issues, became an economist. This occurred because he viewed material concerns as constituting the principal arena for our social nature and ethical conduct. Smith first identified what he regarded as the chief attribute of human nature, which is self-love directed at bettering one's condition through the human propensity to "truck, barter, and exchange," and then he deduced a model of the good society and from this model derived suggestions for the conduct of government.[5]

To Smith, society represented a vast marketplace in which the political order must act primarily to protect the individual's liberty and property. Economic advantages, competitively gained, then create the efficient and progressive economy that Smith identified with the good community. Thus, the moral question of whether the individual is being selfish or unselfish becomes irrelevant. The very nature of a free exchange economy, disciplined by competition, Smith believed, forced people to behave cooperatively through exchanging the surplus of their labor. In short, citizens promoted the common good and perhaps even a moral community by pursuing their individual interests. This beneficent design Smith regarded as universal and objective—an expression of God's eternal order.

In pursuing this reasoning, Smith developed so effective and elegant a paradigm of how a market economy worked that it still dominates much of economic thought. Even Karl Marx, whose conclusions differed diametrically from Smith's, relied on the Scotsman's economic analysis to advance his own. It may even be that Marx was influenced somewhat by passages in the book that call attention to the workers being exploited and abused by dishonest traders, manufacturers, and idle landlords. But certainly there is no trace in Smith's work of what Marx depicted as the internal contradictions of capitalism.[6]

To understand Smith's economic thinking, we need to know about the British economy of his era. For much of the eighteenth century, the demands for British goods had challenged the ability of manufacturers to meet them by traditional means of production. Eagerness to profit from this demand by increasing output contributed to the explosion of innovations that transformed Britain in the century's second half—it has been estimated that productivity in that country doubled from 1760 to 1801.[7]

Innovations in production took two directions that in time converged into a powerful force for change. At the time that Smith was writing, most commercial manufacturing occurred in small workshops, as artisans and mechanics relied on hard-learned skills and simple hand tools to painstakingly produce a limited output. A major exception was the all-important textile industry, which, starting in the sixteenth century, used the "putting-out" system, in which merchant capitalists—a contemporary term used for merchants who dealt with numerous independent artisans—acquired the raw wool, which they then distributed among farm families to work at home. In their spare time, mainly during the winter months, family members processed the wool, spun it into thread, wove it into cloth, and often dyed and softened the cloth. However, by the end of the eighteenth century, the manufacture of cotton imported from India had superseded woolen goods to become Britain's leading industry, and this too relied on the putting-out system.

By the time Smith published *The Wealth of Nations*, little change had occurred in the prior decades in the implements employed in handicraft production. But an increasing amount of production now occurred in what Adam Smith called "manufactories." Here, to increase output, a relatively large group of men assembled and worked out new divisions of labor. At the very beginning of *The Wealth of Nations* Smith offered his celebrated description of a pin factory. Ten workers, he stated, each responsible for a distinct step in a process "divided into about 18 distinct operations," could collectively make 48,000 pins a day through this specialization of labor. "One man draws out the wire, another straightens it, a third cuts it, a fourth points it, a fifth grinds it at the top for receiving the head." If each worked alone, according to Smith, ten men could not produce together more than two hundred pins. The description of this manufacturing illustrates one of Smith's central ideas—that the division of labor is the key to improved productivity, as increased "dexterity" gained through repetition improved "the quality of the work [a man] can perform." Although Smith expressed concern that repetitive labor would lower the worker's intellect, he did not consider the possibility that the division of labor could diminish the importance or the wages of workers.[8]

Industrialization, the application of powered machinery to production, had already begun to transform manufacturing, mining, and transportation. This development, however, did not receive notice from Smith, who was firmly convinced that economic progress came from greater labor specialization. A series of mechanical inventions (the spinning jenny in 1764, the water frame in 1769, and the mule in 1779) soon offered an alternative to the putting-out system in the manufacture of cotton cloth. Powered machines led to the construction of factories located near free-flowing water—a source of power—that occasionally used workforces as numerous as several hundred by 1800.[9]

As the possibilities for increased output at lowered costs became evident, other industries, such as iron, sought to develop an industrial technology. Merchants with capital and business connections joined with the artisans and mechanics, who in turn provided the inventions and know-how to promote the "factory system." The machines of these early factories were not sophisticated inventions that broke conceptual barriers. Instead, they usually resulted from painstaking trial and error and much practical knowledge of an industry and its manufacturing process by a self-taught mechanic or engineer.

With the advent of the factory system's new scale of production, capital became increasingly important to manufacturing. After the middle of the nineteenth century, manufacturing and the factory owner supplanted commerce and the merchant as formative factors in the shaping of capitalism. The term "Industrial Revolution" is presently regarded by scholars as misleading in suggesting abrupt change based on technological innovations. They stress the complexity and unevenness of the industrial process as it slowly advanced through fits and starts. The Industrial Revolution should be viewed accordingly as a continual building of small improvements whose history shows the difficulty of achieving regular growth. The explosion of technology came only late in the nineteenth century, well after many incremental gains. In any case, the nascent industrial technology of his day apparently did not interest Smith.[10]

Instead, he focused on the importance of market demand in advancing the division of labor. But the English experience influenced Smith in another direction as well. The fact that the English economy suffered from a shortage of manufactured goods meant that important commercial groups lacked compelling reasons to support government policies protecting home industry. A school of thought critical of mercantilism flourished in eighteenth-century England.[11]

Sir Dudley North offered one such early criticism of mercantilism that warrants prominent placement in every U.S. congressional office. He advised that merchants seeking special laws "usually esteem the immediate interests of their own to be the common Measure of Good and Evil." To remedy special interest lobbying, North advised the elimination of laws that bestowed special privileges. In 1714, Bernard Mandeville published *The Fable of the Bees: or Private Vices, Publick Benefits*, a scathing satire intended to shock as well as inform. Mandeville theorized that selfishness and greed (using these terms as interchangeable with rational self-interest), if universally practiced, must lead to feats of individual industry which would benefit all. In Mandeville's defiantly paradoxical assertion, it was precisely the vices of selfish individuals that made not only themselves but others prosperous.

England's rising commercial ethos severely challenged traditional Christian values of compassion as well as paternalistic norms inherited from feudalism. A calculus based on rational self-interest challenged an older, communal-minded ethos as the guiding principles of social action. The ethical problems that resulted from this tension understandably intrigued the holder of the chair of philosophy at Glasgow University. In his *Theory of Moral Sentiments* (1759), Smith wrote: "To feel much for others and little for ourselves . . . to restrain our selfishness, and to indulge our benevolent affections, institutes the perfection of human nature."[12] Two decades later, Smith resolved the moral quandary very differently in *The Wealth of Nations.*

Here he asserted that the self-serving individual who competes with others effectively advances the nation's wealth. In Smith's famous statement: "He . . . neither intends to promote the publick interest, nor knows how much he is promoting it. . . . He intends only his own gain and he is in this . . . led by an invisible hand which was no part of his original intention."[13] Thus Smith created an ethic of production in which the acquisitive individual serves the design of Divine Providence, who ordered the Universe for exactly this end. A nation interfering in any way (the book was an attack on mercantilist policies restricting international trade) impeded the most efficient use of resources.

To Smith, government should limit itself to maintaining the police and the courts and undertaking only those generally useful activities, such as public education, that offer no profit incentive. Smith's work provided the ideology we know of as commercial capitalism. Its eternal appeal lies in the thesis that the market mechanism allows individuals to exercise their freedoms and self-interest while—effortlessly and without sacrifice—benefiting others. The "invisible hand" mediated the interests of all parties and guaranteed a self-regulating economy devoid of the internal contradictions and class conflicts Marx foresaw as causing capitalism's eventual destruction. To Smith, a natural harmony of interests flowed from the free play of the laws of supply and demand.

That the Declaration of Independence and *The Wealth of Nations* appeared in the same year is certainly coincidental. Their appearance in the same epoch, however, is not. Joseph Schumpeter believed that Adam Smith's ideas and proposals reflected the mood of his time. The same may be said for

Jefferson. Both men extolled the importance of individual freedom at the moment when powerful currents of change were breaking through older barriers. Jefferson provided the moral foundation for democracy; Smith supplied the theoretical basis for free enterprise. Together, their ideas represent a synthesis that envisions an economic order of freely enterprising individuals, a synthesis that would eventually become the ideology of the new nation. Each expressed views that are part of the Age of Reason's broad attempt to expand the range of individual freedom and collective well-being. Does their linkage at the birth of the nation mean, as is so often suggested, that democracy and free enterprise are as inseparable as two sides of the same coin?

Smith urged not free enterprise alone, but an extreme laissez-faire version. Few would argue that his vision is applicable in its entirety to the modern world. Even in the mid-nineteenth century, John Ruskin charged Smith with teaching that "thou shalt covet thy neighbor's goods," and Smith's fellow Scotsman Thomas Carlyle ridiculed his views as "anarchy plus a constable." Adam Smith, it must be remembered, wrote before the Industrial Revolution had dotted England with infamous Coketowns, with their choking, filthy environments and "dark satanic mills and tall factory smokestacks" bemoaned by Dickens and William Blake. Nor did eighteenth-century technology confront Smith with industrial pollution or massive social dislocations. And although he was well aware of the "mean rapacity, the monopolizing spirit of merchants and manufacturers," he could not anticipate the complexity, scale, and consequences of modern manipulations by international cartels, insider trading on the stock exchange, or price-rigging holding companies.[14]

Smith's primary concern was, understandably, the misuse of state power. He believed that business activity posed little menace when the competitive forces of the market enjoyed full play. Our present concerns, however, must include the potential for corporate abuse in an age of huge multinational businesses. In this regard, it is well to recall Smith's warning that "people of the same trade seldom meet together even for merriment and diversion, but the conversation ends in a conspiracy against the public or in some contrivance to raise prices." Smith's ideas, stressing the efficiencies fostered by competition and the unintended social benefits of self-seeking action, do not constitute uncritical praise for the commercial classes and individual selfishness. But any dangers were effectively controlled, he argued, by the "invisible hand" of the market that reconciled supply and demand. Competition and the market necessarily brought about economic well-being without the intrusive hand of government. It is here that Smith's reasoning is open to challenge.[15]

THE CONSTITUTION AS A COMMERCIAL INSTRUMENT

The Wealth of Nations quickly influenced scholarly thinking and achieved a lasting significance, while the Declaration of Independence initiated a difficult five-year war. At its end, the new American states confronted the need to establish their relationship with one another, as well as the issue of how to sustain their economies. Rivalries among the states and a legacy of suspicion of Parliament led in 1781 to the creation of a feeble central government under the Articles of Confederation: a unicameral legislature authorized to conduct foreign affairs, control maritime matters, and coin national money. More important was what the national government could not do. Unable to raise revenue directly, it needed to rely on the states for funds, and the central government could not compel the states to heed its decisions or act adequately to foster foreign trade.

Under the Articles of Confederation, the United States failed to promote favorable commercial developments, either domestic or foreign. The severe dislocation caused by the loss of markets for American goods in the British empire (although Americans continued to buy English manufactures dumped at low prices to discourage the rise of American rivals) led in 1782 to a severe depression that lasted five years. In an effort to compensate for the loss of traditional colonial connections, a new trade was opened with China. However, the Confederation government's inability to assist in furthering trade, among other weaknesses, led to doubts about its value. Several of the states, under popular pressure, had enacted extremely lenient debtor-relief laws, and all casually printed paper money, which later caused future Chief Justice John Marshall to assert at the Virginia Convention ratifying the Constitution, meeting in June 1788, that under the Articles the state governments had "render[ed] property insecure and unprotected."

The Constitutional Convention that met in Philadelphia from May to September of 1787 intended a central government capable of furthering economic development by securing property rights. Writing in 1913, the historian Charles Beard asserted that the resultant Constitution also reflected a hidden agenda. He charged that the delegates wanted to redeem at face value the various bonds and paper money issued by the states and the national government since 1776 to enrich speculators who had acquired the paper at a discount. One does not have to accept the thesis expressed in Beard's *An Economic Interpretation of the Constitution*—and few historians at present do—to accept his famous conclusion that "the Constitution was essentially an economic document based upon the concept that the fundamental rights of property are anterior to government and morally beyond the reach of popular majorities."[16]

The businessmen, lawyers, and planters who drafted the Constitution intended to promote trade and manufacture by safeguarding private property and the sanctity of legal contracts. Connecticut representative Roger Sherman categorically stated: "The right of property is the guardian of every other right." Alexander Hamilton declared: "One great object of Govt. is personal protection and the security of Property." John Rutledge of South Carolina remarked: "Property was certainly the principal object of Society." And James Madison wrote in *The Federalist Papers* No. 10: "Government is instituted no less for protection of the property than of the person of individuals." But it is also clear that to the Founding Fathers property represented not merely the possession of goods as such but the ownership of "work resources" (such as land or tools) that provided the holder the wherewithal for that independence of action deemed essential to a citizen of a republic.[17]

Aside from squabbling between the North and the South over the counting of slaves for purposes of taxes (resolved by the "three-fifths of a man" rule, both to apportion taxes and to allocate representatives in the House among the states) and the southern demand that its exports be guaranteed against tariffs, little controversy occurred over economic principles as such. The clauses in the Constitution granting Congress power to regulate commerce between the states and with foreign governments, to draft national laws of bankruptcy, to control the issuance of patents and copyrights, to pay debts, to borrow money, and to provide for the common welfare gained adoption with surprisingly little discussion. Most of Article I, Section 10, was designed to limit the abuse of business and private agreements by state legislatures. But its critical section is "No state shall . . . pass coin money; emit bills of credit; make anything but gold and silver coin a tender in payment of debts; or pass any . . . law impairing the obligation of contracts."

This justly famous contract clause (Article I, Section 8), a keystone of American capitalism, is one of the few protections against state actions given to individuals in the body of the Constitution. The Founding Fathers shared the view stated by Roger Sherman, the Connecticut delegate: "The right of property is the guardian of every other right" and essential to economic progress. Tucked away in the Fifth Amendment is the passage often referred to as the taking clause: "Nor shall private property be taken for public use without just compensation." Delegates feared that a people's government, unless sufficiently safeguarded against, might protect debtors or take property to equalize wealth. Yet, as historian Charles Sellers has pointed out, the contract clause's inflexibility toward small debtors must be contrasted to a bankruptcy clause "mandating relief for large debtors," since "bankruptcy was understood as a process whereby large debtors were freed from their debt by surrendering their assets."[18]

In *Federalist Papers* No. 10, James Madison praised the Constitution for providing a government that would secure the general rights of property against the claims of the propertyless but noted another concern. "The regulation of . . . various and interfering interests," Madison warned, "forms the principal task of modern legislation, and involves the spirit of party and faction in the necessary operation of the government." Only a federal government, well designed in terms of checks and balances, could effectively limit the organized use of political power to pursue parochial economic interests at the public expense. To Madison, a major part of the art of lawgiving consisted in balancing different interests to allow an effective control of their rivalries.

INVENTED COMMUNITY

The Revolution created the possibility of a new nation. It is, however, the year 1787 and the drafting of a Constitution that truly opens the national history. Most important for the future economy, the Constitution unified the contentious thirteen states into a common market destined to grow by the addition of new states to span a continent. A state under the Constitution could not, as previously it could under the Articles, levy tariffs or impose quotas or other barriers on the products of the other states, and therefore goods would freely cross state lines. A contract written in one state was binding in all others. A strengthened central government could promote trade and commerce by providing a federal post office, postal roads, a national currency, and uniform standards of weights and measurement. James Madison had even wanted the federal government authorized to charter corporations. But it was argued that federal charters smacked of royal perquisites like those employed by the

East India Company. Therefore it was left to the states to grant charters of incorporation, a decision still affecting American business in important ways.

The major defects of the Articles of Confederation in regard to commerce and industry had been remedied. The adoption of the Constitution provided the political and legal framework that has ever since undergirded the American free enterprise system. In most major ways, the Constitution offered a brilliant solution to the needs of the new nation.

The Constitution is more than an economic document; it is in effect a commercial instrument designed to promote economic growth. The ultimate test of a government in regard to business is how it provides for the safety of persons and property, the economic freedom it allows, the soundness of the currency, and the effectiveness of its legal system. As numerous Third World nations demonstrate, a written constitution, even when closely modeled on the American example, is not sufficient to guarantee these, and much depends on what economists refer to as the "institutional matrix" of economic activity. Alexis de Tocqueville found the expanse of the American continent and the richness of its soil "extraordinary" but then said that geography explained less of the nation's distinctiveness than did its laws and mores.[19]

This includes such factors as family structure, religion, inherited moral habits, educational standards, and attitudes regarding property and doing business. Clarity of private property rights and standards of honesty are as much a symptom of the underlying health and stability of a society as they are means to achieve these ends. For the first half century of national existence, Americans shaped their political and legal culture as a synthesis of custom and reason and with an eye toward favoring enterprise and promoting rapid development. But this did not occur without dissent. Thomas Jefferson, in his *Notes on the State of Virginia* (1787), argued against developing large-scale domestic manufactures on the grounds that this would lead to large cities with an unruly shiftless urban proletariat, whereas a republic needed to rest on a population of landowning, independent, and virtuous yeomanry rooted in an agrarian way of life.[20]

FEDERAL COURTS AND THE ECONOMY

The probusiness principles present in the American Constitution would be greatly enhanced in the early national period by John Marshall, Jefferson's distant relative and political opponent. In his long tenure as chief justice of the Supreme Court (1801–35), Marshall determined to make the Constitution a binding contract among the American people rather than a compact among sovereign states. As a young man, he had fought as a rifleman in the major battles of the Revolutionary War. Like Washington, he had developed a deep distrust of local and state governments that had promised much during the fighting while delivering little and desired a strong national government based on a written constitution. Thomas Jefferson said of Marshall's steel-trap mind: "You must never give him an affirmative answer or you will be forced to grant his conclusion. Why, if he were to ask me if it were daylight or not, I'd reply, 'Sir, I don't know. I can't tell.'"[21]

Marshall's federal courts interpreted laws to favor rapid economic growth. His Supreme Court vigorously blocked state actions that impeded interstate commerce or hindered development. Even property rights were not allowed to interfere with commercial progress. Eminent domain often forced reluctant private landowners to surrender their land for the purpose of building roads, bridges, and canals in return for a stipulated compensation. And when a property owner's erection of a water mill or dam adversely impacted his neighbor's property downstream, the courts usually supported the party whose use of property encouraged economic improvement. Marshall's successor as chief justice, Roger Taney, in 1837 in the *Charles River Bridge* case, denied that a charter given to one bridge company implied a monopoly preventing the construction of rival bridges. Noting the city of Boston's need for a second bridge, he stated: "While the rights of property are sacredly guarded, we must not forget that the community also has rights." He then added that property rights should not deprive the people of "the benefit of those improvements which are now adding to the wealth and prosperity." American federal and state courts preferred development, property in motion, to the status quo.[22]

Federal judges generally, and state judges frequently, labored to adapt the common law to the needs of a fluid market society. Ideally, the law was to be reliable, transparent, and consistent. It was to encourage, not obstruct, new opportunities for expanding wealth and profit. According to Charles Sellers, "With a fusillade of momentous decisions . . . the Court established the critical constitutional bulwarks required by the emerging capitalist order."[23]

In his 1803 decision in *Marbury v. Madison*, Marshall decisively established the Court's right of judicial review—a power to invalidate any legislation or court decision judged contrary to the Constitution. He then used this power to shield the rights of contract and charters from challenges by state legislatures in several landmark cases. Marshall wrote, in *Dartmouth College v. Woodward* (1819): "If business is to prosper, men must have assurance that contracts will be enforced." Marshall in his decisions used the contract to forge a strong link between capitalism and constitutionalism: the contract clause in the nineteenth century figured in more Supreme Court decisions than any other section of the Constitution.[24]

Gibbons v. Ogden (1824) was the first major case construing the commerce clause of the Constitution ("The Congress shall have Power . . . To regulate Commerce with Foreign Nations, and among the Several States"). Marshall's decision took a broad view of Congress's powers to legislate all "commercial intercourse" between the states: "No area of interstate commerce is reserved for state control." Under Marshall and his immediate successors, the Court assumed a special responsibility for protecting property rights from governmental actions, even warning the states that their laws regarding corporations had to be consistent with constitutional protection of contract and commerce.[25]

Starting with the Marshall Court, the federal judiciary contributed greatly to shaping nineteenth-century America's probusiness legal climate. Law had become an instrument for furthering individual economic freedom, and the federal courts led the way for the state courts to transform a conception of property derived from a past rooted in a relatively static agrarian economy to legal doctrines appropriate for nascent industrial capitalism. In 1808, John Hall established the nation's first law journal, *The American Journal and Miscellany Repertory*, claiming that "every merchant must sensibly feel the inconvenience and perplexity which result from his ignorance of those laws by which his dearest and most important privileges are regulated."[26]

Most important, the federal system of divided powers gravely impeded the federal government's response to change. The Constitution had given the states, not the federal government, latitude in supervising economic activities and their consequences. In England, for example, the appalling working conditions of the factory system resulted in Parliament passing factory inspection laws in 1832 to protect workers; Congress could not act comparably. The Constitution authorized the states to enact laws involving the health, safety, and welfare of their populations. Working conditions and business activity in general remained the near-exclusive responsibility of the states until the twentieth century.

Change occurred in America without the legal hindrances experienced elsewhere, but also without the protection to the populace offered by many other countries. As initially interpreted, the Constitution gave the national government power to further the progress of a national economy but not to attend to the sometimes negative consequences. That the social implications of a preindustrial economy are generally limited in impact contributed to an anomaly in the federal system that became obvious in the light of later developments. Much of preindustrial business was parochial—small in scale and concerned with a local market—and thus of concern only to the immediate communities. This changed dramatically in the second half of the nineteenth century with the rise of a national economy. Practices benign in a largely rural nation became troublesome or worse in an urban-industrial setting.

SECTIONAL DIFFERENCES AND THE RISE OF PARTIES

Frederick Jackson Turner's famous 1892 essay "The Significance of the Frontier in American History" has depicted the impact of westward movement on nineteenth-century Americans. As in the colonial period, new settlements symbolized the rich potential of continental expansion and Americans' association of growth and change with progress. Between 1791 and 1820, the United States added ten states to the original thirteen, with the purchases of the Louisiana Territory (1803) and Florida (1819) doubling the nation's land size. A partial listing of the new states indicates the rapidity of westward settlement. Kentucky became a state in 1792, Tennessee in 1796, Ohio in 1803, Louisiana in 1812, Mississippi in 1817, and Illinois in 1819. National policy promoted westward movement, favoring rapid settlement over the careful sale of federal land. "Doing a land office business" became a common phrase. Land speculation with cycles of boom and bust encouraged farmers to evaluate acreage in dollars and cents terms, not as a family patrimony with sentimental ties.[27]

Acquisition of new territories and the addition of new states exacerbated the sectional conflicts present from the beginning of the nation. These, joined to differences over foreign policy, created two factions in national government that soon resulted in the two-party system of American politics. Conflicting visions of the federal government's role and the nation's economic future further deepened the divide between "Federalists" and "Democratic Republicans." Federal funding of internal improvements and tariffs were central to a debate between advocates of a strong central government and their opponents. Those favoring a role for the federal government usually supported using this power to advance business activity.[28]

Alexander Hamilton, secretary of the treasury in Washington's administration, led the business-oriented Federalists. He hoped to further trade and industry by establishing "the ligaments" between government and business for the "pursuit of a common interest" in a prosperous economy. Hamilton wanted federal assumption of the Revolutionary War debt, to reassure all that the new nation would honor its public debt. He also asked Congress to charter a Bank of the United States, modeled closely on the century-old Bank of England, to fund the national debt by selling securities to investors. Hamilton's objective here was to win support among the wealthy and influential, who held the bonds.

Owned jointly by private banks and the national government, the Bank of the United States would act as a depository for federal funds and as the new government's fiscal agent. In ensuring an adequate medium of exchange, the Bank of the United States could act to check the activity of private banks. Hamilton's policies further looked to the creation of a large fund of domestic credit to lift the economy and provide investment in trade and industry. Clearly, Hamilton intended to place the new nation firmly on the road to very rapid economic growth.

A question arose, however, as to whether Congress had constitutional authority to charter a national bank. Thomas Jefferson and the Democratic Republicans thought not; James Madison, the "father of the Constitution," explained that the Constitutional Convention had rejected a clause empowering Congress to issue corporate charters. Hamilton replied with what became known as the "broad constructionist" view, or doctrine of "implied powers." He argued that Article I, Section 8, of the Constitution (the famous elastic clause) delegated to Congress the power to "make all Laws which shall be necessary and proper for carrying into Execution the foregoing powers," and that a national bank facilitated the carrying out of responsibilities given to the federal government.

The strict constructionists insisted that "necessary" meant that Congress was forbidden to act simply in terms of expedience but must demonstrate actual necessity, but Hamilton suggested instead that Congress could choose any "useful" means not specifically forbidden to it by the Constitution. With Hamilton's reasoning prevailing, and an important precedent established, the Bank of the United States was chartered for a twenty-year term with the possibility of renewal. In 1812, the Bank was not extended. But a Second Bank was chartered in 1816, once again for an initial twenty-year term.

WESTWARD MOVEMENT AND INTERNAL IMPROVEMENT

In 1790, 90 percent of Americans lived within 100 miles of the coast. The population grew from a little under 4 million in 1790 to 10 million in 1820 and to 17 million in 1840—an increase of a third each decade—and the center of population shifted westward. By 1840, nearly 40 percent of all Americans lived west of the Appalachian Mountains. Pioneers relocated, often more than once, to better themselves. Economic historian Stanley Lebergott has remarked: "Particularly after the formation of the United States of America, [internal] migration became the model means for adjusting an imperfect market and a limited supply of labor to the intense possibilities of economic gain."[29]

Pioneer farmers slashed and burned forests to achieve tillable land for subsistence farming and hopefully a marketable crop. Viewing the fertile country in and around the Illinois River Valley in 1819, optimists rhapsodized over moneymaking prospects. However, reality often offered a bleaker picture of a rugged frontier culture: isolated farmsteads, poor roads, and a "social life thin and harsh." Many settlers never intended to farm and went westward to locate in rapidly growing cities. Linked with the older cities of the East, the new aspiring metropolises extended far-reaching commercial tentacles. Transportation and its improvement concerned all settlers, whether in the city or on the farm. Private corporations built turnpikes along the more important routes of travel, but few ever turned a profit. A pattern of dispersed settlements and small local markets, combined with an American aversion to taxes, presented substantial problems for funding internal improvements. However, in 1811, the federal government financed the construction of the National Road, which extended from Cumberland, Maryland, to Vandalia, Illinois.

Until the advent of the railroads in the 1830s, travel by water, including inland river and canal travel, had always been cheaper, safer, faster, and more reliable than land travel. (In the 1770s, the learned Londoner Dr. Samuel Johnson had even theorized that the human frame could not withstand a motion of more than twenty-five miles an hour on land.) When settlement was along the seacoast in the eighteenth century, with trade conducted mainly by vessels plying the coastal waters or crossing the ocean, the problems of land travel could be surmounted. Even as settlement approached the Appalachian mountain range running roughly parallel to the coast, Americans could take advantage of streams and rivers that flow in a west-to-east direction. On the far side of the western slope of the Appalachians, however, rivers and streams run north to south. Rafts and flatboats allowed downward passage at reasonable cost, but the return upriver on foot or horseback or by keelboat was time consuming and expensive until the arrival of the steamboat in 1807.

THE TRANSPORTATION REVOLUTION

Few factors are as critical to creating new markets and to determining where and how people do business as the ability to move people and goods quickly and cheaply. Secretary of the Treasury Albert Gallatin had written in his official *Report on Roads and Canals* (1808) that "good roads and canals will shorten distances, facilitate commercial and personal intercourse, and unite, by a still more intimate community of interests, the most remote quarters of the United States." By 1815, some progress in surmounting the overland transportation barrier had occurred. Yet the great distances involved posed problems costly to solve in a nation of limited capital resources. In the United States, unlike in most of Europe, the national government played only a secondary role to private enterprise in establishing the nation's transportation and communication infrastructure—a difference important in shaping the rise of American enterprise and its corporations.[30]

After 1790, Western Europe experienced a frenzy of canal and road building. America joined in the enthusiasm with the end of the War of 1812. Private companies built toll roads and bridges, occasionally employing a technique of all-weather hard surfacing invented by the Scottish engineer J. L. MacAdam in the early nineteenth century. Other private companies built canals, but the amount of capital required for such ambitious projects forced the canal companies to turn to state and local governments for assistance in buying their stocks and bonds. State governments invested nearly $100 million in canals in the years 1815 to 1860. The most expensive of the canals, the 364-mile Erie Canal, begun in 1816, received $5 million from the New York legislature toward its total cost of $7 million, but a request for financial help from Congress was refused.[31]

Linking Lake Erie with the Hudson River Valley, the Erie Canal placed

New York City firmly astride the growing agricultural trade of the American West. With its completion in 1825, the cost of transporting freight from Buffalo to New York City plummeted from twenty cents to less than two cents per ton. "Gotham" now surged forward as the most populous and wealthiest of American cities. The Erie's success sparked a frenzy of canal construction. Not until the 1840s did this enthusiasm ebb, and not until the next decade (when more miles were abandoned than built) was it obvious that canals had been surpassed by a new marvel, the railroad. In all, 4,400 miles of canals had been constructed in three decades at a cost of over $125 million.

New technology played a minor role in canal building—the first phase of the transportation revolution. Then, as commercial pressure built for ever better and faster ways to transport people and goods, mechanical inventors scurried in a whirligig of tinkering to win fame and fortune by developing transportation breakthroughs. Robert Fulton's 1807 development of the *Clermont*, a steam-powered paddleboat, capable of a top speed of five miles per hour, demonstrated the potential importance of new technology to improving transportation.

Steamboats soon became a commonplace of American river and coastal trade. Designed for speed and carrying a bulky cargo, steamboats tied the agricultural economy of the West to the rest of the nation by means of a network of natural waterways. The expression "letting off steam," referring to releasing pressure before a ship's boiler exploded, became a valuable addition .to the English language. With the railroad's advent in the 1830s, followed by Samuel Morse's invention of the electric telegraph in 1844 with its ability to make near-instantaneous transmission of coded messages, the long-desired technological breakthroughs in land travel also began to materialize. With the railroad, the country would have a form of transportation that could be built almost anywhere, could operate in all seasons, and would prove able to stay on schedule even in severe weather.

TRANSPORTATION AND THE CONDUCT OF COMMERCE

Transportation innovations soon transformed the conduct of commerce. Lower transportation costs allowed for larger markets, opening up new inland markets for manufactured goods. After 1815, the all-purpose merchant, so important to colonial trade, faded in the face of ever-more-voluminous and varied types of commercial activity. Even the versatile merchant ship owner faltered before the rise of specialized shipping, or "packet," companies.

In 1818, the newly formed Black Ball Line, with four ships, introduced posted departures between New York and Liverpool, a ship sailing in each direction during the first week of each month "full or not." A typical cargo of a ship leaving New York might consist of "provisions, oil, lard, oilcakes, cheese, coals, and sundry Yankee" manufactured products. Other companies soon followed suit, using small and fast ships to carry mail, passengers, and goods regularly on a fixed route. Though started by merchants, the owners of the Black Ball Line quickly discovered that it required all their time. By sailing on a fixed schedule they had sharply reduced the uncertainty of ocean-borne commerce. As ship size increased in the next several decades, carrying capacity rose and freight tariffs fell. The Black Ball Line operated successfully for sixty years, until 1878.

Faced with a growing volume of trade, merchants after 1815 became increasingly specialized. Greater scale meant that fewer activities carried on intensively allowed for a more efficient and profitable operation. General merchants lacked the specialized knowledge or facilities required to do a good job in providing information and to broker goods at low cost, the two main functions of a middleman. Some merchants remained in export-import as wholesalers or redirected their activity as wholesalers to the domestic market. Others devoted themselves to retail; still others became brokers, auctioneers, jobbers, soliciting agents, and commission merchants in an ever-expanding web of commercial operations. Jobbers, as middlemen, provided warehousing services, often extended credit, and bought goods in bulk, only to break them into smaller lots for resale to their customers. Sometimes young men were employed as peddlers to wander country lanes with carts of merchandise. These new types of activities required a new word. In the 1830s, the older term "merchant" was joined by the word "business-man," an American contribution to the English language.[32]

Horatio Seymour wrote in 1852 of this new businessman: "He can now take advantage of the principle which lies at the heart of success in commercial and manufacturing pursuits, of doing one thing: doing it extensively and well. . . . It enables him to methodize his business." By the early 1830s, this new network of specialized wholesalers could avail itself of such sophisticated services as freight forwarders, credit reporting agencies, and commercial newspapers and trade magazines.[33]

Glenn Porter and Harold C. Livesay have written of the integrative importance of wholesalers in tying the economy together, at least through the Civil
War. Located in the larger inland cities as well as on the East Coast, they
usually dealt in a full line, such as hardware or dry goods. But some specialized in selling specific products such as hats or shoes or books, and the
same was true for retailers—the smaller the market served, the more general
the store. Almost all goods provided by wholesalers were unlabeled commodities, flour, sugar, or kegs of nails, although a very few branded products,
such as nationally known patent medicines, were carried.[34]

DOMESTIC MANUFACTURING AND THE FACTORY

The Embargo of 1807–8 and its culmination in the War of 1812 diminished
dependence on imported British goods. By the war's end, domestic manufacturing had increased to meet the growing American market. Surging demands for manufactured products led merchants to shift capital from countinghouse to the new factory. "The Americans," wrote the English traveler
Fanny Wright in 1819, "were fashioning a world within themselves."

In 1792, a young English mechanic, Samuel Slater (1768–1835), immi-
grated to the United States. To prevent the loss of England's industrial lead,
Parliament had barred the shipping of any textile machinery or its plans
abroad. But Slater had memorized the details of Richard Arkwright's cotton
spindles and knew how to construct them. Other British mechanics did the
same in France, Holland, and Belgium, indicating the difficulty even then of
keeping industrial secrets. In partnership with Moses Brown, owner of a
prosperous Rhode Island mercantile house (Brown University is named
after the family), Slater built America's first true factory along a waterfall in
Pawtucket, Rhode Island, containing seventy-two spindles—worked by nine
children, seven boys and two girls, aged nine to fourteen. Once spun, the
cotton was then "put out" to be woven in the old way by hand loom weavers
laboring at home. This combining of machine work in a factory with putting
out long remained a common if dwindling practice as textile production
grew greatly. Between 1820 and 1831, the capacity of American cotton mills
increased sixfold, and by the latter year a majority of textile workers labored
in factories.[35]

Indeed, several industries combined older practices with new factory
methods during the period from 1790 to 1850. Preliminary work was performed in factories by machine, and the finishing was done elsewhere using

hand tools. In traditional craft manufacturing, a master craftsman had to train, educate, and possibly lodge his apprentices and journeymen, whose skill, energy, and diligence largely determined the workshop's profit. He also led his helpers in the manufacturing and design of products, while in addition attracting business, handling sales, and keeping books. It required an exceptionally intelligent master craftsman to handle all these activities adroitly.[36]

In comparison to craft production, the factory system offered substantial savings through labor specialization and the use of unskilled workers to handle repetitive tasks done by machines. Factory production of an entire item also eliminated the high transportation costs associated with putting out. Most important, employers in the factory system exerted greater control over both the worker and the productive process, such as a greater ability to match worker skills to job requirements.

Along with these advantages, the early factory owners had their own peculiar problems. They needed to learn to use machines efficiently; to recruit, train, discipline, and retain their workforce; and to plan and maintain work schedules and calculate costs. Finally, they had to secure a market for their goods and ensure their delivery. Often, as most of the factory owners were merchants, they relied on their trading connections to sell their output. Because the scale and nature of their businesses tended to be considerably grander and more complex than the usual commercial or craft business, early factories suffered from undermanagement. Factory owners required experience with the new type of industrial organization before they could fully realize the advantages of factory over craft production, and this came only with time. From this perspective, the combining of workshop and factory production in the period from 1790 to the Civil War was a necessary transitional or intermediate stage between old and new manufacturing processes.

Centered in New England—where an abundance of waterfalls on rivers provided the means to turn the waterwheels and thus the drives that powered the machinery—the infant American textile industry gained impetus from the disruption of trade with Britain prior to and during the War of 1812. Pioneer mill owner Francis Cabot Lowell was descended from the most prominent of Boston families during a time when such connections represented the key to commercial success. From age eighteen to age thirty-five, he worked as an all-purpose merchant. He then visited England from 1810 to 1812, studying Lancashire textile mills with the full cooperation of owners—who did not realize his intention of setting himself up as their Yankee rival.

Returning to America, Lowell worked with a talented American master mechanic to assemble a power loom. His family connections provided him with financial backing in the Boston mercantile community, and he soon organized a group of ten men, known as the "Boston Associates," to incorporate the Boston Manufacturing Company in 1813. Within a year and a half, Lowell's company had constructed America's largest factory in Waltham, Massachusetts, at the then-staggering cost of $400,000. By the time of Lowell's death at forty-two, he had shown the way for a successful American textile industry capable of competing even with the English. The Waltham mill by 1825 had already paid dividends in excess of the original investment. Subsequently named the "Waltham System," Lowell's method employed an integrated factory production of cotton (spinning, weaving, bleaching, dyeing, printing, and cutting) under unified management, with substantial capitalization to allow for large-scale operation. After Lowell's premature death in 1817, the Boston Associates opened nine factories within fifteen years, each factory specializing in a particular textile product. The only part of the process not integrated was sales—for this the owners relied on commissioned agents. One mill that was placed in a pastoral setting near Boston and named for Lowell became the celebrated site of a model community that drew thousands of visitors, but its history awaits the next chapter.[37]

The movement of capital from commerce to industry only slowly transformed a market revolution into an industrial revolution before the Civil War. A growing home market nurtured infant American industries, and manufacturers won protective tariffs from Congress as early as 1816 and 1817. They encountered, however, opposition from agrarian interests, which understandably resisted paying more for imported goods while gaining nothing in return.

With the expanding market economy came a constant pressure to increase production. An increasing variety of goods had to be manufactured in large enough amounts to encourage and satisfy growing demands, while making them affordable to more of the population. A key to advancing the new industrial order was mass production based on interchangeable parts, an approach that would in time lead to the assembly line. Its beginnings are found at the end of the eighteenth century in the work of one man, Eli Whitney (1765–1825). A New Englander, Whitney had graduated from Yale

University at age twenty-seven, in 1792. He then went to South Carolina to tutor the children of a large plantation owner.[38]

ELI WHITNEY'S VISION OF MASS PRODUCTION

At this time, tobacco sat on the throne of southern agriculture amid anxiety that soil depletion would prove ruinous to the region. A small amount of sea-island cotton was raised along the coast of South Carolina, but it could not be grown inland. Another variety of upland short-staple cotton could, but its thistle contained a green seed. This had to be removed at an average rate of a pound a day per worker, making it uneconomical. Demand for cotton had been fed by the new mechanized mills of England, as people eagerly sought the greater comfort and washability of cotton clothing. Indigenous to India, cotton was not important in Europe until the late eighteenth century, when Indian cotton known as "calico" become more than a luxury.

Whitney solved the seed problem in 1793 by designing a mechanical "gin" (engine) to separate the fiber from the seed. Consisting of a wooden cylinder turned by a crank, with wire teeth that revolved around slots in a bar, the gin replaced the labor of ten workers when hand-operated and fifty workers when horse-operated. This invention, by lowering the cost of preparing the raw fiber, opened the way for short-staple cotton cultivation in the interior of South Carolina and Georgia, and later, after 1810, in the rich southwestern lands extending from Alabama to Texas. The South possessed the soil and climate to grow the raw stuff that the British textile revolution had made one of the world's main commodities. Cotton production rose from 3,135 bales a year in 1790 to half a million bales in 1820.

After 1815, King Cotton reigned over the South's economy. It soon accounted for more than half the value of American exports—the domestic textile industry purchased about a fifth of the South's cotton crop. (Cotton textiles coincidentally also made up about half of Britain's export trade.) Cotton revitalized the southern economy, making slavery once again highly profitable for the planters. Raising cotton demanded sustained attention over a long growing period, and this lent itself to the use of slave labor. A characteristic of American slave labor was the high rate of labor force participation: women, young children, the elderly, and the infirm as a rule worked long and hard hours. The price of slaves at auction soared; the South's entrenched "peculiar institution" of human chattel property (the value of which some southerners had questioned on economic, and less frequently moral, grounds) assumed a greater regional importance than before. Increasingly, southern writers would defend their highly profitable "peculiar institution" in a variety of ways.

An economic system nakedly based on human exploitation and the laying on of the lash increasingly rested on the ideological assumption that the African race was rightfully regarded as an inferior race. In this manner, slave owners rationalized their benefiting handsomely from the enforced labor and suffering of other human beings. The racism that the planter class thus appealed to was endemic in white society.

Domestic cotton growing also encouraged the American arrival of the factory system in the form of textile mills. Whitney, however, did not make a fortune from his invention of the gin. Others manufactured this relatively simple machine and refused to compensate him. When the courts failed to protect his patent rights, a disappointed Whitney looked elsewhere for his fortune.

In 1776, George Washington ordered the building of an arsenal to manufacture guns and ammunition for his army, and the town of Springfield, Massachusetts, was selected for the site. The Springfield Armory helped to arm Washington's troops and in so doing began the industrialization of the Connecticut River Valley, which in turn became the nursery of the American machine tool industry. Learning in 1797 that the army intended to place a large order of muskets with the Springfield Armory, Whitney wrote to the secretary of the treasury requesting a contract "to Manufacture Ten or Fifteen Thousand Stand of Arms" in twenty-eight months, a very brief time if one used traditional artisan production.

In 1798, the government advanced Whitney money toward building the innovative jigs for the guiding tools that he had designed as the key to production. But from the first, snags were encountered in meeting the deadline. In one letter to the secretary of the treasury, Whitney explained that his still-crude machines presented problems but insisted that when perfected they would replicate the various components of the musket so uniformly that all units of the same part would be interchangeable. The whole musket could then be readily assembled by unskilled workers.

Such was Whitney's plan. In practice, the precision tools his process required proved beyond the primitive state of the mechanic's art, and this remained largely true until well after the Civil War. To fill the order, Whitney's workers, or "fitters," needed to combine machine production with conventional craft techniques, finishing the work by hand and taking ten years to fulfill the contract. Whitney's ideas on standardization and inter-changeable parts, initially called the "armory practice," after 1850 became known as "the American System." Whitney received greatly exaggerated credit as its inventor; but, as David Hounshell has written, his real contribution was in promoting mechanization and interchangeable parts. The effective execution of these ideas required the involvement of many anonymous mechanics over a considerable period of time. Standardization was a way of simplifying tasks to make them repetitive, allowing quickly trained workers to be highly productive. Moreover, as David Landes has perceived, an American "market free of the local and regional preferences and the class and status distinctions that prevailed in Europe . . . [was] ready to accept standardized articles."[39]

Other firearms manufacturers, including Simeon North of Middletown, Connecticut, and Samuel Colt of Hartford, Connecticut (inventor of the revolving pistol, which bore his name), and the federal armories in Spring-field and Harpers Ferry, Virginia, employed the American System in producing reliable, inexpensive guns marveled at by European gunsmiths. As Colt boasted, "There is nothing that cannot be made by machine." The effort to employ interchangeable parts spread quickly, for it met the needs of an American industry short of skilled craftsmen. From weapons to mechanical harvesters to sewing machines to typewriters and, by century's end, bicycles —uniformity of parts became the goal. More important than the question of Whitney's role in the development of interchangeable parts, or even the recent questioning of whether he actually did invent the cotton gin, is the fact that Americans elevated him to their pantheon of heroes. Every nation creates the heroes it wants and believes it deserves, and Americans, in lionizing Whitney as an icon of ingenuity, celebrated the inventor as businessman. The message was clear: the United States valued inventors as practical innovators rather than as searchers for abstract knowledge. Not afraid to dirty their hands, they affirmed the values of American individualism. For Americans, inventing was not to be an intellectual exercise but an effort at personal enrichment through designing the proverbial better mousetrap.[40]

The expense of American labor compared to European labor caused American manufacturers to be eager to develop machines and tools to enhance productivity. Americans prided themselves that their workers were more inventive and resourceful than European workers, although admittedly not the equal of the European craftsman. There is more support for the latter claim than for the former in the early national period; the United States long benefited greatly from borrowing advanced European technology. But Americans did exhibit a special fascination with laborsaving gadgets, resulting from the high cost of labor. Nathan Rosenberg, in *Technology and American Economic Growth*, has stated: "Much of American inventive activity in the first half of the nineteenth century aimed at substituting abundant natural resources for scarcer capital and labor."[41]

Moreover, he noted that the American patent system encouraged technological advances by ordinary people, with the result that the nation's productivity advanced rapidly. However, it was in technology's commercial applications that Americans displayed a national genius that gave them their competitive edge, demonstrating early on an undeniable prowess in making inventions and ideas pay off. A mechanic in a Lowell mill invented the sewing machine in 1846; but it was Isaac Singer who in 1852 added a treadle operation, freeing both hands to guide the cloth and thus commercializing such machines. Opening a factory in New York in 1853, Singer went on to pioneer such sales techniques as installment buying and customer service. His name is memorialized by history, while the luckless inventor from the Lowell mill, Elias Howe, is all but forgotten.[42]

MERCHANT TO BUSINESSMAN

American businessmen knew well the importance of adjusting quickly to their markets. America's economic future by 1820 clearly lay with its large and growing home market, which within a few decades would be the world's biggest. Historians often point to the years between 1815 and 1830 as the time the agrarian household economy gave way to a market economy in the North. To prosper, American industry needed to meet this market's special needs. The domestic demand for cheap standardized goods speeded the transfer of capital from mercantile activity to manufacturing. The growth of capitalism had long been primarily commercial, and before 1820, as already noted, it was comparatively rare to find production organized on a large scale. Industrial manufacturing grew in response to a ready mass market for inexpensive goods, and the domestic American market, with its large number of middle-class farm families, gave American-made products a characteristic style: a stress on simplicity in design and structure and an avoidance of ornament and ostentation. The absence in America of a strong craft tradition, of commitment to fine workmanship, encouraged this development. In

France, as economic historian David Landes has noted, a craftsman derived his status largely from that of his customers. In America, however, his counterpart could concentrate on making money through emphasizing quantity, not quality. The distinctly American expression "making money," in fact, dates to the 1830s.[43]

American circumstances assured a bright future for business in the early national period. The population had scattered to find new opportunities. An entrepreneurial culture permeated American life, along with a triumphal optimism that celebrated the individual's ability to make his own economic destiny. A sustainable conviction of American identity as individuals of enterprise and innovation, egalitarian and freedom loving, had been created early on. The United States was a nation with an abundance of natural resources and a stable government whose laws protected property while also promoting commerce and economic change. Few entrenched interests or social forces—excepting the slave-owning planter class of the South, a handful of New England intellectuals, and a few radical workingmen—challenged the society's strong commercial values.[44]

An 1854 report on American and British manufacturing by Joseph Whitworth commented that British workers with fewer opportunities for employment than Americans had organized to resist new technology, which threatened their jobs. But in the United States, change, although destabilizing, only seemed to be perceived as offering new opportunities. Henry Clay, in 1832, referred to the United States as the "land of the self-made man," the first recorded use of that quintessential Americanism. Confronted with massive depressions in 1819 and 1837 as the economy began to exhibit boom-and-bust cycles, a few Americans enthused over ideas of a cooperative commonwealth based on the mutual interests of all producers. Some of them even formed short-lived communitarian colonies. Most Americans, however, regarded self-interest and competition as engines of economic progress. They remained satisfied with the nation's individualistic get-up-and-go materialist culture. Already, in an 1836 article in *Knickerbockers' Magazine*, Washington Irving referred both reverentially and disparagingly to "the almighty dollar."[45]

CHAPTER FOUR

Antebellum America, 1820–1860

It may . . . be safely affirmed that industry can only be found where artificial wants have crept in, and have acquired the character of necessities.—JOHN PENDLETON KENNEDY, Miscellaneous Papers *(1849)*

It is strange to see with what feverish ardor the Americans pursue their own welfare. . . . Everyone wants to either to increase his own resources or to provide fresh ones for his progeny.—ALEXIS DE TOCQUEVILLE, Democracy in America *(1835)*

In 1855, P. T. Barnum (1810–91), America's first great impresario, traveled to London and delivered a lecture, "The Art of Money-Getting," to thousands of Englishmen eager for "Hints and Helps; or How to Make a Fortune." With their nation only a little more than a half-century old, Americans believed they had something to teach the world about success and business. Remarkably, others agreed. In 1851, the British government sent a mission to the United States to study the American "armory system" of manufacture.[1] The possibilities of profit in cheap cotton fabrics, simple tables and chairs, and inexpensive shoes and clocks reflected the increasing importance of factory mass production in consumer goods for a domestic market. Westward movement and the rapid growth of the domestic economy turned America increasingly inward. Rapidly declining costs of transportation and communication set the stage for a dramatic restructuring of the economy. With the advent of the railroad and the telegraph Americans raced to meet the future. The darkest cloud on the horizon was slavery and the profound contradiction it represented to American ideals of freedom as tied up with economic independence and ownership of one's own labor.

COMING OF AGE

Numerous changes from 1820 to 1860 signaled a quickening pace in the movement toward an industrial economy. The nation's population grew in these decades at six times the rate of Europe's; its economy expanded at an even faster rate. Alexis de Tocqueville, the celebrated French observer of the New World, wrote in the 1830s of America's "unprecedented release of energy" and remarked: "What astonishes me in the United States is not so much the marvelous grandeur of some undertaking as the innumerable multitude of small ones."[2] Americans often found themselves uprooted from familiar occupations and ways of life as cities and factories thrust forward. By midcentury, railroads already challenged the rivers and canals as the dominant inland transportation system. The factory system was replacing both craft and home production as manufacturing strove to keep pace with market expansion. The generation of the 1830s and 1840s, a "breathless generation," regarded with awe and astonishment the advent of the railroad, the sewing machine, the Colt revolver, the telegraph, the mechanical harvester and reaper, and numerous other useful devices. Nevertheless, mechanization had not taken full command. Industrialization before 1860 occurred primarily in textiles, the milling of paper and flour, and what was known as "small ware" or machine tools.

Commercial capitalism connected farm to city, worker to employer, and consumer to manufacturer and middleman in an ever-expanding network of tightening interdependencies. Americans, eager to switch from homemade goods to newly available commercial ones, were prepared to sell farms for profit and move on, change occupations, or start bootstrap businesses to earn the wherewithal for consumerism. P. T. Barnum, in his lecture "The Art of Money Getting," reflected a strain of American optimism when he noted as his opening remark that "in the United States, where we have more land than people, it is not at all difficult for persons in good health to make money."[3]

The nation experienced an industrial transformation even as it moved west, the two processes feeding on each other. Capital and people could be imported from Europe. Immigrants from Ireland, Germany, and England landed on the docks of eastern cities; Americans from the established East traveled westward. Between 1820 and 1860 the economy grew more regionally specialized, as the vastness of the United States with its varied climates and resources encouraged regional differences in a way few European nations could experience. Manufacturing expanded in the Northeast, while the South continued to cultivate staple crops for export. The West of the Upper Mississippi River Valley and the Ohio River Valley engaged in commercial agriculture oriented to urban markets, and its population rose from under 1 million at the period's start to over 9 million at its end.

In emphasizing the momentum of change, attention must be focused on developments occurring in the North and the East of the United States. As Tocqueville discerned in 1831, the Americans of enterprise and progress were those who inhabited the regions where slavery did not exist.[4] This is not to deny the significance of distinctive developments in the West and even the South; but these are related in the main, though not exclusively, to agriculture. That the South's slave-grown cotton financed much of the North's industrialization, as well as represented a critical factor in the latter's commerce, banking, insurance, and shipping, cannot be overstated. Slave labor, as historian Charles Sellers has noted, "extended the market and multiplied capital, [as] wage labor became more profitable." But, as the same historian also observed, "a free self-motivated labor energized growth, [and] bound labor both offended liberal morality and impeded capitalist progress."[5]

It is in the North, not the South, that protean changes occurred. In 1861, for example, the South accounted for only 15 percent of the nation's factories, with most located in a few urban areas, such as the ironworks at Richmond, Virginia. While cotton growing remained relatively unchanged, the mechanized reaper and the steel plow allowed a farmer in the West to greatly expand land under his cultivation by the 1840s. Still, much of the Mississippi Valley and the South retained the frontier-rural style of life dominant in the early republic.[6]

Agriculture remained key to the nation's economy, but with the advantage of hindsight we can discern its slow retreat from center stage. Between 1840 and 1860, the percentage of the workforce engaged in agriculture declined from 63 to 53 percent, and Americans employed in manufacturing rose from 14 percent to 19 percent of the workforce—the cutting edge of occupational change. Work for wages, a relative rarity at the century's beginning, would by midcentury become the norm in the rapidly growing urban areas of the Northeast and the Midwest. Regional differences offered economic advantages while heightening sectional tensions over the future of slavery. Sectional strife that threatened to erupt after the Mexican War led to the acquisition of the Southwest in 1848. The new territories posed the question of shifting sectional power; as they became states they would inevitably alter the close political balance of North and South.

THE MODERNIZATION OF OUTLOOK

Historian Richard D. Brown has described the "modernization of outlook" that occurred among Americans in these years. He cites an Englishman visiting New England in 1844, who, to his amazement, found that every home, including rural households, prominently displayed a mass-produced clock in a mahogany case with a "looking-glass plate front" turned out in the Connecticut River Valley factories of Eli Terry, Seth Thomas, and Chauncey Jerome and sold near and far by Yankee peddlers for five dollars. The overseas traveler also remarked that the residents used the phrase "I reckon" or "I calculate" as synonyms for "I believe" or "I think." A growing industrial economy placed greater emphasis on the structuring of time. The New York diarist Philip Hone reported that 500,000 clocks were made annually in Connecticut in the early 1840s. Even farmers, involved in a market economy, found it increasingly necessary to think and act differently. They recognized that the practical value of an idea lay in its use. Americans were learning to live in a rapidly changing environment that required new ways of adapting. But this, of course, had been true from the moment of their arrival in a strange continent.[7]

Tocqueville observed as early as 1831 that Americans were relentless in pursuing material gain. The many groups in Europe, ranging from poets to aristocrats, that despised commerce and moneymaking had few counterparts in the United States. Five years later the Reverend Thomas Hunt published a best seller, *The Book of Wealth: In Which It Is Proved from the Bible That It Is the Duty of Every Man to Become Rich*. As a people who relocated often in search of new opportunities, Americans regarded change as progress and did not cling to the familiar. Ralph Waldo Emerson, in the essay "Self Reliance," advised his countrymen that "a foolish consistency is the hobgoblin of little minds."

Railroads and packet shipping lines made travel and shipping more predictable, and by midcentury, only a few years after its introduction in 1844, messages using Samuel Morse's ingenious code were being sent over 3,000 miles of telegraph lines to coordinate far-flung business operations. By 1861, the first transcontinental telegraph connection was established. Daily life, especially in the cities, came to be increasingly dictated by scheduled working hours, as the imperatives of a market economy made themselves increasingly evident in daily life. The sixty-year-old New York merchant Philip Hone plaintively entered in his diary, on November 28, 1844: "This world is going too fast. Improvements, Politics, Reform, Religion—all fly. Railroads, steamers packets, race against time and beat it hollow. . . . By and by we shall have balloons and pass over to Europe between sun and sun. Oh, for the good old days of heavy post-coaches and speed at the rate of six miles an hour."[8]

What was truly revolutionary in transportation, however, was that innovations allowed for remarkable regularity and even scheduling of long-distance travel, even as costs declined dramatically. Commercial expansion accelerated with improvements in transportation, population gain, westward movement, and urbanization—and the railroad played a critical factor in these developments. A trip to Chicago that had taken Hone nearly three weeks in the early 1840s could be done by rail in less than three days in 1860. By the 1850s railroads served as a catalyst to the opening of vast new possibilities for business activity.

Movement west of the Appalachians revealed rich new resources, especially in anthracite coal, lead, copper, iron, and oil. In 1849, the discovery of gold in California fanned a feverish westward rush as would-be miners crossed the plains or took coastal ships to an isthmian portage in Nicaragua. The transatlantic trade continued in importance past midcentury, but it no longer dominated the economy. By then, America's domestic economy nearly rivaled in size that of Great Britain, the world's greatest industrial power, and it was growing at a much faster rate. The structure of the economy was being transformed.

By 1812, Jefferson would write: "Our manufacturing are now nearly on a footing with those of England. She has not a single improvement which we do not possess, and many of them [are] better adapted by ourselves to our ordinary use."[9] Jefferson overstated. Britain at the time of his writing was still the "world's workshop," accounting for a quarter of the globe's industrial production as late as 1850. By 1860, however, the United States was among the world's leading industrial nations and was possibly second, to

Britain. In the half century after 1810, the total value of manufactures had increased tenfold, from $200 million to roughly $2 billion.

Confident about their country's future, American businessmen readily adapted their business practices to rapidly swelling markets. American merchants and industrialists turned inward to focus on the domestic market, developing networks to facilitate this trade. The general merchant primarily oriented to the maritime import and export trade who traded in a broad range of goods and services—so long essential to the colonial economy—yielded to more narrowly focused commercial agents. An increased volume of activity forced them to specialize by either commodity or function. Some traded in specific commodities; others offered services, such as shipping or finance. Over time, large wholesale houses opened up regional and local offices to facilitate the sale and movement of goods and to provide reliable information to the central office.

The historic parochialism of American business can be traced in origin to the decades preceding the Civil War. A pattern soon emerged, which persisted until the 1970s: American business oriented to a relatively self-sufficient and rapidly growing home market. The rise of cities, with their networks of middlemen linking together established eastern cities, mushrooming western towns, and the cotton markets of the South, had established a new type of American economy free of its colonial roots. In 1830, there were twenty-three cities with 10,000 or more inhabitants; by 1860, there were over a hundred. A visitor to St. Louis in June 1847 was astonished to find along the riverfront or levee some fifty large steamboats taking on and discharging cargoes from New Orleans and other cities on the Mississippi: "The whole of the levee is covered as far as the eye can see with . . . thousands of barrels of flour and bags of corn, hogsheads of tobacco, and immense piles of lead."[10]

LOWELL: FROM MODEL COMMUNITY TO FACTORY TOWN

A less-picturesque scene than the levees along the Mississippi but one more telling for the future was provided by the dense black smoke issuing from factory stacks in the numerous mill towns of New England. One mill town in particular warrants a closer look. As noted in the previous chapter, the Boston Associates, in 1822, constructed a complex of cotton mills and dormitories twenty-five miles north of Boston and named it Lowell. A single canal was built parallel to a river that had a large drop in elevation and four-story-high factories—twenty-two by 1835—laced in a line on the land between the canal and the river. Water from the canal entered the factories, dropped through the power-producing wheels or turbines and exited into the river below. To attract a reliable low-cost workforce, the decision was made to employ the unmarried daughters of New England farm families—and since these families would not risk their daughters' morals and health in an ordinary industrial setting, Lowell was built as a model community. Mostly between the ages of eighteen and twenty-two, the girls were expected to work only a few years in the mills before returning home with their savings as a dowry.

At Lowell, they resided in carefully chaperoned company dormitories with facilities for religious and cultural training and published their own literary magazine. The model mill town received considerable praise from both American and foreign visitors, including Anthony Trollope, Alexis de Tocqueville, Harriet Martineau, and Charles Dickens, Trollope going so far as to praise Lowell as "the realization of a commercial Utopia." But Lowell's life as a model community proved short-lived. In 1834, the mill management slashed wages by 25 percent, and the workers struck: "It was not the reduction in wages," said one of the strikers, "but that haughty overbearing disposition, that purse-proud insolence, which was becoming more and more apparent."[11] Over time, working conditions deteriorated and fewer and fewer young women sought work in Lowell.[12]

FACTORY HANDS AND WAGE OPERATIVES

Irish and French Canadian immigrants supplemented the "rosy cheeked farm maidens" in Lowell's factories in the 1840s. By then the Boston Associates had sold Lowell to outsiders, who were determined to squeeze out profits. The few visitors now found more to fault than to praise. In 1846, Lowell, with a population of 30,000, was the nation's leading textile center, and it was reported that the workers worked thirteen hours a day in the summertime and from daylight to darkness in the winter for a six-day work week averaging seventy-two to seventy-eight hours per week, with a mere half hour a day allowed for the noonday meal, the major meal of the day. The six-day week remained the general rule until the century's end—the diurnal workday, from dawn to dusk, simply perpetuated the norm of a preindustrial society.

But what made the long hours of the Lowell worker noteworthy was the tension and the exhausting labor conditions. In mill work, labor occurred under highly confining and supervised circumstances and often involved such unpleasantness as forced "speed-ups." Farmwork, in contrast to factory work, was seasonal, intermittent, varied, often casual and self-regulated, and usually done in a familiar family environment. Even the craftsmen's workroom with its camaraderie of a small group of peers lacked the grinding labor of the mill factory. From the late 1820s onward, the labor movement fought for the introduction of the ten-hour day, which the Martin Van Buren administration (1837–41) gave federal workers in 1840. When, in the late 1880s, this became the general practice, organized labor demanded an eight-hour day.

The tyranny of the factory clock and whistle demanded a new regularity on the part of the laborer. Specialized machine work required a disciplined and coordinated labor force, capable of integrating production between different "task gangs." Nor would time-pressured performance remain restricted to factory production—"time discipline" also became increasingly critical, as new forms of communication and transportation structured and routinized commerce and transportation. Even the average night's sleep of nine to ten hours at the start of the nineteenth century declined to a little over eight by its end, as increasingly inexpensive and effective artificial lighting dispelled darkness for purposes of both work and play.

E. P. Thompson, a preeminent historian of the English laboring class, has chronicled how the rise of an industrial system profoundly altered people's notion of time, from one based on the calendar to one based on the clock. He termed the dominant feature of work prior to the industrial economy as a "task-orientation," based on the worker's own sense of a customary pacing in his or her activity, as well as seasonal demands such as seeding or harvesting. Intermittent activity alternated with periods of lassitude, when much socializing occurred. The industrial era introduced, according to Thompson, a "time discipline," characterized by a machine-like pattern of regular work—incessant and tension creating—with little opportunity for relief. Factory workers were increasingly paid wages in terms of hours worked rather than the piece rate of the putting-out system.

Although possibly overdrawn, Thompson's analysis depicts the dramatic transformation of work in the modern world and helps explain the Western world's preoccupation in the nineteenth century with standardizing time. The gathering of a large number of workers in one place, such as a mill or a factory, certainly offered new possibilities to control costs and to demand a regularity of output, and, as the American sociologist Thorstein Veblen commented, the machine "compels the adaptation of the workman to his work, rather than the adaptation of the work to the workman." Under these conditions, it is understandable that careless work practices, absenteeism, and quitting became common in factory work as a way of resisting imposed discipline.[13]

Even in labor-short America, unskilled factory hands could be easily hired —and fired. Factory owners complained about the lack of reliable workers and the high wages they needed to pay, but they demonstrated little interest in the welfare of the workforce, and the 1830s witnessed widespread labor unrest, as collegial craft relationships between master and journeyman based on the old apprenticeship system with its familial-like connections weakened. Skilled craft workers, still largely outside the factory system, often organized unions, and in the 1830s local trade unions in large eastern cities occasionally created short-lived "radical workingmen" political parties. But unskilled workers had little leverage. Hired by the hour, wageworkers were let go when they became a liability due to illness, old age, or lack of work. A reliance on women and children, who could be paid considerably less than adult males for routine mill work, persisted until the turn of the century. But until the Civil War, only a relatively few Americans worked for wages, and many who did still labored as part of a small workforce of several people who retained intimate ties with the owner, though not necessarily as one big happy family.

As early as the 1830s, Thomas Carlyle bemoaned the weakening of traditional, paternalistic ties between classes in Britain, denouncing the relationship between mill owners and their "hands" as a "cash-nexus" based only on self-interest. Many Americans, however, welcomed the cash-nexus. They viewed paternalism, with its clear distinction between superior and subordinate (and demands for the latter's cap-doffing deference), as contrary to the republican principles of the Revolution. For them, the impersonal business arrangement of the "contract for wages"—with the worker always free to accept or reject the offered wage and working conditions—established a "voluntary" relationship of two "willing parties" suitable for a democracy. This view soon prevailed in the courts.

By the 1830s, judges had begun to regard employer-employee relations as a "free labor contract," and, as with all contracts, they considered the voluntary agreement of the parties, not the merits or fairness of their arrangement, as the critical test of legal validity. As long as both parties had "willingly" entered into an agreement in good faith, it was legally enforceable.

The assumption was that all parties were peers, even when this was manifestly false. A worker accepting employment under vile conditions might simply be making a choice between starving and surviving. Only a half century earlier, with a paternalistic ethos still lingering, judges might have scrutinized a contract in terms of fairness and merit, but no longer, as an increasingly laissez-faire legal system ignored the fact that one party to the labor contract was ordinarily less free to refuse such a "contract." All that mattered now was that both parties "willingly" entered into a relationship.

In the historic *Commonwealth v. Hunt* (1840), the Massachusetts Supreme Court held that unions as such were not illegal organizations and that collective action by labor did not necessarily constitute a crime. This overturned the reasoning behind decisions in Philadelphia in 1806 and 1815 and in New York in 1810 convicting strikers for engaging in a criminal conspiracy to compel others to join their union. Yet the view that labor and capital were partners whose well-being was codependent generally prevailed.

A few labor radicals employed the rhetoric of class conflict. However, many, if not most, Americans regarded this as a foreign import irrelevant to a nation of "self-made men," where wage work represented the bottom rung on a ladder climbed to self-employment. The apprentices and journeymen who labored in the small workshops of the industrial system still hoped to acquire the skill and capital to go out on their own, viewing wage earning as only a temporary stage. Partly due to this entrepreneurial vision of free labor, union membership lagged far behind such countries as Great Britain and France. This was reinforced by the white workers' sense of superiority to blacks, regardless of whether they were slave or free. As David Roediger has written in an important study, "Working class formation and the systematic development of a sense of whiteness went hand in hand."[14]

A NEW INDUSTRIAL SYSTEM

The importance of the factory system to the pre–Civil War economy should not be exaggerated. The great bulk of production still occurred outside the factory gates, in artisan workshops and in a proliferation of small and medium-sized manufactories or by the putting-out system. Raising capital for large manufacturing ventures posed problems, and factories with inadequate capital often lacked the reserves to withstand the sharp business downturns that occurred in 1837 and 1857. Ambitious mechanics with technical knowledge found that banks were reluctant to extend loans without collateral, which the aspiring entrepreneurs often lacked. The capitalization of the early factory system rested on money derived from mercantile activity. Many manufacturing firms represented a partnership of merchants and mechanics, with the former providing the required capital and using their trading connections to purchase supplies or sell the end product. Firms managed by several owners often suffered from poor definition of authority and consequent friction. Sometimes a merchant financed a new factory by incorporating and selling stock to close personal acquaintances, but until well after the Civil War this was the exception rather than the rule. Most factories still did not involve huge investments. As late as 1860, the average number of workers in factories other than textile mills was fewer than ten.

Only slowly did the new industrial system spread through the economy. After 1820 the factory system dominated the textile industry, a decade later it transformed carpet manufacturing, and by the 1840s factory operatives prepared metal works and iron. Moreover, American manufacturers of small arms, located chiefly in the Connecticut River Valley, had developed specialized milling machines to cut out components to a prescribed shape at high speed so as to have interchangeable parts.[15]

The pace of industrialization gained momentum by midcentury. The competitive pressures of enlarging markets and the growing supply of unskilled labor gave master craftsmen and merchant capitalists incentives to reduce labor costs by dividing tasks and sometimes assigning production quotas to foremen subcontractors. Skilled craft workers often found their ability to either protect their job security or to go out on their own greatly diminished. As the industrial system advanced, a new terminology entered the language. According to the *Oxford English Dictionary*, the term "employer" can be found in Shakespeare but was only infrequently used until the second quarter of the nineteenth century, the very time the word "employee" is first introduced.

Important sectors of American manufacturing, such as shoemaking, clung tenaciously to traditional artisan and putting-out production until the Civil War, and in many cities, the factory system coexisted with traditional small-scale manufacture and the putting-out system. Rapidly swelling populations created demands for the products and services of traditional crafts. Flour milling, with an average of only two workers per mill, produced as late as 1850 an output valued greatly in excess of the value of textile production of threads, yarn, and cloth done in factories. In 1860, the average value of the capital invested in an American cotton textile factory was just under $109,000 and the average number of employees was 130. The sharp increase in volume of production in the period from 1790 to 1850 was largely due, as already noted, to an expansion of traditional craft and putting-out production. But the potential for profit in meeting the market's rising demands for mass-manufactured products created a powerful incentive for innovation. The result was an increasing reliance on a new machine-oriented technology, much of it derived initially from English or other European examples.

For their part, workers clung, when possible, to traditional craft practices, even when placed in a factory setting. The shoemakers of Lynn, Massachusetts, had begun their local industry late in the eighteenth century on the basis of the domestic outwork or putting-out system. But between 1830 and 1860, shoe production in Lynn became increasingly centralized in factories relying on machinery. Still using the artisan tradition, the workers struggled vainly to retain control over their tools and the product of their labors, failing to fathom the vast changes in manufacturing and its financing under way. Their thinking clung to an older model of a relatively simple master-workman relationship. This tendency to persist with past practices remained so widespread that at the end of the nineteenth century Frederick Taylor, the founder of "scientific management," began his factory studies primarily to end it.

The "new labor history" of the 1970s demonstrated that what Taylor considered "soldiering" or dawdling often represented efforts by craft workers to protect their sense of self-worth by clinging to customary work arrangements and craft traditions—a desire that clashed with the need for control over the manufacturing process on the part of factory owners eager for cost-cutting innovations. Difficulties experienced by all involved in adjusting to the radical transformation of the workplace are understandable, as new machinery increasingly acted as an agent of sweeping and even violent change. As early as 1829, Harvard professor Jacob Bigelow coined the word "technology" to denote this new process of industrial transformation.[16]

America remained an agricultural country and economy well into the nineteenth century, and agriculture easily remained the nation's most important business until the 1890s. But farmers increasingly bought many of the goods they consumed or used from an impersonal marketplace instead of producing them on the farm, and even farming was changing. Improvements in farm machinery increased the amount of acreage a farmer could cultivate. In 1831, Cyrus McCormick invented his mechanical reaper, and four years later John Deere perfected his steel plow. Greater productivity, improved transportation, and distributive networks spreading from large cities to small cities to towns and villages increasingly linked farmers to national and even international markets and made them major consumers of manufactured goods.

THE RISE OF AN URBAN ORDER

The growth of American cities had exceeded the growth of the national population as a whole prior to 1820, but only slightly—increasing from 5 percent of the total American population in 1790 to 7 percent thirty years later. In contrast, the rise of cities after 1820 occurred at a speed and magnitude inconceivable to the preceding generation. As manufacturing became more important to a market economy, low transportation costs provided the impetus for concentrating things in cities. By 1860 nearly one out of every five Americans resided in cities, and almost one out of ten lived in the "great cities" of 100,000 inhabitants or more. Large cities could be found in all parts of the nation, including the gold rush boomtown of San Francisco, nestled on a bay near the Pacific coast, and the cotton town of Mobile on the Gulf of Mexico. As the volume and velocity of trade soared after 1820, the merchant as jack-of-all-trades retreated before the rise of more specialized business types: jobbers, commission merchants, retailers, brokers, exporters, insurers, bankers, and many others.

Adam Smith had carefully considered the essential role cities played in promoting labor specialization. He noted that city dwellers had to manufacture goods to exchange for food, fuel, and raw materials; the larger the city, the greater the market area or hinterland that was needed to draw upon. Market size, in turn, largely determined both task differentiation and the division of labor, and urban centers provided clusters of populations that were dependent upon shopkeepers and tradesmen for their consumer goods.[17]

Smith believed that the growth of cities was indispensable for the extension and development of an exchange economy and labor specialization. He was right. Cities offered a mass market allowing economies of scale, pools of skilled labor, easy communication of technological and business innovations, and other benefits that come from having people concentrated in one area. When many people doing business together are gathered in one place, information is easily shared or simply observed. The benefits of density explain why cities acted as vital centers of economic activity, despite high costs and added social problems.

Cities played very different economic roles, depending on their size and location. William Tudor, editor of *North American Review*, commented that American cities were of two kinds: "The first . . . are the depots for the sale of the domestic produce of the district. . . . The second class consists of those cities which, in addition to those branches of trade, are . . . convenient marts for general commerce."[18] In other words, small cities dominate a local market and trade with larger cities, which control regional markets. To add to this analysis, a few cities that are most advantageously located in terms of transportation (which also meant that they attracted a very large population seeking employment) are at the market apex, servicing and integrating local and regional markets in terms of national and international business. A city's role in this urban network determined whether its future was one of growth or decline. In the 1820s most economic activity still remained of a local nature, but the rush of change exerted a broadening influence, although this awaited technological innovations. Thus, fresh produce and many dairy products, to use obvious examples, were grown, processed, and eaten locally until the introduction of refrigeration and pasteurization in the latter half of the century.

A city's commercial leadership could not rest content with a local economy and a limited hinterland when possibilities existed for extending trade. Complacency, these leaders knew, invited urban decline and business failures, while growth offered the path to success. Fear that a rival city might make gains motivated leading citizens to promote the local economy. "Boosterism" led to the formation of chambers of commerce by the 1830s, and rival urban elites competed to sponsor canals and railroads. In turn, new transportation enterprises prompted metropolitan businessmen to form civic associations to divert trade away from urban rivals by establishing their own better connection with the hinterlands. Not to boost one's own city revealed both a lack of civic spirit and a deficiency in business shrewdness. In 1841, New York merchant and fervent abolitionist Lewis Tappan established the Mercantile Agency to provide credit information on firms involved in an ever-growing web of far-flung business relations. The Mercantile Agency (renamed Dun and Bradstreet in 1933) was the forerunner of industry-specific business journals whose purpose was to provide needed information for businessmen to make informed decisions.[19]

In this urban competition, cities specialized in activities and industries. During the 1820s, Boston was strong in insurance, Philadelphia in banking, and New York in printing. An industry's concentration in a city led to the creation of service industries and an infrastructure tailored to its needs. Most industries required a pool of skilled workers and sophisticated networks of specialized middlemen, as well as the informal exchange of knowledge swapped at meeting places and in the street. An industry would concentrate in one location, act as a magnet to attract others in the trade, and then find it easier to expand its scale of production. In turn, this advantage encouraged even greater regional concentration.[20]

The field of "economic geography" has attracted considerable interest, and several economists, including Michael E. Porter of the Harvard School of Business, have argued that networks, or "clusters," are a critical source of competitive advantage by offering "external economies of scale." A cluster of related firms provides a large market for people of specialized skills, which means that workers are attracted because they have some insurance against unemployment, and business in consequence has some protection against labor shortages. Furthermore, a local industrial cluster supports providers of specialized services and facilitates the exchange of information (and thus the advance of technology) as well as deal making. As the great Cambridge economist Alfred Marshall explained in the 1890s: "The mysteries of the trade become no mystery; but as if it were in the air. . . . If one starts a new idea, it is taken up by others and combined with suggestions of their own; and thus becomes the source of further new ideas."[21] It is difficult indeed for an isolated competitor elsewhere to reproduce single-handedly the advantages provided his rivals by an urban or regional "cluster."

The rapidly growing cities of the first half of the nineteenth century developed a new type of urban spatial order to accommodate the emerging industrial order, one of increasingly specialized land use by function. Older city centers became places of commerce and industry, surrounded by residential neighborhoods. An 1833 guide to New York reported that South Street, running along the East River, contained the warehouses and offices of most of the principal shipping merchants. Wall Street was occupied by banks, insurance companies, merchants' exchanges, newspapers, and brokers' offices, and "Canal-street . . . is a spacious street, principally occupied by retail stores."[22] Already town life purveyed a consumer ethos, with shop windows —plate glass was introduced in the 1840s—enticingly displaying goods.

The residential location of an individual, family, or social group in the new spatial order of the city often reflected status. Newly built-up areas at a distance from the business center offered the more desirable residential neighborhoods. Older areas tended to become the blighted and undesirable neighborhoods of the poor.

The adoption of coal-derived steam power, starting in the 1840s, freed factories from their former dependence on free-flowing streams for power. The geographic mobility thus gained allowed them to relocate in or near cities where urban labor, transportation, and markets offered them advantages over the previous rural locations. Urban infrastructure eliminated the need for a business to provide housing, stores, water supply, and waste disposal for its workforce; newly arrived immigrants came to the cities seeking employment; and coal could be delivered by rail or ship. Though the cost of land and rent was greater, cities provided industry with advantages rural locations could not match. Like a magnet, successful cities drew in resources from the outside and, transforming them, profitably distributed them to places near and far.

The increasing scale and complexity of trade between older and newer cities required the development of a new type of support network. The merchants of New York, Philadelphia, Baltimore, and Boston invested in manufacture, finance, mining, insurance, and transportation to facilitate servicing the rapidly expanding inland markets of Pittsburgh, Cleveland, Cincinnati, Chicago, and St. Louis. Among the offshoots of the old general merchant role were investment and commercial banking, as established urban centers —in addition to attending to local needs—provided capital for the settlement and development of new regions. In addition, merchants financed the rapid rise of banking after 1814. To facilitate intercity transactions, banks deposited with each other and sometimes borrowed from each other as well. By 1850, banks had acquired an important new role: they discounted promissory notes merchants received from customers, thus greatly expanding the merchants' ability to extend credit. Until the time of the first "greenbacks" during the Civil War, the federal government produced no paper money—only coins —paper money being left for banks to issue in the form of banknotes.

STATE BANKS AND "SHINPLASTERS"

Commercial farmers and small businessmen needed ready access to credit, and they found it in thousands of state-chartered banks. An eagerness for easy credit encouraged most states to permit the casual establishment of both chartered and private banks. This often resulted in shaky and mis-managed banks, many of which operated chiefly for the purpose of issuing paper currency—often of such dubious value that the notes were referred to as "shinplasters." Directors, having put up little in the way of capital, avidly divided the quick profits, while recurrent efforts by the banking community to engage in self-regulation proved ineffectual. The First and Second Banks of the United States (1796–1811 and 1816–36) briefly acted as restraints to excessive note issues.

But after the demise of the Second Bank of the United States, rampant land speculation fueled by unsound banknotes quickly created a volatile situation. The Specie Circular Act of 1836 sought to remedy the problem by requiring that federal land sales be paid in specie. The resultant Panic of 1837 caused widespread bank failures and a severe business downturn, which persisted until 1843. The dismayed New York diarist George Templeton Strong wrote of the banks: "So they go—smash, crash. Where in the name of wonder is to be the end of it."[23]

Many states belatedly passed tougher banking regulations, and several western states expressed antibank sentiments by temporarily prohibiting the chartering of new banks. By the Civil War, however, the decentralized banking system and bank-issued currency seemed so unreliable that arranging for banknotes to be exchanged in business transactions often posed a formidable hurdle to completing a deal. An independent treasury was established in the 1840s to meet the federal government's needs. All money owed the government now had to be paid in gold or silver with federal funds kept in the vaults of the treasury. This primitive and awkward system limited the ability of the treasury in Washington to offer assistance to banks during occasional "bank panics" or to properly meet the business community's need for a flexible supply of money. Yet the Independent Treasury system, in one form or another, remained largely in place until 1913.

Despite, or perhaps because of, the weakness of the banking system, great fortunes could be easily made and just as easily lost. From the colonial period onward, land speculation represented to Americans a quick way to "make a buck." This was not only true on the frontier but also in settled urban areas. Money could be made in building America's burgeoning cities. Speculators often bought land in or near a town, platted it into lots, and then turned them over to other eager speculators, some of whom might even be builders eager to put up a house in anticipation of a sale.

John Jacob Astor (1763–1848) emigrated from the German town of Waldorf to New York City in April 1784, with $200 to his name. By 1800 he had amassed a fortune of a quarter of a million dollars in the northwest fur trade and had started trading with China and investing in Manhattan real estate. At his death, nearly a half century later, he was worth an estimated $20 million to $25 million. Astor had initially developed unimproved Manhattan property for sale, subdividing country estates into small building lots. In time, however, he preferred to build and rent. After 1820, Astor rarely sold property he had acquired, preferring to lease it out. When the value of the location appreciated, he renegotiated rents at ever-higher rates. As New York evolved into one of the world's great cities, the Astor estate, the city's largest landlord, profited handsomely. On his deathbed at age eighty-four, America's wealthiest citizen was supposedly asked if he had any regrets. He reportedly replied: "Could I begin life again, knowing what I know, and had the money to invest, I would buy every foot of land on the Island of Manhattan."

Only the great size of Astor's fortune was unusual. By 1840, some sixty Americans were credited with being "millionaires," and every large city counted at least one among its citizens. However, there was greater wealth among the southern planters than among the northern merchants and manufacturers. Nearly two out of every three males with estates of $100,000 or more in 1860 lived in the South. Yet the once popular view that, aside from the South, Jacksonian America had no extremes of rich and poor has long since been disproved. Older eastern cities possessed a sizable wealthy elite in 1825, and in the next twenty years the members of this elite and their heirs would greatly increase their fortunes, despite the severe business recession in the years 1837 to 1843. According to Jeffrey G. Williamson and Peter H. Lindert, the richest 1 percent of the population owned well over a quarter of the wealth in 1860, and the top 10 percent held 73 percent. At the other extreme, the bottom one-fifth of the nation, excluding slaves, owned little more than the clothes on their backs and the few coins in their pockets.[24]

It is therefore understandable that George Bancroft, the nation's first notable historian, could write in 1834, "The feud between the capitalist and the laborer, the house of Have and the house of Want, is as old as social union and can never be entirely quieted," and then add hopefully, "But he who will act with moderation, and remember that every thing in the world is relative and not absolute will see that the violence of the contest may be stilled." This, of course, remains the prevailing American credo.[25]

THE VICTORIAN FAMILY: SEPARATE SPHERES

A new type of middle-class family emerged in the first half of the nineteenth century in response to the rise of cities. Alexis de Tocqueville even perceived a close connection between the American emphasis on individualism and this family: "Individualism . . . disposes each member of the community to sever himself from the mass of his fellows and to draw apart with his family and friends, so that after he has thus formed a little circle of his own, he willingly leaves society at large to itself."

A breadwinner father increasingly worked away from home in the outside world while the mother raised the children and attended to household needs. The importance of the new emerging urban middle-class family is that its domestic values and behavior—child-oriented and showing a greater concern with household comforts—would gain acceptance as the socially approved norm. But it also marked the family's redefinition in economic terms. Less and less a unit of household production, the urban middle-class family and its household increasingly served as a vehicle for purchase and consumption of market-bought goods and less and less as the site of home production. A redefinition of the proper roles of men and women, known to social historians as the "ideology of separate spheres," had occurred.[26]

STATUS AND RESPECTABILITY

The home was the woman's sphere, to order and control. *Ladies Magazine*, started in 1828, and a few years later *Godey's Lady's Journal*, provided useful advice on how to shop, how to decorate a home, and how to supervise a domestic staff—including helpful hints on how to keep a husband at home and happy in his leisure time. In 1852, *Godey's Lady's Journal* even offered its readers a buying service from which readers could choose bonnets, dresses, and jewelry to be mailed to any address in the country.

By midcentury, the parlors and sitting rooms of middle-class homes featured stuffed chairs, heavy wooden furniture, draperies, carpets, potted plants, mirrors, and often a piano. Economic growth fostered a commercial spirit that encouraged both specialized and standardized work. To acquire a sofa in 1830, for example, you first had to have a joiner build a frame. Then an upholsterer purchased the necessary leather, horsehair, and feathers to finish the work in the house. A similarly involved procedure was followed for most important pieces of upholstered furniture; but a decade or two later "furniture stores" carried an extensive line of ready-made pieces in various sizes, shapes, colors, and price ranges.

Urban retailing was still based on specialization and a distributive network of wholesalers and commodity dealers, but changes were under way. During the 1830s, New York's Broadway, for example, was lined with stores specializing in wallpaper, dry goods, or "gents' furnishings." A. T. Stewart, an Irish immigrant who had started in business with a small dry goods shop in 1823, some twenty years later in 1846 opened his "Marble Palace" in a huge commercial building, which encouraged customers to browse freely while examining goods with set prices based on low markups. One awed New Yorker observed: "Several of the windows on the first floor are formed by plate glass, six feet by eleven, which must have cost four or five hundred dollars each."[27] In 1862, Stewart built an even-larger building, which is widely regarded as America's first department store.

Often businessmen sought to profit by making and marketing (for a downscale market) cheaper mass-produced versions of more expensive middle-class consumer goods. Power-loom weaving in the 1840s brought down the price of carpets dramatically, and new furniture factories in the 1850s manufactured bedsteads at five dollars to twenty dollars apiece. An observer in 1860 noted with approval that the same mass-produced clocks that had cost twenty dollars two decades earlier now sold for three dollars. Preoccupation with domestic "comfort"—the word did not acquire its modern sense of physical well-being until the late eighteenth century—had become a huge new presence, not only in the home but also in the marketplace.

To the middle-class urban housewife, "the sphere of domestic economy" meant attending to household expenditures, supervising servants, and child-rearing. Her life was very different from her grandmother's, who had been very actively involved in home production. But it also differed greatly from those many housewives without servants, who spent upward of twenty hours a week just washing, drying, and ironing an average-size household's laundry. The ideology of separate spheres never described the actual lives of the overwhelming majority of American women. But by identifying the home as the proper arena of a women's thoughts and goals, it posed many problems, economic and psychological, for the vast multitude of women for whom it would only prove a chimera.

Nor was it necessarily beneficial for the privileged few who were able to realize the ideal. Feminist historians argue that the increasing reliance by the middle-class urban family on the marketplace—and therefore the husband's cash earnings—left the "fortunate" middle-class wife vulnerable. Some historians have even suggested that the role of women in selecting, purchasing, and displaying consumer goods altered their historic function as preservers of traditional culture to become agents of its transformation as they eagerly chased after the latest styles.[28]

CLASS AND CONSUMERISM

Before the Age of Advertising, the most powerful creator of consumer tastes remained the timeless desire to emulate those a step higher in status: sociologists call this phenomenon "stratified diffusion." The nicer the house, the better the location, and the more complete its furnishing, the higher a family's status. Stuart Blumin has written that "consumption . . . was a family strategy, a more or less deliberate attempt to shape the domestic environment in ways that signified social respectability, and that could favor the acquisition of habits of personal deportment that could set a family apart."[29] A family had to employ at least one general maid, preferably live-in, to be considered middle class. On the lower end of the social scale, a clean and well-ordered home signified respectability. Domestic consumption had clearly a comparative or even competitive character; at the very least, families wanted to keep up with their neighbors.

British sociologist W. G. Runciman remarked in the 1960s that the English seldom feel relatively deprived by reference to members of more fortunate groups with whom they have no reason to compare themselves. Americans thought differently. Frances Trollope, an Englishwoman visiting in the 1830s, noted that Americans were an "I'm-as-good-as-you" people. Such an attitude challenged sumptuary class distinctions. Foreign travelers often noted the difficulty of distinguishing an American's class by dress, as Americans did not overly concern themselves with limiting their desires according to their station in life. Tocqueville thought that "democratic institutions most successfully develop sentiments of envy in the human heart."[30]

The historical study of consumerism must involve critical concepts like class and societal values. A Boston religious paper of the 1840s, *The Christian Disciple*, thought it necessary to encourage thrift and saving among the working class, and philanthropists often started savings institutions to teach children the value of thrift and deferring immediate gratification. However, the most effective reins on material appetites were the lack of wherewithal to satisfy them and the need to provide for a rainy day. But some historians of the period believe that Victorian exhortations to practice self-restraint are evidence in themselves of the rapid growth in this period of a consumer market of considerable seductive powers.

Raising middle-class children in cities involved significant expense. Unlike children on a farm, they did not contribute to their own keep through early labor. In the 1830s, northern and western cities introduced public school systems, although most southern cities did not follow suit until long after the Civil War. In 1846, American educator Horace Mann wrote: "Intelligence is a primary ingredient in the wealth of nations."[31] Foreign travelers in the North often commented on the high literacy among Americans and thought this made for a superior American workforce.

As the expense involved in child rearing rose, a noticeable decline in the birthrate occurred among the urban middle class; the modern practice of regulating procreation by economic calculations had taken root. By the 1840s, statisticians in Massachusetts had documented the decline in birthrates for native-born American families residing in that state. The very large families of the colonial period became the exception in middle-class neighborhoods of the American city, although they were still common among farm families or among immigrants residing in urban slums.[32]

The demographics of a nation, such as its age distribution, profoundly affect its productivity and shape its consumer spending. However, in the nineteenth century, declining birthrates were offset by large-scale immigration and the drop in the mortality rates after 1840. Between 1820 and 1860, nearly 5 million immigrants entered the country, with 90 percent coming from the British Isles, Germany, and Scandinavia. By the Civil War, immigrants totaled nearly a fifth of the American population, with the vast majority living outside of the slaveholding South.

As the population grew increasingly diverse, the economy also became accordingly complex with new economic arrangements and business relations. There was Main Street and Wall Street, cotton mills and slave-worked cotton plantations, railroads and family farms. The young republic had become a mature and wealthy nation, but one deeply and increasingly divided along sectional and ideological lines.

CHAPTER FIVE

The Unstoppable Engine

A railroad is like a lie—you have to keep building it
to make it stand.—MARK TWAIN, San Francisco
Alta California, *1867*

Ralph Waldo Emerson, surveying the changing America of his day, wrote reprovingly in 1847 of an advancing materialistic civilization where "things are in the saddle and ride mankind." A few years earlier he had entered in his journal that the "invasion of nations by Trade with its Money, its Steam [and] its Railroads, threatens to upset the balance of men and establish a new universal Monarchy more tyrannical than Babylon or Rome."[1] The associations among trains, trade, and industrial profit were clear, and to Emerson and his small circle of friends they were menacing. The young Henry Thoreau worried that "when the conductor shouts 'All aboard!' when the smoke is blown away . . . it will be perceived that a few are riding, but the rest are run over."[2]

TRAINS AND MODERN TIMES

Others, however, were of another mind. They rejoiced at the speedy introduction of novel and inexpensive goods and celebrated America as a "country of beginnings, of projects, of vast designs and expectations." "Progress" was fastest in the cities, but revolutionary developments in transportation encouraged change to radiate rapidly outward, as a market economy with its purchasable necessities and creature comforts extended its range and depth.

Many looked to these fast-moving developments as opportunities to make their fortunes. Towns and cities vied for the coming of a railroad.

One man's career exemplifies these changes. Cornelius Vanderbilt (1794–1877) succeeded Astor as the wealthiest American. Barely educated and somewhat crude, Vanderbilt began his business life by operating ferry lines sailing to and from Manhattan Island and nearby communities. Many who used the "Commodore's" ferry commuted on a daily basis to Manhattan's businesses, while residing away from its high urban density. Later Vanderbilt acquired transatlantic steamship lines. In the 1850s, the *New York Times*, describing Vanderbilt's hard-fisted approach to business, likened him to a feudal robber baron—apparently the first use of this term in connection with American businessmen.

In the early 1860s, Vanderbilt sold his maritime businesses to invest in three inefficiently run railroads, believing the time right to leave an already-mature industry for one more promising. Vanderbilt joined his three railroads together as the New York Central, which was destined to become one of the nation's great commuter lines. Americans remember the nineteenth-century railroad for opening the Far West to settlement, but it was only after the Civil War that transcontinental railroads pioneered the settlement of the trans-Mississippi West. Well before this the railroads played a critical role in facilitating the integration of local into ever-larger regional economies.

The railroad provided the world with an inexpensive form of land transportation to handle low-cost, high-bulk goods and high-cost, low-bulk goods with equal speed and reliability all year-round. Adna Ferrin Weber, in his 1899 classic study, *The Growth of Cities in the Nineteenth Century*, called the train the most important invention of the nineteenth century. The importance of the railroad to all facets of life and business in the nineteenth century cannot be overstated. To Weber, the railroad had indeed "ushered in the modern world" and was the reason for that "most remarkable social phenomenon of the present century . . . the concentration of population in cities."[3]

In 1825 a small British line, the Stockton and Darlington, used a steam locomotive designed by George Stephenson to introduce the first commercial railroad. Stephenson's "Locomotion No. 1" could pull a ninety-ton train of thirty-four wagons at a speed of ten to twelve miles per hour—news that excited the Western world and evoked immediate emulation. In many nations the high cost of railroad development required government ownership of the railroads. In the United States such action was never considered. Nevertheless, railroad building never would have progressed beyond its primitive stage without considerable governmental assistance received from local entities, the states, and (after 1850) the federal government.

Merchants in cities, unable to compete effectively with the canals of rival cities, pioneered railroads as an alternative, and a few short lines developed in the early 1830s, led by the cities of Baltimore, Charleston, and Boston. In 1833, land developers interested in selling home plots in the northeastern part of Manhattan Island organized the New York and Harlem as a commuter and freight line. Philadelphia business interests soon ran several rail connections to the coalfields of eastern Pennsylvania. By 1840, there were more than 300 railway companies in the United States. But the average railroad had thirteen miles of track, laid at a cost of $17,000 per mile. Rarely did a company exceed twenty miles. Gauges on the tracks of the various lines ranged from four feet eight and a half inches, all the way to a six-foot gauge.

At first railroads did not compete effectively with canals. Lines were laid as an alternative to canals, or often to join with and complement canal systems. It soon became apparent that the first railway promoters had grossly underestimated the expenses and difficulties involved. As the pioneer lines fell short of expectations, initial enthusiasm yielded to concern that the iron horse's role would be modest and peripheral at best. Then, in the early 1850s, a second wave of railroad investment fever occurred, permanently ending interest in canals.[4]

In 1840, the cities of the East were loosely joined by some 3,300 miles of rails, and in the next two decades railroad construction progressed by leaps and bounds. By 1850, 8,879 miles of iron roads had been laid, and by the eve of the Civil War, over 30,000 miles of rail connected all major eastern and midwestern cities. Long-distance passengers, however, often had to travel by several different lines. Each change required the passenger to leave a train and station, cross town to another railroad's station, purchase new tickets, and then wait for the next train. Speeds of less than twenty miles an hour were typical, derailments were common, and traveling conditions were crude and uncomfortable. Lines used different gauges and even disagreed over a standard time to be used in schedules. The "miraculous decade," the 1850s, experienced a movement toward consolidation of individual lines into what within three decades would become integrated trunk lines, part of a national rail system employing a uniform gauge and, beginning in 1883, standard regional time zones.

The railroad industry's rapid progress in the 1850s resulted from untangling a cat's cradle of mechanical and technical problems. A wide range of possibilities was explored, and a steep takeoff replaced the former pattern of gradual incremental changes. Safer manual brakes and stronger rails in the 1850s allowed for heavier rolling stock and fewer accidents. However, not until the decade after the Civil War did George Westinghouse's air brake and George Pullman's sleeping and dining cars make safe and pleasant train travel possible.

The railroads provided a workshop for American industry, training several generations of engineers. American mechanics learned to work with precise measurements to high standards of reliability for the sake of safety. An ancient respect for leisurely craftsmanship surrendered to a need for quick servicing and repairs as well as knowledge of the right parts and tools: what impressed English observers about American mechanics was "the application of special tools to minute purposes." A nascent machine-tool industry for the textile industry had sprung up in the 1820s in Windsor, Vermont, and Providence, Rhode Island. "Yankee tinkers" became celebrated for their versatility in devising the light, accurate, machine tools needed to manufacture tiny clock parts, gun components, and pieces for the newly invented sewing machine. Now machine shops for the railroads took their places alongside the older tool shops. The railroad industry spurred the development of machine-tool factories to build milling machines, engine parts, boilers, frames, axles, and wheels as well. Other shops manufactured the specially developed tools and machines necessary to make these parts. By 1860, Britain's long-enjoyed lead over the United States in machine tools had been reversed.

A rapidly changing railroad industry provided new problems and opportunities that challenged managers and workers alike. Requirements of safety and efficiency prompted innovations. The peril of collisions and derailments posed by the common single-track lines necessitated careful coordination. "This is no way to run a railroad" became the standard American reproof against inefficiency or unreliability.[5]

THE WAY TO RUN A RAILROAD

The decade from 1850 to 1860 witnessed important changes in railroad organization and management as small railroads merged to form large "trunk" lines. In these mergers, the dominant partner was the company that serviced the main trunk line and owned the principal terminal stations. Putting down lines, buying rolling stock, and constructing stations and depots required large amounts of capital—as did creating trunk lines consisting of hundreds (and then thousands) of miles of track.

From the start, the railroads, as incorporated companies, received considerable assistance from state and local governments. This took the form of charters, tax abatements, and grants of eminent domain to acquire rights-of-way at reasonable prices. State and local governments also issued nearly $90 million in bonds between 1845 and 1860 to further railroad construction; for its part, the federal government from 1850 to 1876 provided handsome grants of public land to support interstate and then—after the Civil War—the great transcontinental lines. Justification for such public assistance to private companies rested on the view that the importance of railroads as common carriers rendered them public utilities.

Railroads by the 1850s promised handsome profits for those prepared to take risks. This was true not only for railroad builders but also for those with the know-how to raise money. The volume of railroad building required access to vast amounts of capital, including acquisition capital for mergers. The promise of political stability offered by the Compromise of 1850 (which initially eased the regional tensions over the issue of slavery in the territories) encouraged business optimism.

STOCK JOBBING ON WALL STREET

An institution eager to bring the railroads together with investors and lenders already existed. Starting in 1792, a group of New Yorkers met daily on Wall Street to trade in government notes and the securities of public corporations. Until 1815 only a very limited number of issues were traded. But an upturn in activity occurred with the formation of numerous canal and toll road companies, and this increased business led in 1817 to the formal organization of the New York Stock and Exchange Board. By 1827, the exchange was handling eight government securities, twelve bank stocks, nineteen marine or insurance companies, and a few other miscellaneous companies. Then, in 1830, the stock of the Mohawk and Hudson Railroad became the first railroad security traded on the exchange. A journalist described Wall Street in the early 1830s as "the seat of heavier moneyed transactions than any other place in America."[6] Brokers managed their affairs like a loosely run gentlemen's club governed only by a few scant house rules. Already by

1848 the anonymously authored *Stocks and Stock-Jobbing in Wall Street with Sketches of Brokers and Fancy Stocks*, by a "Reformed Stock Gambler," warned of sharp traders who coolly fleeced widows and orphans of their savings.

The shortage of sufficient American capital to finance railroad building forced Wall Street to turn to Europe. From 1830 to 1860 British investors and lenders purchased nearly a quarter of a billion dollars in American railroad and canal securities. European investors, as indeed did Americans, preferred the more secure bonds to railroad common stock, which fluctuated wildly in price and rarely paid substantial dividends. The American economy's rapid growth permitted payment of higher interest rates on bonds than Europeans found at home. Foreign banks and investors, however, had good reason to approach American railroads with caution.

British banking houses controlled most of the capital flowing to Wall Street. But European investments in American railroad bonds represented a passive involvement in distant companies operating in an unfamiliar business and legal environment; foreign investors needed to be concerned about risks and shady practices. "Cornering," the hoarding of a supply of stock by traders, who manipulated its sales or planted rumors and "news" of the stock to rig its price, was a common practice. A more serious danger to investors was a lack of reliable information about a company and its activities and an inability to ensure that the company's directors acted in the interests of stockholders. On one well-publicized occasion in the 1850s, the New York and New Haven Railroad's president printed and sold $2 million of false stock, fleeing to Europe with the money in a suitcase.

In 1837, N. M. Rothschild & Sons of London sent twenty-one-year-old August Belmont to reside in New York to report personally on American financial prospects. Belmont found them sufficiently promising to start a firm as the Rothschild agent in America. A few years later a Baltimorean, George Peabody, moved to London, where he established his own banking house and took on as a partner the Boston dry goods merchant Junius Spencer Morgan. On Peabody's retirement in 1861, the firm reorganized as J. S. Morgan & Company. The British investment houses, with Wall Street brokers and bankers as their agents, pressed the American railroads to provide reliable and adequate disclosures of financial operations. Winslow, Lanier & Company of New York proved highly active in monitoring railroad behavior for its clients, even placing representatives on corporate boards to safeguard their interests.

Investment banks did not accept deposits or make loans to merchants.

Their business consisted of marketing on commission large blocks of securities for private corporations and local, state, and even the national government. They frequently used their own capital in floating an issue. Financial institutions also often provided "call loans" for brokers and stock gamblers interested in high-risk, short-term speculation. Henry Varnum Poor's *American Railroad Journal*, published from 1849 to 1862, printed trade news and other information that aided investors. By then, the investing public had learned to expect the large investment firms to vouch for the soundness of their offerings and especially the accuracy of information the issuers provided the prospective buyers.[7]

CHARGING WHAT THE TRAFFIC WILL BEAR

Apart from pressure from creditors, railroads had good reasons of their own for developing effective management skills. Business record keeping had been initially developed in response to the merchant's need to keep ledgers, with the classic double-entry system having hardly changed since its introduction to Europe by fourteenth-century Venetian merchants, who had learned it from Muslim traders. A mid-nineteenth-century textbook commented that "book-keeping implies a systematic arrangement of mercantile transactions[,] the purpose of which is to afford at all times ready access to Resources and Liabilities of the party whose operations are recorded."[8]

Such an approach could not guide the establishment of railroad "pricing policies" for freight shipment or passenger travel. For the first few decades of railroad history, a superintendent, selected on the basis of his practical experience and reporting to the company president and board of directors, took overall charge of operations. His decision making tended to be pragmatic, relying heavily on nonsystematic impressions and observations—"rule of thumb." Indirect costs represented a very large part of total costs in the railroad industry, and assigning costs among the various productive factors had to be worked out. Such calculations required sophisticated and reliable information on the railroad's activity. Then principles of cost accounting had to be developed as an essential instrument of control.[9]

It has been suggested that managers of large American railroads initiated nearly all of the basic techniques of modern accounting in the 1850s and 1860s. A new type of innovative auditor appeared, one seeking to design analytically informative financial statements. Methods were developed to track costs and improve the flow of supplies; balance sheets attempted to present a financial picture that went beyond the merely descriptive to serve as a useful tool in making decisions and then assessing results. The accountant's handiwork was expected to expose problems and even suggest their solutions. Accounting became differentiated from bookkeeping as a specialized profession, and accountants responsive to their clients' wants increasingly defined the expectations, practices, and training of their field.

What railroad companies required, as does any complex organization, was a way for relevant information to move from the bottom ranks to top management for analysis, and for decisions to be communicated accurately and quickly downward. In a small business, this can be managed by a boss with a hands-on intuitive approach who personally supervises all activities and speaks to everyone. As a business grew larger, this ability was inevitably lost, and inefficiencies unimportant in a small company escalated in seriousness in large ones. Big business required a sophisticated theory of organization. Railroads in particular could not afford mistakes, which could result in the loss of lives and expensive equipment.[10]

American trunk lines in the 1850s were already too large and complex—the details too many, too varied, and too technical—for one man to master. In 1855, the general superintendent of the Erie Railroad, Daniel McCallum, described the great difference between managing a fifty-mile line, fairly standard in the early 1840s, and the new trunk lines of two hundred or more miles that appeared in the next decade. The key to operating the short line, he believed, was simply capable leadership; managing a trunk line required "a system perfect in its details, properly adapted and vigilantly enforced."[11] McCallum suggested that internal reporting systems be devised to provide all required information, that the performance of all employees be routinely evaluated, and that managers should be permitted decision-making powers appropriate to their responsibilities. Ad hoc ways of doing things needed to yield to impersonal and formal administrative structures.

Daily decision-making operations involved people, stations, offices, warehouses, car barns, trains, tracks, and telegraph lines. A schedule of train movements had to be established and kept to. Invented in 1844, the telegraph, with its lines strung alongside the tracks, quickly became absolutely indispensable in coordinating complex train movements of both passenger and freight cars and communicating news. Long-term planning involved anticipating future operations, purchasing, capital improvements, route expansion, leasing or owning equipment, and financing in its myriad aspects. With the rise of the trunk lines, a primitive type of system management approach emerged, employing quantitative calculations of cost and benefits. Borrowing from the model of the army's chain of command, the trunk lines by the 1870s developed functional organizations that distinguished between line operations and staff support. Activities were now increasingly organized around specialized departments such as finance, purchasing, traffic, sales, real estate, engineering, and law. The search for "system" became the holy grail of railroad management in the second half of the nineteenth century.

In their search for a perfect system (and, in an age that thought in mechanical terms, this was generally thought of as something that could be essentially achieved once and for all), trunk lines pioneered in dividing their operations into various departments based on activity and region. Separate operational departments were established, each under its own head, for freight service, passenger service, and regional divisions. A superintendent in charge of a general office then supervised and coordinated the activities of the operational departments and regional divisions. This general superintendent reported to the line's president, who in turn was responsible to its board of directors.

Historian Alfred D. Chandler Jr. suggested in the 1960s that railroads were the first private enterprises in the United States with modern administrative structures and that they provided useful precedents for organizational structuring when the industrials grew to be of comparable size and complexity. A change of such magnitude did not happen overnight, but important changes in the legal nature of the corporation and its charter even before the Civil War laid the groundwork for such change.[12]

CORPORATIONS

Most industrial expansion in the nineteenth century occurred in traditional types of proprietary and partnership firms. By the very end of the nineteenth century, however, the corporation had become the basic instrument of large-scale private collective action. The rise of American big business at the end of the century could have occurred without the corporation. As a business type, corporations certainly played a lesser role in Europe than in the United States, but the imperatives of modern business scale and complexity would have eventually required complex organization. The corporate form with its legal advantages facilitated this.

The Constitutional Convention of 1787 had denied Congress specific power to create corporations, leaving them the creatures of state government, and the usual corporation of the late eighteenth century was a private company created by and acting as agent of the state. Under this "grant" theory, the act of incorporation was a privilege conferred on private individuals for the pursuit of public purposes. As late as 1800, there were fewer than fifty business corporations chartered in the new United States.[13]

Eager to promote economic development and often open to influence peddling or bribes, state legislatures soon acted more generously in chartering business corporations. By 1820, some 1,200 such businesses had been incorporated. Most charters were for companies involved in public works, such as bridges, water works, turnpikes, and canals. Incorporation normally involved a pro forma vote by a state legislature, and in theory this vote represented the negotiation of a contract between private interests and government—with the resulting charters often vague in detailing limitations and responsibilities, although usually quite explicit in defining permissible activities.

Resistance toward accepting the corporation as legitimately and exclusively representing private profit rather than the public good was expressed in an 1809 judgment of the Virginia Supreme Court. In a decision involving a corporate charter, the court stated: "It may be often convenient for a set of associated individuals to have the privileges of a corporation bestowed upon them; but if their object is merely private or selfish; if it is detrimental to, or not promotive [sic] of, the public good, they have no adequate claim upon the legislature for the privileges."[14] Reluctance to fully accept the corporation as a profit-oriented business was due to its association with legislatively granted privileges, especially monopoly rights for valuable franchises.

Before the 1840s, most corporations involved public service enterprises in banking, insurance, turnpikes, canals, and railroads. By then, however, the corporation already enjoyed court-given advantages over other types of business organizations. In 1811, New York State passed laws limiting the liability of stockholders of all corporations to their equity investment, and all states followed suit by 1830.

Chief Justice John Marshall, in the *Dartmouth College* case of 1819, established the legal principle that charters were protected by the contract clause of the Constitution from revision by state legislatures. But Marshall's decision went even further. Marshall legally defined the corporation as an "artificial human being. . . . Being the mere creature of law, it possesses only those properties which the charter of its creation confers upon it. . . . Among the most important are immortality and, if the expression be allowed, individuality." Marshall's decision conveyed a clear message to state legislatures to include "reserve clauses" in the charters, clauses that specifically gave legislators the right to "repeal and amend." His "artificial-entity theory" meant that a corporation had no power or rights except for those explicitly given or necessarily implied by its charter.[15]

States acted accordingly. Tightly drawn charters of incorporation carefully enumerated privileges and responsibilities. In Pennsylvania, the 1849 General Manufacturing Act set a twenty-year limit on the life of manufacturing corporations. Many states limited the business that could be conducted, especially by manufacturing corporations. Ordinarily, authorization to borrow money or issue bonds was not given in the original charter but required supplementary legislation.[16]

Most important, in declaring corporations persons before the law (albeit in the limited sense of artificial entities created by the state and subject to special constraints), the Supreme Court created impressive new legal advantages. Empowered with a code of "natural rights," such as the rights of the due process clause and the contract clause, the corporations could effectively beat back legal attacks.

Moreover, by the 1870s, the view that a corporate charter conveyed a specific public responsibility had been largely replaced. The corporation had gained recognition as a strictly utilitarian business device whose contribution to the public welfare consisted of advancing economic development. In *Gibbons v. Ogden* (1824), the Supreme Court held the federal power over interstate commerce to be inviolable by the states. Building on this decision in *Bank of Augusta v. Earle* (1839), the High Court affirmed the right of corporations to do business in any state unless expressly forbidden by law. State legislatures also moved to enhance the attractiveness of the corporation as a business arrangement. Preeminent among the advantages of the corporation were, of course, its ability to facilitate the raising of capital and the fact that freely marketable shares made equity highly liquid.[17]

As part of a move against established interests in the 1830s, a demand arose that state legislatures be deprived of the right to vote charters of incorporation. Those wanting "free" or general incorporation, a pro forma procedure governed by statute law, argued that legislatures often acted corruptly and showed favoritism in granting charters. In 1837, Connecticut passed a General Incorporation Act: a charter could be obtained by anyone meeting the requirements and paying a fee. Several other states soon enacted general incorporation acts; by 1870, the remaining states had followed suit, making incorporation throughout the United States a simple bureaucratic act. The new laws made the limited-purpose charter a thing of the past and set the stage for the growth of genuinely national enterprises. General laws of incorporation strengthened the growing view of corporations as merely private businesses having limited liability but without special public responsibilities.

Railroads, as common carriers, however, remained an exception. Although state rules for chartering and operating a corporation varied greatly, most businesses did not shop around to incorporate in the state offering the best terms. This would be a later development.[18]

In the Jacksonian era (1828–40), the corporation as such—despite its historic association with monopoly and special privilege—did not convey an exclusively undemocratic connotation. Some even hailed the corporation as a democratic device, with stockholders electing a board and its chairman, and many of the numerous utopian communities of the time were themselves chartered as joint-stock corporations. The antipathy that did exist toward corporations reflected a deep-seated fear that government might favor entrenched interests at the expense of the majority. It was in this vein that President Jackson in his farewell speech as president castigated "the multitudes of corporations with exclusive privileges which they have succeeded in obtaining in different states."

ANDREW JACKSON'S WAR ON THE SECOND BANK OF THE UNITED STATES

The single most momentous action in Andrew Jackson's eventful presidency, 1828–36, was his destruction of the Second Bank of the United States. Most economists credit the Second Bank with providing the United States with its best banking system prior to the twentieth century. Acting as a clearinghouse for state banks, the bank restrained them from issuing their notes as freely as they wished by accumulating them and then presenting them for redemption in specie. The bank could also establish branches across state lines, while state chartered banks could not.

But the bank's power guaranteed it enemies. Senator Thomas Hart Benton of Missouri, speaking for many farmers and small merchants, declaimed in 1831, "I object to the renewal of the charter of the Bank of the United States because I look upon the bank as an institution too great and powerful to be tolerated in a Government of free and equal powers. Its power is that of the purse; a power more potent than the sword."[19]

The source of Jackson's own hostility to the bank remains uncertain. He may have been genuinely concerned that the bank was a "monster," a "hydra of corruption" representing a dangerous and undemocratic concentration of power. Then again Nicholas Biddle, its president, a man of unquestionable ability and integrity, possessed a strong personality that clashed with Jackson's iron will. Biddle committed the fatal mistake of letting Jackson's political rivals use the bank's rechartering as an issue in the presidential election of 1832. Congress voted to recharter the bank but failed to override Jackson's veto. In his veto message, Jackson charged that rechartering would grant the bank "exclusive privileges to make the rich richer and the potent more powerful."

Jackson then articulated what is probably the most powerful of American social ideals. Americans, he said, desired a society that offered no unfair and artificial advantages but where all could rise according to the best of their abilities. Jackson's goal espoused an equality of opportunity but not an equality of outcome. In his second term, Jackson crippled the bank by removing its federal funds, and when its federal charter expired, it became just another private bank. From then until 1862, the "era of free banking," the United States lacked a national system.

In the absence of a central bank, thousands of state banks issued notes of often spurious value and refused to exchange these notes for specie on demand. This, of course, led their notes to depreciate, but at different rates in different locations, resulting in a widespread reluctance to hold banknotes. The transaction cost of negotiating banknotes soared. Receiving cashiers had to discount from the face value when the creditability of the lending institution was uncertain—which was often. In 1859, Samuel C. Thompson began a weekly issue of *The Bank Note Detector* to list bogus and shaky banknotes. Despite the woeful inadequacy of the nation's banking and monetary system, the inflow of foreign capital allowed for sufficient investment capital to permit continued economic growth. The American economy was increasingly inward looking, but in the important matter of investment capital needed for rapid development it would rely on European sources until the next century.

AMERICA ON THE EVE OF THE CIVIL WAR

The attention we have given thus far to the corporation is clearly out of proportion to its actual importance in the Jacksonian era. Nevertheless, this period set the stage, legally and otherwise, for the remarkably rapid rise of corporate America by the century's end. As late as the 1840s, the traditional enterprises remained virtually ubiquitous in industry and commerce. In nearly all cases, businesses were a family affair. When and if they acquired a legal form, it was normally that of a partnership.

As late as the 1870s, this still remained largely true. But the signs of change had become evident decades earlier. Already in the years 1850 to 1860, state legislatures issued more corporate charters than in the previous sixty years of national history combined. Each succeeding decade in the century established a new record, only to be topped in turn.

The British periodical *The Economist* foretold in 1851 that the "economic superiority of the United States to England is ultimately as certain as the next eclipse."[20] In the period 1825 to 1860, we observe the planting and sprouting of the seeds of this change. If a decisive break with the past had occurred, the extent and nature of this rupture remained uncertain. A common theme of landscape painters of the period offered an overhead, bird's-eye view of a railroad traversing a rural valley, slips of smoke issuing from the locomotive to gently blur with low-hung wisps of clouds in an otherwise blue sky. The new railroad in a pastoral setting seemingly complemented rather than conflicted with a rural way of life. Industry's potential to transform the old order was still not fully comprehended.

After seventy years of national life, the United States in 1860 ranked after Great Britain and possibly France as a manufacturing nation. Manufacturing had accounted for barely 10 percent of the value of the American economy in 1840; by 1860 this figure had reached 17 percent. Industry was the most dynamic sector at midcentury and already dominated the activity of the Northeast. Subsistence agriculture had largely yielded to farming of a highly commercial nature, with farmers in all sections increasingly tied to major markets by an extensive system of rivers, roads, canals, and railroads. Composing a fourth of the nation's population, a large urban market for industrial and consumer goods now existed.

After the Mexican War, 1846–48, and the acquisition of much of the present West, the United States straddled a huge continent unchallenged, and with little need to spend money on a sizable army or navy. Rich in natural resources, the nation boasted a youthful, rapidly growing population imbued with a vigorously entrepreneurial ethos. A flood of immigrants and foreign capital speeded economic growth. By 1860, industrialization had occurred in textile manufacturing and in machine tooling—and was well along in shoemaking and paper and flour milling. The celebrated "American system" of interchangeable parts was effectively used in the production of firearms, sewing machines, farm implements, and clocks. But industry was concentrated primarily in the northern section of an increasingly divided country.[21]

Americans liked to believe that they had created a society that rewarded talent and individual initiative instead of class and bloodlines. How could such values be reconciled with the South's "peculiar institution," slavery? The question of whether the increasingly northern-dominated national government in Washington, D.C., could prohibit slavery in the new federal territories prepared the tinder for the coming conflict. A fierce debate over states' rights versus centralized power raged on several levels, reshaping the party system as the antislavery Republican Party emerged.[22] Delegates at its convention in 1860, which nominated Abraham Lincoln as the party's presidential candidate, enthusiastically sang "Get Off the Track," a song about the unstoppable engine "Emancipation" barreling across America. This metaphor of industrial power transforming and troubling a nation was certainly appropriate. But five years later, a grimmer symbol of power and strife could be found scattered around Georgia in the form of the "Sherman Bowtie"—an iron locomotive rail, pulled from its tracks, heated, and left twisted around a tree in the wake of Sherman's avenging union army.

CHAPTER SIX

Entrepreneurial Leaves
from the Gilded Age

Joy sat on every countenance, and there was a glad, almost
fierce intensity in every eye that told of money-getting schemes
that were seething in every brain and the high hopes that held
sway in every heart.—MARK TWAIN, Roughing It (1872)

The thirty years that followed the end of the Civil War are often cited as the Golden Age of the American entrepreneur. Entrepreneurs are generally thought of as innovators who energize and reshape an economy by developing new products or services or introducing new techniques of production, distribution, or business organization. But Austrian economist Ludwig von Mises has provided a more evocative description: "The real entrepreneur is a *speculator*[,] a man eager to utilize his opinion about the future structure of the market for business operations promising profits. . . . He judges the future in a different way. . . . He is directed by an opinion of the future which deviates from those held by the crowd."[1]

The role of the entrepreneur in the rapid rise of big business in the quarter century after the Civil War has produced more controversy than any other theme in American business history. No one questions the importance of entrepreneurs in the economic life of the times, but at issue is whether they were the primary cause of the coming of big business or only the instrument of adaptation to powerful forces related to changes in technology and the market. Contemporaries certainly closely identified entrepreneurs, especially Andrew Carnegie, John D. Rockefeller, and J. P. Morgan, with the transformation of the American economy, and this chapter will consider these three men and the consequences of their actions before returning to the theme of the role of the entrepreneur and a debate without a foreseeable end.

THE GILDED AGE AS PRELUDE

The Civil War forever ended slavery and altered the balance of power between the federal government and the states. The South's defeat also ended the most formidable ideological challenge to the advance of untrammeled industrial capitalism in American history. But the Civil War was not the clean-cut dividing line between an earlier agrarian America and a new industrial nation; the pace of industrialization, even with the voracious demands of war, did not quicken as fast as once generally thought. The 600,000 fatalities of the war caused a labor shortage only remedied through internal and external immigration and the quickened pace of mechanization. The great leap actually occurred almost a decade later. However, the war and its aftermath did create a political climate that released pent-up forces of change. The country, or at least the North and West, now entered a period of intense competition and economic growth, promoted and sustained by national values and policies supportive of enterprise and novelty.

In 1866 the first transatlantic telegraph cable was laid; three years later the first transcontinental railroad opened for business. Soon the nation's rapidly evolving railroad system serviced a continent-wide market; the size of this national marker created an explosive demand for goods and services, offering incentives for technological advance. In the ten years between 1865 and 1875, the nation's industrial output rose 75 percent. The escalating breakneck pace of change in the next several decades signifies the advent of a technology of mass production based on steam power and steel—the Machine Age. The immense fortunes of the final third of the century, the fabled wealth of men such as John D. Rockefeller and Andrew Carnegie, came from industry, not commerce or real estate. Industrial America had arrived.[2]

The dominance of the business-oriented Republican Party finally permitted the creation of a national banking system. After establishing a uniform national currency of banknotes in 1864 (the controversial "greenbacks"), Congress placed a heavy tax on state banknotes a year later, effectively driving them out of circulation. A series of laws created a system of federal banks, with banks required to hold specified amounts of federal bonds and a capitalization of at least $150,000. Nor could the defeated South prevent the rise of a high protective wall of tariffs shielding largely northern industry. Federal subsidies to transcontinental railroads, along with the Homestead Act and other actions, speeded the settlement of the West. All this legislation contributed greatly to the development of a national economy and a subsequent movement to "big business." In 1886 Andrew Carnegie bragged of his adopted land, "The old nations of the world creep on at snails pace; the republic thunders past with the rush of the express."[3]

THE REPUBLIC THUNDERS PAST

For the North, the war's clearest consequences were political. The Union victory established the primacy of the national government over the states, redefining the nature of the federal system. Ratified in 1868, the Fourteenth Amendment to the Constitution, initially intended to defend the rights of the new freedmen in the former Confederate states, would be used after 1886 and the Supreme Court's decision in *Santa Clara County v. Southern Pacific Railroad* to protect corporations in their fictive form of "legal" persons from state and local regulatory actions.[4] The Supreme Court, now dominated by northern interests, adopted what has been called "laissez-faire constitutionalism." The judges carefully scrutinized state efforts to regulate business, striking down purported interference with interstate commerce.

THE SOUTH

The section of the country most deeply affected by the war was, of course, the stricken South. In 1860, the South's 4 million slaves were valued at $2.7 billion, nearly three times the amount invested either in manufacturing or in railroads nationwide. The plantation system ended with the freeing of slaves without compensation to their owners—or, more poignantly, any economic provision for those freed. As white southerners sought to limit the potentials and the consequences of freedom, the ex-slaves soon found new forms of subjugation and exploitation imposed on them. Racial segregation, or "Jim Crow," evolved as part of a pattern of legal and economic inequalities, including disenfranchisement, inferior education, discrimination in the labor market, and unequal justice. Southern racial stereotypes convinced whites of black inferiority while seeking to persuade blacks of the same. These practices were enforced by state and local governments, community norms, and private employers, as well as by the ultimate intimidation of vigilante justice or lynch law. The end of slavery did not end the profound contradiction between the stated national conviction that "all men are created equal" and the harsh treatment, with governmental tolerance or approval, of blacks, Indians, Chinese, and certain other minorities.[5]

A cash-poor South had to reconstruct its economy. Former plantations were divided into small parcels and leased out. Tenant farmers agreed to pay a specified quantity of cotton to the landlord, while the "sharecropper" yielded a share, anywhere from half to two-thirds of his crop, to the land's owner. Cotton growing became more, not less, important to the South's agricultural economy between 1865 and 1900. This was especially true for black farmers, who had more than 80 percent of their crops in cotton, as compared to less than 70 percent for white farmers. Poor farmers, almost always short of cash, bought goods from a local country store, which extended credit in return for higher prices. Often the owner of the general store was also the owner of the land the sharecropper worked, a situation of total dependency allowing for gross exploitation. To make their situation graver, the global cotton market became savagely competitive with increased production in India, Brazil, and Egypt. Prices were forced down for the remainder of the century. Many cotton growers, vulnerable and powerless, remained in chronic debt peonage to the landlords.[6]

Despite impressive efforts to encourage industry, the South, lacking capital for development, fell even further behind the North in 1900 than it had been in 1860. The region's per capita income declined from 72 percent of the national average at the Civil War's beginning to 51 percent forty years later. The southern industries that did do well were extractive (lumbering and mining) or were devoted to processing regional agricultural products (tobacco and cotton manufacturing). Many blacks and whites left the region to seek greater opportunities elsewhere, and immigrants from abroad largely avoided the South. Thus the great demographic and social divide in the South remained that of race, with whites and blacks alike tracing their American ancestry to the eighteenth century or earlier. This divide, the notorious "race problem," influenced all aspects of southern life: economic, social, and political.

Historian C. Vann Woodward's classic view of the "New South"—as a region ground down under colonial economic rule—has been modified somewhat by recent scholarship, which has depicted the post–Civil War rise of southern cities and towns as linked by an improved transportation network and often attracting industry. Yet the South weaned itself only slowly from its dependency on agriculture and cotton. Standing apart from the rest of the nation, preoccupied by painful racial tensions (90 percent of all American blacks lived in the South in 1900 and 75 percent as late as 1940), and desperately short of capital, the South reentered the mainstream of American economic life only after World War II, when the region finally transformed its low-wage economy.

IN THE LAND OF THE DOLLAR

Economic prospects in postbellum America inflamed the imagination of Americans eager for wealth and progress. An emotional letdown followed the end of wartime sacrifices, but a rampant materialism soon glorified the aggressive pursuit of wealth. The two decades following Appomattox witnessed an era in which greed and corruption weakened government on all levels and fed a speculative mania in business circles. The lure of immense wealth led to overbuilding, fierce competition, widespread corruption, and frequent financial panics. Overblown expectations provided the theme for Mark Twain and Charles Dudley Warner's 1873 novel, *The Gilded Age*, a phrase that historians later used to name the epoch.

In the financial district of lower Manhattan, runners, traders, and speculators engaged in frenetic activity, and investment pools manipulated share prices to fleece the unwary. Wildcat promoters peddled "watered" and worthless securities to investors blinded by greed. Some investors consulted their horoscopes before investing, and Commodore Vanderbilt hired a medium to communicate with the dead for advice before buying or selling. Others, however, relied on the stock ticker invented by Edison in 1872. James K. Medbery, in *Men and Mysteries of Wall Street* (1870), complained: "All the worst evils of stock manipulation have their birth and abiding-place in the secret counsels of the Rings and Cliques—of that association of railway, steamship and telegraph directors, presidents who . . . do everything which will keep them outside of prison bars by means of shrewd lawyers and complaisant judges, if only in doing all this, they can manage to make three dollars grow where but one grew before." Mark Twain wryly asked in 1871: "What is the chief end of man?—to get rich. In what way? dishonestly if he can; honestly if he must."[7]

Such eras—the 1920s, the 1980s, and the 1990s were similar times—often occur during periods of exploding opportunities, rapid growth, and major business reorganization. Bursts of technological advances act to fuel an upsurge in investment and keen competition between firms. Much is achieved economically but at a high price to civic morality and business stability. Moreover, these periods exaggerate disparities of income and wealth, with a greater clustering at both ends of the class spectrum. Economic woes in the 1870s, for example, forced overbuilt railroad lines to slash the wages of their workers, bringing about the first national strike and riotous confrontations in several cities between labor and the National Guard.

The *New York Tribune*, in an 1892 list of millionaires, calculated that in the years between 1860 and the 1890 the number of millionaires in the United States had risen from less than a hundred to over 4,000. The newspaper summed up the era: "The late nineteenth century was the heroic age of the forceful individual personality in American enterprise."[8] Railroad barons reportedly worth more than $10 million in 1880 included Jay Gould, Leland Stanford, and the heirs of Cornelius Vanderbilt. In 1900 the U.S. Senate alone counted twenty-five millionaires among its members, leading critics to deride this august body as a "Rich Man's Club" and the "House of Dollars." Luxuriating in vast mansions and traveling by rail in private "palace" cars, these new rich, with their opulent ways, fascinated contemporaries. Supposedly, when a young reporter asked J. P. Morgan the cost of his yacht, the banker condescendingly replied: "If you have to ask, you can't afford it." The vast fortunes of the age stirred both ire and envy.[9]

Youth indulged its fantasies and found inspiration in the 130 dime novels (an estimated 200 million copies sold) written by Horatio Alger between 1867 and 1895. His heroes were usually orphan boys who turned pennies into the American dream of wealth and success with hard work, honesty, cheerfulness, and more than a little luck. In Alger's books, success was measured by opulent materialism competitively achieved. It was to be won on an urban battlefield. From the fields and farms of America and the fields, villages, and towns of Europe, young men and women flocked to America's cities. As Matthew Josephson has written in the foreword to the 1962 reprint of *The Robber Barons*, "The expanding America of the post–Civil War era was the paradise of freebooting capitalists, untrammeled and untaxed," who acted "nevertheless, [as] agents of progress." American capitalism with few institutional restraints has never seemed more an arena for ruffians and speculators.[10]

From this eruption of ambitions rose the world's greatest economy. Samuel J. Tilden, New York railroad lawyer, politician, and Democratic presidential candidate in 1876, addressed a group of millionaire guests at a fund-raising dinner with words suggestive of Adam Smith: "You are, doubtless in some degree, clinging to the illusion that you are working for yourself, but it is my pleasure to claim that you are working for the public. [Applause.] While you are scheming for your own selfish ends, there is an overruling and wise Providence directing that most of all you do should inure to the benefit of the people."[11] Most of his contemporaries supported Tilden's self-congratulatory view that you aided your fellows by lining your pockets. The English writer G. W. Steavens visited the United States in the 1890s and caustically entitled the resulting travel book *In the Land of the Dollar*.

All Americans, and indeed many others, knew the celebrated names Carnegie, Morgan, and Rockefeller and much about their wealth and princely possessions. The economist Robert Gallman has estimated that the amount of the national wealth owned by the richest 2,000 families increased from 3.6 to 9.6 percent between 1860 and 1890—a gain that came at the expense of those on the bottom of the income ladder. Although highly skilled workers and the salaried middle class usually fared well, for others the Gilded Age offered only irregular employment, low wages, and inadequate housing.[12]

In September 1869 the *New York Times* reported that small workshops had recently decreased in numbers, as many experienced difficulty in competing with the larger firms able to afford new labor-saving machines. Small business, however, remained the mainstay of the American economy for the remainder of the century. The newspaper was nevertheless right in believing that small manufacturers had reason for concern.

Only a few times in American history has the economy experienced such a wild roller coaster ride as the final three decades of the nineteenth century. All businessmen, big or small, shared a common anxiety about untamed business cycles that whip lashed between boom and bust. Moreover, two of the three downturns in these years rank only below the Great Depression of the 1930s in severity. During the "panic" years of 1873–78, 1883–86, and especially 1893–97, businesses failed frequently and unemployment soared as the nation experienced "hard times" and often violent labor unrest.[13]

But the last third of the century was also, paradoxically, a period of great gains in capital and productivity, and a time in which the intense competitive pressures buffeting businessmen benefited consumers, as wholesale prices declined nearly 50 percent between 1869 and 1897. Increased output and falling prices propelled demand, with a wide variety of manufactured goods affordable for the first time. In 1864, glass goblets, for example, were made by hand and cost $3.50 a dozen. Within twenty years, the introduction of bottle-making machines had dropped the price to 40 cents a dozen. Inexpensive western beef became nationally accessible, thanks to the refrigerated railroad freight car introduced in the 1870s. Real gross national product (GNP) grew at a very impressive annual rate of over 4 percent in the three decades after the war.

KINGS OF AMERICA

In 1868, as the first transcontinental railroad neared completion, Harvard-educated Charles Francis Adams Jr., great grandson of the nation's second president and grandson of the fifth, pondered its implications: "Here is an enormous and incalculable force . . . exercising all sorts of influences social, moral, political. . . . Yet with the curious hardness of a material age, we rarely regard this new power otherwise than as a money-getting and time saving machine." Adams's interest in railroads led him to serve briefly as president of a line, but he never respected the railroad magnates, summing them up in 1912 shortly before his death as a "coarse, realistic, bargaining crowd."[14] By 1880, Adams's unsavory "crowd" had created a network of four transcontinental railroads, allowing for the integration of regional markets into a truly national economy. The railroad system opened the trans-Mississippi West to rapid settlement and made such cities as Chicago, Denver, Seattle, Kansas City, and Minneapolis and St. Paul into great and prospering metropolises.

Throughout this period, railroads remained America's most important industry. The capital invested in American railroads rose from $2.5 billion in 1870 to $10 billion by 1890, and it was estimated that by then the railroads owned a fourth of the nation's wealth. Of the steel made in the nation's steel mills, 80 percent went for rails—with the railroads owning many of the mills. Indeed, the 30,000 miles of iron rails that were laid by 1860 had multiplied to nearly 200,000 miles of steel rails by 1900.

An astute British observer of the United States, James Bryce, referred to the railroad magnates as "kings of America." Adams, though, never altered his low opinion of them. He confided in 1882 to a friend his loathing for William H. Vanderbilt after the latter publicly stated: "The railroads are not run for the benefit of the dear public. That cry is all nonsense. They are built for men who invest their money and expect to get a fair percentage of the same."[15] But Vanderbilt's sentiments received a very different reception on Wall Street.

A generation of financiers had cut their teeth trading in national bonds during the Civil War. Their firms dominated the security markets for the next sixty years, but the nature of their activity changed. By the 1880s the business of Wall Street's new investment bankers consisted nearly entirely of railroad securities. Even before the war, American railroads had become dependent on investment bankers affiliated with European money centers to issue securities (mainly short-term negotiable bonds) for construction, expansion, and even operation. New York journalist Charles Dow constructed the forerunner of his celebrated Dow Jones Industrial Average in 1884, devising a market measure using railroads as nine of the eleven companies used in its computation. Only in 1896 did Dow, by now founder and publisher of the *Wall Street Journal*, create a second index, based on daily changes in the stock prices of twelve industrial firms.[16]

In his 1870 best seller, *Ten Years in Wall Street*, William Worthington Fowler wrote reprovingly: "The moralists and the philosophers look upon [Wall Street] as a gambling den—a cage of unclean birds; an abomination where men drive a horrible trade, fattening and battening on the substance of their friends and neighbors." At this time, big corporations represented a novelty. Even the scoundrels needed to learn their trade. The economist Richard Ely believed that the sharp practices of the railroad industry had provided Wall Street's speculators and crooked management with lessons on how to fleece any corporation.[17]

A speculator versed in New York City's geography described Wall Street "as having a river at one end, a graveyard at the other, and a school for thieves in the middle." In 1888 the English visitor James Bryce described the "Street" more prosaically in the *American Commonwealth* as the center for finance and transportation, the two determining powers in business. An awed Bryce, later appointed British ambassador to the United States, predicted that within a generation Wall Street would become the world's financial capital.[18]

The New York Exchange was rife with dirty tricks. In addition to "stock-purchase pools," there were "corners," in which a group of investors bought up most of the available supply of a stock or a commodity to drive up its price. The simplest method of "plucking the goose," the stockholder, involved stock "watering," the deliberate issuing of certificates well in excess of assets. Lack of reliable information placed stock buyers at great risk, and there were many other ways to "milk" a railroad.

A corrupt management and board of directors could sacrifice the stockholders' interests for their own personal gain. One sophisticated type of operation involved creating a subsidiary corporation, either for land development or construction, owned by the railroad's board of directors. This subsidiary then charged an exorbitant fee for its services, allowing the directors and other "insiders" (often influential politicians) to profit at the expense of the railroad's ordinary stockholder and bondholder. Erastus Corning of Albany, the first president of the New York Central, forced the railroad to buy all its iron at exorbitant prices from a company he owned.

A weak railroad could continue operation by issuing securities, as long as investment bankers were willing to market them. Well into the twentieth century, railroad stocks, with the exception of a handful of high quality railroads (the foremost being the Pennsylvania), were avoided by the prudent as too speculative. Bonds long remained the preferred form of long-term investment. Investing in a railroad was risky, but so too was operating one.

SHORT HAULS—LONG HAULS

A long shadow was cast by the erratic practices of the railroad industry. American values of fairness appeared threatened by railroad practices that favored big shippers over small shippers and large cities over towns. Western farmers and small-town merchants were vocal in complaining about the industry. They disliked the tendency to charge more for short hauls over noncompeting routes than for long hauls where competition existed and objected to the railroad's practice of granting secret rebates on the published tariff to large shippers. Faced with overbuilding (often due to speculative frenzy) and the resulting excessive competition, railroads in the 1870s often arrived at arrangements known as pools. These restricted competition in order to avoid "rate wars" but tended to collapse under the weight of aggressive lines reverting in time to price-cutting to gain a competitive edge. Pools and other questionable practices of the railroads created a demand for state regulation of the industry.

Railroads, with their flagrant abuses, made the public aware of the peril that big business could pose to ordinary people and small businesses. And since almost all American businesses were small, including the millions of family-owned farms, it is not surprising that railroads would soon become the nation's first regulated industry.

The American entrepreneur of the Gilded Age played a more important economic role than did entrepreneurs in other countries, in part because there were so many of them. This is true even when differences in national populations are taken into account. H. J. Habakkuk, in *American and British Technology in the Nineteenth Century*, commented that in Great Britain the social system limited social mobility, offering as much if not greater status and power to landowners, the military, and the professions as compared to business. In America, however, the businessman as entrepreneur was unchallenged. Moreover, he was encouraged to differentiate himself from the crowd. Money was to be made not only by designing a better mousetrap but also in producing it cheaper and broadening its market. As the architect Daniel Burnham told a group of Chicago businessmen: "Think big because small ideas do not have the power to move men's minds." Americans were prepared to think big because society's values and attitudes encouraged them to be bold. Schoolchildren learned their ABCs, as well as lessons on character, enterprise, and success, from the famous *Readers* of William Holmes McGuffey, who advised them:

> Once or twice though you should fail,
> Try, Try Again;
> If you would at last Prevail,
> Try, Try Again.[19]

Change was in the air, and it was eagerly embraced. Railroads dramatically reconfigured the domestic market in the last third of the nineteenth century, and many Americans were prepared to take risks and seize opportunities. The great names of the era still have a familiar ring: Armour, Pillsbury, Duke, Westinghouse, Stanford. For those who succeeded the rewards were occasionally staggering. This was especially true for the three men most closely identified with the rise of the American economy in the last third of the nineteenth century: Rockefeller, Carnegie, and Morgan.

ROCKEFELLER AND STANDARD OIL

The railroad's critical role in the rise of American big business is demonstrated by the career of John D. Rockefeller (1839–1937) and his Standard Oil Company of Ohio. Sometime after the War of 1812, whale-oil lamps, offering a source of lighting that was superior to feeble candlelight, came into wide use; but within forty years the supply of whale oil fell short of demand. By midcentury many urban dwellers relied for lighting on coal oil, a product derived from the "squeezing" of coal, though it produced a dark smoke with an unpleasant odor.

Petroleum, or "rock oil," known to be beneath the western slopes of the Appalachians in Pennsylvania, offered an alternative to whale oil or coal oil. But petroleum's use required learning how to refine or distill crude oil into kerosene, as well as developing techniques for drilling wells and bringing the oil to the surface. In 1859, with these technical problems solved, a remarkable boom occurred after drilling started at Titusville, Pennsylvania, on the western slope of the Appalachian Mountains.

The city of Cleveland, on Lake Erie, a natural transport depot, quickly became a refining center. And within a decade, the oil industry loomed large in the nation's new industrial economy. Technological advances came quickly in the young industry, driving prices down and leading to the creation of new by-products. However, efficiency depended on maintaining a high volume of output in the production, refining, and distribution of oil by-products. As early as 1880, kerosene was the nation's fourth-largest export. For nearly a century, the United States led the world in producing, refining, using, and exporting oil and its by-products.[20]

In 1862, a twenty-three-year-old Cleveland commission merchant, already known to his acquaintances for his formidable self-control and shrewdness, invested $2,500 in the new industry. Three years later, young John D. Rockefeller wisely decided to limit his activities to the refining of crude to produce kerosene and by-products, with his company being one of Cleveland's thirty-one oil refiners. Rail-thin, tireless, and quick in thought and speech, he appeared to others as always in motion, clearly a man in a hurry. In 1867, Rockefeller acquired capital for expansion by joining with a partner, Henry Flagler; within two years the growing firm owned two refineries, a barrel-making plant, and a fleet of tank cars. Critical to a competitive edge in the new industry was reducing the expenses of transporting crude oil to the refineries and transporting the finished by-products to purchasers. With his business large enough to exert pressure on the railroads, Rockefeller demanded—and received—secret rebates on transportation charges for his oil shipments. Rockefeller soon won even more favorable freight rates by guaranteeing minimum shipments to railroads eager to use tracks and rolling stock fully and efficiently. Using his collusion with the railroads as leverage, Rockefeller then forced the oil producers who owned the wellheads to submit to his will.

In 1867 Rockefeller incorporated Standard Oil of Ohio. He kept half the voting stock in his family's hands and used the remainder to create an alliance of Cleveland refiners. Standard Oil grew as a company by internal expansion and through mergers, often secretly acquiring rivals. By April 1872, Rockefeller's corporation had acquired twenty-two of twenty-six Cleveland competitors and accounted for a fifth of the nation's output of refined oil. In the next five years, it moved forcefully against rivals in Pittsburgh, Philadelphia, and New York. Efficient competitors were granted favorable terms to combine; others, forced to their knees, sold for what he offered. Employing questionable and sometimes clearly illegal practices—including predatory pricing, frivolous lawsuits, and outright bribery—Standard Oil gained control over more than one hundred companies before century's end. But Rockefeller later claimed that he had allowed a few rivals to survive to refute charges of Standard Oil's monopoly of the industry.

POOLS AND TRUSTS

Never having a controlling share of the stock personally, Rockefeller dominated his associates by his proven business sagacity and strength of personality. Working with the Pennsylvania Railroad, Rockefeller acquired in 1872 a defunct Pennsylvania corporation, the South Improvement Corporation. Its loose charter allowed almost any business activity. Rockefeller's growing alliance of refiners, some of whom themselves had only recently been brought to heel, now coordinated their actions through the South Improvement Corporation to intimidate oil producers and the railroads. An ingenious stratagem was concocted to pressure the railroads to increase carrying rates on both crude and refined oil; all additional new charges—including those paid by competitors—were to be remitted to the South Improvement Corporation. By 1874, with over a thousand employees and a net worth of $1 million, Standard Oil was the world's largest refiner of crude.

Oil producers fought back, refusing to sell their crude to the Rockefeller combination. As news of Rockefeller's "drawback" scheme on the shipments of competitors became known, the railroads, under public fire, backed out of their agreements. The Pennsylvania legislature had no choice but to revoke the South Improvement Corporation's charter. This widely reported scandal fed Standard Oil's growing reputation for squeezing out competitors and corrupting public officials. In 1879 a grand jury in Pennsylvania indicted Rockefeller and other Standard Oil officials on charges of conspiring to extort railroad rebates and predatory pricing to destroy rivals. A federal commission, headed by Republican senator Shelby Cullom of Illinois, charged in 1886 that Standard Oil Company sought to crush all rivals by any possible means.

Despite these reversals, Rockefeller remained firmly convinced (if self-servingly) that without combination the petroleum industry faced chronic problems of excess capacity and overproduction. The capital-intensive refineries needed a high-volume, low-cost production flow. This "continuous flow production" inevitably meant periodic oil gluts, especially during business downturns, along with cutthroat competition and predatory price slashing. The resulting chaos, Rockefeller claimed, only harmed the industry and the consumer. The solution, he believed, required refiners to cooperate in setting prices and limiting competition.

As Standard Oil could not, under Ohio law, hold stock in out-of-state corporations, or even own plants in other states, Rockefeller had to find a replacement for the defunct South Improvement Corporation. For a while he relied on a trade association, the National Refiners Association, to informally arrange "pools"—the contemporary term for extralegal agreements among ostensibly competing firms to control production and prices to the satisfaction of all involved parties. But these "soft" arrangements quickly collapsed during hard times when firms struggled for survival. By the end of the 1870s, Rockefeller had concluded that the pool, being legally unenforceable, was useless or, in his own words, "a rope of sand."

Within a few years, a shrewd Rockefeller lawyer, Samuel C. T. Dodd, thought up the ingenious legal device of the "voting trust." Rockefeller had continued to use his influence on the railroads and the rebates they paid him to limit competition, while secretly exchanging stock with other refining companies. By 1881 the Rockefeller interests had tentacles in forty-two companies, controlling nearly 90 percent of the nation's refined oil. Representatives of these companies conferred frequently to coordinate prices and production. But this alliance lacked a central board to provide formal control at a time when rapid changes unsettled the industry and when oil producers, who had organized to strengthen their own interests, threatened to move into refining. An industry observer in 1880 compared oilmen to cats, since "you can't tell from their screaming whether they are fighting or making love."

Dodd needed a legal, or at least not illegal, way to centralize control over the Rockefeller associates. In 1882, employing an instrument found in estate law, he created the Standard Oil Trust, with nine trustees, headed by Rockefeller and Flagler. The companies, or more precisely their shareholders—led of course by Rockefeller and his associates—exchanged a controlling interest of their stock for trust certificates in the new creation. The nine trustees, holding effective decision-making control, established policy for all member companies. Lacking a charter, Dodd's "voting trust" constituted only a legal fiduciary arrangement—but that seemingly sufficed. Dodd's device effectively achieved corporate consolidation while, it was hoped, avoiding state laws designed to prevent collusion among rivals.[21]

The trustees met weekly in Standard Oil's New York headquarters, a six-story office building at 26 Broadway near Wall Street. From here, they directed far-flung operations. They created subsidiary companies in several states—for example, Standard Oil of New York and Standard Oil of New Jersey—with management of operations handled by the executives of the individual corporations. But the trustees kept tight control of planning and policy functions. To further their central control, uniform accounting and reporting were adopted. The trustees soon acted to consolidate refining operations, closing small plants to concentrate work in several large ones. This done, the Standard Oil Trust moved to integrate operations in the purchasing of crude oil, the transportation of both crude and refined oil, and, finally, the marketing of refined oil and by-products to wholesalers. Oil fields were crisscrossed with efficient pipelines, and important innovations in oil tankers and tank wagons were introduced. By 1890, the trust, moving into crude production, had acquired wells in newly discovered fields in Ohio to achieve full vertical integration. By then, the industry, following Standard Oil's lead, had lowered the price of retail kerosene to seven cents from the twenty-five cents of two decades earlier.

Petroleum prices stabilized, and profits of participating companies rose. Standard Oil's policy set its prices high enough to earn a handsome profit but never so high as to lure competitors back into the field. Its foes claimed that the trust controlled over 90 percent of the country's refined oil and 70 percent of the world market. But a shocked public could only stand by as Rockefeller's trust ran roughshod over opposition to integrating one of the nation's leading industries. Even many who shared the trust's view that consumers benefited from its leadership of the industry distrusted its ruthlessness and monopoly position.

John D. Rockefeller relinquished personal control over the company in 1899, visiting his office only infrequently. By then he had achieved his goal of building a fully integrated organization, complete with marketing and distribution networks and capable of effectively exploiting economies of scale in its rough-and-tumble industry. A deeply religious Baptist, he increasingly devoted his time in retirement to philanthropy. To the public, however, Rockefeller epitomized the rapacious monopolist who ruined competitors by using deep pockets to engage in predatory practices. Journalists and politicians would long seek to make their mark by bringing down a man whose very name had become synonymous in many of the world's languages with vast wealth—"as rich as Rockefeller"—and immense power.

Dodd's model of a trust soon appeared in nearly a dozen other industries. As giant trusts emerged to control the production of sugar, cotton, linseed oil, matches, tobacco, cordage, lead, and whiskey, the public seemed threatened. Almost overnight the trust problem had emerged as the nation's central economic concern, and by 1890 nearly half the states had either enacted antitrust statutes or incorporated clauses into their constitutions aimed at restoring competition. Indeed, six states brought legal action to revoke the charters of corporations involved in trusts. The most famous of these involved suits by Ohio against Standard Oil and New York against the sugar trust. Dodd's strategy of avoiding involvement with the corporate laws of states by means of the trust had not worked, and the trust as a strategy for consolidation had proven vulnerable. In 1892, the Supreme Court of Ohio ordered Standard Oil of Ohio to dissolve. For a few more years, the combination was sustained by interlocking directorates among the major refining companies that had been set up by the trust in various states before its dissolution. But this arrangement, too, was legally suspect. A new way to achieve consolidation had to be found, and this would assume a new form, that of a holding company—Standard Oil of New Jersey.

THE HOLDING COMPANY

In 1889, the New Jersey state legislature, influenced by corporate lawyers (including Samuel Dodd, who helped with drafting the legislation) passed a new law, which allowed incorporation "for any lawful business or purpose whatever." The law permitted manufacturing companies to freely own stock in other companies and offered them wide latitude for exchanging stock between companies. Thus, the New Jersey Corporation Law of 1889 created, in effect, the modern holding company. Two years later, a noted corporation lawyer stated his belief that New Jersey had already earned enough from corporate fees to pay nearly all the state's annual expenses. But all talk of illicit money paled before the significance of the legislature's action. By 1901, a staggering 71 percent of American firms of over $25 million in capital had incorporated in New Jersey—the most prominent being Standard Oil of New Jersey.

Before New Jersey's action, most states had limited share ownership in corporations to individuals. This meant that the corporations were not permitted to own and exchange shares in other companies without a special act of the state legislature. Eager to attract corporations and incorporation fees, other states quickly rushed ("charter-mongering") to make their legislation more attractive to corporations, amid entirely accurate charges of a "race to the bottom." In 1899, Delaware's legislature approved laws so favorable to a corporation's board of directors—at the expense of its stockholders—that it became, and remains, the preferred state for incorporation.[22]

Under political and legal attack and no longer necessary, Dodd's ingenious "voting trust" faded into oblivion as a business stratagem—but the term "trust" continued in wide usage to broadly denote holding companies, as well as looser business alliances such as pools and trade associations. Most often, it was employed simply as a synonym for monopoly and even as a catchall pejorative for big business.

ANDREW CARNEGIE: FROM RAGS TO PHILANTHROPY

Rockefeller's relations with the railroads explained much of his success. The same held true for Andrew Carnegie (1835–1919), the immigrant boy with a soft Scottish burr who amassed a great fortune only to give away over 90 percent. To his contemporaries, the diminutive, five-foot-three-inch Carnegie epitomized that archetypal American hero—the rags-to-riches, self-made man, whose drive and talent led to fame and fortune. But Carnegie's fabulous accomplishment was not the norm. Most successful businessmen at the time started their careers well positioned: affluent parents, American birth, Protestant religion, and far better than average education. Nineteenth-century mobility for the average man was very modest; his chances of rising over the course of a career or enjoying a better job than his father's were good. But the advances tended to be small, as from unskilled to semiskilled laborer.[23] But faith in the possibility of "rags to riches" has long been a powerful idea in the American psyche.

Carnegie, the son of a Dunfermline, Scotland, weaver left unemployable in his trade by the introduction of power looms, emigrated with his impoverished parents to America and a Pittsburgh slum in 1848. At age thirteen, he went to work as a $1.20-a-week bobbin boy in a cotton mill and soon devoted his meager spare hours to training himself for work as a telegrapher. Until the advent of the telephone, the electric telegraph provided the surest means of transmitting information quickly over long distances, conveying in minutes messages that had previously required days and even weeks. At first the principal user of the telegraph was the railroad industry, with the lines usually strung alongside the rails. A dispatcher, informed by telegraph instructions and using trackside signals, could control rail traffic to avoid accidents and increase the rail system's carrying potential. The new invention proved essential to railroad management, and in 1851, young Carnegie, agile of mind and with a forceful personality, became the personal telegraph operator of Tom Scott, superintendent of the Pennsylvania Railroad's western division.[24]

Founded in 1846, the Pennsylvania was the nation's largest corporation and its best-managed trunk line, providing a yardstick for measuring the performance of other roads. Yet, in 1865, the shrewd thirty-year-old Carnegie, now superintendent of the railroad's Pittsburgh division, declined Scott's offer to become general superintendent. Believing he knew enough about business to succeed on his own, Carnegie resigned his position with the railroad to explore new opportunities. Carnegie later commented that if his family had stayed in Scotland he would have lacked the ambition to go out on his own. To Carnegie, as he never tired of saying, America represented opportunities and a culture that encouraged acting on them. In a talk, "The Road to Business Success: A Talk to Young Men," delivered to students of a commercial college in 1885, Carnegie advised: "Say to yourself, 'My place is at the top,' Be King in your dreams." Always the rugged individualist, Carnegie dealt with the world largely on his own terms.

IRON AND STEEL

From 1865 to 1872, Carnegie, to quote him, "had many eggs in many baskets." Most of his early dealings related to the railroad industry, but in 1873

Carnegie decided to concentrate on the iron and steel business. This decision reflected his awareness of the newly developed Bessemer process and the railroad industry's potential market for inexpensive steel—and, as important, the fact that in 1870 Congress had enacted a high tariff on steel, offsetting the competitive advantage of the British steel producers. Establishing himself in steel, Carnegie brought to his operations the managerial skills acquired as Scott's protégé as well as his own intuitive genius. By 1879, at age forty-four, thirty-one years after arriving as a poor immigrant boy without trade or skill, he owned with his partners a company that produced 75 percent of America's crude steel.

In 1860, the United States produced less than a million tons of iron and a negligible 20,000 tons of steel. The iron came in two types—cast and wrought; neither type possessed sufficient tensile strength for versatile use. Making steel from iron required the labor-intensive removal of carbon and silicon impurities, always an expensive operation. The small amount of steel produced went largely for small items, such as knives, straight razors, and springs. Developed in 1856, the Bessemer-Kelly process "drove" out impurities by blowing cold air through molten iron in a cone-shaped "converter." This allowed for large-batch production methods that turned out a superior grade of steel at low cost. Annual production of steel rose from less than 70,000 gross tons in 1870 to 1,247 million gross tons ten years later. By 1900 output exceeded 200 times the 1860 production. By then the output of Carnegie's mills exceeded that of Great Britain. A major new industry had arisen. As a "producer goods industry," it was representative of other major sectors (power machinery, copper, explosives) of the late nineteenth-century economy in selling a product used by businesses rather than the public directly.

Carnegie early recognized that cheap steel meant that railroads would speedily replace brittle iron rails then commonly used since stronger steel rails permitted greatly increased load-carrying capacity. Indeed, almost all U.S.-produced rolled steel went initially to the railroads. By 1880, 50 percent of the nation's rails were steel, and a decade later virtually all. In the booming 1880s alone, 75,000 miles of new steel track was laid, more track than in any prior decade.

In 1875, Carnegie erected the huge Edgar Thomson steelworks in Pittsburgh. Hundred-foot-high smokestacks towered like the spires of a cathedral of industry over plants that spread over several hundred acres. Steelmaking was a capital-intensive industry with high fixed costs, and before a profit could be made, a company had to achieve high-volume, low-cost levels of output, with mills running at full capacity. But steel as a "producing good" was sold to manufacturers whose orders reflected the business cycle, and these circumstances led to drastic price slashing during hard times.

"WATCH THE COSTS"

Knowing nothing about metallurgy or steelmaking, Carnegie employed experts to design the Edgar Thomson works and organize its operations. He claimed to be the first steel man to hire university-trained chemists. Engineers and scientists knowledgeable in the principles of physics, chemistry, and mechanics tested material and designed production flow. Carnegie's own strength lay in management, especially the astute selection of top personnel with the needed technical skills. One of Carnegie's concerns was to devise strategies to deal with the industry's problem of maintaining production and prices during slack times, and another was to cut costs to the bone. One of his associates observed: "Carnegie never wanted to know the profits. He always wanted to know the costs."[25] Striving ceaselessly for cost cutting, Carnegie proved the hardest competitor in a bare-knuckles industry where competition continually pushed down prices and profit margins. Every expense was examined and bottlenecks in production ruthlessly eliminated to cut costs. In Carnegie's own celebrated and often-quoted words, "Cut the prices; scoop the market; run the mills full. . . . Watch the costs, and the profits will take care of themselves." Newer scholarship, however, has suggested that his emphasis on competition and price cutting may have been exaggerated and that considerable collusion among steel manufacturers often allocated market shares among themselves.[26]

By retaining tight managerial control, Carnegie underbid competitors while earning a profit. He based his prices not on market rates but on his own costs and gained a reputation for saving pennies by setting his managers at each other's throats to cut expenses. Carnegie eagerly entered price and production pools with his rivals but was the first to quit when it seemed no longer advantageous. Always the opportunist, he reportedly acquired the Duquesne Steel Company at a fire-sale price after spreading libelous stories about its management.

Carnegie eagerly sought to increase his company's market share. He boasted that others increased their plants and capacity in good times, but he preferred to expand when a depressed economy brought down costs. This positioned him to undersell competitors, taking their markets when the business cycle turned upward. He also maintained full production during downturns, cutting prices and even occasionally selling below cost. A former vice president of his mills noted: "The advantage of Carnegie's management was that even at reduced prices a profit can still be made, and decreased earnings were regarded as preferable to suspended operations. It was the recognized Carnegie policy—'take orders and run full.'"[27]

This strategy reflected the reality of an industry whose high fixed costs put a premium on economies of scale. As he phrased it, "Cheapness is in proportion to the scale of production. To make ten tons of steel a day would cost many times as much per ton as to make one hundred tons." Machines and their tenders were both "hard driven full blast" and replaced as they broke under the strain. When an English chemist demonstrated that the open-hearth furnace, in which hot air and coal gas are blown over molten iron in a large shallow bath, produced steel more economically than the Bessemer converters, Carnegie did not hesitate. Despite heavy investment in the Bessemer process, he quickly installed six open-hearth furnaces at his Homestead plant situated in the vicinity of Pittsburgh.

The Carnegie Steel Company provided one of the earliest and largest examples of vertical integration. Starting with the mills where steel was manufactured, Carnegie soon acquired the mines where iron was extracted. Then he moved on to add coal mines and even the ships that transported iron ore and the railroads that brought coal to the coke ovens in his factories. In all these operations, Carnegie steadfastly lowered costs.

Rivals scoffed at his "scrap and build" approach to buying the new, but Carnegie knew that a small savings per ton at very high volumes justified the policy. When a British steelmaker told Carnegie that English companies relied on twenty-year-old equipment, Carnegie replied, "That is what is the matter with the British steel trade. Most British equipment is in use . . . after it should have been scrapped. It is because you keep this used up machinery that the United States is making you a back number."[28]

Eager to economize on raw materials, the most important aside from iron ore being limestone and coke (or coal baked to remove sulfur and phosphorus), Carnegie acquired his suppliers. He recruited Henry Clay Frick (1849–1919) as a partner because Frick owned mines that provided the soft coal needed to heat blast furnaces; in the 1890s, Carnegie acquired extensive holdings in Minnesota's Mesabi Iron Range, rich in high grade ore. Now fully integrated, his company owned limestone and coking coal quarries, coal mines, railroad lines, and Great Lakes freighters, as well as four great mill complexes. The efficiencies and innovation of Carnegie's company provided the driving force for turning steelmaking into one of the nation's basic industries and for making steel into the building material of industrial America.

Carnegie always retained over 50 percent of the Carnegie Brothers limited partnership, an unincorporated private company. Actively involved in running the company, his "general partners" had unlimited liability for its debts. Carnie recruited his partners for their capital, connections, and talent, but only if they signed an "ironclad agreement" that on leaving the company they sold back their interests. Despite his partners' objections, Carnegie insisted that profits be used for expansion and improvement and always boasted that not needing to heed either stockholders or bankers allowed him to pay more attention to long-term strategy.[29]

Highly social and an inveterate traveler, Carnegie used his trips to make connections with important politicians and businessmen. In his long absences from Pittsburgh, he insisted on accurate reports and pressured his accountants to develop sophisticated systems of cost sheets, modeled on railroad practices, to expose unnecessary expenses and potential inventory problems. But the changing nature of the steel market also had to be considered. In 1875 the railroads used over 90 percent of rolled steel, but by 1890 they required only 50 percent. As this market diminished, Carnegie quickly found other purchasers for steel—in building construction, shipbuilding, and elsewhere. But here he encountered new competition. A rival described Carnegie as "one of those rare characters who can see the drift of things, and was always to be found . . . swimming in the main current where movement was the fastest." Now his mettle would be tested severely.

At the dawn of the new century, Carnegie faced a fight in the rapidly changing steel industry with the combined Rockefeller and J. P. Morgan interests. Yet he ended his career on his own terms. In 1901 the Carnegie partners received $492 million to merge their holdings into Morgan's newly created U.S. Steel. Always the wily Scotsman, Carnegie insisted on being paid his share, $225 million, in 5 percent gold bonds, politely declining the overvalued shares of U.S. Steel offered him. On closing the deal, J. P. Morgan supposedly said to Carnegie: "I want to congratulate you on being the richest man in the world."[30]

Long an advocate of what he termed the "gospel of wealth," Carnegie believed the rich had a responsibility to use their wealth while alive for social benefit, rather than hoard up riches to be apportioned by the executors of their wills. ("He who thus dies rich dies disgraced.") Prominent among his many causes was the American public library system, and he funded over 2,500 libraries in all states of the union. An adept self-promoter, the highly vain Carnegie also tried to fashion a reputation as an enlightened capitalist. In this regard, a long-standing embarrassment had been the Homestead Strike of 1892, one of the bitterest industrial conflicts of the era. Seemingly, wage cuts caused the strike—the company, after making mechanical improvements in the production process, reduced wages for skilled workers. Yet some historians believe that management considered wages less important than their desire to break the steelworkers' union and assert complete control over work rules. Leaving his tough-minded partner and general manager Henry Clay Frick in charge of negotiations, Carnegie conveniently left in early spring for a "vacation" in Scotland.[31]

Frick promptly locked the men out of the Homestead steelworks, a Dickensian place where green and orange flames from molten steel leapt high into the sky. Frontage on a navigable river or seacoast was (and is) crucial to controlling transportation costs at a steel mill, and Homestead stretched for miles along the banks of the Monongahela River. To break the strike, Frick brought in by barge several hundred rifle-toting hired Pinkerton "detectives." In the ensuing pitched battle with workers waiting along the banks, deaths occurred on both sides. Pennsylvania's governor called in the state National Guard to reopen the factory, and after a five-month standoff the union collapsed. The beaten men now returned to work. Public sympathy shifted from the workers after an anarchist, unconnected to the strikers, shot and wounded Frick. Remaining in Scotland until the strike had been broken, Carnegie sought to distance himself from industrial strife at a time when it had reached levels in the United States that were among the highest in the Western world. But to many workingmen, the Homestead strike came to symbolize a conspiracy in which industry and government linked arms to deter unions or any other threat to the power and profit of big business. Carnegie's critics bitterly dismissed his talk of social responsibility as hypocritical. Many of his workers angrily charged that he had forgotten his own humble background to gain the approval and company of the world's rich and titled.

The career of J. Pierpont Morgan (1837–1913) was also intimately tied to the railroad industry. His father, Junius Spencer Morgan, had moved the family to London in 1854 to sell American government bonds and a few railroad securities, as a partner in a private merchant banking firm. The mechanism for foreign investment then consisted of banking arrangements for transferring funds from one country to another. The elder Morgan soon established his own firm of Dabney, Morgan & Company, and in 1860 his son returned to the United States as his father's agent, providing him information on political and economic developments. The young man's early career would be largely spent obtaining capital in Europe for U.S. government securities and increasingly selling the stocks and bonds of American railroads. When the North introduced military conscription in 1863, Morgan legally hired a substitute for $300 to serve out the Civil War in his stead and bragged that he had earned $55,796 for the year. In later years, Morgan humorously referred to the man as "the other Pierpont Morgan," giving him occasional gifts of cash.[32]

The young Morgan joined the old Philadelphia banking house of Drexel in 1871 to challenge the supremacy of another venerable firm, Jay Cooke and Sons. After the Panic of 1873 ruined Jay Cooke, Drexel, Morgan & Company acted as the principal conduit for European investment in American railroad securities. This mostly involved bonds, stocks being favored only by speculative investors. After British investors lost heavily when the Erie Railroad declared bankruptcy during the Panic of 1873, Morgan redoubled his efforts to rehabilitate the name of American railroad securities. His firm acted as New York agent for his father's firm in London, now known as J. S. Morgan & Company, with many of the same directors on both boards. The huge need for capital for American railroads presented profitable opportunities for Morgan to bring together European investors and American companies —if foreign investors could be confident that their investments were reasonably safe.

In 1873, J. P. Morgan's firm moved into the Drexel Building at the corner of Broad and Wall Streets, kitty-corner across the street from the New York Stock Exchange. Reconstituted as J. P. Morgan & Co. in 1895, it remained housed in the Drexel Building until World War I. Morgan's private office, separated from clerks and customers only by a frosted-glass partition, was located on the first floor close to the entrance. A reputation for icy brusque-ness protected Morgan's privacy, as did his imposing six-foot stature and withering glance when irked. According to his son-in-law, "Anyone who called could speak to him, but anyone who interrupted him unnecessarily or stayed too long was not encouraged to do so again." The journalist Lincoln Steffens observed: "His partners did not go near him unless he sent for them, and then they looked alarmed and darted in like office boys."[33] He worked his partners hard but richly rewarded those who demonstrated worth and survived.

Morgan prided himself on remaining imperturbable in a crisis. He invari-ably dominated negotiations, with his reserved presence and highly orga-nized intellect. A big, burly figure with piercing black eyes and a prominent nose disfigured and reddened by a skin disease, Morgan's visage easily lent itself to caricature by cartoonists after he acquired fame as the nation's lead-ing banker.

During the Civil War, many commodity houses, such as Lehman Broth-ers, which had traded in antebellum cotton, moved into the securities field to become investment banking firms. Railroads and their financing occupied center stage of the capital market by the 1870s. Investment bankers, after studying and approving a proposed security sale, would agree to take the securities on commission, to underwrite them (guarantee their sale), or to purchase them outright. With large issues, banks organized a syndicate to spread the risk. Investment bankers thus acted as the intermediary between lenders (including commercial banks, insurance companies, wealthy inves-tors, and foreign sources) and borrowers. As such, they needed to protect the lender's position, which often involved exercising oversight over a borrow-er's use of the acquired funds. Then, as now, investment banking demanded good judgment—and above all steady nerves. In 1912, Morgan told the Pujo Committee of the House of Representatives in all sincerity that "the first thing in [finance] is character."[34]

Morgan informed one journalist: "The fact is that bankers are in the business of managing risk. Pure and simple, that is the business of bank-ing." His lifelong strategy was to avoid highly speculative ventures, and his business philosophy rested on that simple premise: "The kind of bonds which I want to be connected with are those which can be recom-mended without a shadow of a doubt, and without the least subsequent anxiety, as to payment of interest, as it matures." He directed much of his energy toward sheltering his companies and clients from the chaotic business cycle and chicanery.

"MORGANIZING" THE RAILROADS

Morgan advised clients on how best to invest their funds. Here he tried to recommend solid properties. Given the shady bookkeeping and other ethical lapses of railroad lines, this posed problems. Moreover, Morgan tried to protect the investments once they were made. Along with other investment bankers, Morgan acted to tame destructive warfare among rival roads. He acknowledged his "moral responsibility" for companies he underwrote, scrutinizing every aspect of their operations and if necessary restructuring their finances and hiring and firing managers. To Morgan, excessive competition wasted resources by unnecessary duplications, and he tried to persuade lines to avoid rate warfare.

Excessive competition, however, can be partly explained by the nature of the railroad industry. The primary costs of running a railroad were fixed costs—including the costs of servicing the debt incurred in laying the track and buying the rolling stock. Indeed two-thirds of operating costs were fixed. With such high fixed costs, large railroads had an inherent advantage since they had a lower total cost per shipment. This well-recognized rule spurred heavy investments in increasing capacity, which in turn led to heightened competition for passengers and freight. Pushed to the wall by excessive capacity, railroad lines often declared bankruptcy.

Some railroad managers made money through financial stratagems rather than by operating a transportation business. A few, though, most notably Jay Gould of the Erie Railroad and Cornelius Vanderbilt of the New York Central, managed to do both. Cornelius Vanderbilt (1794–1877) consolidated eleven small railroads in the 1860s to form the giant New York Central, while greatly adding to his own wealth by watering its stock. At his death, at age eighty-three, Vanderbilt's estate was valued at $100 million. He left 87 percent of his railroad stock to his eldest son, William H. Vanderbilt, despite the fact that he openly called him a dunce.

The New York Central operated a well-run network of 4,500 miles of track, which branched north from New York City to Albany and then swept west to the Great Lakes, opening the nation's interior to eastern ports. In contrast to Vanderbilt's system were the actions of his rivals in one of railroad history's titanic wars: the struggle for the Erie Road (1867–71). Daniel Drew, Jay Gould, and Jim Fisk—the winners in the war—soon engaged in a series of criminal machinations in pursuit of short-term trading profits that left the Erie crippled for decades. The Erie—the "harlot of the rails," the "Scarlet Woman of Wall Street"—could not use the market to raise capital for needed improvements until reorganized by Morgan in 1895.[35]

In 1876, two-fifths of all railroad bonds defaulted and many lines were in receivership. London investors, badly burned by the Panic of 1873, would not buy American railroad stocks. Morgan was painfully aware that the railroads needed to get down to business and earn a profit from the day-to-day operations.

American railroads' weakness stemmed from ruinous overbuilding, high capitalization, and the costly floating of bonds and stocks. Cutthroat competition forced down rates, and rival roads struggled to attract sufficient business to service debt. Morgan acted to consolidate competing lines. He believed that uncertainty had to yield to the rational, conflict to cooperation. Working with other investment banking houses, Morgan pressured the railroads to use their regional industrial associations to act as a pool, regulating fares and rates. His lieutenants on the boards of railroads actively worked with the railroad associations; in several celebrated instances, Morgan personally intervened to end rate wars between rival lines.

Morgan reorganized the major eastern railroad lines, bolstering their shaky capital structure by scaling down fixed liabilities and exchanging them for stock—almost the opposite of what would occur in the 1980s. If bondholders proved unwilling to accept stocks for their obligations, he tried to persuade them to exchange their bonds for ones of lesser yield. When such remedial action did not suffice, Morgan promoted mergers and acquisitions to construct viable systems. Often he would create a "voting trust" composed of his handpicked representatives to control a bankrupt company.

Morgan frequently described his policies as creating a "community of interest" among rival lines; the stronger "Morganized" lines now effectively resisted the large shippers with their constant demands for rebates. Bankers and railroads persuaded bondholders to cut interest charges, and Morgan used Wall Street to raise new capital for railroad improvements. In all, rational collective decisions had to replace "blind competition" as the guiding force in the railroad industry; long-term profits and the interests of bondholders and stockholders had to be paramount. He dressed down a railroad president talking of "his" roads by exploding, "Your roads, your roads belong to my clients!"[36] Morgan had a pronounced love of order and system—some believed it an obsession—and the instability of the railroad industry appalled him.

MORGAN AS AMERICA'S TREASURER

Until late in his career, Morgan's activities centered on the railroads. In 1890, Morgan interests controlled one-sixth of the nation's railway system; it was time to diversify his interests. In April 1892 Morgan engineered the merger of two companies to create the General Electric Company. During a financial panic in 1895, the federal government borrowed $62 million in gold through Morgan's banking house to replenish the treasury's dwindling reserve, averting a serious crisis and gaining Morgan the reputation as the most "powerful private citizen in the world." He had served as America's unofficial central banker, stopping a Wall Street panic by single-handedly keeping the treasury solvent.

The nation's railroads emerged from the 1890s a mature industry. The major lines had been consolidated by decade's end into six huge systems controlled by groups organized through Wall Street banks, principally J. P. Morgan and Company and its formidable rival Kuhn, Loeb. No longer a pioneer industry or catalyst for the economy, its importance would be as a provider of transportation. Investment bankers widened their nets and looked elsewhere for new opportunities.

Initially, the rise of big business in manufacturing had largely relied on personal funds, transferred mercantile capital, and reinvestment of profits. Some industrial stock was traded, but with a few exceptions investors regarded industry suspiciously. As a rule, utility companies and industrial stocks were judged too speculative for insurance companies and savings institutions to own. In fact, most manufacturing enterprises had remained small private companies as late as the 1880s, with net worth seldom reaching $2 million.

Then, in the 1890s, industrials began to be freely traded on the floor of the New York Stock Exchange. The number of manufacturing firms issuing shares rose from 30 in 1893 to 170 in 1897. But these numbers reveal only part of the change: the size of the involved firms completes the picture. The total value of industrial stocks and bonds listed on the exchanges jumped from $33 million in 1890 to nearly a billion dollars in 1898 and then rose to exceed \$7 billion in 1903. Wall Street and big business working together had entered a new stage.

CULTURE, THE ENTREPRENEUR, AND THE RISE OF BIG BUSINESS

Big business happened first and more quickly in the United States than elsewhere. In assessing the reasons for this it has been suggested that America had created a new kind of businessman who wanted to do things in a big way. He thought and worked in ways conducive to large-scale enterprise. Businessmen similar to Morgan, Rockefeller, and Carnegie, however, were present in Great Britain and Western Europe, and this complex process cannot be explained by a single factor or a simple explanation. German industrial development, for example, took the form of cartels of suppliers and manufacturers rather than vertically integrated firms. Certainly the size of the American market played a role in the rise of giant integrated firms.

Nevertheless, it appears that an American value system and culture, which identified change with progress, caused the rapid pace of economic activity and helped shape it. What people believe possible has much to do with what they achieve. The American economy possessed an energizing entrepreneurial ethos fueled by American cultural values. Common sense suggests that such a business environment must encourage more risk takers and innovators than one that emphasizes tradition and continuity. Every society is capable of producing exceptional individuals. What is truly startling about America in the last decades of the nineteenth century is the number of entrepreneurs and the extent and scope of their activities.

American values and behavior supported competition with a relative absence of social constraints. In a society where everyone looked for his main chance, American businessmen eagerly sought opportunities to grow big. However, national character can offer only a partial explanation for the remarkable revolution that occurred at the end of the nineteenth century.

Many economists and historians believe that technological changes at the end of the nineteenth century made the rise of big business inevitable. According to this view, a new type of capital-intensive industrial firm was needed that would be capable of benefiting from economies of scale so as to lower costs and broaden its market. No less a contemporary observer of the rise of big business then Andrew Carnegie thought this to be the case. The historian Alfred Chandler developed a sophisticated version of this interpretation and minimized the importance of the individual entrepreneur. Instead, he stressed the role of transportation, technology, and market forces as the catalysts of business change.

Pressed too far, however, such a view regards history as an unraveling or evolutionary process rather than as in part the creation of human choice reflecting individual creativity and strength of will. Great men and women do influence history. In an article for the *Atlantic Monthly* of October 1880, Harvard philosopher William James commented on the power of individual initiative: "The formative influence of geniuses must be admitted as, at any rate, one factor in the changes that constitute social evolution."[37] It says much about American society that its best and brightest are drawn to business to develop and express their strengths. It is hard to explain the dynamism of American capitalism in the Gilded Age without celebrating the role of the entrepreneurial adventurer in propelling the emergence of an industrial economy characterized by the rise of big business.

CHAPTER SEVEN

A Changing Workplace
and Society

None of the processes in the mechanical industries is self-suffcing. Each follows some and precedes other processes in an endless sequence, into which each fits.—THORSTEIN VEBLEN, The Theory of Business Enterprise (1904)

Sometime in the 1890s the United States surpassed Great Britain to become the world's leading industrial nation. This development had long been expected. What had not been anticipated was a new trend in business. The size of business enterprises had grown greatly in the last two decades of the nineteenth century. A large-scale transformation of business enterprise occurred in important sectors of the economy in the form of giant incorporated managerially directed firms that increasingly coordinated mass production and distribution to sell standardized and branded goods to a national market. According to the brilliant iconoclastic sociologist Thorstein Veblen, the metamorphosis of business was due to the "modern concatenation" of industrial process and markets. The new scale and scope of activities, he recognized, required far-reaching business strategies based on this new interplay of production and distribution, rethinking older business practices now demonstrated to be inadequate.[1]

The value of products manufactured in 1880 was $5 billion; this figure rose to $11 billion by 1900, by which time the United States produced more iron and steel than Great Britain and Germany combined. The disruptive era of industrial capitalism on a national and even international scale had arrived. The thrust of the economy was toward churning out commodities faster, cheaper, newer, more. The movement in business was away from the locally oriented family firm and toward the publicly owned and professionally managed national firm.[2]

To contemporary observers, the most visible expression of economic change was the greater variety and volume of products offered consumers and made affordable by modern industry. Mass marketing of brand-name goods and advances in meatpacking and canning changed the way Americans shopped and ate. Swift meant packaged meats, Campbell meant canned soup, and Singer meant sewing machines. As William Leach has written of the years after the Civil War, in *Land of Desire*, "American capitalism began to produce a distinct culture, unconnected to traditional family or community values, to religion in any conventional sense, or to political democracy. It was a secular business and market-oriented culture."[3]

The emergence of this culture was not smooth. The last two decades of the century experienced major recessions, massive labor conflicts, and strident political battles over gold versus silver and tariffs. The economy grew quickly but with an unevenness that made for desperation for those being left behind and a general sense of insecurity for many others. Conflict between capital and labor became strident and at times violent. Even the telling of time became a matter of practical concern as well as a search for certitude. Business leaders took the lead in a push for standardization and coordination now made possible by telegraph lines and underwater cables. In 1880 Britain adopted Greenwich mean time as its standard, and three years later American railroads, voting according to how much track they controlled, divided the nation into four time zones. In 1884 the World Time Conference in Washington, D.C., established Greenwich Observatory in England as the prime meridian from which world time is reckoned.

PHILADELPHIA CENTENNIAL

Nearly one in six Americans, 8 million in all, visited the Philadelphia Centennial International Exhibition of 1876. Enthusiastic crowds thronged exhibits displaying Singer sewing machines, Yale locks, Otis safety elevators, McCormick reapers, Pullman sleepers, and Remington typewriters. The startled Brazilian emperor, Dom Pedro II, listened to the newly invented telephone and exclaimed, "My God! It talks!" An industrial age, started a century earlier in England with primitive shuttlecocks and flying jennies, had by now transformed the lives of ordinary Americans. Before the eyes of the fairgoers stood evidence of their country's industrial prowess, with many of the inventions not yet in common use. The unsettling pace of change was increasingly driven by technology. Within twenty-five years, many of the major features of the modern age had emerged, from a nascent global economy to the vertically integrated industrial corporation to a consumer culture soon to be propelled by sophisticated advertising firms. As early as the 1880s, however, the "throughput" of business, meaning the amount of goods and services passing through the national economy, had grown so large that a new type of business organization was needed to handle the vast traffic of goods resulting from the accelerating velocity and complexity of industrial change.

MECHANIZATION TAKES COMMAND

The showpiece of the Philadelphia Exhibit was the gigantic Corliss steam engine, the world's largest. Forty feet tall and weighing 680 tons, the Corliss —driven by twenty boilers that worked two double-action vertical high-steam pressure engines—powered every machine in the Hall of Machinery. The Corliss was an awesome display of a perfect mechanical system of interrelated cylinders, flywheels, cogs, pulleys, shafts, and belts, all assembled by man to achieve almost unthinkable power and efficiency. "An athlete of steel and iron with not a superfluous ounce of metal," rhapsodized the novelist William Dean Howells.[4]

The Corliss engine symbolized for a generation the rise of a powerful mechanized technology as the foundation of an unprecedented scale of production that some historians have called a second industrial revolution. Such industries as petroleum, chemicals, primary metals, transportation equipment, and food processing sought economies of scale—high fixed costs meant that increasing the volume of production decreased cost per unit. Andrew Carnegie observed, "In an age noted for its inventions, we see the same law running through these. Inventions facilitate big operations, and in most instances, require to be worked upon a great scale." Factories had to be run at or near full capacity. To Carnegie, this fact sufficed to explain "an overpowering, irresistible tendency towards aggregation of capital."[5]

In the last quarter of the century, large industrial companies arose in significant numbers for the first time. With small and fragmented markets coalescing into an expanding national market, the potential for companies capable of utilizing new technologies to achieve an unprecedented scale and speed of production became clear. However, it also became obvious, as Veblen had noted, that a company, in order to fully profit from economies of scale, had to integrate production and distribution. Shortages of raw materials or a backup of finished products could not be tolerated. From start to sales, the possibility of holdups needed to be minimized. In the rush to grow bigger, companies joined not only with competitors but, increasingly, also with suppliers and distributors. A process was under way that has been variously described as the "rationalization" of the industrial corporation, or, in less evaluative terms, the concentration and consolidation of leading sectors of the economy. The forces unleashed by this push toward business consolidations in the final decades of the century struck the business world with an impact a Morgan associate likened in 1898 to a powerful hurricane broadsiding a small Caribbean island.

A usual early step in the formation of this new type of industrial firm was to increase output and lower costs by long runs of a single item. After this elementary step, the firm had to reorganize in order to master the sheer scope and complexity of its own activities. This often required attempting to establish control over all aspect of operations, from the acquisition of raw material to delivery of finished products to the consumer—from managing personnel to developing new techniques of cost-based accounting. By itself, the Corliss engine, and the technology it represented, remained a sleeping giant until it was harnessed to a complex business system (managerial and financial as well as technological) able to efficiently channel its potential for profit. Success required building a business organization capable of effectively exploiting the economies of scale. English biologist Thomas Henry Huxley informed reporters at the Philadelphia Exhibition: "I am [not] in the slightest degree impressed by bigness. Size is not grandeur. . . . The great issue, about which hangs a true sublimity . . . is what are you going to do with all these things."[6] Yet in the United States bigness would soon become synonymous with a new business strategy, Veblen's "concatenation" of industrial process and of markets that sought to shift from reacting to the market to a systematic effort to master market forces.

THE ORGANIZATIONAL INFRASTRUCTURE OF BUSINESS

As industry after industry pushed technological breakthroughs to achieve and maximize high-volume production, entrepreneurs had to exploit new business opportunities in a timely fashion. The successful innovator of technological advantages could often reap large short-term profits until competitors caught up with him, a phenomenon economists refer to as the "first mover" advantage. Basic inventions often resulted from a recognized demand, the proverbial better mousetrap, in which many sought to develop a product that met a recognized need. Some inventions, however, resulted from serendipity and individual genius. In any case, to be profitable entrepreneurs had to transform inventions into innovations people were prepared to pay for. Innovation is different from invention. Business people are rarely inventors. Generally, they turn the inventions of others to profitable use. Indeed, many "big businesses" resulted from successfully combining technological innovations with marketing systems.

Americans proved ready consumers of standardized mass-marketed goods. Enlarged markets, in turn, required large-scale operations to sustain them. Transcontinental railroads spawned a national market, and business rushed to profit from new opportunities. In 1866, Cyrus Field laid a transatlantic telegraph cable between New York and London. Indeed, after 1870, innovations in information technology acquired a breathtaking pace. The telegraph and later also the telephone allowed the speedy transmission of business information and conveyed the decisions derived from this information. Steam-powered freighters and liners replaced sailing ships in the last third of the century, and in 1876 Alexander Graham Bell invented the telephone. (When offered the patent on Bell's telephone, the telegraph company Western Union reportedly declined, replying that "the device is inherently of no value to us.") By 1900, Manhattan had 20,000 phones, all but a handful used for business, with 20 percent located south of City Hall in the financial district. Inventions had so compressed space and time that the financial and commercial markets of America and Europe were by now in constant communication with one another every moment of the day.[7]

Important innovations always suggested—or even required—new ways of organizing things. In 1874 the Remington Company began selling large numbers of the first practical typewriter and in doing so pioneered three features of the office machine industry to come: low-cost manufacturing of complex machines, the need for a widespread organization to sell and maintain the product, and training to enable workers to use the technology effectively. Remington stores and typing schools spread around the country, and typewriter sales within a decade reached 20,000 a year. By 1875 the rotary printing press made it possible to print on both sides of a sheet of paper simultaneously. Edward Barbour invented a calculating machine in 1872 that provided for printed totals and subtotals, and an eccentric crank named John Patterson devised a cash register and then founded the National Cash Register Company. When shopkeepers resisted buying this expensive novelty, Patterson established a sales training school whose students memorized a scripted sales approach. By the end of the century, businesses produced large volumes of information efficiently and distributed it quickly.

By century's end, the self-taught, amateur, mechanical-tinkerer inventor characteristic of the early nineteenth century was being challenged by university-educated scientists trained in a rigorous methodology. As capital demands increased and adequate financing became more difficult for individuals to obtain, large companies increasingly took over the role of generating new technologies. The career of Thomas Edison (1847–1931) exemplified this transition. The self-taught Edison had conducted crude experiments at his parents' home as a youth. After his initial success as an inventor-businessman, he designed and constructed a large industrial laboratory in New Jersey in the late 1870s. Here he hired academically trained scientists to research inventions adaptable to commercial use. Edison numbered among his inventions the lightbulb and the phonograph and a pioneer movie camera known as the kinetoscope. Edison also organized commercial companies, among them Edison Light Company, Edison Illuminating Company, Edison General Electric, and Edison Biograph Films. To make the use of electrical inventions more practical, in the early 1880s he worked out the design of a complete light and power system. A central dynamo station pumped an electric current through underground wires to homes and offices. This system was demonstrated successfully in the Morgan-bankrolled Pearl Street station in lower Manhattan, America's first central power station. A compulsive worker, Edison insisted that persistence brought success, telling interviewers that "genius is 1% inspiration, 99% perspiration."[8]

What set Edison apart from other inventors was a lifelong interest in building systems, not merely individual devices. His Edison General Electric Company, predecessor of General Electric, manufactured and installed everything required to illuminate the night—from the bulbs to the huge coal-fired generators known as dynamos. The introduction of the electric dynamo in the early 1880s opened the way for the commercial use of electricity. Its concentration of immense energy in high-capacity power stations provided a powerful metaphor for a miraculous industrial technology capable of transforming night's darkness into seeming daylight and emitting a flow of energy that traveled great distances over wires.[9]

At century's end, the production of high explosives and the creation of new alloys (such as aluminum) opened possibilities for the application of physics and chemistry to the industrial process. Academic institutions expanded programs for training scientists and engineers, and farsighted corporations involved in areas that were technologically challenging gave thought to opening their own laboratories. The flowering of the chemical and electrical industries in the late nineteenth century demonstrated the importance of applied sciences to the creation of new industries.

Sleeping car king George M. Pullman made it a practice in the 1870s to open his office doors for an hour or two Thursday afternoons to any inventor with a patent to sell. But a more deliberate and systematic linkage between science and technology had to be forged. A fortune awaited the inventor of the metaphorical "better mousetrap," and there was no shortage of aspirants. From 1790 to 1860, the U.S. Patent Office had granted 36,000 patents; in the three years between 1886 and 1889 it issued 38,000. Overwhelmed, the U.S. Patent Office could not process patents fast enough. Technology had become a self-generating force, with one invention providing the impetus for others. Big business no longer could afford to wait for inventors to show up. Instead, scientists were hired to work in industrial labs on specified projects. Begun in 1900, General Electric's research lab was proudly named "The House of Magic" and soon employed several hundred college-trained scientists.[10]

CONTINUITY AMID CHANGE

Some historians of business, writing in the 1990s, have put forth a revisionist view of big business's ascendancy at the end of the nineteenth century, challenging the interpretation of the rise of the modern industrial corporation as pushing small family-owned industries to the margins of the economy where they remained of relatively little interest and importance. Philip Scranton, of the University of Pennsylvania, in his 1997 study *Endless Novelty*, suggested a very different picture. He has shown that firms engaged in specialty and custom production played important roles in such areas as machinery and machine tools and in such consumer fields as apparel, jewelry, styled textiles, and furniture. Firms in these fields had to be nimble and flexible, quick to shift product line and output as demand and market fashions required. Scranton argues that small companies in the twentieth century accounted for much of America's manufacturing. Big business was neither as efficient as once thought, nor were small industrial firms as marginal or backward as portrayed.

This new line of thinking is a valuable corrective in pointing out that thinking about industry and business cannot be shoehorned into overly simplistic categories. Historians no doubt have a tendency to emphasize change at the expense of continuity. This said, it is still imperative to recognize the advent of modern industrial corporations, as did contemporaries, as the cutting edge of the future. Their practices and products have shaped modern America.

FACTORY FLOOR AND FACTORY OFFICE

A self-righteous John D. Rockefeller testified to investigators for the Ohio Supreme Court, which was trying Standard Oil Company of Ohio for conspiracy against trade in 1898: "I ascribe the success of Standard Oil to its consistent policy to make the volume of its business large. . . . It has not hesitated to sacrifice old machinery and old plants for new and better ones."[11] Rockefeller obviously intended to rebuke critics who claimed that his success was due to unfair business practices. Yet there was truth in Rockefeller's remarks. Continuous-process machines in such varied activities as meatpacking, cigarette rolling, soap manufacturing, and foodstuffs canning reflected a new type of industrial technology geared to high-volume production. Technology had acquired an irreversible momentum, and business practices and organizations needed to adapt. The goal was to coordinate the processes of manufacture and distribution under the unified administration of a hierarchy of managers in order to lower costs and minimize snags in a continuous flow of production from raw material to the finished product offered for sale.

The new scale of production required major business reorganization from factory floor on up. The average workforce in a steel mill, for example, jumped from 220 to 412 in the ten-year period after 1879. Old ways of doing business had to be reexamined. Greater complexity demanded a greater effort at control. The informal "rule of thumb" had to be supplanted by a reasoned procedure on the basis of the systematic knowledge of the forces employed. A few years later Thorstein Veblen would expand on this thought:

"None of the processes in the mechanical industries is self-sufficing. Each follows some and precedes other processes to an endless sequence, into which each fits and to the requirements each must adapt its own workings."[12] Alfred D. Chandler Jr., a leader in the institutional school of business history, would provide a fuller description and explanation of changes in the organization of manufacturing and distribution. Integrated firms, he premised, needed to develop professional salaried managerial hierarchies. Once established, these hierarchies would seek to extend and perpetuate their power. Essential to their role was the need for information to maintain control and coordinate activities.

The way the people worked and what they made had to be taken into account and systematized. Technology's potential had to be coordinated with corporate marketing strategy. Industries oriented to mass production required people trained in engineering skills, management, and finance, as well as skilled and semiskilled labor. Speed, punctuality, and routine became important as operations expanded in scale and scope. Provision had to be made for the rapid and integrated flow and the record keeping of materials and information, all the way from the lowest laborer's workbench to the desks of upper management.

By 1900, carbon paper, time cards and time clocks, typewriters, file folders, telegraphs, phones, paper clips, staplers, switchboards, and filing cabinets were standard office equipment in large firms. The once-ubiquitous all-purpose male clerk perched on a high stool and wearing eyeshades gave way to a typist, switchboard operator, and filing clerk, who were soon joined by the receptionist—all increasingly female. It required experience for a company to identify the organizational changes necessary to cope with bigness and complexity. Moreover, it took Americans time to understand the profound social changes resulting from new ways of doing business.

Appearing before a New York State Industrial Commission in 1888, John D. Rockefeller bluntly asserted: "It is too late to argue about the advantages of industrial combinations. They are a necessity . . . and require the agency of more than one corporation."[13] Big business was a jinni, released from a bottle. By the late 1890s most large manufacturing firms had incorporated. Economies of scale dictated business concentration, and incorporation facilitated integration. Industrial combinations would provide goods and services on a scale previously unseen while requiring the employment of vast amounts of human and financial capital.[14]

The advantages of a corporation in raising capital, achieving limited liability, and acquiring permanent life paled before its growing importance as the foundation for complex business organization. The management or institutional school of business historians has challenged the once commonly held view that industrial combinations resulted primarily from the need to raise capital or from the desire to reduce competition by means of mergers. Although not rejecting these as contributing factors, these historians propose as their explanation the "efficiency hypothesis": that the rise of the integrated corporation represented the necessary integration or "rationalization" of production and distribution within a single corporation.

According to Alfred D. Chandler Jr., a leader of the management school, big business—in the form of the modern corporation—occurred when the process of mass production and the process of distribution were joined within one business firm. Stated in more familiar terms, Chandler suggested, as Thorstein Veblen and Ronald Coase had earlier, that the placing of activities formerly handled by different companies under one corporate roof resulted—in certain industries—in greater efficiencies. Even more important than the desire to eliminate competition and achieve a dominant market position, horizontal and vertical integration resulted from a search for managerial control and transactional efficiencies, which were made possible by a revolution in transportation and communication that lowered the cost of and made feasible "administrative coordination."[15]

Management's goal was for the corporation to be impervious to market forces and fluctuations. In Chandler's words, the "invisible hand" of the marketplace had yielded to the "visible hand" of managerial decision making. Adam Smith's perfect competition had been replaced by managerial usurpation of market forces. This was done by assembling various business operations under one corporate roof. Integrated firms arose because managerial control inside the organization allowed for the production and distribution of goods at lower cost than in the wider marketplace. Moreover, such large firms were well positioned to diversify their activities into other industries, expanding both their scope as well as their scale.

Requiring as they did a steady flow in order to operate with high efficiency, industries oriented to high-volume output remained vulnerable to interruptions in manufacturing. The velocity of throughput—the rate at which raw material flows through production—was of course a key to efficiency and lowered business expenses, because with capital equipment the biggest cost is the cost of not working, periods during which interest and other overhead must be paid but the equipment does not earn. Problems in production might result from difficulties outside as well as inside the plant. The former might include holdups in the delivery of basic supplies needed to manufacture the product or snags in the distribution or sale of the finished product. Thus difficulties at either end of the process could result in an intolerable backup of inventory.

For these reasons and to control costs companies reached out beyond the factory gate—to seek ownership of their sources of supplies and the distributive network for their products. Such a strategy is known as vertical integration, and it occurred in two ways: forward or backward. A manufacturer integrated forward toward the consumer by entering directly into distribution or sales. Backward integration required acquiring ownership of needed raw materials and parts.

Each of these strategies has broad implications for business operations and organization. Forward integration dispenses with independent distributors: commission agents, wholesalers, and retailers. Backward integration replaces the supplier. Even more than horizontal integration (with its dreaded specter of monopoly), vertical integration—especially forward integration—transforms the nature of both the corporation and the economy. Only a very few companies, notably railroads, steamship lines, and telegraph companies, exhibited tendencies toward this pattern before 1880, but during the 1880s vertical integration became increasingly common in oil, steel, meatpacking, and tobacco. Early in the twentieth century, certainly by 1910, almost all major American industries were vertically integrated. It was this aspect of the big American corporation that largely distinguished it from big German or Japanese firms, which relied on informal long-term associations of suppliers, manufacturers, and distributors.

FINANCE CAPITALISM

This rise of big business in the form of the integrated corporation occurred too quickly—in less than three decades—to be explained only in evolutionary terms. The role of Wall Street in encouraging business consolidation was also significant. Some companies went public to raise capital for mergers and acquisitions or simply to expand; others did so to gain profits for founders and their investment bankers. The highly contagious development of what has been termed "finance capitalism," the remarkable torrent of private firms going public in a brief period, suggests that their owners had discovered that converting to equity shares in their business made their wealth more marketable and hence more valuable. Furthermore, investment bankers eager to profit from brokerage fees gladly acted as their teachers. By 1900, Henry Clew, president of the New York Stock Exchange, could report a new interest, even obsession, among financiers. They lusted after "the profits to be made . . . and powers to be gained in arranging mergers and acquisitions."[16] Carnegie's retirement in 1901 is often taken as symbolic of the passing of the era of the entrepreneurial firm, for this consummate entrepreneur and rugged individualist sold out to a corporation, U.S. Steel, created by a financier, J. P. Morgan.

The growing need for capital increased the importance of financiers in the affairs of industry. Business expansion had formerly occurred through reinvestment of profits to build new factories and acquire additional machinery, but expansion now increasingly relied on the selling of stocks and bonds to finance mergers and acquisitions. The number of industrial firms trading shares on the New York Stock Exchange rose from 30 in 1893 to 170 in 1897, while the total value of industrial stocks and bonds listed on the exchange jumped from $33 million in 1890 to nearly a billion dollars in 1898. But even these figures do not do justice to the transformation that occurred in leading sectors of American industry and finance. Close and powerful links between investment bankers and big business disturbed those who feared the "money power" of Wall Street.

MAKING CONSUMER MARKETS

The integrated corporation needed to develop mass-marketing operations to expedite "economies of speed." Manufacturers used the new national railroad network to "ship" brand-name products from coast to coast. Richard S. Tedlow of the Harvard Business School has contributed greatly to our understanding of the mass-marketing revolution that started at the end of the nineteenth century. Until the rise of national companies prepared to handle coast-to-coast distribution, the American marketplace was regional and fragmented, with very few nationally known products and little national advertising. The usual strategy for the small businessmen engaged in producing, wholesaling, or retailing was to compensate for low volume by keeping prices high. All of this now changed.

Large firms arose to market nationally advertised, standardized, branded products to 76 million Americans. A population unaccustomed to branded products had to be trained first to accept and then to prefer them. Tedlow described the process, which he has called "unification": "Through advertising and publicity, through forward integration into company-owned wholesaling, through franchise arrangements with retailers, through the creation of sales programs and their implementation, and through the systematic analysis of carefully collected data, the large firm came to exercise an impact on the market. . . . The market still played a key role in the sense that consumer acceptance was essential, but the firm's power to shape and mold the market was greatly increased."[17]

A new era in marketing emerged that changed not only how Americans bought, but what they bought and, in due time, their sense of well-being. In the traditional main street shop or at the general store at a country crossroads, almost everything from sugar to soap to crackers was sold without a brand name as a generic. Placed in barrels or bins, items were wholesaled and retailed by weight or volume and often carried away in the customer's own container. Prices were not necessarily uniform, and customers often haggled. Many of these practices represented the way things had been bought and sold from time immemorial, but revolutionary changes were under way. Shopping by brand was to be the quintessential modern experience.

As early as the 1880s, corporate logos were introduced, attached to mass-produced products. Soon basic commodities came packaged and identified with a company's brand. The consumer no longer asked the grocer for a pound of flour but instead requested a pound of Pillsbury's packaged flour. The color of a box or the familiar figure of Aunt Jemima was sufficient to identify the contents and convey a subliminal message.

Brand-labeled products of national firms—like Campbell's soup, Heinz beans, and Ivory soap—appeared on store shelves in Boston, Omaha, and San Francisco and in small towns in between. New industries came forward, ranging from processed and packaged foods and beverages to pharmaceuticals and advertising. The arrival of factory packaging, and such conveniences as waxed paper, offered a potential for predictable quality and encouraged the emergence of national brands; buyers helped themselves to premeasured branded bags. Nonperishable foods, such as crackers, sugar, and oatmeal, which had been marketed in bulk from barrels, were now sold under brand names in boxes of standard size and weight. Whatever their other differences, almost all Americans, with the exception of pockets of the rural poor, were exposed to an increasingly shared universe of uniform consumer goods. By century's end, advertising billboards festooned country roads and cluttered the urban landscape.

The closing years of the century witnessed an avalanche of appealing and enduring products: Coca-Cola (1886), Log Cabin syrup (1887), Aunt Jemima pancake mix (1889), Fig Newtons (1893), and Animal Crackers (1900), as lawyers registered over 10,000 trademarks with federal authorities in Washington, D.C. With greater choices opening up to consumers, businessmen needed to influence what they purchased. Advertisements urged consumers to bathe with Pears' soap or eat Uneeda biscuits. The older view that the businessman's skill lay in finding out who wants what and satisfying that market need now also often included the ability to shape and even create markets. The active promotion of brand names became a major function of American business. Giant national firms worked hard to introduce and improve products and to gain name recognition for them. Special packaging or different formulas were employed for product positioning and market segmentation in order to appeal to particular groups of potential customers. In 1900 companies paid nearly a $100 million for advertising space in newspapers and magazines.

PALACES OF CONSUMPTION

Department stores first appeared in the 1870s and quickly established a policy of uniform prices. Offering a wide variety of goods at fixed prices, these "palaces of consumption" took advantage of a concentrated urban market to profit from high-volume sales. Downtown department stores—Marshall Field's in Chicago, Macy's in New York, Wanamaker's in Philadelphia, and I. Magnin in San Francisco—attracted middle-class women with money to spend and time to shop. The stores' genteel tearooms provided customers with "quiet elegance" for dining and decorous socialization. Neatly dressed shopgirls staffed the counters to handle transactions politely and efficiently. Marshall Field coined his store's snappy slogan, "Give the Lady What She Wants." Indeed, much time and preparation went into encouraging women's wants, with eye-catching decorations and enticing displays of a cornucopia of ready-made merchandise carefully displayed to produce a maximum effect. For many middle-class women, shopping now represented a social occasion and even an adventure, but not everyone approved. Sunday sermons by the 1880s frequently denounced the idle and expensive "vice of shopping" prevalent among female parishioners. But for other parishioners, department stores provided an important new source of female employment.[18]

By the 1890s, mail-order houses like Sears, Roebuck and Company and Montgomery Ward, famous for their hefty catalogs, were shipping goods by rail to small-town and rural America. New products appeared sooner in cities than in the countryside, but the mail-order houses speeded their appearance in the hinterlands. Sears distributed its first general catalog for home delivery service in 1894. Early catalogs offered customers the chance to examine purchases at freight offices before paying COD, or customers could use products like musical instruments for a trial period, with a token down payment of a dollar; the freight was paid by Sears on returned goods. The Sears founder promised customers to add only the smallest percentage of profit possible to the actual cost. Enthusiastic recipients referred to catalogs as "wish lists."

Chain notion and grocery stores like Woolworth's and A&P also appeared by century's end to spread the largesse of economic growth downward. Founded in 1859, the Great Atlantic and Pacific Tea Company (A&P) began as a tea importer but stocked groceries as early as 1859. By 1900, A&P, as it was then known, had 600 stores nationwide. But they were of the old-fashioned type, with clerks fetching requested items from high shelves. In some of the high-volume mechanical industries, such as the manufacturing of sewing machines and agricultural implements, the producing firm took over marketing responsibilities and built dealer organizations, which were the prototypes of modern direct marketing operations. The Singer Sewing Machine Company, a pioneer since the 1850s in manufacturing's retail selling, claimed 2,000 stores worldwide by 1905. Each store featured not only salespeople but also mechanics to service repairs.[19]

These developments benefited consumers by offering a constantly expanding variety of goods and services at lower prices. They posed a threat, however, to jobbers and commission merchants and also, of course, the small independent stores that dominated the nation's retail trade. Companies such as Procter and Gamble and the National Biscuit Company developed products with brand loyalty. With customers requesting them, they could sell directly to retailers, dictating terms and prices and bypassing middlemen.

Department stores and chain stores not only often forced out small retail competitors but they developed integrated systems of purchasing, sometimes involving the acquisition of factories to produce desired items, which they then branded with their private label. As with many of the changes described in this chapter, the interests of consumer and producer, of big business and small business, often clashed. Developments in retailing especially fueled fears that the coming of big business diminished entrepreneurial avenues for the small businessman. Many of the changes, moreover, were of such a complex nature that it is difficult to evaluate them in terms of winners and losers. What can be said with certainty is that business operated in an environment of constant change that offered many opportunities and perils.[20]

ENTREPRENEURS AND MANAGERIAL CAPITALISM

The rise of big business altered the nature of the workforce from top to bottom. Until the closing years of the nineteenth century, nearly all enterprises were managed at the top, in a personal entrepreneurial fashion, often having been started by a founder inspired by a new invention or idea to provide something otherwise unavailable. Businesses, even ones as large as Standard Oil or American Tobacco, were usually closely identified with a single man whose style and reputation provided the corporate image or personality. Henry Adams described such masterful businessmen as Carnegie and Rockefeller when he wrote that "the new American . . . must be a sort of God compared with any former creation of nature."[21] Family involvement and sons succeeding fathers in the business still counted greatly; but appearances of continuity at century's turn only obscured the important changes now under way. The world of owner-managed firms had yielded in major sectors of the economy to a new type of professional management administering a hierarchic organization. In major segments of the economy, small firms had been pushed from the center of the economy by the advent of giant businesses organized along new lines. To oversimplify, a two-tier economy of large corporations that dominated key industrial sectors and small proprietary family businesses mainly on the periphery of business activity now seemingly existed.

Professionally managed integrated corporations represented the leading edge of the new American industrial economy. Chandler wrote of the modern business enterprise:

This institution appeared when managerial staff were able to monitor and coordinate the activities of business units more efficiently than did market mechanisms. It continued to grow so that hierarchies of increasingly professional managers might remain fully employed. It emerged and spread, however, only in those industries and sectors whose technology and markets permitted administrative coordination to be more profitable than market coordination. Because these areas were at the center of the American economy and because professional managers replaced families, financiers, or their representatives as decision makers in these areas, modern American capitalism became managerial capitalism.[22]

In 1878, William H. Vanderbilt, who a year earlier had succeeded his father as president of the New York Central, told a state committee investigating Standard Oil he had never encountered their equals as businessmen: "One man could hardly have been able to do it; it's a combination of men."

When Vanderbilt made his remarks, Standard Oil and the railroads— exemplars of big business and the modern corporation—were still rarities in a world where most firms remained proprietary. In 1880, most manufacturing still occurred in small or medium-sized factories, an owner almost always personally managing his business. In the next two decades, as industrial corporations became the rule and pushed for "bigness," salaried managers took the owner's place. These managers were professionals with special skills who were expected to create a "system" suitable to the nature and scale of the enterprise. Ownership and management had been separated in other ways as well.

Stock ownership could be widely dispersed among passive observers, whose only concern was the dividend check or share value on the exchange. Obscuring these changes at the top was the lingering tendency to regard a great business firm as an expression of the personality of some dominant entrepreneurial figure, usually the founder. Big business in the form of the professionally managed integrated industrial corporation was becoming increasingly impersonal and bureaucratic, but many in the public clung to an older view of business as identified with an owner.

GEORGE M. PULLMAN, HIS COMPANY AND TOWN

George M. Pullman (1831–97) was the sort of iron-willed, hard-driving American entrepreneur who was regarded as characteristic of the period.

Andrew Carnegie, a shrewd judge of people who had briefly been Pullman's partner, wrote of him in 1886: "He monopolized everything. It was well that it should be so. The man has arisen who could manage, and the tools belonged to him."[23] By the end of his career ten years later, however, Pullman neither managed well nor owned the tools, and his death in 1897 actually caused the stock of his company—of which he owned by then shockingly little—to rise appreciably.

A contemporary said of Pullman that he invented "comfort in railroad travel." Starting in 1865 with a luxury sleeping car with upper-berth beds, Pullman within a few years introduced the dining and salon cars to rail travel. Buying out his initial partners, he incorporated Pullman's Palace Car Company in early 1867 with an initial offering of $1 million in stock. Pullman acted as general manager while serving as both company president and chairman of the board of directors. He ran the company bearing his name with an iron hand and also was a domineering presence over rivals and the railroads who leased his cars. Leading competitors either merged with him or left the business. To the public, George M. Pullman embodied a company identified with luxury, efficiency, and uniformity in product and service.

The Pullman Palace Car Company operated a variety of sleepers and other service cars on railroad lines owned by others. Passengers first bought a ticket from the railroad for travel; then if they wished to avail themselves of Pullman's services they paid a surcharge to his company. In operating the cars, Pullman's company strived for consistently high levels of performance by all employers. (With its fabled Pullman porters, the company for over half a century was the country's largest private employer of African Americans.) The company soon entered the railroad car building business, producing cars not only for its own use but also for the railroads. But as late as 1873 the company had only 300 workers manufacturing and repairing sleeping cars. Pullman could deal directly with his shop foremen with little need of layers of middle management standing between him and his men.[24]

Pullman was as brilliant a promoter as he was a businessman. Working to convince the public that the services he provided in travel truly represented a luxury worth paying extra for, Pullman not only made his name synonymous in several languages with elegance and comfort (in Italy and Greece luxury tour buses are still called Pullmans), but also made it shorthand for modern industrial efficiency. French observers at the Philadelphia Centennial Exposition of 1876, awed by the American products on display, called them "Pullman style." Asked often by reporters the secret of his success, the sleeping car king usually referred to the "Pullman system"—order, efficiency, and planning.

In 1880, Pullman decided to build a new railcar manufacturing shop several miles south of Chicago, though the scarcity of housing in the selected area was an obstacle to attracting the skilled workforce needed. Pullman acted boldly to solve this problem, building a complete, planned "model town" for a population of 10,000 that reflected the high standards and efficiency already associated with his name. Not prone to modesty, he bestowed his name upon the town. Pullman intended the town to guarantee a supply of good labor and to free these workers and their families from the many social problems of the cities, elevating them in health, reliability, and behavior.

A company brochure explained to the many visitors attracted to this unique and attractive social experiment that "the Story of Pullman naturally divides itself into three parts—the building of the car, the building of the operating system, and the building of the town." To Pullman, building a model town was not to be regarded as philanthropy. Instead, he described his intentions as an exercise in enlightened self-interest. The factory's car-building facilities were carefully designed so that manufacture could be done in sequence. As a car was constructed, it moved along rails, foreshadowing the future assembly line, to subassembly points; at each of these a work gang under a foreman completed a specific job.

Pullman expected all nonfactory facilities in the town, including even the church, to return a rate of 6 percent, and he set rents accordingly. The happy and healthy workers of the model town would, he believed, provide a stable, sober, industrious workforce, immune to both the blandishment of union organizers and the lure of saloons. Nor did Pullman allow either union or saloon in his model town. Pullman intended his "experiment" to demonstrate that a company acting strictly in its own interests could also benefit its workers and solve many social problems of an urban-industrial society: the conflict between capital and labor, the housing of the working class, and even the crowding of cities. The town would, he predicted, demonstrate the natural harmony of interests between employer and employee; and in attracting attention it would also act as a showplace for the company.

Pullman's fame and praise for his model town soon traveled throughout the world. An English journalist wrote in 1883 of "the clean workplace, the care bestowed on the homes and comforts of the work people and their families." By the end of the 1880s, however, Pullman had lost his once-tight control over company affairs. This had not resulted from internal challenges, for here he remained impregnable. But after 1884 Pullman no longer owned a controlling interest, nor was he the biggest of the company's several thousand stockholders. Pullman's real problem, however, was that the company's operations had become too varied and its scale too large for him to manage in the personal style he had used for so long.

By 1889, the Pullman Palace Car Company employed over 11,000 workers, divided into two divisions. One serviced the sleeping cars as porters, cleaners, and conductors. The other built and repaired cars. Its factory in the model town was reportedly America's biggest plant, with a workforce of nearly 6,000; in addition, there were two other car works and some seventy-six repair shops and warehouses scattered across the country. Company office buildings were maintained in Chicago and New York, and the company (and George Pullman personally) had invested in a score of other companies, including New York's new elevated Third Avenue steam railroad. By now spending more than half of each year away from his Chicago home, Pullman devoted himself almost exclusively to handling the company's investments, extending its operations to Europe, and supervising major contract renewals with the railroads. A superintendent was in charge of car production in the model town; other company officers and clerks attended to the town's management. Pullman's visits to the town had become infrequent.

In 1894 the factory workers of the model town went out on strike, for the interests of capital and labor could diverge as well as converge. Pullman's vaunted theory of a harmony of interests had proven naive. Wage cuts by the company due to a depressed economy had brought on the strike. The workers resented the company's authoritarian control of their lives in the town and Pullman's refusal to lower rents while slashing wages. But it is also clear that poor lines of communication between management and the workers promoted mutual suspicion. (When Eugene Debs's American Railway Union engaged in a sympathetic boycott of all trains carrying Pullman cars, rioting erupted in Chicago. U.S. troops were ordered in to break the boycott and restore order. Debs, convicted of violating the recently passed Sherman Antitrust Act, went to prison.)

Intended to showcase the harmony of interests of capital and labor, Pullman's model town instead became infamous as the site of one of America's most important strikes and as a demonstration that paternalism, however well-intentioned, invites hostility. For a generation, the Pullman strike symbolized an America fraught with labor unrest and even, many feared, succumbing to the European disease of class conflict. Not a few thought federal interventions in the strike demonstrated once again a political order based on an alliance between big business and the national government.

After Pullman's death, his successor, Robert Todd Lincoln, son of the martyred president, quickly divested the company of the town. Lincoln, a lawyer by training, was strictly a management man. He ran the Pullman Company in a highly businesslike way that brought profits but showed little daring, and neither the company nor its president ever again captured the public imagination as it had done repeatedly with George Pullman's bold entrepreneurial style. The Pullman Company had moved from an initial stage of corporate organization, dominated by an entrepreneurial founder, to a second stage in which executive power resided in a salaried upper management.

When a congressional committee heard Pullman testify in 1895 about the cause of the strike, the members expressed astonishment. His reputation was as a leader in total control, but an uneasy Pullman reluctantly admitted he knew little of his business's day-to-day operation. This had been delegated to others, while Pullman devoted himself to the larger picture and financial matters. It soon became apparent to the congressmen that much of the factory superintendent's authority in the shops had been delegated to largely unsupervised foremen or "straw bosses."[25] Foremen often acted as inside contractors who took responsibility for an operation at a set price, paying their crew and pocketing the profit. Car production had not been effectively systematized and coordinated by the company executives in their offices miles away in the headquarters building. Instead, it was handled ad hoc by the foremen. Pullman's well-publicized "system," at least as far as the plant was concerned, was more show than substance.[26]

The dispersal of authority found at Pullman was characteristic of much of nineteenth-century industry. Craft traditions based on the autonomy of the worker and his solidarity with his mates flourished. Autonomous craft workers often owned their tools, set their own pace, and sometimes even established a "stint," or a self-imposed limit on production. With ethnic clustering in particular jobs or skills the rule, worker solidarity, often based on shared ethnicity, bolstered labor's bargaining position with employers and foremen. Efforts in the late 1880s to control costs, increase the productivity of workers, and transfer control from foremen to management had proven largely ineffectual.[27]

The practice of "inside contracting" was common wherever complicated operations existed, used by companies as different as the R. H. Macy's Department Store and the Winchester Repeating Arms Company, famous for its lever-action rifles, but it was most commonly employed by firms that made custom-designed products. The Winchester factory floor was organized into departments and subunits, the latter being run by foremen acting as job contractors with considerable discretion in hiring and assigning schedules. Foremen were expected to deliver a finished product to the company at a set price and were responsible for quality control, although an assistant superintendent signed off on each satisfactory "subassembly." Until the very end of the nineteenth century, reliance on subcontractors existed in many big companies side by side with attempts at new systems of centralized control.[28]

Always eager to demonstrate that his company stood at the forefront of progress, George Pullman in 1880 had purchased the famous Corliss engine from the Philadelphia Centennial for $130,000. Thirty-five cars had carried the dismantled pieces to his model town, where they had been reassembled and placed behind a giant plate glass window at the main factory. Facing the tracks of the Illinois Central and visible to rail travelers coming to Chicago from the south and east, the engine stood tall as the physical expression of the power of the so-called Pullman system. Yet the strike of 1894 revealed that Pullman's system had not taken into account either the human factor or the complexity of modern business organization and industrial operations. "Scientific management" of the workplace would become a major concern of the next generation of company managers. This was especially the case as professional salaried managers inherited (or took) the reins of power away from the hard-driving and often intuitive entrepreneurs who had founded America's giant corporations.

FASTER, CHEAPER, NEWER, MORE

Between 1870 and 1900, America experienced what has been described as a second industrial revolution, one based on the dynamo and steelmaking. This was the "technology of steel girders and whirling gears."[29] The harnessing of electricity and the industrial uses of chemistry began to amplify an industrial production originally based on steam power transmitted through belts and pulleys. Annual industrial productivity increased at a rate of an unprecedented 3 or 4 percent annually. These spectacular gains had resulted from a huge capital investment in industrial technology. Agricultural implements, typewriters, bicycles, and some types of railroad cars were assembled from standardized parts. Over time, the machine tools used to cut, drill, and grind the metal became more specialized ("dedicated") as they did the same job over and over to produce long runs of the same item.

Watching developments unfold, economist David A. Wells wrote: "Combinations of capital on a scale hitherto wholly unprecedented constitutes one of the remarkable features of modern business methods."[30] A new industrial order oriented to mass production—with its novel tools and machines—required a rethinking of the organization of the factory floor. The persistence of traditional craft work and weak management practices demonstrated the need for a new management style to reduce confusion and inefficiencies.[31]

SCIENTIFIC METHOD AND SCIENTIFIC MANAGEMENT

British philosopher Alfred Lord North suggested in 1891 that the century's most important invention was the scientific method itself. A way of "scientific thinking" soon merged with the search for progress and efficiency in almost all aspects of life: from the bedroom (eugenics), to the kitchen (home economics), to the factory (scientific management). The movement toward greater industrial efficiency was profoundly influenced by a new educational emphasis on the importance of science and scientists. A self-conscious modernity, based in large part, ironically, upon faith in the scientific method, influenced the thinking of the educated classes. Everything was to be questioned and subjected to rigorous and methodical scrutiny.

In May 1886 a paper entitled "The Engineer as Economist" was read to members of the American Society of Mechanical Engineers. Its author, Henry Towne, president of the Yale and Towne Manufacturing Company, remarked: "The management of works has become a matter of such great and far-reaching importance as perhaps to justify its classification also as one of the modern arts," and he called on his colleagues to involve themselves.[32] Even as he spoke, members of the American Society of Mechanical Engineers engaged in methodical studies of just how workers went about a task. One of them, Frederick W. Taylor (1856–1915), confirmed the costly inefficiencies resulting from workers clinging to familiar ways of working, or "soldiering" as it was called, despite the new industrial technology. Born to a prominent Philadelphia family, after receiving an engineering degree, Taylor did the unusual. He worked for six years on the factory floor of the Midvale Iron Works. Starting as a lowly mechanic, he quickly rose to foreman, and then, after becoming an expert on metal-cutting methods, to the plant's chief engineer. While at Midvale, the slight, boyish-looking Taylor developed his ideas about reorganizing factory work. According to Taylor, there was a right way to do things and a wrong way of doing things and nothing in between; by the right way he meant increased production, lower costs, higher wages, and bigger profits.

Taylor regarded industry's customary reliance on foremen using rule-of-thumb practices—derived from an older craft tradition of work and personal experience—as a serious impediment to effective control. The foreman's discretionary authority needed to be replaced by a "shift system of functional foremen" responsible only for a specific job done in a manner set by upper management. To Taylor, the key to business success was a "carefully woven network of system. . . . It is the lack of this system which . . . constitutes the greatest risk in manufacturing." For twenty years, Taylor toured the country, lecturing with evangelical enthusiasm on his vision of scientific management.[33]

To Taylor, management needed to determine scientifically the best way of doing things. It could then impose a rigid command-and-control system by means of "carrots" and "sticks." As the system had to be imposed from the top down, the entire corporate structure needed to be "centralized, standardized, and rationalized." All practices and policies had to be methodically scrutinized and reviewed in terms of efficiency—with all manual operations timed and record keeping and improved accounting systems set up. Taylor was sure his system—which included wages based on piece rates—would reduce tension by demonstrating that "men will not do an extraordinary day's work for an ordinary day's pay." However, from labor's perspective, Taylor's call for systematizing posed a "newfangled type of speed-up." It would strip the men of any vestige of autonomy while forcing them to work harder.

In 1898 the Bethlehem Steel Company hired Taylor as a consultant at a salary of fifty dollars a day plus expenses. He immediately undertook an experiment, the "Pig Iron Study," which came to be the most celebrated demonstration of his principles. With a stopwatch, its dials marked off in tenths of a minute, he timed a gang of men carrying ninety-two-pound "pigs" of iron up a ramp onto a freight car. The men averaged 12.5 long tons of iron a day, which earned them on average $1.15. Taylor thought it possible to quadruple this output. He selected from the workmen a "small Pennsylvania Dutchman." For the purpose of writing up the experiment, he named the man "Schmidt." Taylor had picked "Schmidt" as his subject because the man was energetic and "mentally sluggish," characteristics Taylor considered ideal for the job at hand.

Schmidt was told that he would be paid $1.85 a day if he complied fully with the instructions given him by Taylor's assistant. The assistant followed Schmidt about for several days ordering him about: "Now pick up the pig and walk. Now sit down and rest. Now walk—now rest." By the end of the experiment, Schmidt was averaging a daily load of 47.5 long tons of iron. Using the results as a norm and factoring in time for delays and rest, Taylor came up with a set of instructions. The science of pig-iron handling had now, he believed, been determined. Taylor had substituted a mechanical work pace based on repetitive motions for the worker's freedom to use his body and his tools as he chose.

Analyzing the results of his experiment, Taylor concluded that a pig-iron handler should lift only 43 percent of the time and be entirely free from any load the remainder of the time. More important, while under load, a handler should never be permitted to just stand still, as merely holding the ninety-two-pound pig caused nearly as much fatigue as moving it. Using Taylor's ideas, the Bethlehem Steel Company cut its workforce of pig-iron shovelers from 600 to 140, reportedly reducing its costs of handling the material by more than half. The full implications of Taylor's work awaited the twentieth century, when he gained international stature as the founder of the scientific management movement whose goal was streamlining the industrial workplace.

Though understandably regarded as the enemy of workers and unions, Taylor was also critical of management. He wanted a new type of businessmen, one trained in analytic skills. He once bluntly told an audience of Bethlehem management: "You haven't got any brains, you haven't got any ability." Taylor indeed antagonized more than he converted. He thought both management and workers tended to oppose change even when it meant greater efficiency. At the end of his life, he wrote, "In the past man has been first; in the future the system must be first."[34]

CLERKS, SECRETARIES, AND WOMEN'S WORK

Only the "scientific system," Taylor argued, could handle the complexity of big business. The new age required leadership based on professionalized skills and team management, with hierarchical layers of middle management interposed between workers and upper management. The quill pen and hand copy book of a clerk perched on a stool before a pigeon-holed desk in a countinghouse had long since yielded to the typewriter, telephone, and filing cabinet of the corporation office. The company clerk prized for his penmanship had multiplied in numbers and been transformed into a white-collar employee who, increasingly, was a woman. An important and revealing social change was under way. Clerical positions that when held exclusively by men often represented an apprenticeship for management now tended to be dead-end. American employers did not generally believe that women could effectively supervise men or should make a career out of business. Many corporations held down or lowered wages by hiring only single women and firing those who married. Race, religion, ethnicity, and gender all operated as distinct criteria in hiring. This, of course, worked to the disadvantage of blacks and, to a lesser extent, of certain ethnic and religious groups. Indeed, black women generally could not find clerical employment outside of black-owned businesses until the 1960s.

In 1890, there were already 33,000 stenographers and typists, and by 1900 this figure had increased to 134,000, including a new occupation listed by the census as "secretary." Women in 1900 made up 77 percent of all typists and stenographers, but they represented only 5 percent of physicians and 1 percent of lawyers. Just how jobs came to be defined by gender is not always easy to explain, but certain occupations quickly became identified as women's work. These were usually occupations that involved little hard physical labor, offered poor pay and low status, and required little investment of time and money in education. It was assumed that women should earn less than men since they could count on family support. Moreover, a woman working was still regarded as a temporary stage before she started a family, a woman's true calling. In 1900, only 6 percent of married women worked outside the home. The most respected professions fully, and almost exclusively, open to females were primary school teaching and nursing.

In 1900 there were nearly a million domestic servants, by far the largest job category for women. The right race, religion, and age were considered legitimate requirements for even the most poorly paid and low-status positions as housekeepers and chambermaids. Classified ads of the period clearly demonstrated America's social and ethnic consciousness. New York newspaper ads commonly included such phrases as "Neat Colored Girl," "Refined Girl, white," "German preferred," "Girl, light colored."

Yet M. Carey Thomas, president of Bryn Mawr College, after recounting the difficulties and self-doubts she had overcome in aspiring to a higher education and a career in the 1870s, could conclude in 1908 that social changes were preparing the way for the coming economic independence of women. These changes reflected in large part the new needs for women workers and the opportunities thus created.

SYMBOLS OF AN AGE

The modern corporation, along with the Corliss engine, was a symbol of the age. But the corporation was a social invention, not a mechanical one, and its parts and their arrangement could not be determined with finality. This allowed adaptation to changing circumstances. In 1897, the twenty-year-old Corliss, made obsolete by the electric dynamo, was sold for scrap. But the modern business corporation demonstrated viability. Its enduring value is as a flexible business form that allows for the creation of complex communities of business interests, replacing the informal personal ties that no longer sufficed in a modern economy.

By 1900 the United States stood supreme as the world's greatest industrial and economic power. It was the world's leading producer of coal, natural gas, oil, copper, iron ore, and silver, and its factories produced more goods than those of Britain and France put together. America's economic advantages included geographic expanse, natural resources, and a national market of 76 million consumers. The annual value of the nation's manufactured goods in constant dollars had increased from $2 billion in 1870 to $11 billion in 1900. For the average American, progress was not an abstraction but a commonplace of experience.

America's great corporations spearheaded new industrial technology and pioneered new forms of business organization. In the years between 1865 and 1900, capital formation as a proportion of national income rose an average of 20 percent each year. Productivity gains delivered by technological advances reduced prices, while real incomes, demand, and production all rose. In the final thirty years of the nineteenth century, wholesale prices fell by at least a third; yet annual real growth in the period still averaged around 4 percent. American workers enjoyed a standard of living superior to that of Europeans. The German sociologist Werner Sombart, upon visiting the United States, wondered why American workers did not become socialists and concluded that they did not because they could afford to eat apple pie and roast beef.

One could argue that the late nineteenth century experienced more change affecting greater numbers of people in basic ways than any other comparable prior time in history. Historians have focused on the last two decades of the nineteenth century as the time of the emergence of full-scale urban-industrial society.

By 1900, two of five Americans lived in cities. For the most part, city building was an exercise in private enterprise, and eagerness for profit spurred urban innovations. Everywhere could be seen countless signs of change, from towering skyscrapers employing steel-frame constructions and safety elevators to tabloid newspapers whose editors sensationalized their pages and added comic strips and supplements to increase readership and attract advertisers. Electric-arc street lighting in the 1890s created "great white ways" in city "downtowns," sustaining business (and pleasure) late into the night. Cable cars, electric trolleys, and elevated railroads moved masses of workers, shoppers, and pleasure seekers into and out of crowded urban business districts. Stand-up lunch counters became popular in accommodating eating habits to the new fast-paced tempo of an urban-industrial era. The main meal of the day, dinner, eaten around noon on the farm, became the evening meal in the late nineteenth century, and mechanical refrigeration for the food industry changed eating habits.[35]

Between 1880 and 1900, the standard work week for nonagricultural workers declined from sixty hours a week to fifty-four; two weeks of paid holiday in the summer became fairly common for salaried workers—but not for wage earners. A leisure culture was emerging as crowds attended professional sporting events; amusement parks attracted throngs by offering roller coasters, racetracks, dance halls, and fun houses with air jets in the floor. The introduction in the 1880s of a bicycle with two wheels of equal size (as a safer version of a model with high front wheels) made cycling for fun a popular craze. Penny arcades with primitive projectors lined Chicago's State Street and New York's Broadway in the early 1890s, and in 1896 the first projection of a "motion picture" occurred at Koster and Bial's Music Hall in New York.

Machinery and the Corliss engine had dominated the Philadelphia Centennial of 1876. Two decades later, at Chicago's Columbian Exposition, the exhibited machines were placed in a building more than three miles away from the main fairgrounds and were relatively unvisited. The crowds at the fair in 1893 gawked instead at a giant Ferris wheel and admired the "White

City" coordinated by architects and landscape designers as an expression of planned civic order. The Heinz Company distributed a half million miniature pickle pins to be worn on the lapels of fairgoers, and crowds were scandalized or titillated by the belly dancing of Little Egypt. People could capture the moment with George Eastman's inexpensive Kodak box camera. Named the Brownie after a cartoon character of the day, the camera was first marketed with the catchy slogan "You press the button, we do the rest" in 1888. One historian has optimistically concluded, "Telegraph and telephone, electricity and press increased public knowledge, business efficiency, and political debate."[36]

THE DOWNSIDE OF CHANGE

It is easy to paint a rosy picture of the era of "progress." But aspects of the economic and social transformation profoundly disturbed contemporaries. American capitalism expressed an intense preoccupation with the amassing of personal wealth. Noted English legal scholar Sir Henry Maine marveled at the vast contrast in conditions among the classes in America: desperate poverty for many and the staggering luxury enjoyed by the rich. Sociologist Thorstein Veblen chronicled the "conspicuous consumption" of America's wealthy at the turn of the century in *The Theory of the Leisure Class* (1899), noting Americans' extravagant spending (for example, gold-handled walking sticks), designed to call attention to their wealth and thus gain social status. However, most Americans remained concerned with necessities, not luxuries. In 1900, nonfarm families spent an average of 43 percent of their income on food, as compared to 17 percent at the end of the twentieth century.

Economic growth had been accompanied by wild economic fluctuations. Severe depressions, known as "panics," struck in 1873, 1884, and 1893—causing numerous business failures, widespread unemployment, and great hardships. At such times of crisis, many, no matter how determined, found their ability to control their own lives overtaken by impersonal forces, while technological changes associated with industrialization often made existing skills and businesses obsolete.[37]

Labor unrest, often marked by violence, characterized the last quarter of the nineteenth century, as workers organized in the face of employer opposition. Organized labor sought through collective bargaining to gain the leverage with giant corporations that eluded individual workers. But workers who organized unions were often uncertain about the proper path to take. Initially, many hoped to replace capitalism with a so-called cooperative commonwealth. This was the stated goal of the Knights of Labor, originally organized as a secret fraternal order by Philadelphia garment workers. But by the 1880s it had become a national federation of unions, plus interested individuals. Harking back to a radical tradition that dates to the English utopian socialist Robert Owen and the 1820s, the Knights of Labor sought to promote employee ownership of shops and factories until both the economy and society would be totally transformed.

A more practical tack was adopted by a number of trade unions that in 1886 formed the American Federation of Labor (AFL), with Samuel Gompers as its president. Gompers accepted the existing system but demanded that labor have the right to organize and engage in collective bargaining, with the calling of a strike (or threat thereof) as the workers' ultimate weapon. His concern was bread-and-butter issues, such as wages, working conditions, and job security. The AFL organized trade unions representing the skilled trades and largely ignored the unskilled. Barely surviving the depression and labor turbulence of the mid-1890s, AFL membership surged from 256,000 in 1997 to 1,676,000 in 1904. This sudden consolidation of labor, coming at a time of a massive movement toward business mergers, troubled many, who feared that strikes and violence would tear the social fabric. Gompers, however, rejected the European model of a socialist political party for workers. Workers were to provide for themselves, not look to government.

America lagged behind other industrial nations in providing for worker welfare. Its backwardness was clearly demonstrated in the area of industrial safety. The United States experienced by far the highest rate of industrial accidents of any Western nation. At this time, industrial relations were the exclusive responsibility of lax state legislatures. From 1880 to 1900, the nation averaged over a half million industrial accidents per year, including 35,000 fatalities annually. Newspapers of the day were filled with accounts of brakemen losing limbs in railroad accidents and steelworkers tumbling into vats of molten metal. Most state labor laws required an injured worker or his survivors to demonstrate direct employer negligence to receive compensation, not an easy matter. Cost-conscious corporations knew they could safely spend little on employee safety and comfort.[38]

The great economic gains of the time came at a high cost. Mining, timber, and other extractive industries plundered natural resources to exact a quick profit with no concern for the landscape or the needs of future generations, and uncontrolled market forces promoted business behavior indifferent to larger social goals. Congested, filthy, and disease-filled slums stood next to mansion-lined streets in all large American cities, with more Americans dying of tuberculosis in 1900 than of cancer. Nor did most state legislatures address the sort of conditions that obliged boys of thirteen to work sixty hours a week in the notoriously dangerous coal mines of Kentucky's infamous Harlan County.

Between 1877 and 1895, the nation feared the possibility of class war. Rumblings of discontent heard during the depressed mid-1890s did not ease completely with the return of prosperity in 1898. The nation exhibited so many ominous signs of social conflict that some, including George Pullman and Andrew Carnegie, even doubted democracy's survival.[39]

ROBBER BARONS AND MUCKRAKERS

Americans expressed a strong ambivalence toward the entrepreneurs of the Gilded Age, regarding them with both awe and distrust. As historian Glenn Porter has noted: "For the first time, whole industries came to be identified with the names of powerful individuals who dominated them—Cornelius Vanderbilt, E. H. Harriman, and James J. Hill in railroads, Cyrus McCormick in reapers, John D. Rockefeller in oil, J. P. Morgan in finance, James B. Duke in tobacco, . . . Carnegie in steel."[40] Reformers and crusading journalists (Teddy Roosevelt derisively called them "muckrakers") denounced rapacious "robber barons" indifferent to the public interest. Henry Demarest Lloyd, a Chicago writer, in *Wealth against Commonwealth* (1894), charged that behind big business's rise lurked a tale of ruthlessness and corruption. Critics depicted the Senate as a "millionaire's club" run in the interests of plutocrats, while Jay Gould of the Erie Railroad testified before a congressional hearing that "it was the custom when men received nominations [for office] to come to me to make contributions and I made them and considered them good paying investments for the company."[41]

A chasm between reform-minded elements of American society and big business had opened—never to completely close. Henry Demarest Lloyd would write: "What we call Monopoly is Business at the end of its journey. The concentration of wealth and the wiping out of the middle classes are other names for it." The Darwinian impersonality of big business ran counter to that grain in American thinking that identified success with a moral order based on good character. In 1896, social scientist Charles B. Spaur roughly calculated that 1 percent of the population owned more than half of all the national wealth, while the 44 percent at the bottom owned only 7.2 percent. This tension between older values and new realities challenged the laissez-faire tenets that had long prevailed not only in business but in government.[42]

For many reformers, the economic power of large corporations meant that they could corrupt democracy, reducing state governments and Washington to minions of Wall Street. In rebuttal, friends of big business argued that its rise reflected industrial progress. Big business had to be a good thing because it produced better, cheaper, and more varied goods and services. That it arose first in the United States, many concluded, testified to American virtues.

New industrial corporations—Standard Oil, General Electric, DuPont, American Tobacco, National Biscuit Company, and many others—firmly straddled a huge national economy stretching from ocean to ocean. Many believed that changes of such magnitude mandated a major reconsideration of the role of government. This questioning took place in the context of a general awareness that traditional certainties no longer sufficed either to explain developments or to offer guidance for action.

PART TWO

From Theodore Roosevelt
to Reagan

Washington Comes Forward, 1900–1912

Here is not a nation but a teeming nation of nations.

—WALT WHITMAN, Leaves of Grass *(1855)*

Historian Henry Adams testified to the overwhelming speed of change in his lifetime in his autobiography, *The Education of Henry Adams* (1907). Writing of the inadequacy of his own classical education to prepare him to understand a world of science- and technology-driven change, he asserted that the education of "the American boy of 1854 stood nearer the year 1 than to the year 1900."[1] Even those who viewed change favorably had reason for second thought. A national transformation of startling magnitude required a response in the form of new institutions and new social thought. By 1900 reform activity reached an intensity that was sustained until World War I, a period that historians refer to as the Progressive Era. Conventional thinking had trusted to competition to protect the consumer and to secure a relationship between resources that assured progress. With the ascendancy of big business, questions arose as to the viability of competition and even its value. Reformers looked to government for purposeful action to control a market and its business activity that they no longer believed to be self-regulating.

FIN DE SIÈCLE AMERICA

Henry George's *Progress and Poverty* (1879) posed the penetrating question of how, in a democratic nation so bountifully endowed, could so many lead lives of want and toil, while a privileged few flaunted their princely existence.

Americans accustomed to thinking of change as good had reasons for grave concerns and even pessimism as the nation pulled away from its agrarian republican roots. An American value system that prized self-reliance and personal achievement as paramount had to be reexamined in terms of a society and economy where impersonal forces increasingly dwarfed individual efforts.

Developments beyond any individual's control fed psychic anxiety and encouraged a movement toward collective action—from business mergers and labor unions to professional, civic, and fraternal organizations. Historian T. J. Jackson Lears has even suggested that an early strategy of the emerging advertising industry at the end of the nineteenth century was to connect consumption with "an emerging therapeutic ethos of self-realization—an ethos rooted in Americans' feeling that their sense of selfhood had become fragmented, diffuse, and somehow 'weightless' or 'unreal.'"[2] With a new century, Americans, startled by the pace of social, economic, and technological change, wanted reassurance both in their personal lives and in their electoral politics.

A classic consideration of this period by historian Robert Wiebe is tellingly entitled *The Search for Order* (1967). This sense of a need for greater social controls and cohesion took many forms, but the dominant theme was acceptance of the need for increased reliance on government. By the 1890s, the foundation was being laid for a new regulatory role for the federal government. Industrialization had thrown up social and economic issues clearly beyond the resources of individuals and even state governments. The weakening of traditional American fears of government reflected growing concerns about social and economic problems. The older Jeffersonian ideal of the American as a freestanding individual seemed overtaken and overwhelmed by the rise of an urban-industrial order in which no individual could be in full mastery of his (or her) destiny.

Frederick Jackson Turner's celebrated essay "The Significance of the Frontier in American History" noted in 1893 the passing of an older America of wilderness, pioneers, and farmers, which had forged a distinctive national character and value system. To Turner, the frontier experience had created a distinctive American type: a reality-oriented, nonintrospective individual of practical bent, free of inhibitions and eager for adventure. Now the frontier no longer existed. Implicit in this celebrated essay was the foreboding question of how these assumed attributes would fare in the newly urban-industrialized America. Whether one accepts Turner's theory or not, it revealingly exposes American concerns at the turn of the century. The country had been transformed almost overnight.

Waves of immigrants from Southern and Eastern Europe augmented, and after the turn of the century dwarfed, the older flow from the British Isles, Germany, and Scandinavia. In 1900 three American cities—New York, Chicago, and Philadelphia—each numbered in excess of a million souls. New York in 1900, with 4 million people, was second only to London in population size among the world's cities. America grew ever more diverse—alarmingly so some thought—in religion, ethnic origins, and even employment as the industrial age created new occupations.

By 1900, 76 million Americans had been joined into a national economy. Nationally advertised branded products bought off store shelves or ordered from mail order catalogs were the same whether purchased in Iowa or Massachusetts. Geographically mobile and without the strong local loyalties or class-specific habits of consumption of Europe, Americans proved ready consumers of standardized, mass-marketed goods. But no less a critic of superfluous and excessive consumerism than Thorstein Veblen recognized, in *The Theory of Business Enterprise* (1904), that advertising was increasingly providing useful information to guide consumers in making choices.

Growing market unity did not soften regional tensions, which were exacerbated by the rise of big business. Small-town businessmen threatened by the erosion of their local markets bitterly attacked the great corporations for stifling opportunity. State legislatures sometimes heeded these cries for help, enacting laws to limit corporate enterprises' ability to compete with local businesses. The wheat farmers of the newly settled plains and the cotton farmers of the South struggled against an international market that determined crop prices with total indifference to the producers' welfare. Aspiring businessmen complained that a handful of New York banks controlled interest rates and credit. Middlemen felt threatened as corporations integrated toward the consumer. The radicalism of farmer discontent expressed in the Populist Party of 1892 helped spawn an agenda of political change that demanded an active and caring national government. A loss of confidence in the self-regulating market eroded traditional faith in laissez-faire.

Even Divine Providence needed rethinking. Darwin's theory of natural selection called into question the literal acceptance of the Bible. Religion as expressed in the mainstream Protestant churches' Social Gospel movement became less demanding and more compassionate; but post-Darwinian nature seemed crueler, at least in this world. In the hands of thinkers seeking to apply natural selection to the sociology of nations and to "races," Darwin's misapplied concepts justified the imperial dominance of the strong races over the weak, while social Darwinism, developed chiefly by the English sociologist Herbert Spencer, provided a pseudoscientific rationale for the suffering of the poor as the necessary price of economic progress. (It was Spencer, not Darwin, who coined the phrase "survival of the fittest.") Governmental action to alleviate distress, according to Spencer, contravened evolutionary laws of social progress and thus only harmed the nation.

But no modern society could long subscribe to Spencer's harsh credo. When Spencer visited the United States in 1877, Andrew Carnegie feted him at a gala dinner attended by hundreds of the nation's leaders. American businessmen were more likely, however, to justify their behavior by references to market forces than to social Darwinism. They had learned the basic Darwinian principle—adapt or die—firsthand from their own business experiences, a theme effectively employed by William Dean Howells in his 1885 novel about the travails of a businessman, *The Rise of Silas Lapham*.[3]

THE CORPORATION AS "MASTER INSTITUTION"

To Thorstein Veblen, the corporation had come to be "the master institution of civilized Life," while a journalist complained in 1891 of an America that resembled an industrial company in which every action is taken "with profit in mind."[4] With the astonishing growth of the trusts, the unmatched power of big business received blame for the nation's economic inequalities. To critics, the giant corporations symbolized the ominous transformation of an economy of small farms and family businesses into an industrial order marked by economic concentration. Concentration of economic power appeared antithetical to republican virtues, challenging the survival of American democracy. One oft-told joke held that Rockefeller's Standard Oil Trust could do anything it wanted with politicians except refine them. The weakness of state governments in the face of national corporations, whose budgets and number of employees often greatly exceeded their own, underscored the need for a federal role.

Americans felt ambivalent toward the large corporations and their canny "captains of industry." The notion that the corporation represented an "artificial human entity" troubled its critics. In the debate over the merits and role of the corporation, the word "soulless" constantly recurred. There is irony in corporations often treating individuals as things, because one can more easily coordinate things than men. As purely legal creations, the corporations transcended the moral and natural laws binding mere mortals, for corporations had no organic limits to size and life. In contrast, small businessmen competing with a corporation appeared frail and vulnerable; the corporation's own employees seemed powerless and dependent. The large corporation's impersonal power threatened the American worker, the small businessman, the consumer, and, it was feared, democratic government itself. Eugene V. Debs lamented that the corporation, lacking both body and soul, could not be kicked in the seat of the pants nor "damned to blazes." In a similar vein, satirist Ambrose Bierce, in *The Devil's Dictionary*, defined a corporation as "an ingenious device for obtaining individual profit without individual responsibility."[5]

Ethics and laws originally designed for simpler circumstances could not be easily applied to corporations involved with other corporations through pools, trusts, or mergers. Dwarfed by the power of big business, individuals turned to government to check growing corporate power. A resolution creating a special committee on small business of the New York legislature in 1897 warned that economic concentration had resulted in production and price being determined by combinations operating together to destroy competition and exact "unreasonable charges from the people." But such political efforts to control big business amounted to a puppy snapping at the heels of a striding Goliath. Governmental response to the rise of big business, on both the state and national levels, tended to be confused and confusing. But it greatly perturbed business leaders, who increasingly had to devote resources to their political and legal environment. Currying favor with politicians and regulators would soon become an important business skill.

REGULATORY ROLE FOR GOVERNMENT

In a groundbreaking 1886 case, *Santa Clara County v. Southern Pacific Railroad*, the U.S. Supreme Court held a corporation to be a person under the Fourteenth Amendment and thus entitled to protection as such from actions by local and state governments. Corporate lawyers now used the amendment to cripple the states' ability to effectively regulate. In doing so, however, they inadvertently demonstrated the need for a new federal regulatory role. Federal actions toward business in the final decades of the nineteenth century never constituted a clear or consistent policy. Their significance lies in exposing the erosion in the faith that market forces, left alone, will inevitably prove self-regulating.

Railroads became the first industry to be nationally regulated, for they often behaved badly and evoked an old American dread of monopoly. "Charging what the traffic will bear" was well-known railroad terminology. Starting in the early 1870s, many states created commissions to oversee and regulate railroads. Those formed in midwestern and western states satisfied irate farmers by severely restricting the industry's freedom, provoking the railroads to fight back in the courts. The Supreme Court ruled in *Wabash v. Illinois* (1886) that the federal government alone had the constitutional right to regulate interstate commerce, thus striking down state regulations of railroads crossing state lines. State regulatory bodies, in any case, had not been adequate to the job of regulating powerful trunk lines linked into national systems. Under public pressure, Congress moved to fill the resulting vacuum.

In 1887, the Interstate Commerce Act created the first independent federal regulatory agency, the Interstate Commerce Commission (ICC), but the commission's weaknesses soon became evident. It was mandated to maintain "reasonable and just rates" within the industry and to prohibit unfair practices and pooling arrangements. But the law allowed for numerous exceptions. Unsure of their authority, the commissioners were overwhelmed by the weight of detail, much of it highly technical. The passage of the Hepburn Act in 1906 greatly strengthened the ICC by giving the commissioners the power to establish maximum rates, using as their yardstick a "reasonable rate-of-return" on investment. But although the ICC eliminated practices regarded as injurious to the public, it also discouraged innovation in a mature industry facing decline. Historian Albro Martin has argued that the ICC did not allow the railroads to raise rates sufficiently to replace rolling stock and facilities in a timely fashion and that after 1916 federal regulation of prices—and featherbedding by unions—crippled the railroads' ability to defend themselves from the new competition of trucks, buses, and private cars. Others, however, fault poor railroad management and its failure to integrate services with the new trucking lines.[6]

THE SHERMAN ANTITRUST ACT

The Sherman Antitrust Act of 1890 represented the nation's boldest effort to confront the problems of business concentration. Englishman James Bryce described them clearly in *The American Commonwealth* (1888): "New causes are at work. . . . Modern civilization has become more exacting. It discerns more benefits which the organized power of government can secure, and grows more anxious to attain them. . . . The power of groups of men organized by incorporation as joint stock companies . . . has developed in unexpected strength in unexpected ways, overshadowing individuals and even communities, and showing that the very freedom of association which men sought to secure by law . . . may, under the shadow of the law, ripen into a new form of tyranny."[7]

By 1890, twenty-one states had enacted antitrust statutes. But federal action remained necessary. Passed with only one dissenting vote in a conservative Senate and none in the House, the Sherman Antitrust Act codified existing common law (the historic body of Anglo-American judicial decisions) for interstate trade and commerce. Senator Orville Platt of Connecticut claimed his colleagues had desperately "look[ed] for a 'Bill to Punish Trusts' to go to the voters with."[8] But although some congressmen wanted to halt the drift toward big business, others, possibly the majority, regarded the law as merely a measure against collusive behavior, notably price-fixing that curtailed competition. Designed to be vague by its framers, the Sherman Antitrust Act intentionally left much to the discretion of the Justice Department and the federal courts. Indeed, it has often been suggested that the law's principal benefit was its symbolic reassurance that Washington could protect the people from the abuses of business consolidation.[9]

The Sherman Act initiated a national antitrust policy that over time has proven inconsistent, difficult to enforce, and open to shifts in political power and public mood—but nonetheless highly important. Enforcement of the act has ebbed and flowed, an indication of both its ill-defined nature and the ambivalence that judges, politicians, and the public have had toward big business over the years. The question of whether "bigness" alone, as represented by market share, can constitute a violation of the act (and, if so, what percentage of market share) still perplexes. Antitrust policy from its inception represented a somewhat conflicting statement of philosophy, which acquired specific and changing form as the courts and governmental agencies applied its generalities to the facts of individual cases in the economic, political, and ideological setting of the time—a setting, of course, that too often reflected the influence of special interests. A voluminous literature devoted to the subject of competitive industries has evolved, with continuing disagreement on basic terms and concepts, although it is generally accepted that at least seven to ten large companies in any industry represents ideal competition.

The Sherman Antitrust Act of 1890 prohibited any combination or conspiracy "in restraint of trade or commerce among the several states or with foreign nations." Those involved in these ill-defined crimes could be fined up to $5,000 and sentenced to a year in jail, while individuals and businesses suffering losses because of illegal actions could sue for triple damage. Application of the law was left to the attorney general, with the Department of Justice prosecuting violators in the federal courts.

Cynics who sneered at the Sherman Act as a toothless ruse to quiet public demands for action against the trusts soon had their skepticism confirmed. In *United States v. E. C. Knight Company* (1895), the Supreme Court ruled that the American Sugar Refining Company had not violated the Sherman Act in acquiring several competitors—even though this increased the company's 65 percent control over the nation's refined sugar industry to an astonishing 98 percent.

The judges' remarkable reasoning stated that as a refinery the American Sugar Refining Company only "incidentally and indirectly" involved itself in commerce. Thus the Sherman Act did not apply to the company. By offering this very narrow view of commerce, the Supreme Court appeared to void the Sherman Act—which rested constitutionally on the interstate commerce clause—when applied to any industrial combinations, thus largely denying Congress the power to prohibit monopolies in industry. Yet legal historian Charles W. McCurdy has argued that the view of the decision as a victory for laissez-faire is wrong. To McCurdy, the judges had only affirmed the authority of the states to police the corporations they had created; even he, however, does not deny that the decision posed a serious stumbling block to federal regulation under the Sherman Act and that it implied that the act did not preclude large firms from growing by merger or acquisition.[10]

The controversial *E. C. Knight* decision needs to be placed in its historical context. In a series of decisions from 1880 to 1937, the Supreme Court formulated what legal scholars have called a "dual federalism approach." Decisions in this period generally reflected the view that vast areas of economic life (for example, regulation of child labor) should be left to state regulation and other areas should be left to the federal government. The concern was that the state and federal jurisdictions should not overlap; an area should fall either to the states or to the Congress, but not both. In *E. C. Knight*, then, the court upheld the right and responsibility of the state to regulate "local" activities that had no "direct logical relationship with commerce." The one dissenting judge, John Marshall Harlan, pointed out the absurdity of the view that a major national monopoly did not have a "direct logical relationship with commerce." He noted, moreover, that the Court had not considered Congress's powers under the interstate commerce clause since *Gibbons v. Ogden* in 1824, and that the rise of a new type of economy required a reconsideration of what constituted "commerce."

The Court soon backed away from the extreme position of *E. C. Knight* in a series of cases from 1897 and 1898, most notably *U.S. v. Addyston Pipe and Steel Company*. In this case and others, the Court ruled that agreements by manufacturers to fix prices and divide markets violated the Sherman Act if they resulted in "substantial economic effect" upon interstate commerce.

A dramatic upturn in the American and world economies occurred after the depression years of 1893 to 1897. Discoveries of gold in Alaska, Australia, and South Africa in the years 1898 to 1901 fed recovery by dramatically increasing the hard money supplies at a time when all important nations were converting their currencies into a fixed amount of the precious metal—the United States having adopted the gold standard in 1873. World and American deflationary trends and tight money, which had prevailed for three decades, were now reversed, boosting business optimism. American wheat farmers of the plains states and cotton farmers of the South, who had suffered falling prices from 1873 to 1896 (and whose discontent had profound political consequences, including the startling rise of the radical Populist Party in the 1890s), found their fortunes improving.

RISE TO GLOBALISM

From a global perspective, the last decades of the nineteenth century saw the rise of the modern age. International trade rose dramatically, facilitated by the laying of telegraph cable along ocean bottoms and fast-moving ships. The United States was surpassing Europe in population size and technology. America assumed a new global role with the building of a modern steel navy and the securing of bases and protectorates in the Caribbean, Central America, and the Pacific. The United States had clearly acquired both the requisite force and the will to act as a world power.

America's increasing role in world affairs received dramatic demonstration in the Spanish-American War of 1898. An easy victory resulted in a peace treaty, which established a strong U.S. presence in the Pacific and the

Caribbean. Walter LaFeber has asserted that American commercial ambitions contributed greatly to the declaration of war on Spain, depicting President McKinley and Congress as influenced by businessmen who regarded overseas markets as necessary to absorb American excess production. But LaFeber may have exaggerated the importance of commercial motivations for expansionism. Strategic considerations—the desire to obtain naval bases —combined with an excess of jingoistic flag-waving, weighed heavier than trading considerations in the decisions to acquire territories.[11]

In a more general way, it seems inevitable that as a nation grows wealthier it redefines its interests in more expansive terms, casting about to extend influence. America becoming a global player in the 1890s at the same time that it emerged as the world's largest economy is not surprising. Yet, for some, the economic hard times of the 1890s did make foreign markets appear indispensable to the nation's future prosperity. As influential American naval theorist Alfred Thayer Mahan often noted, "Trade follows the flag," and military success in 1898 certainly encouraged American businessmen to look overseas. American desire to hold on to the Philippines did indeed rest in large part on the view that it might provide an effective stepping stone to Chinese markets.

Although foreign trade grew greatly after the Civil War, its significance for the American economy is easily overstated; the domestic market retained its primacy. In contrast, the impact of American corporations, such as the United Fruit Company, on the small nations of Central America and the Caribbean was profound. Tracing its start to a group of canny Boston businessmen in 1885, United Fruit Company made the previously rare banana a staple of the American diet and even of the Western European diet. The world output of bananas rose from 30,000 tons in 1880 to an astonishing 1.8 million tons in 1910, and slipping on a banana peel became a routine seen in vaudeville acts in American theaters and in early silent films. By World War I, United Fruit may have controlled the governments of four Central American countries through bribes and intimidation.

American exports worth $450 million in 1870s exceeded $1.2 billion in 1900; imports also increased, but at a slower rate. The United States traditionally had exported raw materials and imported manufactures. But with American farm machinery, firearms, sewing machines, typewriters, cameras, electrical equipment, and other products dominating the world market in the 1890s, the terms of trade soon changed. By 1900, the United States shipped abroad more manufactured goods than it imported (a situation not reversed until 1985), and in 1913 the value of American manufacturing exports surpassed for the first time the value of its agricultural exports. A powerful lobby ensured that a wall of high tariffs limited foreign competition with American manufacture for the home market, although raw materials and specialized goods (such as German dyestuffs) were still imported in vast quantities to satisfy the needs of American industry.

On the eve of World War I, U.S. investments abroad, mainly in Canada, Latin America, and the United Kingdom, neared $3.5 billion. European investments in the United States stood at double this amount but consisted mostly of passive bond and stock holdings. In contrast, market-oriented American manufacturers invested overseas in subsidiary companies to escape tariffs and other trading restrictions. The Singer Sewing Machine Company, for example, operated a huge plant in Scotland to produce for the U.K. and continental European market, while smaller plants employing local labor supplied Canada and Australia. Important industries derived a substantial portion of their profits overseas, with Standard Oil, International Harvester, and New York Life—to name only three giant firms—depending heavily on foreign earnings. At the onset of World War I in 1914 the United States ranked third among the world's exporters, behind the United Kingdom and Germany.

Taken alone these facts may mislead. They accurately demonstrate America's growing role in the world but exaggerate the importance of foreign trade to its own economy. Countries with large domestic markets are rarely great traders, and the United States was less dependent on the rest of the world than any other major power. Aside from a few highly specialized items and industries, such as rubber and coffee, foreign trade did not usually involve matters of economic life or death. Between 1900 and 1915, foreign trade represented the same percentage, 7 percent, of the GNP as thirty years earlier. In contrast, the GNP for the United Kingdom in 1910 was 26 percent. Increased scale, then, reflected American economic growth and industrial prowess. It did not indicate an outward-looking restructuring of the economy.

Colossal size and power alone sufficed to make America important in world trade. By the turn of the century, the United States boasted the world's leading economy while continuing to expand at a faster rate than its competitors. It had become an imposing force, capable of accelerating and on occasions depressing the world's trading system. The huge domestic market and enormous reserves of raw materials made the United States less dependent upon foreign trade. Most American businessmen, unlike their British,

Dutch, and German counterparts, worried less about the world market than their domestic market, since American industry—protected by high tariffs—could achieve economies of scale without the need to look abroad. This important fact, true of no other major nation, profoundly shaped American business practices and habits until the 1970s.

MERGER MANIA, 1897–1904

As important to the economy as the increase in foreign trade was the feverish consolidation occurring at the end of the nineteenth century. A rush toward mergers of unprecedented magnitude occurred in the years 1897 to 1904, totally transforming the economy and the nation as 4,227 firms consolidated into 257. Indeed, by 1904, 318 "trusts" reportedly owned 40 percent of the country's manufacturing capacity. Naomi Lamoreaux, in her study of this merger movement, contended that the primary cause was the desire to decrease price competition and that it occurred mainly in the form of horizontal integration, challenging Chandler's view of mergers as a form of rationalization to take advantage of technological and market changes. But the two views need not be mutually exclusive, and both certainly contributed to mergers—as indeed did the self-interest of investment bankers.[12]

With railroad activity slowing in the 1890s, investment bankers had moved strongly into industrial stocks. In the years between 1896 and 1907, the number of shares traded annually on the New York Stock Exchange exploded, rising from 57 million to 260 million. Besides charging fees for advising on stock and debt structure and financing, investment houses also charged for underwriting the new issues of stocks and bonds. Acting sometimes as both principal and agent, bankers put together deals that created large holding companies. One house alone, J. P. Morgan and Company, arranged in the period from 1898 to 1903 the financing of General Electric, International Harvester Company, the ill-fated International Mercantile Combine, and U.S. Steel Corporation.

Morgan created the U.S. Steel Corporation in 1901 by combining Carnegie Steel with its eight largest competitors. U.S. Steel was the world's first billion-dollar corporation—capitalized at a greatly watered $1.4 billion dollars (or roughly $30 billion in 2008 dollars when adjusted for inflation). The significance of this figure is conveyed by the fact that only three years earlier the capitalization of all U.S. manufacturing had totaled only $9 billion. At its birth, U.S. Steel, in reality a holding company, controlled nearly 70 percent of the nation's steel and iron production capacity and manufactured more tonnage than Britain and France combined. Owning 149 steelworks, it employed nearly 200,000 people. J. P. Morgan's agent, Elbert H. Gary, became the new corporation's president, and when the company began constructing a huge plant in Indiana just south of Chicago, the resulting city received his name. J. P. Morgan and Company realized an estimated profit of $60 million in fees for underwriting, syndicating, and promoting U.S. Steel. But the largest corporation in the world was over-capitalized, lacked proper coordination, and functioned poorly.

"Promoters," or speculators, standing outside the established investment banking system—notably Charles R. Flint and John "Bet-a-Million" Gates—often led the charge in initiating high-risk mergers; more cautious investment banking houses trailed behind. "Money pools," or syndicates of underwriters, were assembled to buy an issue of securities for the purpose of its sale at increased prices, in part or in whole, to the public. Speculators profited quickly in stock operations, moving rapidly in and out of a company. But, by 1904, the enthusiasm for mergers ebbed amid a mood of business uncertainty. Early success had bred excess: optimism soared and stock prices followed. As some combinations faltered and stock prices declined, investors grew wary.

The bubble had burst, but the merger movement of the period 1895 to 1904 left a permanent legacy in a dramatically restructured economy. A new form of large-scale corporate organization relying increasingly on vertical integration had come of age. By 1905, fully integrated corporate giants were leading sectors of the economy. In hindsight, it appears that the Sherman Act contributed to the merger mania, for reasons shortly to be explained.[13]

ROOSEVELT'S BULLY PULPIT

President William McKinley's tentative policies in regard to business concentration contributed to a sense of political drift. But after his assassination in September 1901, his successor, Theodore Roosevelt, quickly displayed drive and a strong streak of unconventionality as he strove to make his presidency a "bully pulpit." He would later say that "when the interests of the American people demanded that a certain act should be done and I had the power to do it, I did it unless it was specifically prohibited by law."[14] In refashioning the role of the presidency to exert legislative leadership, Roosevelt sought not only to adjust the balance between the executive and legislative branches, but also between Washington and the states, and between big business and government.

A discernible shift in the distribution of power within the American political system was already under way, but Roosevelt hurried it along. As early as 1890, the Supreme Court had greatly strengthened the presidency by holding that the executive branch possessed all powers needed to enforce "the rights, duties, and obligations growing out of the Constitution itself." And in the next century, beginning with Roosevelt, presidents were expected to be assertive, as the executive branch agencies grew bigger and as the federal government extended its influence relative to the states.

Even before Roosevelt's presidency, federal antitrust policies had inadvertently encouraged merger activity. Supreme Court actions in several cases from 1897 and 1898 appeared to uphold the legality of holding companies along the lines permitted by New Jersey's 1889 law, while looking askance at cartels and "soft combinations" aimed at sharing markets or setting prices. Accordingly, lawyers encouraged corporate clients to join in "hard" combinations through mergers and acquisitions. The usual pattern was to begin as a loosely constructed holding company and then reorganize, with the constituent companies brought together into a single operating company. This was the intended approach for the founders of the Northern Securities Holding Company.[15]

J. P. Morgan had created the Northern Securities Holding Company, in order to end a battle in 1901 between two railroad titans—James Hill of the Great Northern Railroad and Edward Harriman of the Union Pacific—for control of the Northern Pacific Railroad. Hill counted on the support of Morgan, and Harriman relied on the Rockefeller interests and the investment banking house of Kuhn, Loeb. Newspapermen, having a field day with the struggle, called it the "War of the Magnates." With the stake being control of the nation's western railroads, both sides bid the stock up into a range that unsettled the stock market, threatening a panic. But at this critical point, in the fall of 1901, Morgan set up the Northern Securities Company, a holding company capitalized at $400 million (roughly the equivalent adjusted for inflation of a little more than $8 billion in 2008) for the involved roads. Its stock was then divided between the two competing groups, reassuring the stock market. However, the American public, especially westerners, trembled at the specter of a giant monopoly controlling a region of the nation. Even before the advent of Northern Securities, many had warned that six groups of investors controlled two-thirds of the nation's rails. The new trust would greatly increase concentration.[16]

Recognizing a political opportunity, the astute Roosevelt moved against the Northern Securities Company, ordering the Department of Justice to bring suit. A surprised Morgan rushed to the White House and purportedly told Roosevelt, "If we have done anything wrong, send your man to my man and they can fix it up,"[17] treating the president of the United States as merely another magnate. Roosevelt, however, intended to demonstrate the federal government's power over big business. The Supreme Court upheld the government's order for divestiture of Northern Securities. The jubilant Roosevelt soon acquired the politically evocative appellation "trust buster" and easily won the presidential election of 1904. (The Democrats attempted to capitalize on business's fears of Roosevelt by nominating as their candidate a conservative Wall Street lawyer.) Ever the loyal Republican, even J. P. Morgan contributed $150,000 to Roosevelt's 1904 campaign—or perhaps he simply sought to buy influence, as did the Rockefeller interests.

Using the revitalized Sherman Antitrust Act, Roosevelt's administration ultimately instituted forty-four actions and secured twenty-six indictments. At the president's urging, in 1903 Congress created the Bureau of Corporations, forerunner of the Department of Commerce, to investigate questionable corporate activity, and the president also supported the passage of the Hepburn Act, which strengthened the powers of the ICC, and the Pure Food and Drug Act of 1906, the nation's first consumer protection bill. The 1906 act forbade the manufacture and sale of adulterated and fraudulently labeled products. Roosevelt also actively championed a federal program to conserve and protect natural resources.

Roosevelt's active involvement in both economic and social matters won him plaudits from many reformers. But all the while Roosevelt reassured big business that he was not its enemy. To the president, the ascendancy of big business indeed represented progress. He wrote in 1913 in his autobiography: "Business cannot be successfully conducted in accordance with the practices and theories of 60 years ago unless we abolish steam, electricity, big cities, and, in short, not only all modern business and modern industrial conditions, but all the modern conditions of our civilization."[18] Believing big business progressive and beneficial, Roosevelt intended only its effective regulation. Moreover, he preferred ongoing "continuous administrative action" to "necessarily intermittent lawsuits" by the federal authorities.

On Roosevelt's instructions, the newly established Bureau of Corporations reached agreements with U.S. Steel, International Harvester Company, and Standard Oil. Each corporation agreed to open its records for examination on the condition that uncovered abuses could be corrected without legal action. Only after Standard Oil reneged on this agreement did the Department of Justice indict the Rockefeller interests in 1906 for violating the Sherman Antitrust Act. A five-hundred-page document detailed a laundry list of charges against Standard Oil. The other two corporations, allied to Morgan, remained conciliatory toward Uncle Sam and escaped prosecution.

Roosevelt wanted an empowered federal government to rein in or break up only what he called the "malefactors of great wealth," giant corporations whose actions endangered the public. Bigness as such did not constitute a threat when properly supervised by government. To Roosevelt, it was essential to distinguish between good trusts, such as U.S. Steel and International Harvester, and bad trusts, such as Standard Oil. However, even businessmen prepared to accept antitrust laws were troubled by their vagueness. They (and their lawyers) often remained uncertain about the legality of actions taken until there was a judicial ruling, which required, at the very least, high legal fees and considerable paperwork. Business organizations therefore pressed for a federal mechanism by which "advance advice" could be provided.

After the Northern Securities decision, corporate executives had to take the Sherman Antitrust Act seriously. In this and other ways, pressure, legal and otherwise, mounted for big business to conduct itself in a circumspect manner. Editorials in leading newspapers demanded that public corporations provide both government and the public with periodic information on their operations, structure, and profits. Muckraking journalists scrutinized business activity for evidence of wrongdoing to expose. Standard Oil, under attack from state and national officials and the subject of Ida Tarbell's exposure of its ruthlessness in a widely read *McClure's Magazine* series, hired its first public relations man in 1906. The need to manage public opinion had become part of the business environment. The era of freewheeling robber barons had yielded to more discreet corporate behavior. Corporations still wanted their way, but they had to give greater consideration to both government and public opinion and how to influence both.

"RULE OF REASON"

William Howard Taft, assuming office in 1909, insisted that the Sherman Antitrust Act be vigorously applied. A former Ohio judge and solicitor general of the United States, Taft regarded Roosevelt's "gentlemen's agreements" as relying unduly on presidential discretion, and in his four years as president, there were forty-six federal suits and forty-three indictments—a more impressive record than Roosevelt's entire seven-year administration. Taft also discarded, at least rhetorically, Roosevelt's distinction between good and bad trusts: "Certainly under the present anti-trust law," he informed Congress in 1910, "no such distinctions exist."[19] In 1911, the Supreme Court ordered the dissolution of Standard Oil of New Jersey and of the American Tobacco Company, forcing Standard Oil to split into thirty-four companies. (Exxon, Mobil, Amoco, and Chevron all resulted from the breakup.) Between the issuance of the court order and the breakup, the price of Standard Oil stock rose over 100 percent, and reformers fumed that Rockefeller and his associates had seen their fortunes double.

These high-profile decisions introduced the principle of the "rule of reason" as a new constraint on antitrust action. This required a case-by-case approach where only combinations that "unduly restrained" trade would be deemed in violation of the Sherman Act. Business actions for legitimate economic ends that only "incidentally led to a restraint of trade" could be considered "reasonable" and lawful. Both Standard Oil and American Tobacco were found, under the "rule of reason," to have engaged in predatory pricing—temporarily establishing prices under cost to drive out rivals. In his solitary dissenting opinion, Justice John Marshall Harlan predicted that the "rule of reason" would "throw the business of the country into confusion and invite widely extended and harassing litigation, the injurious effects [of] which will be felt for many years to come."[20]

What did the "rule of reason" mean in practical terms? U.S. Steel's Elbert Gary requested to no avail that the Department of Justice provide a precise distinction between "reasonable" and "unreasonable" restraints of trade. George Perkins, a Morgan associate and Roosevelt political confidant, warned that without a clear understanding "chaos in business was upon us." Lawyers and accountants might have been delighted with the "rule of reason" and the work it created; corporate businessmen decidedly were not.[21]

The 1911 decisions left much to the courts' discretion. Each case had to be decided in terms of its specifics, with little in the way of general principles— mere bigness or market share could not decide the outcome. Mountains of documents had to be carefully examined for relevant information, which then needed to be analyzed for significance. Taft had wanted a federal law that could allow Washington to review and approve or disapprove proposed mergers and acquisitions in advance. No such bill was passed during his presidency, but it would be acted on shortly after.

As previously discussed, the first decade of the twentieth century had witnessed a remarkable transformation of the economy. After 1904, with the decline of merger activity, a period of settling down and sorting out occurred, and the weakness of many newly created corporate giants became apparent. Several foundered and declared bankruptcy or dissolved into several smaller companies. Others sailed on as flagships of the new corporate America, but even they tended to retreat from the market share they had initially enjoyed. Mergers and acquisitions are certainly good for investment bankers and Wall Street but not always for the new corporations. In 1906, the U.S. Bureau of Corporations found that U.S. Steel's market share of the nation's steel had slipped from nearly 70 percent in 1901 to 55 percent and calculated the real value of the company's stock at less than half its initial $1.4 billion capitalization. The investment climate now turned sharply against mergers; enthusiasm was not to revive until the 1920s. But the profound changes in corporate structure and the economy that resulted from Wall Street's whirlwind activity between 1895 and 1904 endured. As late as 1955, nearly half of America's forty largest corporations traced their births to those years.

A new type of corporate giant had arisen to dominate the national economy. In 1905, 95 percent of American corporations were capitalized at less than $1 million and owned only 4 percent of the nation's private wealth. In stark contrast, a mere 300 corporations, mostly created by new mergers, owned over 40 percent of all private wealth. By then an estimated seventy-eight industrial sectors (meaning by this a division of an industry, as, for example, the production of naphtha as a by-product of petroleum refining) had a third or more of their total production controlled by only one or two corporations. This thrust toward concentration dramatically reshaped business strategy in affected industries.

By 1910, a definite pattern had emerged. Several of the nation's major industries—oil refining, railroad car production, steel, chemicals—were controlled by a handful of companies. These "rivals" usually coexisted harmoniously, enjoying higher profits than in nonconcentrated industries. The company with the largest market share, the "market leader," tended to set prices for the industry. The others went along and refrained from price wars. Thus the cutthroat competition experienced in the late nineteenth century was effectively curbed in these industries. This development resulted not from monopoly, which might have invited federal action, but through oligopoly—a term often defined as applying to any industry made up of fewer than seven firms. The large corporations controlling capital-intensive industries cooperated to impose a stability and order seen as being in their mutual interest. When one company dominated an industry, it would act as the price setter. In the absence of a leading firm, price and marketing arrangements required more complex and often legally doubtful arrangements.[22]

To a remarkable extent, important industries had moved away from market discipline. The managers of a vertically integrated company worked out the "in-house" transactional relationships between the suppliers of raw material and the manufacturers and between producers and distributors. Administrative decision making by management—rather than competitive market forces—thus determined prices and often market share. Oligopolistic big businesses usually avoided undercutting rivals through price cutting because too dominant a market share in an industry by one company could invite antitrust action.

Instead, major companies knew that the key to success was to identify a mass market and then develop a national enterprise capable of serving it. The vertically integrated firm, absorbing the function of many small, specialized enterprises within a single operational organization, sought to reach forward to the consumer. Manufacturers sought to create distribution systems that provided services to the customer that won his or her loyalty not only to specific brands but to a company's products, both present and future. To achieve and ensure consumer loyalty, however, management resorted to outside assistance.

MADISON AVENUE AND THE SOFT SELL

Modern advertising arose at the end of the nineteenth century to mold demand for the branded goods of national manufacturers. In the new century, it soon played a critical role in shaping the relationship between commerce and the consumer. Although Jackson Lears surely exaggerated in suggesting that advertising largely replaced religion at century's end as the major force in redefining personal values, many contemporary accounts have described shoppers, besotted by advertising, approaching consumerism with almost a religious fervor.

Oligopolistic tendencies in the economy expedited the industry's progress, as product promotion often substituted for price competition in these industries. With major corporations selling products that often differed little in price, quality, service, or usefulness, newly created "ad agencies" were paid handsomely to sustain market loyalties for familiar products and enthusiasm for new ones. As early as the 1910s, advertising accounted for 1.5 percent of the GDP.

The larger agencies formed before World War I—J. Walter Thompson and Barton, Durstine and Osborn—developed sophisticated strategies for influencing public wants and public attitudes. Their shaping of modern consumer culture expedited introducing new products and establishing market demand for them, while also influencing domestic behavior and other activities. For many, especially the young, advertising played a role in defining reality and a sense of self. No matter the breadth of its influence, the ultimate goal of advertising always remained, of course, to provide commercial advantage to clients.

Advertising played an important role for the packaged food industry. The public initially had to be convinced that standardized, advertised brand-named goods were superior to unbranded merchandise. Only then would small "mom and pop stores" (resistant to carrying national brands because of their lower profit margin) be forced to stock them because of customer demand. Advertising copywriters, using jingles, poster-style displays, and hard-selling copy, tried to fashion a binding loyalty to their sponsors' products, while nationally advertised, branded packaging allowed manufacturers to bypass retailers and "speak" directly to consumers.

Packaging, no longer a mere container, emerged as a sophisticated communication and advertising device, with design departments using the packaging as an important part of campaigns. A skillfully designed package could transmit overt and subliminal messages of price, value, quality—and even class and gender attitudes and aspirations. A popular consumer culture closely connected to new social values as well as market needs had become one of the defining features of modern life. Karl Marx depicted at capitalism's core a "Faustian conflict between the passion for accumulation and the desire for enjoyment."[23] Advertising's job was to champion enjoyment.

Entrepreneurial activity had been historically directed to meeting market demand for the better mousetrap. Advertising, however, now went well beyond this. It demonstrated that great profit could be made by creating or manipulating demand. This was especially true of such novel inventions as the phonograph. People had to be initially convinced that owning them would improve their lives.

An economy organized for efficient mass production needed a correspond-ingly high "velocity of flow" in consumer purchasing. Mass merchandising emphasizing low prices was practiced by chain stores, notably A&P and Wool-worth's, as well as the mail-order houses. Department stores, however, still preferred to rely on services rather than discounts. In 1916, Clarence Saun-ders opened the nation's first "supermarket," in Memphis, Tennessee. In his Piggly Wiggly store, customers helped themselves to goods displayed on shelves along long aisles rather than being waited on by clerks. Saunders soon added improvements such as putting price tags on every item and equipping adding machines with rolls of paper. Piggly Wiggly's advertised business policy was "high-volume, low-profit margin." Success soon invited imitation.

A close relationship evolved in the early twentieth century between mar-keting, advertising, and the developing field of public relations: the dual strategy of promoting a firm's image as well as its products soon emerged. In a skillfully orchestrated campaign launched in 1917, advertisers turned ciga-rette smoking by women from a taboo into acceptable and even fashionable behavior. Indeed, smoking was promoted not only as chic and pleasurable but also as a beneficial way to reduce tension. Madison Avenue, in New York City, the street where several leading advertising agencies located after 1900, played a critical role in eroding an earlier social code based on self-restraint by advancing a newer code of self-gratification.

Advertising firms and their client corporations equated their wares with progress, good taste, and, whenever possible, health and wholesomeness. Style, not durability, dictated how long you should keep an item, and adver-tising's core message was that the new was always preferable to the old. To keep abreast of fashion and progress required double timing to the rapid drumbeat of change, with Madison Avenue playing the drums. It soon be-came axiomatic among large manufacturers that their products needed con-tinuously increasing advertising to stay competitive and appear "brand new."

MASS PRODUCTION ECONOMY

In industries with stable prices, corporations increased profits by lowering costs through increased efficiencies. By the outbreak of World War I in 1914, improvements in machine tools and new techniques of management, as well as the increasing use of electric power, had produced considerable advances in productivity. Several factors contributed greatly to extending the mass production economy that had taken shape by World War I: the organizational hierarchy and centralized control advocated by "scientific management," the assembly line's intensive specialization, and Madison Avenue's midwifery of a consumer culture. Most of all, the American market was ready-made for standardized mass-market goods. With no national boundaries to impede the flow of goods and with a soaring population, the United States provided manufacturers a vast and accessible home market for their products. The paradigm of corporate organization oriented toward mass production that arose between 1880 and 1925 would prevail for most of the twentieth century.

THE ASSEMBLY LINE

First introduced into factory production in the 1880s, electric power accounted in 1914 for 25 percent of all machine power and made possible the introduction of the modern assembly line in 1913.[24] As David Hounshell has observed, the assembly line represented the culmination of a century-old process leading to mass production begun with the work of Eli Whitney and others on interchangeable parts early in the nineteenth century.[25] As technology evolved, the goal of innovators had remained constant: mass production relying on uniformity to increase output and lower costs. Electric power's potential for rearranging the factory floor to facilitate the flow of production revealed itself slowly. Primitive types of assembly lines began to be used in the 1880s in flour milling, vegetable canning, and meat packaging—activities that required "flow" production or "continuous process" manufacturing. Even railroad car production had moved along indoor tracks to work gangs stationed along the line. But the assembly line as a ubiquitous tool of industry required an awareness of electricity's potential for freeing machines from a necessary proximity to their source of power. This did not occur until the second decade of the twentieth century.

In 1913, Michigan automaker Henry Ford introduced a crude assembly line using a rope and windlass in his Highland Park factory; within three years, the entire line would be electrified and Ford's system perfected. The key to the assembly line lay in assigning each worker on the line a repetitive and simple specialized chore. At each stage, the product came to the stationary worker, and all transport was done mechanically. The conveyor belt's constant motion, rather than any worker's habits, set the pace of production by the speed at which it moved the work in progress, such as an engine, from one worker to another until it became a completed unit. The belt organized the flow of work to a final assembly line from which emerged a completed Ford car.

Previously, cars had been built in several different shops, between which they were dragged: one for paint, another for the engine, and so on. The new assembly line thus saved energy, materials, and time, cutting costs greatly. According to a visiting engineer, "Each individual worker and each feature of the plant is fitted into the factory whole with planned expediency."[26]

The old-fashioned, multistoried, cramped factory buildings of the nineteenth century, with their shafts and countershafts, pulleys and belts, all to allow a massive steam engine to power many machines, had become a relic. Its replacement was a single-story, interconnected structure—long, but with high ceilings allowing overhead space for traveling cranes—designed around electric power with an open plan of few interior walls. Moreover, the single rail spur originally relied on to deliver raw materials and take away shipments soon began to be supplemented or replaced with road transport.

Within five years, the time involved in putting together a chassis for Ford's famous Model T dropped from 12 hours 20 minutes to one hour 33 minutes. "Every time I reduce the charge for our car by one dollar," Henry Ford said, "I get a thousand new buyers." By 1924, his original Highland Park plant encompassed over 50 acres and employed 68,000 workers. A second plant at River Rouge constructed from 1917 to 1925 in Dearborn, Michigan, had 160 acres of floor space spread over 93 buildings with 27 miles of conveyor belts. Iron ore, coal, and other raw materials went into one end of the factory complex—and finished autos came out the other.

Although none of Ford's ideas were revolutionary, and often they were not original, their impact on productivity was. He had demonstrated that the assembly line made possible more products at lower cost, hence yielding greater profits.[27] The assembly line's size, its tempo, and the standardization of product and process seemed quintessentially American: the culmination of the American fascination with mass-producing serviceable goods that the common man could afford. The inexorable flow of parts and materials typical of the assembly line as workers repeated their actions became characteristic of the way heavy industry operated. The possibility of bottlenecks at the point of assembly due to the scale of production had been greatly reduced. Soon swarms of foreign visitors in their quest for efficiency came to Ford's factory to admire and learn from it. Ford had entered the pantheon of American heroes of industry.

TOP-DOWN LEADERSHIP

Along with Frederick W. Taylor's scientific management, Ford's assembly line was part of a general effort by management to increase centralized control over production and, in part at least, to bring about the deskilling of labor. The pressure for "speedup" and the punctuality demanded of assembly workers placed great emphasis on routine and system, leaving little if any room for personal initiative or a sense of accomplishment.

Efficiency experts often addressed businessmen's clubs on the need for uniform controls imposed from top to bottom. By now Taylor had spoken and written on the subject for over a decade, publishing his classic *Principles of Scientific Management* in 1911. A year later, shortly before his death, he testified before a congressional committee to refute accusations that scientific management techniques created a brutal work environment. His disciples took the lead in establishing and staffing the new fields of personnel work and industrial psychology. The considerable autonomy once enjoyed by many workers who had practiced their craft on a factory floor had very largely been eroded as factory work took on a new meaning.[28]

As factory workers on assembly lines largely lost their sense of craft, a new profession emerged in the offices above the factory floor. Already by 1903 nearly half of America's largest industries were led by men who had climbed the corporate ladder. In part, this shift to professional managers as industry's leaders reflected the importance of sales and management for large industrial corporations, which required the understanding of sophisticated business systems. A high school diploma or better had become the usual prerequisite for a starting position with management. The desirability of "top-down" leadership to impose "system" became an article of faith for big business. The assumption was that optimum states for all operations could be devised "scientifically" and then be locked in place by management.

Changes on the factory floor required changes all along the corporate hierarchy. In 1904, a young Frank Lloyd Wright designed Buffalo's Larkin Office Building on an "open plan," one huge space where secretaries and clerks performing simple and repetitive tasks were easily overseen by supervisors—an architectural manifestation of Taylor's "scientific management." The white-collar and the blue-collar workers were clearly shown as the two arms of the industrial machine. Henry Ford described his business strategy —sometimes referred to as "Fordism"—as focused upon "the principles of power, accuracy, economy, system, continuity, and speed."[29] The human factor needed to be trained and harnessed to advance these goals.

THE ALTERNATIVE ECONOMY

The emphasis on the rise of the integrated corporation in this book conforms to the conventional view that this development was the most significant business occurrence of the period and of great importance to the shaping of twentieth-century America. But from the vantage point of the twenty-first century, the giant corporations appear less awesome than they did either at the twentieth century's beginning or during the 1970s when Alfred Chandler celebrated their efficiencies. Reflecting this, historians are pointing out that much of industrial production throughout the period from 1880 to 1920 (and indeed since) continued to be handled by businesses that remained relatively small and often family-owned and that engaged in activities that do not lend themselves to mass production techniques. Such activities often involved the ability to shift output quickly, attributes presently regarded as highly important. In short, we are becoming increasingly aware that big business did not take over industry as thoroughly as long portrayed.

PROGRESSIVISM RECONSIDERED

The period between the outbreak of war with Spain in 1898 and U.S. entry into World War I in 1917 is referred to by historians as the Progressive Era. Until the late 1950s, historians viewed the period as a time when democracy reasserted itself against the power of corporations by enacting regulatory laws. This interpretation is now regarded as simplistic. Historians, however, do agree that the federal government did indeed become more active.[30]

Gabriel Kolko, in an influential 1963 study, *The Triumph of Conservatism*, argued that business leaders actively promoted federal government intervention in order to curb competition and to limit even more regulation by the states. Federal regulations, he believed, were controlled by the leaders of the regulated industry and largely served their interests. A similar thesis was advanced in Martin Sklar's *The Corporate Reconstruction of American Capitalism* (1988). One lesson safely drawn from both studies is that business and the markets need governments to set and enforce the rules, but once government is involved, well-organized private interests will, not surprisingly, try to tilt the rules in their favor, and in this they often succeed.[31]

The anti–big business animus once assumed to be the major motivation for Progressive reforms has been effectively downplayed by recent historiography. The Progressive Era is now considered to be a period of adjusting to structural changes in the economy and the society. There was, it is agreed, a widespread acceptance by contemporaries that American institutions and social thinking were out of step with the new realities of urban-industrial America. The importance of the individual as a social force gave way in many aspects of American life to an organized group response, government being but one of the members of the group.

Powerful businessmen had shaped a national economy dominated by giant integrated firms and understandably sought to influence developments that affected their interests—including the actions of the federal government. But so did their critics, who regarded the federal government as the people's bulwark, to be influenced and strengthened as protection against big business. To implement their reforms, Progressive reformers championed the growth of the administrative state. As Morton Keller has stated, "Modern American economic regulation emerged from an expanding, roiling, aggregate of interests, issues, institutions, ideas: in sum, an increasing pluralistic American polity."[32]

Washington, D.C., has always been a happy hunting ground for lobbyists, and Americans have long looked to government to pump up the marketplace (and more than occasionally their own coffers). As early as 1852, James Buchanan described Washington as so full of lobbyists that a "brick couldn't be thrown without hitting one."[33] If no nation has ever practiced a pure laissez-faire approach, the United States of the period 1865 to 1890 came closest. But even then the federal government actively promoted business interests through heavy protective tariffs, land grants to railroads and settlers, and a legal system conducive to industrial and corporate development.

Where the federal government had indeed practiced laissez-faire was in its belated responses to profound economic and social change. The government exercised little direct influence over developments in the last third of the nineteenth century, except to facilitate economic change by actions sympathetic to corporate business. One exception to this was the granting of generous pensions for Civil War veterans. Suspicion of powerful government and a federal system were all factors that contributed to limiting Washington's influence. But while deeply ingrained attitudes persisted into the new century, the nature of the debate over Washington's role in the economy changed dramatically after 1900.[34]

By this time, some form of federal regulation of business was accepted as necessary. However, new relationships between government and business needed to develop within a tradition that frowned on intrusive interference with enterprise, even while recognizing the need for regulatory protection. The rapid rise of an economy dominated by powerful corporations challenged lingering visions of a self-regulating market economy presided over by a "night-watchman" state.

The election of 1912 highlighted contradictions still puzzling to the historian. The two leading presidential candidates, Theodore Roosevelt and Woodrow Wilson, offered voters two contrary visions of American society and business reform. As federal involvement in the economy and society grew, the whirligig of competing interests intensified. Through a fractious political process, Americans sought to adapt their system to the realities of the modern age.

As Theodore Roosevelt noted, the new industrial order had created a "riot of individualistic materialism under which complete freedom to the individual . . . turned out in practice to mean perfect freedom for the strong to wrong the weak."[35] The proponents of federal regulatory powers regarded its development as essential to guarding the public against the abuses of business. But this regulatory function could also impede positive change by stifling innovation and limiting the options open to business.

CHAPTER NINE

The Age of Organization

A pragmatist . . . turns away from abstraction . . . from . . .
closed systems and pretended absolutes. He turns towards
concreteness . . . towards facts, towards action and power.
—WILLIAM JAMES, Pragmatism *(1907)*

An American economy once locally rooted had been unified into a continental common market with a handful of giant corporations dominating
major sectors of the economy. Large corporations, with multiple dispersed
plants and thousands of employees, did business nationally. Change rever-
berated throughout almost all aspects of American life. The new imbalance
among social institutions filled many Americans with anxiety that the free-
standing individual seemed powerless before sweeping changes. Social theorists in the new discipline of sociology offered a new emphasis on collective
activity of all types and often stressed the need to regard groups as having an
organic existence apart from their individual members. The American government, previously largely a patchwork of states held together loosely by the
Constitution, would in the Progressive Era be refashioned by the initiatives
of a strong executive. For organizations seeking power to advance economic
interests there was an increasing need to influence Washington.

BROKER-STATE MODEL

Political scientists have viewed the political implications of this "organizational revolution" in various ways. Radical critics of the American system
argue that, not withstanding rhetoric to the contrary, big business made

all important decisions. Many scholars, however, lean to the "broker-state model." In this model, highly organized interest groups sought the support of government, while policy makers brokered between competing interests. They posit that there were too many organized interests for any one group or even a coalition of several to prevail for long.

The latter view will be advanced here. This is not to deny that the power of big business provided decisive advantages in influencing government. Nevertheless, it is useful to bear in mind that businessmen disagreed about such issues as trade unions, banking reforms, and various types of governmental regulation of products and activities. Indeed, these issues often even divided management within a corporation. In an ultimate sense, however, the dominating domestic issue faced at the beginning of the twentieth century, as at present, was how government could curb brutal tendencies in competitive capitalism while allowing its productive energies to flow. The early decades of the twentieth century considered different approaches, and this is, as it should be, still the case.

TWO VISIONS OF REFORM

In the aftermath of the Spanish-American War of 1898, a nation born in a struggle for colonial independence acquired far-flung territories, including Hawaii, the Philippines, and Puerto Rico. The country had drifted far indeed from Jefferson's vision of a nation of self-reliant yeoman farmers. Many expressed grave concern that conflicts between capital and labor and the crowding of American cities with new immigrants from Southern and Eastern Europe threatened the democratic principles of the American Republic. The awesome power of small groups of men standing at the head of Wall Street firms added to this unease.

An older mechanistic view of the social order as the sum total of autonomous individuals was challenged by a competing vision of society as an organic web of economic and social linkages. Very early in the twentieth century, the word "system" had lost its once-static meaning and now referred to a "fluid social process that at peak efficiency remained in dynamic equilibrium."[1] Faith in a self-regulating market gave way to a growing belief in the need for purposeful control managed by public-spirited experts trained in the "scientific method" to reduce waste and misuse of natural and human resources. Some reformers (and even businessmen who were not reformers) believed that excessive competition led to economic inefficiencies. In his well-received book *The Promise of American Life* (1909), the writer Herbert Croly proposed that the federal government should come forward to reshape the economic order. To reformers like Croly, an activist state should serve as the instrument of democratically controlled progress.

Croly and other American intellectuals were influenced by thinkers in Europe, notably German institutional economists and English Fabian Socialists, who advocated far-reaching state intervention to ameliorate grave economic and social dangers. These American social thinkers had concluded that the free-market economy was an unstable system, prone to excesses of speculation and cutthroat competition. They preferred to trust the future to the presumed rational approach of state technocrats. Few Americans were prepared to go so far, but an increasing number now thought Washington must attend to business.

Progressive reformers did not agree on the form intervention should take. Those who thought the problems of the economy resulted largely from concentration wanted antitrust action to guarantee a competitive marketplace. Others, however, believed excessive competition to be the problem. But all agreed that something had to be done. For reformers, strengthening Washington's role in the economy was the order of the day.

Antitrust policies loomed large in the 1912 election. Democratic candidate Woodrow Wilson called for "the destruction of monopoly not by regulation, but by the enactment of specific legislation."[2] Allied with the antitrust wing of his party, Wilson wanted the economy returned as much as possible to the highly competitive activity of smaller economic units that had long characterized the nation. His opponents, Taft on the Republican ticket and Theodore Roosevelt as the Progressive Party candidate, thought differently. Both were prepared to accept big business, but Roosevelt specified conditions.

The 1912 contest between Roosevelt's "New Nationalism" and Wilson's "New Freedom" offered voters a choice between two very different visions of government and business. One sought to decentralize economic concentration; the other aimed to control business by enlarging the national government's regulatory role. Wilson urged the use of government to limit big business to curb its influence. He exhorted that "no country can afford to have its prosperity originated by a small controlling class. . . . Every country is renewed out of the ranks of the unknown, not out of the ranks of the already famous and powerful in control."[3] Roosevelt, consistent with his views as president, called for a federal presence sufficient to guard against business misconduct: "All we wish to do on behalf of the people is to meet the na-tionalization of the big business by nationalized government control."[4]

Wilson's message harked back to an older and more individualistic vision of America as a nation of small-scale competitive capitalism. Viewing anti-trust action as a way to redistribute power, he believed that economic compe-tition was as fundamental to American democracy as the freedom to express competing ideas. Federal regulatory involvement had to be carefully limited to protecting the marketplace from unscrupulous operators and monopolis-tic practices. In contrast, Roosevelt envisioned a corporate society of orga-nized interests supervised and possibly coordinated by Washington. An in-terconnected elite of business managers and civil servants imbued with an ethos of public service would administer a stable economy, welcoming and encouraging the efficiencies of big business. Taft warned, however, that both his opponents promoted false expectations, for "a national government can-not create good times. It cannot make the rain to fall, the sun to shine or the crops to grow."[5]

Conflicting answers to two very important questions—how to limit private economic power and how to protect the individual—pulled American reform in two directions. Wilson noted in one 1912 speech: "There is one proposi-tion upon which this campaign turns. . . . That proposition is this: is monop-oly inevitable. . . . If monopoly is inevitable, then the thing to do is for government to take hold of monopoly and to regulate it. If monopoly is not inevitable, then the thing for the law to do is to break it and prevent it forming again." As president, he would call for antitrust legislation to "make men in a small way of business as free to succeed as men in a big way."[6]

Both men presented themselves as reformers, but their differences posed a dialectic without synthesis. Should American reform, as Roosevelt had it, center on an administrative state and society: the cooperative integration of all interests, including those representing otherwise powerless groups? Or should it focus on Wilson's concern to promote small business and competi-tion? There is a third possibility. Reform might involve the use of the balanc-ing approach espoused by the philosopher William James, who noted that when faced with different alternatives, "the pragmatic method" is to consider each possibility by weighing its respective consequences. The question of the proper scope and nature of state action should not be answered in the ab-stract but must be continually determined anew in terms of ever-changing circumstances and needs.[7]

As early as 1912, such leading industrialists as George Perkins and Frank Munsey noted that "enlightened businessmen" had a social conscience that was responsive to the new needs of an urban-industrial society and that these socially responsible business managers, with minimal governmental supervision, could be trusted to work, through trade associations and other business organizations, to avoid ruinous competition and improve business ethics and generally to handle the nation's social problems through their collective actions. The classical liberal ideal of a sovereign state with limited powers atop a self-regulating market was yielding to a new sense of a managed capitalism, where government was only first among equals in a network of interlinked organizations.

Presidential elections are, of course, determined more by political realities than philosophical discourse. Wilson's victory in 1912 resulted from a division within the Republican Party that split the party's vote. When Roosevelt failed to wrest his party's nomination from the incumbent Taft, his supporters had organized the Progressive Party for him to run for the presidency and drafted a platform calling for wide-ranging reform. Wilson, supported by less than 42 percent of the electorate, won an overwhelming victory in the electoral college.

REFORM OF THE BANKING SYSTEM

Roosevelt had handpicked Taft as his successor in 1908, yet he soon found reasons to criticize his presidency. Taft, however, precipitated the final break between the two by authorizing an antitrust suit against U.S. Steel in October 1911, an action regarded by the irate Roosevelt as a personal attack. The details behind this incident yield insight into the close working connections among business, banking, and government in the early Progressive years. More important, they provide the background for important legislation passed in 1913 and 1914.

The heart of the government's case against U.S. Steel in 1911 was the corporation's acquisition four years earlier of one of its smaller rivals, the Tennessee Coal and Iron Company. But U.S. Steel had in fact obtained Roosevelt's prior approval before the 1907 takeover. To Roosevelt, the antitrust action implied that he had been duped into consenting. Furious, believing his successor was playing "small, mean, and foolish politics," Roosevelt determined to run for the presidency himself in 1912.

Behind Roosevelt's acquiescence to U.S. Steel's takeover lay a story exposing critical weaknesses in banking and finance. After a 50 percent fall in the value of Wall Street stocks in a six-month period, panic had struck the banking world in October 1907. Starting with a run on several important New York trust companies, it spread overnight to the stock exchange as speculators found themselves unable to borrow money to meet their obligations. The federal government responded by placing federal funds in New York banks, while J. P. Morgan called together the city's top bankers to a meeting in the opulent library of his mansion on Manhattan's East Thirty-sixth Street.

Over a two-week period, Morgan organized a "money pool" to lend funds to endangered investment firms. This assistance came almost too late for one prominent Wall Street firm. Moore and Schley had played a leading role in promoting industrial mergers between 1898 and 1902. In 1907, however, the firm owed $35 million to various banks, with shares of Tennessee Iron and Coal Company (TI&C), an independent steel producer, as collateral for these "massive loans." With TI&C's stocks sliding in value, Moore and Schley faced bankruptcy as creditors called in their debts. To save the firm, Morgan proposed that U.S. Steel acquire Moore and Schley's TI&C stock. But since TI&C competed with U.S. Steel, legal problems could be encountered. To forestall trouble, Henry Clay Frick and Elbert Gary raced to the nation's capital in a special train, a single Pullman car hitched to the locomotive, to gain Roosevelt's approval. Persuaded by them that the action would prevent a market collapse, the president verbally guaranteed that U.S. Steel would not be prosecuted under the Sherman Act. In 1909, however, a Senate Judiciary Committee investigated the takeover of TI&C. It concluded that U.S. Steel had gained assets worth several hundred million dollars at a bargain price, while eliminating a "strong and growing competitor." An angered Morgan replied that his intention had been only to head off a crisis.

The Bankers' Panic of 1907 underscored the inadequacy of the existing financial system. Public opinion rightfully concluded that the government's reliance on informal stewardship of private bankers such as J. P. Morgan could no longer be condoned. For over two decades, Morgan had wielded a power no other private citizen has ever exercised before or since—powers that led reform-minded Senator Robert La Follette of Wisconsin to denounce Morgan as a "thick-necked financial bully, drunk with wealth and power [who] bawls his orders to stock markets, Directors, courts, Governments, and nations."[8]

A banking system dating to the Civil War era needed to be replaced. There existed in 1907 more than 20,000 state and national banks with no coordinated management or pool of common reserves. Bankers among themselves disagreed sharply on what was needed; small-town and rural bankers wanted to weaken the influence of the large city banks, while most of the country sought to lessen the power of Wall Street.

The Aldrich-Vreeland Act of 1908 provided a system of federal credit as a stopgap measure in times of fiscal crisis and created the National Monetary Commission to study the banking system. The Democratic-controlled House of Representatives, fearing that this commission's Republican chairman, Rhode Island senator Nelson Aldrich, was under Wall Street influence, established the Pujo Committee to investigate the "money trust." The well-publicized Pujo hearings documented the immense concentration of power in the financial world—reporting that twelve banks in New York, Boston, and Chicago held a total of 746 interlocking directorships in 134 other banks, railroads, public utilities, and industrials. The Morgan bank alone accounted for 341 directorships in 112 corporations and owned major shares in the nation's three largest life insurance companies.[9]

THE ELECTION OF 1912 AND ITS AFTERMATH

The election of 1912 dramatized the increased involvement of the federal government in the economy. Voters had to choose between contrasting proposals by Wilson and Roosevelt for changing the tariff, the national banking system, and antitrust policies. Wilson decried "the curse of bigness"; Roosevelt's platform, although asking for political and social reforms well beyond those of the Democratic platform, including a federal child labor law, accepted big business when properly regulated. With the conservative Taft and the reform-minded Roosevelt splitting the Republican vote, Wilson carried the election, and his party won both the Senate and the House. Political circumstances and the public mood joined to break the legislative logjam that had prevailed since 1908.

Tariff reduction headed the new president's agenda. The Underwood Tariff Act of 1913 passed by a special session of Congress called by Wilson dramatically lowered most duties. More important, it provided for a graduated income tax (up to 7 percent on the personal incomes of the wealthy and 1 percent on corporate incomes) to compensate for the loss of tariff revenue.

An earlier effort at an income tax had been declared unconstitutional, but the ratification of the Sixteenth Amendment in 1913 removed this obstacle. With new power to tax incomes, the federal government developed far-reaching tentacles. A few reformers suggested that federal tax powers provided the means for transferring wealth away from the rich to the less fortunate. Apprehensive conservatives warned that the ability to levy income taxes made it inevitable that the federal government's power over the economy would escalate rapidly—anticipating P. J. O'Rourke's celebrated wisecrack: "Giving money and power to government is like giving whiskey and car keys to teenage boys." Phrased in the less colorful language of political science, the income tax added immensely to that portion of "national power the government can extract for its purposes." Washington, as it became confident of its ability to command greater revenues, often found reasons for new programs to spend it on. The issue of raising or lowering the federal income tax soon became a perennial of American election year campaigns.

FEDERAL RESERVE SYSTEM

With the tariff attended to, banking and currency reform assumed priority. On December 23, 1913, nine months after the death of J. P. Morgan, the Federal Reserve Act created a central system. The intention was to provide a more elastic currency responsive to both regional and business-cycle needs. To meet its responsibilities of supervising the nation's banking, the Federal Reserve could issue notes backed by the "full faith and credit" of the United States, set reserves for member banks, and under certain circumstances intervene directly in the market. Unlike the relatively simple institution of the Bank of England, the model for the First Bank and Second Bank of the United States, the new system was from the start jerry-built and cumbersome.[10]

Consisting of twelve regional banking districts and a national Federal Reserve Board in Washington, D.C., the new system combined private and federal interests. It represented compromises between those desirous of a strong central system and those fearful of undue federal control, between those seeking easier access to credit and those preferring a stable solid currency. Even though viewed by bankers as an improvement, few were truly happy with the new Federal Reserve System. Conservatives worried that the system could provide leverage for governmental control of the private economy. Others feared that it would permit undue influence by private bankers over the nation's money.

Each district bank (with its stock owned by the member banks) was a separate corporation with nine directors, six elected by their member banks and the remaining three designated by the Federal Reserve Board. All the national banks created under the Banking Act of 1862 had to join a district bank, while state banks willing to meet certain standards could apply for voluntary membership. The twelve district banks monitored their local banks, distributed currency, processed checks, and settled interbank payment. Operating with great independence, they supervised the day-to-day operations of the nation's banking system while facilitating their local banks' response to regional needs.

The Federal Reserve Board, in Washington, D.C., consisted ex officio of the secretary of the treasury and the comptroller of the currency (Wilson having insisted on this latter inclusion to guarantee the president a voice), as well as five paid members appointed by the president and confirmed by the Senate. Though excluded from the board, member banks sent representatives to a Federal Advisory Commission that met regularly with the Federal Reserve Board to make recommendations.

On paper, the Federal Reserve Board possessed impressive powers to set policy and oversee the operations of the regional banks. It bought and sold government securities, established the reserve requirements for member banks, and set the rediscount rate for member banks borrowing from the system. But until important changes were enacted in 1935, it was New York's Reserve Bank under the leadership of the formidable Benjamin Strong that dominated Washington.

In part, this development reflected the imposing resources of the New York banks and Strong's own commanding personality. Other factors also contributed to New York's retaining control of an estimated 50 percent of the country's banking. The desire to avoid an overly centralized system had led to a feudal realm of twelve dukedoms not effectively controlled by the federal government. The most powerful of the twelve district banks, the New York Reserve Bank, filled the power vacuum and policed the other eleven. Furthermore, the sophisticated understanding required for meaningful centralized direction and control of the Fed's power (both actual and potential) did not exist. It would only be acquired the hard way at the hands of a ruthless taskmaster, the Great Depression. In fact, some economists, notably Milton Friedman, hold the Fed's mismanagement of interest rates in 1930 responsible for turning a business downturn into the worst depression in American history.

The final items on Wilson's reform agenda concerned business behavior and antitrust. He supported the Clayton Act of 1914, which tightened restrictions on uncompetitive practices. Some were specified as illegal. These included interlocking directorates in competing firms, "tying" agreements (in which a retailer had to restrict itself to one company's product as the condition for receiving it), and pricing practices or agreements that discouraged competition. Most important, section 7 of the act prohibited mergers or acquisitions where "the effect . . . may be substantially to lessen competition or to tend to create a monopoly." Wilson supported the act despite his disapproval of its exemption of labor unions and agricultural organizations from antitrust laws.

Shortly before passing the Clayton Act, Congress created the Federal Trade Commission (FTC) to replace the Bureau of Corporations. Wilson wanted a regulatory agency that enforced antitrust laws but also worked with industry to anticipate trends and needs. The FTC was empowered not only to investigate but also to regulate and to issue desist orders to corporations engaged in "unfair methods of competition." Observers pointed out that the FTC was more in line with Roosevelt's administrative regulation of big business than Wilson's philosophy. Although antitrust laws had been strengthened, too many critical questions remained unanswered. Little guidance, for example, was provided on the central issue of at what point a company's market share deterred meaningful competition and therefore warranted curtailing.

Businessmen who were worried about the anti–big business rhetoric of Wilson's "New Freedom" soon received reassurance. Wilson appointed FTC commissioners sympathetic to the corporations. After a business downturn in the fall of 1913, corporations were permitted to work out informal agreements with the Department of Justice—as had been the practice in the Roosevelt administration. Seemingly powerful new tools had been fashioned in 1913 and 1914 to allow the federal government to protect the consumers and small business, but these did not necessarily threaten big business. The underlying assumptions of Roosevelt's New Nationalism had prevailed despite Wilson's election. America continued to move toward an economy marked by concentration. With the outbreak of war in 1914, antitrust sentiment quickly waned.

In fact, Martin Sklar has claimed that both the FTC and the Clayton Act represented the victory of big business over small business, "end[ing] the debate over the legitimacy of the large corporation." This view may be challenged, but there is no doubt that the Clayton Act and the act creating the FTC were indeed drafted in consultation with representatives of the business community. However, this does not necessarily prove undue influence.[11]

A decisive shift to a mixed system of public and private controls over the American economy occurred in the years 1901 to 1914. The timidity of much of the federal government's regulatory actions in this period reflected real concern that public actions should not curtail economic growth nor exceed constitutional powers. Nevertheless, the new federal involvement in the economy indicated at the very least a waning of faith in a self-regulating market economy.

Big business warily accepted these developments as useful—to a point. But its spokesmen remained vigilant that government's role not threaten what they regarded as management's prerogatives. In the view of most businessmen, government had to restrict its role so as not to unduly interfere with profits or stifle innovation. Big business, despite its frequent complaints, proved until the Great Depression to be more than a match for government on all levels.

PROFESSIONALS AND TECHNOCRATS

As noted earlier, many in the Progressive Era regarded the volatility of the nineteenth-century society and economy as unacceptable. A prevailing sentiment among those who shared such a view was that most major social and economic problems could be at least managed if not solved. All that was required was for highly educated technicians to work within well-designed bureaucratic structures to ensure stability and order by applying the scientific method to problems.

This new concept of responsible and "scientific" professionalism, with its faith in the possibility of harmonizing public and private interests, was a central tenet of Progressive reformers. Reformers looked to the schools and colleges to provide the technicians needed by the economy and government. For them, fact gathering and problem solving by well-trained professionals could, if properly handled, constitute a true science free of subjective or self-interested judgments. They either overlooked or largely ignored the concept now referred to as the "principal agent," which notes that agents have their own agenda of self-interest that they will often pursue even when it comes at the expense of the client whose interests they have been hired to serve.

The turn of the century brought a dramatic expansion in the number of Americans engaged in administrative and professional tasks. Corporations needed a hierarchy of managers, technicians, and accountants, while all levels of government required trained professionals to replace patronage appointees in a reformed civil service. Universities and industrial laboratories required scientists. Some scholars of the period regard these developments as creating a distinct new social group, a rising professional middle class based on higher education. Olivier Zunz, for one, has suggested that the corporation helped to create a new class of middle managers from Americans migrating from farm to city.[12]

Thomas Cochran has estimated that by 1915 a quarter of a million Americans could be classified as middle managers. As corporate bureaucracy expanded and its hierarchy became more defined, the delegation of managerial responsibility became an ever-increasing necessity. More and more professionals who provided advice on law, accounting, engineering, or science were added. To Chandler, these changes involved a critical transition from "entrepreneurial" enterprises—which he defined as "manager-manned but owner-controlled" firms—to manager-dominated enterprise, a theme to be returned to.

As late as 1880, less than 3 percent of eighteen-year-olds graduated from high school, and most of these attended college. By 1920, nearly a fourth of eighteen-year-olds had graduated from high school, but only 8 percent of these graduated from college. Several states passed laws that required all children to stay in school till the age of sixteen, and high schools which had previously taught Greek to an elite student body destined for college now trained large numbers of students in the art of reading blueprints and training manuals. Education had become a vocational necessity, and the more you had the better.

Parents interested in their children's mobility urged them to remain in school so that they could find employment in a secure job paying a salary rather than a wage. In lower-income families, this might mean that the older children and the daughters left school early, providing financial help by working in order to allow younger sons to complete high school—and possibly even go on to college. Private "commercial schools" offered intensive short-term training in typing and bookkeeping to prepare their students for office work, and two-year community colleges were introduced shortly before World War I to help the children of less financially fortunate families to climb the ladder of middle-class respectability.

A new stage of life had emerged—adolescence. Beyond childhood but before full adulthood, adolescents were increasingly expected to prepare themselves through education for their future lives. Along with this new stage, there began to evolve a distinct sense of a youth culture, as adolescents increasingly looked to each other as models for dress, behavior, and even values.

WHITE-COLLAR WORK

Colleges and universities trained the vast army of technical experts and administrators employed by large corporations. Most found their future in middle management, while a fortunate few advanced into the new "managerial elite." For both groups, however, a proliferation of professional and technical societies existed to hone skills and provide opportunities for networking and generally to advance the interests of their members. Businessmen supported the creation of schools of business administration and created their own national organizations, the National Association of Manufacturers in 1895 and the United States Chamber of Commerce in 1912. Both bodies had as their stated purposes promoting the cause of organized business and furthering American civic progress.

The Progressive Era's impulse toward organization and expertise received expression in the ideas of "scientific management," the term itself coming into common usage around 1910. Frederick W. Taylor's ideas were advocated after 1911 by the Society to Promote the Study of Scientific Management (later known as the Taylor Society), and the enthusiasts included Taylor's most important disciples—Henry Laurence Gantt and Frank and Lillian Gilbreth. The latter were a husband-and-wife engineering team whose children later chronicled their "scientifically ordered family life" in the popular book, twice made into a movie, *Cheaper by the Dozen*. Another of Taylor's disciples, Melville Dewey, "rationalized" the nation's libraries with the Dewey decimal system and wrote his own name as "Melvil Dui" in the interests of spelling efficiency. In 1912, Christine Frederick, in a much-discussed article in the *Ladies' Home Journal*, brought "scientific management" into the home. In a truly modern society, it would seem that everything that was traditional or accidental or even intuitive had to be scrutinized and then discarded if deemed wasteful or obsolete. But scientific management's most important application was to the corporation.[13]

By 1911 and the publication of *The Principles of Scientific Management*, Taylor had extended its scope to offer operational principles for the office operations of a complex organization. These included purchasing and inventory control systems, cost accounting, and production planning. Within ten years of its publication in 1911, Taylor's organizational primer had been translated into all major European languages, as well as Japanese.

Some labor historians have regarded Taylorism as stripping factory workers of the last vestiges of craft pride. The alienated worker without his sense of self-worth and autonomy could then be molded to meet management's needs. The Marxist scholar Harry Braverman advanced this thesis in his provocative study *Labor and Monopoly Capital: The Degradation of Work in the Twentieth Century* (1974). However, Braverman greatly exaggerated the extent of Taylor's acceptance by American companies. Management approached Taylorism cautiously, believing it had limited applicability. The few firms that tried to introduce Taylorism as a complete system encountered opposition from old-line management, which felt as threatened as workers on the faculty floor. Yet Taylor's ideas did contribute to the formulation of the classical input-process-output (IPO), which dominated management training from the 1920s to the 1970s. Such an approach emphasized clockwork production lines capable of mass-producing products in very large numbers.

By World War I, a woman's expectations regarding work had changed dramatically from the late 1890s. Women now expected to work until marriage and often after. Many middle-class women worked until the birth of a first child and occasionally longer. As a result, working women composed a third of the nonfarm labor force in 1916. Race, ethnicity, and class, in addition to gender, continued to define work possibilities. Black women typically worked in domestic service. Immigrant women often worked in factories, including the infamous sweatshops of the garment trade. The cleaner and more respectable jobs as salesclerks, office workers, or teachers were usually reserved for native-born whites.

With increased opportunities for unskilled women workers in factories and shops, the supply of servants declined sharply in the early years of the twentieth century. Married middle-class women sometimes had to do without live-in help, a situation that encouraged the development by 1907 of a primitive washing machine. Stay-at-home mothers became less a manager of household help and devoted more time to household chores, shopping, and the handling of household expenditures.

Progressive reformers sought legislation regulating the working conditions of women (and children), "to protect the family and America's future." Between 1906 and 1974, for example, a New York state law prohibited women from working as bartenders, because a saloon was deemed morally inappropriate for the "weaker and more vulnerable sex." (Ironically, feminists in the 1970s led the fight to eliminate a law that women reformers had strongly advocated in 1906—an instance of how one generation's reform often becomes another generation's problem.)

In the pathbreaking 1908 case, *Muller v. Oregon*, the "people's lawyer" and future Supreme Court justice Louis D. Brandeis successfully defended state laws limiting hours of labor for women before the Supreme Court by emphasizing the negative effects of long working hours. His brief, a classic of what became known as "sociological jurisprudence," contained two pages of legal argument and ninety-five pages of social science data, all to demonstrate that social reality, not precedence, had to dominate the life of the law. Several years later, on March 25, 1911, a fire at New York City's Triangle Shirtwaist Company killed 146 young immigrant girls, many of whom jumped from the upper floors of a ten-story factory building because the fire exits had been locked. Nearly 200,000 marchers paraded up Fifth Avenue to express their outrage at "sweatshop" safety conditions and to demand reforms.

THE ECONOMY OF PLENTY AND FORD'S "$5 DAY"

Despite the problems of the time, optimists eagerly anticipated national affluence and a new civilization. The influential economist Simon Patten, in *The New Basis of Civilization* (1907), asserted that modern science and technology invalidated ideas of scarcity that underlay classical economics. He believed that excessive competition was responsible for unemployment, business cycles, and labor conflicts. Patten called for an activist government to tame the marketplace, creating an economy of plenty with high wages for the working class. Patten was not alone in calling for a new way to think about the economy and the related role of government. Writers like Walter Lippmann and Herbert Croly stressed the importance of a broadly distributed material abundance in easing social tensions and achieving a more comfortable and egalitarian society.[14]

On January 5, 1914, Henry Ford announced to an audience of reporters that his assembly-line workers would receive a "$5 day" wage for an eight-hour work shift in place of $2.34 for nine hours. The following morning, 12,000 men lined up to seek employment at Ford's Highland Park plant. Within two years, the company reported that the value in savings and property of the average Ford worker had risen from $196 to $750. The "Age of Affluence" had seemingly been born—with Ford, not the social theorists, acting as midwife.

Ford explained his actions strictly in terms of cold calculation. American industry's self-interest, he stated, required that employees be paid enough for them to afford to buy what they produced. It would now take an assembly-line worker only about five months' pay to buy the new Model T he had helped make. Ford had seemingly arrived at a seminal formula for modern American capitalism: an industrial economy's success depended on designing standardized products, lowering costs to make them affordable through mass-production, and then paying high wages to the workforce to stimulate productivity and sales. Selling millions of automobiles at a small profit per car allowed Ford to keep prices low and wages high while profiting handsomely—the perfect formula for a mass-consumption market.[15]

There was, however, more to the "$5 wage" than Ford disclosed. Before introducing the assembly line, he had anticipated that workers would welcome the repetitive work because he assumed they disliked jobs requiring intelligence or physical exertion. Developments soon proved otherwise. In 1913, labor turnover reached an astonishing 380 percent at Highland Park. The tediously exacting nature of assembly-line work had led to a dramatic rise in absenteeism and turnover. Labor problems explained Ford's innovative wage policy: the need to recruit, retain, and motivate his large workforce. The "$5 day" represented, he told reporters, "efficiency engineering" and resulted in "one of the finest cost-cutting moves we ever made."[16] (Economists use the term "efficiency wages" for pay that is above the minimum level required to hire and retain workers.)

Ford's workforce consisted mainly of immigrants from Eastern Europe, who often had personal habits the company considered undesirable. Ford ordered that only workers exhibiting the "right behavior," on and off the job, could earn the "$5 day." Accordingly, the company's so-called sociological department checked on workers' savings, drinking habits, and moral conduct by questioning the men's families, neighbors, and clergy. A company school taught English and personal hygiene to immigrant workers, who faced a wage cut unless they demonstrated a willingness to become "Americans" and subscribe to "American values." Ford's emphasis on the assembly line and high wages was often contrasted favorably to Taylor's stress on time-and-motion studies, piece rates, and functional foremen supervising the laborer's every move. Ford himself claimed to have increased productivity without intensifying work by analyzing and improving all factors of production rather than simply demanding more effort from the worker. More accurately, Taylorism and Fordism represented complementary systems of harnessing relatively unskilled labor to mass production in such a way as to keep raw materials and workplace both steadily in motion, with management controlling the pace of work. Both constituted bold experiments in imposing managerial control to eliminate unproductive time and labor.[17]

PATERNALISM, WELFARE WORK, AND LABOR UNIONS

Ford's overt paternalism represented an extreme instance of "welfare work," an interest in employees' welfare and their productivity exhibited by many large corporations after 1900. The National Civic Federation (NCF), founded as a reaction to class tensions evident at the time of the Pullman strike, sought to promote an "enlightened capitalism," harmonizing the interests of labor and management. By 1903, the NCF counted among its members many leading figures in American industry and finance, prominent civic notables, and the heads of the most important labor unions, including Samuel Gompers, president of the American Federation of Labor.

The NCF urged business acceptance of the trade union movement as a logical development of the modern economy. To encourage peaceful resolution of labor conflicts, the NCF made mediation services available whenever both parties were prepared to accept them. Many influential members who supported the NCF's program in theory, however, continued to fight union activity in their own firms. Nevertheless, the American Federation of Labor's membership in 1917 reached 2.5 million, roughly 15 percent of the non-agricultural workforce—a higher percentage than union membership at the beginning of the twenty-first century.[18]

Despite growing numbers, Gompers's organization, which was based on trade unions, refused to organize the unskilled or semiskilled, who constituted the great mass of American workers. By the end of World War I, unions were largely confined to skilled crafts in the brewing, building, metal, mining, railroad, and garment industries. The history of labor in the early decades of the century revealed that the Progressive ideal of harmonizing various interests had proven elusive.

After 1905, the NCF devoted its energies to welfare work. Here it encouraged management to develop employee pension, health, insurance, and savings programs, theoretically strengthening the ties between capital and labor. Not the least appeal of welfare work programs to management was that they in no way diminished its power. In time, the NCF acquired a reputation for directing its energies to reducing labor unrest and combating socialist sentiment among workers. Indeed, historian David Noble has dismissed the NCF's interest in welfare work as an effort at improving worker efficiency by "transform[ing] the energy of potential conflict into a constructive, profitable force within a larger corporate framework."[19]

Welfare work relied on the goodwill of management and reflected management's needs. Often it represented an effort at offering workers an alternative to unionization. But by its unilateral nature, the powerful doing for the powerless, welfare work was prone to paternalism and even outright manipulation and coercion. Management, in seeking to inculcate certain values, such as sobriety, hard work, and self-discipline, served society's ends, but it did so for its own purpose—to increase productivity and profit. The two, of course, need not be mutually exclusive. However, welfare work could easily lead to unacceptable intrusion into the private lives of workers, and too often did. The next decade, to jump ahead briefly in our chronology, experienced a further development in labor relations.

During the 1920s, the "personnel" field experienced a struggle between industrial engineers practicing Taylorism and the emerging discipline of industrial psychology pioneered by Elton Mayo and Harvard's Chester Barnard. The psychologists faulted Taylorism for viewing workers as motivated only by economic gain, arguing that employees needed a sense of self-worth and accomplishment in the workplace. Between 1927 and 1932, Elton Mayo conducted a study of fatigue among workers in the relay assembling test room of a Western Electric plant in Hawthorne, Illinois. The study involved women assembling telephone components in a setting he described as hot, dirty, and dark. To determine the effect of working conditions on productivity, Mayo had the lighting improved. As he expected, productivity increased. But when, in a subsequent phase of the experiment, the lights were lowered, productivity again increased. Mayo concluded that both times the workers had responded positively to the attention they received from observers: a theory known since as the "Hawthorne effect."

Mayo then studied workers who were allowed greater initiative. He found that they worked more efficiently when monotony was reduced and when trust between workers and foremen existed. Mayo concluded: "The desire to stand well with one's fellows, the so-called human instinct of association, easily outweighs the merely individual interest and the logic of reasoning upon which so many spurious principles of management are based." Along with Mayo, industrial psychologists in the 1920s emphasized workers' morale and motivation as key factors in production. However, Taylor's disciples, the efficiency experts, continued to stress impersonal systems in which workers merely did what they were told. The clash between these two very different philosophies of management continues to this day.[20]

COMPETING INTERESTS

Advocates of Roosevelt's New Nationalism underestimated the ability of organized interests to influence politics for their own ends. Their view of an active involvement by a government staffed by experts in the economy assumed that the federal government could act as an honest broker and mediate the needs of competing interest groups. Such an approach with its emphasis on disinterested professional civil servants largely ignored the importance of political factors based on self-interest in determining national policy. But as the governmental role increased, organized interest groups had increased reason to influence public action through lobbying efforts.

Although history records that big business fared well in the Washington arena, its leaders knew that neither American government nor American politics could be totally controlled by them. A deep strain of populism, with its marked antipathy toward big business and great wealth, could always erupt in unexpected and—from business's perspective—undesirable ways. For this reason, big business, though prepared to accommodate itself to an active government and eager to use the government for its own advantage, wanted clear limits to federal power. Small and medium-sized businesses felt even more threatened by state and federal regulatory action. The important legislation passed in the first two years of Wilson's administration exhausted a Congress already under pressure to consider such controversial social issues as Prohibition and female suffrage, while World War I diverted attention from domestic reform.

When the outbreak of war in 1914 threw the Western world into tumult, Wilson proclaimed America's neutrality. Hostilities offered American businessmen rich opportunities to increase trade with the belligerents, but British control of the seas guaranteed it would be one-sided. Direct American trade with the Central Powers declined from $169 million in 1914 to $1.2 million in 1916 as trade with the Allies rose from $825 million to $3.2 billion. With foreign holdings of American assets soon liquidated to pay for this flood of materials, the extension of commercial credit by private American banks and businesses to Allied governments exceeded $5 billion by 1917. Once short of capital, the American economy emerged almost overnight as a cornucopia of surplus funds. After 1919, nations needing to rebuild war-damaged economies sought financing from American banks.

American sympathy for the Allied cause mounted as the war dragged on. The conviction grew that economic interest required Germany's defeat; even before the U.S. entry into the conflict, committees had been appointed in Washington to prepare for its eventuality. Once war was declared in early April 1917, the Wilson administration recognized that the need to equip and send a large American expeditionary army to France while also assisting the Allies required the economy's mobilization. In July 1917, the War Industries Board (WIB), one of several hundred agencies to manage the nation's wartime economy, was created to allocate key raw materials to industry.

Transportation bottlenecks and profiteers interfered with the smooth management of the war effort. To correct the situation, Wilson appointed Wall Street speculator Bernard Baruch to head the WIB in March 1918. At war's start, the United States had largely lacked an armaments industry. The little money spent on the military had gone mainly to the navy. Baruch insisted on broad powers to establish production quotas. To facilitate this, he created some 350 industrial associations that ranged from casket makers to producers of asbestos. By war's end, Baruch controlled the production of almost all consumer goods and claimed to have shifted a quarter of the economy from consumer to war production. The ladies' shoe industry, for example, reduced its styles to a few basic models. Baruch even bragged that enough metal had been saved by removing unnecessary stays from women's corsets to construct two large battleships. According to Baruch, "If the war had lasted much longer, the civilian population would have been clothed in serviceable, if drab, apparel."[21]

It had been hoped that national planning would rely on voluntary cooperation. In reality, many companies and industries either proved reluctant to take on war work or sought undue profits. Two major industries offered serious problems. Automakers preferred to continue civilian production; steelmakers expected windfall profits. Baruch coerced the industries through a variety of threats, such as withholding vital raw materials or limiting their use of the rails. Even so, he admitted, many steel companies had profited excessively during the war. His enemies, and there were many, believed that Baruch had permitted collusion on price setting. Indeed, after 1916, the government had virtually suspended antitrust action. Organized labor, however, also gained from the war effort. Gompers and other labor leaders served on industry boards, and union membership rose from 2,000,000 in 1916 to 2,726,000 at war's end.[22]

But America's mobilization effort accomplished a remarkable outpouring of war matériel. To an unprecedented degree, the Wilson administration had successfully managed key sectors of the economy. And now reliance on decision making by experts rather than market forces appealed to some as the better way to run the postwar economy. The apparent success of the WIB reinforced the view that the government could act effectively. Corporations also emerged from the wartime experience with high marks for expanded industrial capacity. Only faith in Adam Smith's "invisible hand" had suffered. The wartime experience appeared to demonstrate that the twentieth-century economy required public policies that promoted industrial cooperation and restrained excessive competition.

The war's cost had exceeded twice the total of all federal expenditures since 1789 and was ten times the price of the Civil War. For many businessmen, their wartime experience with the WIB demonstrated the difficulties of dealing with the governmental bureaucracy. Businessmen did not want to lose independence or surrender power. Yet World War I also suggested the advantages of sailing within the relatively sheltered harbor provided by government-supported trade and industrial associations in limiting business uncertainties. Federal regulations were preferable to a bewildering array of state regulations and, perhaps more important, offered the advantage of clarifying the rules of legal competition.

Wartime controls, with the exception of those on the railroads, ended abruptly in early 1919. The problems of conversion to a peacetime economy produced severe labor turmoil, as unions demanded higher wages and management fought back by organizing company unions and expanding welfare work. Rampant inflation in 1919 was suddenly followed by a sharp deflation in 1920–21, brought about by excess inventories, a drop in exports, and a tightening of credit by the Federal Reserve. Union membership now plummeted sharply, and by decade's end the unions had surrendered the membership gains of the war years.

A SWING TO THE RIGHT

The 1920s represented a decade of triumphant conservatism. The Republican presidential candidate in 1920, Warren G. Harding, promised Americans a return to "normalcy," and voters responded by giving him nearly 60 percent of the vote in the first national election in which women cast ballots. Very briefly, in 1919 and 1920, Wilson's Department of Justice had revived an active antitrust policy. But by 1920 the national mood called for a retreat from federal activism. What the people wanted was less governmental involvement in their lives. They wanted shoe manufacturers to offer a wide variety of stylish models, not a few. Nor were they concerned with skimping on materials or costs. Fun not frugality proved to be the theme of the 1920s.

But the decade did not wholly wash away the changes of the preceding two decades. A time of governmental retrenchment, the 1920s was also a period of ongoing governmental involvement in the economy. What had altered was the public's view of the nature of the relationship between the government and big business. Progressives had hailed government staffed by experts as a watchdog against wrongdoings in the private sector. The FTC and the Clayton Act dampened anti–big business sentiment by seemingly offering protection from large corporations. In the 1920s, the public mood swung in favor of business. Business promised progress. President Calvin Coolidge laconically asserted that brains "are wealth and wealth is the chief end of man." To this he added: "The man who builds a factory builds a temple, the man who works there worships there, and each is due . . . reverence and praise."[23]

COMPETITION TAMED AND HARNESSED

The Progressive themes of reliance on experts and scientific management of complex organizations were skillfully employed by corporations. This in itself was not startling. Many Progressive reformers had long hailed the model of big business rationality and spoken of the need for government to operate in a businesslike way.

But these shared themes were in the 1920s firmly embedded by corporations in the image they wished to convey, as well as a corollary projection of corporate public service. Leading industrialists spoke of the need to provide high wages and more leisure hours to workers so that they and their families would have time and money to purchase the products their plants turned out in increasing variety and numbers. If allowed latitude, big business promised in return both economic growth and social responsibility. Further involvement of the government, they argued, could for the most part be avoided, because business itself would correct the problems of a market economy. Moreover, governmental involvement obstructed business efficiency—and possibly represented creeping socialism. What business wanted was encapsulated by Calvin Coolidge's oft-quoted statement that "the business of America is business."

The conservative turn of the 1920s did not constitute a return to the past. Instead, trade and industrial associations of leading corporations formed networks to exchange information to eliminate waste and to limit competition. In an important antitrust decision in 1918, *United States v. United States Steel Corp.*, the Supreme Court, after stating that bigness as such was not a violation of the law, noted with approval the "company's cooperation with competitors . . . in the expedients of pools, associations, trade meetings, and finally in a system of dinners inaugurated in 1907 by the president of the company." If still praised, competition was to be made all the more beneficial for being tamed. Many in the corporate business community feared that a freely competitive economy led to instabilities and business inefficiencies. Wasteful and vicious cutthroat competition had to go.

A seeming consensus held that management had to be made "scientific." As they expanded, corporations frequently moved away from their core activities. Centralized organizations sometimes proved inadequate to the task of managing this greater scope of operations. Organizational innovation was required to allow for the flexibility required to handle diversified activity.

The DuPont Company had profited handsomely from producing munitions during the war, and after the Armistice the company expanded into new areas offering the potential for growth in peacetime. But its organizational structure soon faltered under the increased load. After a period of experimentation, DuPont reorganized itself into a multidivisional (M-form) form of organization along product lines. The head of each division was its chief executive with full authority to run the operation independently. The

DuPont board held each head accountable for profit-and-loss performance, on the basis of which it allocated resources to the divisions.

By 1921, DuPont had become the largest owner, 43 percent, of General Motors shares, and here too a multidivisional organization would be introduced. Alfred P. Sloan (1875–1966) was placed in charge. His mission was to replace the risk-taking, entrepreneurial style of William C. Durant, the General Motors founder, with central oversight of multiorganization corporations. The responsibility for introducing innovations, Sloan believed, should be a matter of decision making by teams of managerial specialists. Sloan, frequently described as the first modern CEO, played down the value of personal leadership and emphasized corporate structure and strategy. Cost accounting, rather than intuition, was to be decisive in decision making involving the various divisions, and Sloan was definite about the purpose of General Motors: "The primary object of the corporation . . . was to make money, not just to make motor cars."[24]

However, few other corporations adopted the multidivision organization in the 1920s, and movement toward it slowed to a halt during the Depression years. Only after World War II, as corporate America again diversified, did the M-form become the paradigm for America's largest companies.

To simplify somewhat, the 1920s would be the Progressive Era minus the emphasis on innovative governmental reform. The technocratic and bureaucratic thrust of the earlier period continued, as did the zeal for the efficient use of resources. But these now occurred principally in the "scientifically managed" and "public-spirited" world of America's corporate giants. The theme of a powerful efficient government as a counterbalance to big business and organized labor or as a goad to social and economic progress had been largely shelved. American business, thank you very much, did well enough on its own. Few doubted that corporate America had performed well for Americans. Even the radical journalist Lincoln Steffens, who had built a muckraking career on attacking American business, conceded in 1921: "Big business in America is producing what the Socialists hold up as their goal: food, shelter, and clothing for all."[25] But the question remained, Could the masses pay for this flood of goods?

The Consumer Decade

Across the courtesy bay the white palaces of
fashionable East Egg glittered along the water.
—F. SCOTT FITZGERALD, The Great Gatsby *(1925)*

In the 1920s, Americans provided the market for the lucrative rise of professional sports, the motion picture industry, tourism, and health care. Mass
advertising created new wants and styles, skillfully working to undermine
traditional habits of thrift. The icon of the decade was the automobile. Between 1921 and 1929, the number of cars registered in the United States rose
from 9 million to 26.5 million, and half of all American families owned at
least one. An economy performing splendidly did not need much in the way
of political reform, or so many thought.

Scholars now view the 1920s as the decade in which modern life, with
its mass consumption and demand-driven economy shaped by advertising
agencies, became recognizably our own. During the 1920s, the United States
became the world's financial power, and the country's energy and creativity in
entertainment, marketing, and science influenced the way people shopped
and acted in metropolitan centers around the world.

ALL THAT JAZZ

The 1920s threw into clear focus changes that had long been under way,
foreshadowing much of the pattern of twentieth-century American life. The
emergence of a consumer culture oriented to the masses was the decade's
most dramatic development. But although popular stereotypes of the de-

cade ("The Roaring Twenties," "The Jazz Age") have long dwelt on the frothy and the frivolous—flappers, bootleggers, flagpole sitters, Babbitts, and bohemians—beneath the tinsel and the titillation, the world's first true consumer society required innovative business practices.

Advertising budgets more than doubled in the decade, to an annual $1.5 billion. Madison Avenue entered the lexicon as a synonym for advertising agencies, as its copywriters and artists depicted an idealized world populated by slim, beautiful people who doted on the product being huckstered. The intricate connections among advertising, consumerism, and popular culture had clearly emerged. To historian of advertising Roland Marchand, advertising men and women had emerged as the "apostles of modernity," who heralded new products, styles, and tastes as the essence of progress and happiness.[1]

New technologies and increased reliance on electric power led to a surge in productivity. Between 1921 and 1929, production nearly doubled as demand rose to meet output. After recovering from a brief but sharp recession in 1920 and 1921, the U.S. economy expanded at a healthy annual rate of 3.3 percent. Americans fared so well that the 1920s was soon dubbed, albeit only until October 1929, "the prosperity decade."

In response to a strong demand for new varieties of standardized mass-produced goods, America became the world's incubator for consumer service industries. It pioneered techniques of modern marketing, as an economy oriented to a massive consumer market truly came of age. Innovative product lines aimed at middle-class consumers promoted an image of an America at the cutting edge of the future, and frequent style changes and built-in obsolescence made last year's products seem dated.

According to standard economic models, consumers look over available wares and then select those that they prefer. In the 1920s, however, firms often decided which goods were most profitable to produce and then employed marketing to convince consumers to buy them. Advertising encouraged a commercial hedonism. Consumers were conditioned to choose products that expressed a desired lifestyle. Marchand commented on the enveloping totality of advertising: "By the 1920s advertisers had come to recognize a public demand for broad guidance—not just about product attributes, but about taste, social correctness, and psychological satisfactions."[2]

"We were the most powerful nation," wrote F. Scott Fitzgerald in 1931, summing up the postwar generation's satisfaction at America's preeminence. "Who can tell us anymore what was fashionable." Indeed, America increasingly acted as modernity's embodiment. Advanced technology, new and more-inclusive consumption patterns, movies, sports, jazz, the emancipation of youth, the displacement of traditional cultural leaders, the rise in divorce, the "new woman"—all spoke of an American energy ushering in a problematic modernity for all the world.

Nor were Americans inclined to be modest (and some were well paid to be immodest). Marchand has observed that "modern styles and ways of life needed their missionaries. Advertising men were modernity's 'town criers.' They brought good news about progress."[3] Madison Avenue broadcast the message that America was all about tomorrow and what's new and what's next. Agency advertisements heralded the latest products and styles. As a service to clients, the agencies provided market research, suggested product names, and designed packaging. All of this was in addition to planning and conducting the actual advertising campaign.

English economist John Maynard Keynes sneered at America's obsession with material success, at "the horrid fact that every American has ten motorcars and a wireless set in every room of every house." German Marxist Moritz J. Bonn claimed that "the almighty dollar and its use" are the meaning and goal of American life. But Americans were not inclined to heed European critics, or American ones for that matter. Madison Avenue offered a more cheerful message. What one purchased, Americans were told, added to a sense of status and self-worth. Consumerism was an exercise in self-expression and personal development, with advertising as an indispensable guide. For their clients, ad agencies proffered a different message: advertising would train buyers to prefer their products over those of their competitors.

Advertisers in the 1920s sought to convince Americans that the nation had discovered the secret of permanent prosperity. If advertising did not create the optimism of the decade, it certainly contributed greatly to it. A speculative enthusiasm during the decade encouraged people to purchase land in Florida (often under water) and to invest in Wall Street's stocks (often overvalued). For the first time in history, a populace was encouraged to live today fully without worrying about tomorrow. The nation had come a long way from Franklin's humble homily: "Waste not, want not."

THE NEW CONSUMER ECONOMY

A Victorian view of character as based on self-restraint was being challenged by an ethos of consumerism. The traditional view of the worker as a producer now also had to encompass the worker as a consumer. The average American household had spent $79 a year between 1899 and 1908 on consumer durables; that rose to $267 a year from 1919 to 1928. The 1920s witnessed a revolution in consumer taste. Americans not only increased their buying of consumer durables but switched from (or added to) buying china, furniture, and pianos to such newly mass-produced items as cars, radios, and refrigerators. Mass consumption had joined mass production as factors in the nation's spectacular economic success.[4]

America had evolved into a society centered on the modern marketplace of seductive products and the never-ending search for commercial novelty. A 1929 study by a governmental agency noted that "scarcely less characteristic of our period than unit cost reductions is the rapid expansion in the production and sale of products little used or wholly unknown a generation or even a decade ago." It then provided a list of some two dozen new consumer items, including not only the obvious automobiles, radios, and rayon but also "propeller lead pencils," wristwatches, and cigarette lighters—the latter two popularized by their use in the muddy trenches of World War I. In a brief aside, the report also noted that oil was beginning to be used as a substitute for coal as a heating fuel.[5]

Consumer spending acquired greater recognition as being key to the economy's progress. The study stated that although fifty years earlier only one-third of factory products (as measured in dollar value) had been intended for consumer use, this had now increased to two-thirds. It also noted that nine of the twenty leading American corporations specialized in consumer goods in 1928, as compared to only one in 1919.[6]

By 1929, chain stores, defined by the government as any company with four or more units, accounted for one-fifth of all retail sales and nearly 40 percent of all grocery sales. The Great Atlantic & Pacific Tea Company (A&P) increased the number of its stores from 4,600 in 1919 to nearly 16,000 in 1929. With their advantage in low operating costs and bulk discount buying operations, chain stores represented a formidable threat to small retailers, who sometimes in self-defense organized themselves into collective buying organizations to obtain cheaper prices from quantity purchases. Similarly, fast-food chains pioneered by White Castle and Howard Johnson gave owners of Main Street diners sleepless nights.

One company's actions illustrated how the America of the 1920s anticipated our own. Robert E. Wood, vice president in charge of retail stores for Sears Roebuck, faced an important decision in 1925. Started as a mail-order house three decades earlier, Sears Roebuck had achieved annual sales of over $230 million by 1920, with millions of rural families, distant from any city stores, thumbing through its hefty catalogs, humorously referred to as "The Farmer's Bible." But the absolute number of American farmers declined after 1910, and their percentage of the workforce fell by 1920 to 25 percent. The census of 1920 indicated that for the first time a majority of Americans lived in cities, and during the course of the decade additional millions left rural areas. Furthermore, the automobile put many farm families within driving distance of city stores.[7]

Everyone knew that these trends were irreversible and that Sears Roebuck needed to open retail stores. Wood had to decide where to locate these future stores. A pioneer of market research, he presciently decided to construct stores in low-density areas on or just outside the urban periphery. Provided with parking facilities, hundreds of stores would be placed near major traffic intersections throughout the nation. The expansion of the middle-class suburbs, which had started in the last third of the nineteenth century with the commuter railroad and the electrified streetcar, had accelerated with mass ownership of automobiles; suburbs in the 1920s grew at a faster rate than cities.

In recognizing the automobile's importance to the future American lifestyle, Wood assured Sears Roebuck, the "Great American Company," fifty years of growth and prosperity. As the American suburb became the residence of choice, Sears Roebuck emerged in the 1960s as the world's largest merchandising operation. Even before World War II, the company, pushed by its great size, pioneered the use of autonomous territorial divisions for its far-flung operations, and as late as 1972 Sears accounted for over 1 percent of America's GNP. Its business strategy, which was based on the circumstances of the 1920s, had remained viable for half a century.[8]

Important new industries came of age in the 1920s, including radio and film, but none had a greater overall impact—economically or culturally—than the automobile. At the end of the decade, the production of cars, trucks, and buses constituted America's largest industry, and the industry contained three of the country's largest companies. In 1929 it employed one-tenth of all nonagricultural workers. The automobile quickly reshaped America's transportation and residential patterns, severely undermining the railroads in the process.

With a farm boy's distaste for urban life, Henry Ford boasted in 1922 that "the automobile frees us to leave the city" for the suburb. The automobile spawned subsidiary businesses, such as service stations, repair shops, motor cabins or "motels," and garages, and became the principal market for enamel, steel, plate glass, and rubber. The powerful oil industry, which had experienced difficult times as Edison's lightbulb replaced the kerosene lamp, was rescued by the automobile: gasoline, formerly a little used by-product, now fueled the internal combustion engine. The automobile also promoted new methods of consumer finance. The social and spatial changes were equally profound; the automobile transformed almost overnight the whole pattern of the real estate market, broke down the barrier between urban and rural America, promoted suburban development, and altered not only lifestyles but also values.

By 1929, the United States possessed over 80 percent of the world's automobiles. The Sunday family drive with a stop at a diner symbolized a consumer society increasingly oriented to leisure time. New road systems provided scenic routes for family outings as well as quick ways to get to beaches and state parks. Encouraged by funds offered by the Federal Aid Road Act of 1916, the states created highway departments to build a network of paved interstate systems crisscrossing the nation and inspiring their own lore and legend, such as Route 66, which was fabled in song and extended from Chicago to Los Angeles.

Detroit's astonishing yearly production of millions of the "people's chariots" attracted world attention but required a hard sell to empty the dealers' lots. General Motors advertised the automobile as "a great contributor to human effectiveness, an enlarger and enricher of human life."[9] Immigrants long lured to America by stories of "streets paved with gold" now came in search of streets lined with cars, but in fewer numbers as the decade progressed. The immigration quota acts of 1921 and 1924 for the first time severely curtailed entry into the United States, while expressing preference for immigrants from Western Europe over those from Southern and Eastern Europe in establishing national quotas.

The automobile is not an American invention. French and German mechanics had developed the internal combustion engine and the automobile in the last quarter of the nineteenth century, and the United States lagged behind until the first decade of the 1900s (explaining the use of the French terms "limousine," "garage," and "chauffeur"). Initially the automobile was envisioned as a plaything of the wealthy. The first automobile show in New York City in 1901, when the city's speed limit was nine miles an hour, invited carefully screened guests to attend in black tie.

The first automakers were mostly small operators—carriage makers, bicycle manufacturers—who enthused about the new technology of the horseless carriage. Between 1904 and 1908 more than 240 companies entered the new industry. Some operators specialized in parts supplies and some in assembly, but their fortunes were often joined since the supplies were usually custom made. Production was limited and the product expensive. As late as 1906, Woodrow Wilson, then president of Princeton University, fretted that automobiles might heighten class tensions by arousing working-class envy. But he need not have worried. The United States soon led the way in pioneering inexpensive automobiles affordable to the masses.[10]

America's circumstances of broad expanses, low density, and high per capita income provided a natural market for an inexpensive car used as basic transportation. By 1908, no fewer than twenty-four companies produced low-cost automobiles, and in that year Henry Ford introduced his Model T, a simple, boxlike vehicle. Available in "any color as long as it was black," Ford's "Tin Lizzie" quickly dominated the field and remained in production nearly unchanged in appearance for nineteen years, with some 15 million sold.[11] The automobile for the people had become a reality. Ford was a pioneer in demonstrating that maximizing production while minimizing costs would result in maximum profit. Deservedly, Henry Ford entered the pantheon of American folk heroes.[12]

Unable to match Ford's price and quality, many of his rivals failed. By World War I, Ford was producing nearly half the automobiles sold in America. In 1918, Henry Ford bought out minority stockholders in the company he had incorporated in 1903. With the giant firm now family owned and managed, the egocentric Ford's autocratic ways increasingly antagonized top executives. Close associates either quit or were fired. In 1923, Henry Ford published his ghostwritten *My Life and Work*, in which he presented himself as the quintessential American entrepreneur always eager for a better way of doing business. The book quickly became a runaway best seller. But after 1924, sales of Ford cars stumbled badly, and by 1926 seven out of ten Ford dealers were operating in the red. The market for the Model T had become saturated. Car buyers, many of them second-time purchasers trading up, now wanted style and the status they wanted a new car to convey. The public had tired of the same basic model being offered year after year. On May 27, 1927, all Ford plants closed down production.

Six months later, a new model rolled off the reopened assembly line. The Model T was history. But change came too late; ineptness in adjusting to a new market was symptomatic of the company's mismanagement. Ford became increasingly overbearing and erratic in his actions as he refused to recognize the changing nature of an industry he had once easily dominated. By 1925, General Motors overtook Ford as the nation's largest automobile producer; five years later its assets of $1.5 billion made it twice as large as Ford. Of the more than 180 companies competing in the infant automobile industry, only a handful now survived, and three—General Motors, Ford, and Chrysler—accounted for over 90 percent of all production. But GM was the leader.[13]

GM'S CHARIOTS OF STEEL

Yet GM had started the 1920s with very serious problems. Its wheeler-dealer founder, William C. Durant, had run the company aground. Fortunately, the firm had a brilliant manager in his successor, Alfred P. Sloan. The contrast between Sloan and Durant (or between Ford and Durant) provides insight into changes under way in the type and style of American corporate leadership as the automobile industry matured.

"Billy" Durant delighted in operating intuitively in high-risk ventures. After heading the Buick Motor Company for four years, the live-wire Durant incorporated GM as a New Jersey holding company in 1908. But when Durant predicted that someday 500,000 automobiles would be produced annually in the United States, the powerful banker George Perkins, of the House of Morgan, advised him "to keep those notions to himself if he ever wanted to borrow money."[14] Determined to pursue a strategy of rapid growth, Durant engaged in an aggressive and risky policy of merging with rivals. With Buick as his base, he soon added, among others, Cadillac and Oldsmobile and even made a failed attempt to acquire Ford. Borrowing heavily, Durant was forced in 1910 to surrender voting control over his stocks to a supervisory trust of Wall Street bankers.

Undaunted, Durant took control of the Chevrolet Motor Company, only to trade its stock in 1915 for sufficient GM shares to regain control. Dissolving his New Jersey company, he reorganized GM as a Delaware-based operating company. But GM's divisions consisted of its former subsidiaries largely functioning as independent companies and with the same people in charge as before. Durant paid little attention to their operations, preferring to play the stock market and make deals. Moving in many different directions at the same time, he acquired new companies, several of which had little to do with the automobile industry. His erratic behavior resulted in a rapid turnover of top executives and a chaotic corporate structure—thrashing arms and legs with little in the way of torso or head.

On the edge of bankruptcy in 1920, GM came under the control of the Du-Pont company. Pierre du Pont was named president, with Durant pushed out for a final time. He lost his remaining fortune through stock market speculation in the 1929 crash, and at his death in 1947 at age eighty-six, Durant was managing a small bowling alley in Flint, Michigan, the GM company town. Durant's successor, MIT-trained mechanical engineer Alfred Sloan, prided himself on being a professional manager whose responsibility was to manage prudently other people's capital. Although admiring Durant's entrepreneurial genius, Sloan considered his actions inappropriate in a giant corporation, which needed to behave predictably. Methodical and deliberate in his actions and distant in his personal relations, Sloan had the analytic outlook of a systematizer, rather than an empire builder's intuitive taste for risk. With Sloan in charge, Durant's impulsiveness gave way to decision making by committees, with Sloan carefully soliciting all views. This systematizing, rather than curtailing innovation, actually promoted daring changes.

Sloan, who came to GM in 1916, watched carefully as Durant's erratic style resulted in a floundering and failing industrial giant and even considered leaving prior to the DuPont takeover. In late December 1920, Sloan, then forty-five, presented the now DuPont-dominated board of directors a scheme for line-and-staff reorganization that remains a classic document of American business history. His initial concern was "to determine the functioning of the various divisions . . . not only in relationship to one another, but in [their] relationship to the central organization." This analysis provided the key to delegating authority to and within the divisions while retaining centralized control.[15]

Sloan then reversed his analytic perspective, examining GM's organization downward from the central office to the divisions. His intention was "to centralize the control of all the executive functions of the Corporation in the President as its chief executive officer." Freed from operating tasks, top management could then concentrate on overall coordination. In 1925, GM introduced "forecasting" to provide a vision of the future to be tested against later developments, and a more effective system of budgeting became top management's primary device for controlling the divisions. At least in theory, top management now could creatively and systematically execute entrepreneurial policy making.

Sloan called this organization "federal decentralization." It is better known, however, as the "M-form." He had pioneered a systematic approach to multidivisional organization. GM's success indeed guaranteed that Sloan's leadership and organizational innovations would in time be valued as a paradigm by leading industrial corporations. Sloan had done for management what Ford and Taylor had achieved on the shop floor, the imposition of a rational system. His strategy allowed divisional chiefs considerable working autonomy, even over marketing and engineering, while a central administrative staff (composed of lawyers, accountants, and other experts) monitored division operations and handled such common concerns as capitalization, investment policies, research, planning procurement, and advertising. An executive committee of staff administrators developed company-wide policies and had final approval of divisional plans.

A design department responsible for research and development—including annual style changes in models to promote the policy of obsolescence—was soon introduced. Charles Kettering, head of the research division, frankly defined his goals as the creation of dissatisfaction with the old, and beginning in 1927 GM introduced yearly model changes. The historian Daniel Boorstin has written of the introduction of annual model changes as teaching "that Americans would climb the ladder of consumption by abandoning the new for the newer."[16]

Sloan carefully positioned the various divisions to minimize overlapping markets, even as they continued to compete with each other. According to the GM idea, a young first-time car buyer purchased an inexpensive Chevrolet. With greater affluence, he worked his way up the GM "ladder" to the moderate-priced Pontiac, Oldsmobile, or Buick. Finally, he purchased the luxury and status of a Cadillac. *Fortune* described the marketing targets: "Chevrolet for the hoi polloi. . . . Pontiac . . . for the poor but proud, Oldsmobile for the comfortable but discreet, Buick for the striving, Cadillac for the rich." Less gratingly, GM hired the Madison Avenue firm of Barton, Durstine and Osborn, which advertised GM products as "a car for every purpose and every pocketbook." The research department developed a quick-drying spray paint so that cars could be offered in different colors to buyers. The journalist and social pundit Walter Lippmann, in admiring Sloan's handiwork at GM, reflected that Sloan's comprehensive plan of production actually included a plan of marketing and consumption. He recognized that, with only two rivals in the industry, GM did not really have to compete in terms of price for market share but only through market strategy.[17]

Sloan's leadership demonstrated his mastery of all aspects of the company: from manufacturing to management to sales. It also revealed his insight into human nature and its desires. Unlike Henry Ford, who had emphasized mass production to manufacture a single inexpensive model, Sloan had made GM responsive to changing demands and market pressures. Ford had focused single-mindedly on the car and its production. Sloan looked instead to the customer and the car market.

Sloan's strategy of a proliferation of products to both meet and create consumer demands succeeded brilliantly. Chevrolet was the GM model in most direct competition with Ford. Its production rose from 280,000 automobiles in 1924 to a million in 1928; the next year the Chevrolet engine was increased from four to six cylinders, and annual sales soared to nearly 1.5 million cars. This success of the low-priced Chevy proved a godsend for GM during the decade of the Depression.[18]

Historian Stuart Piggot, in a history of the Assyrian war chariot, has remarked that fast and dashing vehicles always conferred on their possessors social prestige and even sexual allure. Madison Avenue was teaching manufacturers that they had to sell the psychological benefits of a product as well as its more obvious ones—the customer had to be made fully aware that he or she purchased prestige with the car. Ford manufactured inexpensive automobiles to transport the masses; Sloan produced automobiles to confer status for a few years, until style changes made them outmoded. A carefully orchestrated market strategy persuaded the consumer that newness and novelty, as well as price, conferred status. Sloan recognized GM's real business as selling cars, not building them.[19]

Sloan claimed that the centralized power he had exercised as head of GM was "exercised with discretion; I got better results by selling my ideas than by telling people what to do." Commendable advice, but advice that cannot be entered on an organizational chart. Peter Drucker, in his classic *The Concept of the Corporation* (1946), told another story. He faulted GM for its rigidity and its discouragement of employee input on ways of improving operations.[20] The intangibles of individual personalities and values influence a corporation in critical ways, no matter how it is bureaucratically organized, to achieve what we now term a "corporate culture." Brilliant and innovative as a leader, Sloan paradoxically championed a management style that sought what Joseph Schumpeter has called "mechanized" progress: a bureaucratic organization that transforms corporate strategy into routinized management.

BUY NOW, PAY LATER

The automobile showcased the new consumer society, and the years between 1920 and 1930 familiarized Americans with other important novelties. The increasing availability of electricity (by 1929 only about a third of the population, almost all rural, did without) allowed families to acquire electric irons, washing machines, electric stoves, fans, vacuum cleaners, and the refrigerator (replacing the icebox, which had been introduced only forty years earlier as a wonder of modern convenience). In 1922, only 60,000 households had a radio. By 1929, 10.25 million households, nearly half of American families, owned radios. The family gathering about the large console in the living room to be entertained (and to absorb commercials) became a nightly ritual. The proliferation of "consumer durable goods" created a new retail niche. Many of these products required electricity, propelling the electric power industry, led by such giants as General Electric and Westinghouse, into new areas of growth and investment.[21]

"Buying on time," formerly reserved by the middle class for such expensive purchases as pianos or furniture, now became routine, as families rushed to enjoy products offered to the masses and elite alike by the genius of industry. Consumers reached for the good life, spending above their means, in confident expectation that tomorrow would be better. Nonfarm consumer credit, including home mortgages, rose from $32 billion to $60 billion, and by decade's end 60 percent of all cars and 75 percent of all radios were purchased on the installment plan. It has been estimated that between 1919 and 1929 installment purchasing was used in 15 percent of all goods sold. Terms for the average installment purchase in 1925 was one-third down, with the balance and interest charges to be paid in twelve equal payments.[22]

If consumers hesitated or faltered in their shopping, advertising agencies spurred them on. An increasingly sophisticated Madison Avenue skillfully nurtured the association between the good life and consumption. In the best-selling 1925 *The Man Nobody Knows*, advertising executive Bruce Barton, the son of a preacher, portrayed Jesus as a super salesman of Christianity who had "picked up twelve men from the bottom ranks of business and forged them into an organization that conquered the world." Barton described the parables as "the most powerful advertisement of all times."[23] Stuart Ewen's *Captains of Consciousness* (1976) doubtlessly overstated the argument that mass consumption rested on manipulation through advertising. But the fact that Ewen's extreme position appeared plausible to reviewers underscores a general acceptance of advertising's critical role in the rise of a consumer society. Certainly by the 1920s ad agencies worked not only to sell individual products but also to promote a positive image of the client company itself, establishing its "corporate consciousness" with the public.[24]

American business—concerned that it might produce more than people would buy—sought to enlarge markets through advertising, built-in obsolescence, and frequent style changes. Items still useful were rendered psychologically obsolete by being portrayed as out of fashion. Sociologists Robert and Helen Lynd, in their 1929 study of Middletown, actually the town of Muncie, Indiana, remarked that the ads of the 1920s were focused upon a type of copy that aimed to make readers emotionally uneasy. The ads bombarded people with the notion that respectable folks had to live up to a certain standard: decent people ride on balloon tires, have a second bathroom, and so on. Sinclair Lewis's novel *Babbitt* so effectively depicted a salesman's compulsive devotion to acquiring the latest fashionable products that it added a word to the English language—"Babbitt," a mindless conformist whose sense of worth depends on owning the right things.

Americans in the 1920s were taught to identify lifestyle with status and progress. The days of buying sturdy clothes for a lifetime of use had ended. Still wearable clothes and other durable consumer products were discarded only because they appeared out-of-date. Consumers replaced, traded in, and up-scaled products because they had lost their ability to impart pleasure or status. The term "dated" to convey this meaning may indeed have been first used in a newspaper ad that appeared in 1926.

Women who had formerly gone to hairdressers two or three times a year to cut long tresses now went weekly to the proliferating new beauty parlors to have their hair bobbed, cut, and colored in the styles sported in their latest films by Gloria Swanson or Louise Brooks. Off the screen, the handsome and dashing young movie couple Mary Pickford and Douglas Fairbanks demonstrated to awed admirers by way of "screen magazines" that expensive clothes, luggage, and jewelry provided an enviable way to live.

A Hollywood makeup artist named Max Factor discerned that women would eagerly buy the lipstick, eye shadow, and pancake makeup (terms that he either coined or popularized) that he had initially prepared for actresses. His company advertised: "Make-up in seconds, look lovely for hours." Max Factor made it acceptable for "nice" girls to wear makeup. An entirely new market quickly emerged; despite the Depression, the cosmetics industry was the twelfth largest in the United States in 1936. Twenty years later, Max Factor Inc. was selling cosmetics in more than 100 countries.

Film studios and their associated industry of thousands of "movie houses," "screen magazines," and "movie columnists" came of age as big business in the 1920s. The industry had its beginnings in the early 1900s in working-class neighborhoods. After World War I, the studios, which also owned the theaters, made a concerted effort to broaden their films' appeal—using marketing to establish heartthrobs and sirens and erecting lavish movie palaces. In the late 1920s, American Telephone and Telegraph (AT&T) developed methods of synchronizing the sound and film tracks, and the "talkies" were born. By decade's end, 90 million Americans attended the movies weekly, an average of three attendances for each American household. The product value of the movie industry by 1935 was third in the United States and the fourth largest of any industry in the world.[25]

Hollywood had emerged as the world's dream factory and served as a cultural ambassador for the desirability of the American way of life—30 percent of the studios profits came from overseas. Audiences in Athens and Sofia, as well as in Topeka and Chicago, thrilled to the elegant dancing of Fred Astaire or the manly good looks of Clark Gable. As had the auto industry, the film industry evolved into a few large producers, the studios. Locked in an intense consumer-oriented competition, they sought to control not only the actors, directors, and screenwriters under contract but also the industry's distributors and exhibitors. Nor were the studios alone in chasing the discretionary dollars Americans spent on entertainment.

As the work week moved from a six-day to a five-day week (weekly working hours for manufacturing workers declined from 47.4 hours in 1905 to 42.1 hours in 1925), leisure-time businesses—the entertainment industry—provided amusement for a price. Attendance at sporting events soared, with crowds flocking to see Jack Dempsey maul his opponents in the ring or Babe Ruth swat homers into the stands. Weekly moviegoing was a ritual for many Americans, with city children attending Saturday matinee programs especially designed for them. New restaurant chains, such as Howard Johnson and Horn and Hardart, sought to persuade the American family to "give mom a break" and eat out on a regular basis. Not surprisingly, cultural conflict between those welcoming changing values and those resisting them loomed large during the decade.

SICK INDUSTRIES

New industries often grew at the expense of older ones. Alongside the growth industries of the consumer society existed "sick industries," ones plagued by aging plants, overcapacity, low returns, and often labor troubles. Cotton textiles faced competition from new synthetic materials such as rayon. Experiencing hard times, New England mills moved south in search of cheaper nonunionized labor.

The bituminous coal industry shrank amid desperate efforts by the miners to keep their jobs. Railroads, encountering competition from trucks and buses for passengers and freight, proved incapable of the innovative strategies needed to restore their competitive position. The industry that had long served as the engine of progress experienced a painful decline.[26]

American farmers represented a notable exception to the general prosperity of the 1920s. High farm prices during World War I, when warring nations desperately required American farm products, could not be sustained in peacetime. Yet wartime needs had encouraged increased production, and the government had promoted the use of chemical fertilizers and farm machinery. A postwar drop in agricultural prices led in ten years to a decline of nearly 50 percent in the farmers' share of the national income. Understandably, between 1919 and 1929, some nineteen million people fled the farm for the city. Even with this great migration, many of the remaining farmers barely held on to their land.[27]

On the whole, the economy of the 1920s achieved remarkable success. Chemical and pharmaceutical firms invested millions in research laboratories, which produced such wondrous new products as cellophane (invented in 1926) and synthetic vitamins. After a sharp but brief recession that lasted from spring 1920 to summer 1922, industry boomed. Production nearly doubled in the following six-year period, and the GNP rose 40 percent. As unemployment sank to negligible levels and price levels remained constant, real wages increased some 22 percent, even as hours of work declined. Two decades earlier, the German sociologist Werner Sombart had asked rhetorically why American workers did not, like Europeans, become politically radicalized and then answered his own question—that Americans remained content with a system that meant they could eat well. In the 1920s many middle-class American families could afford vacations, extended schooling, and other experiences reserved in Europe for the privileged few.[28]

Compared to other nations, America had achieved the highest standard of living for the greatest numbers of citizens. On the other hand, more than a fifth of American families had incomes of under $1,000 a year, and 70 percent of families fell short of the $2,500 that was estimated as necessary for a decent lifestyle. Based on these figures, less than a third of the population experienced fully the decade's affluence. Many Americans could only press their noses to the shop windows and gaze longingly at the merchandise inside—or surrender to temptation and buy on credit.[29]

As long as the economy grew rapidly, there was confidence that prosperity would trickle down. Coolidge's secretary of commerce, Herbert Hoover, in accepting his party's nomination for the presidency in 1928, claimed: "We in America are nearer to the final triumph over poverty than ever before in the history of any land."[30] In the meantime, one could always consider buying on time. Satisfied with the pace of progress, many Americans regarded the decade as the beginning, in Hoover's words, of a "New Economic Era."

In a probusiness climate, credit for prosperity largely went to "forward-looking corporations." Manufacturing was increasingly dominated by industries that relied on mass production and bureaucratic organization and that strove to appear progressive and socially responsible. Acceptance of large enterprise by the federal courts after the Clayton Act meant an antitrust policy extremely sympathetic to bigness. With an upbeat economy few cared.

If business was good for America, science was good for business. The new industries of the 1920s depended on high capital investment and sophisticated technology. Many corporations started research laboratories during the war years, and by 1927 some 1,000 large businesses—mainly concentrated in the electrical, chemical, pharmaceutical, metals, and rubber industries—supported laboratories seeking to improve existing products and develop new ones. During the 1930s, a flood of products came to market that resulted from research first started in the 1920s. The DuPont laboratories, for example, successfully developed Freon for refrigerators in 1932 and nylon in 1938.

Corporations sought to vary their product lines and to adapt to regional market differences. "Scientific management" seemed essential to handling increasingly complex decision making, involving product and corporate diversification as well as the operating of the business. The high corporate profits allowed management greater freedom from dependence on bankers or the stock market. Though accountable to the stockholders and boards of directors in theory, the reality in most cases permitted them full discretion without serious challenge.

·ABSENTEE OWNERS AND MANAGED FIRMS

In 1928 two young men, lawyer Adolf A. Berle Jr. and economist Gardiner C. Means, began a study of the modern corporation that led in 1932 to the publication of a seminal work, *The Modern Corporation and Private Property*. By then, the authors observed, all types of business had adopted the corporate form. The critical difference was between the large corporations and the others. Their statistics showed that the 200 largest corporations controlled about 20 percent of the nation's wealth and about 40 percent of business wealth, and the authors noted that in large corporations, unlike in small ones, there was a prevailing pattern of separation of ownership and control of property, with management in total charge. In many large corporations, stock ownership was so widely dispersed that not even a substantial minority interest existed.[31]

They cited the world's largest corporation of the time, AT&T, as a dramatic example. AT&T had an estimated value in 1928 of nearly $4.5 billion. More to the point, none of the 469,801 shareholders owned even as much as 1 percent of its total shares. The largest, the Sun Life Assurance Company, held exactly .6 percent and was itself a company with broad shareholding.

The multiplication of ownership allowed management to use the proxy system of voting, which allowed directors to become, in effect, self-perpetuating. For all intents and purposes, the literal owners of the company had little real role. Corporations exhibiting significant separation of ownership and management the authors termed "quasi-public corporations," and in these the interests of owners and of management often diverged, and too often with weak restraints on the actions of the latter.

Management usually owned only a small share of stock. Thus managers could be casual toward profits, even regarding them as a secondary objective. Other factors, such as increasing and retaining power, personal income, or professional reputation, might be seen as more important. The consequence of separation of ownership and management, the authors thought, was to challenge the assumption that the quest for profit guaranteed business efficiency.

This development represented a novelty in business behavior whose implications the authors viewed as outside the scope of their study. Their focus was on establishing the rise of a new type of complex social organization, the public corporation, and the division it created between ownership and control. The full consequences of management's new importance remained unclear but appeared to suggest that a handful of corporate managers of 200 firms dominated American wealth and power. The authors did not doubt that the phenomenon they had described would long remain important. Time has, of course, proven them right.

Management's importance in corporate affairs had attracted considerable comment throughout the 1920s. By and large, it had been hailed as a positive development. Professional management was generally credited with adopting a long-range perspective, investing in research and product development, and avoiding the speculative forays that had unsettled the market. In contrast to entrepreneurial firms, managerial firms often emphasized a committee system as a means of effectively utilizing middle management and consensus building, and the well-managed organization appeared to represent a stabilizing force. Alfred Sloan would even claim that a great strength of the corporation was that it was designed to be an "objective organization," in contrast to the personality-driven proprietary firm.[32]

In the 1920s, nearly all larger corporations hired professionals to conscientiously cultivate a favorable public image. Public relation firms like Lee and Parker, N. W. Ayer and Sons, and that of the charismatic guru Bruce Barton had been engaged in institutional advertising well before World War I. The line between promoting a product and contriving a corporate image was being erased. Corporations created public relations departments to deal with the press and the public, hired consultants to advise them on their dealings with politicians and government, and worked through trade associations (as well as such umbrella organizations as the Chamber of Commerce and the National Association of Manufacturers) to project the image that business heeded the public interest. Edward L. Bernays, a nephew of Sigmund Freud, would make an exaggerated claim to have fathered the field of corporate public relations. In 1928, the American Tobacco Company hired Bernays to promote cigarette smoking as beneficial to health, with the company depicted accordingly as a public benefactor. Bernays paid the well-known dance instructor Arthur Murray to appear in ads advising women that they should smoke so as not to overeat, gain weight, or embarrass themselves socially.[33]

HOOVER'S ASSOCIATIVE STATE

Trade and industrial associations became a prominent part of business life in the 1920s, proliferating from 700 in 1919 to 2,000 in 1929. This development received the enthusiastic support of Herbert Hoover as secretary of commerce under Harding and Coolidge and later as president. He told an audience of businessmen in 1925:

> We are passing from a period of individualistic action into a period of associational activities in business. . . . I think we are in the presence of a new era in the organization of industry and commerce with infinite possibilities of moral progress. . . . We have perhaps twenty-five thousand associational activities in the American economic field. . . . The total interdependence of all industries compels trade associations in the long run to go parallel to the general economic good. . . . I believe through these forces we are slowly moving toward some sort of industrial democracy. . . . With these private collective agencies used as the machinery for the elimination of abuses and the cultivation of high standards, I am convinced that we shall have entered a great *new era of self-governing industry* [emphasis added].[34]

Hoover, a Progressive Republican, considered himself to be a staunch advocate of American individualism. Trained as a geologist and engineer at Stanford University, Hoover had acquired a sizable fortune as consultant to international mining interests before devoting himself in 1915 to public service. Not until 1920, after having served in the Wilson administration, did Hoover identify himself as a Republican when seeking the party's presidential nomination. By then he enjoyed a national reputation as a great humanitarian and statesman. Interested in national economic efficiency, he assumed that business could largely regulate itself—with a little help from government. His vision would encourage cooperation among businesses and between businesses and government to achieve a stable and growing economy.

Never a believer in laissez-faire, Hoover was prepared to use the constitutional powers of the federal government to further the public good. But he distrusted any coercive role or what he called "collectivism," "statism," and "socialism," preferring that government act solely as an enabler. Voluntary associations by the business community were the foundation stones to Hoover's progressive capitalism. Hoover wanted to avoid "Waste in Industry"—the title of an influential paper he delivered in 1921 as secretary of commerce. For this reason, he wanted major industries organized around self-governing trade associations, which imposed controls on competition and business behavior for the sake of stability and greater efficiency.[35]

In reality, trade and industrial associations did involve themselves in a variety of activities, from facilitating intercompany cooperation in research to establishing industry-wide standards and engaging in public relations and lobbying activity on behalf of their members. Some, acting as a cartel, sought to stabilize prices and market shares among their members. In general, the Republican administrations of the 1920s encouraged such activities, even when of questionable legality under the antitrust laws.

According to Louis Galambos and Joseph Pratt, the authors of an excellent study of business and public policy, the trade and industrial associations "took the lead in forging in the 1920's a more cooperative form of capitalism," which historians have termed the "associative state."[36] Hoover, a single-minded technocrat, emerged as the most influential spokesman for its philosophy. This "associative state" sought to substitute a framework of cooperation among rival businesses and between them and government. His intention was to impose a rational cartel-like pattern on the economy, encouraging a stability for long-range corporate planning. Market disciplines, tamed and controlled, would remain the guiding economic force, with government's role largely that of catalyst; the powerful machinery of business, along with enlightened self-interest, would thus pull the United States into a "new scientific and economic frontier."

Hoover, as secretary of commerce, established a Division of Simplified Practices and a Bureau of Specifications to promote standardization and to encourage voluntary business "cooperative work." When he approved of them, Hoover publicly endorsed agreements among businessmen, thus offering semiofficial standing and protection to private compliance efforts.

Corporate efforts at presenting an image of public responsibility did not, of course, foreclose contradictory behavior. Speculators and corporate predators continued to be very much a part of the business picture, as did efforts at market rigging. Holding companies would take over many small operating companies and use their own dividends to pay off the very bondholders who had financed the takeovers in the first place. This permitted an infinite chain of acquisitions. Pyramiding, or erecting huge holding company empires based on little capital investment, occurred with astonishing frequency in public utilities.

Organized labor lost a quarter of its membership from 1920 to 1930 as businesses sponsored company "unions." These company unions busied themselves with welfare programs and working conditions but avoided issues of wages, hours, and job security. Management in the 1920s continued to resist collective bargaining, thus denying labor a meaningful role in decision making. Instead, what has been termed "welfare capitalism" represented a major development in American management in the 1920s, and a 1926 survey of America's largest firms found that 80 percent had at least one form of "welfare" program and nearly half ran fairly comprehensive programs. Although ostensibly concerned with the worker's welfare, most companies also sought through welfare programs to increase productivity and company loyalty, often also with the aim of keeping real unions out.

Foreign observers frequently noted the informality of American workers in their relations with management and the seeming absence of class consciousness and class politics. Explanations of the apparent absence of class tensions usually mentioned America's high wages, fluidity of class structure, and a value system that encouraged individualism and optimism. But much of this informality reflected style, not substance. These visitors might indeed have received a very different impression if they had visited the factory floor during the tense times of the 1930s. Then labor unrest often spilled over into violence. Indeed, when hard times came and business tightened its belt, the labor gains of the prosperous 1920s and many company welfare programs were quickly jettisoned.

From 1922 to late summer 1928, the New York Stock Exchange experienced a heady jump in stock prices: over 200 percent between 1925 and 1928. With greed in the air, speculation ran high. Margin rates, the amount one had to have in cash, sank on occasion to as low as 10 percent (although more typically it was about 33 percent). Brokers extended credit for the balance, retaining the stock as collateral. In turn, the brokers often borrowed from the banks. Brokerage houses introduced an exciting new investment instrument, leveraged mutual funds called "investment trusts." Easy money appeared "ripe for the picking" as stock prices soared. By 1929, some 500 trusts had combined assets of $11 billion, the equivalent of $800 billion in 2000.

Whispered tips and sly winks promised quick profits, as investors, including many first-timers, rushed in record numbers to join the party. The well-regarded Yale economist Irving Fisher predicted in 1929 that the market had reached "what looks like a permanent high plateau." Fisher believed that "it was only as the public came to realize . . . that stocks were to be preferred to bonds . . . that the bull market began in good earnest to cause a proper valuation of common shares."[37]

Investing in the market, formerly an arena for the relatively well-off, now broadened as the bull market kept its legs; small investors numbered in the millions by decade's end. The exaggerated view that many ordinary Americans owned stock has for a long time been widely accepted. But, according to David M. Kennedy, 3 million Americans, or only 2.5 percent of the population, owned stock in 1928, and the number owning stock fell to a little more than 1.5 million in 1929. Between the end of 1926 and June 1929, the Standard Statistical Index of common stock nearly doubled. It then rose a further 30 percent by September 1929 (the Dow reaching its high point on September 3) before showing signs of weakness.[38]

If by its end the bull market was powered by speculative fervor, the earlier increases had been fueled by solid factors. Much of the decade's affluence had been funneled into business profits that led to higher dividends and greater corporate equity. Stocks certainly seemed the place to be. The August 1929 issue of the *Ladies' Home Journal* featured an article ("Everybody Ought to Be Rich"), which advised readers to hurry and buy stocks.

A merger movement occurred in the 1920s that offered knowledgeable buyers ample attractive investment opportunities. Berle and Means have estimated that roughly 20 percent of the growth of large corporations in the decade resulted from mergers. Of the 200 largest American corporations in 1919, they reported, 12 percent had merged by 1929; activity involving medium-sized corporations was more frenzied, with some 10,000 mergers during the decade. A common pattern saw a corporate giant buy out a small entrepreneurial firm that had pioneered a new product. Utility holding companies pyramided trolley lines and electric companies, often only to milk the underlying operating companies. A one-time assistant to Edison, Samuel Insull, built an empire based on utilities centered in and around Chicago. Well into the last stock market run-up, which began in 1927, there existed sound reasons to be bullish.[39]

The American economy's strength in the 1920s propped up the world's. In the aftermath of World War I, Europe confronted strong inflationary forces and unsettled international trade, the flow of American capital and goods becoming critical to nations seeking to rebuild and modernize. This was especially true for Germany, where American bank loans became the means to meet the huge reparation payments exacted by the Versailles Treaty.

The value of American manufactured exports in the 1920s consistently exceeded that of agricultural exports for the first time. In the immediate postwar years, the U.S. trade surplus averaged the then-colossal sum of $2 billion annually. Before the war, major European nations had run a trade deficit with the United States in goods and commodities that was more or less evened out by their earnings on "invisible exports" (returns on foreign investments and various commercial services offered). However, most of their American investments had evaporated during the war, and unfavorable postwar trade balances placed inflationary forces on most European currencies. One important consequence was a weakening of the position of the overvalued pound sterling, with the dollar replacing it as the yardstick of international currency.

The remarkable rise of the United States to economic dominance underscored the postwar instability of the old economic order. By 1929, the United States accounted for about 25 percent of the world's GNP. The United Kingdom's decline made the United States Britain's successor as linchpin of the global financial market, and during the 1920s American bankers probably attained their peak of influence in American history. American capital flowed to Europe in the form of loans and investments (the latter averaging about a billion dollars a year), while the reliance of most nations on the gold standard led to the reverse flow of European gold to the United States. New York now overtook London as the world's financial capital.

Despite European concern about the "gold flight," world trade seemed safe as the decade neared its end. It depended on the well-being of the American economy, and surging confidence in American private enterprise pushed the stock market to dizzying heights. The Dow Jones average set records in each of six consecutive years—the longest such string on record until the bull market of the 1990s. Edgar Loren, a New York investment banker, urged Americans, in his 1924 book *Common Stock as Long-Term Investment*, to buy stock to provide for their old age, and using margin they often did.

Perhaps a million Americans owned stock on margin in 1929, and heavy speculation using margin leverage contributed greatly to the coming of the 1929 crash. The Dow peaked at 381.17 in September 1929. But even as early as the spring of 1929 shrewd speculators—such as Bernard Baruch and Joseph Kennedy, or so they later bragged—had questioned the market's direction and repositioned themselves. Timing was key as the market turned volatile. One speculator, Jesse Livermore, correctly anticipated a downturn but went short too early—costing him his fortune.[40]

The Bank of England raised its rediscount rates in late September, forcing British investors to pull large sums from the American market. As the stock market index declined, frightened investors panicked. Prices rose in early October, and investors eager to recoup losses and greedy to gain from a "buying opportunity" raced to reinvest. By mid-October, institutional investors again began to withdraw, even as small investors continued to buy. On October 24, "Black Thursday," large sell orders in the morning turned into an avalanche by early afternoon. J. P. Morgan Jr. and other New York bankers created—on the spot—a bankers' pool of $240 million to calm the panic, and the next day, a Friday, President Hoover reassuringly declared the economy to be on a sound and prosperous basis.[41]

When the market reopened after the weekend, brokers repeated Hoover's message as a talisman to steady shaky nerves. Monday passed uneventfully, and Tuesday's market also started calmly. But after the first hour it became apparent that a feverish pitch of activity was destroying fortunes. In the wildest trading ever seen on the exchange floor, 16.5 million shares changed hands before the final bell on "Tragic Tuesday." (This stood as a record until the late 1960s.) By the end of 1929, the exchange's listed stocks had lost $40 billion in paper value, a quarter of their early October worth. A cartoon in the

New Yorker magazine depicted a well-dressed Wall Street type checking into a hotel and the desk clerk inquiring whether the room would be needed for the night or only to jump from. Wall Street suicides were, in fact, rare, but black humor had much to feed on in the next years. Not until 1954 did the Dow Jones average regain its 1929 peak.

FREE FALL

On July 8, 1932, the Dow Jones average dropped to 41.22, its lowest point after the crash and a point above where the "average" had begun when first started in 1896. Well into 1930, however, most believed that what had happened was the familiar cyclical business downturn, which would soon bottom out. For a brief time in 1930 the stock market even turned bullish. President Hoover urged businessmen to refrain from cutting wages or their workforce, insisting that an economic turnaround was at hand.

Between 1929 and 1933, over 85,000 businesses failed, unemployment rose from just over 3 percent to nearly 25 percent, and more than 5,500 banks closed their doors. The GNP fell by half within five years. Seemingly overnight, America had plunged from the world's most prosperous nation to a land of breadlines and bank failures, a drag on the global economy. Talk of the "new economy" and American business genius vanished. This shift in public mood from exuberance to deep pessimism traumatized many and confused all. To the popular mind, then and now, Black Thursday and its aftermath caused the Great Depression of the 1930s.

There is truth to this, but it oversimplifies. The collapse of security values in late October 1929 did indeed lead to a massive failure of confidence in the future of the economy. The erosion of business confidence stifled investment as business cut back. Americans lost much of their wealth, making it harder for them to buy goods and services. This does not, however, answer why the Depression—by far the worst in our history—became so severe, or why it had such dire impact on the world scene, or, most important, why it persisted for over a decade.[42]

Economists still do not provide definitive answers to these questions. The list of possible explanations includes tight money due to high interest rates, low prices for commodities, the psychology of fear, and speculative excess. What is definite, though, is that several different factors came together with unfortunate consequences. These factors collectively produced a downward spiral difficult for contemporaries to understand or react to effectively. Efforts to unravel one line of problems often led to tightening other snarls, creating ever more intractable knots. The economy had been pushed downward at the very time it needed a lift—the Federal Reserve Board raised the rediscount rate from 3.5 percent in January 1928 to 5 percent by July 1928 and again to 6 percent in the following year. In part, Fed actions reflected a desire to burst the inflationary stock market bubble; but the Fed's real concern was the dollar's standing in the international currency markets. A wave of bank failures in the Midwest in 1930 radiated outward to other regions. Yet the Fed maintained its high rates policy, even as frantic banks called in old loans and refused new ones.

Withdrawal of international credit caused a crisis and trade war among nations no longer able to finance their war debts or meet reparations schedules. Maintaining the gold standard became a top priority of central banks throughout the world. Collapsing American wholesale prices had a deflationary effect on other nations. In turn, American exports were negatively impacted by the collapse of trade abroad, which helped abort signs of a U.S. turnaround in 1930. Nations seeking to prop up their economies and currencies now emphatically moved toward protectionism.

In many oligopolistic industries, prices continued at high levels for the first years of the Depression (GM provided an often-cited example of this), compounding the difficulties for less-concentrated areas of the economy obliged to respond to competitive pressures. As the situation worsened, pessimism about short-range business prospects deepened into serious concerns about the long-range viability of the economy and even the nation's political stability. Many of the same people who a few years earlier had celebrated a miraculous "New Era Economy" now predicted capitalism's imminent demise.

All of this is intended not as a complete analysis of the Depression but only as an indication of the complexity of factors that fed it. Peter Temin, an MIT economist, has concluded that "the Depression was started by an unexplained event," but its persistence resulted from "some combination of factors which cannot be disentangled."[43] Perhaps the fundamental weakness of the economy was discerned in early 1929 by Wesley C. Mitchell, who warned: "The incomes disbursed to consumers, and to wage earners in particular, must be increased on a scale sufficient to pay for the swelling volume of consumer goods sent to market." This view of the critical weakness of capitalism—its inability to provide a sufficiently broad distribution of wealth to allow for indefinite growth in consumption—led reform-minded economists in the 1930s and for long after to argue the need for corrective action by government.[44]

However, a very different view of the Depression was offered by the multi-millionaire Andrew Mellon, Hoover's secretary of the treasury, who advised him: "It will purge the rottenness out of the system. High costs of living and high living will come down. People will work harder, live a moral life. Values will be adjusted, and enterprising people will pick up the wrecks from less competent people."[45]

One thing is definite about the Depression's early years. The continuing economic slippage cannot be blamed on President Hoover's passivity; research over the last decades has rescued his reputation from this long-standing calumny. Hoover's initiatives actually represented a significant departure from the behavior of his predecessors during hard times. He indeed rejected Mellon's view that economic downturns had to be left alone to run a natural course. His Farm Board sought to prop up wheat prices, and the Reconstruction Finance Corporation set up in early 1932 tried to rescue failing banks. Unfortunately, his actions proved of limited effectiveness.

Monetarists, following the thesis of Milton Friedman and Anna Schwarz's important study *Monetary History of the United States*, have faulted the Federal Reserve System for failing to save the banks by use of a sound monetary policy, which would have loosened credit. Instead, in mid-1930, the Federal Reserve Board raised the rediscount rate and drastically shrank the money supply to stop the flow of gold to Europe. On December 11, 1930, the Bank of the United States, New York City's fourth-largest bank, with nearly a half million depositors, shut its doors in the face of a crowd hysterical with grief. Nevertheless, the Fed held to its tight money policies.[46]

THE POLITICS OF DEPRESSION

For Hoover, ending the Depression required active stimulation of the economy. But he wanted government's role in this fight limited to providing a resource for private actions. Voluntary cooperation free of coercion continued to be the centerpiece of Hoover's policies. Circumstances had changed, but Hoover's thinking had not. As the economy rolled and creaked in a storm-tossed sea, Americans lost confidence in his seamanship. Hoover, a stolid, solitary, humorless man who day in and day out wore the same somber suits and ties, lacked the personal qualities needed to rally the nation. His glum persona only lengthened the shadows cast by the bad news conveyed daily in the nation's press.[47]

But Hoover kept on trying. He met with businessmen and labor leaders, reassuring them of the economy's soundness. He asked state governors to increase expenditures on public works while the federal government did the same. By the spring of 1930, the president pointed to hopeful signs of recovery, including a turn up in stock prices. Then, in June, a downturn occurred that persisted and deepened. Leading business leaders now abandoned any lingering optimism and scaled back on capital investments and production. Hoover, seeking to balance the budget, took the disastrous step of persuading Congress to pass a tax increase.

Even worse, Hoover signed the highly protective Smoot-Hawley Tariff Act in June 1930, despite a letter from 1,200 economists urging a veto and arguing that the proposed tariff constituted an economic declaration of war amid a worldwide depression. The United States Tariff Commission estimated that Smoot-Hawley raised U.S. tariff rates on average by more than 20 percent. Twenty-five nations furiously retaliated, and U.S. exports plummeted nearly 40 percent in two years. A chain reaction of trade wars ensued, as the "made in America" Depression spread throughout the globe. In the early 1930s, both the world's production and its trade fell by 5 percent to 10 percent annually, as retaliatory trade actions by nations became the rule. A strong case can be made that had the United States promoted international cooperation in the crucial years from 1930 to 1933 the Depression would have ended sooner.[48]

National politics turned increasingly partisan and nasty as the Democrats won impressively in the 1930 congressional elections. With the economy deteriorating, congressional Democrats took legislative initiative away from the White House. The president did work with Congress to create the Reconstruction Finance Corporation in January 1932 with a capitalization of $.5 billion to prop up failing banks, insurance companies, and other large businesses. But Hoover resisted congressional efforts to introduce wider federal relief and welfare programs. This opposition, given the circumstances, was inevitably viewed as hard-hearted.

In 1931, strained international monetary systems further complicated the worsening trading crisis. The world stock markets experienced their worst year ever. Few now doubted the seriousness of the situation, and Hoover blamed the collapse of international trade for "shock[ing]" the nation into a prolonged crisis. The economy that a few years earlier had promised a "New Era" for ordinary Americans now failed to provide their essential needs. The acrimonious relations between Hoover and the man elected to succeed him in November 1932 combined with rumors of currency devaluation and a general mood of despair to lead to a further downturn before the new president's March inauguration. Photos of breadlines and reports of bank failures in the morning papers and movie newsreels even led to fear of the possible rise of a dictator, as had recently occurred in Germany.

By February 1933, some 13 million Americans were jobless. Bank failings accompanied by riotous mob scenes occurred daily. Desperate Americans demanded that Washington act. The basic difference between Hoover and Franklin Delano Roosevelt lay in the new president's flexibility in the face of a crisis he knew warranted extraordinary measures. In a letter sent on February 18, 1933, Hoover advised his successor: "It would steady the country greatly if there could be prompt assurance . . . that the budget will be unquestionably balanced"—and Hoover had supported a tax increase in 1932 to achieve this. Hoover trusted to a balanced budget and voluntarism, but the pragmatic and sanguine FDR did not hesitate to employ direct federal intervention and deficit spending.

In rejecting Hoover, in November 1932, Americans expressed skepticism about the paradigm of reform that he exemplified and shared with many Progressive reformers. This paradigm believed in a commonality of interests among all Americans and assumed that the problems of an urban-industrial society could be solved by means of technocratic expertise and the voluntary cooperation of leaders of industry without the need for direct governmental involvement in the economy.

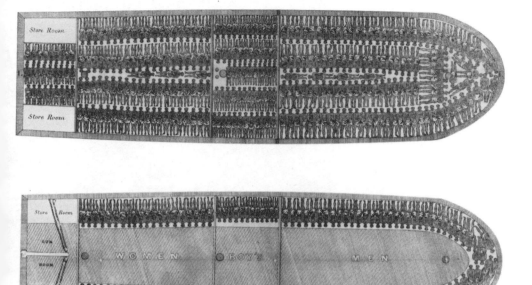

SLAVE SHIP The highly profitable and economically important transatlantic slave trade lasted for over three centuries. Slave ships were loaded according to a cost-cutting calculus for a voyage taking two and a half months in the eighteenth century. If any proof is required that rational economic behavior in response to market demands does not necessarily include a moral compass, this diagram provides it. *(The Granger Collection, New York)*

COLONIAL CLOTH MAKERS
Women are here engaged in
carding, spinning, and weaving
wool in the putting-out system
of part-time domestic labor,
which usually occurred in the
winter months. The distaff—
the rod attached to the spinning
wheel—was long used as an
adjective to describe a group
of females but has nearly fallen
out of use for this purpose. *(The
Granger Collection, New York)*

NEW YORK RAILROAD, 1831 The train was rightly regarded by many
contemporaries as the most important invention of the nineteenth century.
For the first time it was possible to travel by land faster than by water.
This 1831 etching reveals that the first coaches were designed to resemble
stagecoaches. (*The Granger Collection, New York*)

TITUSVILLE OIL WELL, 1859 This crude homemade rig began a new industry that changed the world when in 1859, in Titusville, Pennsylvania, it drilled seventy feet and came up coated with oil. The man on the right is Edward L. Drake, who built the rig. *(The Granger Collection, New York)*

CORLISS STEAM ENGINE, 1876 The steam engine—an indispensable tool of industrialization—allowed for the location of heavy industry in cities, furthering the urbanization characteristic of the modern economy. The Corliss engine, forty feet in height, was the world's largest steam engine. For twenty years, the Corliss engine, displayed here as the principal attraction at the Philadelphia Centennial of 1876, served as an icon of the steam age, only to be discarded as the electric dynamo replaced the steam engine. *(The Granger Collection, New York)*

MACY'S, NEW YORK, 1884 New Yorkers looking at a Christmas display window in Macy's department store in 1884. The department store as a near-universal provider of most goods and many services represented a new world of retailing. Patrons were offered elegant restaurants, restrooms, and reading rooms, as well as wrapping, home delivery, and mailing services. Shopping was made enticing, convenient, and pleasurable. (*The Granger Collection, New York*)

WOMEN WORKERS, METROPOLITAN LIFE INSURANCE COMPANY The rise of the modern office required a new type of workforce and accordingly offered new opportunities for some women workers. The women shown here in the actuarial room of the Metropolitan Life Insurance Company were young, white, probably single, native-born Americans of "acceptable" ethnic and religious back-grounds. The only man present is clearly in charge. (*Postcard in author's possession, circa 1910*)

LUNCHROOM, METROPOLITAN LIFE INSURANCE COMPANY This gender-segregated lunch-room of the Metropolitan Life Insurance Company indicated the concern that women be provided a work situation that did not "endanger their reputation" or place them in temptation's way. *(Postcard in author's possession, circa 1910)*

WALL STREET When the United States surpassed the United Kingdom as the world's leading industrial nation, around 1900, it was apparent that Wall Street would soon challenge London's The City as the world's financial hub. The multistoried towering commercial structures seen here were made possible by the relatively recent introduction of the safety elevator and steel frame construction. *(Postcard in author's possession, circa 1905)*

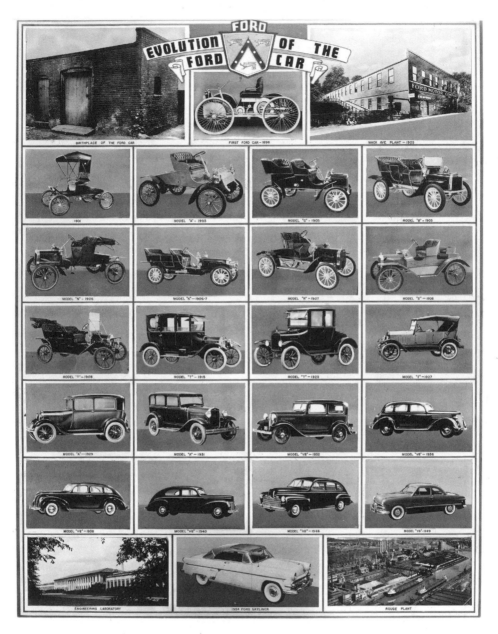

FORD AUTOMOBILES The automobile transformed the nation's economy and life in the first half of the twentieth century. This Ford advertising poster from the mid-1950s tells the pictorial story of the automobile—from concept in the 1890s, to reliable form of transportation in the 1910s, and, by the 1920s, to the American Dream of style, status, and power. *(The Granger Collection, New York)*

IBM SYSTEM COMPUTER By 1970 individuals at large corporations and universities were using computers, which were still too expensive and bulky for individual use. Innovations in that decade brought down the size and price to make the personal computer accessible to the masses. An information technology revolution had started whose momentum is still building today. *(The Granger Collection, New York)*

CHAPTER ELEVEN

Hard Times, 1933–1945

The social objective . . . is to try to do what any honest government . . .

would do: to try to increase the security and happiness of a larger number

of people in all occupations of life and in all parts of the country . . .

to give them assurance that they are not going to starve in their old age.

—FRANKLIN D. ROOSEVELT, *press conference, June 7, 1935*

America led the world into depression in the 1930s, and it was more severe and longer lasting in the United States than elsewhere. The Great Depression changed profoundly how Americans viewed their social contract with Washington. A tectonic shift occurred in the view of government's responsibility for the welfare of its citizens and the state of the economy. The New Deal sought to chart a middle course between free enterprise and a government-directed economy, a managed capitalism, with results and implications that continue to be controversial. In critical ways, the New Deal remains a major benchmark in American history. National politics ever since has largely centered on a struggle over whether to continue or reverse the course set by Roosevelt—whether to make the federal government's role in domestic affairs bigger or smaller.

ACTION NOW

With the exception of Lincoln, no president of the United States assumed office under darker clouds than did Franklin Delano Roosevelt on March 4, 1933. With the Depression deepening by the day amid a heightening national mood of anxiety and near despair, he entered the White House without a clear program of action. Once in office, he would try various approaches in the expectation that at least some might work. Business failures, bank closings, and massive unemployment necessitated immediate federal government intervention to halt the national economy's slide into economic chaos. As Ellis Hawley has carefully documented, a critical dividing line ran through the New Deal—an internal struggle between the two conflicting visions of reforms, which had surfaced in 1912. The ideal of a planned economy based on the coordination of business competed with a vision of an antitrust policy reinforcing the roles of small business and competition in the economy.[1]

In his inaugural address, Roosevelt requested authority "as great as the power that would be given me if we were in fact invaded by a foreign foe." He promised in return "action, and action now." He delivered fully on this commitment. "The country demands," he observed during the campaign, "bold persistent experimentation." On taking office, he called Congress into special session. The torrent of legislation enacted has entered history as "the Hundred Days."

The mood of paralysis and hopelessness that gripped the nation started to lift. Walter Salant, a young Harvard-trained economist, who came to Washington to join a new agency, sensed "energy, a feeling that something was being done, that there was leadership when leadership was needed, that there was a relationship between the government and the people in which the government was the citizen's friend."[2] The Washington reporter for the *New York Times*, James Reston, remembered in his memoirs the city's changed mood: "The New Deal had begun and you could feel its electricity wherever you went."[3]

THE NEW DEAL AND THE POSITIVE STATE

Roosevelt brought to the White House a forceful and charismatic personality, brilliant communication skills, and a contagious sense of self-confidence embodied in the jaunty tilt of his cigarette holder. He immediately instructed Congress that "government has a final responsibility for the well-being of its citizenship." His response to the Great Depression set in motion the interventionist economic and social policies that have ever since characterized the federal government.

For critics on the right, the New Deal commenced what the one-time liberal Democrat Ronald Reagan termed in 1980 a "half century of creeping socialism." To those on the radical left, however, the New Deal never seriously challenged the distribution of wealth or power in the United States. It instead propped up "corporate capitalism," establishing new linkages between government and business while palliating popular discontent with superficial reforms. Ironically, one may agree with both sets of New Deal critics without sharing their conclusions. Certainly, the New Deal never intended to radically transform the American economy and society, and Washington's role in the economy and the society has not been without problems. The present consensus among historians is that the New Deal did not significantly alter the free enterprise system or the distribution of economic power. It was, at most, a "half-way revolution."[4]

The Progressive ideal of a greatly strengthened and active government came to fruition in the New Deal's response to the problems of the 1930s. The helplessness felt by people in the Great Depression supported Charles Beard's claim that "the cold truth is that the individualistic creed of everybody for himself . . . is not applicable in an age of technology, science, and rationalized economy." Many by 1933 thought that an industrial economy required stabilization, planning, orderly procedure, prudence, and the adjustment of production. Accordingly, the New Deal initially sought a controlled capitalism that promoted business stability by confronting the excessive capacity and competition that even many prominent business leaders believed were at the core of the problem.

The New Deal bureaucrats recruited to Washington were certainly not, for the most part, the disinterested experts envisioned by Progressive Era reformers. Too often they were political players with their own agendas. The technocratic vision of a mandarin state run strictly by rational principles proved illusory. The American population and economy proved too diverse, with too many conflicting interests, for politics by consensus, as some New Dealers initially hoped. The New Deal must be judged on the basis of achievements accomplished and not by a utopian yardstick proffered by its critics on the right or left without reference to the politics or other circumstances of the period. At first concerned with urgent questions of relief and recovery, the New Deal would after 1935 redirect its energies. In doing so, it profoundly defined American thinking about modern "liberalism"—the belief that government must provide a social welfare system and accept responsibility for the economy.

One hard truth about the New Deal remains beyond dispute. It did not succeed in ending the Depression. The harshest of hard times occurred in the winter of 1932–33, after which the economy experienced halting recovery to 1937. A contraction of the economy in 1937–38 witnessed a stock market crash, an industrial nosedive, and a jump in unemployment, without quite returning to its low point of 1933. Yet the economy never fully regained health until American involvement in World War II began. Even in late 1940—when the American economy first began to feel the stimulus of the war in Europe—unemployment still hovered at an unacceptably high 10 percent.

The pathbreaking ideas of Cambridge economist John Maynard Keynes must be considered in any discussion of the welfare or "positive state" pioneered by Roosevelt—but not because they profoundly influenced New Deal policies, for they did not. However, Keynesian ideas do provide a conceptual framework with which to analyze the achievements of the Roosevelt administration. Keynes's followers argued that if federal spending had been greater and more adroitly administered, the economy could have recovered earlier than it did. Here they applied Keynes's premise that economic downturns are caused by a lack of overall demand in the economy, which could be prevented or remedied by cutting taxes even while increasing public-sector spending.

FIGHTING FEAR

Roosevelt's inaugural address on March 4, 1933, assured the country that "the only thing we have to fear is fear itself." But was this indeed true? Since the election four months earlier, the economy had experienced a virtual free fall. A banking system near collapse posed the most immediate problem; some 5,500 banks had already failed, costing depositors $3 billion in lost savings.

Panic and confusion ruled the day. Thirty-eight states had temporarily closed their banks to forestall frantic depositors from withdrawing savings. Even the New York Stock Exchange prudently shut its doors on Inauguration Day to forestall panic selling. On March 6, the new president declared a four-day national bank holiday. Federal auditors were rushed to check bank records, permitting only "strong" banks to reopen. Congress, called into emergency session, gave the president broad powers over the Federal Reserve System and enacted an Emergency Banking Act to provide banks with access to funds. In the first of his famous Fireside Chats, broadcast by radio on March 12, Roosevelt assured the American public of the solvency of the remaining banks. Amazingly, on the following day the value of deposits exceeded withdrawals.[5] But a radical restructuring of the banking system still lay ahead. Within two years, banking emerged from its ordeal a highly regulated industry, stable and secure but also, as time showed, unimaginative and static.

FINANCE AND BANKING

The Glass-Steagall Act, also known as the Banking Act of 1933, limited stock speculation by banks. Within the year, banks had to choose either investment or commercial functions exclusively, thus ending the practice of using depositors' accounts to finance their own security dealings. J. P. Morgan and Company responded by becoming a commercial bank, spinning off Morgan Stanley and Company as an investment bank; the First Boston Company was carved from the First National Bank of Boston. Goldman Sachs, Lehman Brothers, and Kuhn, Loeb & Co. all chose to be investment banks.[6]

In fact, over 90 percent of the banks that had failed were one-office banks in small towns, and hardly any closed because of security holdings or activities. They simply went under as their local communities' economies collapsed. Few banks involved in securities operations—as a rule the larger banks—actually failed. Nevertheless, it was thought with some justification that the banks' underwriting and trading of securities had contributed to the banking collapse. Hearings conducted for the Senate Banking Committee in early 1933 by Ferdinand Pecora, a former New York prosecutor, heard startling testimony of banker wrongdoings. The popular columnist Heywood Broun commented: "The only thing that some of our great financial institutions overlooked during the years of boom was the installation of a roulette-wheel for the convenience of depositors."[7]

Congress, in order to reassure the public, created the Federal Deposit Insurance Corporation, with savings deposits insured to $10,000. A few of Roosevelt's advisers had worried that without proper supervision the banks might rashly invest the newly insured deposits, knowing that they could not be permanently lost. To discourage this, Congress established maximum interest rates on savings accounts. For hard-pressed home owners, Congress created the Home Owners Loan Corporation in June 1933 to refinance mortgages. Finally, Roosevelt took the nation off the domestic gold standard. To inflate the dollar, the price of American gold on the international market was deliberately set at a high thirty-five dollars an ounce.[8]

With the banking crisis under control, the first changes in the Federal Reserve System since 1913 commenced. There had been much criticism of the Fed's handling of interest rates, and its inability to respond to the run on the banks had been painfully obvious. Drastic changes in the system appeared necessary.

The Banking Act of 1935 created the centralized banking system that Congress had avoided when it established the Federal Reserve System. The power now given to the central board in Washington, renamed the Board of Governors, was enormous. Federal Reserve districts could no longer conduct open-market operations on their own; the Board of Governors through its powerful Open Market Committee set interest-rate policy for all. The Board of Governors was given power to curb margin loans. To free the Fed from short-term political influences, both the secretary of the treasury and the comptroller of the currency were removed as ex officio members of the Board of Governors; the chairman received a four-year term, the start of which was so planned as to never coincide with the first year of a presidential administration. The unintended consequence of this was, and is, that presidents tend to be held politically accountable for actions by a Board of Governors over which they have only limited control.

In his fascinating study of the Federal Reserve System, *Secrets of the Temple*, William Greider asserted that in mission and methods the modern Federal Reserve System really began in 1935. Marriner Eccles, whom Roosevelt appointed as chairman of the new Board of Governors, pursued policies aimed at providing orderly money and securities markets, rather than making more imaginative efforts to stimulate the economy. Thus Eccles gave top priority to eliminating speculative practices in banking. Powers given the Federal Reserve System for this purpose included placing ceilings on interest rates paid by the banks on savings deposits and the prohibition of interstate branch banking. Under this regime, the banking industry remained remarkably secure and stable until the deregulation activity of the 1980s.[9]

SECURITIES MARKET REFORM

Americans blamed Wall Street and the stock exchanges for the Depression. Reforming the shaky securities market was a high priority on the agenda of the New Deal. The Truth-in-Securities Act of 1933 and the Securities Exchange Act of 1934 kept stock exchanges in private hands while requiring that "full publicity and information" be given the public on securities and their underwriting. Manipulation of stock prices by insider pools had been commonplace before the market crash, and the Securities and Exchange Commission (SEC) sought to guard against this by requiring full and open disclosures of vital information—transparency—by public corporations.

Stock exchanges had to register with the newly established SEC, with their practices subjected to scrutiny. The SEC required that periodic corporate reports certified by public accountants be provided to the public. Insider trading was defined as a punishable wrongdoing for the first time, and the SEC was empowered to prosecute market manipulations.

Many of the regulatory responsibilities remained with the exchanges, and the over-the-counter market and the commodities exchanges were not subject to the law. The Public Utility Holding Company Act of 1935, however, did require all utility holding companies, an area rife with scandals, to register with the SEC, which had the power to limit a utility holding company to "one system." In 1937 the Maloney Act reorganized and further strengthened the SEC, while also creating the National Association of Security Dealers (NASD) to oversee the over-the-counter market.[10]

The SEC's first head was the canny speculator Joseph Kennedy, father of the future president. Roosevelt supposedly told intimates that he chose him "because it takes a thief to catch one." Joseph Kennedy made a superb SEC chairman, as did his successor, William O. Douglas. In 1937, Douglas, then a Supreme Court justice, criticized American stock exchanges as private clubs—inappropriate bodies for a "business so vested with the public interest"—and argued forcefully for the SEC to act as the investors' advocate.

Stated simply, the objectives of security market regulations were to provide stability and equity by ensuring a level playing field for all players. Despite these changes, public confidence in the stock market did not recover fully until 1949. Too many small investors had been badly hurt for the memory of October 1929 to fade quickly.

A FLAWED EXPERIMENT IN ECONOMIC PLANNING

On June 16, 1933, a hundred days after Roosevelt took office, Congress passed the National Industrial Recovery Act (NIRA). This act provided Roosevelt and his so-called brain trust of academic advisers with what they envisioned as the major weapon to win the war against the Depression. Signing the bill, Roosevelt called it "the most important and far reaching legislation ever enacted by the American Congress."[11] But the NIRA proved a short-lived victory for a school of reformers led by Rexford Tugwell, a Columbia University economist, who believed national planning essential for an efficient modern industrial economy.

The NIRA created a National Recovery Administration (NRA) to restore prosperity by the unprecedented means of establishing controls over industrial output and prices. The act was clearly intended to be inflationary; it sought to increase profits by inflating prices and thereby to expand business activity while also encouraging workers to unionize and benefit from higher wages. Closely modeled on the example of Bernard Baruch's War Production Board of 1917–18, the NRA encouraged industrial and trade councils to prepare codes governing behavior. It was headed by Hugh "Iron Pants" Johnson, a rugged, publicity-seeking ex-soldier who supposedly worked twenty-hour days while traveling the country. Industries lacking industrial organizations, such as the shoulder-pad industry, were told to create them forthwith.[12]

The NRA intended that "rational planning" would replace the "competitive chaos" and deflation (the wholesale price index had declined 33 percent) that were pulling the economy down. Antitrust laws were suspended for two years while industrywide codes were drafted to control wages, prices, and labor practices. In many ways, the NRA approach resembled Hoover's "associative philosophy." It differed in giving the federal government a greater role than Hoover thought constitutional, and he had opposed the NRA. Some economists objected to the goal of cartel-induced scarcity. They argued that the only limit upon output should be the absence of profitability, not government-sponsored quotas.

From the start, Roosevelt's advisers differed on the NRA's intent. Rexford Tugwell wanted a permanent corporate economy in which various interests cooperated for mutual benefit. Raymond Moley, author of the act's first draft, sought only to combat deflation through a temporary curb on competition. Indeed, the NIRA had been deliberately written so that it could be read to mean different things. This vagueness explained the initial enthusiasm for the act by groups inclined to be opposed to government intervention, such as the National Association of Manufacturers and the American Federation of Labor (AFL). But confusion also laid the groundwork for future controversy.

The NRA staff supervised the enactment and implementation of each industry's code. In practice, however, the larger corporations established the codes for most industries. These codes set production limits, prescribed wages and working conditions, and forbade price-cutting and unfair competitive practices. Often an effort was made to establish guidelines for product quality and consumer servicing. The nation's burlesque houses even adopted a code specifying the degree of permissible on-stage nudity.

By 1935, the Blue Eagle logo of the NRA adorned flags, placards, and ads ("We Do Our Part"), which were displayed by over 700 industries employing 23 million workers. Soon, however, small firms claimed that the codes favored their large rivals, while irate consumer organizations blamed the NRA for higher prices and restricted competition. Labor leaders generally supported the policy, especially a requirement for collective bargaining, but a few warned that restricting production would eventually lead to layoffs.

To satisfy the complaints of small business, the NRA encouraged the redrafting of a few codes, winning it few new friends and angering corporate America. As opposition to the program mounted from all quarters, its defenders could point to very few accomplishments. The economy improved in 1934 only slightly—prices increased but not employment.

The NRA rested on the premise that overproduction caused the Depression. American consumers in 1933 and 1934, however, lacked the financial ability to turn the economy around. The problem was not one of supply but of demand. The NIRA had indeed allocated $3.3 billion for a federal public works program to employ the jobless; however, this fell far short of the need. By the summer of 1934 the NRA represented a clear political liability. Its days were numbered.

The NIRA died formally in May 1935 when the Supreme Court declared it unconstitutional. Roosevelt expressed his concern to intimates that the conservative Court might soon undo other New Deal legislation. The experiment with national planning did not, however, disappear without a trace. Antagonism toward the NRA introduced an adversarial element into both big and small business's relationship with the New Deal, and this hostility persisted after the NRA and its industrial codes had been dismantled.

A SAFETY NET

Roosevelt initially tried to create a national consensus of business, farmers, and labor to fight the Depression. But by the middle of 1934, this coalition had unraveled. Leading industrialists, such as Jacob Raskin of DuPont, had by now concluded that the New Deal posed dangerous "socialistic" tendencies. Meanwhile, the demagogic senator Huey Long of Louisiana and the popular "radio priest" Father Coughlin complained that Roosevelt was shortchanging the average family. In 1935 Roosevelt moved to secure his popularity among ordinary Americans. Legislation he proposed to Congress soon reflected this tactical change. In 1935 the president urged the enactment of the Utility Companies Holding Act to break up holding companies that had allowed a handful of individuals to control far-flung networks of local power companies. A year later he broadened his populist appeal, calling for higher income, estate, and corporate taxes while denouncing big business as "economic royalists."

The Social Security Act of 1935 is regarded as the most important domestic bill ever passed by Congress. It laid the foundation of our present system of old age pensions, unemployment and disability insurance, and the American welfare system as it existed until 1996. But initially an estimated one-third to one-fourth of the labor force remained uncovered by the program's benefits.[13]

The United States had lagged well behind other industrial nations in accepting responsibility for its citizens' minimum welfare. By enacting the Social Security Act of 1935 the federal government acknowledged the need for a federal "safety net" against the hazards of an industrial economy, even though the nation had not acted until a depression taught Americans the hard lesson that self-reliance could be impossible during events beyond their control. A modern urban-industrial society demonstrated that problems formerly regarded as personal in nature now required a societal response and that poverty might not reflect shortcomings of character but might instead result from the failure of the economy to provide jobs or living wages.[14]

Even more controversial than the Social Security Act was the National Labor Relations Act of 1935, also known as the Wagner Act. The decline in union membership suffered through the 1920s by organized labor continued during the first several years of the Depression—indeed union membership generally declines in hard times. By 1935 nearly as many American workers belonged to company-sponsored unions as to independent labor unions.[15]

The Wagner Act created a permanent National Labor Relations Board to oversee elections in which employees voted for or against union affiliation. The act outlawed "unfair labor practices" by employers, including firing workers because of union membership or activity, creating company unions, or refusing to bargain collectively with a duly certified union. The act, which Roosevelt supported only reluctantly, came at a time of great turmoil within organized labor.

Insurgents within the AFL had started organizing the nation's major industries, notably automobile and steel, but encountered opposition from advocates of the craft unionism. The rebels left the AFL and created the Congress of Industrial Organizations (CIO) to crusade for a more inclusive unionism. By 1941 union membership had increased 40 percent to 4.5 million, more than half of whom belonged to CIO affiliates, including the United Automobile Workers and the United Steel Workers.

Strongly allied with the Democratic Party, unions now bargained from a stronger position because management was required to "negotiate in good faith." The Wagner Act brought a semblance of order and stability to labor relations, although bloody battles still occurred. Achieving new legal rights, labor turned increasingly to the political arena for additional gains. Union support contributed greatly to Roosevelt's landslide reelection, and union members became an important element in the "Roosevelt coalition" that turned the Democrats into the nation's majority party with the election of 1936. Organized labor's growth in numbers and political power stands as one of the decade's important developments.[16]

In 1938 the Fair Labor Standards Act set a national minimum hourly wage of forty cents and established a maximum forty-hour work week, with time and a half to be paid for overtime. This bill is usually regarded as the New Deal's last major piece of legislation, and after its passage growing conservative strength in Congress led Roosevelt to move away from initiating further reform. A congressional alliance had been forged by Republicans concerned with federal deficits and mounting business regulations and southern Democrats apprehensive about federal involvement in civil rights. This alliance dominated Capitol Hill for the next quarter century.

The New Deal's vulnerability in 1938 had many causes, not the least being Roosevelt's "court-packing bill" of 1937. As already noted, Roosevelt had taken the Supreme Court's striking down of the NIRA as a warning bell that other New Deal legislation resting on the commerce clause would meet a similar judicial end. This impression was reinforced in 1936 when the Court ruled against a recent federal law establishing maximum hours and minimum wages for coal miners.

Roosevelt waited until after the elections of 1936 to attack the Court. His assault took the form of proposed legislation that allowed a president to appoint additional federal judges to a maximum number of fifteen judges to the Supreme Court. Roosevelt's court-packing scheme provoked a political storm and went down to defeat in Congress. His actions were not, however, without results. An apparently intimidated Supreme Court "reformed itself" in a 1937 decision that provided the precedent to uphold the constitutionality of "commerce-based laws" with only a loose relationship to interstate commerce. Thus in 1941 the Court upheld the 1938 minimum wage and maximum hours laws. But even as Roosevelt had his way with the Court, he encountered mounting opposition in Congress.

THE NEW DEAL ENDS AND THE DEPRESSION CONTINUES

Compounding the New Deal's political vulnerability after 1938 was its failure to bring back prosperity. A partial recovery had indeed occurred after Roosevelt's second inauguration, which lasted until the winter of 1937–38. But Roosevelt, who was always uncomfortable with the large federal deficits forced on him by fighting the Depression, took the occasion of the upturn in 1937 to slash federal expenditures. This either caused or contributed to a sudden severe downturn, the "Roosevelt depression." Recently improved stock values plummeted by a third in a two-month period, and more than 6 million more people joined the jobless rolls. Hasty resumption of federal spending eased the situation somewhat in late 1938, but the economy remained sluggish, with unemployment exceeding 10 percent, until stimulated by defense spending in 1941 as the United States prepared itself for war. With American entry into World War II, "Dr. New Deal" had become "Dr. Win-the-War."

Keynesian economists, notably Nobel Prize winner Paul Samuelson, have argued in retrospect that the effective use of federal deficit spending by the New Deal would have revitalized the economy. From their perspective, not enough federal money was spent and the expenditures made were not targeted properly. Keynes himself had visited the White House in a futile effort to offer advice and to persuade the American president of the importance of his recently developed theories of countercyclical spending.

A Cambridge University–trained economist, John Maynard Keynes had studied under Alfred Marshall, a pioneer in the development of the theory of "marginal utility." Keynes first attracted public attention as a critic of the heavy reparations imposed on the defeated Germans. As a junior member of the British delegation at the Versailles Peace Conference, Keynes correctly predicted that the severity of the treaty's terms would result in economic and political instability, leading to another world war within a generation. During the 1920s, Keynes rose to prominence as a gadfly of the monetary and trading policies of the major powers, and in 1936 he published *The General*

Theory of Employment, Interest and Money. This, his major work, attacked a critical premise of classical economics, namely, that the market responded to business swings by means of a self-adjusting mechanism. Keynes also rejected Say's Law, a theory that held that economic recession could not be resolved by changes in demand. Jean-Baptiste Say, a French businessman and economist of the late eighteenth century, believed that production generated its own demand, thus implying that the focus of policy should be on developing conditions conducive to promoting supply.

Keynes argued instead that a deflationary economy could decline so steeply that equilibrium would be established only at so low a level as to mean permanent depression. The demand for goods and services would accordingly fall far short of a nation's capacity to produce them, even with very low interest rates. Such a combination of underemployed resources and high unemployment would be economically disastrous and politically dangerous. A despairing populace might turn away from democracy, as had happened in Germany in 1933. But Keynes believed he knew the answer to this problem. Deflation should be remedied by powerful "countercyclical" actions on the part of government. Keynes believed that the principal cause of depressions was underconsumption—that the economy could produce more than people could buy—which meant that businesses were unable to find sufficient investment opportunities. As his biographer, Robert Skidelsky, has written, "Keynes was the first leading modern economist to focus analytic attention on the level of demand, or spending, as the determinant of activity." (An English autoworker, quoted by Skidelsky talking about his declining industry in 1992, illustrated this point simply: "When no one's buying cars there's no point in making them.")[17]

According to Keynes, government had to respond to a bottomed-out economy's slack by employing "demand-side" policies. Such action could assume many forms. Reducing taxes would increase the amount of money in the hands of consumers. Buying back government securities, or lowering the interest rates for loans, would do the same. So too would direct governmental spending on the construction of useful public works such as schools, roads, hospitals, and parks. The critical factor was for government to spend more than it received in taxes, thus running a deficit to push inflation.

After the publication of his book, economists heatedly debated the merits of Keynes's theories. Indeed, some supporters questioned the survival of capitalism without the permanent application of public deficit spending. But Keynesian ideas did not significantly impact New Deal policy. During World

War II, it was defense spending that led to prosperity, full employment, and an estimated 50 percent increase in the nation's productive capacity. Many economists and others now became convinced that the wartime experience demonstrated conclusively the correctness of Keynesian economics. Government spending had proven its worth and would be required periodically in a postwar economy to maintain consumer demand and employment.[18]

Keynesian ideas increasingly influenced American policies and politics for the first several decades after 1945, leading to the famous remark of Richard Nixon in 1971: "We are all Keynesians now." Keynesian economists in the 1950s and 1960s argued that the federal government's application of his policy prescriptions in the 1930s would have ended the Depression, accepting as axiomatic that informed governmental fiscal policies regarding taxing, borrowing, and spending could calibrate or "fine-tune" an economy to permit the sustained growth and high employment they regarded as highly desirable. This assertion is easier to state than support. It assumed that Keynesian policies could be applied in a political vacuum by disinterested technicians indifferent to public opinion. It is clear that additional massive federal deficit spending in the 1930s was not only distasteful to Roosevelt but perhaps politically impossible. Whether Keynesian policies could have worked remains an open question. But there is room for skepticism.

The historian Alan Brinkley has argued in *The End of Reform* (1995) that by accepting countercyclical policies as the key to economic growth New Deal liberalism moved away from a more vital tradition of American reform. In effect, it had retreated from a concern with economic concentration and other structural problems of American capitalism. The result was that the view that Washington could manage the economy without managing the institutions of the economy had emerged as important elements of liberal thought. Whether the later New Deal represented, as Brinkley believes, a rupture with a more radical public philosophy of reform that profoundly altered American reform is for a new generation of historians to answer. But economists remain concerned with older questions related to Keynesian deficit spending and to whether sufficient demand will exist to make use of a nation's savings and resources.[19]

ASSESSING THE NEW DEAL

Recent economic thinking stresses that in capitalist economies key investment decisions are made by private investors and institutions on the basis of many different factors. Deficit spending will not necessarily stimulate a sagging economy if the dip in the economy is regarded as dangerous because then people reduce spending. A decline in private investment may thus offset the stimulus created by the deficit, leaving conditions unchanged or worse. The New Deal undoubtedly antagonized business interests, contributing to a crisis of confidence that discouraged the capital investment desperately needed to revive the economy. Certainly in Roosevelt's second presidential campaign, he denounced "economic royalists" and espoused a rhetorical radicalism clearly intended to win votes. His critics fault him for politically motivated demagogic recklessness; his supporters believe he told it as it was.[20]

Two members of his original brain trust offer strikingly different explanations for Roosevelt's public antagonism toward big business after 1935. Breaking sharply with his president, the conservative Raymond Moley regarded Roosevelt's actions as a politically motivated betrayal of his earlier overtures to business. But the more radical Rexford Tugwell believed Roosevelt's class rhetoric to be a political smoke screen to disguise his capitulation to the economic establishment. There is little doubt that many of the bright young men brought to Washington by the New Deal tended to be hostile toward big business, which the latter fully reciprocated.

Still not adequately explained is the reversal of the NRA approval of cartels and the revival of strong antitrust policies in the second Roosevelt administration. When Roosevelt turned to the "little man" as his core political constituency, he returned to Woodrow Wilson's fears of big business. In 1938 Roosevelt spoke publicly on the dangers of monopoly power and requested from Congress "a thorough study of the concentration of power in American industry." In June 1938 Congress created the Temporary National Economic Committee (TNEC) to find examples of undue concentration and other abuses by big business and to recommend corrective measures. In the next several months the TNEC scrutinized important industries, including petroleum, steel, and the motion pictures, with inconclusive results. But the public expressed little interest in the hearings, and no new laws resulted from its findings.

Also in 1938 the Antitrust Division of the Department of Justice, newly headed by Yale law professor Thurman Arnold, greatly expanded operations. A year earlier, Arnold had written that the true significance of antitrust actions was as a type of folk ritual to express the superiority of government over big business. Businessmen now, however, complained that Arnold pursued them for actions that the NIRA a few years earlier had requested. A few charged that the Justice Department's actions were intended to punish Roosevelt's political opponents. But recent scholarship suggests that Arnold sought to use antitrust law primarily to protect the consumer from noncompetitive pricing. Arnold also sought to promote economic efficiency, being particularly concerned about those industries in which a handful of companies could set "administered prices" and thus operate insulated from supply and demand. "If the antitrust laws are simply an expression of a religion which condemns largeness as an economic sin," he wrote, "they will be regarded as an anachronism in a machine age. If, however, they are directed at making distribution more efficient, they will begin to make sense." Soon defense needs fostered an alliance between government and the major corporations; after Pearl Harbor, the antitrust efforts of the Department of Justice flagged, and Arnold resigned in 1943 for a federal judgeship. The conduct of the war, or so it was claimed, demanded a tightly controlled economy tolerant of economic concentration. In March 1941 Roosevelt ordered the suspension of all antitrust suits.[21]

Did business, either big or small, have reason to fear the New Deal? In retrospect, it appears not. Despite the fulminations of critics who denounced Roosevelt as a "traitor to his class," he certainly did not intend to move the economy to socialism. It is true that with the Tennessee Valley Authority and the Rural Electrification Agency government moved directly into generating and providing energy to consumers, but these were part of a limited vision of state-promoted economic development and technological diffusion. What the New Deal intended and achieved was a mixed economy, with controls to promote a stability, which businessmen, once recovery occurred, found highly satisfactory. No doubt many businessmen found their lives greatly complicated by the red tape and regulations introduced by New Deal agencies, and certainly the labor legislation of the 1930s required an adjustment to a new relationship with their workers and organized labor. Employers now had to heed governmental regulations in decision making regarding wages, hours, and work rules formerly the sole prerogative of management. But business had much to gain from these arrangements, annoying as they appeared. In its new institutionalized form, labor relations soon became relatively stable, predictable, and usually peaceful.

Above all, the mixed economy promoted by the New Deal stabilized the workings of what had been a relatively unregulated capitalistic economy, moderating social conflict and lessening an unrealistic reliance on "rugged individualism." The antecedents of the New Deal's mixed economy can certainly be traced to the turn of the century, but it burst forward in the 1930s. New forms of relationships between government, business, and labor usually allowed room for accommodation rather than the unending strife some businessmen had predicted in the 1930s. Indeed, a frequent problem was presented by relationships that had grown too cordial and comfortable.

Many regulatory agencies acquired over time a sympathetic attitude toward the industries they supervised, especially since their administrative personnel were frequently recruited from precisely these industries for their expertise and returned to them after a few years of government service. Cozy arrangements between regulators and corporate management were not uncommon. These often protected the interests of the businesses involved rather than those of consumers. Yet the mutual animosity of New Deal and business left a lingering legacy of suspicion, which flared up in the Truman administration.

Overall, the policies of the New Deal evolved in an improvised, piecemeal fashion. Roosevelt's political opponent Huey Long joked with some truth that two people ran the government: Roosevelt and the last person who had spoken to him. But underneath the tentative and the contradictory, a pattern is still discernible. The New Deal gave a greater priority to returning the economy to prosperity and stabilizing it than to efforts at striving for social justice or promoting industrial efficiency or economic growth. Economic and political circumstances made this understandable. Above all, Americans wanted to be reassured that the system could provide them with jobs and necessities, while the American Dream of material progress was temporarily deferred. In the 1930s, many thoughtful individuals indeed viewed the United States as a mature economy, with rapid economic growth no longer possible. A very few even concluded that capitalism had self-destructed. As late as 1941, James Burnham informed readers of *The Managerial Revolution* that the continuing massive unemployment made inevitable market capitalism's replacement by a more efficient "managerial" state based on the models of the Soviet Union or Nazi Germany.

Given the overriding concern with economic security and stability, the politics of the 1930s promoted the dramatic extension of governmental controls. The free market economy of the late nineteenth century had never really been faulted for an inability to produce or innovate but only found wanting in its excesses of speculation and cutthroat competition. These flaws, many believed, had led to instability, panics, and inefficiencies. To liberal reformers, including Roosevelt, the critical need was to safeguard the economy against extreme business cycle swings.

BIG GOVERNMENT

To correct weaknesses in the economy, the "Roosevelt revolution" created what political scientists have referred to as the "positive," "interventionist," or "broker state." The federal government, imposing new controls on market capitalism, played a role in all aspects of what was fast becoming a "mixed economy" by 1941. Washington's growing involvement can be illustrated by the rise in the number of federal civilian employees, from 601,319 in 1930 to 1,042,420 in 1940. During this decade the federal budget roughly tripled, from a little over $3 billion to about $9 billion. More important, the percentage of the GNP that was federal expenditure rose from 3.7 percent in 1930 to 9.9 percent in 1940. (In 2004, this stood at over 25 percent.) The New Deal did not end hard times, but it contributed greatly to the emergence of the big government that we know today.

With government's growing role in American life, the question of how federal power would be used became increasingly important. A conventional view of historians favorable to the New Deal is that it promoted the organizing of relatively powerless groups and involved them in the political process, creating a "broker state." It was more difficult for business to simply have its way, as organized lobbying interests grew more numerous and American politics more pluralistic. But big business still retained considerable influence in Washington, and the New Deal's antibusiness bark had proven worse than its bite. Wall Street still dominated the financial sector; corporate concentration even increased. The key characteristics of the economy thus remained unchanged, despite the fulminations of Roosevelt's conservative critics.

Small businessmen did not fare well in the 1930s. Often operating on small margins and with little capital, they proved vulnerable to hard times. The expense of complying with new governmental regulations came hard to businesses operating on the edge and with little ability to raise prices. Two pieces of legislation passed in the 1930s had the ostensible purpose of protecting small business from big business, particularly small retailers from chain stores. The Robinson-Patman Act, "the Magna Carta" of small business, passed in June 1936, allowed states to pass legislation to limit manufacturers' and wholesalers' discounts to mass marketers. In 1937 Congress modified the Sherman Act and passed the Miller-Tydings Fair Trade Act, which legalized resale price maintenance. A manufacturer could now require all retailers to sell at or above a set price. Although both bills are often viewed as antitrust acts, Jonathan J. Bean has pointed out that they were intended to aid small retailers in their struggle against chain store supermarkets, such as A&P, by limiting price competition, and thus they came at the expense of the consumer. (In the 1970s Robinson-Patman became a dead letter, ignored and unenforced; and Miller-Tydings was repealed in 1975.)[22]

This effort to win small business support for the president did not succeed. In 1938, the Roosevelt administration invited 1,000 small businessmen to a White House conference, which proved embarrassing when these guests complained bitterly about New Deal economic controls. Other groups had also been harmed by New Deal policies. Tenant farmers in the South found that federal subsidies were directed to the landowners and not to the tillers. But most Americans did benefit from New Deal programs, especially the new security it offered the individual.[23]

The story of the suffering and shock caused by the Great Depression in the 1930s has often been told. Often overlooked, however, are the long-range effects it had on an entire generation. Those born between 1910 and 1920 who entered the depressed job market of the 1930s often had their work lives permanently stunted. Many would opt in later years for job security, limiting their opportunities for mobility. A generation of Americans had reason, at least for a time, to question the American assumption that change is always for the good.

It is now inconceivable that any American government could ever again adopt a passive attitude toward a depression. The political costs would prove too high. The New Deal created a profound sense of entitlement for Americans: government was expected to help. This change in thinking must be counted among the important accomplishments of the New Deal. The passive regulatory role for the federal government advocated by mainstream Progressive reformers early in the century had been transformed into a view of Washington as an "enabler" or catalyst, both in the economy and in the larger society. Even the vigorous attack on big government by some conservatives has not challenged the general consensus that the federal government must ensure the health of the economy and the welfare of its citizens.

Before leaving this discussion of business in the 1930s, we must point out that the pace of technological advance and the introduction of new products remained, despite the Depression, truly astounding. The chemical industry introduced Lucite, Bakelite, synthetic rubber, and nylon; the electronics industry developed the fluorescent light and readied television for the market; Eastman Kodak perfected Kodachrome color film in 1935. By 1941, 10 million Americans had already been prescribed the new "miracle" sulfa drugs introduced to the market only six years before. Antibiotics quickly advanced this pharmacological revolution—especially penicillin, which began to be used widely during World War II. It is true that most of these developments resulted from investments in research and development begun in the prosperous 1920s. But the impressive expansion of commercial airlines— including Pan American, TWA, United Airlines, Eastern, and American Airlines—and the companies that provided their planes—Martin at Baltimore, Boeing at Seattle, Douglas at Santa Monica, and Grumman on Long Island—can only be taken as evidence of the incorrigible optimism of American business. The availability in 1941 of a large body of trained commercial pilots and the facilities for producing modern aircraft proved a godsend as the nation girded for total war.

THE ECONOMIC CONSEQUENCES OF THE WAR

The United States mobilized for World War II at a time when the economy had sizable idle capacity. Early in 1941 over 10 percent of the workforce was jobless. Deficit spending to fight World War II combined with draft call-ups to quickly end unemployment, as the civilian labor force rose from 54 million to 64 million between 1940 and 1945—despite the fact that 12.5 million Americans served in the armed forces. The labor shortage soon brought married women with small children into the workforce (a few plants even provided accommodations for the children of workers) in great numbers. "Rosie the Riveter" was hailed as a patriot during the war only to be told at its end to go home and attend to her family.

Blacks, traditionally "last hired and first fired," also benefited greatly from the wartime labor shortage. The migration from farms to cities and from the South to the North, ongoing since the century's start, now accelerated. Full employment during World War II improved the position of those on the bottom rungs of income distribution significantly—a fact pointed to by postwar supporters of full-employment policies. The war years also witnessed a substantial narrowing of wage differentials paid to men according to their skills and education, as the United States transformed its economy to serve as the "arsenal of democracy." Hourly earning in industry went up 60 percent between January 1941 and January 1945. By 1945, America's factories, many of them newly built with federal funds, were turning out 90,000 tanks and a staggering 300,000 airplanes a year, while production of new automobiles and other consumer goods, such as typewriters, dropped dramatically. Consumers also had to deal with the rationing of such staples as gasoline, meat, and sugar.[24]

Despite an initial fear of Axis saboteurs, inflation represented the main wartime domestic threat. Disposable personal incomes rose from a total of $92 billion in 1941 to $151 billion in 1945, while the value of available goods and services remained nearly constant. The War Production Board established in early 1942 was the principal agency to coordinate war production. The Emergency Price Control Act of 1942 empowered the head of the Office of Price Administration (OPA) to fix maximum prices and rents in many areas and even to pay subsidies to producers if necessary to forestall price increases. Controls curbed inflation, but efforts to limit wage increases were less successful. Richard Nixon, as a young lawyer, worked briefly for the OPA. When confronted with a troubling inflation in 1971, President Nixon relied on policies of price and wage controls employed earlier at the OPA.

By 1945, the OPA served as the hub of a web of agencies that mobilized the economy for the war effort while minimizing domestic hardships. A fully employed civilian workforce put in long hours of overtime. Unable to buy big ticket civilian goods such as automobiles and refrigerators, Americans deposited record personal savings in banks, tripling the totals of these accounts in four years—this despite war bond sales and wartime tax reforms, which subjected ordinary Americans for the first time to the personal income tax. (Payroll withholding, a "temporary measure," had been introduced in 1942.) A significant redistribution of income occurred during the war years. The bottom 40 percent of wage earners increased their share of the pie to about 20 percent, while that of the top 5 percent declined from 28 to 19 percent.

The swelling of government in wartime made the changes brought about by New Deal domestic reforms appear minuscule. A greatly enlarged federal government in 1945 counted 3,816,310 civilian employees, compared to 1,042,420 five years earlier. During the same period, federal government budget expenditures swelled nearly eleven fold—$98 billion as against $9 billion—and federal spending in the war's final year was 43.5 percent of the GNP. Wartime prosperity seemed to prove that government could spend the economy back to robust health.

Impressively free of partisan politics, the wartime effort was, of course, never intended as a permanent solution to America's economic troubles. After Japan's surrender in August 1945, Washington's foremost concern was a quick and smooth return to a peacetime economy. Between 1940 and 1946, the federal government spent annually over $2.5 billion to build new factories to meet defense needs; at war's end these facilities were sold to private industry at a fraction of the cost, greatly expanding the nation's industrial base. It was feared by many that a halt in defense spending would bring the reappearance of the economy's prewar weaknesses, as overproduction forced deflation and a slide into depression.

Fortunately, this did not occur. A surge in consumer spending after years of wartime rationing combined with the needs of a war-ruined world to forestall a postwar depression. Both the nation's economy and America's position in the postwar world had been permanently changed. Key to these changes was an awareness that the federal government would employ monetary and fiscal policies to fight an economic slump. American politics would now involve a struggle between those committed to an activist, socially conscious state and advocates of a sharply limited role for Washington. Most American had views somewhere in between, moving from one side to the other on occasion but usually hovering close to the center. But circumstances as well as beliefs influence the flow of politics.

The federal government did not retreat from the postwar economy as completely as anticipated. The advent of the Cold War meant that federal defense spending, which had dipped dramatically in 1946, rose greatly after the Korean War in 1950, tripling in three years. From 1950 to 1973, defense spending regularly absorbed nearly 10 percent of the nation's GNP and almost 50 percent of the federal government's budget. Defense spending and New Deal entitlement programs meant that Washington continued to play a formidable role in the postwar economy. For example, low-interest GI loans combined with Federal Housing Administration mortgage insurance to subsidize thousands of new suburban real estate developments. Indeed, the huge defense expenditures from 1940 to the end of the Cold War in 1990 created what some called a "permanent war economy."

The fragmented competitive market economy of nineteenth-century America had given way by 1910 to oligarchic formations in leading industrial sectors. This pattern continued, but new possibilities for accommodation within an industry occurred after World War II. Near the midpoint of the twentieth century a very different type of economy had emerged from the one in 1900. Businesspeople still wanted profit, growth, and increased mar-

ket share, but they paid greater attention to stability and security than previously and thus often tended to be more cautious. Government's control of
economic behavior to meet social needs had to be accepted. The actual policies implementing these goals, however, reflected political reality, and here
the number of organized interest groups involved in lobbying Washington
grew greatly.[25]

Various branches and agencies of government act daily to influence the
actions of small businesspeople and giant corporations, consumers and labor unions, local government and international banking houses. Each in
turn seeks to influence public policies that affect their own welfare. Moreover, as sociologist Theda Skocpol has observed, the people staffing government also have their own interests to serve. Fifteen years of the New Deal and
World War II had made for the interventionist state, and the advent of the
Cold War expanded this role. Increasingly, the federal government brokered
between various organized interest groups seeking benefits and power.

The volatility of market capitalism was to be monitored and moderated
by the federal government. Washington had definitely assumed responsibility for mitigating the system's social and economic disruptions. Exactly
when, where, and how intervention is warranted was and is a controversial
political issue disputed by the political parties. That Washington has bottom-
line accountability for the functioning of the economy, however, remains
indisputable.

CHAPTER TWELVE

The American (Quarter) Century, 1945–1973

A refrigerator. You can live without it. A yellow convertible car.

You can live without it. A television set. A Chippendale chair. . . .

You can live without any or all of these. But who in America wants to?

In America these things represent LIFE *rather than mere subsistence.*

—BURLINGTON MILLS ADVERTISEMENT, New York Times,

September 19, 1952

A Washington journalist noted in 1897 that it was possible for him to drop in at the White House and simply ask a clerk whether President McKinley had time for an interview. Less than fifty years later, both the White House and the federal government operated very differently. Washington now was in the middle of the major issues confronting the nation and the world. Those who expected that its role would recede with peacetime's return were mistaken. World War II reinforced the new era of government intervention in economic affairs and seemingly affirmed the correctness of Keynesian deficit-spending policies.

Power was firmly centered in the nation's capital and not in the nation's statehouses, and Washington's role continued to grow. The expansion of the federal government's role in the economy since 1945 had two main causes. One was the postwar extension of the "positive state." The other resulted from the interventionist role played after 1945 in the Cold War and the world. But it is necessary to keep in mind that these two causes arose from different roots, received nurture from different political circumstances, and competed with each other for their share of the federal budget. More important, federal money spent on welfare or defense influenced the economy and the society very differently.

Among the many changes experienced by American business life after 1945 none exceeded in importance the greatly expanded power of the federal government. Washington's new role in the world gave American businesses a unique opportunity to expand their global operations. At home, American business needed more than ever to influence Washington.

For ordinary Americans, however, life centered about obtaining and enjoying the "good life." From 1948 to 1973 productivity grew at an annual rate of over 3 percent, doubling the living standard in that period. Free-spending consumers bought the American economy a quarter century of unprecedented prosperity. A 1946 Commerce Department study correctly predicted that the new television, with its potential for advertising, would create new consumer desires and needs.

FROM ANGST TO AFFLUENCE

The United States emerged from World War II the world's preeminent power. All other major powers experienced massive destruction and ended the war deeply in debt, but America's industrial base had been augmented and modernized. The scientific and technological know-how that had produced the atomic bomb and the resourcefulness of business leaders who had organized the war effort appeared to guarantee American leadership for the indefinite future. As early as February 17, 1941, Henry Luce, the editor-owner of *Life* magazine, had predicted the onset of the "American century." "The time had come," Luce wrote in the magazine, to exert "the full measure of our influence, for such purpose as we see fit." Few in 1945 found reason to question this expectation.

American foreign policy's declared goals supported self-determination and democracy, freedom of the seas, and an absence of barriers to investment. Even before the war's end the United States had led an effort to create an international monetary structure capable of promoting trade and international stability, in part by avoiding the currency manipulations governments had used to promote exports. The Bretton Woods Agreement of 1944 sought a global economic system based on free trade, convertible currencies, and fixed exchange rates. All international currencies were to have fixed rates (which would be occasionally adjusted) and be convertible to dollars backed by gold to facilitate foreign trade. The agreement also called for an international stabilization fund, the International Monetary Fund (IMF), and an International Bank for Reconstruction and Development (World Bank). This new system represented a compromise between the rigid gold standard of the nineteenth century and the uncertain floating exchange rate of the 1930s. Experts hoped that the new institutions, and the three-quarters of the world's gold stock in the vaults of the U.S. Treasury, would prevent or minimize currency instability, competitive devaluations, protective tariffs, and import quotas. The U.S. dollar had replaced gold as the anchor of the international monetary system. It would act to fix exchange rates and be realigned only in instances of "fundamental disequilibrium."[1]

These goals expressed American principles—while also serving American interests. As the world's strongest and most prosperous nation, the United States would profit from a stable international order based on an "open door." As the country rapidly stood down from its war footing (American forces in Europe had been reduced from 3.5 million at their peak to under half a million by spring 1946) and lifted wartime economic controls, there was reason for worry. Conversion to a peacetime economy could prove difficult, engendering labor disputes and other social conflicts. Moreover, the future did not look bright. Productive capacity had been greatly expanded, perhaps doubled, during the war years, with the federal government financing five-sixths of total major new plant construction. Who would soak up this increased capacity? The demographics of the market did not look promising.

The long-declining American birthrate had fallen for the first time below the replacement figure in the 1930s, and quotas enacted in the 1920s curtailed immigration. Harvard economist Alvin Hansen, often referred to as the American Keynes, believed that a leveling off of population had contributed to the Great Depression. Before the war, government demographers had predicted that America's population would peak in the range of 140 million in 1943 and then decline. Combined with this concern was the further worry that the population would "age" rapidly. America's expanded postwar industrial capacity thus appeared to confront a contracting market. Many economists feared that the United States had reached a mature economy with no place to go but down.[2]

Important factors in earlier American economic growth, such as the building of American cities and the arrival of multitudes of immigrants, no longer appeared important. Adding to the anxiety, Austrian-born Harvard economist Joseph Schumpeter warned that the rise of corporate capitalism with its bureaucratic organization meant the end of a risk-taking "creative entrepreneurship," which he regarded as vital for a dynamic economy. To Schumpeter, entrepreneurs, by the force of new ideas, wrought change that pushed the economy to ever-higher levels of performance. Without the strong presence of entrepreneurs in an economy there could be only stagnation. Schumpeter's ideas reinforced the fear some had that the United States had lost the vitality characteristic of its history.[3]

POSTWAR PROSPERITY

The nation did indeed enter a new phase after 1946. But confounding the pessimists, the United States experienced a long and sustained period of economic growth. The prosperity widened in the late 1940s, accelerated in the 1950s, and reached impressive heights in the 1960s. As early as 1947, Americans concluded that economic growth was once again possible. From then on, optimism rose with each decade. Harold Vatter wrote: "Around 1964 many thought it more or less inevitable. The business cycle, it seemed, had been abolished."[4]

In 1956, *Fortune* magazine defined a middle-class family annual income as starting at $5,000 and predicted that half of American families would soon attain this level, thanks to an "economy of abundance." For many Americans, the years between the late 1940s and the early 1970s were the best years of their lives economically. Innovations and material gains altered lifestyles in numerous ways. In 1945, crossing America by train took three days, and most shopping was still done in mom-and-pop stores on Main Street. By 1970, the journey from one end of the country to the other took five hours by plane, and groceries came from efficient supermarkets located in about 7,800 suburban malls. Americans once again believed in the American Dream.[5]

Pent-up demand for consumer goods fueled by stored-up savings spurred on postwar production and capital investment. When wartime Office of Price Administration (OPA) controls ended, prices rose 15 percent between 1945 and 1947. The unanticipated baby boom between 1946 and 1963 propelled population growth. Governmental policies promoting home ownership, along with societal emphasis on family values, encouraged Americans to move to the new suburbs. By 1953, 19 percent of Americans lived in suburbs, and this group accounted for 29 percent of consumer spending. Home ownership rose from 44 percent in 1940 to 62 percent by 1960. By 1970, nearly two out of five Americans lived in communities outside (but close to) the central city, with an affluent lifestyle of free-standing houses, station wagons, country clubs, and patios and barbecues that reshaped popular culture.[6]

Harvard economist James Duesenberry popularized the phrase "keeping up with the Joneses" in his classic description of consumers matching their neighbors in the purchase of dishwashers, televisions, second cars, and the like.[7] Betty Friedan, in her seminal work *The Feminine Mystique* (1963), complained correctly that although women's magazines in the immediate postwar years had celebrated women entering male careers, this had altered by the 1950s of the Eisenhower administration. Magazines of that time encouraged readers to devote themselves to advancing their husbands' careers while tending their suburban homes and carpooling their children.

THE GRAY-FLANNEL DECADE

Organized labor was restless and strikes were common in 1946 as workers tried to consolidate gains made during wartime and to ensure job security in the transition years. In 1947, a Republican Congress, the first in twenty years, enacted the Taft-Hartley Act to curb union power. The law outlawed the closed shop (the requirement of union membership before employment) and declared illegal certain "unfair labor practices," such as secondary boycotts. Unions had to file financial statements with the federal government. Most important, the president was authorized to seek a court injunction to prevent strikes he regarded as dangerous to the national interest. Such an injunction would block a strike for an eighty-day "cooling-off" period, during which time a presidential fact-finding board could make recommendations. If the dispute persisted past this period, the president was to advise Congress on appropriate action.

In turn, organized labor became increasingly involved in politics as a constituency of the Democratic Party. Raising large sums for campaigns and capable of mobilizing an army of volunteers, the unions became a formidable force. In 1955, the American Federation of Labor and the Congress of Industrial Organizations merged to form the AFL-CIO, which represented more than 90 percent of the nation's unionized workers. In return for labor stability and the avoidance of strikes, management often offered contracts that provided job security and raises topped off by cost of living adjustments for inflation (COLAS). Organized labor participated fully in the new pros-

perity, and union membership rose as a percentage of nonagricultural workers to its historic high of 33 percent in 1953.

American society basked in self-confidence. With only 6 percent of the
world's population, Americans accounted for almost half the world's total
GNP in the years immediately after the war. Massive federal defense spending after 1950 benefited some areas of the nation more than others, particularly supporting the development of cities in the West and the South.
Military bases and defense industries, as well as the research and development facilities linked to the latter, fueled the economies and population
growth of Albuquerque, Atlanta, Houston, San Diego, Los Angeles, San
Francisco, Portland, Phoenix, Tucson, and Seattle.[8]

Americans assumed that they could be as mobile as they wished, both
physically and socially. Physically, their choice was often the suburbs of their
own cities, but many packed up and moved to the Sunbelt, especially after
1951 when the Carrier Corporation began to market home air conditioners
and, a few years later, central air conditioning. (Although invented in 1902
by Willis Carrier, the air conditioner had been used mainly in movie theaters
until after World War II.)

The GI Bill provided tuition-free education for veterans. Hailed as the
path to success and social mobility, education was generously supported, and
community colleges proliferated. Traditional values appeared strong. Americans seemingly believed strongly in organized religion and the family and
the virtues of hard work and honesty. Society's rapid postwar social and
economic changes appeared to be reasonably trouble-free progress.

American business easily—perhaps too easily—established a position of
world leadership, as Washington encouraged corporate activity abroad in
order to increase the nation's influence and complement national strategic
interests. Opportunities seemed limitless. The economies of erstwhile international competitors—debt-ridden England and defeated and occupied Germany and Japan—lay in shambles. Sheer bigness in business appeared an
incontrovertible good that allowed for the efficient use of vast resources in
the research and development of new products. Large firms maintained their
dominance of the economy; the antibusiness sentiment of the Depression
years receded. The Democrats, who had intended to use antitrust legislation
as a campaign issue in congressional elections in 1950, largely abandoned
the idea when they discovered that voters were indifferent to this once highly
divisive issue.[9]

College seniors no longer regarded small business as the promised land.

Young Americans of the 1950s planned careers in terms of climbing the corporate ladder. Social critics chided a "silent generation" in gray-flannel suits, who mindlessly marched to the beat of corporate norms. Sociologists debated whether the new white-collar life of middle America came at too high a price to individual freedom, but most Americans, intent on pursuing this life, ignored them.

As prosperity continued, fear of a depression faded. Americans increasingly thought of severe economic downturns as relics of a bygone age. Disneyland opened its doors in Anaheim, California, in 1955—with an inspirational speech by movie star Ronald Reagan—and thereby created a uniquely American symbol of the pleasures of affluence. Disneyland itself posed an interesting paradox. A squeaky-clean, small-town Main Street reflected nostalgia for an older and simpler America. To this was added a futuristic Tomorrowland based on a vision of a better life that American business promised—including a House of the Future made of plastic and a Carousel of Progress. After ten years of operation, one-quarter of the U.S. population had visited the park and Disneyland had earned $273 million.

Americans, flocking to have their children shake hands with Mickey Mouse, never had seemed more family oriented. A higher percentage of Americans married than in the 1930s, and they also divorced less. From 1946 to roughly 1963, the nation experienced the remarkable phenomenon of a rapidly rising birthrate. Businesses profitably met the need for diapers (disposables did not appear until the end of the 1960s) and nursery room furniture, and communities floated bonds to build new schools and to hire teachers.

The 1954 birthrate of 25.9 per thousand was the highest since 1924, and three years later a historic high 4.3 million births were recorded. By then, the first baby boomers were watching television's "Howdy Doody" and "Father Knows Best." Even President Eisenhower, as everyone's avuncular grandfather, played a role in celebrating the strength of the middle-class family. Legendary radio talk show host Jean Shepherd caustically warned listeners about "creeping meatballism"—a conformist society where happiness meant a big station wagon and an ice-cold bottle of Coke.

In 1958 John Kenneth Galbraith published a study of the American economy significantly entitled *The Affluent Society*. By 1956, six out of ten American families owned their home, eight out of ten owned a car, and nearly nine out of ten had at least one television set. (A decade later, Americans owned some 20 million color televisions, and a fourth of American families drove two or more cars.) The real income of the American worker stood a third higher in 1960 than in 1945.[10]

Life appeared better, or perhaps merely more convenient. Easily prepared frozen dinners, first developed by Clarence Birdseye, considered the founder of the frozen food industry, occupied whole sections of the supermarket. Advertising, a $6.5 billion industry in 1951, hawked the nation's wares and thought up some of the classic American ads, such as the Marlboro man and M&Ms that "melt in your mouth, not in your hand." From 1945 to 1973 real wages experienced the most rapid and sustained rise in American history, with median family income doubling. Discretionary income—income above that necessary to meet basic needs—soared. By 1973, three-quarters of all American families enjoyed at least some discretionary income, as compared to only one-fourth in 1929. Consumers enjoyed more free time to spend their money, with a standard forty-hour week and a minimum two weeks of vacation per year.

But there remained reasons for concern—most dramatically explosive tensions involving race and involvement in Vietnam in the 1960s. But the United States did not experience serious economic problems, at least as far as most Americans were aware, until 1973. As the world's leading super-power, the United States became accustomed to trading economic conces-sions for geopolitical advantages. It was commonplace for the media to refer to the second half of the twentieth century as the American Era or the American Century, or even Pax Americana. Very few, only an occasional Cas-sandra such as Walter Lippmann, sounded the alarm that the nation's econ-omy faced new challenges. But in 1973 an oil embargo suddenly stunned Americans into awareness of their vulnerability.

Until nearly the end of Richard Nixon's presidency the American econ-omy appeared capable of working miracles: providing its people with a stan-dard of living envied by all, supporting the defense of the Free World, aiding in the rebuilding of friendly economies damaged by World War II, and assuming a major role in the economic transformation of underdeveloped nations. A consideration of the American Era must begin with the immedi-ate postwar years.

As already noted, pent-up buying power in 1946 after seventeen years of the Depression and wartime shortages quickly solved the problem of conver-sion to a civilian economy. Returning servicemen found employment or went to college on the GI Bill, and working mothers experienced pressure to leave the workforce to make places for these returning servicemen. The female percentage of the labor force, 36.3 percent in 1944, dropped to 31.8 percent in 1947 and then began to rise slowly. Organized labor strove to retain and expand gains made during the war years, leading to considerable industrial unrest until the late 1940s. But the national mood became progressively upbeat as fears of a depression receded. In part, the new confidence rested on faith in the government's power to manage the economy.

GOVERNMENT AND THE ECONOMY

In February 1946 Congress enacted the Employment Act of 1946. The law formalized the government's role—to promote economic growth while overseeing that growth benefited all. Government, in short, was "to promote maximum employment, production, and purchasing power."[11] And the Council of Economic Advisers was created to assist the president in implementing these goals. Federal ability to fuel the economy through spending seemingly had been conclusively demonstrated in the war years. Most academic economists endorsed the ideas of John Maynard Keynes, and the Council of Economic Advisers made clear its commitment to a Keynesian countercyclical approach: "The agents of government must put a brake on at certain points where boom forces develop and support purchasing power when it becomes unduly depressed."[12]

The bill's passage appeared to represent Washington's embrace of "macroeconomic" planning. However, changes in the original bill as it made its way through Congress revealed conflicting views. A conservative coalition of southern Democrats and Republicans weakened the original bill by eliminating a mechanism for establishing specific trigger points for governmental action and mandated responses. The resulting ambiguity made the bill's significance largely symbolic.

Weakening the bill carried important consequences: federal participation in the economy would not take precedence over a free-market approach. Moreover, many members of Congress did not share the Keynesian casualness toward unbalanced federal budgets.

With the Truman Doctrine of 1947 the United States ended its traditional global isolationism. A bipartisan foreign policy now evolved that was devoted to the containment of Soviet expansion. In 1949, the United States, for the first time in its history, became a signatory to a permanent military alliance with the creation of the North Atlantic Treaty Organization. In April 1950 a top secret report by the recently created National Security Council (NSC 68) recommended a massive American military buildup regardless of cost. Defense contractors and electronics companies benefiting from military spending became the 1950s hot stocks. The Cold War's immense financial costs strongly influenced American economic developments for half of the twentieth century as collective defense served as the guiding principles of American foreign policy.

From the Korean War in 1950 to the end of the Cold War in 1991, military spending averaged 7.7 percent of the GDP, or about one-fourth of the total federal budget. This had a profound influence on the domestic economy. Localities, cities, states, and even whole regions grew highly dependent on military spending. In his farewell radio and television address on January 17, 1961, Eisenhower grimly warned Americans about the political power of a "military-industrial complex."

By military-industrial complex, Eisenhower meant an alliance between the Pentagon, large corporations, and politicians to influence the size and distribution of defense appropriations. He noted ominously in his address: "We annually spend on military security more than the net income of all United States corporations. . . . In the councils of government we must guard against the acquisition of unwarranted influence."

Defense spending could be facilely justified in terms of national security, in contrast to social welfare programs where questions always arose about who gets what at whose expense. Nor did defense spending displace private investment. Instead it enjoyed popularity with those in the business community who profited from it. Political lobbying, not competitive bidding, often determined the issuance of defense contracts, which generally guaranteed contractors costs plus a profit.

Between 1946 and 1969, the military spent a trillion dollars. Defense contracts were critical to several important industries and influenced the well-being of nearly all major corporations. From 1940 to 1965, the fifty largest corporations in the country received annually more than half of all prime military contracts.

Big businesses' involvement with defense is explained in part by a strong drive to diversify. Defense research spending focused on critical new technologies in electronics, computers, and aerospace. In these areas, commercial spin-offs proved easy and profitable. The commanding lead long enjoyed by the United States in aviation reflected the research and economies of scale resulting from huge long-term defense contracts. Spending on theoretical research that private enterprise would not find profitable to undertake, the military often spearheaded important technological advances. Indeed, the Pentagon sponsored the development of the Internet in the 1960s as a communication system intended to survive a nuclear attack.

CORPORATE AMERICA

With important exceptions, most major American corporations had re- stricted activities prior to 1950 to a limited range of traditional products. And they had not entered foreign markets in a major way. All of this changed rapidly in the late 1940s as American companies diversified and looked toward new markets. The growth of a military-industrial complex of enor- mous size and the expansion of consumer culture both domestically and abroad offered a myriad of new possibilities for growth and profit. Firms initially diversified into activities closely related to their main product line but in time moved further afield.

As they diversified, many adopted Sloan's M-form, with its autonomous operating divisions, as a model for their own organizations. Carefully pre- pared line-and-staff organizational charts with multicolored flow lines epito- mized the rationality and efficiency of American corporations.

Corporations with executives cocky after their highly praised wartime performances searched for new opportunities. Newly hired young execu- tives, often coming from the military, eagerly raced to make up for lost years with a can-do attitude. Their military experience, moreover, often inclined them to unconventional business approaches. They sometimes sought to apply military concepts of tactical and strategic planning to running a busi- ness and spoke of "attacking markets" and "defeating" rivals. Following their lead, large firms often created specialized departments to formulate an an- nual strategic plan. Most of these were essentially efforts to tell a firm where it wanted to go and how it could get there efficiently.

Nowhere was the changing of the generational guard more dramatic than at the Ford Motor Company. In the fall of 1945 the legendary founder's twenty-eight-year-old grandson forced the senile autocrat to relinquish the tight-gripped control that had caused the company to lag behind its ri- vals. The young Henry Ford II then selected forty-seven-year-old Ernest Breech, the head of Bendix Aviation, a General Motors supplier, as board chairman. A "finance man" rather than a "car man," Breech had been trained in Alfred Sloan's managerial approach. He quickly moved to over-haul his new company.

Meeting resistance from entrenched management, Breech reached out-side to recruit a new team. He hired the "Whiz Kids," ten former U.S. Air Force statistical control analysts who had pioneered applying quantitative analysis to military operations. In one early effort, they had impressed the Pentagon brass by devising an impressive and cost-effective way of transport-ing a million tons of military cargo from San Francisco to Australia. In 1955, eight years after the death of its founder, the Ford Motor Company, the world's largest family-owned industrial business, went public. The stock sold quickly. Ford was once again hot. By retaining 40 percent of voting shares, the family kept control. (Wall Street experts assume that holders of 10 to 20 percent of a company's stock are usually able to exert control.)

By the time Breech left Ford in 1960, he had transformed the automaker into a highly profitable company admired for innovative boldness. One gam-ble, the unpopular Edsel, earned a celebrated place in the annals of car design and business fiascos but was quickly followed by the extraordinarily successful Thunderbird.

Breech's Whiz Kids exemplified a new type of professional manager that rose to prominence in America's larger corporations during the 1960s. These included Robert McNamara (CEO of the Ford Motor Company, 1960–61; secretary of defense, 1961–68; and head of the World Bank, 1968–81) and Tex Thornton, the architect of the Litton Industries conglomerate. The ideal CEO in the late 1950s came to be viewed as one with no special attachment to either product or functional activity (sales, production, or corporate finance).[13]

Robert McNamara, for example, a graduate of the Harvard Business School, defined himself as a professional problem solver. For McNamara, running any large organization was the same, whether it was the Ford Motor Company or the Department of Defense. This new breed of professional managers prided themselves on being jacks of all trades but not specialists. They argued, to use the terminology of management studies, that "generic" analysis could substitute for "situational" analysis. Since they believed that the substance of a business was not overly important, they moved freely from employer to employer and industry to industry. The key to advancing careers was a toolbox of analytic skills believed applicable to all large corporations: the systems management approach.

One key technique, matrix planning, was borrowed from econometrics and involved the use of statistical analysis of data to predict future projections. Confident of their abilities, number-crunching executives claimed that they did things differently. Eager to diversify and grow, they often combined companies from unrelated industries. As one scholar noted: "It is very likely that managers—armed as they were with the latest portfolio techniques developed in consulting firms—felt especially confident of their abilities to manage a diverse portfolio of businesses."[14]

A tendency in larger corporations toward diversification, multinational operations, and even the occasional conglomerate had existed since the turn of the century. After 1950, however, what had been merely a trend became the norm. The prestigious Boston Consulting Group urged companies to place the businesses they owned into three categories: "stars," with high growth potential; "cash cows," having slow growth but with strong market position; and "dogs." Companies were told to shed their "dogs" and transfer resources from "cash cows" to "stars." This "strategic vision" encouraged the wave of mergers and conglomerate building during the 1960s.

In the 1960s, 25 percent of major American corporations diversified. Firms acquired firms unrelated to their core activities, reasoning that it was desirable to produce goods with "different time periods of demand." Often the way to take control of another company was to buy it. This was commonly done by issuing nonstock securities, which would later be converted into common stock. Since initially these securities did not count as stock, the existing company appeared more profitable than it really was, and the inflated stock prices made more acquisitions possible.

A good example of diversification was provided by General Mills, a flour-milling business started in 1928. Between 1950 and 1959, as the milling business matured and growth slowed, General Mills shifted to a consumer orientation, emphasizing packaged foods. By the 1970s, the company competed in thirteen different industries, including chemicals, furniture, luggage, toys, and wallpaper. It by now bore little resemblance to its earlier self. Milling, once its core business, played only a minor role. The story of General Mills demonstrated, at least for a time, the advantage of a firm drawing capital from slow-growing divisions to build up high-growing divisions and with no need to disclose sensitive information to outsiders.[15]

Foreign market growth and business diversity were now assumed to be yardsticks of corporate success. In 1960 only a handful of companies relied heavily on corporate income from outside the United States, but in that decade overseas business became increasingly important. By its end, many of America's leading companies had 30 percent or more of their sales overseas. Market growth and technological changes had driven companies to stress greater diversity in their products and markets.

With diversification and growth, large corporations found it necessary to restructure. They often adopted some variation of the standard decentralized multidivisional organization (M-form) pioneered by DuPont and General Motors in the 1920s. This type of organization became the dominant corporate model by 1960. Restructuring, in turn, called for a new set of management roles and relationships that emphasized the decentralization of responsibility and created operating divisions whose activities were controlled and coordinated by a central corporate office that made entrepreneurial decisions about resource allocation.

The M-form was especially well suited to managing conglomerates. The conglomerate represented the most extreme instance of movement away from a core product and its related line. By the early 1960s, for example, General Motors manufactured locomotives, refrigerators, and washing machines and General Electric produced jet engines, computers, and synthetic diamonds. Conglomerates by now had become highly attractive to investors, a trend that further fed the movement away from core businesses.[16]

Diversification can take several forms. The simplest involves a company acquiring new but related products that rely on the firm's existing technology or distribution system or both. Examples of this are when a chemical company moves to produce rayon or Orlon or a firm involved in mass marketing sells unrelated but nationally advertised and branded consumer goods by employing its mass-marketing facilities and expertise. Further afield— because it neither employs nor emerges from a company's own area of special competence—is the strategy of branching into products that require new skills and technology: for example, a steel company attempting to sell electronics by acquiring companies that already possess these assets. This approach requires recruiting, training, and assimilating new management and poses formidable problems of integrating the old and the new. Indeed, a highly regarded study has suggested that at any point in time a "management team has an inbuilt limit to the extent of diversity it can manage."[17]

In the 1960s, many companies plunged into totally unrelated fields and industries. It sometimes seemed that the motive in buying a business was simply that it seemed cheap. Understandably, companies whose core businesses had lost profitability initially led the movement. It is not always easy to distinguish a diversified company from a conglomerate. The rule of thumb, according to a writer for the *New York Times*, was "the high contribution of mergers to . . . asset growth." In the diversified company, the figure was usually under 10 percent. In conglomerates, this figure went much higher, often 40 percent or higher.[18]

The Eisenhower era witnessed vigorous antitrust action, a policy that encouraged the development of conglomerates. Congress had passed the Celler-Kefauver Anti-Merger Act in 1950. This act sought to prevent the purchase by a company of the stock and assets of other companies—usually its suppliers or distributors—if the result would substantially lessen competition. The Department of Justice won two notable cases. In 1953, DuPont was forced to divest itself of the ownership of 23 percent of the stock in General Motors. A year later, Eisenhower's Justice Department stopped Youngstown Sheet and Tube Company from a merger with Bethlehem Steel Corporation that would have increased concentration in "substantial relevant markets."

But the government's position on "market power" allowed a presumption of immunity for large enterprises whose behavior did not threaten preexisting patterns. Combining unrelated businesses was a prudent way to bypass antitrust restrictions. With large fees to be made for arranging "marriages," no matter how mismatched the pair, investment bankers strained to promote business romances, and Wall Street analysts pushed conglomerates as a safe form of investment. Tex Thornton's Litton Industries, Charles Bludhorn's Gulf and Western Industries, and James Ling's Ling-Temco-Vought became, as we shall see, the hot ticket stocks of the 1960s.

COLD WAR IMPERATIVES AND BUSINESS INTERESTS

The rapid proliferation of American multinational corporations reflected the diversification that occurred after World War II. It was promoted by a policy after 1948 that American foreign aid required purchases in the United States. Certainly, the government used its powers in the postwar world to enhance the global influence of American business. But these efforts, neither systematic nor consistent, failed to represent a comprehensive strategy. Instead containment of the Soviet threat overrode all other national concerns.

Reflecting Cold War strategic priorities, U.S. policies did not effectively represent America's long-range business interests; no tight coordination existed between national strategic policy and economic policies. Referring to American policies concerning foreign trade, Michael Porter of Harvard's Graduate School of Business has asserted that "while government policy yielded benefits that flowed to industry, these were rarely the primary motivating force. Instead, American economic strength was used to advance other goals."[19] Until the 1960s, however, American business needed little federal government assistance in their overseas operations.

MULTINATIONALS

The growth of multinational activity reflected the desperate need of much of the postwar world for American goods, capital, and technology. In 1953, nearly a decade after war's end, the United States produced 70 percent of the world's motor vehicles. The country enjoyed an overwhelming lead in industries employing advanced technology, notably telecommunications and electronics, and American business was the center of innovation for the world. As late as 1967, well-known French journalist Jean Jacques Servan-Schreiber warned of American global economic and cultural dominance in his influential *The American Challenge*. He reported that although U.S. companies controlled less than 5 percent of Western Europe's total business activity, American companies accounted for 80 percent of all computers, 95 percent of integrated circuits, and 50 percent of semiconductors. The danger was clear to Servan-Schreiber: the United States controlled the industries that were key to Europe's future.

American companies became multinationals because a large overseas market existed for their products. To perform effectively, however, they needed to create foreign subsidiaries and establish plants abroad, following a trail that a few American companies, such as Singer Sewing Machines and the Pullman Palace Car Company, had blazed at the end of the last century, followed, in the 1920s, by Ford and General Motors. Concentrating their efforts in Canada, Central and South America, and the Caribbean, other American companies at the turn of the century had invested in such areas as mining, agriculture, and oil. United Fruit, with huge coffee, cocoa, and banana plantations in Columbia, Honduras, and Nicaragua, provided an egregious example of a powerful American corporation corrupting native politicians and officials with bribes.

But, for the most part, America's abundant natural resources and large domestic market provided most of the opportunities that American businesspeople needed. Foreign resources and markets alike had been left largely to others, especially such historic trading peoples as the Dutch, the English, and the Germans.

After World War II, the multinational path widened into an eight-lane expressway, with most of the traffic moving eastward across the Atlantic. One student of this postwar development, Jack N. Behrman, suggested that the best criteria for defining a multinational corporation was centralization of policy and the integration of key operations among the foreign affiliates. Applying this test, he found that 85 percent of the Fortune 500's leading American corporations qualified in 1967 as multinationals. According to Behrman, the degree of centralization varied from company to company, with the chief determining factor being the nature of an industry. In general, however, the parent American company controlled capital expenditures and product lines, with local management allowed discretion in matters of personnel and marketing.[20]

Despite the great gains made in international markets after 1945, American companies still regarded overseas activity as secondary to their home markets. Executives tended to regard foreign postings as something to be avoided by the ambitious. The domestic market remained the place to make a mark.

America's postwar boom at home and abroad probably came too easily for the nation's good. In the 1950s, U.S. companies faced feeble foreign competition. This very ease contributed greatly to the loss of the competitive edge that American industry had displayed throughout the 1960s. Lulling many business leaders into a false sense of superiority, it blinded them to the rising threat of foreign competitors.

As their economies recovered, Europeans expressed concern about the power of American multinationals. By the end of the 1960s, foreign governments had placed restrictions and taxes on multinational operations that made them less attractive, and American overseas acquisitions slowed as foreign competitors leveled the playing field.[21]

THE TIME OF THE CONGLOMERATES

The 1950s tremor in mergers and acquisitions between companies operating in totally unrelated markets became, as already noted, an earthquake in the following decade. Conglomerates represented 60 percent of all large mergers in the 1960s. The craze remade the corporate landscape seemingly overnight. In 1968 conglomerates represented eighteen of America's one hundred largest companies.

Diversification into new products and markets is a reasonable action for companies whose core industries have peaked. However, the "urge to merge" carried this response beyond its logical limits. Many conglomerates were acquisitive upstarts that financed takeovers with the inflated share prices of the conglomerates themselves. Conglomerates often used accounting systems—"pool accounting"—that produced a rosier corporate picture than warranted. Expansion was commonly done by pledging stock as collateral for loans or by selling bondlike instruments ("convertible debentures") at a prearranged price, which were in time convertible to common stock.

Conglomerates were pressured to raise the price-earnings ratio of their stock. A financial reporter observed, "The need for maintaining a rising P/E ratio never ceases so long as the conglomerate continues to make acquisitions. And in order to avoid a decline or slowdown in per share value, it should seek to merge with companies whose P/E's are lower than its own."[22] This financial logic soon trumped earlier business strategies. The role of aggressive investment bankers in conglomerations is indisputable.

The thrust toward conglomerate formation initially represented a hedge against corporate eggs being in one basket. A company involved in a secure and stable business might thus acquire a high-risk venture, or vice versa. Later, the company might join companies representing complementary types of activities, such as airlines, hotels, or auto rentals. This type of linkage was said to create "synergy," bringing opportunities that otherwise would not have been possible for any one company on its own (a belief often expressed as the sum of the corporate whole being equal to more than the sum of its parts).[23]

But, in some cases, companies were acquired only because their deductible losses offered useful tax breaks to the takeover party. Schools of business graduated accountants and financial managers eager to explore the possibilities offered by conglomerates—including combinations that did not even offer a product. Fast profits for management through quick turnovers often figured prominently in deal making. Neil Jacoby, writing in *Center Magazine* in July 1969, observed that "promoters and bankers take advantage of the optimism of the public . . . to generate profits for themselves. Thus the above game can continue until the public recognizes that there is no growth in the operative earnings of acquired companies."[24]

James Ling, a high school dropout, assembled Ling-Temco-Vought (LTV) in the early 1960s, and its stock increased from around $10 a share to more than $160 in 1967. According to *Fortune* magazine, LTV was the fastest-growing company in the United States from 1961 to 1966. At its peak in 1969, LTV employed 29,000 workers and offered 15,000 different products.

Ling, a good old boy from Texas with political connections to the Johnson administration, lived in a home described as a palace with the décor of a Holiday Inn.

Much of this rapid rise was due to defense contracts, and along the way Ling acquired electronics, missiles, sporting goods, chemicals, meatpacking, and audio sound companies, as well as Braniff Airlines. Ling focused on "creatively deploying" an acquired company's underlying assets. He split off divisions into separate companies and then sold shares in these companies for more than the market had valued the parent company. He spelled out his philosophy in LTV's 1966 annual report: "Most importantly," acquisitions "must meet the test of the 2 plus 2 equals 5 (or 6) formula."

Ling's empire fell apart, however, after he acquired money-losing Jones and Laughlin Steel Corporation in May 1968 and had to sell subsidiaries to stanch the financial hemorrhage. His dazzling financial acrobatics no longer availed. Ling resigned, and in 1971 LTV, its stock worthless, declared bankruptcy.

The flagship of the postwar conglomerate movement, however, was International Telephone and Telegraph (ITT). Under the leadership of hard-driving Harold S. Geneen, an accountant by training, ITT grew from a middle-sized telecommunication company in 1959 into a highly diversified multinational giant. In 1972, the "Geneen Machine" employed 400,000 employees in some 350 companies in 80 countries, and ranked eighth in size among American corporations. In that year, ITT reportedly sought to influence a Justice Department antitrust suit against its acquisition of the Hartford Fire Insurance Company through political contributions to the Nixon administration.

A supremely confident Geneen boasted to the press that "good managers can manage anything." He predicted that conglomerates were "the business of the future." For a time in the late 1960s, the workaholic Geneen held monthly telecom meetings around long tables both in New York and Brussels with up to 150 division chiefs. A man who wanted to know everything, he required his many managers to provide him with detailed weekly reports totaling thousands of pages. He often told reporters that his business philosophy was to stay as close as possible "to what is happening." In *Managing*, a book he coauthored in 1984, Geneen claimed he gave managers overlapping responsibilities so that checks and balance always existed on everyone.[25]

To Geneen, the real challenge in creating an effective conglomerate was in finding the right mix of apparently unrelated product and service companies. To the outsider, such a structure might seem jerry-built, lacking rhyme or reason. But according to Geneen, the successful conglomerate contained an inherent logic based on creating synergy. What exactly the logic of his acquiring companies was—companies whose activities varied from baking bread, to renting cars, to building homes, to making grass seed, to writing insurance and running hotels—was never precisely spelled out. Nevertheless, Geneen's successes seemed to support his claim.

Once he stepped down as chairman in 1979, however, the weaknesses of ITT's strategy became readily apparent. Its size and diversity slowed down decision making and sowed confusion—not the synergy Geneen boasted of. His successor, known as "slash and burn Araskog," kept busy shedding companies and real estate, with the result that ITT by the mid-1990s was a pale shadow of the company in its Geneen days, and what remained of the firm was split in 1995 into three independent companies.[26]

Other impressive examples included J. Peter Grace Jr. of W. R. Grace & Company; Charles Bludhorn of Gulf and Western; Royal Little of Textron; and Charles Tex Thornton of Litton Industries. Most of these men stood outside the corporate establishment and criticized its "bean-counting" ways. They regarded themselves as throwbacks to an older and more virile entrepreneurial ethos—swashbuckling adventurers and empire builders. In truth, the more decentralized their conglomerates became, the less of a role they usually played in management. Their concern was voraciously gobbling up corporations and persuading investors to buy their stocks at high prices.

Fueling the heady merger mania of the late 1960s' bull market, conglomerates contributed to the erosion of American business efficiency. Both the Securities and Exchange Commission and the Department of Justice began to pay increasing attention to conglomerate activity at the very time it showed signs of waning. A concern was that conglomerates could cross-subsidize lines of business, by using profits from one subsidiary where their position was strong to cut prices and drive out competitors in another market.[27]

Conglomerate managers prided themselves on picking the right acquisitions and negotiating the highest price for a subsidiary. Financial gamesmanship proved exhilarating and profitable, and the best and brightest of the young managers quickly learned to play. Fewer and fewer managers evinced any interest in the traditional apprenticeship of learning a company's operations from the ground up. Such expertise might even limit mobility. It could tie you to one industry or one company. The ladder to the top had been switched. An ability to produce the well-made and reasonably priced proverbial widget did not seem to matter.

A few Cassandras warned that managers were engaged in a "paper chase for profits" and that they downplayed the product, which threatened the long-term well-being of their companies. Scholars of management generally agree that there is a loss of competitive advantage the further a firm diversifies away from its core business. Yet corporations, in their enthusiasm for mergers and acquisitions, moved further and further afield. The result was that at the end of the 1960s American capital investment and gains in productivity lagged behind those of other advanced nations.[28]

A BEAR MARKET

Most conglomerates did not work out well for shareholders. LTV, for example, fell by the wayside because of its high debt and heavy exposure to a contracting steel market. A few, however, did well. Time Warner, under the leadership of Steve Ross, went from parking lots, electrical contractors, burglar alarms, and movie production to become one of the nation's largest and most-diversified information firms.

The end of an era came with the start of the bear market of 1973–74. The same buccaneers who had once lauded the synergy of the conglomerate now asked if the value of the sum of the parts could be greater than the value of the whole. This view, known as "reverse synergy," became fashionable in the 1970s as assets were sold off for quick profit. An uncertain business picture combined with high interest rates to discourage capital investment. High inflation exacerbated the situation. Stock prices dropped, and investors moved away from stocks, buying gold or art work or other commodities as a hedge against inflation.

THE CORPORATION AS A SOCIAL INSTITUTION

Between 1941 and the mid-1960s, corporate America encountered little significant criticism. Wartime mobilization, the advent of the Cold War, and the domestic repercussions of McCarthyism all had subdued American radicalism, largely silencing its antibusiness rhetoric. In the 1950s, Americans celebrated the accomplishments of an economy that served as the model for the Free World. Well-financed and slickly designed public relations campaigns associated big business with civic virtue, selling to the public a "corporate image" of good neighbor and good citizen. The corporation, in Peter Drucker's phrase, served as "America's representative social institution."[29]

There were exceptions to the chorus of praise. Sociologist David Riesman, the principal author of *The Lonely Crowd* (1951), charged that Americans had forsaken individualism to embrace the bland conformity demanded for success within the corporate bureaucracy. According to the authors, the "inner directed" Victorian American had become an "other directed" twentieth-century corporate climber. The theme of corporate conformity was also explored in Sloan Wilson's popular novel *The Man in the Gray Flannel Suit* (1953) and in William H. Whyte's best-selling sociological study *The Organization Man* (1956).

To Whyte, as to Riesman and Wilson, the rugged individualists of entrepreneurial folklore had yielded to bureaucrats obsessed with safety and conformity. A more radical indictment was presented by Columbia University sociologist C. Wright Mills in his influential *The Power Elite* (1956). Mills charged that American society in the Eisenhower years was governed in reality by a very small elite of businessmen, military leaders, and political leaders.

Vance Packard's *The Hidden Persuaders* (1957) critically dissected Madison Avenue's advertising agencies. He warned that Americans as consumers and even as voters were more and more psychologically conditioned to respond to commercial stimuli as a conditioned reflex. Academically trained psychologists employed social science research methods to analyze consumer decision making. Major advertising agencies hired "motivation research experts," and corporations contracted with firms that specialized in focus group studies.

Critics of business constituted, however, only a small minority. America in the 1950s seemingly celebrated a remarkable consensus on values: the importance of education, work, family, and patriotism. Adolf A. Berle and John Kenneth Galbraith published books dismissing the charge that big business posed a threat to American values. Galbraith theorized a pluralistic political system of "countervailing powers" that checked and balanced each other. His only concern was that the United States needed to devote more funds to the public sector—the building of schools, hospitals, public housing, and the like. Galbraith's proposed worst case scenario for corporations was higher corporate taxes.

The 1960s would be a decade of fast-paced social change. John Kennedy's brief presidency raised expectations of reform, but his assassination in November 1963, amid mounting racial tensions and involvement in Vietnam, cast a shadow over initial hopes. In the course of the decade, America lurched from consensus into divisiveness. Corporate America's values now underwent scrutiny. The twenty-one-year-old student commencement speaker at the Wellesley graduation in 1969, Hillary Rodham, spoke for many of her generation: "We feel that our prevailing acquisitive and competitive corporate life is not the way of life for us."[30]

In response, "corporate social responsibility" emerged as one of the 1960s "buzz words" (a phrase coined during that decade). Balancing the needs of company and society was regarded as the goal of enlightened management. However, much of this vaunted corporate "social responsibility" took the form of symbolic rhetoric or programs that cost little and represented no serious commitment.

A WATERSHED DECADE: THE 1960S

Slow economic growth at the end of the Eisenhower era contributed to Kennedy's election, and as president he tried "to get the country moving again" while avoiding inflation. To this end, he persuaded the reluctant United Steel Workers of America to settle for an annual wage increase of 2.5 percent over the previous contract, but then major steel companies broke a promise to raise prices only moderately. "My father always told me all businessmen were sons of bitches," Kennedy informed his advisers, "but I never believed it until now." Threatened with antitrust suits, the steel corporations rolled back prices. The public applauded, but the administration's relationship with business showed strain. The stock market began a slide that would take it down 26 percent from the middle of March to the middle of June 1962, and a startled White House signaled that the president was not hostile to big business.[31]

In 1962, with a sluggish economy, Kennedy needed to act. His Keynesian-inclined adviser Walter Heller, the chairman of his Council of Economic Advisers, urged a large cut in personal and corporate taxes. But the proposed tax cut did not pass Congress until after Kennedy's assassination. Lyndon Johnson came to the presidency determined to make his mark as a great reformer. His domestic program, the Great Society, assumed that Washington had the ability to rectify profound social problems. Amid an outpouring of important legislation, Johnson signed a tax cut into law in early 1964. It seemed to work, and low inflation and high employment made the 1960s one of the most prosperous decades in American history.

Economic growth in the decade averaged a robust 4.7 percent a year. Keynesian policies had apparently performed as predicted, and the Englishman's macroeconomic planning gained credibility. Keynesian economists referred to their approach as the New Economics. They taught that government should fine-tune economic performance to ensure satisfactory levels of growth and employment, and some even spoke of taming the business cycle.

But, in the early 1960s, a small group of economists formed around the University of Chicago's Milton Friedman, who retained the view of a self-correcting market. Known as "monetarists" because of their emphasis on the importance of the money supply, Friedman and his followers, the Chicago School, remained voices in the wilderness until events in the 1970s mandated a reconsideration of Keynesian tenets.

In the mid-1960s, however, all seemed well with the economy. Workers experienced substantial increases in real income. Plastic credit cards became commonplace in the decade. Introduced in the 1950s by the Diners Club, credit cards were an instant success; Visa appeared in 1963 and MasterCard two years later. In anticipation of increasing corporate profits, the stock market soared; changes in the laws allowed institutions greater freedom to invest in Wall Street. In the bull market of the late 1960s, institutional investors accounted for a quarter of total shares.

Economists warned of inflation as Vietnam and domestic reform increased the national debt. Cuts in federal spending and increased taxes were called for, but politicians did not want to antagonize voters. Johnson's effort to provide "guns and butter" was proving costly. Inflation, already at 6 percent in 1968, now accelerated.

Great Society activism impacted business in many ways. A plethora of regulatory legislation revolutionized the business climate. The Civil Rights Act of 1964 established the Equal Employment Opportunity Commission (EEOC) to end discrimination in employment in firms with more than twenty-five employees. Any individual who believed himself discriminated against on the basis of race, religion, sex, or national origins could call on the Department of Justice to initiate a suit on his or her behalf.

When black urban neighborhoods throughout the nation erupted in riots from 1965 to 1969, the federal government initiated what became known as "affirmative action." Federal contractors were required to keep track of the numbers of women and minorities employed at various job levels. If the percentage fell below that in the hiring pool, companies had to institute special recruitment and career development programs. Affirmative action by 1970 required business to establish quotas for recruitment of minorities and women. This approach prevailed until the *Bakke* decision of 1978. In *Regents of the University of California v. Bakke,* the Supreme Court ruled against a state medical school admission program that set aside a fixed number of places for black and other minority group applicants. But even as it disallowed quotas, the decision did permit schools and employees to take race and gender into account as factors to achieve greater diversity.

George Davis and Glen Watson, in *Black Life in Corporate America* (1982), wrote that a policy of the EEOC in the 1960s was to make an example of the largest companies in several industries, thereby frightening the others into line. Companies that failed to design and implement acceptable affirmative action plans could be declared ineligible to receive federal contracts. Businesses, large and small, found that the government now required more in the way of records and paperwork. Some companies, however, offered only token compliance. Refusing to provide women and minorities with adequate support and guidance, they set them up for resentment on the part of coworkers and failure.

THE ECOLOGICAL MOVEMENT AND THE RUSH TO REGULATE

The social ferment of the 1960s brought forward public interest groups to press for legislation protecting the consumer, the environment, and the health and safety of workers. Rachel Carson, in *Silent Spring* (1962), sounded the alarm about the dangers of DDT and other insecticides. The chemical industry spent over $150,000 on public relations in the year after the book's publication attempting to counter Carson's message that certain insecticides poisoned the soil and water. A number of writers—David Brower, Barry Commoner, Paul and Anne Ehrlich, and René Dubos—brought environmental concerns to public attention, demonstrating that the environmental crisis was directly traceable to fossil fuels, industrial waste, and consumer profligacy. In 1970 Americans observed the nation's first Earth Day. A vital movement had come to life.[32]

New governmental regulations, environmental and otherwise, added to the cost of doing business in America. In important ways, they differed from previous regulatory practices. With some exceptions, federal regulations of business had involved "single industry regulation." Each regulated industry had its own agency, for example, the Federal Communications Commission for radio and television. Most of the regulation of the 1960s, however, assumed a new form—the "cross industry regulation." Single-industry regulatory agencies too often establish close ties with their particular industries, viewing the regulated companies as clients rather than adversaries. Personnel often moved back and forth between the agency and the industry. Such cozy arrangements did not thrive with cross-industry commissions, and they soon encountered sharp criticism for harming business.

Congress, in eight years, from 1964 to 1972, enacted thirty-five separate regulatory programs creating new regulatory agencies. These included the EEOC in 1964, the Consumer Product Safety Commission (CPSC) in 1966, the Environmental Protection Agency (EPA) in 1969, and the Occupational Safety and Health Administration (OSHA) in 1970. New regulations covered a wide range of potential hazards—from specifying the proper handling of toxic chemicals to restrictions on storing inflammable materials to the safe design of children's toys. Confronted by costly new regulations, some industries, notably automobile manufacturing, requested delays in implementation or an easing of standards.

The regulatory enthusiasm of the late 1960s occurred as the American economy weakened, inflation soared, and American companies fell behind foreign competitors. It was charged that regulatory rules often inhibited business initiative and innovation. The inevitable cost, inconvenience, and occasional arbitrariness also rankled. Business complained about being disadvantaged in regard to foreign competitors. But other major industrial nations were moving, and usually faster, in a similar direction.

From a business point of view, the timing of new regulatory legislation was decidedly unfortunate—though for some opponents of regulation no time would have been right. Corporate America often spoke with two voices. Collectively, it was hostile to what it regarded as governmental interference. But individual corporations often demanded that government restrain their rivals. As one lobbyist said: "Sometimes a highly regulated administration is useful and sometimes it is not. What I would really like is regulations for my competition and none for me."[33]

The EPA acted vigorously. Its first act had been a ban on DDT and seven other of Rachel Carson's "elixirs of Death." Major new construction required advance approval after the submission of an "environmental impact statement." Construction slowed, became more expensive, and even occasionally halted. In one well-reported instance, a New York state utility's planned electric power plant on the Hudson River north of New York City had to be shelved after a failed eighteen-year effort to get EPA approval. Previously, the power plant would have required three years from conception to completion.

The new array of environmental, workplace, and product regulations resulted in a safer and environmentally cleaner America, but at a price. A temporary loss in business efficiency and innovativeness resulted in higher costs and slower product development and other disadvantages for the public. Environmental and safety efforts and affirmative action accomplished much that is positive, but American business in the 1970s operated in a demanding regulatory world. The economist Murray L. Weidenbaum warned that the extensive new regulations had shifted decision making from businesspeople to government, with, he believed, disastrous consequences for efficiency.[34]

NIXON AND THE 1970S

In 1968 Richard Nixon narrowly won the presidency. The supposedly conservative Nixon proved surprisingly pragmatic in his domestic policies. His real interests lay in foreign affairs, but issues of inflation, rising interest rates, and a slowing economy could not be avoided for long. As interest rates rose, the economy weakened. To gain control over inflation, Nixon, on August 15, 1971, imposed a wage and price freeze. This initial freeze of ninety days was followed by three months of less stringent controls and then by a six-month period during which the government closely monitored price and wage increases.

In a related series of actions, Nixon ended the dollar's guaranteed convertibility to gold, allowing the international currency market to set its value. Nixon's new "floating dollar" unilaterally ended the Bretton Woods Agreement of 1944. Herbert Stein, chairman of the president's Council of Economic Advisers, later admitted that these momentous decisions resulted from a weekend of brainstorming at Camp David.

Nixon's actions, which also included a 10 percent surcharge on imported goods, were in response to a record high balance-of-payments deficit in 1970. This deficit required increasing the value of American exports. Instead, the reverse occurred. American exports declined and dollars flowed overseas to fill the trade gap. Only bold action by the United States kept gold prices (under pressure from speculators seeking to sell dollars for gold) stable through the 1960s. But mistrust of the overvalued dollar grew, and by 1970 a crisis loomed. Something needed to be done quickly. However, Nixon's unilateral ending of the Bretton Woods structure without first consulting other governments angered the international financial world.[35]

The Smithsonian Agreement, arrived at by ten nations in December 1971, retained the dollar as the standard for the currency of most important industrial nations, though it was no longer convertible to gold. The sense of a weakening of America's postwar prominence was growing. Foreigners frequently criticized American products as overpriced, poorly designed, and low in quality. In 1963 the United States accounted for over 17 percent of the world's exports of manufactures. Ten years later this had declined to 12 percent.

The limits of American economic and military power also had become evident in Vietnam. In January 1973, the Paris Accord ended America's direct role in Vietnam. The end of U.S. primary involvement, however, did not lift the national mood of unease; Americans had other reasons for concern. Throughout 1973 the Watergate scandal distracted Washington until a disgraced Nixon resigned in August 1974. Distrust of government, the "post-Watergate syndrome," remained evident for the rest of the decade. No one any longer talked of an American century.

Inflation soared to 8 percent at the beginning of 1973 and then to 10 percent by year's end, as the federal budget's annual deficit jumped to $40 billion—an astonishing sum for the time. A battered economy reeled as a distracted president fought to remain in office. According to Keynesian New Economics, high unemployment would reduce inflation. In 1958 the English economist A. W. Phillips indeed premised a precise mathematical inverse relation between inflation and unemployment: the Phillips curve. Government simply had to choose the right balance by balancing the two. But contrary to Phillips, inflation and unemployment rose in tandem for the 1970s. A newly coined term, "stagflation," referred to a sluggish economy of high unemployment and rampant inflation.

Milton Friedman and the monetarists of the Chicago School suddenly gained a wide hearing. Friedman's central premise was that a change in the money supply led to a change in total demand. Thus, he argued, "inflation is always and everywhere a monetary phenomenon." By this he meant that inflation is generally caused by government creating a situation where "too much money chas[ed] too few goods." Faced with inflationary problems, the best policy was to slowly reduce the rate of growth of money in the economy. Interest rates and the budget deficit should be allowed to fluctuate passively as automatic stabilizers.[36]

In the aftermath of the war against Israel fought in October 1973 by Egypt and Syria, Arab states belonging to the Organization of Petroleum Exporting Countries (OPEC) imposed an oil embargo. OPEC had been created in 1960 as an effort to push up oil prices by producing nations after major oil companies reduced the prices paid them. Until the 1973 embargo, the world had little reason to pay attention to OPEC.

The United States relied on the Middle East for only 12 percent of its oil consumption (another 20 percent came from Mexico, Venezuela, and Canada). Accordingly, experts initially expected the boycott to end before America suffered significantly. The boycott's impact on the United States, however, was more direct than anticipated. It lasted five months, causing worldwide shortages; crude oil prices jumped from two dollars a barrel to eight dollars. Long lines of impatient drivers formed at service station gas pumps. Inexpensive energy had long been taken for granted, but no longer.

Higher petroleum prices resulted in greater costs for heating, lighting, fertilizers, airline tickets, clothing made out of synthetics, and anything made from plastics, while higher freight charges brought up prices in general. The rate of inflation reached 12.2 percent in 1974. Americans expressed dismay, but double-digit inflation afflicted most of the world. In fact, rising oil prices served to distract attention from a general increase in the price of most raw materials during the 1970s.

Americans sensed a dire economic environment for the first time since the Great Depression. The "finely tuned" permanent prosperity promised by Keynesian New Economics had proven illusory. The hippies of the counterculture, who had railed at decadent American materialism a few years earlier, scrambled in the 1970s to find their place in the sun—a sun that seemed to be setting. A growing conservative sentiment gathered momentum as social norms once taken for granted eroded.

Nevertheless, many social changes identified with the counterculture of the 1960s gained acceptance. Social movements such as feminism, gay rights, and environmentalism moved steadily ahead. But the liberal credo of reliance on government began to be challenged by those who argued that Washington's social engineering had weakened the nation. Economists also had their critics, who noted their apparent inability to predict the course of the economy.

The Turn of
the Millennium

Coping with Decline, 1974–1980

In the 1950s and 1960s when you could sell anything we used obsolete machines and paid the unions what they asked. We were too greedy and too lazy. The Germans and Japanese invested in new technology. Now we're in deep trouble.—ANONYMOUS AMERICAN BUSINESSMAN, New York Times, May 11, 1977

In many ways the "sobering seventies" was a transitional decade. Western economies lost their self-confidence in the face of an Arab oil embargo that showed the vulnerability of industrial nations. Many Americans expressed discontent with the present and apprehension about the future. Amid this gloom and pessimism, however, a major shift in American culture, society, and politics had occurred. Until the 1970s the United States had remained relatively self-sufficient with respect to fuels and foods. This would now change, with important consequences for national power and industrial competitiveness. The nation moved politically to the right as Keynesian economics appeared ineffectual, and in its place came a call for deregulation, privatization, federal fiscal conservatism, and tax cuts.

Leadership was in short supply as "stagflation" was fed by soaring oil and commodity prices. The nation recoiled from the raised expectations and social activism of the Great Society, with its often ineffective programs. A bear market brought stock values down sharply for the decade, and American business experienced a steady decline that some believed was irreversible. The national sense of general malaise was startling; Americans had reason to doubt their future and the competitive prowess of American business. American companies even lost much of their own home markets in such diverse industries as textiles, electronics, and auto manufacturing to highly efficient Japanese firms, which could rely on cheap capital, protected home markets, and other government support.[1]

STAGFLATION AND SLIPPAGE

Throughout the 1970s Americans sensed "slippage," as the American economy slowed. The real income of American workers declined after 1973. American business lost market share and profitability in the face of the revitalized economies of Western Europe and Japan. In retrospect, it is clear that the "slippage" that troubled contemporaries largely reflected structural changes in the American economy. The share of the nation's employment accounted for by manufacturing industries fell from 30.3 percent in 1962 to 22.9 percent in 1977. American dependence on exports rose from an estimated 6.34 percent of real GNP in the 1960s to 10 percent in the late 1970s. As the quotation at the head of this chapter indicates, the roots of the problems of the 1970s can be traced to earlier good times when American business, complacent and out of condition, started to lose its competitive edge.[2]

There was no easy explanation at hand for America's fall from grace in the 1970s. Not only did the United States slip in terms of past performance, but it lagged behind other nations that were pressing forward while the American economy stalled. Most Americans did not understand what had happened and why. The raging inflation, high interest rates, and depressed business conditions of the 1970s discouraged capital investment. These developments also puzzled economists and policy makers, who shifted almost overnight to a more market-oriented perspective. Dissatisfaction with what many viewed as high taxes and excessive regulation gained momentum as the decade advanced. As the economy exhibited weaknesses, Americans preferred to blame Washington, not Wall Street.

THE FORD PRESIDENCY AND POST-WATERGATE

Gerald Ford succeeded Nixon in August 1974. He first needed to restore confidence in government and the presidency, which had been severely shaken by Watergate. As political life returned to normal, the economy experienced a sharp downturn. Both inflation and unemployment rose in late 1974. President Ford, focusing on inflation, urged citizens to wear the widely ridiculed WIN (Whip Inflation Now) buttons. Despite his efforts to depict occasional signs of upturn as evidence of better times, the situation worsened, with inflation standing at over 11 percent and unemployment at 9 percent by late 1975. As Nixon's successor had modestly informed the American public, he was indeed "a Ford not a Lincoln."

The great post–World War II bull market reached a peak in January 1973 as the Dow Jones reached 1,051. Then came a crescendo of bad news— stagflation, oil embargo, Watergate, recession. By December 1975 the Dow had fallen to 577. It had lost 45 percent of its value, and pundits facilely found similarities with 1929. A business journalist noted a bright spot: "The current bear market may have . . . put to rest the overworked and misapplied thesis that the stock market offers a consistent hedge against inflation." The decline of the stock market particularly battered those conglomerates that had borrowed on their overpriced stock. Investor enthusiasm for conglomerates dropped sharply, and analysts noted that excessive diversification away from core competences had severely weakened managerial control and corporate performance.[3]

As stagflation worsened, White House advisers could not decide whether to focus on inflation or unemployment: fighting one meant fueling the other. Even as Americans replaced the WIN button with the "smiley face"—a smiling face made by an upturned line in a circle thought up by an advertising man—and hailed each other in the morning with "have a nice one," they worried about job security and the cost of getting by. With a presidential race ahead in 1976, Ford judged unemployment the more troubling of his concerns.

Confidence in America's economic prospects underpinned the nation's faith in progress, and the long postwar prosperity served to bolster this belief. But in the early 1970s the accepted indicators of economic health showed sharp declines. From 1972 to 1978, gains in industrial productivity slowed to 1 percent per year, less than half of the previous decade's rate of increase and only a third of the period from 1948 to 1955. To compound the problem, high interest rates discouraged the capital investment needed for significant improvement. The GDP decreased in several of the years of the 1970s and exhibited only sluggish performance even in better ones. Four Western European nations (Denmark, West Germany, Sweden, and Switzerland) threatened to surpass the United States in per capita GDP in the mid-1970s. As exports shrank and imports soared, the nation's balance of trade fell deeply into the red. Ordinary Americans found their paychecks shrinking yearly as their wages lagged behind the quickened pace of inflation.

Moreover, Americans failed to agree on the causes of their problems. Some blamed greedy Organization of Petroleum Exporting Countries (OPEC) nations; others worried that the United States had contracted the "British disease" of over-powerful unions, complacent management, and an obstinate refusal to adapt to change. The sociologist Daniel Bell, in *The Cultural Contradictions of Capitalism* (1976), explained that a consumer-oriented economy had made Americans hedonistic and soft; as a result they spent the capital needed to invest in their futures on immediate gratification. Americans by mid-decade generally agreed that Keynesian policies could not restore or sustain economic growth.

POST-KEYNESIAN ECONOMICS

After 1974, Keynesian economists experienced a crisis in self-confidence and backpedaled from their earlier views. Their conviction that low unemployment could be combined with moderate inflation to benefit the economy had to be reexamined in terms of the stagflation of the 1970s. Most critical, economists debated the ability of public policy to both stabilize the economy and promote full employment. As the Great Depression had called into question the conservative belief in the efficacy of market forces, stagflation in the 1970s challenged the liberal faith in the New Economics and its usefulness in fine-tuning the economy. Frustrated by the inability of fiscal policies to end the recession, economists increasingly questioned reliance on government interventionism.

Respect for market forces emerged as a powerful theme of economic and political thinking in the 1970s. Even liberal economists now conceded the inevitability of the business cycle and the limits of governmental response. The Keynesian position that market economies are chronically depression-prone also fell out of favor. Many economists moved to the view (in a way, a return to older pre-Keynesian thinking) that in the long run market forces kept an economy on track. The interventionist policies favored by the president's economic advisers in the 1960s now appeared highly problematic, often leading to unwanted results, and federal actions tended to reflect political rather than strictly economic considerations—especially in presidential election years. Even the most ardent Keynesians admitted that they had overestimated the possibility of rational economic management and ignored the decisive importance of politics in governmental decision making. Economists had learned the hard lesson that governmental policies required a political process to be implemented, and political considerations in turn introduced numerous factors that were difficult to anticipate. These often produced unexpected and even unwanted results.

Almost all economists came to agree that Nixon's efforts to fine-tune the economy in the early 1970s had contributed to business uncertainty and instability. Actions involving taxes or federal spending had to be used sparingly and be reserved for circumstances requiring drastic measures. By the late 1970s, advocates of the New Economics acknowledged that stagflation's intractability illustrated the difficulties of macroeconomic management. Market disciplines needed considerable freedom from governmental interference in order to energize and redirect economic activity. Keynesian fiscal policies to fine-tune the economy seemed an idea whose time had come and gone.[4]

As the decade drew to a close, Milton Friedman's monetarist approach won increasing support. Friedman believed that monetary policy (control over the supply of money) profoundly influenced business performance and expectations. However, monetary policies required a year or two to be fully felt. Thus, reasoned Friedman, monetary policies should avoid responding unduly to temporary market conditions. Instead, they should aim for stable prices by steadily decreasing or increasing the money supply, and nothing else. Whereas erratic postwar monetary policies had unsettled and hurt the economy by trying proactively to create jobs and high growth, economic stability required that the money supply be carefully increased to equal the economy's rate of growth over the long run.[5]

Monetarists did not dispute the importance of government's role in the economy but merely argued that Washington's limited ability to anticipate and direct developments meant that federal policy should rely principally on the Federal Reserve Board's control of the money supply by means of open market operations and the setting of interest rates. A healthy market-directed economy required an adequate money supply and balanced federal budgets. Then a self-regulating market would perform efficiently without need of further macroeconomic management. Unfortunately, the market did not perform efficiently in the 1970s. Although Friedman's followers refused to lose faith, others did, as events failed to follow his predictions. Moreover, electronic financial transactions and money market accounts meant that economists found it increasingly difficult to define or measure the money supply. New forms of monetary exchange were being created regularly by the financial world. How then, Friedman's critics asked, could money supply be targeted for controlling inflation? Monetarists found their basic theory in tatters, and once inflation eased in the 1980s they soon fought among themselves over how it might be applied. Alan Greenspan, chairman of the Federal Reserve, made its death seemingly official in 1993, announcing that he no longer paid real attention to the money supply.

Dramatic jumps in the price of oil and other commodities largely explain the economy's poor performance during the second half of the 1970s. Other factors also contributed to the wage-price spiral. The role of unions in raising wages and labor costs came under scrutiny, as did the inflationary impact of federal regulations, which curtailed innovation while raising prices for consumers. The call for a return to market discipline became the hallmark of the 1970s' drift to conservative thinking; big government and powerful unions had distorted market forces and pulled down the economy. The mantras of privatizing and deregulation resonated from conservative think tanks and corporate executive suites. Corporations had to be free to innovate, restructure, and, if need be, relocate and outsource.

Generous labor contracts, including automatic cost of living adjustments (COLAS), had been the rule in industries with strong unions, thanks to what was termed "pattern bargaining," which had first occurred in the automobile industry in the late 1940s. At that time the United Automobile Workers (UAW) had won an agreement with Ford that provided COLAS and, using this contract as leverage, had gotten General Motors and Chrysler to go along. Wage increases won by the unions at the bargaining tables came on top of the COLAS, fueling inflation. Companies in industries characterized by oligopoly, like auto manufacturing, could usually pass on higher labor costs to consumers. This ability inclined them to buy labor peace through generous contracts to their own unions.

Two powerful unions, the UAW and the United Steel Workers, paved the way for other strong industrial unions. Wages for unionized American industrial workers rose at a much faster rate than those of the workforce as a whole. Moreover, by the early 1970s, many leading American companies had contractually locked themselves into high labor costs, a situation feeding inflation. High labor costs also worked against American products on the international market.

Many argued that labor costs needed to come down for inflation to be checked and the economy strengthened. This meant that companies should force "givebacks" from unions and end labor's ability to limit cost-saving innovations. The new conservative mood in the country, plus organized labor's vulnerability, encouraged management in many industries to go on the offensive. Since the 1970s, relations between corporations and organized labor in the United States have been markedly more adversarial than in other advanced nations. By the end of the decade, organized labor was reeling from union busting, "give-back contracts," and shrinking membership. Even the once mighty UAW gave up substantial concessions to obtain job security. The impressive political and economic muscle organized labor had flexed in the postwar decades had atrophied.

Largely unnoticed by pundits and public, organized labor had been losing membership as a percentage of the workforce for over two decades. In 1953, at its peak, a third of the nonagricultural workforce belonged to unions. This figure dropped below 20 percent by 1980. (In 2007 only 12 percent of the workforce belonged to unions and as few as 7.5 percent of these came from the private sector.) Moreover, the nature of union membership had altered greatly. Membership in the powerful industrial unions declined due to job losses in industry caused by automation and foreign competition or multi-national companies transferring production to nations with a cheaper labor supply. As the pool of industrial workers dwindled, existing unions reached out to organize other sectors of the economy. This included the public sector, as well as airline pilots and well-paid athletes. By 1980 nearly two-fifths of all union members worked in the public sector. Industrial unions thus ended the 1970s ill-prepared to fend off management's efforts to downsize the workforce and cut back on wages and benefits.[6]

Widespread dissatisfaction with union leadership contributed to sagging membership. The entry of baby boomers into the workforce in the late 1960s and early 1970s triggered what Walter Wriston, CEO of Citicorp, described as a movement from "the willing worker to the questioning worker." One of the most publicized labor conflicts of the 1970s involved a wildcat strike in the Lordstown, Ohio, plant of General Motors. Young Lordstown workers, with an average age of twenty-four, struck without union authorization in 1973 to protest not low pay or hazardous conditions but the alienation of the assembly line and a hierarchical corporate bureaucracy. The Lordstown plant, which had been built only a few years earlier, boasted the world's fastest assembly line. Workers, who had forty seconds to complete their job on each moving auto, were being pressed to speed up the operations. The strikers complained that this resulted in shoddy work. But the wildcat strike soon raised broader issues, of how management would deal with baby boomer workers who demanded greater say in how a job should be done.

A General Motors vice president angrily complained that among younger workers "the traditional motivations of job security, money rewards, and even opportunities of personal advancement are proving insufficient." Workers needed to be reminded, one corporate executive lectured a journalist, "that a job is the most important thing they can have." If American workers were spoiled by affluence and "no longer could cut the mustard," then, some argued, applying the lash of economic adversity and job insecurity would return discipline to the workplace. Popular country music singer Donald Lytle, or "Johnny Paycheck," advised employers in 1978: "Take This Job and Shove It." A decade later the singer Rodney Lay captured a more subdued mood in "I Wish I Had a Job to Shove."[7]

DOUBTS AND DEREGULATION

Many businesspeople criticized government regulatory behavior as excessive and costly. A 1975 study by the liberal Brookings Institution estimated that safety and environmental standards enacted since 1965 had diminished annual productivity by nearly 1.5 percent, a loss that fueled inflation and cut in half the projected productivity gain for 1974. A citizen concerned about escalating prices could learn from a follow-up Brookings study in 1977 that the costs of regulations added an estimated 5 percent to the price of most articles purchased. Simply adding antipollution devices raised automobile prices by some $700, and drivers paid an extra $200 annually for the required no-lead gasoline.

But there also were immeasurable costs. Businesspeople and conservative economists believed that excessive regulatory requirements discouraged innovation and business expansion. One businessman compared himself to Jonathan Swift's fictional Gulliver, who awoke to find himself pinned to the ground by hundreds of six-inch-tall Lilliputians—in the businessman's case, government regulators, lawyers, and insurance companies. He complained that the Equal Economic Opportunity Commission scrutinized his personnel records, the Occupation Safety and Health Administration was watchdog of his factory floor, and the Environmental Protection Agency claimed responsibility for almost everything else.

OSHA alone mandated over 2,100 regulations, including specifications for the shape of toilet seats and even the height of toilet paper dispensers, as well as more understandable rules for the handling of inflammable liquids. And not only had the newer cross-industry regulations experienced criticism. Studies of traditionally regulated industries regarded as essential services or "natural monopolies" (airlines and telephones) concluded that the lack of competition, combined with bureaucratic red tape, usually resulted in poor services at high prices. Free-market enthusiasts often found themselves allied with radicals in advocating deregulation, the latter having concluded that single-industry regulatory agencies largely served the interests of corporate America. Insulated from competition, regulated industries had little reason to lower costs or innovate but instead concentrated on influencing their regulators to make favorable decisions.[8]

Even consumer advocates Mark Green and Ralph Nader defended recently enacted automobile safety standards by pointing to regulatory abuses. "Where is the free enterprise system?" they asked. "Is the oil oligopoly, protected by import quotas? The securities market, that bastion of capitalism operating on fixed commissions, and now provided with socialized insurance. . . . Businessmen are the true radicals in this country. They are taking us deeper and deeper into corporate socialism—corporate power using governmental powers to protect it from competition."[9] Deregulation, a term formerly used mainly by a handful of economists and academicians, entered everyday parlance in the 1970s.

As the debate over the reasons for the economy's problems continued throughout the 1970s, so did high inflation and unemployment. When the economy became the major issue in the 1976 elections, Jimmy Carter's campaign strategists devised a clever little gimmick they termed the "discomfort index." To compute the index, Carter simply added the percentage of unemployed in the workforce to the annual increase in the cost of living. Thus in 1975 the "discomfort index" stood at nearly 16 percent. Dissatisfaction with the statistics behind the "discomfort index" contributed greatly to Carter's slim victory. (Four years later the discomfort index proved to be an embarrassment, as Republicans gleefully reported the 1980 index as being over 20 percent.)

CARTER AND THE POLITICS OF LOWERED EXPECTATIONS

Jimmy Carter took office in January 1977 with reducing unemployment as a priority, and he succeeded in bringing the jobless rate down to 5.8 percent by early 1979. But Carter, as had Ford, confronted an economy that offered only a choice between a rock and a hard place. Fighting unemployment heightened inflation; consumer prices climbed by 6.8 percent in 1977 and by 9 percent in 1978. A Democratic-controlled Congress in 1978 passed the Humphrey-Hawkins Act, which charged the Federal Reserve System with maintaining both low inflation and high unemployment but offered little in the way of useful instruction on how to achieve these goals. By now Carter must have felt like Harry Truman, who, frustrated by hedging advisers, once said that what he needed was a one-armed economist, who would be unable to say, "On the one hand this, on the other hand that." In 1979, under the impact of an oil crisis triggered by the revolution in Iran, inflation rose to 13.3 percent. Foreign governments and investors warned of a collapse in the value of the dollar. Curbing inflation now became Carter's overriding domestic priority, and that July he named Paul A. Volcker to be chair of the Federal Reserve Board to lead the fight.[10]

In October of 1979, Volcker began to reduce the money supply, an approach he termed "operational monetarism." The discount rate—the rate at which banks borrow from the Federal Reserve—was raised a full percentage point to a record 12 percent. Volcker's strict controls forced interest rates to an astronomical 20 percent, slowing the pace of inflation but also throwing the economy into deep recession. Businesses and consumers could not afford to borrow. The brakes had applied to an economy already in recession. The jobless rate rose to 7.8 percent by summer 1980, and, although the recession eased in late August, the turnaround came too late to help Carter win reelection. Despite the fact that unemployment stood at 7.4 percent when he left office, economists continued to regard inflation as the battle that needed to be won. Most everyone else thought so too.

How critical was the situation at the end of the 1970s? A 1981 analysis by John Palmer and Isabel V. Sawhill of the Urban Institute compared the decade to its predecessors, reporting that inflation (as measured by percentage increases in the Consumer Price Index) had risen 20 percent in the 1950s, 31 percent in the 1960s, and 112 percent in the 1970s. By the same token, unemployment also ran higher in the 1970s, averaging 6.2 percent, as compared to 4.8 percent in the 1950s and 4.5 percent in the 1960s. These figures demonstrate the undeniable economic hardships of the decade. But what of long-range consequences? Here we need to look at statistics on economic growth and productivity.[11]

The rate of real economic growth in the 1970s was a third slower than in the 1960s, adjusted for inflation; the GDP rose 49 percent in the 1960s and 36 percent in the 1970s. Moreover, America's performance had declined relative to other industrial nations. The great advantages enjoyed by American industry and economy in the first two postwar decades had been all but erased. A widespread sense of a deteriorating economy led many to think that the United States was in a long-term, perhaps permanent, decline.

The *Harvard Business Review* of July 1980 published an article entitled "Managing Our Way to Economic Decline." The first paragraph bluntly stated: "During the past several years American business has experienced a marked deterioration of competitive vigor and a growing uneasiness about its economic well-being." According to the article, the most troubling fact of all was that gains in productivity (measured as output per hour in the private business sector) had slowed dramatically in the 1970s. Productivity had risen during the 1970s, but at a rate of little more than 1 percent a year, while in the previous two decades the yearly average had been almost 3 percent.[12]

The decline in the increase of productivity cannot be measured solely against a historical yardstick. During the 1970s most advanced industrial nations increased productivity at a higher rate than the United States. Japan, for example, averaged an annual 4 percent. American workers still outproduced all others, but the difference had narrowed. This decline continued well into the 1980s. According to the Bureau of Labor Statistics, U.S. productivity increased only 50 percent between 1960 and 1990; Germany's doubled for the same period, and Japan's rose a remarkable 400 percent. During the Carter years and after, economists lectured Americans that only handsome increases in productivity would allow for real wage gains without feeding inflation or damaging America's international trade standing.

Several factors explain America's slowdown in productivity in the 1970s. A prime culprit was high inflation, which pushed interest rates skyward and thus discouraged capital investments. Highly competitive Japanese and European firms, often with more up-to-date equipment, made major inroads into the American market. With declining profits and slow domestic growth, American manufacturing firms often allowed their plants and machinery to deteriorate. The Midwest, with its older smokestack industries, began to be referred to as the Rust Belt. Another explanation for America's failure to invest adequately in new plants and equipment was that, unlike other nations such as Japan, the United States did not experience a labor shortage in the 1970s. American firms found it cheaper to hire more workers than to invest in new equipment or find new ways of doing things.

Those born in the baby boom years of 1945 to 1960 became employable in the 1970s, while the women's movement—and economic pressure—combined to cause mothers of young children to enter the workforce in record numbers. In 1960 around 30 percent of women with school-age children worked; by 1980 the figure had risen to nearly two-thirds. And as the divorce rate rose rapidly (along with the number of children born out of wedlock), many women could no longer afford to remain at home. An increasing number of women raising children in single-parent households had to work to earn their family's bread. One reason American employers felt free to hire is that they, unlike their counterparts in most other nations, felt free to fire without the need to worry about laws protecting the workforce.

The good news of the 1970s was the great number of jobs created; the bad news was that most occurred in the low-paying service areas of the economy. The workforce increased by 27 percent in the 1970s as compared to 11 percent in the 1960s, but this was balanced by a higher unemployment rate. The large increase in the workforce, then, reflected social and demographic factors more than it did the economy's health. (New entries by women and the young accounted for a large part of the increase in unemployment statistics in the 1970s, as well as gains in the workforce.) Workforce increase also must be viewed in terms of an important shift in employment in the sectors of the economy (namely the movement away from manufacturing and toward service activities), as well as the changing role of women and minorities in the labor force. Moreover, the enlarged labor pool available to management in the 1970s contributed to the decline in real wages experienced by unskilled workers.

Changing employment opportunities reflected these ongoing structural changes in the nature of the American economy, as the service sector gained at the expense of manufacturing. Between 1940 and 1980, employment in service occupations grew from 46 percent of total employment to 82 percent. Manufacturing jobs declined both in absolute numbers and as a percentage of total employment. There were reasons, of course, for this development.

Competition from countries with low labor costs forced American firms producing consumer goods into retreat, even as the revived industries of Western Europe and Japan battled American manufacturers for a whole new range of electronic consumer goods. The shrinkage of industrial employment meant the loss of many well-paid union jobs, while the jobs created often involved, or so many feared, flipping hamburgers at fast-food franchises. A large percentage of women and minorities who entered (or reentered) the workforce in the 1970s found themselves in jobs that offered little potential for advancement—despite the fact that the Equal Economic Opportunity Commission (EEOC) was authorized to prohibit discrimination on the basis of race, gender, nationality, or religion.

Throughout the 1970s, the EEOC sought to enforce affirmative action. The number of women and blacks and other designated minorities employed by larger corporations in middle management did rise in the 1970s, but many complained that corporations tended to place affirmative action recruits into "velvet ghettos." Minorities and women so ghettoized would be assigned low-risk, low-prestige positions in human relations, public affairs, and other staff positions, limiting their opportunities to rise within the corporate hierarchy to higher positions of real influence and power. Subverting the spirit of the law, many bean-counting corporations focused on having the "right" number of blacks and women rather than truly creating opportunity. (Even in the 1990s executives of the oil company Texaco were secretly taped talking of African American employees as "black jelly beans.")

SLICES OF THE PIE

Calling for economic growth in 1961, John F. Kennedy had once remarked famously, "A rising tide lifts all ships." Enlarging the economic pie to provide a greater slice for all has been the preferred American way of ensuring general progress without risking painful social conflict over redistributing income. In the late 1970s, for the first time since the Great Depression, social commentators worried about the future of a society whose culture encouraged optimism and promoted consumerism amid a reality of little or no economic growth. Despite Johnson's Great Society programs to improve the circumstances of the less fortunate, the gulf between rich and poor widened after 1972, and the identification of the Democratic Party's liberal wing with high taxes to finance programs for poor Americans largely explained the party's weakness in presidential elections after 1968.

To most Americans, the important economic question was simply this: Will I have more or less money to pay the bills and buy something extra? It turned out that many indeed had less money but bought the extras anyway.

Personal indebtedness rose rapidly as the average worker experienced a decrease in real wages. Per capita weekly income in constant dollars (with 1977 used for the index) fell from $187 in 1970 to $173 in 1980, and only the increase in two-paycheck families due to mothers of school-age children entering the workforce allowed real family income to rise. By 1979, working wives living with spouses accounted for 24 percent of their household's income; their paychecks often permitted a family to pay the bills and perhaps enjoy a few luxuries.

In 1963, the long-retired Alfred Sloan confidently stated in *My Years with General Motors* that his company "could hardly be imagined to exist anywhere but in this country, with its very active and enterprising people; its resources, including its science and technology and its business and industrial know-how."[13] Ten years later, his less-confident successor at General Motors warned that the American people had lost confidence in government, big business, and even the work ethic. Vietnam and Watergate eroded traditional values and respect for authority, and the economic problems of the 1970s undermined habits of saving as well as confidence about the future. High inflation taught a generation that it was more rational to borrow and spend than to save money that in time would only lose value. By the end of the decade, nearly two-thirds of the population feared a future of declining living standards. Matters only became worse when a revolution in Iran in 1979 overthrew a friendly government and replaced it with one that banned oil shipments to the United States. As oil prices skyrocketed, a crowd stormed the U.S. embassy in Teheran and held its staff hostage for 444 days.

A TIME OF LIMITS

As Americans endured an oil shortage and rising prices at the gas pumps, Carter's popularity rating, as measured by polls, plummeted to a distressing 26 percent. He reacted by withdrawing to the presidential retreat at Camp David for ten days and then, on July 15, 1979, delivering a remarkably doleful and demoralizing television address known as the "malaise speech." In it Carter complained of a "crisis of confidence" striking "at the very heart and soul of our national will." Carter announced that he was lifting controls imposed earlier on domestic crude oil and would ask Congress for a tax on any windfall profits that would result.

In stern terms, Carter then declared that Americans would have to change their living and working habits and that they must be prepared to be colder in the winter and warmer in the summer, to drive less and in smaller cars while paying more for oil.[14] Carter and many others accepted that oil as a scarce commodity would eventually run out and that its price must accordingly rise over time.

Indeed, a continuing theme of the 1970s was that industrial economies relied upon a finite supply of natural resources and might very soon experience a crisis. Some scholars believed that industrial economies did face immediate shortages and higher commodity prices for essential raw materials (often obtained from Third World nations of uncertain political reliability), leading to "zero growth" and an "age of limits."[15] Actively pursuing a national energy policy based on conservation, Carter became identified with views most Americans dismissed as the counsel of gloom and doom and urged the nation to learn to live with narrowing expectations. In what turned out to be a serious political blunder, Carter in his April 5 talk called on Americans for sacrifices necessary to survive in a world of limited natural resources.

At the president's request, the State Department undertook a study, published in 1980 as the *Global 2000 Report*, which predicted that the world would be more polluted and crowded in 2000 and more vulnerable to disruptions unless the United States and other nations acted to deter these developments.[16] Carter would soon learn that Americans prefer leaders who project optimism.

American business at the beginning of the 1960s had "stood tall at home and abroad." But twenty years later Americans had to measure their performance against others, and for the first time in the twentieth century, American business needed to worry seriously about foreign penetration of its home markets. After 1971 the United States consistently purchased more manufactured goods from abroad than it sold.

In the 1970s, Third World producers of raw materials gained leverage over the pricing of their resources. All the nations of the industrial world experienced some instability and declining growth. Other advanced economies, however, handled the situation better than did the United States: both the federal government and American business leaders had failed to provide the leadership required by the times.

Conservative economic thinking started to come into fashion in the second half of the 1970s, along with a substantial shift in the political mood. Well-funded think tanks such as the Hoover Institute and American Heritage became centers of intellectual conservatism. They faulted a heavy-handed federal bureaucracy for the economy's problems. Research reports proliferated on such issues as the effect of taxation on personal motivation and governmental restrictions on business innovation and on how social problems created by the crumbling of traditional institutions affected the workforce. Led by Ronald Reagan, the right wing of the Republican Party aggressively challenged the New Deal's public philosophy of the "interventionist state." As the elements of the coalition that had made the Democratic Party the majority party since 1932 (in elective offices, party identification, and voting patterns in both local and national elections) unraveled in the 1970s, pundits speculated on whether a political realignment had occurred, with the Republicans the nation's new dominant party.

The poor performance of American business generated considerable anxiety. Business leaders could not, of course, be held directly responsible for the inflation and rising national debt of the late 1970s; instead, criticism tended to focus on a lack of capital investment and a related slowdown in labor productivity, measured as output per unit of labor. A ratcheting down of business profits depressed stock prices throughout the 1970s and, along with high interest rates for loans, discouraged capital investment ("the engine of the economy"). In 1982, MIT economist Lester Thurow reported that few companies had much cash to spend, and that those with money preferred mergers and acquisitions to investing in new plants and equipment.

Wary of a recession and worried about profitability, a wide variety of corporations cut spending on research and development. By the end of the Carter presidency, the percentage of national income invested in research and development, not including military research, was nearly identical for Western Europe, Japan, and the United States. An analyst in 1980 expressed concern that American business failed to sufficiently plan for the future. America had moved rapidly from a "nuts and bolts" economy to one centered on the less tangible commodities of money and information. Manufacturing industries declined, and some products born and bred in the United States—phonographs, radios, television—virtually ceased to be made in America. Even businessmen referred to manufacturing as "the forgotten industry."

A dramatic example of America's industrial downturn in the 1970s is provided by Detroit. The Big Three automakers—General Motors, Ford, and Chrysler—had grown wealthy in the 1950s and 1960s by selling big expensive cars to Americans who were then persuaded to pay extra for add-ons. Along the way the Big Three had misplaced their concern for quality and even safety. Detroit's guiding precept was that "$10 worth of chrome did more for sales than $100 worth of engineering."[17]

In 1965 Ralph Nader published *Unsafe at Any Speed*, a damning indictment of General Motors' Corvair model, claiming that the car's defective suspension system could cause loss of control during turns.[18] By 1970, 10 percent of the cars driven in the United States were foreign imports, with the small and inexpensive Volkswagen Beetle by far the best-selling foreign car. Detroit, nonetheless, preferred to continue to produce large cars with high profit margins. As the price of gasoline soared throughout the 1970s, Americans in increasing numbers bought inexpensive and well-made Japanese compact cars that used gas efficiently. By 1980, 30 percent of American auto sales were imports. A bankrupt Chrysler needed a federal bailout to survive, and Detroit was begging the federal government to impose a quota on Japanese imports.[19]

Detroit's story was not unique. Americans, since very early in the nineteenth century, had pioneered in producing standardized goods in huge volumes. This was indeed the profitable hallmark of America's manufacturing giants in the 1960s. Now, in the late 1970s, some large manufacturers worried that their markets were becoming increasingly segmented ("niched"); customers tired quickly of products and styles and sought novelties to express their own tastes and personalities. This market segmentation threatened to erode the comfortable profits that came from manufacturing products by traditional high-volume, assembly-line production methods. Its reputation for high-quality production plummeting, American industry needed to adopt more flexible and sophisticated methods required by the segmenting of the market; but American manufacturers frequently responded slowly and ineffectively to the technological forces reshaping production.

The hierarchical management style that had been so effective in mass production often proved unwieldy in meeting the growing demand for segmented production. In the 1970s the foreign challenge was essentially limited to manufacturing and not significantly to research or distribution. Nevertheless, American industrial giants often found themselves reduced to the role of followers of foreign competitors, especially the Japanese, who often copied (with cultural adaptations) earlier American examples.

GLOBAL COMPETITION

Americans had long regarded their way of doing business as special. They identified "American exceptionalism" with free enterprise, believing American entrepreneurs more innovative than businessmen elsewhere. Business, after all, had long been the genius of America, and Washington had actively crusaded to export the American economic system throughout the world. By the late 1970s, however, America's ideological message sold better than American products, and the country had perhaps become more adept at fighting the Cold War than in waging economic warfare. Industrial America —including the auto, steel, electronics, and machine tool industries—lost market share and profits to the Japanese, the Germans, and other rivals. Productivity growth declined to a 1 percent annual rate as concern grew that the United States had fallen into a long-term decline. From world leader, the United States was now in a horse race that some believed it would lose.

Postwar students of the corporation had believed that the leading firms with competent management could endure figuratively forever. Longevity was an accepted goal of management. But many corporate giants would not survive the coming decade. A short attention span and a tendency to manipulate assets rather than provide capital investment to improve plants or product lines were increasingly seen as weaknesses of American corporate management in the late 1970s. Henry Thoreau's observation in *Walden,* that "one generation abandons the enterprises of another like stranded vessels bleaching on a beach," now seemed apropos of companies deemed only a short time earlier to be as solid as the Rock of Gibraltar.

Previously esteemed as the "motive force of American progress," large corporations were scrutinized in the 1980s for easy pickings by "corporate raiders." Adding insult to injury, raiders boasted of returning the economy to health by eliminating stale management and injecting a fresh and much-needed entrepreneurial energy. Disgruntled stockholders, unhappy with the performance of their shares in the 1970s and early 1980s, were often eager for runs on their own companies. One raider, Carl Icahn, spoke contemptuously of the lack of managerial talent and the strangling bureaucracy that existed in most of corporate America. Many of the CEOs of the 1970s had been trained in the gray-flannel days of the 1950s and 1960s, when corporate routines were relatively fixed and a hierarchical style of leadership was expected. At a time of challenge, a more charismatic and personal style of business leadership seemed necessary. By the late 1970s, such influential management experts as Peter Drucker and Warren Benis urged corporations to abandon the standard "command and control" corporate structure for a more interactive leadership and organization.

However, Thomas J. Peters and Robert H. Waterman's widely read 1982

In Search of Excellence still celebrated the traditional big company. As Peters later wrote, "We implicitly endorsed humungous American technocratic enterprise in general—the institutions that John Kenneth Galbraith and business historian Alfred Chandler had not so long before declared almost perfect institutions for achieving America's manifest destiny. Bob Waterman and I, who came of age in the '50s and '60s, were Galbraith's and Chandler's children."[20] *In Search of Excellence* sold over 5 million copies and became the decade's most influential business book. Two years after its publication, however, several of the forty-three companies the two authors had designated as "excellent" were struggling. In 1988, Tom Peters, in *Thriving on Chaos*, no longer thought big was beautiful.[21]

Calls to break corporate inertia grew, as the nation, still suffering stagflation, yearned for rejuvenation. Ronald Reagan rhetorically asked Americans in the campaign of 1980: "Are you better off than you were four years ago?" An insecure America responded by voting into office the most conservative president in half a century. For the first time since the Great Depression, most Americans had ended a decade perhaps poorer and certainly less confident than they had started it.

In retrospect, it is evident that pessimism over the economy of the 1970s was excessive. Many of the problems of the 1970s related to the structural change from an industrial base to a postindustrial or service-oriented economy. Often overlooked in accounts of the decade are important advances in the fields of electronics and information technology that only had major impact in the following decade. In short, to examine a time period, in this case some ten years, without placing it fully in the context of later events invariably leads to an incomplete account. Nevertheless, what is distinctive about the 1970s is an economic anxiety matched in recent history only by the Great Depression. This mood of malaise had consequences in pushing both economic and political thinking in a more conservative direction. Of perhaps greater significance, however, is that during the 1970s the disparities in wealth and income among Americans, which had been lessening since 1928, widened perceptibly.

CHAPTER FOURTEEN

Restructuring and Rebirth, 1980s

Greed will save America.—GORDON GEKKO
(Michael Douglas), in Wall Street *(1988)*

With high inflation and a faltering economy, the 1980s began on a shaky note. Dissatisfied Americans soon elected a president who promised to return the nation to economic preeminence. Much would be heard of new companies, such as Microsoft, Apple, and CNN. Americans soon learned such new terms as "leveraged buyout" (a purchase made with borrowed money that is secured by the assets of the company bought) and "hostile takeover" (a takeover against the wishes of the target company's management and board of directors). Nearly half of all big U.S. companies received a takeover offer in the decade as Wall Street called the shots for corporate reorganization. A new era in American business opened—the Cold War ground to a halt and CEOs were exhorted to provide innovative leadership for global competition. In 1990 Harvard Business School's Michael Jensen and Kevin Murphy of the University of Southern California urged greater incentives for CEOs to be entrepreneurial. Noting that "corporate America pays its most important leaders like bureaucrats," he asked, "Is it any wonder, then that so many CEO's act like bureaucrats?"[1]

A CALL FOR CHANGE

On the unseasonably springlike morning of January 20, 1981, Ronald Reagan delivered his inaugural address to the guests and dignitaries assembled on Capitol Hill. In a confident voice, he asserted: "In this present crisis government is not the solution to our problem; government is the problem." Reagan arrived in office with a straightforward agenda: to pry the federal government off the backs of the public and the business community. The new president's election campaign had trumpeted a philosophy of a strong military, a scaled-back federal government, and, not least, a return to traditional values.

Reagan sought to reverse the rise of the "positive state" with its strong governmental role. "Our aim," he proclaimed in his inaugural address, "is to increase national wealth so all will have more, not just redistribute what we have, which is just a sharing of scarcity." By the time Reagan concluded his presidency in January 1989, faith in federal programs as the master key to handling social and economic problems had received serious challenge.

A new president traditionally selects a predecessor's portrait to hang in the Cabinet Room of the White House; Reagan selected Calvin Coolidge, who had joked that the presidency was the easiest job he had ever held. Despite an undergraduate major in the subject, Reagan knew little about economics. Neither, of course, did most of his predecessors, but the supremely self-assured Reagan felt little need to learn more. David Stockman, Reagan's first director of the Office of Management and Budget, later wrote that the president dozed at budget meetings, relying on advisers and his intuition, while rarely looking at the figures placed before him. His focus was the broad picture, the sharp reversal of a fifty-year drift toward a welfare state. Big government had to be rolled back, individual and corporate taxes had to be slashed, social programs had to be cut, industries had to be deregulated, the budget had to be balanced, and the role of state governments had to be strengthened. But Reagan also believed that a Soviet military buildup in the 1970s required vast new American defense expenditures. In many ways, the Reagan years would be an era of striking contradictions. More, not less, federal spending occurred during his presidency, as the national debt tripled.

SUPPLY-SIDE ECONOMICS

The new president quickly announced a bold program of "supply-side" economics, a term economists use broadly for any policy seeking to increase the economy's capacity to produce. Reagan and his advisers employed it more specifically. They believed that excessive taxation had discouraged hard work and left inadequate capital available to investors. Slashing taxes on the wealthy would stimulate investments since they would invest this windfall. The benefits of a robust economy would in time "trickle down." Opponents derided his ideas as simplistic, "voodoo economics," or "Reaganomics."[2]

As a fiscal conservative, Reagan intended to balance the budget. But how could this be done while cutting taxes? Here again his advisers offered a simple solution. They claimed that the "Laffer Curve" demonstrated that lowered tax rates would more than pay for themselves by stimulating growth. Increased growth would return greater tax revenues, even at the lower rates. For the short term, however, loss in federal revenue resulting from a tax cut could be matched by cutting government spending. White House advisers even promised a balanced federal budget as early as 1984.[3]

The Economic Recovery Tax of 1981 gave individuals in the highest tax brackets a 23 percent cut over three years, and the rate on capital gains (the profit from investments) declined from 28 percent to 20 percent. Most important, the new law indexed yearly income for inflation, meaning that Washington would no longer collect an "inflation creep." However, the new tax law had barely been signed before Congress voted tax increases to offset lost revenue. Social Security taxes were also raised substantially in 1983 in an effort to put the shaky retirement system back on sound footing. But the tax system in the mid-1980s provided loopholes that allowed many of the nation's largest corporations (and wealthiest individuals) to avoid paying any taxes. Dissatisfaction with such inequities led to the Tax Reform Act of 1986, the most comprehensive overhaul of the country's tax structure since World War II.

The Reagan administration had inherited Federal Reserve chairman Paul Volcker's tight money policy, with the prime rate reaching an astonishing 21 percent in late 1980. The economy responded with a deep recession. Inflation dropped from 12.4 percent in 1980 to 4 percent in 1982, and unemployment in that year reached 10.7 percent—higher than in any year since 1940. Fortunately, the recession proved short lived, but, more important, the inflationary fever had been broken. Business expansion occurred in 1983 without reigniting inflation. After fifteen years, stagflation had finally ended. Unfortunately, not all benefited from "recovery." Real wages for ordinary workers showed little improvement. Nor could their unions help. In 1982 Reagan fired air traffic controllers (members of the Professional Air Traffic Controllers Organization [PATCO]) for violating a law prohibiting federal workers from striking. A weakened labor movement faced with a hostile

White House and fearing corporate downsizing showed greater concern for staving off demands for givebacks than for gaining wage increases. How one viewed this development depended on perspective and self-interest. Weak unions often make for flexibility and rapid growth in productivity. However, weak unions also squeeze wages at the bottom, worsen inequality, and create economic insecurity.

The economy's turnaround assured Reagan's reelection. In 1984 real GDP growth reached 6.8 percent—the highest growth for a single year since 1951. Democratic critics complained that the so-called Reagan prosperity represented only an illusion based on "borrowed time and borrowed money" due to federal deficit spending. However, Reagan offered hope for better times as he extolled the virtues of a free market and downsized government.

MORNING IN AMERICA

Republican campaign ads in 1984, "It's Morning in America," highlighted the theme of renewal. But Reagan's policies had produced mixed results. Mushrooming defense budgets had contributed greatly to domestic prosperity but had increased the annual deficit and the national debt. Nevertheless, Reagan presided after 1982 over an economy blessed by high employment, stable prices, and one of the great bull market runs of modern times. Moreover, he had come to office at a time when the United States had fallen behind in the Cold War. The Soviets had invaded Afghanistan, financed Cuban troops in Angola, and assisted Marxist governments in Nicaragua and Ethiopia. But Reagan's second term would see the Soviets showing signs of internal collapse as the Cold War entered its final stage.

Reagan had planned to cut nondefense federal spending. This proved difficult. Apart from defense, the federal budget consisted primarily of entitlement programs such as Social Security and Medicare that could not be easily cut. Thus massive defense spending between 1982 and 1986 overwhelmed reductions elsewhere. Federal government borrowing forced interest rates upward. High interest rates attracted billions of dollars from overseas, and the dollar skyrocketed over 50 percent in value, making U.S. business uncompetitive abroad. In 1984 the United States became a debtor nation for the first time since 1915. The rapid growth during the 1980s of foreign ownership of American companies and real estate spurred highly exaggerated and widespread concern that the nation had lost control of its economic destiny.

In 1990 a "Wall Streeter" described the Reagan years to a reporter as "a dirty decade. . . . All [Wall] Street misbehavior was to the 1980's what bootlegging was to the 20s—the crime that defined the era."[4] Inflation and declining business earnings severely depressed stock prices in the 1970s. By the early 1980s stock prices registered far below the book value of tangible corporate assets, such as real estate, buildings, and machinery. Furthermore, high start-up costs for a new business now reflected the long inflationary run-up after 1973. Companies with cash to spend preferred to engage in mergers and acquisitions rather than investing in new plants and equipment. Depressed corporate assets attracted bargain hunters, triggering the fourth major merger movement in American history. It would differ from the others, however, in the large number of hostile takeovers.[5]

The intent of some threatened takeovers was simply for the raider in question to be paid off to go away. Carl Icahn, the product of a tough working-class Detroit neighborhood, made more than $100 million by accumulating enough stock in a company to become a nuisance, then allowing himself to be bought out by a corporate board. This practice, known as "green-mail," was used by Icahn on such companies as Phillips Petroleum, Marshall Field's, and Hammermill Paper. In 1985, Icahn acquired Trans World Airlines in a hostile takeover and then broke its union before running the airline into bankruptcy. Bold raiders, who made money but often left the wreckage of a company in their wake, exemplified the aggressive side of capitalism. The consequences to corporate America of their fox-in-the-henhouse antics remain uncertain and controversial. Was it a healthy stimulus for change or a destructive onslaught on worthwhile companies?

The apparent prosperity of the 1980s concealed a strikingly schizophrenic quality in American life. The Republican political analyst Kevin Phillips, noting its excesses, called the decade a second Gilded Age. Others quoted Charles Dickens's famous opening line in *A Tale of Two Cities*: "It was the best of times; it was the worst of times." The rich certainly got richer, but, notwithstanding Reagan's touted trickle-down effect, the poor became poorer and the middle class went nowhere in particular. According to the Congressional Budget Office, the richest 20 percent of families gained almost 100 percent of the 1980s' growth in average family income—because the bottom 40 percent continued to lose ground; the remaining 40 percent of Americans, at best, barely recouped the previous decade's losses in real wages. Frequently, families experienced gains in living standards only because a working wife compensated for the husband's decline in real wages.[6]

Even many among the decade's winners expressed concern about America's weakening position in the global economy as Japan's sun continued to rise. Much of the decade's affluence resulted from Americans spending instead of saving. The host of the popular television program *Lifestyles of the Rich and Famous* signed off by wishing his audience "champagne wishes and caviar dreams." Some deep thinkers pasted stickers on their car bumpers with the words "He who dies with the most toys wins," provoking the retort "If you die with the most toys, you're still dead." Financier Ivan Boesky told a graduating class at the University of California at Berkeley School of Business in 1986: "I think greed is healthy. You can be greedy and still feel good about yourself." Shortly after, Boesky received jail time and paid a $100 million penalty for illegal insider trading—after implicating others to lighten his sentence.

Self-serving behavior became the basis for the proliferation of jokes about yuppies (young urban professionals) and their status cars and expensive watches. Juliet Schor suggested, in *The Overspent American*, that sometime in the 1980s the national penchant for stylish consumerism ratcheted up into a "national culture of upscale spending." Americans were no longer content to just keep up with the Joneses but were likely to choose as a reference group people whose incomes were three, four, or five times their own. For millions of Americans, a mentality of "shop till you drop" had become an opiate. Pollsters and marketing experts grouped people according to consumption patterns, which (even more than Marx's view of relationships to the means of production) indicated class structure in contemporary America. If money hadn't bought you happiness, according to one joke, you just hadn't shopped at the right stores.[7]

ASCENDANT CONSUMERISM

British literary critic Raymond Williams criticized American consumer culture as one in which "the dominant mode of human perception and interaction is very generally mediated by commodities."[8] Market researchers coined the term "psychographics" to describe their compilation of demographic and psychological characteristics to ascertain or describe a particular market niche. A study commissioned by an ad agency in 1998, "The Nag Factor," even analyzed how children under the age of six badgered parents into buying products they had seen in television commercials.

For too many Americans, shopping had become a quest for meaning and identity. Consumers sought to flaunt, or at least dissimulate, their desired lifestyles by wearing clothes with chic labels on the outside and T-shirts advertising fashionable resorts. As artists, notably Andy Warhol with his Campbell's Soup painting, had recognized, consumerism had become a driving cultural force. Even the museums and concert halls became merchandizing venues as they opened retail stores in malls. The ubiquitous influence of mass consumerism has been described by historian Lizabeth Cohen as the "central defining engine, not simply of the American economy but of its politics and culture as well."[9]

Advertising and "branding strategies" sought to differentiate and give meaning to otherwise interchangeable and frequently unnecessary products. In many product categories, handsomely packaged commodities sold for premium prices as status symbols. Restaurant patrons accustomed to a glass of tap water with ice were now asked if they preferred, at a price, "still" or "sparkling" bottled water. By 1997 the name-brand bottled water industry had catapulted to sales of $3.4 billion annually. Marketing was increasingly about taking the ordinary, everyday product and changing it from something useful into something upscale, at a higher price. It was about creating the illusion of luxury and well-being for the masses, with "aromatherapeutic" household cleaners that supposedly smelled of thyme or coriander.

Market researchers used lifestyle preferences to help identify target markets or to find the customers most likely to switch brands. "Marketers," starting in the 1950s, had categorized census tracts in which various income groups resided. Now they developed techniques of databases and "psychographics" to sort consumers into over forty lifestyle categories, such as "money and brains" or "young affluent suburbia," in order to match products with market segment. Consumers were encouraged to think that tastes in music, art, cars, clothes, and even food were related to social position. In a world of blurring social hierarchies, consumerism became the way to define who you were and what group you wanted to be identified with. A "sophisticated" consumer in Kurt Andersen's 1990s novel *Turn of the Century* drinks "$10.95-a-pound Starbucks coffee" while the clueless make do with the "$7-a-pound Chock Full o' Nuts brand."[10]

Not all consumerism resulted from manipulation of consumers by advertising. Teenagers and young adults often dressed in styles introduced not by commercial houses but by youth in inner-city ghettoes. Merchandisers, however, then acted speedily to co-opt "ghetto wear" for a broad national and even international market. In a similar vein, retail stores employed buyers to anticipate what customers wanted. Frequent sales, however, by retail and discount outlets demonstrated that buyers did not always guess right.

Consumerism, moreover, had its defenders. The economic historian Stanley Lebergott, in *Pursuing Happiness: American Consumers in the Twentieth Century*, asserted that the great American shopping spree represented an essential part of a remarkably successful pursuit of happiness. The masses had been invited to a banquet formerly reserved for an elite.[11]

Not everyone in the 1980s could engage in upscale consumerism. Seemingly overnight, countless numbers of homeless people roamed the streets of American cities. Increased crime made the United States the most dangerous of all developed nations, and American cities sometimes resembled the Third World in their disorder and menace, as the middle class retreated to gated and guarded "communities" on the urban periphery.

WALL STREET: THRIVING ON CHAOS

As the bull market gathered momentum, the Reagan administration showed greater interest in Wall Street than in Skid Row. Corporate takeover raiders and leveraged-buyout firms hunted vulnerable businesses, encircling their prey until weakness signaled the moment to attack. Speculators then swept up the stocks of takeover candidates, setting the stage for a feeding frenzy. Management often sought to deter hostile takeovers by issuing preferred stock or bonds, a technique known as a "poison pill," to make the costs of a takeover prohibitive. In the event that a hostile takeover went through, management frequently provided itself with "golden parachutes" in the form of generous severance pay. The cost of takeovers, or the expense of fighting them off, left many corporations at decade's end deeply in debt, their futures mortgaged and uncertain. Nearly half of all big U.S. corporations received a takeover offer in the 1980s. In 1986 alone, 20 percent of the Fortune 500 corporations disappeared through merger and acquisition.[12]

Critics charged that pursuit of overnight gain had undermined long-term corporate planning. Corporate raiders had overwhelmed traditional managers, who no longer could afford to focus on fundamentals. Management increasingly fixated on next quarter's bottom line and its impact on stock prices. High finance was no longer an activity principally related to financing the operations of industry. Instead, Wall Street provided fiscal stratagems for changes in the ownership of industry to benefit nonproducing raiders and brokers. Proponents of change argued the opposite: that Wall Street's financial churning expressed "the creative destruction" needed for economic growth.

Reagan enthusiastically endorsed the decade's pursuit of wealth. To Reagan, the rich became rich because of virtue and talent. White House advisers came to work wearing green ties decorated with Adam Smith's profile and dollar signs. Knowing what he wanted, Reagan skillfully enacted most of his programs despite a Democratic Congress. Reducing the federal role in the economy was his personal crusade. No other issue, except perhaps tax cuts, received higher priority on Reagan's domestic agenda than shrinking government's regulatory role.

DEREGULATION

Critics of the Civil Aeronautics Board (CAB) had long regarded the agency's policies as contrary to the public interest. Until the 1970s, the CAB regulated fares and routes, while permitting striking differences in regional rates and services. These often resulted from political pressure by underpopulated regions and cities to shape a national system that met their own needs, while shifting the costs to large urban markets with heavily traveled routes. In the 1970s, the airline industry became a test case for those urging the advantages of deregulation.

Industry analysts pointed out that under regulatory rules America's existing airlines lacked incentive to improve. Carriers could only fly routes awarded them by the CAB, an agency that did little to encourage new airlines. However, in the mid-1970s, several ambitious small carriers, with support from consumer groups, launched a campaign for deregulation to facilitate expansion. In 1978, the Airline Deregulation Act weakened the agency, and in 1985 Congress eliminated it. An explosion of entrepreneurial activity reshaped the industry and the way it did business.

Deregulation led to substantial savings for the public. Domestic airfares, adjusted for inflation, declined nearly 40 percent by 2000. Airlines now came and went in an industry where the players changed frequently. One year's record profits often were followed in the next year by disastrous losses. The industry attracted hard-driving and difficult men who could build an airline but often proved to be lackluster managers—men such as Frank Lorenzo, who leveraged tiny Texas International into an empire of Continental Airlines, New York Air, Eastern Airlines, and Peoples Express but then parachuted out before it crashed.

Nearly uncontrolled open entry and pricing freedom soon created an industry rife with contentious labor relations. Competition between rival lines was often cutthroat. Deregulation transformed the airlines from high-priced transport to an inexpensive system for the masses. But passengers complained about poor and even unsafe service as well as bewildering pricing policies. The fundamental problem of the industry has never been solved: too many seats for too few passengers. Critics of deregulation argue that the industry is a natural monopoly and that only governmentally regulated capacity will allow for the long-run return on capital necessary to support the reinvestment requirements of the industry.

The Motor Carrier Act and the companion Staggers Rail Act initiated the deregulation in 1980 of interstate trucking, and the Reagan administration eagerly pushed it along. Truckers and railroads, previously required to provide service over unprofitable routes, could now act freely in terms of their own bottom lines. Some small communities suffered, but deregulation of the industry resulted in substantial savings to shippers. Freight rates (adjusted for inflation) dropped over a third between 1980 and 1993.

In 1982 the Department of Justice finally settled out of court an antitrust suit initiated eight years earlier against the American Telephone and Telegraph Company. Over a million stockholders owned shares in AT&T, the world's largest company. Grandparents gave grandchildren at birth a gift of "Ma Bell," because its stocks retained value and paid regular dividends. With a celebrated research laboratory whose scientists had won more Nobel prizes than any single university, AT&T provided the nation with the world's best telecommunications system in the form of a publicly controlled monopoly. Indeed, as Roland Marchand demonstrated, in *Creating the Corporate Soul*, the company had, at great expense, carefully nurtured for nearly a century, with Madison Avenue's help, the view that the telephone was a "natural monopoly" and thus only a single "universal" system could provide maximum service.[13]

The Justice Department believed otherwise, claiming that AT&T's privileged position impeded progress in a vital industry. AT&T controlled nearly all long-distance service and 80 percent of local telephone service, with high long-distance rates subsidizing low rates on basic local service. The company, government lawyers argued, blocked competition and thus curtailed innovative forces in the expanding area of telecommunications, even as an evolving new technology of cable, microwave relay, and satellites foretold a major change in the structure of the industry. After suffering a series of legal reversals, AT&T agreed in 1982 to the creation of seven new and independent "Baby Bell" companies to provide local service. AT&T, however, retained long-distance operations, its Bell research labs, and the Western Electric subsidiary, which manufactured phones and other equipment. An excellent system had been dissolved in the hope of encouraging rapid innovation in telecommunications. The results proved remarkable. New companies proliferated, long-distance rates dropped, and innovations, such as the cellular phone, the fax machine, and the modem, occurred at breakneck speed.

By 1995, AT&T, vying with MCI and Sprint among other rivals, controlled less than 50 percent of long-distance service—this as the industry under the wide-ranging Telecommunications Act of 1996 continued deregulation. Changing the rules of an entire industry, it allowed free competition in most of the national communications market, including local and long-distance telephone service and television, so that a single company could now provide all of these across the country. In fact, the rules seemed to favor firms that offered the biggest package of services to the largest number of customers, and several Baby Bells immediately merged and entered into the long-distance and cellular fields amid fears that mergers pointed to the rise of new monopolies. In turn, AT&T entered the local telephone market and acquired cable companies, with their coaxial and broadband networks, while spinning off its manufacturing division. Fed by stock market speculation and rapid innovations, the telecommunications industry radically transformed itself during the 1990s. Excessive growth and unreasonable expectations of profit, however, set the stage for a disaster waiting to happen—and it did in 2000.[14]

Deregulation in banking and other financial institutions also brought unforeseen and troubling consequences. The impetus for deregulation of financial institutions had actually developed within the industries themselves. Federally fixed interest rates of 3 percent for savings accounts had led bank depositors in the 1970s, facing runaway inflation, to transfer their money to more attractive forms of holdings. Deregulation in 1981 allowed banks to offer truly competitive interest and loan rates as well as new services and even to branch out across state lines. However, they continued to be part of a system in which losses were underwritten by the government—which continued to insure deposits—while profits accrued to managers and owners.[15]

Savings and loan banks, critics had complained, conducted business according to the "3-6-3" principle (pay 3 percent on passbook savings accounts, charge 6 percent on mortgages, and be at the golf course by 3 in the afternoon). With deregulation, the savings and loan banks, with little to lose, moved recklessly into highly speculative commercial real estate development. A real estate downturn in 1988 brought the savings and loan industry to near collapse, and a quarter of them eventually closed. In August 1989, Congress enacted a bill to bail out the savings and loan industry, establishing the Resolution and Trust Corporation to handle the salvage job. At the same time, deregulation of financial institutions continued apace, as the walls erected by New Deal agencies to separate banking, securities, and insurance industries crumbled.[16]

Deregulation in all industries brought down prices and encouraged competition. This was accompanied by much confusion and hardship to those involved in a deregulated industry. The deregulation process was intensely political and sometimes provided cover for abuse—but, of course, the same can be said for the regulatory process. Certainly, deregulation speeded the restructuring of corporate America in the 1980s. Deregulation provided ambitious risk takers with the opportunity to transform staid industries into exciting new entrepreneurial ways of doing business. It also gave unscrupulous management opportunities for fleecing the public and even their own employees and stockholders. As financier Felix G. Rohatyn complained: "Deregulation became a kind of religion—it was supposed to enable people to get better product or services more competitively. But it doesn't mean wiping out all the protection of consumers to respond to some kind of dogma."[17]

As Reagan left office in January 1989, the uneasy coalition of liberals and conservatives working for deregulation unraveled. With the regulatory deadwood inherited from the past now greatly thinned, some thought the pendulum should swing back, and even George H. W. Bush, Reagan's successor, subscribed to this mood. Bush beefed up regulatory agencies deliberately understaffed by Reagan and supported the passage in 1991 of both the Clean Air Act and the Americans with Disabilities Act. Nevertheless, as the economy picked up momentum in the 1990s, deregulation continued, most notably in the energy, finance, and telecommunications industries. The new information technology and globalization had altered the way financial markets needed to operate, and the regulations that governed them had to be modified to allow rapid change.

Reagan's Department of Justice placed few obstacles in the way of the merger mania of the decade. The Hart-Scott-Rodino Antitrust Improvement Act of 1976 (commonly known as the HSR Act) required companies planning mergers above a specified size to alert the Justice Department and the Federal Trade Commission (FTC) and to provide the two agencies with any information they requested—giving antitrust enforcers great leverage and also much discretion. In the Reagan years, "merger and acquisition activity" almost always received the benefit of the doubt. The United States had gone from being the most vigorous country in antitrust enforcement in the 1960s to one of the least aggressive in the 1980s. Antitrust had become a largely unnoticed issue; it now attracted little public interest, with rare exceptions, like Microsoft in 1998.[18]

There is irony in the fact that an administration that pledged to a vision of a highly competitive market economy downplayed the importance of antitrust action. But the Reagan administration's antitrust policies relied on the work of the Chicago School, led by Robert Bork and Richard Posner. The Chicago School argued that the market, if left alone, would self-correct for monopolistic tendencies and practices to restore competition. This philosophy challenged the then conventional wisdom—sometimes referred to as the "Harvard School"—that large companies commonly employed the practice of pricing below cost to drive out competitors and establish market dominance. Bork's influential 1978 book, *The Antitrust Paradox*, applied neoclassical economic theory emphasizing the determination of prices by market factors of supply and demand to argue that below-cost pricing was actually extremely rare. This was, he argued, because the would-be monopolist who forced competitors out of business by price cutting and then raised his prices would only attract new competitors into the market. Most monopolies accordingly were only temporary, short-lived rewards for superior corporate performance.

Bork reasoned that only through constant innovations and relatively cheap prices could a company sustain a monopoly. And in that case what would be the harm? Accordingly, when courts acted against presumed predatory pricing, they only deprived customers of the benefits of lower prices. Bork concluded that "the only legitimate goal of American antitrust law is the maximization of consumer welfare," not the "survival or comfort of small business." He believed market forces benign and any concern groundless that unless regulated they led to concentration of wealth and monopoly.[19]

With the Reagan presidency, the spirit of laissez-faire reigned—and nowhere more than in the field of antitrust. "Merger mania" characterized the 1980s, and its ultimate impact on American business proved profound. Not since the 1920s had corporate mergers enjoyed such tolerance from Washington.[20]

MERGERS AND ACQUISITIONS

"Doing mergers" was the growth business of the 1980s. Between 1981 and 1988 some 2,000 mergers and leveraged buyouts (LBO) of large firms occurred. In an LBO a public company's shareholders are bought out using the company itself as collateral. Students in prestigious graduate schools of business enrolled in overcrowded courses in investment banking—while courses geared toward training chief financial officers or comptrollers had seats to spare. Investment banks and brokerage firms offered glamour and six-figure starting salaries. Manufacturing companies all but stopped trying to recruit MBAS from prestigious graduate schools into line management positions, turning instead to in-house training and promotion—this, despite the fact that in 1960 some 40 schools graduated fewer than 4,000 MBAS annually— in 1989 over 800 schools produced more than 70,000.

Making it on Wall Street became a rite of passage for graduates of the better colleges, as yuppies became the subject of such movies as *Wall Street*. Among undergraduates, the number of business majors dwarfed those enrolled in either liberal arts, the sciences, or education. In 1986 one out of every ten Yale College graduates applied for a job at First Boston, a leading merger and investment bank.

The stock market's principal function is to provide a means for investors to channel their savings into productive enterprise. In the 1980s companies preferred selling stock to borrowing because they then would not have to repay the money gained. With equity capital cheaper in the high interest decade than borrowed funds, corporate managers could use it (at least in theory) more effectively in planning long-term strategy. Reality, alas, did not correspond to theory.

The Reagan boom of the 1980s, with its raiders, hostile takeovers, and leveraged buyouts, whetted appetites among managers and stockholders for quick annual profits at the 30 percent–plus levels. By the end of the 1990s, corporate management had taken on the values of the raiders. Managers became as rich as the raiders by giving themselves stock-related incentives.

Corporate management quickly learned that survival as well as profit from stock options required an eye to the short term: the Form 10-K (annual reports required by the Securities and Exchange Commission) had to look good.[21] The conventional view of an excellent company as one that lasted forever and performed in a superior way to consistently reward its stockholders over time with better than average returns appeared obsolete. All that mattered was the here and now. Any sign of weakness, such as a drop in the market value of stocks, attracted takeover raiders, who pored over spreadsheet databases looking for undervalued companies to buy—and bust up. Even defeating a takeover bid usually proved financially and emotionally draining. Much of top management's activities in the 1980s involved simply fending off or making acquisitions. Reflecting this, the background of corporate executives was increasingly in law and finance; previously it had been marketing, engineering, and sales.

THE HUMAN FACTOR

Management consultants with backgrounds in Human Resources, as Personnel Departments were now called, expressed another view of the weakness of large corporations. They believed that management tended to ignore the two most important factors of a business: the human element and the product. They often urged the breaking down of the traditional corporate "command and control" structures, discarding organizational charts and thick rule books. An influence on the Human Resources approach was the work of statistician W. Edwards Deming (1900–1993). In the 1930s Deming had studied statistical quality control (SQC) in the manufacturing process under the influence of Walter A. Shewhart of Bell Laboratories. Deming had the opportunity to use this knowledge professionally during World War II when he and other scholars provided a government-sponsored training course for defense plant managers. He concluded that most problems resulted from design flaws, not worker error, and that inspection for flaws after the fact was not the answer. Workers had to be encouraged to use initiative to correct problems as they occurred. During the 1950s, Deming traveled to Japan, where his ideas attracted considerable interest. William M. Tsutsui, however, has suggested in a study of scientific management in Japan that, although Deming made useful suggestions about small-group dynamics and management on the factory floor, he provided little useful guidance to senior executives in how to integrate this new knowledge with such important functions as performance assessment and planning.[22]

In time, Deming's message was distilled down to fourteen points, which became the commandments of the quality movement (for example, "8. Drive Out Fear"; "9. Break Down Barriers Between Staff Offices"). By the end of the 1980s, some dozen books extolled the virtues of "quality circles"—with an emphasis on worker initiative and group cooperation. Ford, Dow Chemical, and Procter and Gamble employed Deming as a consultant, as team building became all the rage in management circles. For the most part, however, American corporations tended to rely on traditional management techniques. It would take more than books to transform American business.[23]

The impetus for radical change arose from accelerating merger and acquisition activity. As noted earlier, the merger movement had started in 1981 for solid reasons. An underpriced stock market offered good buys. Many corporations had understated book assets in the form of real estate, plants, and equipment, their replacement or market value having risen due to inflation. However, depressed stock prices did not reflect this gain. Companies seeking to expand or diversify found it cheaper to merge with or simply acquire undervalued corporations than to start de novo.[24]

When the market after 1982 turned bullish, speculators acquired companies to make a killing on stock gains. Analysts looking at corporations soon realized that, for some companies, the various parts if sold separately—the "breakup value"—had greater value than the company as a whole. A smart corporation or investor could acquire the company with borrowed funds, sell some of its subsidiaries—"de-integration"—to reduce debt, and manage the remainder for a profit. Companies with a clean balance sheet, little debt, and loads of cash strongly warranted the interest of raiders—unless, that is, management actively discouraged them by loading up on debt.

With the Department of Justice looking on benignly, the merger movement swelled as investors searched tirelessly for profit through innovative types of financial activity. Investment bankers and brokerage houses—no longer satisfied with the usual returns made from advising clients and arranging the financing of deals—began to put up their own money to become active participants. An older term, "merchant banking," was redefined to encompass management buyouts, taking equity stakes in takeovers, or making bridge loans to finance takeovers. The scale of change in corporate America was evidenced by the fact that hostile takeovers represented nearly 50 percent of all large mergers by 1990. Even America's largest corporations were not safe from raiders. As a financial journalist noted, "A hostile take-over is raw capitalism where decisions are based on immediate returns to individuals," adding, "maybe there is a need for a kinder, gentler capitalism that has a morality beyond the marketplace."[25]

JUNK BONDS

A quarter of a trillion dollars of so-called junk bonds fueled the takeover spree of the 1980s. Junk bonds, or more precisely high-yield bonds, are the securities of companies too young or too loaded with debt to receive invest-ment grade ratings by rating agencies such as Standard & Poor's. Junk bonds, though not yet named, existed well before the 1980s. Michael Milken, however, demonstrated that junk bonds promising high yields, properly packaged and promoted, would be eagerly purchased by institutions, banks, pension funds, and insurance companies. By creating a market for these securities, Milken made a source of funding available to high-risk businesses that otherwise would have been denied credit.

Milken ingeniously linked the junk bond to the decade's takeover frenzy. The highly creative financier recognized rich possibilities in acquiring trou-bled firms that held undervalued assets. Debts could be used for tax write-offs, and less efficient parts could be sold off. Valuable operations would then be retained, merged, or even sold to form a profitable new entity for "in the know" investors who got in early. One journalist wrote of "companies being cracked open like piggy banks or split up like pizzas." Another compared the wheeling and dealing to the stockyards, where every part of a slaughtered pig but the oink was put to profitable use. Using junk bonds to finance manifold financial operations brought even more profit to the broker.[26]

To his many defenders, Milken was a financial genius. He had single-handedly demonstrated how to use junk bonds to leverage a "restructuring revolution." The bonds supplied the wherewithal for hostile takeovers, lever-aged buyouts, and other debt-financed maneuvers that transformed cor-porations as raiders launched runs on icons of American business. It was claimed that "Milken's magic" had shifted power to shareholders unhappy at low equity returns. Management faced the choice of actively pursuing greater profitability by shaking things up, thus raising share value, or risking losing control. Even Milken's critics have conceded that too many American companies were run by an over-perked, stodgy management indifferent to the shareholder. Now, thanks to Milken and his junk bonds, rapid change was the name of their game. Management learned that they had to play with new rules and perform as entrepreneurs.

Milken's brokerage house, Drexel Burnham Lambert, dominated the junk bond market until his arrest in 1987 for insider trading. Milken had worked with such Wall Street raiders as T. Boone Pickens, Henry Kravis, Ronald Pearlman, Sir James Goldsmith, and Carl Icahn. When Drexel Burnham Lambert declared bankruptcy in February 1990, Wall Street observers knew an era had ended. Sentenced to ten years in jail in 1991, Milken received parole in 1993, still insisting that he had not acted improperly. He had paid over $.5 billion in fines and settlement costs, while retaining a fortune of comparable worth. Arguably not since the days of J. P. Morgan had any financier left so deep a mark on the corporate terrain or stirred such conflicting passions.[27]

Along with the junk bond industry, the 1980s experienced the creation of a market in stock index futures. Stock futures consisted of speculative financial instruments traded in the commodity exchanges of Chicago; futures allowed their buyers to bet on the future up-or-down movements in the stock market without buying or selling the actual stocks. When stock prices fell, large portfolio managers could retain their stocks, selling instead the index futures. Sales of the futures defrayed losses on the underlying stock values, which would be retained in hope of a rise in value.

RESTRUCTURING CORPORATE AMERICA

The full consequence of the restructuring of corporate America provoked by the hostile takeovers and leveraged buyouts unfolded slowly. Critics complained that LBOs and hostile takeover attempts often left companies crippled by debt. The paying off of high corporate debt required some combination of the sale of assets, workforce reductions, and cutbacks in research and development. Many companies failed; others limped along for years. The only obvious and consistent gainers, critics argued, were speculators, lawyers, and brokers. But supporters of restructuring painted a very different picture.

They suggested that the restructuring had revitalized American business, creating a business culture that encouraged and rewarded innovation. America's corporate management (and not only the raided corporations) had been forced to change or to yield to more dynamic successors. The clear message had been sent out: act boldly or lose your job. This often meant restructuring the workforce, breaking up bureaucratic logjams, focusing on core competencies, and shedding peripheral businesses while introducing cost-saving innovations. The decade's most influential business book, *In Search of Excellence*, by Tom Peters and Robert Waterman Jr., instructed businesses to "stick to their knitting"—figure out what they did well and build on it.[28]

Mature companies transferred capital from declining activities to thriving ones and adjusted to technological flux while seeking new opportunities. Executive compensation, especially through stock option incentives, became increasingly tied to Wall Street's performance. According to this reasoning, restructuring, with its emphasis on entrepreneurial and innovative activity, benefited not only the handsomely rewarded CEOs, but stockholders and the economy at large. That companies needed to foster constant innovation became ideas ubiquitously enshrined in management books throughout the 1990s.[29]

Threat of a takeover by corporate raiders was not the only force for change. Business efficiency became an obsession of financial analysts and management in the late 1980s as they scrambled to cut costs. Factory productivity had stalled in the high-inflation, low-growth 1970s, and it had failed to improve in the 1980s. Improving productivity became the ultimate justification for types of behavior that might otherwise have been challenged on moral grounds. A utilitarian hardness increasingly dominated top management's thinking. "We are not in business to conduct moral activity," IBM chairman John Akers declared in 1986. "We are in business to conduct business."[30] National leaders saw gains in productivity as the only way to raise the living standards of Americans and to stem a mounting foreign debt.

THE END OF THE 1980S

The Dow Jones ended the decade 228 percent above where it had stood in 1980. This impressive bull market was not fueled only by merger mania. Much of the decade's high-riding activity was in new tech companies. A company called Microsoft went public in 1986 with shares offered at twenty-six dollars. Microsoft acted as the lead company in a new industry that promised to change the way American business functioned—and even to revolutionize daily life as dramatically as the railroad and the automobile had.

In 1946 the U.S. Army had revealed that it had secretly developed a remarkable machine called Eniac, which performed complex mathematical calculations with lightning speed. Two years later, Bell Laboratories announced the invention of a device called a transistor. By the 1980s there was a veritable explosion in the technologies of electronics, especially computers. In August 1981, IBM introduced a personal computer that used the operating system MS-DOS. This system was owned by a six-year-old firm called Microsoft headed by a twenty-five-year-old Bill Gates, a college dropout. Ten years later, Microsoft Corporation, controlling the key operating software for personal computers (PCs), had grown into the world's largest software company and was ranked among the fifty most valuable corporations in America. Gates's personal fortune, $4 billion in 1991, made him the richest American. His company was working on developing a new system known as Windows, which would feature such applications as Microsoft Word and Excel.[31]

By then, the highly competitive Gates had broken with IBM (which had ruefully discovered that software was more important than hardware in computers) and antagonized almost everyone in the computer industry. Rivals complained that Microsoft had contributed very little to the industry, either following the lead of others or acquiring programs through purchase. But even they conceded Gates's brilliance at anticipating change, shaping an appropriate strategy, and then precisely executing it. Once again, it was demonstrated that it was not the basic invention but the ability to commercialize it that brought success. Competitors would either make their applications compatible with Windows or go under.

As Microsoft shares soared in value, so did the importance and prestige of the new market it was listed on, the NASDAQ. Created in 1971 as a quote source, NASDAQ had quickly evolved into a global electronic stock exchange, with new companies in industries such as electronics and biotechnology that promised rapid growth. The 1980s witnessed the introduction of videocassette recorders, compact disc players, cellular phones, and inexpensive fax machines. Mergers and acquisitions of established companies dominated the financial news of the 1980s, and many shrewd investors recognized that the real action in the immediate future would be in the tech stocks.

The New Economy, the Burst Bubble, and an Economy in Trouble, 1990–2008

All wealth is power, so power must infallibly draw wealth to it by some means or another.—EDMUND BURKE, *speech to Parliament, 1780*

Good things happened to the United States in the 1990s. The Cold War that had shaped American foreign policy and influenced domestic developments for half a century ended. Corporate profits powered by an information technology explosion doubled in the decade, and the stock market soared over 400 percent. After 1995, productivity, corporate profit, and real wages all rose handsomely. Then the new century began. Americans were suddenly shocked and sobered by a sharp correction of the market and more ominously by the events of September 11, 2001.

Americans in the 1990s became fully aware of changes that had long been under way. Half of all new marriages were ending in divorce and a third of all children were born out of wedlock, and people married at an older age—or more than ever before did not marry. Married couples with children indeed represented less than a fourth of all households in 2000. The nuclear family, long perceived as the building block of the society, seemingly was shifting.

A flood of legal and illegal immigrants from Asia, Africa, and Central and South America visibly altered the composition of the population. Mosques opened in Cleveland and Sikh temples opened in Chicago. A population once perceived as either black or white now included every ethnicity and race. The black inner-city ghettoes were now joined by barrios, Chinatowns, and Koreatowns. A sharpening of social and political tensions over issues such as multiculturalism reflected these issues.

American business also experienced dramatic change. Large integrated corporations had dominated the business landscape for most of the twentieth century, producing and marketing the flood of standardized and affordable goods that sustained the modern consumer society. Their supremacy, however, was challenged, as some downsized corporations became network-based organizations. In an effort to think out of the box and be nimble, some corporations increasingly relied on shifting alliances, borrowing and collaborating with other firms. Here, often-specialized small units would come together for only a limited time and for a specific purpose—to make a deal or restructure a company. Other large companies, however, continued to grow, and even in many companies that had become smaller, the power and authority of their CEOs was not noticeably diminished.[1]

Increasing pressure would be put on this process of change in the last decade of the twentieth century and the first decade of the new century. Economic developments would be hastened by the increased competition of a global economy and the revolution in information technology that encouraged and often required changes in corporate organization. Information moved instantly and decision makers had to act quickly. Fortunes would change hands and jobs would be created and lost as individuals and companies scrambled to capitalize on change. The Schumpeterian theory of growth—as driven by continuous innovation and "creative destruction"—would never appear more applicable. Investment bankers and others would try to make sense and profit out of new opportunities by creating ever-more-creative and complex financial instruments.

THRIVING ON CHAOS

After a recession in 1990–91, a resurgent American economy gained steam for the remainder of the decade. In the years 1974 to 1994 America's productivity had averaged only 1.4 percent annually. From 1994 to 2000 it climbed over 2.5 percent a year. The long-awaited renaissance of American business had materialized. Once more Americans viewed their free market as an exemplar of entrepreneurial energy. Market forecasters focused on the remarkable strengths of what they called a "New Economy." The key to this new economy was perceived to be a technological revolution that allowed for great gains in business efficiency, enabling high employment without inflation.

Nevertheless, concern for job security topped the list of worries for many Americans throughout the 1990s. Even with a strong economy, in the years 1993 to 1997 one out of every twelve job holders left their jobs involuntarily. Many indeed lost employment as a result of corporate downsizing. Wall Street talked about the "seven percent rule," that is, when a company announced a layoff its stock price jumped 7 percent. In the 1997 *The Ax*, crime novelist Donald E. Westlake depicted a chillingly humorous portrait of a desperate downsized middle manager who turns serial killer simply to eliminate rivals for any possible future position. With less humor, a management scholar summed up the change succinctly: "The old employment system of secure, lifetime jobs, with predictable advancement and stable pay is dead."[2]

New antitakeover laws passed by many state legislatures and a drying up of funds for corporate acquisitions had, by 1990, reduced the threat of hostile takeovers, as merger activity temporarily subsided. But the pressure for Fortune 500 corporations to reinvent themselves continued. The bywords of American business by the end of the 1980s had become "lean and mean." America's blue-collar workers had been hard hit earlier, as corporations turned to cheap labor abroad to manufacture or assemble their products. In the 1990s, middle management had its turn to be held over the fire. Layers of middle management made corporations much more top-heavy in the United States, compared to other nations. Management theorists now urged a "flattened hierarchy."[3]

Downsizing in the early 1990s represented a strategy for structural reorganization. Firms doing well downsized to improve efficiency and productivity while investing heavily in the new information technology. A survey by the American Management Association claimed that middle management, although making up only 8 percent of the nation's workforce, accounted for nearly 20 percent of the downsizing in 1992. Those still employed often had to do the work of the discharged as well as their own.

Entrepreneurial CEOs became the cult heroes of the 1990s, but only insofar as they boosted equity value. The 1990s was the decade of the "imperial CEO." Companies looked for chief executives with big ideas about aggressively increasing the scale of business. CEOs had their boards generously grant them and upper management stock-related incentives, "to align their interests with the share holder." The new mood of corporate America was captured by Rakesh Khurana, a Harvard Business School professor, in the apt title he chose for a critical study of this subject, *Searching for a Corporate Savior: The Irrational Quest for Charismatic CEOs*. Often flaunting wealth and flashy lifestyles, they replaced corporate raiders as the pop icons of Wall Street. However, the view that the best way to motivate managers is to link their pay closely to performance through stock options worked better in theory than in practice. Frequently, a company's performance rose or fell for reasons unrelated to any particular executive's performance. And, more critical, stock options tended to encourage a short-term focus on a company's share price instead of a long-term strategic vision.[4]

REENGINEERING THE CORPORATION

Much of the restructuring of the mid-1990s occurred under the banner of a management theory known as "reengineering." Michael Hammer and James Champy, in their best-selling book *Reengineering the Corporation* (1993), called for radical changes in a corporation, based on rethinking all aspects of a business, in order to move away from organization by departments to organization by process. Their basic idea was that organizations needed to identify their key processes and make them as lean and efficient as possible. In 1994, corporate America eliminated 516,000 jobs, even as its profits rose 11 percent. A labor market where employers hired and fired freely was hailed as an American strength—contrasting favorably with labor policies elsewhere—that allowed for the shifting of resources to meet changing needs.[5]

Management consultants advised corporate clients interested in reengineering that their relations with employees had to be transformed. McKinsey & Company, with 6,000 consultants, confidently stated its philosophy: "Everything can be measured and what gets measured can be managed." A leading management guru, Michael Hammer, wrote that "the company expects flexibility and initiative from the employee, and offers in return an opportunity to learn and to grow."[6] As modern technology advanced rapidly, this required educated and motivated workers capable of quick adaptation to change. Therefore corporations should not encourage workers to expect lifetime employment. Instead, employees had to be treated as subcontractors: hired to accomplish a task, financially rewarded for quality performance, and told to move on when their skills were no longer needed. The goal was to achieve a "participative workplace."[7]

In a fast-changing economy, more and more companies sought to become agile by farming out tasks to contractors, downsizing, and concentrating on core activities. Corporate loyalty, which depended on the sense of mutual obligation and responsibility between upper management and employees, suffered accordingly. Scholars discerned that this trend had been under way for much of the 1980s. Constantinos C. Markides wrote in 1995: "The trend toward diversification that began fifty years ago is now reversing itself. In particular there [is] a significant increase in the single-business firms and a decrease in the unrelated-business-firms within the population of Fortune 500 firms." By then he estimated that 25 percent of American corporations had "refocused" to reduce their diversification.[8]

At the turn of the twentieth century, vertically integrated corporations coordinating mass production with volume distribution had set the standards and pioneered the way for the American economy. Indeed, vertical integration became synonymous with big business. According to Alfred D. Chandler, the preeminent historian of the industrial corporation, it was their multi-investment in marketing and management that created large enterprises capable of sustaining themselves. Now this paradigm of vertical integration was being called into question as corporations furiously downsized and outsourced.

General Motors, for example, in 2000 employed less than a third of its 1979 workforce. By then, the company, locked in a losing struggle for dominance of the global automotive industry with Toyota, had discarded the famous model of the "modern multi-divisional corporation" created in the 1920s by Alfred Sloan. Moving away from Sloan's ideal of a vertically integrated company, GM increasingly bought its parts from suppliers and focused on auto design and marketing. As much as possible, it relied on suppliers; some, like Delphi, an auto parts maker, were spin-offs from GM created to preassemble "modules," such as entire instrument panels.[9] Smaller, less labor-intensive, "robotic" factories had been built, in which GM workers put together the modules to arrive at a finished product.

Moreover, these new factories were very different from the old. They employed the "lean production" management approach pioneered by Toyota, the benchmark for assembly-line efficiency. Information technology allowed "just-in-time" systems that facilitated the manufacture of a wide variety of products in short runs, while still allowing for economies of scale, so that instead of making one product or model by the tens of thousands on a single assembly line, new electronic machinery allowed for "limited batch" production. Workers on the factory floor were organized into teams. Using computers to change tooling, an assembly line was now capable of turning out small volumes of many different models. Discarding Sloan's concept that Cadillac, Pontiac, Buick, and Chevrolet should function as autonomous divisions, GM centralized sales, servicing, and marketing. The era of high volume production had ended in much of American industry, and the corporate organizational forms it had spawned had to be rethought. Unfortunately, GM's problems had not ended.[10]

THINKING AS AN ENTREPRENEUR

As previously noted, a "cult of the CEO" had developed whereby a company's performance and share price was assumed to be determined almost exclusively by the actions of the CEO or lack thereof. Rakesh Khurana's study of the CEO selection process found an overemphasis on charisma and forceful personality that often led to the selection of an outsider over an in-house-trained manager. Increasingly, the chief executive also chaired the board of directors, strengthening the role greatly.

CEOs were encouraged to "think outside the box" and were paid handsomely to do so. CEO pay packages jumped between 1980 and 2000 from 42 times the average worker's salary to 531 times the average worker's salary.[11] A key part of this pay package consisted of stock-related incentives. This was especially true after 1995. In that year Congress passed a law limiting the tax-deductibility of corporate salaries of more than $1 million but allowed exemptions for incentive-related bonuses. Stock options now offered substantial tax advantages for the executive, and the corporation benefited by not having to charge them against earnings.[12]

Options gave executives the right to buy stock in a company at a given favorable price, the "strike price," on a certain date in the future. Options were used extensively by cash-poor start-up companies in the nation's Silicon Valleys to attract and retain talent, a practice usually continued after the company became successful. They were far from alone in this practice. By 2000, on average, more than half the pay of a chief executive of a company in the Standard & Poor's 500 was stock-price related. According to those who favored stock options, the practice aligned management's and stockholders' interests: both now gained directly from increasing shareholder values.

CEOs replaced the raiders of the 1980s as catalysts of corporate change. American companies justified high compensation for top officers, much higher than any other nation, as necessary "to attract, energize, reward superior talent." It was even suggested that stock options were cost free to companies and their shareholders. A particularly American cult of the business superstar led to bidding wars for executive talent. The model of the CEO as a "statesman of business" overseeing the welfare of their employees and customers and socially involved in the community, which had been fashionable in the 1950s and 1960s, had long since been discarded. Nor did CEOs act in the 1990s in terms of a long view to safeguard corporate stability and longevity. They now looked for quick returns with immediate financial rewards. In contrast, companies run by a founder or a founder's family generally retained a sense of stewardship and a concern for the corporate future. But only 3 percent of America's large corporations were family held in 2006, a dramatically lower figure than the rest of the Western world.[13]

NEUTRON JACK

The 1990s' most esteemed chief executive was Jack Welch of General Electric. Welch, perhaps more than any other CEO, reshaped the popular perception of the chief executive—from a somewhat gray, impersonal figure to a larger-than-life personality. Welch took an industrial company with a market value of $12 billion in 1981, and by retirement, two decades later, he had turned it into an immensely successful conglomerate worth $500 billion. Along the way, Welch—whose celebrated epigram was "fix, sell, or close"—sold off underperforming divisions and fired about 100,000 people, thus earning the sobriquet "Neutron Jack." Before Welch, GE had been known for its layers of sector managers, department managers, and supervisors, all thought to be essential to strategic planning and quality control. Defying this assumption, and borrowing ideas and systems from companies like Hewlett-Packard and Toshiba, Welch eliminated all but four of nine hierarchical levels. The heads of GE's various businesses were directed to report directly to him and encouraged to think for themselves and to question corporate culture, a management style he called the "boundaryless organization." Although not without his detractors, Welsh generated enormous wealth for his company's stockholders. Admirers even ranked him with Alfred Sloan as an icon of managerial innovation. Welch explained the role of a creative CEO as selecting the right people and training them to focus on achieving a few big ideas.[14]

Not all CEOs exited the arena as honored gladiators. Albert J. Dunlap, a self-proclaimed "turnaround artist," boasted about the thousands he had downsized as CEO of several Fortune 500 companies. Nicknamed "Chain-Saw Al," he described himself as a "Rambo in pinstripes" and preached a "slash-and-burn philosophy" as the way to lift a company's stock. With Sunbeam Corporation in the late 1990s he engaged in overt chicanery: "borrowing" sales from a future period. "Borrowing" was done by inducing retailers to stock up on the company's backyard grills in winter by letting them defer payments and store the grills in Sunbeam's warehouses—all of this to pump up the company's first-quarter earnings forecast. But when the second quarter came around, the seasonal jump normally expected had already been claimed. Sunbeam now fell short of its projections and share value dropped. Dunlap was summarily fired as head of Sunbeam by his own handpicked directors in June 1998. The company eventually sought protection from creditors in bankruptcy court, and the Securities and Exchange Commission in 2001 charged Dunlap with fraud for having given a false impression of its business in order to inflate stock prices and enhance its value as an acquisition target.[15]

WINDS OF CHANGE

Wherever one looked in the world of American business in the 1990s turmoil prevailed. The decade's innovations in technology, productivity, and business restructuring ranked in importance with such other seminal periods as 1895–1905, the 1920s, and the 1960s. Important new companies sprang up overnight and old ones disappeared as corporations merged and "de-merged." Constant innovations in the technologies of production, the computer, and telecommunications changed almost daily the way business was thought about and done. The information technology revolution made it possible to "digitize" the boundaries between design, manufacturing, and marketing and to locate these functions in different places. The result was that companies responded with different strategies. Discount chains, such as Wal-Mart, sought growth; most manufacturing industries downsized. Almost all, however, greatly increased their annual investment in computers as a way of supporting restructuring and cost cutting. Along with globalization and deregulation, the communications revolution and a new information technology transformed America's business environment.[16]

Long-established practices and newly devised management strategies alike required constant reappraisal and adaptation to accelerating changes in relations with suppliers and clients. Accounting firms, business schools, and such high-tech firms as International Business Machines (IBM) and Electronic Data launched consulting units, as corporations sought outside help to restructure. This spurred a surge in new theories and accompanying jargons: "reengineering," "knowledge imperative," "competing through competence," "bundling," "transformation management."

A 1989 report published by the MIT Commission on Industrial Recovery offered a laundry list of recommendations for improvement. The authors advised corporations to eliminate rigid hierarchies and boundaries between departments and to encourage technology transfer with suppliers and customers. Workers and union leaders should be given a greater say in decision making. Industries were urged to promote interfirm cooperative research, training, and product standardization—and, if need be, to press for relaxation of any antitrust laws that posed obstacles to such industrial efforts.[17]

Pressure for change came from large institutional shareholders, like pension funds and mutual funds, who leaned on the outside directors on corporate boards. Outside directors played a prominent role in forcing changes in top management at GM, IBM, and American Express. Michael Jensen of the Harvard Business School predicted that big investors would play an increasingly active role as never-sleeping watchdogs of corporate management. Corporations expressed an eagerness to improve relations with shareholders in order to avoid the turmoil caused by proxy contests. In turn, "shareholder" capitalism pressured management to maximize short-term profits while allowing upper management to reward itself for good performance with stock options and bonuses. As long as stock prices rose handsomely, everyone had reason to be happy. This included stockbrokers, who saw increased activity, as the holding period for stocks traded on the New York Stock Exchange declined from eight years in 1960 to under a year in 2000.

As the twenty-first century began, the message for American management was the need to compete effectively in a new global economy where nothing remained stable or predictable for long. In the stuff of legends, the head of American Airlines came up with the idea of eliminating just one olive from every dinner salad served to passengers. He assumed they would never notice and the company could save $40,000 a year. At a time when the art of long-range forecasting seemed more difficult than ever, American business believed it needed to prepare for the next century by embracing change and paring costs.[18]

A concern throughout the 1990s and into the new century was the outsourcing of jobs abroad. As consumers, Americans benefited from the rise of a global economy, but at what price? They watched as first blue-collar and union-protected jobs in manufacturing disappeared across the nation's borders, and then at decade's end as skilled jobs of the college educated in the information technology industry followed, relocating to India, Ireland, and the Philippines. In 1992, President George H. W. Bush signed the North American Free Trade Agreement (NAFTA) in which, subject to congressional approval, the United States, Canada, and Mexico agreed to make all of North America a free-trade zone. NAFTA was bitterly opposed by labor unions and environmentalists but strongly supported by the business community. NAFTA won congressional approval in November 1993 when Clinton, who supported it, was president. Fifteen years later, it was clear that NAFTA received a mixed report card. It had promoted trade but it had not created the jobs anticipated in any of the three countries.

CLINTON AND A REVITALIZED ECONOMY

Bush's defeat in the 1992 election reflected grave concerns about the economy. In hindsight, economists now date the technical end of the recession to March 1991. Unfortunately for Bush, the upswing did not register with most Americans until after he left office. Bush himself placed much of the blame for his loss on Alan Greenspan and the Fed's failure to lower interest rates. A self-made Texas billionaire, Ross Perot, ran as a third-party candidate, focusing on the mushrooming federal debt and job outsourcing, and garnered a remarkable 19 percent of the vote.[19]

In office, Clinton faced hard choices. If he honored his campaign promises to cut taxes for the middle class while increasing the public works budget he would swell the deficit. This would displease Wall Street and the business community. Fiscal conservatives among his advisers—notably Robert Rubin, the director of the newly created National Economic Council (and in 1995 appointed treasury secretary), and the Fed's Greenspan—urged Clinton to cut the deficit to restore the bond market's confidence and bring down interest rates. This latter course, while pleasing the business world, would antagonize important Democratic constituencies.

BALANCING THE BUDGET

In the spring of 1993, the new Clinton administration proposed a $500 billion reduction in the deficit over five years, to be funded by new taxes on corporations and the wealthiest 1 percent of the population. Clinton narrowly won passage of his budget program. The tax increase (retroactive to the first of the year) and a resurgent economy reduced the federal deficit in 1993 from a projected $300 billion to approximately $190 billion. Robert Rubin, who had previously been a risk arbitrageur at Goldman Sachs, had carried the day for a "bond market" strategy of fiscal discipline and deficit reduction. The reassured financial markets responded by allowing long-term interest rates to fall to their lowest level in over twenty years, stimulating investment and jobs. From a Democratic perspective, the 1993 budget deal freed up hundreds of billions of dollars in capital for private investment, growing the economy and increasing federal revenues, which reduced the deficit and freed up still more capital for private investment.

Understandably, Republicans had a different view. They credited Reagan's policies in the 1980s with having unleashed an economic restructuring that had merely required time to translate into a booming economy and reduced deficits. Many economists, however, saw the turnaround as the result of the deficit-reducing tax increase that Bush and a Democratic-controlled Congress had agreed upon in 1990. Wall Street, however, preferred to credit Federal Reserve chairman Alan Greenspan's willingness to feed economic growth by allowing low interest rates while remaining vigilant against inflation. But Greenspan himself would later give major credit to the unexpected strength during the Clinton years of a remarkable technology-driven economic spurt. No matter which explanation is right there is no doubting the ensuing prosperity. By 1995, productivity and the economy were on a definite upswing.[20]

Clinton soon followed his narrow budget victory in early 1993 with a more impressive showing. Congress voted approval in November 1993 for the North American Free Trade Agreement with Mexico and Canada. A Democratic president, overriding the opposition of many Democrats in Congress and the labor unions, had depended on Republican congressional support for a program initiated by the Bush administration. (This would also be true in 2000 when Clinton pushed through a "permanent normal trade relations" agreement with China.) Encouraged by Rubin, "a free-market internationalist," Clinton reassured Americans that increased trade would lead to a growing world market and more efficient domestic economy.

Passage of a universal health insurance bill had dominated the Clinton administration's second year in office. Medical care, a trillion-dollar-a-year industry, accounted for nearly 14 percent of the nation's GDP. Opponents of universal health insurance argued that the government could not afford to add further to its medical costs. A media campaign by the insurance industry and Republican landslide victories in the congressional elections of 1994 doomed enactment of universal health insurance, leaving the United States the only advanced nation without a program. American business would soon learn the heavy price of offering health care to employees, their families, and retirees; businesses, especially small firms, cut back on health insurance or dropped it completely. The companies that retained it complained that health care costs put them at a competitive disadvantage with countries where this expense was borne by the government.

Clinton distanced himself from his party's liberal wing after 1994. Clinton called himself a "New Democrat" and advanced a vision of a centrist Democratic Party closely tied to American business. He personally worked to develop strong political ties with Silicon Valley. In the defining moment of his administration, Clinton proclaimed the era of "big government" over in his 1996 State of the Union Message. His view reflected an apparent national consensus on the need for an economic orthodoxy based on balanced budgets, stable prices, and a strong dollar. Also in 1996, Clinton signed into law a bill that transferred to the states the responsibility to turn "welfare into workfare," with recipients limited to receiving assistance for a maximum of five years.

THE NIFTY NINETIES

By 1995 the economy was experiencing a strong resurgence. Dot-coms and telecommunications caught investor interest as hot growth industries. Fiber optics, microwave relays, and satellites now transmitted staggering amounts of information to all corners of the globe. The Department of Defense in the 1960s had financed the development of the Internet as a secure communications system in the event of a nuclear attack. In 1991 the introduction of the World Wide Web opened the Internet to an exciting range of commercial possibilities. Businesses and entrepreneurs rushed to use cyberspace to sell their products and services. Highly profitable at first were porn "home pages." But eBay's success demonstrated the Web's potential in matching supply and demand in diverse and widely scattered markets.

Mergers and joint ventures between the Baby Bells and cable companies in the 1990s sounded alarm bells about overconcentration in telecommunications. But proponents of the so-called information superhighway argued that only mega-companies could raise the scale of capital needed for development. The Clinton administration, however, sought to maximize competition. A bill enacted in 1995 eliminated legal barriers that separated the telephone, cable TV, and broadcasting industries. The intention was to stimulate the rapid introduction of a free-wheeling information economy, linking independent networks operating at blinding speeds. Developing broadband required huge investments in such technology as fiber optics and computers. Annual spending by business on computers and their software increased fourteen-fold in the course of the decade. As a result, the information technology (IT) sector grew at a startling rate.

Between 1995 and 1998, as the economy took-off, the IT sector accounted for 35 percent of the nation's economic growth, though it accounted for only 8 percent of the GDP. Moreover, this sector reported an increase in worker productivity that was three times the rest of the economy. Economists began to ponder the possibility that by raising productivity in all sorts of other businesses—from auto manufacturing to medical care—IT permitted economic growth without the inflationary pressure normally accompanying an upturn. Despite rapid developments in IT, the government pursued an antitrust suit against Microsoft for monopolistic practices that it charged hindered innovations.

In November 1999 a federal judge concluded that Microsoft, with a monopoly in operating systems for personal computers, had improperly extended itself into a related market, Internet browsers. He soon after ruled that Microsoft had intentionally violated antitrust laws—and that the remedy was breaking up the company. However, the company with its limitless resources battled successfully to reverse his decision in 2001.

Federal action against Microsoft reflected a concern that the new IT markets had stratified into horizontal layers, with a single player coming to dominate each one: microprocessors (Intel), operating systems (Windows), and browsers (Netscape Explorer). Even the experts did not agree on whether a Microsoft breakup would benefit the consumer; some thought it unnecessary, believing that fast-moving developments would by themselves diminish any monopoly, as home and office users alike increasingly ran their "net appliance" and "personal digital assistants" on stripped-down, non-Window operating systems.

Clinton's first term ended with an economy of low unemployment and remarkably low inflation. Business investments and exports were strong as the stock market continued to soar. In 1997 Clinton had made a sweeping agreement with the Republicans for a balanced budget—with tax cuts—and the following fiscal year a small federal surplus replaced the red ink Americans had learned to expect. Public confidence in market-driven change was high as the twentieth century ended. Between 1991 and 1996, the American economy grew at a comfortable but not overly imposing average rate of about 2.5 percent per year, with inflation also hovering at about that figure, and unemployment moved between 5 and 6 percent. At the same time, the Dow rose from 3,000 to 6,100, mergers and acquisitions occurred at a record pace, and business profits rose handsomely. Conventional wisdom among economists and on Wall Street was that a higher growth rate would trigger inflation. Late in 1996 the economy surged, and in 1997 it grew at an impressive 3.6 percent as unemployment dropped to 4.5 percent and the Dow neared 8,000. At century's end, the Dow passed 11,000. But inflation, contrary to expectations, had remained at 2 percent.

A restructured corporate America had seemingly adapted to a remarkable new era of prosperity. Entrepreneurial activity received much of the credit for this. Many of the fastest-growing companies—Microsoft, Dell, Oracle, Nike, and Amazon—were run by their founders and principal owners. Many were also tech companies. Dazzling gains in the stock market fed the sense of national euphoria. The Labor Department reported that in the middle of the 1990s American workers posted handsome yearly productivity gains in the range of 2 percent to 3 percent, roughly double the annual average increase in the period 1970 to 1990. After years of layoffs and plant closings—as well as billions invested in technology—the nation's factories boasted by 1998 a 4 percent annual increase in productivity, the fastest rate of growth among wealthy nations. In 1999 and 2000, productivity rose to 5 percent, the best performance in nearly forty years. Moreover, some economists thought that the productivity gains in banking and finance were badly understated by these impressive statistics.

Financial-service companies were among the top users of high tech, spending heavily on IT systems. Computers had made capital markets more efficient, allowing for the rapid flow of capital worldwide. This new mobility, however, posed a serious problem when investors and speculators lost confidence in a national currency: the potential for overnight flight of capital. This indeed happened in East Asia in 1997.

Merger activity fueled Wall Street's frenzied activity as the new millennium approached. In 1997 the total value of mergers and acquisitions exceeded a trillion dollars—more than double the value of the peak year of the

1980s, 1989. The following year, worldwide mergers rose to $2.4 trillion. The mergers and acquisitions of the 1980s were often hostile takeovers motivated by a desire for cost cutting or the selling off of assets. Those of the 1990s were frequently amiable arrangements driven by a desire to enhance global reach. In some industries, management saw two choices—becoming a small niche player or going for giant scale and emerging a player in a world market via a growth strategy based on merger and acquisition.

The latter choice powered the wave of mergers that swept the oil industry, banking, computer software, telecommunications, and military contracting. In November 1999 Clinton signed into law the Gramm-Leach-Bliley Act, repealing what little remained of the Glass-Steagall Act of 1933.[21] Sanford Weill of Citigroup, who had lobbied heavily for the repeal, now restructured his company to include an insurance company and a brokerage house and major consumer, commercial, and investment banks. Weill indeed had engineered the creation of the world's largest bank, a financial supermarket. His creation epitomized financial deregulation's role as a catalyst and offered evidence that sheer size counted on the global scene. The financial industry in the United States and abroad grew greatly at the end of the century and was increasingly ingenious in the financial engineering of new instruments.

The desire by upper management to cash in on a booming stock market (and to enhance the value of their stock packages) through merger activity also acted as an important incentive—so too did the ego gratification of doing a big deal. In practice, many of the mergers and acquisitions encountered formidable problems. Blending diverse corporate cultures and systems—such as distribution networks or information technology—which do not easily mesh, commonly provoked conflict between the former employees of one firm and those of the other, and the cost savings and economies of scale often proved elusive. As in past merger movements, the end results were very mixed and sometimes disastrous. The most notorious was the merger of Time Warner with AOL.

A few newly enlarged firms prospered, but the majority, perhaps as high as 70 percent, languished. The only winners often turned out to be the shareholders of the acquired business and the investment bankers and lawyers who profited from fees. But an overall generalization about the usefulness of mergers to American business and the economy remained elusive. One result, however, is indisputable: mergers and acquisitions stirred the pot and forestalled corporate stultification. The old controversy about the pros and cons of mergers and acquisitions stayed alive. But no one questioned that vast fortunes had been made. The tonic of tech wealth was to the 1990s what Wall Street's takeover and junk bond explosion had been to the 1980s.[22]

Did consolidation and concentration pose a threat to competition? Those who said no argued that mergers and acquisitions allowed business to adapt to change by mixing assets or acquiring the scale required for global competition. The friendly takeover in early 2001 of Time Warner by America Online (AOL) seemingly revealed a pattern of new high-tech Internet companies (with few tangible assets but high market valuation) combining with older types of firms that were eager to participate effectively in the new world of e-commerce. In the instance of AOL–Time Warner, the merger soon was regretted by the Time Warner management and stockholders, who believed, with justification, that they had been conned by hype.

THE NEW ECONOMY

The boom of the late 1990s needed a big idea to explain it; the media quickly responded. Pundits spoke of a "New Economy." They pointed to positive developments in the economy. Deregulation encouraged innovation; the rise of venture capital and a start-up capital mentality promoted a climate of risk taking; the aggressive professional manager as entrepreneur occupied center stage; the explosion of the Internet and Web offered great gains in productivity. Scholars and businesspeople alike predicted that American business would never be the same. They foresaw the creation of new business models with little resemblance to the corporate forms of the past.

From their optimistic perspective, productivity gains in the period 1996–2000 heralded a dramatic era of "value creation." This development was traceable to the high-tech innovations of the 1970s and 1980s, which were only now paying off, as new technology required a period of time before producing productivity gains. To Alan Greenspan, increased productivity explained why the 1990s had not experienced inflation even with its low unemployment and rapid growth.[23] The development of the Internet in the 1990s alone, others argued, provided a low-cost communications network that could curb inflation indefinitely.

In 1997, however a liquidity crisis in Asian countries threatened to escalate into a global financial crisis. A major hedge fund, Long-Term Capital Management, lost $4 billion and was rescued at the last minute by a Wall Street consortium amid fears that its failure could provoke a market crash. It seemed time for a reappraisal of the recently hailed "New Economy," and previously ignored weaknesses in the business upturn of the 1990s tempo-rarily attracted attention. Three swift interest-rate cuts by the Federal Reserve reassured Wall Street, and in 1999, the good times returned. The Dow rose above 11,000, unemployment and inflation were low, and business profits soared. By the end of the decade, stocks accounted for more than a quarter of the assets of American households.

Warning of a "speculative bubble," Yale economist Robert J. Shiller, in *Irrational Exuberance* (2000), estimated that the recent run-up had over-valued the market by some $7 trillion and predicted that a day of reckoning was coming. His detractors sneered that he underestimated the role of dot-com and telecommunication companies in creating a vigorous New Econ-omy. Events proved Shiller right. A sudden sharp drop in the NASDAQ com-posite, an index largely based on tech companies, in late 2000 caused many bulls to reconsider their portfolios. As President Clinton left office in late January 2001, the future of the economy was foremost on everyone's mind. His successor, George W. Bush, cautioned of a sluggish economy displaying significant weakness and urged a broad tax cut to encourage capital and consumer spending. Who would have the last word on the "New Economy" had yet to be determined.[24]

Americans looking at the economy at century's end could see the glass as either half full or half empty. Certainly they had reasons to be satisfied with their economic model of entrepreneurial capitalism. Millions of new jobs had been created in the 1990s, unemployment was low, and Western Europe and Japan had stopped gaining on the United States in per capita national income. Two decades of deregulation and unrestricted business practices had seemingly fueled a competitive creative intensity, pushing business reorganization and increasing productivity. A continuous shift in resources from declining to expanding industries occurred. The cutting-edge economy that the United States had appeared to lose in the 1970s had been regained. Once again, other nations talked of using U.S. policies and business practices as the model for freeing up their own economies from constraints that limited the ability to innovate or restructure. Yet real wages rose at a slower pace than expected, and some Americans at century's end worried that in "taking care of business" the United States was eroding a sense of equity and social responsibility basic to American democracy—and that the economic disparities between rich and poor, management and em-ployees, skilled and unskilled, had widened unacceptably in the last quarter of the twentieth century. Such inequities, they feared, could not simply be addressed by market-driven change.

THE BUBBLE BURSTS

In December 1996 Greenspan cautioned investors about the "irrational exuberance" of the market.[25] The Dow Jones average had doubled since 1990 and the NASDAQ had advanced from 800 to 2,500. After a momentary pause, the markets brushed aside Greenspan's cautionary note and soared to dizzying heights. Investors began to think of 15 percent growth a year as normal. Some knowledgeable brokers began in 1999 to whisper among themselves about a "casino stock market." Then, in March 2000, a bull market that had lasted for nearly two decades peaked and started a downward slide. In the next year and a half, the Dow lost 40 percent from its high; the NASDAQ lost 70 percent. Many investors, who had been led to believe that market dips only provided buying opportunities, rushed in, temporarily bolstering the market. Then, finally, in summer 2002 they panicked, deserting the market.

Several factors fed into this decline, but weakness in two related industries, dot-coms and telecommunications, contributed greatly to the market's problems. In early 2000, the Internet boom had faltered, with many dot-com companies failing. Indeed, few had ever made money and most had relied heavily on borrowed funds from venture capitalists and banks. Often, start-up companies on going public had seen their opening share price quadruple in a day. Escalating stock values in turn were often used to facilitate mergers and acquisitions.

GET BIG FAST

The defining strategy of start-up dot-com companies was to get big fast. A business should grow quickly, it was asserted, because the first successful entrant in a category could keep out challengers, thanks to first-mover advantages. Microsoft provided a startling example of this in practice. If a company was successful in getting big, it could then use its position to finesse such questions as how it might make money in the future. The founder CEO of one failed e-commerce company, a toy company with a meteoric rise and fall, recalled his thinking: "Grow, grow, grow. Grab market share and worry about the rest later." His fatal mistake was to overestimate the market and build warehouse space and software that was more than double the company's need. The industry's unrealistic expectations and flawed business models became apparent with a business downturn in 2000. Capital markets now closed them off and, with investor confidence vanishing, stock prices plummeted. The industry remained in serious trouble for years.

A dramatic story from the dot-com fiasco is provided by AOL–Time Warner. In February 2000, AOL announced that it had acquired Time Warner Inc. for more than $130 billion in stock, the largest deal in history. Analysts praised the move, generally accepting the rationale offered that the merger of brick-and-mortar media company—with sizable and profitable magazine, cable, and movie holdings—with an Internet portal giant offered powerful synergies as a firm preparing for the future convergence of telephone and cable Internet communications through a single provider. Two years later, as the new company's stock plummeted, many of the same analysts that had praised the move now concluded that Time Warner, with its solid assets, had been taken in by the mirage of e-commerce and that AOL's bookkeeping used for the merger had been questionable. In the summer of 2002 Time Warner people took charge of the company and dropped AOL from the corporate name.[26]

The public shock at the dot-com collapse was amplified with the telecommunication industry's downfall in the summer of 2002. The Telecommunications Act of 1996 and the commercialization and mass-market adoption of the Internet quickly overheated an already-booming industry. With limitless opportunities, telecoms within five years ran up total debts of over $1 trillion. Excessive capital expenditures resulted in a staggering oversupply of capacity. Less than 5 percent of the fiber optics laid in the United States in the 1990s was in use in 2002. Unrealistic expectations led to devastating consequences for the industry. In the first two years of the new century, telecom stocks fell 95 percent off their high and nearly half a million workers lost their jobs.[27]

When prospects seemed golden the stock value of telecom companies performed well above the market. The problem was that if earnings did not show the high growth levels investors had been led to expect their stock prices dropped until the jerry-built companies were threatened. One way to inflate earnings was through acquiring other companies, and another was to play fast and loose with accounting procedures, exaggerating revenues by various shady and sometimes illegal practices. In the summer of 2002, the chickens came home to roost. The problems included mountains of debt, accounting scandals, inefficient industry structure, low investor confidence, and capital markets that had all but shut down to the industry. Several of its leading companies sought bankruptcy protection.

WorldCom's bankruptcy, at $140 billion, was the largest bankruptcy in history. It had misstated earnings to conceal a loss of nearly $4 billion, and several of its top executives were convicted of fraud. The scandal exposed a system characterized by conflicts of interest, self-dealing, bad faith, and outright criminality and rife with manipulated financial statements and shredded documents. Many had bought stock based on the high praise of a leading telecommunications analyst, whose firm pocketed huge sums in banking fees from the companies it was recommending.[28]

Corporate wrongdoings were not limited to these two industries. The financial markets were rocked in summer 2002 by scandals involving several prestigious corporations. Investor confidence in the "transparency" of public companies understandably was severely shaken. Stock options that were offered to upper management as an incentive to focus on raising equity values often worked in an unanticipated manner. As investors became fixated on earnings reports, CEOs often engaged in a strategy that Wall Street wags called "Beat the Numbers." Various accounting stratagems, some legal, some not, began to be employed to pump up reported profits and thus share prices. A corporate culture that downplayed decency and integrity, a casual governance structure, and a compensation system based on stock options had led at the new century's start to a corporate pattern of reckless behavior, or worse.[29]

As the stock of companies that topped earnings forecasts rose dramatically in the bubble years, CEOs targeted short-term profits and downplayed long-term planning. Stock market gambling—not jobs, profits, or products—provided the basis for business decision making. At worst, it led to deliberate strategies to distort earnings, either by "aggressive" accounting or through outright fraud. Some managers inflated prices by making risky short-term investments and acquisitions. Sometimes upper management sold their holdings in a company for a killing while misleading employees and investors about its health. When the energy company Enron crashed, its employees lost not only their jobs but that part of their pension invested in the company's shares.

Enron had showcased the view that "financialization" and deregulation had spurred the development of a new type of corporation. Formed in 1987 by the merger of two natural-gas pipeline operators, Enron had evolved in the 1990s into a company more interested in maximizing trading opportunities than in producing energy. The economist Paul Krugman in 2001 wrote of the company that it "looks as if it had been constructed to illustrate the end of the corporation as we know it."[30] By then, Enron dominated the energy "spot" market (one in which goods are sold for cash and delivered immediately) and the energy futures market, while it also offered over 3,000 other futures and derivative contracts on everything from fiber-optic cable capacity to the weather. Many of these operations turned out to be criminal scams to enrich a handful of upper management.

To make matters worse, auditing firms and banks had abetted Enron's misdeeds. The accounting giant Arthur Andersen was so closely tied to Enron's efforts to bilk investors that it faced criminal charges and civil suits. In an effort to continue a profitable relationship with Enron, from which it not only received auditing fees but also fees for consulting work, Arthur Andersen disregarded the public interest it was legally obligated to protect. After being found guilty of obstruction of justice for destroying subpoenaed documents, it declared bankruptcy.

The Sarbanes-Oxley Act of 2002, passed in response to corporate accounting scandals as epitomized by Enron, set stricter standards for corporate governance and financial accounting. It required companies to inspect their financial reporting procedures and to fix any problems that could lead to errors or fraud in their financial statements. To try to ensure that auditors are truly independent, the act limits the type and amount of services an outside audit firm can provide and requires companies to change auditors periodically. But the larger issue of whether a firm should be allowed to do both accounting and consulting remained unresolved. A debate soon arose over whether the act was too onerous and costly and in particular whether small companies should be exempt. Critics of such an exemption note that smaller companies tend to rely on weaker internal controls and are therefore more prone to financial errors or fraud.

The practice of major banks also came under scrutiny. A pattern became clear. Analysts connected to investment banks were often under pressure to report favorably on companies that were doing underwriting business with the bank. The striking example of the you scratch my back, I'll scratch your back mentality was provided by telecom analyst Jack Grubman of Citigroup's Salomon Smith Barney. Grubman, as analyst, touted the industry, and his advice encouraged investors to pour money into the stocks he suggested as good buys, especially WorldCom. But he was not offering disinterested recommendations. Grubman, earning a reported $20 million a year, was a highly important player in the industry, not a passive observer. He facilitated mergers and acquisitions and obtained loans for telecom companies, to the tune of billions of dollars, with Salomon Smith Barney receiving underwriting and consulting fees for his labor. When questioned about the ethical nature of his dual role of analyst and player, Grubman told a reporter: "What used to be a conflict is now a synergy."[31] Investors who lost money on his tips, not impressed by this reasoning, sued Grubman, and the Justice Department scrutinized his behavior for possible legal action. On December 20, 2002, Jack Grubman was fined $15 million and was banned from securities transactions for life by the Securities and Exchange Commission for conflicts of interest.

As evidence mounted of misdeeds by corporations and financial institutions, demands for strengthening regulations increased. Stock options for top executives received particular attention. A near consensus appeared that these should be listed as expenses and that some limits are needed on executives' ability to sell options while still employed by the company. But perhaps the most important lesson is that the confidence in the marketplace and the suspicion of government that had prevailed since the 1970s may have begun to reverse. The pendulum would soon swing back to reform after three decades of deregulation.

With the unraveling of many of the high-flying "growth" corporations of the 1990s, the question was raised as to whether the decade's apparent gains would in the end prove to have been a mirage. Much of the increase in productivity and wealth certainly is solid and lasting. A revolution in information technology had indeed occurred. Real wages for the ordinary American did go up between 1995 and 2000, although this improvement did not continue in the first decade of the twenty-first century. Indeed, the beginning of the new century proved volatile and rocky for the American economy, and new scandals made headlines. Financial engineering, or, as some critics suggested, financial alchemy, had created a plethora of opaque and unregulated financial vehicles, a so-called shadow-banking system. The risk-ridden financial markets would collapse at the end of the first decade of the new century even more quickly than they had emerged in the final decade of the last century.

In the wake of the Internet bubble collapse, corporate misdoings, and the traumatic impact of 9/11, the Federal Reserve, led by Alan Greenspan, had gradually cut interest rates to 1 percent in 2001 and 2002. The intent was to stave off deflation and to support the stock markets. These goals were accomplished, and in the short run all looked positive. (Later, critics would blame Greenspan for an overly easy monetary policy stance and also for the Fed's failure to appropriately supervise bank activity.)

Easy credit encouraged consumers to spend and sustain the economy. This was in part because of a stunning asset price rise in the housing market: 80 percent nationally in the five years after 2001, reaching a high in August 2006. This rise was fueled significantly by the sudden availability of mortgage loans to subprime borrowers who previously would not have been eligible. The mortgage market, altering since the banking deregulations of the 1980s, was now transformed. Banks no longer retained mortgages extended to homeowners; instead they securitized them into bond instruments (collateralized debt obligations). This often involved bundling into one collateralized debt obligation mortgages with a wide range—different tranches—of risk, not always fully entered on balance sheets.

Drawing on a worldwide market eager for U.S. bonds, the banks found no shortage of buyers. Money market funds bought asset-backed securities from conduits filled by banks originating loans from mortgage brokers. Profits were handsome. High risks were taken and then passed along the chain to buyers, who often had no way of accurately evaluating purchases. The depth, liquidity, inventiveness, and technology of financial markets had outpaced the ability to easily fathom consequences or to monitor and control excesses. The practices that were revealed brought to mind Franklin Delano Roosevelt's inaugural address of 1933 when he called for "an end to a conduct in banking and business that has given to a sacred trust the likeness of callous and selfish wrongdoing."

By early 2007 the housing industry, one of the economy's most important sectors, was in serious trouble: new constructions faltered, the sale of existing and new homes ebbed, and foreclosures rose. The latter was especially true for subprime borrowers, who too often had been led into adjustable rate mortgages they could not afford. In late summer 2007 two giant and interlinked bubbles burst—one in property, one in credit. Leading banks suffered serious losses and, concerned about the damage of what had become a twofold crisis, contracted their lending activity—the very lifeblood of the economy and the key to its expansion. The resultant credit crunch, combined with consumer retrenchment, increasing energy costs, and falling house prices, threatened by early 2008 to precipitate a recession.

Banks, brokerage houses, rating agencies, bond insurers, and regulators, all were severely damaged by the subprime mortgage crisis. Confidence in the nation's financial institutions plunged with the realization that some of its largest financial institutions had neglected risk management and oversight vigilance in their frantic pursuit of new and highly profitable financial instruments, or "products." As the public struggled to assimilate the plethora of novel acronyms and concepts tossed around in media coverage of the financial crisis, it became painfully clear that financial institutions themselves did not fully comprehend the ingeniously complex operations they had spun. Nor for that matter had monoline insurers, companies that guarantee that if a bond defaults they will cover the principal and the interest. The insurers had seriously underestimated the potential for losses, and their own viability came into question.

On January 28, 2008, George W. Bush delivered his final State of the Union Address. The *New York Times* that morning led with a front-page headline: "Echo of First Bush: Good Economy Turns Sour." It noted that for years Bush had presided "over an economic climate of growth that would be the envy of most presidents." All of that had changed after August 2007. Most of his last address would attempt to reassure the American people that the government was able to act to avert a recession that many analysts predicted would be long and deep and perhaps global. Volatile swings in the stock markets had caused the Federal Reserve from September 2007 to March 2008 to cut its target interest rate multiple times, while indicating it was prepared to slash further to counter a consumer-led recession. Monetary policy was reinforced with fiscal action, as president and Congress rushed through a $168 billion economic stimulus package.

Polls showed that the state of the economy had emerged as the nation's principal concern in a presidential election year. The president of the Economic Strategy Institute, a prestigious policy research organization, warned that the economic problems faced by the United States in 2008 bore strong parallels to the Japanese crisis of the 1990s, which had crippled the Japanese economy for well over a decade.[32] A highly respected academic, Nouriel Roubini, founder of the RGE Monitor website, anticipated in February 2008 the high probability of the crisis descending into a vicious meltdown: a cycle of falling house prices, large losses by banks on all sorts of unsecured consumer debt, a wave of corporate defaults, and a collapse in stock prices. All of this leading to a "catastrophic" prolonged global recession. In late spring 2008, an additional concern had arisen. Soaring commodity prices, particularly of oil, were threatening an unacceptable inflationary trend.

Few predicted such dire developments and most thought that the right policies by Washington could successfully navigate the choppy economic waters. Readers of these pages will, of course, know more about the outcome than an author writing at the end of June 2008. The American economy has historically demonstrated a remarkable resiliency and the nation's business a proven ability to adapt successfully to altered circumstances. That this was true in the past is, however, no guarantee of the future.

CHAPTER SIXTEEN

The Rise of a Global Economy

Standing triumphant at the center of the global teen phenomenon
is MTV, which in 1998 was in 273.5 million households—only
70 million of which were in the United States. By 1999, MTV's
eight global divisions broadcast in 83 countries and territories.
—NAOMI KLEIN, No Logo (1999)

Disagreement over globalization is one of the principal fault lines in world politics. Adding a highly charged emotional note to this debate is its perception as being synonymous with an American-derived global consumer culture and the erosion of local customs and identity. American brands have long benefited from a sense that it is fashionable, chic, and modern to be American. In far-off villages in Africa and Asia, children eagerly flaunt Old Navy or Gap apparel. Sixty-four of the world's one hundred most valuable brands were owned in 2004 by American companies. The other side of the coin is that this identification with trendy change comes at a cost, at a time when American policies and companies are blamed for many of the modern world's problems. Even the phenomenal explosion of English as the universal language of global commerce is regarded as another expression of American cultural imperialism. Americans have their own concerns, most notably the global outsourcing of American jobs to foreign workers and such global issues as global warming, deforestation, and energy production. In many countries, and this includes the United States, the benefits of global integration have been very unevenly distributed. Moreover, the diminishment of American global prestige, power, and possibly even economic dominance in the very early years of the twenty-first century has deeply troubled Americans. The fast-growing economies of Asia and Latin America and the burgeoning wealth of oil- and natural gas–producing nations suggest a transformational phase of globalization with increased competition for limited resources.

THE GREAT DEBATE

Americans have long offered their model of capitalism as an exemplar to the world. For accompanying a general belief in the "exceptionalism" of American values is a paradoxical faith in their universal relevance. Thus Americans not only want others to do business with them, but to act as they do. Americans must consider that there are other workable national models of capitalism and that indeed American business itself is presently experiencing profound changes. The belief that globalization means the emergence of one way of doing business or that there is one set of policies or institutions that will be effective for all societies is at best naive and at worst dangerous. A look backward offers useful perspective at a time of transition to a global economy.[1]

To say that we live in a global economy is a contemporary article of faith, but just what the term means is not clear. It does, however, acknowledge the greatly heightened multilateral level of economic activity in recent decades and the fact that the interconnectedness of the global economy has reached heights previously unknown. The present time is characterized for most Western nations by relatively free trade, limited restrictions on immigration, and hardly any regulation of the flow of capital. Business activity is increasingly less constricted by national barriers, as corporate transnational alliances and mergers proliferate in industries where great market size is imperative. With few exceptions, the world's nations are increasingly dependent on, and sensitive to, each others' decisions, prospects, and troubles.[2]

Where once the core of international trade was in bulk commodities it is now in the organization of production in far-flung networks. A paradigm shift has occurred in the way goods are made, tracked, and transported since the 1960s. Giant containerized ships are loaded by cranes with forty-foot barcoded containers, each with a carrying capacity of thirty tons, and often given a turnaround time of a day or two between voyages. International data services and the brokerage industry now transfer huge sums of money overnight from one national market to another, and firms shift their operations from one part of the world to another with ease. It is presently not unusual for a company to have its research and development in Switzerland, its engineering in India, its manufacturing in China, and its marketing functions and headquarters in the United States. National governments have found their ability to control multinational corporations or the momentum and direction of trade more problematic. Thus the ability of governments to restrict commerce and technology transfers is severely limited. Indeed, a revolution in communication has led to speculation that, in a cell phone and Internet world, a new global consciousness may arise, changing the very meaning of state sovereignty.

Free trade across borders is the ideal of many world leaders and economists who regard it as the touchstone of economic growth and rapid promotion of aggregate wealth: a win-win situation. They believe, as proposed by David Ricardo's theory of "comparative advantage," that all will eventually benefit, as each country through effective use of its resources and skills will in time arrive at a mix of goods and services to sell competitively, while buying from other nations with different strengths. To its critics, and they are numerous, globalization is spreading a culture of greed in which the vulnerable and the poor worldwide are ruthlessly exploited for the sake of corporate profits, while in underdeveloped nations traditional values and social orders are undone by novel ideas and ways. Moreover, they argue that even in advanced nations such as the United States there are no necessary gains for the economy as a whole. Nor does Ricardo's conceptualization, they note, reflect a sophisticated awareness that economic relations between nations set the overall tone and depth of the relationship and that a nation's military power and national well-being and world influence is dependent on a country's economic performance.

BACKGROUND

An estimated 3 percent of the world's workforce in 2008 resided outside the country of the worker's citizenship. The revolution in information technology (computers, telecommunications, and semiconductors) is reducing the cost of communication and speeding the diffusion of technology worldwide. Time and space can no longer hinder far-flung trade or, for that matter, the greenhouse gas effect and atmospheric depletion. Communications technology now allows services to be delivered from afar, and capital chases profit freely around the world. For the first time in history most of the world's people are bound tightly together in a global capitalist system with international institutions, such as the WTO and the International Monetary Fund (IMF), whose purpose is to foster intertwining economic development and trade.

That this development is the result of a long process is evidenced by an arresting passage in the *Communist Manifesto* (1848). In the very decade to which many economic historians date the beginnings of a global economy, Marx and Engels wrote: "In place of the old wants satisfied by the production of [one] country, we find new wants, requiring for their satisfaction the products of distant lands and climes. In place of the old local and national seclusion and self-sufficiency, we have intercourse in every direction, universal interdependence of nations."

As Marx recognized, nations are really political economies whose politics and cultures are largely shaped by the way production is organized, and accordingly countries and cultures must profoundly transform themselves to be players in a global capitalist system. The world has, of course, long been linked by trading routes and mercantile activity. But until recently it had been assumed that countries linked by trade need not share values and a vision. Now, however, it seems to be expected, at least by Washington, that forward-looking nations must embrace not only the free market but also democratic institutions and common policies on human rights and the environment. A United Nations report, "Globalization and the State," in 2001 stated only a few of the profound implications of globalization when it noted that the problems of poverty in foreign lands soon become one's own problem: of illegal immigration, pollution, contagious disease, fanaticism, and terrorism.

Most economists believe the more world trade the better, but an increase in trade also exacts a price—the interdependence of economies poses perils as well as promises. Globalization increases capabilities and vulnerabilities simultaneously. With increased trade, a country certainly grows richer in gaining access to more goods at lower prices, but those domestic sectors of the economy in competition with new imports experience dislocation and job losses that are often harmful to workers and small businesses. For example, the rise of China raises questions about the pressure on American jobs and wages of low-skilled labor. After considering the postwar rise in trade and the role of the United States in promoting free-trade policies as furthering American interests in the context of the Cold War, this chapter will conclude with a discussion of the implications of a global economy for public policy.

It is optimistically argued by supporters of free trade and the global economy that all nations more or less gain from it. However, some scholars have suggested a tripartite theory of segmentation of global capitalism into core, middling, and peripheral economies, with nations having different economic roles that allow some to exploit the others. Much of this work rests on older theories of imperialism. Important as this issue is, it is too complex and controversial to be dealt with except in a tangential fashion in this chapter.[3]

Throughout history, long-distance trade has been critical to developing and sustaining market economies. However, the half century between the Civil War and World War I saw a remarkable and unprecedented free movement of people, goods, and capital. The advent of the steamship and the transatlantic telegraph greatly reduced the costs of transporting goods and people across oceans, and this, combined with loosening trade restrictions, resulted in a vast upsurge in international investment and trade—and immigration. But in the 1930s—with its Depression, trade wars, and currency devaluations—world trade shrank to half of the 1910 figures. As the trade collapse prolonged the Depression of the 1930s, the United States sought to forestall a return to economic warfare, even as World War II reached its final stages. Washington's actions in promoting international trade reflected self-interest but also an ideological commitment to free trade and the exporting of the American economic model to the world. These ideological considerations would be reinforced by the half century of the Cold War. By 1950 free trade and collective defense became the twin beacons of American foreign policy. But it was only in the 1970s that most Americans truly realized the new and growing importance of international trade to the domestic economy and their lifestyles, as they discovered that all sorts of goods they bought—from sweaters to cars—that once had carried a "Made in America" label now came from elsewhere.

EXPORTING THE AMERICAN MODEL

World War II represented a more nearly global struggle than the first and resulted in four times the fatalities. The vast scale of destruction, combined with the political dislocation caused by realigned borders and collapsing colonial empires, suggested a prolonged period of world economic decline. In the aftermath of World War II, the United States sought world leadership in order to fashion a global order compatible with its values and interests. This strategy rested on the belief that pro-American democracies could flourish only in prospering economies. Such economies in turn required market capitalism, free trade between nations, and stable international financial institutions. In the words of Cordell Hull, secretary of state under Franklin D. Roosevelt, "Enduring peace and the welfare of nations are indissolubly connected with friendliness, fairness, equality, and the maximum practicable degree of freedom in international trade."[4] Although this outlook relied on idealistic themes that predated the rise of the Cold War, its postwar popularity and influence in Washington also reflected the world's division into two opposing ideological blocs.[5]

The American postwar worldview rested on assumptions brought forward by the Cold War. Foremost was the need "to stop the spread of communism." Compatible with this in theory (though not always in practice, since the United States often supported reactionary anticommunist regimes) was the American conviction that exporting its political and economic values offered the best hope for a peaceful progressive world. The rest of the world clearly required U.S. trade and help in 1945. Few influential Americans doubted that by helping others they could help the nation's business and foreign trade to flourish in a free-market world. Hopefully, increased exports would forestall a postwar depression.

COLD WAR OBJECTIVES

In pursuing its Cold War objective of containing communism, Washington placed strategic objectives above domestic economic interests. Contrary to the view of Marxists and of other critics, the United States did not conduct the Cold War primarily to advance economic goals. American Cold War policies mainly reflected straightforward geopolitical goals, based primarily on ideological and security considerations; and when economic interests conflicted with these, they often fell by the wayside. A study of Washington's behavior toward the American steel industry after 1945, for example, concluded that "post war problems of international trade in steel were left almost entirely in the hands of agencies and commissions devoted to the restoration of war-torn economies [in Europe], and not with groups seeking to establish any long-term policy or strategy of the American producers."[6] The result by the 1970s was an ailing American steel industry that has never fully recovered.

In innumerable ways, strategic grasp strained resources, and the costs of pursuing America's Cold War policies contributed greatly by the late 1960s to weakening the U.S. competitive position in the world economy. Early in the Cold War, the major American goals were initially the rapid rebuilding of war-torn Western European economies to deter internal communist take-overs, and then later the development of an effective military alliance against Soviet expansionist ambitions. Several of the recipient nations—notably France, Germany, and Japan—had long traditions of state involvement in shaping economic developments, and their governments subsidized (and even sometimes partially owned) the international companies or cartels op-erated by their citizens. Many rebuilding nations managed important sectors of their economies. In contrast, the American practice largely left a quick conversion to a peacetime economy, completed by the end of 1947, to market factors. Robert Kuttner has described this period: "Explicit industrial goals were eschewed as unnecessary, as contrary to our stated ideology, and as a bad example to our trading partners." In any case, such a course would have proven politically unfeasible.[7]

In the 1950s, Washington sought to stabilize what it regarded as satisfac-tory economic performance, rather than to spur change and growth. The one exception was the buildup of a formidable defense-oriented industry in the 1950s, starting with the Korean War, and this followed a logic related to the progress of the Cold War. The view that military buildup and foreign pol-icy contained a hidden agenda—to pump up a sluggish domestic economy and to practice "economic imperialism"—is challenged by the results, even though specific interest groups in the military-industrial complex certainly profited. By the end of the 1950s, massive spending on the military and foreign aid had created problems in the form of an unfavorable trade balance as a flood of dollars was sent overseas.

Overall, America's conduct of its foreign policy received high marks in the 1950s from the American people. The objective of a Pax Americana resting on loyal allies, engaged in an expanding network of free trade, proved largely successful; former enemies had been effectively transformed into allies.

ALLIES AND COMPETITORS

European recovery had relied greatly on the Marshall Plan and other Ameri-can aid programs, which provided $17 billion in assistance to Western Euro-pean governments between 1948 and 1952. Notable among the Marshall Plan's accomplishments was the economic reintegration of West Germany with the remainder of Western Europe, a Cold War priority after 1948. By 1951 West Germany's industrial production stood a third higher than the prewar figure, and spectacular gains, "the German miracle," occurred for the remainder of the decade.

Recovery in Japan initially proceeded at a slower pace. Prewar production figures were not reached until the middle of the 1950s, and only then after Japan acted as a supply area for the American forces in the Korean War. Totally dependent on imported resources and foreign markets, the Japanese confronted more serious challenges than the Germans. With considerable American assistance, the Japanese triumphed over these challenges. The United States, for example, opened its markets to Japanese goods even while permitting Japan to protect its own home markets, a policy not fully ended until 1978.[8]

According to Yale historian Paul Kennedy, real income in Western Europe rose as much in a single generation after 1950 as it had in the previous 150 years. In England plans for government-sponsored planned "new towns" built between 1946 and 1951 assumed that working-class families would never own private autos—twenty years later their choked road systems could not handle the traffic. The economies of Western Europe and, to a lesser extent, Japan had become consumer societies along American lines, where ordinary citizens routinely expected goods and services formerly reserved before the war for the wealthy.

The momentum of Western European postwar growth continued throughout the 1960s at levels higher than in the United States. America's lead in the standard of living slowly dwindled, and by decade's end Western Europe had caught up with America. It is noteworthy that although the Soviet Union and many Eastern-bloc nations with similar state-controlled "command economies" experienced impressive growth in industrial capacity (as measured by such things as tonnages of iron or coal) until the end of the 1950s, they failed in the 1960s to effectively convert to a consumer economy. Khrushchev, the Soviet leader, on a visit to the United States in 1959, dismissed the whole question by claiming: "Russians will never want to own automobiles; cheap taxis make more sense." This failure to achieve a consumer economy based on market factors represented an Achilles' heel, one which contributed greatly to the eventual abandonment of communism by the Soviet Union and Eastern Europe.

The postwar economic miracles of much of Western Europe and Japan were often credited to using forms of mixed economies that encouraged co-operation and planning between government, management, and the unions.

The Japanese in particular placed great weight on social stability and team-work to promote a dynamic economy in the absence of natural advantages. Especially in Japan, but also elsewhere, governmental policies focused on encouraging preferred industries and promoting exports, frequently while imposing restrictions on companies buying from foreign suppliers.

Other nations relied heavily in the postwar decades on American technology, sending observers to American plants to study production techniques and enrolling their best students in American business schools. Investment by American corporations in foreign branches during the 1960s contributed to sustaining high growth levels and in spreading American technology and business organization. Perhaps the most significant American contribution to shaping the postwar economies of the West sprang from its efforts to create a new institutional framework for international trade. Export-led economic growth offered Western Europe and Japan the stimulus for sustained rapid growth, and the advantages provided American business by a large domestic market (which encouraged economies of scale) were now enjoyed by others as international trade increased. Despite day-to-day trade frictions, the world moved from a closed system to one that was increasingly open.

INTERNATIONAL INSTITUTIONS OF TRADE

Starting with the Bretton Woods conference in 1944, the United States shaped the institutional framework for a greatly expanded trade between nations. As noted earlier, in chapter 12, the Bretton Woods Agreement established the IMF and the International Bank for Reconstruction and Redevelopment, commonly known as the World Bank. Both were started initially to help war-torn Europe but shifted their attention in the 1950s to Third World nations. The publicly owned World Bank sells bonds to finance development in needy nations. The IMF is a "club." Member nations agree to abide by a code of economic conduct and can draw on IMF funds. At its start, the IMF maintained fixed exchange rates for foreign currency based on the dollar's convertibility to gold, but in 1971, as noted earlier, the United States ended this policy.[9]

To avoid the trade wars of the 1930s, the United States reduced tariff rates at the end of World War II. At least in theory, the ultimate argument for free trade rested on David Ricardo's theories of comparative national advantages. If all nations specialized in what they did best, each in turn would benefit from an efficient and growing world economy. In theory all gain. But powerful groups within nations (as well as many governments) viewed free trade as dangerous to their interests.

Under UN sponsorship, but on the initiative of the United States, twelve nations signed in 1947 the General Agreement on Tariffs and Trade (GATT). Seven multiyear GATT meetings, known as rounds, occurred between 1947 and 1980, in which countries lowered tariffs in return for concessions from other nations. But the process was so slow, and involved so many trade-offs, that it often entrenched protected industries. The seventh meeting, the so-called Tokyo Round, lasted from 1973 to 1980, and an eighth, the Uruguay Round, started in 1986 and finally concluded with an agreement in 1993.

The Uruguay Pact replaced GATT in 1995 with a new umbrella organization, the WTO. Unlike its predecessor, the WTO is empowered to enforce trade accords and assess penalties for violations in the form of trade sanctions. Two primary principles guide the organization: 1) "most favored nation"—a trade privilege given by one member nation to another must be extended to all members; and 2) "national treatment"—a nation must give the same treatment to foreign goods and services that it gives its own. The agreement also covered areas previously outside the GATT system, including the flow of international investments, trade in patents and copyrights, and trade in such services as banking and insurance. Agricultural subsidies were to be reduced and limited. The new rules required countries to provide less protection for many industries that had been helped by import quotas—such as textiles in the United States. Nevertheless, nations continued to seek advantages over the others by relying on nontariff barriers (import quotas, voluntary export restraints, or various structural impediments) to limit imports.

The WTO is highly controversial (as are the IMF and the World Bank). This is not only because of its policies but also because of its role as an institutional symbol of the global economy. The annual meeting in Seattle in 1999 was greeted by mass protests that have been repeated yearly. To critics on the left, the WTO's policies favor powerful corporations from the rich nations at the expense of workers and poor farmers worldwide. A different line of criticism is that the WTO gives powers to international bureaucrats that rightfully belong to the elected representatives of sovereign nations. The Doha Round was launched shortly after 9/11 to respond to the charges that previous rounds of trade negotiations had treated poor nations unfairly. In May 2008, 151 nations belonged to the WTO.[10]

There is also the possibility that regional trading blocs may someday challenge the WTO as the major organizer of international trade. The European Union, some experts suggest, foretells this anticipated development of formidable regional trading blocs. As an expression of self-assertion and independence from the United States, six nations signed the Treaty of Rome in 1957 to create the European Economic Community (EEC), which in 1993 was again renamed the European Union (EU). By early 2008, membership had increased to twenty-seven. All trade barriers to the free movement of goods, services, people, and money among the member nations, with a population nearing half a billion, has, in theory, ended. To the EU's supporters, the eventual goal is a true common market and possibly a unified political entity. Important steps toward this goal have been the creation of a common currency, the euro, and a European Central Bank. The new European Central Bank has arranged for EU nations to choose to adopt the euro as national currency, and fifteen nations had done so by the end of 2007. Supporters believe the single currency will greatly reduce the transaction costs of buying goods and services among member nations, thus encouraging economic integration and the lowering of costs. Clearly most of Europe is now involved in remaking its, and the world's, political and economic structures.

FLOATING CURRENCIES

Since the United States ended the dollar's convertibility to gold in 1971, most Western nations have permitted the exchange rate of their currency to float. Floating exchange rates have on occasion led to volatility and troubling uncertainty for international business leaders, financiers, and governments. "Fiat money," so-called because it is created by government fiat, is backed only by the promises of central bankers to protect the value of their currencies. The creation of the G-7 or "Group of Seven" at the end of the 1970s (the central banks of the United States, Canada, Japan, France, United Kingdom, West Germany, and Italy) represented an effort to use these central banks to limit extreme fluctuations. After the breakup of the USSR, Russia became an associate member, leading to the organization being referred to as G-7 plus one, or simply G-8.

The central banks of the G-8 coordinate their policies of purchasing and selling currency to stabilize exchange rates. But the inability of the central bankers to defend the dollar against "runs" by speculators in 1994 called into question their relative strength against that of money traders able to move trillions of dollars across borders in hours. Indeed, some have questioned the ability of central banks to manipulate the markets—that in any battle of strength they would lose to market forces. The sudden, sharp movements of "hot money"—funds temporarily invested in a country to make a quick killing—can be destabilizing and can cause financial crises, as indeed happened in East Asia in mid-1997, with ripple effects throughout global financial markets for two years. Central banks and the IMF were uncertain how to react.[11]

THE IMPORTANCE OF FOREIGN TRADE

For most of the country's history the American economy had been relatively self-contained. Manufacturers produced for an American market, and distributors and retailers sold to American consumers. From the Civil War to the 1960s, foreign trade accounted for roughly 3 percent to 4 percent of the GDP, imports and exports each counting for half this figure. The big jump in foreign trade occurred in the 1960s and 1970s, spearheaded by rising Japanese imports, and by 1980 this figure had increased to nearly 11 percent. By the end of the century, it had risen to slightly over 15 percent. The escalating importance of world trade to American business appears irreversible. Nevertheless, compared to other industrial nations, the United States remains relatively self-contained, with the notable exception of oil. Import and export statistics appear modest when measured against those of Germany or Japan, or for that matter when considered in terms of the economy as a whole. But statistics do not reveal the whole story.

Reductions in transportation and communication costs in recent decades have more than enhanced the importance of worldwide markets sectors: they have integrated them so much as to blur former national distinctions. The historic national economy, in which a product was exported from one country to another, has been replaced by a multinational economy in which value may be added to the product in several different nations. So-called transnational companies often design their product in one country, manufacture it in another, and sell it in a third. Alternatively, parts produced in various countries are assembled in one, making it impossible to determine which nation produced the product. Indeed, thanks to globalization and the opening of new markets, it is increasingly difficult to view global corporations as attached to a particular country.

The new global economy is leading to structural changes in the nature of the American economy and corporate organization of profound scale and complexity. A typical large American corporation earned 10 percent to 20 percent of its profit from abroad in 1970; but by 2008 many earned at least half their profit overseas. Indeed, in 2006, Coca-Cola made over 80 percent of its profits outside North America and was becoming more and more dependent on developing markets for business growth. Multinational corporations, with their transplanted factories, create problems regarding regulating standards for workers and the environment, which far surpass in complexity those attending the rise of a national market and big business at the end of the nineteenth century. Globalization also makes it hard to decide the nationality of a company and its subsidiaries and where and how they should pay taxes. Not surprisingly, foreign subsidiaries of American companies report higher profit margins in low-tax countries than in high-tax countries.

This globalization of companies and markets has created problems for American antitrust policies; Washington's decision to block a merger between an American and foreign company, or to prohibit a business practice by either, can potentially cause harm to economies half a world away. Efforts to work out international guidelines by the WTO have been hampered by a general lack of agreement on ground rules. Many countries lack any laws protecting competition, and even those that do have widely differing views about their aims and means of enforcement. Third World nations eager for new businesses and investments are understandably reluctant to do anything that would discourage attracting these.

THE RISE AND FALL OF THE JAPANESE THREAT

American economists tend to accept David Ricardo's theory of comparative advantage, but many other Americans do not. They regard the global economy as a highly competitive world of winners and losers. This view may reflect the fact that Americans first became aware of the global economy in the 1970s and 1980s. At that time, amid fears that their economy was in decline, Americans focused their concern on consistent trade deficits with Japan. As the Japanese created the world's most dynamic auto industry and penetrated the American market, Americans watched with awe and apprehension. The ability of the Japanese to best American industry in its home market during the 1980s—and in such areas of former dominance as electronics and microchips—assumed a transcendental symbolism, above and beyond economics. The United States no longer enjoyed a natural edge in manufacturing because of its natural resources. Intangible factors like technological know-how and organizational skill mattered more than the cost of material, which had once provided America a national advantage.

Michael Porter of the Harvard Business School wrote: "There's a new paradigm of international competition and that paradigm is based on dynamism, on the capacity of firms to innovate and to upgrade the sophistication of how they compete. Now success depends on relentless investment by companies."[12] The frequent use of the term "global competition" in the 1980s suggested a Darwinian world of international trade played as a "zero sum game" in which one country's success comes at the expense of others. And Americans feared they had lost out to the Japanese. Indeed, the nature of the Japanese threat, relying as it did on government's orchestrating of the economy and actively promoting and supporting new high-tech industries, confounded Americans and provoked a debate on whether the United States needed a similar industrial policy.

Some blamed the Japanese for unfair business practices, and Washington demanded that Japan open up restricted markets. The World Bank estimated in 1990 that Japan "formally protected" about one-quarter of its imports. "Informal checks" on imports into Japan were also important and very difficult to prove. A meticulous examination of American trade policy grievances against Japan by C. Fred Bergsten and Marcus Noland in 1993, for the Washington-based Institute for International Economics, concluded that indeed the country's trade barriers had been designed to safeguard its market for Japanese business. Moreover, Japanese companies in the auto industry did not provide the health and retirement benefits that the United Auto Workers had negotiated during the U.S. industry's prosperous days.[13]

Americans also worried that the Japanese had surpassed the country in industrial know-how. Numerous books appeared proposing ways that Americans might learn from the Japanese. A small island nation, deficient in resources, easily defeated by American power and technology in 1945, threatened to surpass America as the world's premier economic power.

Japan's dramatic growth had relied on governmental policies designed to ensure industrial strength. Important in this regard was the powerful Ministry of International Trade and Industry (MITI). The MITI provided Japanese factories and their suppliers in selective industries with export subsidies, trade barriers to protect the home market, and low-cost credit. Banks were encouraged, and even directed, to provide preferential loans to industries offering high growth potential. The MITI promoted the dominance of the economy by industrial-financial cartels, the *keiretsu*. These were loosely knit industrial and banking groups with sprawling interests, which bought mainly from within the group and often owned stock in each other's companies. In effect, they shared a common core of managers and coordinated their activities, including the planning of strategy. Initially, the strategy worked. Investment boomed in industries from steel to shipbuilding, lifting many of Japan's best companies into international competitiveness.

Japanese exports rose from 3 percent of all world trade in 1960 to 8 percent in 1978 and then to 12 percent in 1989. By then, Japan accounted for a third of the world's automobiles and consumer electronics products, and in 1989 seven of the ten largest banks in the world were Japanese. Running the world's largest trade surpluses, Japan was widely hailed as the world's most dynamic economy, and there was considerable talk that Japanese "state-and-network capitalism"—the close linkage of government officials, *keiretsu*, and banks—offered an effective alternative to the market-driven American model.[14]

Japanese culture strongly stressed conformity, the discipline of group norms, and the acceptance of collective authority. Harmonious relations were considered essential to stability, and this was regarded as crucial to progress. In return for total loyalty, employees were guaranteed lifetime employment, with salaries and promotions largely based on seniority. Litigation and lawyers were rarely resorted to—confrontation could lead to loss of face for the defeated party. Decisions were usually reached through the shaping of a consensus in which all accepted that their interests had been accommodated and due deference shown them.

Disadvantaged by the "Japanese system" were consumers, who paid the highest prices for goods in the world, and workers, who had to rely on the good faith of their employers. The result was low consumer spending, high savings and investment, and meager imports. A succession of economic shocks in the late 1980s increasingly led Japanese bureaucrats to shelter inefficient firms. This created, in effect, a dual economy: highly competitive export companies like Toyota and Sony coexisted with weak sectors in agriculture, raw materials, and retailing, which were totally dependent on the domestic market.[15]

In fact, the Japanese government lacked any center of accountability, leaving conflicting bureaucracies to contend for power. Public works projects aimed at stimulating the economy created a highly corrupt "construction-industrial complex," and much of Japan's apparent affluence rested on a bubble economy of greatly inflated real estate and stock values. The remarkable efficiency of its export-driven industrial sector was fused with "crony capitalism," whereby banks loaned money in terms of personal relations and the accounting system generally clouded the true nature of business activity and profits. Once regarded as the world's most efficient industrial producers, the Japanese now fell behind in the digital revolution of the 1990s, unable to keep up with America's adept use of Internet technology.

It took several years for these weaknesses to be fully manifest. Until then Americans remained worried. By the early 1990s Japan was the world's second-richest nation and, with a population half that of the United States, had achieved an economy 60 percent the size of the American economy. As late as the first term of the Clinton presidency, many analysts believed that the administratively guided "Japanese system" represented a superior form of capitalism. Several Clinton advisers, including Laura Tyson, who chaired his Council of Economic Advisers, favored an industrial policy in which specific American industries would be singled out for governmental support through tax policies, direct subsidies, trade protection, and, when necessary, a relaxed antitrust stance on cooperative ventures in research and development. Events, however, soon challenged the view that the United States needed a Japanese-style industrial policy.

Japanese annual economic growth limped through the 1990s at a weak 1.3 percent. Under Ministry of Finance guidance, banks loaned to weak firms, keeping them in business and undermining the entire economy, including the banking system. Stifling governmental regulation combined with weak management to permit widespread inefficiency and a dwindling return on capital. Critics charged that bureaucrats had reacted to the economy's sag by ordering Japanese companies to prop up the stock market with funds provided by banks. The banks in return cooked their books to avoid huge write-offs—in the range of a trillion dollars—on bad real estate–backed debts, that is, until worried foreign governments forced a halt.

The Japanese, once thought to have a genius for adapting to change, did not respond decisively to these systemic problems. The American business system, focused as it was on capital return to increase shareholder value, apparently had proven superior to the Japanese model of stakeholder capitalism.[16]

It was now the turn of American businesspeople, academicians, and politicians to lecture the Japanese on the superiority of American market-driven capitalism with its survival-of-the-fittest business approach. By June 1997 a Clinton administration spokesman bragged that the "United States was the world's only economic superpower." The Japanese model was derided as inviting cronyism, corruption, and sweetheart deals. The declining fortunes of the Japanese economy in the 1990s emphasized the volatility of a global economy marked by strong competition and shifting technology. It also underscored the difficulty in anticipating the winds of change in a modern economy of intimidating complexity in which the unexpected frequently happens. In the first years of the twenty-first century, Americans would soon have reason to be concerned about the remarkable rise of China's economy and what this might portend for America's future.

AMERICAN INDUSTRY IN A GLOBAL ECONOMY

The key to America's regaining competitive effectiveness in the global economy of the 1990s was market-driven discipline. Resources moved quickly from older industries to newer ones, as capital goods and retooling spearheaded the rise in American exports. The most successful factories adopted new technologies, forced union concessions, and outsourced components to cut back on costs and labor. Due to increases in productivity, America, with a greatly reduced industrial workforce, produced more in 2000 than ever. But less and less of what Americans bought was made in the U.S.A.

Once again, it was demonstrated that the genius of the American economic system is its remarkable ability to adapt quickly to changes in the business environment. This, of course, is largely explained by the relative absence of impediments to change imposed on management from government, unions, or other entrenched interests. The debate on the need for a national industrial policy subsided as fear of Japanese prowess evaporated. However, it may be resumed in time for reasons we shall now discuss.

Manufacturing makes up a surprisingly small percentage of American output. In 2001, 78 percent of U.S. output consisted of services rather than goods, although services are only 20 percent of U.S. trade. The service sector of the economy was long thought to be impervious to the challenges of international competition and job losses. With the downturn of 2001, however, American companies began outsourcing white-collar service jobs to lower cost centers in countries such as India, the Philippines, and Sri Lanka. Such jobs typically involved customer service, call centers, help desks, payroll processing, and record keeping. Often this work had been previously domestically outsourced, but increasingly corporations have either set up operations overseas or have used foreign vendors to take advantage of skilled labor at low wages and low regulatory operational costs.

Initially, most of the white-collar jobs lost to American workers were fairly low level, but over time almost all levels of employment may be open to such risks. The cost savings from outsourcing can be considerable, and in a low-margin industry, this could be the difference between profit and loss. Articles in 2003 on overseas outsourcing quoted researchers predicting a loss in the range of 3 million to 4 million white-collar jobs by 2015. Scholars began talking about a new industrial revolution in communication technology that would allow global outsourcing of such well-paying jobs as financial analyst, computer programmer, and film and video editor.

As the economies of China and India and other nations expand greatly on the strength of their low wages, an increasingly skilled labor force, and rising technological prowess, many American workers worry about their job security and wages. Nor will these concerns go away in the near future. Management has acquired greater leverage. It has become a truism in the United Sates and in other advanced economies that a global economy has made capital strong and labor weak. With capital highly mobile, companies tell workers to take what is offered or they will look elsewhere for employees. The old national and geographic boundaries between labor markets have broken down. This development accelerates the pressure on wages across large swaths of the economy, with profound impact on national average wages. And outsourcing is one of a score of controversial issues, many not economic in nature, arising from a global economy. Long-term economic and demographic trends are steadily shifting the geopolitical weight away from the United States and Europe, and Washington has to be increasingly concerned with the security implications of this shift. There has been a sharp diminishment of the world's perception and respect for American power and prestige since 2001. How much of this is temporary and can be explained by inept handling of foreign policy and how much is due to long-range shifts in global geopolitical factors remains to be seen. Certainly the view of America's unchallengeable economic and military primacy that emerged after the Cold War was no longer tenable as George W. Bush ended his presidency.

One development that has caused increasing concern in the United States is the growing prominence of "sovereign wealth funds," a term that came into popular usage only in 2005. Sovereign wealth funds are state-owned funds of financial assets created by countries that have budgetary surpluses and little international debt. They can be used to buy stocks, bonds, and companies anywhere in the world. At the beginning of 2008, it was estimated that their capitalization totaled nearly $3 trillion. Investments may be made for economic or strategic concerns or a combination. It is the use of sovereign wealth funds for strategic purposes, most notably to gain control of important industries, facilities, and information, that is the major reason for worry about their growing importance.

In a world grown small, the policies of one nation or the actions of its companies can profoundly affect other countries and indeed global ecology. The obvious need is for the establishment by international agencies of firm guidelines for international business practices. But this, given the high stakes and the mutual suspicions involved, is a difficult task that cannot be accomplished quickly and easily, if at all. Moreover, as noted, the United States has a less dominant economic position than formerly from which to achieve its foreign policy goals.

The policies of all governments and the practices of all businesses must increasingly reflect international concerns. Wage and work policies affecting the ordinary American must also be considered in terms of how they will influence America's competitive standing in world trade. Americans can no longer measure themselves exclusively by the yardstick "Made in America."

WINNERS AND LOSERS IN A GLOBAL ECONOMY

A report in 2004 by the UN's International Labor Organization, entitled "A Fair Globalization," noted that "globalization is a divisive subject. It verges on a dialogue of the deaf, both nationally and internationally." An impressive panel of experts drawn from academics and government circles explained the growing antagonism to globalization resulting from its uneven benefits. They reported that globalization was not only creating a growing divide between rich and poor countries, but within nations, where the gap between rich and poor was also widening.[17]

Third World nations have correctly charged that advanced industrial nations set the rules for international trade. In agriculture, for example, the latter have dismantled barriers in areas where they have a competitive advantage, while according protection and subsidies to politically powerful agricultural interests. The World Bank estimated in 2002 that an end to farm protectionist policies by rich nations could expand global wealth by $.5 trillion, lifting 150 million people out of poverty by 2015. However, an effort by the WTO in 2003 to improve the situation was foiled by the opposition of the richer nations, including the United States.

The widening gap between rich and poor nations was underscored in the UN report by the statistic that 14 percent of the world's population accounted for over half the world's trade and foreign investment. The report also noted that globalization often promoted child labor, unhealthy working conditions, and industrial abuse of the environment in many of the poorer nations. Nevertheless, the underlying premise of the experts was that with proper safeguards and codes to protect labor and the environment the global market economy has potential for good. They rejected out of hand the view of some pessimists that poor countries stay poor because they often have little that rich countries want or need.

The benefits of the global economy for Americans are also problematic. Globalization, either directly or indirectly, has contributed to growing disparities of income distribution. In 2001 the top 1 percent of Americans earned 17 percent of the gross national income, a level last seen in the 1920s. Increasing reliance on imports, as well as the outsourcing of work to foreign companies or employees, is a threat to American jobs, wages, unions, and environmental standards. Whereas labor costs hovered at an average of about $18 an hour in the United States, Japan, and Western Europe in 2000, the average in most emerging economies was less than $2 an hour. A 1997 study by the World Economic Forum in Geneva concluded: "The temptation to concentrate new industrial activities, or relocate existing ones to low wage nations, to the detriment of high wage nations will be difficult to resist." The Federal Reserve Bank of New York estimated that about 2.9 million American jobs were lost as a result of imports or the shifting of domestic jobs overseas between 1997 and 2003, a figure equal to 2.3 percent of the labor force in 2003. Nor can labor standards be universalized, since differences in cultural and economic conditions among countries will remain. The impact of international trade on the shaping of the economy and the American wage structure requires constant reevaluation and informed public policies. Rising corporate profits for American companies without increases in real wages for the American worker is a recipe for trouble.

"What's good for the country is good for General Motors and vice versa" is a celebrated statement by Charles Wilson, the CEO of General Motors, at his confirmation hearing before becoming secretary of defense in 1953. The remark assumed the alignment of interests of American corporations with their workers and the national economy. Although generally true at the time, it is much less true in 2008.

As corporations expand activities globally, their interests and those of the nation increasingly decouple. For example, a corporation such as Dell has evolved a business model emphasizing information technology and other productivity-enhancing investments, together with global sourcing. As a consequence, Dell employs considerably more people offshore than in the United States and its products contain few American-made components.

Established in 1961, the Office of the United States Trade Representative (USTR) was elevated to a subcabinet level by the 1974 Trade Act. The head of USTR is the U.S. Trade Representative, who serves as the president's principal trade adviser and negotiator. The USTR has responsibility for coordinating the policies of all federal agencies involved in foreign trade and the job of writing and enforcing trade agreements. Yet in 2002 the Office of the United States Trade Representative, with a staff of 200 and a budget of $50 million, was smaller than many international law firms that lobbied it.

It is important to consider trade in terms of its consequences to American industry and its workers. Workers have borne the brunt of globalization, even as many corporations have profited from outsourcing. In an age when the click of a keyboard can move a good job from Seattle to Bangalore, free trade can no longer be regarded as a sacred cow. A poll reported by *Business Week* in the April 24, 2000, issue on the global economy described 10 percent of Americans as favoring free trade, 51 percent as "fair traders," and 37 percent as protectionists.[18] Political support for an open global economy has weakened considerably. Nobel economist Paul Samuelson, once a strong supporter of free trade, startled his colleagues when in 2004 he wrote that workers from rich countries are not always winners from globalization.[19]

Certain sectors of the American economy may need protection or encouragement. But this should not be a crutch to discourage greater efficiency and self-reliance. The danger with managed trade or industrial policies is that declining industries, such as textiles, seek preferential treatment at the expense of consumers, taxpayers, and even rising new industries. Misguided policies reflecting political influence and ignoring economic priorities would actually weaken our competitive position and add to the trade deficit; America cannot fall into the perilous position of the United Kingdom in the 1950s or Japan in the 1990s, when futile efforts to shore up declining industries caused a long lag in economic growth.[20]

Yet the belief that if government stopped interfering with business the economy would grow to benefit all is at odds with our history. In the nineteenth century, as noted in earlier chapters, government actively promoted canal and railroad building, while protective tariffs nurtured infant industries and federal funds financed agricultural research and educational training. In a similar manner, Washington must assist in improving the educational system and perhaps in promoting high-tech industries. The debate over whether the nation should have an industrial policy is far from over.

American workers are, of course, not the only ones to express concerns about the global economy. Many national leaders and others around the world believe that the United States uses the IMF and the World Bank to spread American-style capitalism and to rig international standards. In the Asian currency crisis of 1997, the Malaysian prime minister claimed that Washington had used its leverage to force open local economies so that American companies and banks could overheat them and promote currency speculation.

Other developments must be considered in a discussion of globalization. Since the mid-1980s, some signs have pointed to the emergence of three economic superblocs: one in North and Central America based on NAFTA and dominated by the United States; another the European Community led by Germany; and the third an East Asian group controlled by the Chinese as they surpass the Japanese as the region's economic giant. Some scholars reject the view that economic blocs are actually occurring; others view them as a real phenomena but disagree over their true significance.[21]

The Cold War required the minimizing of basic conflicts, whether political or economic, among the nations opposed to the Soviet bloc and allowed the United States to impose a strategic leadership. With this restraining force gone, national and regional disagreements will intensify. There is little question that the information revolution, in shrinking the planet, has greatly diminished barriers of contact between people divided by fundamental differences in all walks of life—economic, social, and cultural. Many outside the United States already complain bitterly of American "hegemonies," by which they mean efforts to impose a "single cultural model" based on American consumerism and media. Contrary to expectations once widely held, modern technology and the global economy may well be shaping a world of increasing psychological distances among people who occupy an ever-contracting space and who compete for ever-diminishing natural resources. Even as we want many of the same goods, we have different abilities to acquire them. The resulting tensions help explain the identity crises of religion and nationalism that permeate contemporary conflicts.[22]

Economists Jeffrey Sachs and Howard J. Schatz suggested in 1996 a reconsideration of the whole concept of national competition, defining competitiveness as "the ability of a nation's economy to make rapid and sustained gains in living standards" and downplaying the idea that nations gain only at each others' expense. Sachs and Schatz further argue that a nation's competitiveness is based on its openness to trade, commitment to free markets, investments in technology and human skills, and dedication to a rule of law, while maintaining social stability. To advocates of a national industrial policy, Sachs and Schatz are only restating Adam Smith, ignoring the Darwinian realities of a global economy in which only the strong prosper. The national industrial policy proponents note that the threat of jobs moving offshore contributed greatly to the erosion of American job security and nonwage benefits and the serious weakening of trade unions.[23]

THE TWENTY-FIRST CENTURY

At century's beginning, most major American firms are already part of a global economy that is seemingly here to stay. American companies and investors are putting more assets overseas; alliances and joint ventures where expertise is pooled and risks are shared have become the preferred way of doing business abroad. Our exports of goods and services, as they have since 1965, continue to grow at twice the rate of the domestic market, and new markets for our trade are rapidly emerging. The growing presence of China and Southeast Asia is a permanent factor in the world economy, and the region as a whole now rivals Europe and Japan. India, long a sleeping giant, has awakened, as its government has loosened its previous tight control of the economy.

At the beginning of the twenty-first century, the United States remains the world's strongest national economy. It leads the world in a significant number of industries: aerospace, beverages, computers, software, and telecommunications, to name a few. High-tech exports continue to exceed imports. No other country rivals the United States in the fields of communications, capital markets, and entertainment. Two-thirds of the world's top fifty companies are based in the United States; significantly, these include the eight biggest high-technology companies. Still, there are numerous reasons for concern.

As mentioned earlier, the rapidly changing international economy poses many different types of problems. Multinational companies exploit their transnational natures to escape the controls of national governments, and they can play governments off against one another through their decisions about where to locate operations. Global companies very frequently use unrealistic transfer prices to shift income from high-tax nations to low-tax countries, with the result that many multinational corporations often pay little or no taxes in the United States, or anywhere else for that matter.

New technologies, such as electronic transfer systems and offshore financial markets, have made it easy to shuffle money electronically from country to country. Since 1973 and the end of fixed exchange rates, the trend, strongly encouraged by the United States, has been for governments to loosen controls over the movement of currency, with rates largely rising and falling with the market. Approximately a trillion dollars' worth of currency was being traded daily in the mid-1990s, amid a growing concern that this capricious and highly volatile flow could prove destructive as well as beneficial. The global international financial crisis of 1997 demonstrated the fragile interdependence of the world's economies and currencies. The crisis began when speculators collapsed the value of Thailand's currency in July 1997 and caused an outflow of borrowed foreign capital. The "Asian flu" soon cut a wide swath, leaving weakened currencies, struggling stock markets, insolvent banks, failed businesses, and declining economies throughout the region. No less an authority than the brilliant money manager George Soros, of the Quantum Fund, who had made billions by betting against a weak British pound in 1992, warned that financial markets had grown so large and bankers so prone to herd behavior that they could destroy a nation's economy by massive withdrawals—especially when a country tried to defend its overvalued currency, as Thailand had.

When the highly leveraged investment fund Long-Term Capital Management almost collapsed in mid-1998, at the height of the crisis, the financial world in the United States trembled. Long-Term Capital Management was one of the nation's largest and most highly regarded hedge funds. Hedge funds had first appeared in the 1980s. As limited partnerships, the funds had no significant restrictions on the type of investment they could buy or sell—unlike a traditional mutual fund. Many hedge funds, as part of a diversified portfolio, bought and sold futures options on major foreign currencies. When Long-Term Capital Management lost heavily in the summer of 1998, the Federal Reserve System, fearing the fallout from its failure, mobilized more than a dozen private banks to save the firm.[24] As the crisis subsided in 1999, there was considerable discussion among financial experts about ways of avoiding a repetition. Reining in the volatility of the financial markets, all agree, will not be easy. Among the ideas discussed are setting up a global central bank and establishing controls to limit the very volatile flow of huge floating funds of investment capital. These funds promote currency speculation but also, on the positive side, allow countries with limited savings to undertake productive developments. Ironically, one of the ways that the United States is dependent on the global economy is that, having a low savings rate, it imports savings from abroad. This has led to a growing U.S. current account deficit, which is worrisome.

There is a need to continually reevaluate long-established views and the over-simple complacency that open markets, free globalization of national economies, and escalating international capital movements are necessarily good at all times and in all circumstances. Aside from economic issues, it is inevitable that the globalization of national economies must be divisive and even painful. Dissatisfaction mounts as globalization erodes the distinctiveness of communities and societies throughout the world. Often, rightly or wrongly, these changes are viewed as extending America's commercial culture. Cultural imperialism is perceived as connected to and reinforcing the economic exploitation attributed to globalization.[25]

Critics believe that economic disparity and social polarization are growing as the balance of power shifts increasingly to employers away from workers and as rich nations gain at the expense of poorer nations. French economist Daniel Cohen, in *Globalization and Its Enemies*, has suggested that the irony of globalization is that it has universalized the demand for a better life without providing the means to satisfy it. A UN report in 1999 claimed that 20 percent of the world's population possessed 86 percent of the world's GDP and used nearly 60 percent of its energy, while the poorest 20 percent had only 1 percent of its GDP. Most troubling was the report's finding that globalization of the world's economy had showed no signs of lessening the disparity.[26]

Another criticism of globalization is ecological. The global market is a market of rapacious consumption, placing mounting pressure on natural resources and threatening catastrophic air and water pollution. Our industrial technology poses environmental issues that require global regulation of business activity. Perhaps the most pressing long-range problems are related to reliance on fossil fuels and the resulting environmental changes, especially global warming. Here, with very few exceptions, the world's governments have demonstrated little will to deal meaningfully with very serious problems that are worsening rapidly and might indeed lead to large-scale economic dislocation and human disaster. The Kyoto Protocol of 1997 to limit greenhouse gas emissions, for example, has been ratified by 175 nations—it was rejected by the United States—and will expire in 2012, hopefully to be replaced by a more effective policy.[27]

Various groups, for different reasons, share the conviction that economic globalization is presently hurting people. American labor unions protest that free trade lowers wages and causes the outsourcing of jobs; other protesters rally against the use of child labor in developing nations by contractors working for multinational corporations; still others are concerned with ecological issues; and political radicals argue that the WTO, the IMF, and the World Bank all serve the interests of American imperialism—establishing rules and procedures to reinforce U.S. economic, political, and cultural domination—while widening the differences between rich and poor nations as well as between the rich and poor within a nation. Indeed, there is little dispute that in much of Africa, Latin America, and South Asia living standards declined from 1980 to 2000. Concerns about the global economy are coming to the fore very rapidly.[28]

THE PERILS OF GLOBALIZATION

There is reason for concern that the United States is losing mastery of its own destiny. The United Auto Workers, in negotiating a labor contract, must now consider the wage scale received by Japanese, German, and Korean auto workers and the possibilities of subcontracting work abroad. Political instability in small nations can add to the costs of food or clothing or inspire a flood of illegal immigrants to U.S. shores. American dependence on imported oil for two-thirds of its needs clearly is troubling and makes for vulnerability. In setting interest rates, balancing trade accounts, or financing the debt, Washington and the Federal Reserve System will, and must, weigh the policies and reactions of other countries and their citizens, who can create havoc by cashing in their dollars or pulling back from their American investments. Indeed, the negative impacts of globalization, such as outsourcing, may in the near future undermine the belief that globalization works in the national interest and may cause a shift in American policy toward protectionism. Active education and welfare policies are necessary to ease the adjustment of the American labor force to globalization.

Whatever the problems of a global economy, one has to accept that the world's economy has been permanently transformed. As Princeton economist Alan Blinder has noted, "The old assumption that if you cannot put it in a box, you cannot trade it is hopelessly obsolete."[29] Many aspects of globalization appear inescapable and irreversible unless we would have a return to the closed economies of the 1930s. The cheap and easy flow across borders of goods and information indeed suggests that there is much more to come. Capital and corporations quickly move from country to country, and technology is transferred from one nation to another overnight. Yet, even as the world's economy has become increasingly integrated, the world's political system remains fragmented. When the United Nations was formed in 1945, 54 nations enrolled as founding members. The membership in 2008 consists of 192 countries, with most of the new members coming from the European empires broken up after World War II. Some pessimistic analysts predict that nations increasingly competing for dwindling resources will lead to international instability and conflicts. U.S. involvement in Iraq and Iran certainly reflects the pivotal importance of Middle East petroleum in the global economy.

World energy consumption is projected to grow 50 percent between 2005 and 2020. China and India will both need to double their energy consumption to maintain a rapid pace of growth. A growing competition between the United States and China, the world's first- and second-largest consumers of energy, for oil seems inevitable, unless, of course, the United States dramatically decreases its dependence on oil.

Globalization is often associated with the United States. Many in the Third World regard the global economy as driven by America's desire for hegemony and profit. Indeed, iconic U.S. names—Coca-Cola, Marlboro, McDonald's, and Disney—are ubiquitous and constant reminders of America's commercial prowess. In fast-growing cities in East Asia, Africa, South America, and the Middle East, societies are being transformed as their populations are swept into the tumult of a modern world. Highly structured social rituals and long-established hierarchical orders confront raucous new freedoms. There is concern that what is emerging is a form of universal civilization, with the United States as its model. To many, this is simply unacceptable. Indeed, in parts of the Third World, the discourse of anti-Americanism fuels a culture of antimodernity because the key ideas of modernity are associated with the United States.

The currents of globalization are fast moving. The international flow of goods, services, capital, peoples, and information expands daily. Profound shifts occur in the global distribution of economic and political power. Whether the global economy in the future will promote greater cooperation among nations and peoples or provoke conflicts remains to be seen. History has too often demonstrated the power of religious fanaticism and nationalism to override economic considerations for easy optimism. Even without the issue of cultural clashes, it is clear that the United States in the twenty-first century faces the challenges of the rapid rise of China and India, the challenges of aging populations and low birthrates in much of the Western world, geopolitical instability, and, not least, the growth of complex corporate supply chains straddling the globe that no one controls or understands.[30]

Nevertheless, international political considerations aside, as long as communication becomes easier and transport remains cheap, globalization seems sure to continue. But if the era of cheap energy comes to an end—as the result of depletion of oil sources or in other ways—then rising transportation costs can reverse the increase of long-distance trade. In such a case, the material standards of living of Americans and many others will necessarily be lowered. If, however, the pace of globalization continues, we will have to replace a naive belief in the positive benefits of market-driven globalization with national policies intended to promote a vision of how the economy should serve national interests and the values of a good society. Such a vision must encompass a consideration in the post-9/11 world of the overlap of economic and security policies and their strategic integration. Business must also accept that it must be very much a part of whatever solutions governmental and multilateral institutions develop to cope with global issues involving not only economic challenges but also environmental and social concerns of an equally grave nature.

CHAPTER SEVENTEEN

Thinking Small

The day of small concerns within the means of many able men

seems to be over, never to return.—ANDREW CARNEGIE,

The Gospel of Wealth *(1900)*

We have lived through the age of big industry and the age of the

giant corporation, but I believe that this is the age of the entrepreneur,

the age of the individual. That is where America's prosperity is

coming from now, that's where it is going to come from in the future.

—RONALD REAGAN, *remarks to the students and faculty of*

St. John's University in New York, March 28, 1985

Giant, vertically integrated corporations have long been the U.S. economy's most prominent feature, but they have never totally dominated. The world of the small and often family-owned business was never static or insignificant. There have been many types of small businesses, and their nature and roles have varied over time and business sector. In flexible and specialty production, for example, small-scale enterprise has always retained importance. As disenchantment mounted with the Fortune 500 companies in the 1990s, small business, or at least a segment, with advantages of motivation and flexibility, began to be hailed as the new engine of economic growth.[1]

Small businesses accounted for over two-thirds of new jobs in the two decades after 1985. For the first time in nearly a century the importance of small businesses to the vitality of the economy and the entrepreneurial energy necessary for progress received significant attention. Individuals and small companies generated new technologies, which they then often sold to larger firms. Time will tell whether this new perspective on the importance of the role of small businesses will be sustained. Management theorists who promote the idea that competitive advantage presently lies with firms of reduced size indeed may very well be as guilty of oversimplification as their predecessors who hailed large integrated firms as the ultimate business form of the modern economy.

The remarkable rise of Wal-Mart in the last third of the twentieth century demonstrates that bigness still retains advantages in certain areas of the economy. In banking, the lure of size and global scale has not diminished but instead increased. At the start of the twenty-first century, giant enterprises and deep bureaucracies remain an essential part of the contemporary business scene, and no one has conclusively demonstrated that this will change soon. Moreover, it is necessary to keep in mind that the term "small business" encompasses a very big tent, from small companies with limited ambitions to new "start-up" companies based on novel ideas of high technology. Many innovative small enterprises are simply vassal organizations controlled by giant enterprises. Despite this diversity, small business—this very vague category—is highly emotionally charged in the American psyche, with its importance to the economy increasingly recognized.[2]

THE BACKBONE OF DEMOCRACY

Small business, "the little fellow," occupies a special niche in the pantheon of national heroes. Small business is regarded as quintessentially American. To many Americans, the large corporation remains an intimidating and impersonal abstraction. In contrast, small business is identified with familiar faces—the small-town shopkeeper, the insurance broker whom you can call with personal problems. Small business is assumed to have stronger loyalty and local ties, strengthening the social as well as local fabric of the community. It is David confronting the big-box Wal-Marts and Home Depots, which have set themselves up just outside the city limits to menace the Main Street merchants of America.

But above all, small business symbolizes the persistent American ideals of the self-made man or woman, opportunities for social mobility, and, perhaps as important, the Jeffersonian theme of independence gained by being one's own boss. It is in some ways the last American frontier, a psychological safety valve, which represents for many Americans the potential of another chance. In 2004, 8.6 percent of American adults—about 15.7 million people —started businesses. According to the Small Business Administration (SBA), about half of new companies last four years and only a quarter survive for ten years. But this effort epitomizes the American Dream and represents remarkable entrepreneurial energy.

From the earliest years of America settlement, ease of entry into small business characterized the colonies. The colonial situation had presaged the American patterns of scarce labor, high wages, and many entrances into and exits from small business. In June 1904, Henry Stimson, a Wall Street lawyer and future American statesman, in an *Atlantic Monthly* article, even called small business "a school of manhood."[3] To this very day, a privately owned small business evokes a simpler age of small towns and family farms, when the virtues of American civilization appeared self-evident and when an individual's business prowess and character all seemed intertwined.

Too often the talk and writings about the importance of small firms avoids defining this term. To most of us, small business refers vaguely to "the little guys," and by "big business" we commonly mean the large national corporations—in today's terms the Fortune 500. But between mom-and-pop operations and the multinational giants are all sorts of businesses that are difficult to categorize. How do we distinguish between big small businesses and big business? There is no easy answer. Even scholars cannot agree on where to make the distinction. The term "small business" is used for businesses operated exclusively by a proprietor all the way to companies with several hundred employees.

Created in 1953 but made a federal agency only in 1958, the SBA has the professional need and mandate to define this ambiguous term. Even so, its director, in 1988, conceded that there is no standard size definition of small business, but it will "vary from industry to industry."[4] However, statisticians collecting data for the SBA on small business use as their criteria for inclusion a business with a workforce of less than 500 or a net worth of under $10 million. In 2004 the SBA divided nearly 24 million businesses considered "small" into thirty-seven subcategories, based on annual revenues in some cases and workforce size in others—depending on the industry code assigned to a company under a Census Bureau classification system. But in contrast to the SBA's expansive definition, most federal and state laws and regulations place the small business cutoff at fifty employees. Some scholars, unhappy with this quantitative approach to a definition, have tried to replace it with a functional approach. They generalize that small businesses are usually tied to a local market, engage in only one or two operations, and have a simple management structure, with the owner often running the business.[5]

Nostalgia alone does not explain the recent revival of interest in small business. Small and medium-sized businesses are (or at least so it was argued) more conducive to the innovative high-tech activities needed by American business to meet global competition, while new types of communication, information, and control—cheap overnight deliveries, international direct dial, desktop video conferencing—provide the small business person with opportunities formerly reserved for large corporations. This new technology greatly reduces the cost of collecting and analyzing vast quantities of information, taking away a major advantage of management in integrated companies. Thus some management theorists speculate that the vaunted triumph of big business over small for most of the twentieth century may be reversed in the twenty-first. Indeed, in recent years, historians have increasingly recognized that small businesses have always remained critically important to the economy though dwarfed in public attention since the nineteenth century's end by the imposing presence of giant corporations. A brief overview of the relationship between big and small business is in order.[6]

DUAL ECONOMY

With the rise of big industrial concerns in the 1880s, a great divide seemingly separated the American business community. The small proprietary firms, partnerships, and family operations that once constituted all of American business became within thirty years a junior partner in the economy. The publicly owned, professionally managed, integrated "modern-business enterprise" rose rapidly to prominence as efforts to contain this growth through the use of state and national antitrust legislation proved futile. Small business was understandably overshadowed in the public mind by the new behemoth while still remaining vitally important to the economy.[7]

Of the 3 million American corporations in 1997, less than 2 percent of the total constituted the giants that stand in the popular mind as big business. Yet these relatively few large firms, 3,000 to 4,000 in all, account for around half of the American GDP. John Kenneth Galbraith observed in 1967: "The two parts of the economy—the world of . . . technically dynamic, massively capitalized and highly organized corporations on the one hand and of the thousands of small and traditional proprietors on the other—are very different. It is not a difference of degree but a difference which invades every aspect of economic organization and behavior, including the motivation of effort itself."[8]

Big business and small business differed in values, styles, and needs. They also operated in very different market structures. Although small business declined in relative importance in manufacturing after 1900, many small firms found ways to develop market niches through specialization and thus usually avoided head-to-head competition with giant corporations. Because even subtle changes in technology and market structure could quickly undermine even the strongest position held by a small firm, flexibility was a key element of small business survival. Thus while the world of small business was usually highly atomistic and competitive, the domain of big business represented, as Alfred Chandler demonstrated impressively in *The Visible Hand*, a managerial capitalism capable of considerable control over market forces. The end of the twentieth century has witnessed major changes, but much in this picture still remains recognizable. The question some ask is, For how much longer? Highly integrated production and distribution within a single firm no longer is the most profitable way of doing business in sectors of the economy where it once prevailed. Yet much of the faultfinding with big business and its bureaucratic organization downplays the powerful shocks and disruptive effects resulting from increasing levels of global competition. It is simply too early to accept the view that a new business paradigm is about to emerge.

The inevitable tension between big business and small business has often been reflected in the political arena. Antitrust and fair-trade policies have historically been efforts to thwart the improper advantages of bigness. The federal government also provides direct assistance to small business in the form of loans and loan guarantees. In addition, small business in 2001 received $90 billion in prime contracts from federal agencies, which are required by law to award up to 23 percent of these contracts to small businesses. There are also federal and state mandates often requiring large companies to subcontract to small companies. In the twentieth century, political skirmishes within the business community were often fierce, as corporate America and its smaller rival jockeyed for influence on Capitol Hill.[9]

Between 1941 and 1980 most economists strongly believed in the economic superiority of the large, vertically integrated corporation. Its ability to combine large-scale production with mass distribution allowed for long-range planning, economies of scale, ample funding for research and development, and product or service innovation. For these reasons, economists argued that large firms provided powerful engines of technological progress. The individual entrepreneur, closely identified with small business, was deemed of decreased importance. Galbraith, for one, asserted that the individual entrepreneur no longer really mattered as an entrepreneur; this was now the role of the large industrial corporation.

Firmly dominating key segments of the economy, big business was thought to have permanently shunted its smaller rivals to the economy's periphery. Small business worked, it was generally believed, with the economy's least desirable economic resources at its least promising opportunities. Wholesaling, retailing, and service businesses—with their operations usually low in capital requirement and high in labor intensity and frequently requiring a specialized skill—constituted the strongholds of small business activity. But after 1945 even these bastions were increasingly penetrated by big business, using chain stores, franchises, and mail-order houses.

Between 1958 and 1972, for example, the number of retail food stores declined by 26 percent, and large stores (greater than $.5 million per year in sales) increased their share of the market from 51 percent to 73 percent. The rise in the 1980s of big retail discount stores, such as Wal-Mart and K-Mart, and "category busters," such as Staples and Home Depot, stressing low prices and high product turnover, further endangered the retail realm of small business. In manufacturing, small business was generally regarded as operating in niche areas often of little interest to big business and indeed incapable of growing to meet demand when and if the niche expanded beyond the original limited market.

It was generally assumed that America's economic growth after World War II occurred primarily in big business: large corporations provided the new jobs, and job losses came from small businesses in recessions. It appeared that small business had been permanently marginalized—struggling to survive in the backwaters of the economy by living off those meager pickings that large corporations had no interest in.

But with corporate America often in trouble and downsizing in the 1980s, these assumptions received new scrutiny. Joseph Schumpeter's long-neglected views—that the innovativeness generated by the frenetic entrepreneurial energy of individuals lay at the heart of capitalism—gained in popularity. Small business as the vehicle of individual entrepreneurial expression received greater notice.

The assumption that big had to be better began to fall from favor in the 1980s. Between 1977 and 1993, the 500 largest industrial companies shrank their total workforce, even as small business employment increased. The large corporations often appeared confused by change and clumsy in responding to it. Held high by advocates of entrepreneurial activity, the long-furled banner "small is beautiful" reappeared on the economic battlefield in the 1980s.

A generation of students broke with their older siblings' view of success—climbing the corporate ladder and eventually occupying a corner office with a window. They, in contrast, set their sights on starting a business of their own. Two magazines directed at small business people, *Inc.* and *Venture,* began publication in the early 1980s and quickly gained a combined circulation of over a million. The *Wall Street Journal* introduced a weekly column on small business. *Forbes* and *Fortune* have also greatly increased their coverage of small firms. Colleges added courses on entrepreneurship and small business to their curricula. And scholars busily researched the formerly neglected areas of small business and entrepreneurship.[10]

As the baby boom generation took over boardrooms, small business was increasingly hailed as the individualistic, creative side of economic activity. This line of reasoning reflected in part the counterculture values that equated bigness with stifling bureaucracy. But it also reflected new developments, notably in information technology and the Internet, that opened up exciting possibilities for certain types of small business. Developments seemed to suggest that small firms, being more nimble and quicker to change, tended to be superior in the research and development process. American business, pressed hard by global competition in the 1980s, needed creative energy and drive, and this seemed more likely in the informal setting of small business than in the cumbersome structure of the corporation. The notion that small business drove job growth and innovation inspired numerous articles in the press and even economic development campaigns that involved building business parks for small business as "incubators" for entrepreneurs. But this new attention often failed to distinguish between various types of small business and how they differentiated themselves. Nor did it consider the dependency of many innovative start-ups on giant enterprises, as, for example, Microsoft's early relationship with IBM. Indeed, a multiplicity of small biotech firms are tied to giant pharmaceuticals by means of development and marketing contracts and financing arrangements designed to get research and development expenses off the sponsoring company's books.[11]

SMALL-SMALL AND BIG-SMALL

There is, of course, no prototypical small business. Small businesses come in various sizes, organizations, and activities. Yet a critical distinction must be made between the very small business and the medium-sized, or "larger small business." The first consists of at most a handful of employees, with the proprietor working alongside them; the latter may employ as many as 500 people and be a tens of millions of dollars per year type of operation. The SBA in 1998 classified large-sized small businesses as 100 to 499 employees, medium-sized small businesses as 20 to 99 employees, and very small businesses as under 20 employees.

It is the "larger small business" that attracted interest as a powerful generator of new jobs, technologies, and innovations. Such firms sometimes either grow into big businesses or are acquired by a large corporation eager to invest in small, promising companies with research and development potential. Many large biotech and electronics firms have pursued an acquisition strategy for small start-up companies, using them as a way of outsourcing research and development. It may well be that certain types of high-tech research are best conducted in a context of organizational looseness by independent and highly competitive firms (often financed by venture capitalists). Their start-up entrepreneurs are often highly creative risk takers. Most of these ventures fail, but those that make it can provide big buck payoffs.[12]

The divide between the two categories of small business is certainly as great as the one separating them from big business. But the tiny concern that grows to middling size and then evolves into a corporate giant is the proverbial success story of American capitalism. Such forms have provided much of the drive and energy—and the mythmaking—that was essential to economic growth in the 1990s. Cisco Systems, Apple Computers, Oracle, Sun Microsystems, Google—all were created in the past two or three decades out of virtually nothing.[13]

In the 1980s takeover specialists had looked for companies with shares trading far below the value of total corporate assets; in the 1990s the pattern for the information technology companies differed. This new acquisition strategy aimed to acquire young companies with cutting-edge technology, along with their people, at an early stage of development. Cisco Systems, for example, was started in 1990 and began an aggressive strategy of acquisitions in 1993. Six years later, it had acquired a total of fifty-eight companies, and from a one-product company, making routers for the Internet, it had grown to providing switchers and numerous other products powering the Internet communications revolution. By 2000, Cisco had achieved an astonishing market value of nearly $.5 trillion. It was generally believed that this remarkable success had resulted primarily from the strategy of acquiring promising small companies. (The company said that it expected success in eight out of ten investments in other companies, but this was before the tech downturn of 2000, after which Cisco in two years lost 70 percent of its market value.)

THE CHANGING LANDSCAPE OF BUSINESS

The nation's largest corporations collectively downsized their workforces by about 20 percent in the 1980s and by another 10 percent in the first five years of the 1990s. In 1981 an oft-cited report by MIT economist David Birch estimated that small business was creating eight out of ten new jobs, and in a number of articles appearing throughout the decade Birch and others following his lead argued that big businesses' inability to compete effectively in world markets provided new opportunities for smaller, private companies whose activities had become the real strength of the American economy. But other scholars challenged Birch's findings, arguing that his analysis rested on faulty data that ignored the distinction between net and gross job creations. Large firms gained headlines by massive layoffs, but small companies, rather than retrench, often simply went out of business, wiping out jobs without attracting media notice. For this and other reasons, many of the jobs generated by small business had proved to be ephemeral. According to the authors of a 1990 study, the survival rate of new jobs "increase[d] sharply with employer size."[14] Companies with 500 or more employees still accounted for half of the new jobs from 1973 to 1988, a much higher total than generally thought.

The differing views, however, may be due to Birch's failure to distinguish effectively between stolid traditional small businesses and the fast-growing young companies—from upstart retailers to Internet stars like Cisco—that quickly grew into large companies and accounted for much of the job growth of the last decades of the twentieth century. Put simply, new jobs were created mainly in fast-growing companies and sectors of the economy, which, of course, is hardly surprising. What is noteworthy, however, is that many small high-tech companies started with the intention of growing large very quickly and did so. It is these successful companies that are critical in new job creation.

Some facts, however, are not disputed. Many managers who were downsized in the last decade of the twentieth century used their severance pay to strike out on their own. A small army of highly sophisticated redundant corporate veterans augmented the ranks of American small business, often seeking narrow niches that related a new entrepreneurial activity to their older industry. Many of the economy's most creative and "value-added functions," especially software design, became primarily a universe of small informal organizations, as Silicon Valley on the West Coast was matched in the 1990s by places like New York City's Silicon Alley in Manhattan.

Bennett Harrison's *Lean and Mean: The Changing Landscape of Corporate Power in the Age of Flexibility* suggested in 1994 that the worldwide development of networks of corporate cooperation, tying together suppliers and firms and modeled on the Japanese *keiretsu*, meant that "production may be decentralized while power, finance, distribution, and control remain concentrated among the big firms."[15] He believed industrial giants were handicapped by high fixed costs, excessive capitalization, bureaucratic inflexibility, and a general timidity concerning new ideas. In the future, he argued, companies that had once created divisions or subsidiaries to handle new products would choose instead to spin them off to new independent companies.[16]

Shorter product cycles, fewer basic designs, and technologies experiencing dramatic changes in skill and equipment all require firms that are geared to grasp opportunities quickly and that are prepared for organizational discontinuity. Small or midsized firms adapt faster to change than corporate giants. The mass market for the personal digital assistant, for example, occurred in the 1990s as the result of swiftly arranged and complex alliances among the telecommunications, computer hardware, computer software, and consumer electronics industries. "Flexible specialization," the ability to produce a variety of products in small batches and to switch rapidly among them, became increasingly important in many industrial sectors. Some scholars, such as D. Hugh Whittaker and Robert E. Cole, have suggested that the *keiretsu* model, though largely unstructured, might prove too confining if organizational looseness is the key to flexible behavior. Indeed, perhaps the looser the organization, the better. Even now, one-third to two-thirds of all associations dissolve within a decade, depending on the industry. Business school studies, relying on models derived from the academic discipline of population ecology, demonstrated that adaptation is most successfully performed by new companies not weighed down by old ways, equipment, and staff. What might therefore be required, Whittaker and Cole argued, are firms intended and designed to be short lived, or at least capable of virtually transforming themselves, their suppliers, their clients, and even their workforce every few years.[17]

Indeed, Robert Cole's ideas were close to the reality of certain ostensibly large manufacturing companies in the 1990s. Nike, Reebok, Calvin Klein, Benetton, and Tommy Hilfiger did not make the sneakers and clothes they sold but contracted out production or "licensed" production to small workshops located in low-cost-labor Third World countries. No longer involved in manufacturing, they concerned themselves with marketing, focusing on a trendy corporate brand image and constantly creating new "attitude" styles. Calvin Klein's ubiquitous ads did not even stress the clothes as much as sex. Reebok and Nike sought successful sales strategies by signing up athletic superstars. What in effect was being offered was not a product but a fantasy experience. Measured in terms of sales or brand recognition, all were large companies. But the number of employees and facilities gave a different picture. The wall separating big business from small has been frequently breeched in recent decades. Entrepreneurs will inevitably try new strategies and new structures.

The average size of a Silicon Valley software company in 2003 was twenty-six employees. Many Silicon Valley model start-ups involve the temporary coming together of human, technological, and financial resources with different backgrounds and institutional settings to work with ad hoc networks of suppliers and clients. Such ventures are not traceable as an extension of any existing organization, a sharp break with the way production had previously been organized. This flexibility is regarded as especially important given the increasing tendency in business toward accelerated product obsolescence and the development, as a result, of a new type of "quick turnaround" industrial process. But how relevant is this "discontinuity" to other than the high-tech sector? In early 2000, a few manufacturers unveiled plans to buy their supplies via ongoing electronic auctions in which would-be suppliers bid on contracts, and such retailers as Sears and Wal-Mart soon announced plans to follow suit. However, huge mergers occurred in the late 1990s, involving such industries as oil, telecommunications, and financial services. In sectors dominated by a few major producers competing in the global market, size and advantages of scale still counted.

But it could not be denied that small business (long counted out in its battle with big business) had staged a remarkable comeback in the last quarter of the century. Small, it would appear, sometimes offered advantages, and business writers in the early 1990s hailed small business as the nursery of the entrepreneurial ethos, human inventiveness, and creativity. With little to lose and much to gain, small business often plunges in where corporate giants refuse to venture. A period of transition, so bedeviling to the hierarchical structure and bureaucratic mentality, seemingly offered special advantages to small-scale entrepreneurial activity. Small businesses can often achieve better internal communication and tailor their products specifically to small markets. The adaptability of small business represented the very weakness of the integrated corporation.

One hundred years after the rise of big business seemed to signify an irreversible trend, some experts suggested that large corporations in many sectors of the economy will have to downsize greatly and simplify operations. Critics of bigness believe that vested and layered organizational interests tend to retard or block innovation because new ventures must be justified in terms of their place in an overall corporate strategy. The very need for large corporations to only undertake innovations that are significant enough to warrant major investments of time, energy, and capital rules out some possibilities, and the high costs involved also require management to think twice about introducing changes. Smallness and flexibility also offered advantages in the export trade in specialty products.

The celebration of small business in the 1990s was not, however, wholly explicable in terms of business prowess. It was at least partly due, according to three economists who authored *Employers Large and Small*, to the fact that small business had become highly skillful at using the American political system to further its interests. Small businesspeople are less and less the mom-and-pop owners of grocery stores and are increasingly influential citizens in every congressional district. A 1993 survey indicated that households with assets of $1 million or more owned 80 percent of America's small businesses with five or more employees. According to the authors, political action committees representing small business interests contributed one-fourth of all PAC contributions received by Senate incumbents running for reelection in 1994. Small business, then, is far from a youthful David bravely confronting big business bullies, as its supporters want the public to believe.[18]

The image of small business as the nursery of entrepreneurial activity proved to be invaluable when lobbyists sought to influence Congress, and small business effectively gained a wide range of benefits from Washington. These included tax breaks, subsidized loans issued by the SBA, and special considerations in terms of health, safety, and consumer regulations. In 1992, for example, the SEC reduced the red tape that had made it too expensive for small companies to register their securities in order to sell them publicly.

ENTREPRENEURS AND SMALL BUSINESS

The flagship of entrepreneurial small businesses was high-tech companies spun off by venturesome individuals from larger companies or universities. Everyone knows the story of Steve Jobs and Stephen Wozniak, two college dropouts who, while working in Jobs's family garage, developed a personal computer in 1976 with just $1,500 from selling an old Volkswagen van. Five years later, their company, Apple Computer, Inc., approached annual sales of $750 million. Still in their twenties, the two entrepreneurs were multimillionaires, with Apple quickly gaining virtually instant entry into the Fortune 500 companies. More important, the duo catalyzed the birth of an important new industry by forcing giant IBM to develop, in response, its own line of personal computers.

As late as 1977, the chairman of the Digital Equipment Corporation had confidently asserted that "there is no reason for anyone to have a computer in his home." But after Apple's success, venture capitalists rushed to finance college professors and computer hackers whose small companies quickly lined the main roads of Silicon Valley, south of San Francisco, and Massachusetts's Route 128 near Harvard and MIT. High tech would be a bright spot in the economy of the 1980s, and small business did play an important role, though one often exaggerated in the telling. Actually, three-quarters of all high-tech employees work for large companies, with less than 5 percent employed by the laidback, small entrepreneurial firms started by brainy offbeat types, perhaps interested more in intellectual answers than money, whom the public assumed represented the cutting edge of the industry.

Modern research on entrepreneurship has owed much to Joseph Schumpeter (1883–1950). At the age of twenty-eight, in his native Austria, he had published *The Theory of Economic Development* (1911), which set down the ideas he would spend the rest of his life developing. During the Great Depression, as many economists questioned the survival of capitalism, Schumpeter, by then at Harvard, emphasized the importance of what he termed "creative entrepreneurship," the introduction of critical innovations that force significant economic change. Schumpeter stressed the protean bursts of energy that individual entrepreneurs provided for innovation and expressed doubt that this creativity could be replicated in the bureaucratic organization of the corporation. To him, the entrepreneur had to possess "the dream and the will to found a private kingdom."[19]

The standard business text's description of an entrepreneur's role lacks the emphasis on sheer strength of will and originality of Schumpeter's writings. The entrepreneur's role, according to business texts, consists of one or more of the following: (1) introducing better or cheaper products or services; (2) differentiating an existing product or service; (3) opening a new market; (4) obtaining a new source of supply; (5) creating a new organization; and (6) introducing a new system to increase productivity or facilitate decision making. To "institutionalists," all of these can be handled more than adequately in complex organizations by professional management. But in the 1980s Schumpeter's insistence on the central role of the entrepreneurial personality gained a more respectful hearing.[20]

Research on entrepreneurial personality and activity tends to rely on two approaches. One, the behavioral, follows in the footsteps of Max Weber and is concerned with the types of political and cultural environment conducive to innovative behavior. Here the emphasis is on whether a culture stresses individual achievement or social conformity and how much deference it accords authority and tradition. Any consideration of American values invariably suggests that they encourage the individual to forge an identity for himself or herself. Emerson, for example, the quintessential American social theorist, advised: "Do not go where the path may lead; go instead where there is no path and leave a trail." Woodrow Wilson, as president of Princeton University, stated that the purpose of higher education was "to make a person as unlike his father as possible."

The other approach, reflecting Schumpeter's influence, is the psychological and explores the personality characteristics of entrepreneurs. Few of the psychological findings are surprising. Entrepreneurs are said to be optimistic, aggressive, resistant to authority, competitive, achievement-oriented, risk taking, tolerant of ambiguity, and desirous of personal control. Several studies suggest that the very characteristics that make for the entrepreneur's ability to successfully start a business present problems for its long-range management. Entrepreneurial types, they assert, are reluctant to relinquish authority, tend to distrust others, have difficulty in communicating and negotiating, and resist systems that try to enforce conformity, since they prefer to act intuitively.

Put simply, the studies seem to say that entrepreneurs are much like many people who are not entrepreneurs. It has been said that it is hard to define entrepreneurship but that you know it when you see it, and the same may be said of entrepreneurs. Whether a comparative approach to entrepreneurial types in different cultures, say comparing Japanese and American entrepreneurs, would find similar or different personality traits is an interesting question. Unfortunately, we still lack sufficient studies to make a judgment. Most small business people, of course, can hardly be described as entrepreneurs—and there is an important sector of small business, franchise operations, that deliberately limits entrepreneurial activity by the small business person.

FRANCHISE OPERATIONS

In 2004, franchise outlets in the United States employed one in sixteen of the nation's workers and accounted for over $1 trillion of annual sales. The rise of franchise operations since World War II has greatly encouraged small business activity in the United States. Franchising, ideally, represents an alliance between small and big business. Yet franchising isn't entrepreneurship made easy. Franchising comes with its own set of problems and solutions. It is, however, an ingenious approach to modern business invented in America to profit from the widespread desire to share in the small-business dream.

Pioneering this development was the relationship established early in the twentieth century by automobile manufacturers and their dealers, gasoline companies with their service stations, and large soda firms with bottlers. Starting in the 1950s with fast-food and motel operations, the franchise industry exploded, evolving into its modern form: the "business format." The older model had relied on the parent company profiting from the sale of supplies (automobiles, Coca-Cola) to dealers and distributors. According to the "business format," the parent company may or may not sell supplies to its licensed "franchisees." What the franchiser essentially does sell is the know-how of running a business. What the business format limits is the entrepreneurial freedom of the small businessman or woman. Eric Schlosser, in *Fast Food Nation*, has asserted that McDonald's, the nation's largest franchise company, has "homogenized" not only its own restaurants but also many of its suppliers. "What we find with franchises," he writes, "is that the original creator of the franchise had a new idea, was actually quite dynamic and risk taking. But in order to expand the franchise he has to impose total conformity on the franchisees."[21]

Arrangements vary greatly in the business format but usually consist of an up-front payment and a profit-sharing agreement, for which guidance is provided in obtaining a location, building or equipping it, and training for its operations. Typically, businesses move into franchising to grow quickly, and many of the better-known chain operations, such as McDonald's and Burger King, consist of both parent company–owned outlets and franchisee-operated outlets. It is often charged that the better locations are retained for the company or even repurchased, while the less advantageous leftovers are offered to franchisees.

Some operations have, of course, been phenomenally successful. Hard-driving Ray Kroc started McDonald's with a single drive-in in San Bernardino, California, in 1955. Four years later, McDonald's had a hundred franchised outlets and by 1965 a total of 710. In that year Kroc went public. The immense amount of money this brought him aroused others to dream of a double killing: huge profits earned on up-front franchise fees followed by a second whammy with a stock flotation. By 2001, about 28,000 McDonald's operated in some 115 countries on six continents, and the McDonald's brand is the most famous and heavily promoted in the world. A company spokesman claimed that every six to eight hours, somewhere in the world, a new store opened its doors and that the company is the planet's biggest owner of retail property as well as the largest private operator of playgrounds.

About half the company's restaurants are outside the United States. The Golden Arches are nearly ubiquitous and universally recognized, even in remote regions of the world. The folks at McDonald's like to tell the story about the Japanese girl who arrived in Los Angeles, looked around, and said to her mother: "Look mom, they have McDonald's here too." Her surprise that McDonald's is an American company is understandable: in the year 2002 the company had more than 3,000 restaurants in Japan, and 10 percent of the nation's beef was consumed as McDonald's hamburgers.[22]

Contrary to common belief, most franchise systems are not operated by big companies like McDonald's Corporation, and many are both small and short lived. The rapid success of the franchise business in the 1960s and 1970s invited fraud, as companies materialized that sold the right to others to, in turn, sell their franchise operations, in effect, creating a pyramid scam. The franchising boom faltered but did not collapse, and although most franchise operations are honest, thousands of people continue to risk their savings on newly launched operations that they know little about—while small investors are often frozen out by the high cost of franchises in the more successful chains. Blocs of franchises are often controlled by very large investors or syndicates of large investors, and some franchisers even prefer not to sell to individual investors. Thus, despite the claims of the industry, franchises do not always allow entry into private business for aspiring but capital-poor working people. The need for a sizable amount of up-front money frequently freezes out the little guy. In the year 2004, the initial investment for fast-food franchises averaged from $100,000 to $250,000, excluding real estate costs.

Franchising has been extended to an astonishing range of retailing and service operations, including opticians, funeral parlors, and trade schools. In 2003 it was estimated that franchising accounted for one-third of all retail sales and two-fifths of all dining out and that there were 320,000 franchises representing 1,200 to 1,500 companies. These figures will no doubt continue to grow. The pages of the *Wall Street Journal* are filled with ads offering franchise opportunities. There are now even business-to-business franchises, which sell services like accounting or web page design to other small businesses, many of them franchises themselves.

The Federal Trade Commission tries to police the industry under its Franchise Rule adopted in 1979, which requires franchisers to disclose information specified by the Uniform Franchise Offering Circular to prospective franchisees. But it was left up to the states to enforce completeness and accuracy of compliance, and few states do so effectively. Fraudulent sales techniques that understate franchisees' costs while making false promises to refund fees if promised earnings do not materialize are common. An estimated half billion dollars a year continues to be lost to outright franchise frauds. In addition, fees and service charges may be too high, and some parent companies do not live up to their promises, even while the franchisee remains contracted to continue in an unsatisfactory arrangement.

A study of small business start-ups by Timothy Bates appeared in 1998.

Despite the reputation franchising has long enjoyed as a safe way for an individual to own a business, his report concluded that the failure rate of new franchisees was higher than that of independent businesses—35 percent compared to 28 percent.[23] He found that even though new franchisees typically posted higher sales volume, were better capitalized, and had easier access to borrowed funds than independent businesses, they reported lower earnings. This, he thought, was due to the royalties they paid while often being required to buy supplies at prices that were higher than on the open market. For their part, franchisers often grow dissatisfied with franchisees' performance and complain about their own weak operational control. The rise in disputes between franchiser and franchisee has led to a new legal specialty, complete with its own publications. The American Franchisee Association, founded in 1993 as an advocacy group, counsels that franchising is no place for the "ignorant or naive."

AGRIBUSINESS

For most of American history, family farms constituted the overwhelming majority of small businesses. In 1900, farmers represented three out of four of the estimated 37 percent of Americans who were self-employed. Over the course of the twentieth century, the farm population of the United States has declined steadily. As late as the middle of the 1930s, however, there were still nearly 7 million farmers, for a population of 140 million. Seventy years later, less than 3 million farmed, although the country's population had more than doubled. By then, some 300,000 large farms, with holdings of over 500 acres, produced more than two-thirds of the value of U.S. farm goods. Small farmers continued to be squeezed off the land, and many held on only by moonlighting away from their farms. Once regarded as the backbone of American democracy, the American family farm has shrunk even in symbolic significance. The era of inexpensive land has long since passed, and its high cost stands as a barrier, just as its availability once acted as a magnet.

The trend has long been toward concentration, with giant farms owned by corporations engaged in "agribusiness." Such corporations have access to the capital that is elusive and expensive for the family farmer. Easy access to credit allows agribusinesses to keep up with the costly scientific and technological advances dramatically transforming both the growing and the selling of produce since they often are able to afford to combine processing and marketing with producing in their operations. Using sophisticated machinery and powerful chemicals, a farmer in the year 2000 produced twice the corn yield per acre that a farmer had produced in 1960. This increased efficiency has lowered food costs for Americans but has required farmers to work twice as many acres to survive. According to the American Farm Bureau, a typical midwestern crop farm in 2000 required 600 to 700 acres in order to make money. For most Americans, it has been several generations since the hope of a farm of one's own symbolized the essence of the American Dream or when jokes about the farmer's daughter were commonplace.[24]

ALLIANCES OF CONVENIENCE

A new linkage between big and small business became popular in the 1980s. Rather than seek dominance of attractive small companies in a cutting-edge field, such as biotech and information technology, large corporations preferred to purchase noncontrolling interests, leaving the entrepreneur in charge. These alliances of convenience increased dramatically with the quickening pace of technological change. This strategy seemed to minimize the possibilities of mismanaging a promising acquisition, a not-uncommon occurrence. It also allowed for greater diversity of investment, since less is required in resources, both financial and managerial, to establish what might prove to be a valuable connection. The downside is the difficulty in establishing effective relationships based on mutual trust and respect between organizations often very different in personnel types, management structures, and hierarchies.

For big business, this type of linkage is important in allowing it to tap into the entrepreneurial and innovative capabilities of dynamic small firms; the benefit to the small business is in access to the resources of the larger company. Most of the investors have been large U.S. corporations, but Japanese firms quickly recognized the advantages of this arrangement in acquiring expertise in American markets as well as advanced technology.

Indeed, the pattern of loose connection between big business and a huge network of suppliers was once cited as the reason for Japan's economic success and a paradigm for future American development. A study of Toyota done in the early 1980s found that it did business with 168 "first level" subcontractors (close and frequent suppliers), with 5,437 "second level" subcontractors, and with over 40,000 occasional suppliers. These figures were four or five times those of American car manufacturers in 1980, but the differences have narrowed greatly since then, and, given present trends, they will disappear entirely by 2010. Close linkage by a big business with an elite small firm poised on the cutting edge of important new opportunities often involves an exchange of stock between the two. Many of the small firms are listed on the NASDAQ, the over-the-counter electronic exchange, whose listing requirements are deliberately designed to attract small firms needing start-up capital. A listing on a stock market devoted to small-company stocks has proven attractive to venture capitalists, because it increased the possibility of recouping their investments with a profit by selling their stock in a few years.

SMALL-SMALL BUSINESS

Very few American small businesses stand on the cutting edge of the economy. Most are involved in small-scale conventional activities in mature areas of the economy. Very often undercapitalized, small businesses are vulnerable in their early years, with over half never reaching their fifth anniversary. Only one in five lasts ten years. Ventures most likely to fail are most commonly found in retail, followed by services and construction. Restaurants, in particular, are notoriously short lived. Training courses for would-be small business people list the following as major causes for business failures: lack of sufficient capital; a weak business plan (especially lack of knowledge on how to distribute the product successfully); a poor concept, usually involving a product in search of a market rather than the safer approach of a market in search of a product; and, finally, lack of day-to-day experience in the running of the business. Between 1989 and 1995, the SBA reported that 2.9 million new businesses began and, in the same period, 2.6 million businesses ended. Not surprisingly, the larger the small business, the greater its chances of profitability.[25]

As in the past, remarkable individual success stories by small business people are transformed into the Horatio Alger myths. Fred Smith started Federal Express as a small-package, quick-delivery system in 1975. In the 1980s, Tom Stemberg devised a business plan for an office supply "superstore" called Staples. In the 1990s, Jeff Bezos started Amazon.com in the seemingly obligatory garage with a bit of money raised from his family to sell books online. These successes, as well as those of other more modest small businesses, supposedly validate the core American values of self-help and individualism and offer encouragement for would-be entrepreneurs.

For most, however, small business is a hard way to make a living, involving long hours, uncertain income, and much anxiety. As talk of the imminent death of small business was exaggerated in the recent past, the new touting of its renaissance may also be overstated. The diversity and scale of small business activity continues to make its well-being important to the economy. But the recent emphasis on its special role in American employment, productivity, and social mobility is more problematic. The authors of one study, *Employers Large and Small*, remain skeptical.[26]

They concede that small business created the majority of new jobs in the 1980s but believe that this was largely offset by a high rate of small business failures resulting in large numbers of lost jobs. The wages offered by small business are generally lower than those provided by larger concerns, and the fringe benefits of small firms—including job training, working conditions, health insurance, pensions, and job security—lag well behind those of larger firms. In general, small business lags behind big firms in such critical contributions to national standards as investment in research and development, product and service innovation, and spending on capital goods. According to the Bureau of Labor Statistics, in 2003 companies with twenty to forty employees paid their workers, on average, $627 a week, compared to $919 a week at companies with 500 employees, and $1,079 a week at companies with 1,000 or more workers.

MINORITIES AND SMALL BUSINESS

Since the 1960s, the SBA has sponsored special programs to assist women and minorities in successfully operating small businesses. Assistance ranged from low-interest loans to special consideration in the awarding of contracts. Despite these efforts, blacks and some Latinos, such as Puerto Ricans, remain greatly underrepresented in the ownership of small businesses. African Americans, for example, owned only 3 percent to 4 percent of businesses in 2000, although they represented 12 percent of the American population. A common complaint of black and Latino businesspeople is that they encounter greater difficulty in securing capital and credit than whites. Nor has small business ownership played a major role in the development of a black middle class. Nearly half of all middle-class black men and two-thirds of middle-class black women in 2000 had public sector jobs.[27] Moreover minority-owned businesses tend to be less profitable. In 1987 African American businesses accounted for only 1 percent of the nation's gross receipts. Several states have recently undertaken to assist individuals on welfare in starting small businesses, but progress is slow and difficult. On the other hand, some immigrant newcomers, as from China, Korea, and the Indian subcontinent, have been remarkably successful in starting and sustaining small businesses.[28]

Self-employment offers an attractive route up the social ladder for individuals and groups outside the corporate mainstream. About 8.5 percent of the adult American population in 2001 had actually started a small business, more than double that of Western European nations. Small businesses have provided perhaps the most important avenue for women and some minorities to advance economically. Studies of the social background of small businesspeople conducted in the 1980s found that they possessed less education —and were more often Catholics, Jews, and immigrants—than the officers of America's leading corporations. As already noted, self-employment rates differ greatly among racial and ethnic groups, as does the choice of business activity. Economists Robert W. Fairlie and Bruce D. Meyer found in 1997, for example, that 30 percent of Korean male immigrants are self-employed, mainly owning food stores, restaurants, and health services, while only 4.4 percent of West Indian blacks are self-employed, with many owning barbershops, hair salons, and auto repair shops. Women own, on average, about half the number of businesses that men do within any particular racial and ethnic group. These statistics clearly indicate that some groups are more familiar than other groups with a commercial ethos that promotes the starting and surviving of businesses. Often these groups have organizations to facilitate entry by providing capital and contacts.[29]

For individuals who prefer to do it their own way, are alienated by the corporate culture, or lack the background and credentials expected for upper management, small business constitutes a safety valve—an alternative open to anyone prepared to accept the risk, drive, and hard work demanded by ownership. Unquestionably, starting a small business is a gutsy and chancy activity. It puts money, livelihood, and self-esteem on the line. There are certainly easier ways to earn a living, but perhaps few as potentially rewarding. Owning one's own business reaches deep into the individualistic spirit embedded in the American psyche, and often the reason given is not to make more money but to create something on one's own. What remains striking about America is that failure is not a badge of dishonor but part of the learning process. Businesses that fail often provide the new generation of entrepreneurs, and those who want to try again usually can.[30]

TOWARD THE FUTURE

Small business and the family firm are likely to retain their significant presence and symbolic importance well into the future. Firms and industries will continually try different organizations and strategies in response to the escalating process of change in technology and markets. The world of business will, of course, remain full of variation. One size or approach certainly does not fit all circumstances.

How the Internet and e-commerce will ultimately affect businesses remains to be seen. No matter what hypothesis one begins with the opposite appears equally plausible. The Internet allows for dispersal of resources and decision making but also permits the tightening of centralized control over formerly loosely controlled operations and networks. No doubt, the Internet provides new opportunities. In 2003, eBay claimed that some 40,000 new businesses had been created by small entrepreneurs who utilized its Web services.

Some students of business change anticipate the development of a wide range of market-based proprietary small firms, which collectively will produce and market a broad range of products. They also predict that large firms will reorganize themselves into holding companies of "federations" of autonomous business units, with very small headquarters staffs measuring financial performances. The possibility thus exists through exchanges of stock between a large variety of companies (some derived from big business, others tightly held private corporations) for a kaleidoscope of arrangements, which will blur the traditional distinctions between big and small business and may even, in many cases, render them insignificant.[31]

THE SIZE OF THE FIRM

In 1937 a young English economist published a brief essay that theoretically explored the subject of the size of the firm. The "transaction costs" approach that Ronald Coase introduced in "The Nature of the Firm" has been seminal in the development of modern organizational theory. It profoundly influenced Alfred Chandler and the economists identified with the New Institutional Economics school. At the time of the article, classical economic theory, with its premise of "market" efficiency, held that when possible an entrepreneur should contract out work to external specialists rather than hire the necessary personnel to internalize the work within the firm, since costs would be less. The rise of the integrated corporation of course challenged this theory—and Coase's essay seemingly, or so some thought, refuted it.[32]

Coase demonstrated that reliance on the market was not free but involved "transaction costs." As examples of these, he cited search and information costs, keeping trade secrets, and policing and enforcement costs. All of these involve time and money that might not be spent if handled in-house. When these costs exceed the expenses involved in doing the work internally, the firm will add personnel and functions to avoid the external transaction costs. Coase then elaborated several circumstances that would encourage a firm to grow larger, before reaching an optimal balance between transaction costs and those related to internalizing operations. But he recognized, though this point tended to be ignored, that all cost variables will alter over time for a variety of reasons, including technological changes involving communication and information processing. The result is a fluid situation: depending on activity and industry, firms will tend for a time to grow larger or smaller, and vice versa.

Coase's 1937 essay contributed to his winning the Nobel Prize in Economics in 1991. As with all ambitious syntheses, his contains an element of oversimplification. Nevertheless, it offers a useful theoretical framework and insights into why some firms in certain industries grow while other firms in different industries shrink dramatically. Perhaps its most important truth is that nothing regarding firm size is static or forever or even predictable over the long term.

There have been several efforts to build on Coase's work. Most important, Oliver Williamson selected strands of his ideas and elaborated on them in an insightful manner. Williamson noted that both parties to a negotiation always have only partial knowledge of all the factors involved, but one party invariably knows more than the other. This obviously offers advantages and brings the possibility of the more knowledgeable party exploiting the other party. This very possibility acts as an impediment (a transaction cost) in all negotiations. The ability of vertically integrated firms to minimize through managerial coordination the risks caused by disadvantages in information between parties long explained their advantage over firms relying on the market. Williamson recognized, however, that in particular circumstances this advantage would be lost and that market negotiations would involve fewer transaction costs than in-house coordination. Along with Coase's work, Williamson's work offers valuable insight into why the vertically integrated corporation is retreating as a business form in some areas of the economy and not in others and why bigness can be either a positive or a negative factor, depending in any given period on variables that are often in flux.[33]

CHAPTER EIGHTEEN

The Twenty-first Century

There is a great destiny which comes in with this as with every
age, which is colossal in its traits, terrible in its strength. . . .
It is shared by every man and woman, for it is by it they live.
— *JOURNALS OF RALPH WALDO EMERSON (1841)*

In the final quarter of the nineteenth century, modern capitalism, in the form of "big business," sprang up almost overnight. Much of America's history in the last century was concerned with coming to terms with the far-ranging consequences. This concluding chapter explores three facets of American business as we confront the new century. The first is its political and social environment. The second is the nature of the modern corporation and its future. The third concern is the relationship of democracy to the American model of free enterprise. Underlying all is an overarching interest in the responsibilities of business to the community.

In any consideration of the future, one must acknowledge that the speed of technological change alone renders any assessment problematic. It has been said that there are more scientists alive today than there were in all the years of the past put together. To list recent changes in travel, communications, medicine, pharmaceuticals, weaponry, robotics, information processing, and genetic engineering is to chronicle a revolution accelerating daily. The U.S. Patent and Trademark Office issued some 170,000 patents in 2000, representing a 70 percent increase over 1990. The pace of change is such that to predict the future by extrapolating from present trends may be no surer than blind guessing. Even leaving technological change aside, it is difficult to foresee the future; few in 1990 would have predicted ten years later the weaknesses of the Japanese economy and the strength of American business. The accidental, the unseen, and the unpredicted play a crucial and sometimes decisive role in the unfolding of events. As Nobel laureate Niels Bohr observed, "Prediction is very difficult, especially if it's about the future." Still it is useful to sum up the present and in so doing to consider some of the forces that will shape the next century.

THE AMERICAN SOCIAL ENVIRONMENT

The United States, it has been argued, has been a society where the most enduring tensions have involved differences of race, ethnicity, religion, and region rather than the clash of social classes and ideologies. This, of course, is a gross overstatement. Class has always mattered as a powerful factor in American society. It cannot be denied that family, money, and connections commonly pave the way to success. Differences in social and economic circumstances of social groups or classes (often, though not always, related to gender, race, and ethnicity) have produced wide differences in outlook and opportunities.

American politics and culture, as with all nations, are shaped by the way production and consumption are organized. But through most of its history, the United States has avoided the deeply etched class animosities and bloody conflicts long characteristic of most societies. Abraham Lincoln told the Workingman's Association of New York in 1864: "That some should be rich shows that others may become rich and hence is just encouragement to industry and enterprise."[1] To a remarkable degree, even when belied by reality and common sense, Americans have trusted in the promise of American life and the social mobility it proffers.

This promise is first and foremost the expectation of an expanding economy, bringing open opportunity and ever-greater prosperity to all Americans ready and able to work hard. As the population has become increasingly heterogeneous, these bedrock expectations continue to weave the fabric and pattern of an increasingly pluralistic society. Associated with core values, they act to provide a lever for economic change as well as ballast for social stability. Americans thus assume that they need not choose, at least in the long run, between economic growth and social equity, since one is expected to facilitate the other. Recent trends, however, may offer reasons for concern.

It is not only the general success of the economy that ensures social peace but also the distribution of a nation's wealth in a manner accepted by society as equitable and reasonable. This is why too gross a discrepancy in incomes and wealth poses a threat to democracy. Americans are more tolerant in this regard than other Western nations. But even in the United States, great differences in wealth and income could erode public confidence in the economic system, while distorting the balance of political power and influence in the nation. A growing inequality between the earnings of the better-paid and the lower-paid has been discernible for over a quarter of a century, and the gap continues to widen. In 1979, the richest 1 percent of Americans in full-time employment earned 3.6 times as much as the poorest 10 percent; by 2000, the richest were earning over five times as much. In 1999, the *New York Times* began a news story with the lead, "The gap between rich and poor has grown into a chasm so wide that this year the richest 2.7 million Americans, the top 1 percent, will have as many after-tax dollars to spend as the bottom 100 million."[2] The share of national income accounted for by the top 1 percent of earners reached 22.8 percent in 2005—a level not seen since 1928.[3]

John Maynard Keynes observed in his *General Theory of Employment, Interest, and Money* that an "outstanding fault" of capitalism is an "arbitrary and inequitable" distribution of income, and this problem has greatly intensified in the United States since the mid-1970s. A Brookings Institution economist, Gary Burtless, expressed his concern over a "startling increase" in the gap between wealthier and poorer Americans in the last quarter of the twentieth century. The top 1 percent of earners in 2000, he asserted, held 40 percent of the country's wealth, a figure Burtless believed more than double the percentage of only a quarter century earlier.[4] The Bush administration's steep tax cuts in 2001, with the top 1 percent receiving 43 percent of the tax breaks, only further heightened the contrast.

It is argued that there is nothing wrong with inequalities when large wage differentials create incentives resulting in higher productivity. A related argument holds that those who make the most money in a free-market economy merit all they get by effectively meeting the demands of consumers. But such arguments cannot be pursued solely in the abstract. Class distinctions based on economic and social differences have profound implications for health, education, and, of course, movement up and down the economic ladder. Moreover, the rich are getting better at passing their advantages on to their children.[5]

American democracy will never tolerate the small elite of wealth and masses of wretched poor commonly found in the cities of Asia, Africa, and South America. This would be true even when the have-nots are only experiencing deprivation relative to the wealthy. Great disparities in wealth and economic power always pose the possibilities of severe social unrest. The outrageous compensation packages of many corporate managers and the colossal ethical and criminal abuses that were exposed in financial institutions at the beginning of the twenty-first century shook faith in the fairness of the American system and convinced many overseas critics that American-style capitalism and globalization exploit the less fortunate both at home and abroad.

Over a century and a half ago, Ralph Waldo Emerson saw humanity as divided between the "Old World's" party of conservatism-past-memory and the "New World's" party of innovation-future-hope. Americans welcome the new as superior to the old and regard change as the measure of progress. American marketing projects a view of the material world as largely composed of commodities offering only transitory pleasures and easily subject to unsentimental replacement. To pursue profit, America's businesses promote change while proposing the social utility of the profit motive and arguing that their self-interested actions benefit all. Certainly, few nations have enjoyed and indeed celebrated the transformational power of economic activity as much as has the United States.

Nevertheless, structural changes in the economy create social tensions that reinforce the need for effective cooperation. Most men and women are generally least threatened when their way of life sustains familiar customs and habits. This still holds true for Americans, even though their values encourage them to expect and accept disruptive change.

It is both the strength and the weakness of American capitalism that it constantly changes not only the way we do business but also the way we live and think. Nowhere is the rapid pace of change more evident than in the workplace. A generation ago, an ordinary American assumed that he or she would have one career and possibly one employer for his or her entire working life. Now we are told that a worker must be prepared to change careers and employers many times before retirement. Americans have historically done little to impede rapid economic change, believing that a market economy must continually adjust itself to technological advance, new information, and innovation—or risk stagnation and a declining standard of living. More than others, Americans identify change with gain and progress. Americans have always sought to speed up the future and are remarkable in their ability to accommodate to the new. But most Americans still long for some security and stability and look to Washington to provide a satisfactory psychological and economic safety net.

Just as the number of farmers has decreased to less than 3 percent of the workforce, so the percentage of that force employed in blue-collar manufacturing jobs is shrinking. At the beginning of the twenty-first century, only 13 percent of the workforce was engaged in manufacturing goods, as compared to 30 percent fifty years earlier. This does not signify that the United States is producing less now than before; increasing productivity simply means that a smaller percentage of factory workers produce what previously required a much larger percentage. Thus, it was possible for the value of manufacturing in the GDP in constant dollars to be higher in 2000 than in 1960.[6]

The very industries that were regarded as spearheading the economy well into the 1980s—steel, automotive, durable goods—downsized their labor forces the most sharply in the 1990s. Between 1968 and 2000, employment in the steel industry declined 60 percent. Workers at the large industrial firms had assumed that if they were loyal to the company they in turn were guaranteed job security, health care, and a comfortable retirement. The jobs being created as replacements often do not offer this rosy picture. And, indeed, the firms that once offered them frequently find that they can no longer honor these promises.

Services, including government services, now account for about three-fourths of the American economy. As manufacturing's share of the American economy (as measured by the value of its products as part of the GDP) continues to dwindle, American consumers and businesses will spend more and more of their dollars on services rather than goods because the cost of the latter is declining relative to service costs.

The service part of the economy, some 73.6 million jobs in 2004, comprises a broad range of employment. It includes most employees of government, universities, and hospitals; the retail and wholesale trades; real estate; banking and finance; hotels and tourism; and all the activities generally regarded as the professions (for example, lawyers, accountants, doctors, and nurses). Many service activities offer employment at salaries considerably higher than the wages paid by manufacturing. But service jobs also include those at McDonald's and Wal-Mart, and there is concern that the replacement of well-paying (and unionized) manufacturing jobs by service industry employment means the proliferation of dead-end, low-paying jobs. The data on new jobs being created in the service sector does not bear this out. In 1999, according to the Bureau of Labor Statistics, the average hourly wage for service jobs was 92 percent of that for factory jobs, up from 77 percent in 1964. This gap may narrow even further as the numbers of computer support specialists and system analysts grow by leaps and bounds (that is assuming they are not outsourced, a very big assumption indeed), but the discrepancies between high-paid and low-paid employment in service industries are greater than in manufacturing.

Better-paid service jobs almost always require postsecondary education, and most workers without college degrees will be forced into the lower-paid service employment, as the alternative to good wages in unionized blue-collar work fades. The newer style of "flexible manufacturing" requires a highly skilled and educated manufacturing workforce, and this will oblige large employers to greatly expand job training and educational programs. Some large American manufacturers are moving to the development of work teams whose members have interchangeable high-level skills. Many workers may need remedial training to prepare for these advanced programs if the educational system fails to do its job. It is anticipated that Americans in the future will change employers and career paths several times in their working life. Skills that are transferable between industries to maximize mobility will loom large in how individuals plan.[7]

The economic upturn of 1993–2000 created new jobs (an estimated 10 million) and lowered unemployment below 5 percent, but many of the disturbing employment patterns of the 1980s persisted into the new century. Surprisingly few of the new jobs promised a secure future; many offered only temporary or part-time employment in services, especially retail, at dismal wages. Meanwhile, corporate downsizing, once a response to the business cycle, is now regarded as a regular cost-cutting tool of management, even during good times. A letter writer to the *New York Times* (March 17, 1996) described a political cartoon in the late 1990s as depicting an affluent older man making a speech at a banquet and proclaiming, "Last year thousands of new jobs were created in this country," while the thought balloon over the waiter's head reads, "Yeah, and I've got three of them."[8]

As economists argue about the causes, consequences, and cures for these trends, many are moving to a multicausal explanation, one that gives a combination of factors—new global competition with low wage countries, outsourcing, deregulation of domestic industries, lower minimum wages, and weaker unions—as having altered profoundly the balance of bargaining power between management and labor, to the disadvantage of the latter. Arguing from this analysis, liberal economists have suggested that Washington must rewrite the labor laws to fashion an equitable workplace contract. In any dynamic society, layoffs will, of course, be necessary, but it must be noted that most Western nations provide protection for this in the form of generous unemployment benefits and pensions, retraining programs, and universal health insurance. American workers losing their jobs often find themselves without health insurance or pensions.[9]

Structural changes in the economy alter our sense of status and class and determine future American mobility. Shifts in job structure determine how and where we work, live, and educate our children. The nearly 40 percent high school dropout rate among Mexican Americans in Los Angeles in 2004 meant personal difficulties for many of them, as well as attendant anger and frustration, which may seek expression in antisocial behavior. It also means the inevitable exacerbation of other social problems. Public opinion polls indicate that Americans strongly believe that all are entitled to equal opportunity in running the race of life—and when the poverty of any ethnic or racial community deters the education of its youth it is not that group's problem alone. Americans, too, often identify certain groups with a lower class status, an attitude that interferes in many ways with upward mobility.

It is clear that an individual's self-identity and self-respect usually require a positive view of his or her group by others. But when heightening economic stratification between rich and poor also correlates highly with racial and ethnic distinctions—which it certainly does—an explosive mix is created. Sustaining the American Dream, with its powerful implications for social harmony, requires a general belief in a level playing field. The benefits of education and training depend on whether jobs are available on a freely competitive basis or whether access to them is restricted in various ways. When, as in the American past, and even to an extent in the present, certain individuals and groups have limited access to jobs, education, and other opportunities then persistent inequalities, with resulting social tension, must occur.

The elimination of discriminatory practices as well as other policies to enhance minority mobility is the law of the land but remains to be fully defined by the courts. A changing political climate in the mid-1990s, including Supreme Court decisions limiting the use of affirmative action and rul-ing against quotas, caused a significant governmental pullback. Further leg-islation may alter policy and implementation. Voters in both California and Washington State have rejected affirmative action in both higher education and state contracting. The view that affirmative action means an effort to achieve equal opportunity in employment for all Americans while ending discrimination is generally accepted. It is when advocates of affirmative ac-tion move beyond this that they encounter resistance. The issues of minority quotas for employees, set-asides (reserving new employment for minorities), and even the preferential treatment accorded by "goal-timetable" (the hiring of certain numbers or workforce percentages of designated groups within a given time frame) are highly controversial and politically charged. For its supporters, affirmative action is necessary to create a level playing field for all Americans, but opponents denounce it as "reverse bias."[10]

The need for prodding employers to recruit qualified minority candidates has been amply demonstrated. The bipartisan Federal Glass Ceiling Com-mission studying diversity in the workplace reported as late as 1995 that entrenched stereotypes and prejudices acted as barriers to the progress of women and minorities. A majority of chief executives acknowledged in inter-views that federal guidelines and pressure had been essential in maintaining corporate commitment to a diverse workforce. The 1995 federal commission also observed that, three decades after the passage of the Civil Rights Act of 1964, about 91 percent of corporate America's senior executives remained white and male. Blacks accounted for only 3 percent of senior-level jobs—those defined as vice president and above; women held about 5 percent. However, women have begun to move into these jobs very quickly.

In 2004, women accounted for nearly 48 percent of those holding man-agerial and executive positions in big American corporations, and many of these women have reached the age and position to reach for the top of the ladder. In 2003, nearly 16 percent of vice presidents or higher positions of Fortune 500 companies that required board approval were held by women. But, in spite of such progress, many women believe that sex discrimination has impeded their careers. Corporate America is seemingly still a man's game, or more precisely a white man's game. As federal support for recruit-ing and retaining women and minorities weakened in the 1990s, many corporations in turn eased their efforts. In late 2001 the *Wall Street Journal* reported that "a lot of companies are putting diversity programs on the back burner."

The nature of the social responsibility of business to the community is a controversial issue. The indifference of nineteenth-century factory owners to the welfare of the worker and the community provoked Karl Marx's fury at a system he believed inherently exploitative. The major criticisms of capitalism or a free-enterprise system have never been with its ability to create wealth: criticisms have been raised against the way this is done, how it is distributed, and with what consequences. Among the criticisms are capitalism's boom-and-bust excesses, the inequitable distribution of wealth and income, and the possibility for human alienation. Thomas Carlyle expressed the last theme with his classic phrase "cash-nexus"—the reduction of human relations to an impersonal business arrangement based solely on self-interest.

Throughout the nineteenth century, a few employers insisted that self-interest, "properly understood," provided a reason to be concerned with the welfare of workers and the community. "Enlightened capitalists" argued that healthier and happier workers would be more productive and reliable, a theme that fed early twentieth-century "welfare capitalism." However, this too often assumed the guise of diverting workers from supporting unions by offering them benefits. Businesses' involvement in the affairs of their workforces (and their communities) will always be open to suspicion of self-interest and paternalism. American democracy works best, although certainly not perfectly, when companies pursue profit in the marketplace and leave social issues largely to the political process. But there are businesspeople who strongly and sincerely believe that it is "enlightened self-interest," or good business practice, for a corporation to be a responsible member of the community by taking into account the interests of employees, customers, suppliers, and local communities, as well as the society at large.

Large corporations in the 1950s and 1960s, in part out of political and public relations considerations, carefully presented themselves as good citizens. Many funded local cultural events and grappled with community problems, donating money to charitable organizations and encouraging employees to volunteer their time. In the context of the tumultuous 1960s, years of mounting social disorder and distrust, community involvement assumed a new urgency. Eager to distance themselves from antibusiness stereotypes, professional corporate managers rushed to demonstrate social concern and participated in extensive discussions of business's role in meeting community goals. But most leaders of American business still harbored a distrust of "excessive" governmental involvement in society as undermining a free enterprise system, and corporate volunteerism was often seen by this group as a preferable alternative to action by government.

Sensitive to criticism, business leaders reacted sharply to the Watergate revelations in 1974 that at least eighteen companies, in currying favor with the Nixon administration, had violated campaign finance laws. Nor did the press revelations in the early 1970s that many defense-related corporations routinely offered money and jobs to American and foreign officials in exchange for lucrative contracts encourage public confidence in the integrity of big business. No doubt many corporate leaders were truly sincere in their social concerns. But others evinced more interest in a positive corporate image than in substantive actions.

An important 1970 article by the Nobel Prize–winning economist Milton Friedman on the social responsibility of the corporation provoked heated discussion. Friedman's libertarian position echoed late nineteenth-century laissez-faire values. To his way of thinking, management's only responsibility resided in maximizing profits for stockholders and obeying the laws of the nation and the community by playing "within the rules of the game . . . open and free competition without deception or fraud." For management to be involved in social engineering could only detract from economic performance and violate its trust. This could indeed prove counterproductive, since management's major, albeit indirect, contribution to American well-being was an efficient national economy. Thus, to Friedman, business's exclusive concern had to be maximizing profit.[11]

Hard times in the late 1970s encouraged American businesses to end or greatly reduce their social programs. "Social responsibility" now appeared almost an outmoded cliché. In many ways these attitudes paralleled a fundamental political shift away from liberalism, as many in the middle class became hostile to Washington's interventionist social programs. These changes reflected widespread disappointment with Lyndon Johnson's Great Society reforms and a growing cynicism about the political process and politicians. The United States had entered an age of antigovernment sentiment and stronger emphasis on market ideology. This did not, however, stop businesspeople from going to Washington for help when it suited their interests, as in the federal bailouts in the 1970s of the Penn Central Railroad, Lockheed, and Chrysler. Conservative or not, business leaders have rarely hesitated to use and expand government when it advanced their interests.

In the 1990s, corporate America flew the banner "Lean and Mean." The decade's downsizing differed from layoffs in the past in that it was not a temporary response to shortfalls in product demand but a deliberate strategy to keep the workforce at a permanent minimum. The intention was to cut costs by increasing efficiency, and in such corporate cost cutting, a company's community and human relations programs often proved convenient items to slash. American business still contributes several billion dollars to various types of social programs, but contributions have declined as a percentage of profits in recent years. It is usually older firms, with roots in a locality and in slow-growth sectors of the economy that are most generous in their corporate giving. Unfortunately, this also describes companies most likely to have been the targets of takeover bids. This was a theme of the Broadway play and of the later movie *Other People's Money*, which posed the question of whether management's responsibility is to a community that is dependent on a company for employment or simply to the stockholders.

Corporate generosity seeks, in part, to enhance image or even to gain visibility for products. Oil companies sponsored programs on public television in the 1970s to counteract public anger at soaring oil prices. The well-known largesse of liquor, beer, and tobacco companies in inner-city black neighborhoods was understandably suspect. Regarded as a devious form of advertising, this corporate "generosity" in sponsoring community programs is resented by local community leaders concerned with residents' health.

This is not to deny that American business has established an impressive record of generosity to community programs of all kinds. It has indeed aided the development of a vast nongovernmental network of social services that have greatly enriched the nation's social resources. It is this phenomenon that President George H. W. Bush referred to in his famous remark in his 1988 campaign as "a thousand points of light." As frequently noted, nongovernmental associations have played a major role in advancing the common good, especially in the areas of health, education, welfare, and the transmission of moral values. Certainly, American business has been a major provider of funds to volunteer efforts by civil society.

Nevertheless, corporate and other forms of private giving only supplement and cannot replace public programs; the latter has to continue to bear the major burden of providing for the needy in our society. Public policy must be the principal determinant of and the main support for the nation's social welfare system. (Likewise, the political arena will decide how far government will go in redistributing wealth from the top down to middle- and lower-income groups in America.) American business's most important contribution to the national well-being is, to paraphrase Friedman, in providing an economy capable of bearing the burden of social welfare while remaining prosperous enough to minimize the numbers requiring assistance. It is the responsibility of the political process to engage in an ongoing search for the best models for government intervention to support social justice policies and sound environmental policies and provide an adequate social safety net while minimizing restraints on the business community to create wealth.[12]

One cannot define in any absolute sense the responsibilities of the corporation to the community. It must, of course, obey the laws and act in a responsible manner. But the meaning of "responsible" will shift, depending on what the public requires and expects of business.[13]

As Adolf A. Berle observed in *The 20th Century Capitalist Revolution* (1954), "Corporate management . . . knowingly or unknowingly, is constrained to work within a framework of surrounding conceptions which in time impose themselves."[14] It is up to public discourse, then, to establish the level of expectations that corporations will fail to meet only at a loss to their public standing. If the expectations are sufficiently important, they may be mandated as binding laws. In particular, government and the public must be aware that at times of frenzied speculation—when fortunes can be made swiftly—both individuals and corporations tend to relax their moral restraints as greed and arrogance overcome fear and conscience. (Moreover, we have seen this phenomenon played out too often in the past to think the tendency will simply go away, no matter what corrective measures are put in place.)

It would be dangerous to give corporations a major role in establishing social or environmental goals or changing social behavior. Paternalism has had unpleasant consequences in the past and runs against the grain of a democracy. One does not have to accept all of Milton Friedman's views of a free-market economy to accept his contention that businesses' contribution to the national well-being must be evaluated primarily in economic terms. The bottom line for business in a public reckoning is, in very large part, how well it performs its role of manufacturing goods or dispensing services. The corporation's main concerns must be inevitably competitive: to invest, to hire, and to generate profits for its shareholders. This said, we also need companies that are concerned with their employees' welfare and offer ample benefits. Workers must be defined in terms of value they create, not solely, as is too often the case, of how much they cost. Although there is no widely

agreed upon definition of social responsibility, it must include a commitment to behave ethically and to contribute to the overall quality of life.

Many companies currently issue an annual "social accountability" report.
To encourage consistent ways of monitoring and reporting, the U.S. Council
on Economic Priorities has prepared guidelines and models of social involvement for various types of industries. Nevertheless, in the bull market euphoria of 1997, the Business Roundtable, a lobbying group that represented the
CEOs of dozens of major companies, changed its position statement. The
former emphasis on the social role of the corporations was altered to read,
"The paramount duty of management and board is to the shareholder."
Soon after, boardroom scandals only added to an already widely held view
that American corporations are greedy and uncaring. In response, business
schools added courses on ethics and morality to their curricula, and publishers flooded the market with books that carried the message that to focus
exclusively on the bottom line is not the best way to run a business.

What is important to the labor force is the creation by corporations of well-
paying, relatively secure jobs offering opportunities for adequate pensions. It
is the nexus of a market economy with a democratic polity that has raised the
American standard of living consonant with individual dignity and freedom.
There is a justifiable concern, however, that global competitiveness and outsourcing may drag down wages and benefits in a race to the bottom. Whether
Americans will or should tolerate such a situation for long will, it is hoped,
never come to a test. A market economy left alone cannot be expected to
promote long-range societal goals. Such national goals as a reasonably equitable distribution of wealth and income, the preservation of aesthetic or
ecological values, or the maintenance of economic and social stability are
issues of public policy to be addressed by the political process. Just as important as Adam Smith's ideas in *The Wealth of Nations* is his argument in *The
Theory of Moral Sentiments* that a moral community—with its social norms
and governmental institutions—must undergird any viable economic one. It
is clear that we must continue to seek a new form of capitalism, one that
more consciously works for the common good instead of depending on the
"invisible hand" to generate positive results for society.[15]

CORPORATE GOVERNANCE

The problems that arose in the 1990s as a result of what had been called
"CEO capitalism" generated interest in improving corporate governance. The

effort to align the interests of shareholders and management through stock options had to be revisited. The "principal agent" problem—how to ensure that an agent acts in the interest of his client or employer when it differs from his own—required further exploration. Though Adam Smith had recognized that the separation of management and ownership in corporations created divergent interests, the corrective reliance on boards of directors to act as a check on management frequently did not suffice, for reasons to be explored. A historic tendency to minimize the potential for conflict had led to a lax style of corporate governance that needed attention.[16]

As the modern industrial corporation evolved at the end of the nineteenth century, one of its most important characteristics initially received sparse attention and little real analysis. The implications of separating management from ownership in the transition from proprietary firms to public companies were not significantly recognized until the creation of the Bureau of Corporations in 1903. This is, at least in part, because the evolution of the corporation often took place in two stages. In the first stage, the public company was headed by the entrepreneur who had founded it and who generally kept tight control. In the second stage, control was assumed by salaried management. It has been suggested that the creation of U.S. Steel in 1901 was the symbolic occasion upon which managerial organization began to take the place of the classic American entrepreneur as personified by Andrew Carnegie.

The importance of entrepreneurial activity by individuals initially obscured, with the exception of railroads, the revolutionary break between ownership and professional salaried management in the modern corporation. Praised as pioneers or damned as robber barons, such entrepreneurs provided the drive to create business organizations of unprecedented scale and complexity. These entrepreneurs appeared to provide continuity with the older proprietary form of business by associating the public corporation with a human face and name, and many of the first industrial corporations were tightly held, with common or voting stock limited to the founder, his family, and perhaps a handful of associates.[17]

Thus, the evolving corporate system in its initial entrepreneurial stage could retain the appearance of continuity with the traditional proprietary firm. The entrepreneurs who founded the company not only owned the corporation, along with the other stockholders, but also ran it. Very soon, in the twentieth century, however, salaried professional management replaced the founders in running those businesses oriented to mass production and forward integration toward the consumer. This was the "managerial capitalism" that institutional historians have analyzed and that prevailed largely unchallenged at least until the 1980s. Alfred Chandler believed that an effective management would necessarily place priority on its own permanence and prefer long-term corporate stability and growth to short-term gains.

It was assumed that salaried managers, for the most part, would fulfill their fiduciary obligation to serve shareholders by maximizing business profitability. Moreover, management was trained to believe that building assets over the long run guaranteed competitive advantage and was in the best interests of the shareholders. When government regulations and trade unions challenged the freedom of corporations to act as they saw fit, management initially argued in response that a business must be run by managers in the interests of its owners in order to operate efficiently and benefit the economy.

It is true that after the stock market crash of 1929 congressional investigators uncovered widespread insider trading and stock market manipulation that belied comfortable assumptions about management's behavior. In this context, Adolf A. Berle and Gardiner Means published *The Modern Corporation and Private Property* in the midst of the Great Depression. They noted the critical significance of the separation of ownership and management and noted the strong probability of a divergence of interests between management and shareholder. But, with the creation of the Securities and Exchange Commission and new disclosure regulations, this problem seemed adequately addressed.

The prowess of the American corporation in World War II and for several decades after forestalled serious discussion of corporate governance. The relationship between management and the stockholders seemed reasonably straightforward. Stockholders elected a board of directors, including "independent directors" from outside. The directors selected top management, set their pay through a compensation committee, and oversaw their financial reporting and performance through an audit committee. Ideally, the directors were knowledgeable about the corporation's affairs and conscientious in representing the interest of the equity owners or stockholders. Almost invariably, stockholders approved the slate of directors proposed by management. In theory, shareholders could join together to force out directors or managers, but rarely did. John Kenneth Galbraith recorded this phenomenon in *The New Industrial State* (1967), terming it the "euthanasia of stockholder power," but did not perceive it to be a major problem.[18]

By the early 1980s, shareholders had become acutely unhappy with low corporate profitability and stagnant stock prices. Most stockholders of large public corporations had no involvement with or attachment to the corporations whose shares they held. They regarded their stock simply as an investment portfolio, to be bought and sold for gain. Many were speculatively inclined and interested in quick trading. They had little, if any, concern for the long-run operations of a business—but considerable interest in daily share value. The takeover mania of the 1980s reflected and exploited this fact. Takeover experts in the 1980s often argued correctly that management of the targeted firms had feathered their own nests to the detriment of stockholders. Corporate raiders and Wall Street firms, like Kohlberg Kravis Roberts or Hicks, Muse used leveraged buyouts to take over companies and then cut costs to boost their stock prices for quick sales. In their search for quick turnover, arbitrageurs bought shares in targeted corporations, intending to hold them for only days, or weeks at the most. The assumption that long-term corporate planning was the preferred approach now began to be challenged in practice and soon in theory as well.[19]

A perspective commonly heard among management scholars in the 1990s was that the twenty-first century corporation must be predicated on constantly altering strategy and structure. Some even suggested that the public corporation might give way to more transitory arrangements and cease to exist as a recognizable form. Nimbleness and adaptability to ever-changing needs, not longevity, seemed the highest business virtue. Until its collapse in 2001, Enron, the energy giant, seemed to represent the cutting edge of the new corporate strategy. Financial engineering was the way to do business. In consequence, long-term planning no longer seemed necessary or indeed even feasible.[20]

Corporate governance was also being rethought in the 1990s as it became apparent that the self-interest of upper management frequently clashed with the interests of shareholders. One commentator noted, after the Enron shell game unraveled, "For a long time we thought that the fundamental conflict in capitalism was between owners and workers. Enron proves that the real conflict is between insiders and outsiders. The losers in the Enron case are both stockholders and workers."[21]

Tensions between the interests of professional managers and those of shareholders presented an intriguing dilemma. When professional managers own little equity in their companies, there is a tendency for them to lavish perks on themselves and seek job security and freedom from accountability rather than from shareholder value. It was partly to align the interests of professional management and shareholders that stock options became widespread in the 1990s. This development, along with the greater stress placed on entrepreneurial prowess, explains why the 1990s became the decade of the "imperial CEO." In the new century, top executives of many of America's corporations continued to enjoy what their critics regarded as excessive compensation packages, including handsome stock options, while wages of ordinary workers grew slowly if at all.

Instead of aligning interests, however, huge grants of options often only provided self-serving executives an incentive to create short-term bumps in stock prices, which they quickly cashed in on. These executives often got rich, while shareholders who held on lost heavily. Perhaps the most startling aspect of the scandals that rocked the economy in 2002 and again in 2007 was that most executives who deluded and defrauded their clients and shareholders did so without breaking the law. Efforts to strengthen the law, however, encounter powerful resistance from those who argue, often based on self-interest, that the most that is needed are minor changes. It remains to be seen which side will prevail.

The bull market of the 1990s gave corporations further impetus to avoid long-term planning. The increasingly short-term nature of CEOs' jobs, along with the pressure on them to deliver results quickly, did not help matters. The corporate culture that had acted to rein in aggressive CEOs and that encouraged companies to stick with the familiar had fallen out of fashion. Instead, the emphasis was on short-term financial returns to increase shareholder values in a rising stock market. Indeed, the view of the corporation as highly ephemeral as the result of recent technological changes that required shifting alliances rather than durable relations militated against long-term goals or a sense of corporate loyalty. Everything was in play. It was all-important for individuals and companies to recognize opportunities offered by quick change. Professional management (and other employees) sought to resolve the conflict by focusing not on the corporation—and longevity of employment—but upon rising share values and the possibility of a windfall. The great bull market of the 1990s, with its "irrational exuberance" and, to use another Alan Greenspan phrase, "infectious greed," encouraged CEOs and other professional managers to enrich themselves at the expense of the stockholder and for investors to speculate with no real interest in corporate fundamentals or in retaining stock for any length of time. Long-term investments in new plants, equipment, and the research necessary for job creation and corporate longevity frequently became at best an afterthought.

In the first years of the new century, the stock market bubble burst and the public mood radically shifted. CEOs, especially those who had led aggressively, became the villains. Seemingly overnight, what had been lauded as entrepreneurial drive now was derided as risky behavior. Corporate reformers called for greater controls over upper management. They stressed the need for independence of directors, meaning that directors should not have financial or other close ties to the company or its executives and that a company's audit, nominating, and compensation committees should consist completely of independent directors. Other suggested reforms had to do with ways of correcting auditing abuses by accounting firms eager to please clients; these called for automatic rotation of an audit firm involved with a client company and limits on nonaudit services provided by the audit firm to a company. Another major concern became how to rein in the abuses invited by stock options. Here, reforms usually called for time restrictions on the sale of options, requiring them to be held for a period of six months or more after being exercised.

Shareholders, however, also bear responsibility for the excesses of the 1990s. Large stockholders, for example, had joined together early in the 1990s to gain leverage over corporate management. The power of institutional investors had grown greatly as stock holdings by individual investors declined and mutual and pension funds replaced individuals as the biggest buyers of stock. In 2008, institutional investors collectively owned well over half the value of all the nation's publicly owned corporations, as compared to only 16 percent in 1965. Institutional shareholders wanted high stock prices, and CEOs who failed to deliver at IBM, General Motors, and American Express were ousted in 1992–93 as a direct result of pressure applied by institutional shareholders unhappy with CEO performances; the bosses of General Dynamic and U.S. Air were forced to take large pay cuts.

Early in the twenty-first century, TIAA-CREF, one of the nation's largest and most socially aware pension funds, distributed a "Policy Statement on Corporate Governance." This requested that management's incentive awards be tied to performance and be fully revealed. The document also asked for two-thirds of a board of directors to be "outsiders," who were required to personally hold a significant amount of the company's shares. As for the inevitable tension between stockholders' concern with the present and management's need to consider the future, the document stated: "Good corporate governance must be expected to maintain an appropriate balance between the rights of shareholders—the owners of the corporation—and the need of the board and management to direct and manage the corporation's affairs free from nonstrategic short term influences. . . . The primary responsibility of the board of directors is to foster the long-term success of the corporation consistent with its fiduciary responsibility to the shareholders."

Although well-intentioned, this statement did not reflect the behavior of many institutional funds. Large institutional investors by and large joined the gold rush of the 1990s. In *Investor Capitalism*, Michael Useem examined how a mutual fund manager who controlled 5 percent of Chase Manhattan Bank's sluggish stocks forced its 1995 merger with Chemical Bank. Useem concluded that "managerial capitalism," in which top executives were in effect unaccountable, had given way to "investor capitalism," where large-scale institutional investors call the shots in their quest for high rates of return. In March 1995, for example, a large pension fund forced W. R. Grace to reduce its board of directors by half and to fire its chairman. Useem urged a backlash against such newly empowered institutional shareholders with their "share-price-is-all" approach and emphasis on short-term results. He argued that management must have the freedom to act for the long run and not have to worry incessantly that a stock's downturn will trigger a shareholder revolt. If perhaps overstated, Useem's argument points out that CEOs were often pressured by shareholders to pursue shortsighted policies for which they would later be faulted. Indeed, a central question of modern corporate strategy is whether corporations should focus more on short-term share price or on long-term value. As one journalist phrased it, "The question is should we trust managers or markets."[22]

But large institutional investors were not alone in demanding stock price performance. Individual investors, no longer satisfied with modest returns on investments, in the 1990s thought in terms of a quick killing. The dream of the small investor was often of instant wealth, won in a twinkling by audacity and good luck. Few were immune. Speculative frenzy occurred on all levels as the stock prices of high-tech companies—Hewlett-Packard, Intel, Cisco—soared, to be joined soon after by companies unrelated to high tech. As long as share price rose handsomely, few complained. It is, of course, during hard times that probing questions are asked and radical proposals gain a hearing. This occurred at the beginning of the twenty-first century.

A concept that has long been around and may in time attract greater interest is the idea of the corporation being responsible to all stakeholders. This would replace the owner-centered governance structure of the American corporation with a "stakeholder" model, where the rights of the stockholders to a profit would be balanced with the corporation's obligations to management, labor, suppliers, customers, the communities where it does business, and indeed society at large. How exactly such a change can be fully implemented remains vague, except to include each of these constituents on the board of directors.[23]

The German *Mitbestimmung* (co-determination) Law of 1976, for example, required all companies with 2,000 or more employees to have shareholders and workers represented in equal numbers on a supervisory board, which together with a board of managers runs the companies in a two-tier system of governance. Although it was clear that the stockholders' representatives had a greater say, *Mitbestimmung* provided a system for reconciling conflicting interests. But it also lessened the ability of businesses to adapt to economic change or to new technologies, and when the German economy floundered in the late 1990s, it hindered the country's competing in the global economy. German companies by the year 2000 had sought a way around the law by hiring more temporary workers and farming out more work, even as the government watered down the law.[24]

In the United States, the "stakeholder" movement has been greatly overshadowed by efforts to strengthen the shareholder's position. Still, questions of community welfare, worker rights, and environmental impacts have to be addressed in the corporate equation. That a market economy can engage in excesses that require external controls to provide some security for the individual and safeguards for the society has been a lesson relearned time and again; that these controls must be periodically revisited and adapted to new circumstances is obvious. Nothing is forever. One decade's reform is very often another decade's problem.

WHITHER AMERICA

It was difficult at the start of the first year of the twenty-first century to be pessimistic about America's economy. But only a few years later there was real reason for concern. The horror of September 11, 2001, underscored a troubling uncertainty about the world and its future. The ethnic and national tensions present in many parts of the world offer little hope of early resolution. Terrorism, both in the United States and in attacks on American interests abroad, has become an omnipresent danger. The possibilities of hostile adventurism by nations great and small are a serious concern. The role of the American military as a global stabilizing force will remain critical for the foreseeable future, with Department of Defense strategists calling for forces

sufficient to simultaneously handle one major and one minor crisis throughout the world—with sufficient resources left in reserve to handle yet a third
threat. Cuts in defense spending in 2000 had brought its share, at 3 percent
of the GDP, to the lowest figure since 1949; but in the aftermath of 9/11, and
interventions in Afghanistan and Iraq, the Pentagon's spending rose to 4
percent. This is still well below Cold War levels.

Highly decentralized market-based economies, in contrast to Soviet-style
command-and-control economies, have effectively altered and evolved over
time. Capitalism invites change by offering incentives to individuals to conduct business more effectively than their competitors. The ability of market
forces to utilize resources efficiently in an imperfect world while raising
living standards remains impressive. This has never been truer than in the
last half century. But this does not necessarily refute the view that competitive individualism left unchecked weakens the social fabric. It is now generally expected that government will limit, if not abolish, inequalities resulting
from improper ethnic or class domination of an economic system intended
to be open to merit. Indeed, the philosopher John Rawls, in *A Theory of Justice*
(1971), concluded his seminal book by asserting that inequalities of income
and wealth should be tolerated only when they raise the position of the least
well-off.[25]

Modern economic change, with its encouragement of new technology and
new markets, will always be attended by political and social consequences
that are neither anticipated nor intended. A free-enterprise system pushes to
maximize individual flexibility and freedom, and this has implications for a
society's political institutions and value systems. The economic and technological possibilities for widespread access to information contributed greatly
to the dismantling of the police state in the Soviet Union and in the communist system, which rested on force. To keep up with developments in information technology, authoritarian governments have had to loosen tight controls,
as has been the case in Singapore, Taiwan, and South Korea and even,
somewhat, in China.

Yet the collapse of communism should not encourage complacency about
the American system. Capitalism as such does not really seek to offer answers to social questions. As a market system, it does not address the issues
of the distribution of wealth and power, the dignity and security of the individual in an age of rapid change, the relations between individuals and
groups in a multicultural society (such as the United States), or the grave
ecological implications of America's technology and lifestyle. There exist

many types of capitalism, differing profoundly from the American model and each other. These distinctions involve, among other critical issues, the relationships between government and business, between finance and industry, between domestic and foreign policy, and, most important, between business and community. Only the political system, and not the free market, will respond to the thorny social and structural concerns listed above. Faith that business efficiency is identical to progress and that economic growth necessarily trickles down to those at the bottom are bromides, obscuring the absence of relevant answers to questions of national values and policies. For the United States to win the respect of the world, it must demonstrate that it is caring toward its poor and capable of sustaining stable families.[26]

But it seems that social democracies like Sweden and Germany, which once seemed to offer the possibilities of alternative models for the United States, have perhaps reached the limits of the state's ability to pay for escalating social benefits. Indeed, what is striking at the beginning of a new century is a general agreement about the limitations of the state. The facile vision that rose a century ago among some intellectuals—of a technocratic state of sufficient resources and public-oriented bureaucratic expertise to construct a society free of major social ills—has proven utopian, and the view once commonly held that capitalism, through state and corporate planning, would become virtually indistinguishable from socialism also at present appears naive.

No matter the approach, we have to reject two extreme views of free-market capitalism: that it is an unambiguously progressive force or that it is an irrational and destructive one. It is in essence an economic system, to be shaped by laws, practices, and values to serve desired social ends.

We have rediscovered in the last two decades that market forces still matter and that there is a limit to tampering with them without hindering creativity and wealth production. Inequality and turbulence are apparently the price we must pay for material progress. But market forces alone should not determine our lives. Increasingly, electorates are less tolerant of economic disruption, as the spread of globalization increases competition. Most Americans no doubt expect the federal government to guarantee high employment, provide unemployment benefits, and, if need be, offer protection and possibly even subsidies to companies whose failures would drag down the economy. In short, Americans want protection from systemic economic insecurities, especially those not of their own making. Already there is discussion of the need for various types of assistance—well-funded governmental retraining programs and universal health insurance—for individuals adversely impacted by downsizing or outsourcing. Consequently, government's role in economic life increased greatly in the twentieth century and probably will not diminish substantially, if at all, in the twenty-first century. There is no question that the drives toward privatization and deregulation have lost momentum. Thus a balance must be struck between the present emphasis on competition and the opportunity to profit from risk and the desire of some Americans for a society in which loyalty, stability, and some protection against economic instability are also priorities of national policy. As global warming's impact becomes more evident and less a matter of controversy, it is inevitable that public policy will need to respond to this and other environmental concerns.

For answers to questions about policies and values, we must draw upon something other than a narrowly defined cost-price calculus of rational self-interest. We cannot be like Thomas Gradgrind, the utilitarian monster of *Hard Times* who, Dickens wrote, is "a man who proceeds upon the principle that two and two are four, and nothing over." The free market and capitalism are not moral ideals, and they do not possess internal moral compasses. They are primarily arrangements for producing what we need. We must be reminded that the economy is not an end in itself but a means to other more selective ends. An ethical order must be imposed on business behavior. A commitment to human dignity and freedom is essential to our society and its democratic system. To allow market forces to exclusively determine our technology, values, and lifestyle would invite alienation and engender social conflict in a beggar-thy-neighbor Hobbesian war of all against all. The vital essence of our social wisdom and professional ethics is surely contained in the Talmudic aphorism: "If I am not for myself, who will be for me? If I am only for myself, what am I?" The pursuit of a well-lived life turns to the quality of existence and such issues as social awareness and responsibility.

In a utilitarian vein, Robert Putnam has proposed that a democratic society needs a certain measure of "social capital" and a high level of civic engagement to work effectively. This means citizens interacting in trust and cooperation with each other and the community while expecting a certain generalized reciprocity arising from a sense of mutual obligations. Putnam thinks that "a society characterized by generalized reciprocity is more efficient than a distrustful society, for the same reason that money is more efficient than barter. If we don't have to balance each exchange instantly, we get more accomplished."[27]

Indeed, Americans long ago recognized this essential truth. The visiting French magistrate Alexis de Tocqueville found in 1831 that "Americans . . . are fond of explaining almost all the actions of their lives by the principle of self-interest rightly understood: they show with complacency how an enlightened regard for themselves constantly prompts them to assist one another and inclines them willingly to sacrifice a portion of their time and property to the welfare of the state." It is "self-interest rightly understood" that acts to balance what some have called America's "culture of competitive individualism." But Putnam has warned that the nation's social capital has decreased drastically since the mid-1960s, as Americans increasingly turn away from social organizations and even each other, at least in part because they have become more cynical and less trusting.[28]

A "good society" requires a moral authority greater than that of political expedience or the marketplace imperative. Aristotle, the first philosopher to pose the concept of the common good, even suggested that any discussion of ethics must be tied to the idea of what it means to flourish as a human being. Society must encourage concepts of justice and solidarity to shape our value system, and many of these may be derived from America's experience and traditions. The opportunity for gainful and meaningful employment for all Americans represents such a value. Equal opportunity for all regardless of race, gender, national origin, or religion is a second. The need for broad distribution of income, education, and health care throughout the population is another value that almost all can agree on. A healthy democracy cannot tolerate for long a trend toward increasing economic inequalities or an increasingly malign physical environment. The breakdown of social standards is likely to arise when society denies many of its members adequate means of achieving socially approved goals. This is why in modern society the state is called upon to initiate and sustain programs that redistribute wealth from the affluent to those of lesser means.

Conservatives believe that the individual is the best judge of his or her own welfare and the means of securing it. There is not necessarily a contradiction between this argument and the view of liberals that as society grows ever more complex the altruistic and collective sides of our nature must both push forward. American culture emphasizes achievement over conformity—a fact not conducive to deference to community authority—but strong social bonds still limit individualism. The complex interdependencies of modern life require an enlightened self-interest. This recognizes that the individual's well-being ultimately rests on a healthy social foundation, Putnam's "social capital," with its inherent reciprocity and mutual obligation. The same statement is, of course, true for business well-being.

American emphasis on materialism is both a consequence and a cause of our long national prosperity; if, in historian David Potter's words, Americans are "a people of plenty," they are happy to be so. American business has been remarkably successful in generating wealth and meeting material needs. The American business system has remained over time flexible and remarkably innovative. The American economic system promotes change, and the political system provides an arena, albeit imperfect and vulnerable to well-funded interest groups, for articulating, criticizing, and adapting peacefully to change. Every national history has its underside, and the United States is certainly no exception. In its past, slavery was its most notable but far from its only stain. The present is still marked by discrimination against women and minorities and striking economic inequities. But the nation also exhibits a pronounced tendency over time to improve. Reform is not guaranteed by the system (and rarely does it arrive expeditiously), but it is feasible—and in an imperfect world that says much.

The ideal of a growing economy open to talent and industry constitutes the core of a secular American theology. An American ideal has long been the self-made individual, and the American premise has been that everyone can achieve this. Perennial optimism and a belief in the relative fairness of the system are the reasons that social conflict, although undeniably present, has never assumed the ominous nature of a fault line running through all of American history. The ultimate source of legitimacy in a democracy with an educated citizenry is public approval and acceptance, and this means the individual must be joined to the society by an awareness of his or her enlightened self-interest. American democracy has won the support of the citizenry by enfranchising them, and American capitalism has so far bought their approval by its results. Diverse peoples have created a common nationality based on a fund of shared values, including the belief that government must promote openness of opportunity. American political discourse is pervasively shaped by the idea of society as an arrangement for mutual advantage. The loss of faith in the system would change that.

The relationships between a society's economic organization and its political and social systems are complex and not always obvious. A concern of this study has been to consider historically the ways American business has interacted with our values and institutions. It currently appears that the most pressing political debate of the twenty-first century will not be over the economic merits of capitalism, a system without rival since the collapse of communism, but how to combine—or perhaps balance—business efficiency with desired social goals. For this reason, government must provide a countervailing force to market-driven change. This is especially true in new technologies, especially biotechnologies that pose powerful and far-reaching potentials for both beneficial and dangerous changes. A prosperous and dynamic society needs to be buoyed by a strong and shared set of beliefs—societies without shared beliefs eventually falter. The primary purpose of government is not, as some have argued, "to bring about a condition of affairs favorable to . . . private enterprise" but, in the words of the Constitution, to "promote the general Welfare and secure the Blessings of Liberty to ourselves and our Posterity." Government in a capitalist system must sustain the well-being of private enterprise, but it must also ensure that business performance profits society at large. A healthy society needs some uplifting vision of the good life. A laissez-faire view that the general welfare will be enhanced if the market is left alone is rejected by history.

Every successful society must distribute fairly to all its citizens "primary goods" or essentials. What these should be will inevitably be a matter of altering expectations and shifting political discourse. However, any list has to include the social ideal that we are all entitled to dignity and decency even if we differ in material wealth and the power and status that it inevitably confers. In this regard, it may be appropriate to conclude this book with the sentiment with which Adam Smith began his *Theory of Moral Sentiments*: "How selfish so ever man may be supposed, there are certainly some principles in his nature, which interest him in the fortunes of others, and render their happiness necessary to him, though he derives nothing except the pleasure of seeing it."[29]

Notes

INTRODUCTION

1 Even theology and economics have often been closely connected. When Ronald Reagan spoke of the United States as "a blessed land . . . set apart in a special way" as part of a "divine Plan," can one doubt that he included in his vision its free enterprise system, or that many Americans share his view? See Ronald Reagan, "We Will Be As a City upon a Hill," Speech to the Conservative Political Action Conference, Washington, D.C., January 25, 1974.

2 Alexis de Tocqueville, *Democracy in America*, ed. J. P. Mayer, trans. George Lawrence (Garden City, N.Y.: Doubleday, 1969), 413; cited in Tony Judt, *Past Imperfect: French Intellectuals, 1944–56* (Berkeley: University of California Press, 1992), 192. The editors of *Le Monde* were notorious for their contempt for the United States, which they regarded as a nation with a dehumanizing materialist culture lacking in tradition.

3 Comparative examinations of American business values and outlook and those of other capitalist countries are George C. Lodge and Ezra Vogel, *Ideology and National Competitiveness: An Analysis of Nine Countries* (Cambridge, Mass.: Harvard Business School Press, 1987); and Jeffrey E. Garten, *A Cold Peace: America, Japan, Germany, and the Struggle for Supremacy* (New York: Times Books, 1993).

4 The sociologist Seymour Martin Lipset noted in 1963 that 78 percent of Americans in a poll endorsed the view that "the strength of this country today is mostly based on the success of American business" and that 65 percent believed that hard work, not luck, is the key to success. I have found nothing more recent, but I expect a poll now would show a drop in responses to both questions. Seymour Martin Lipset, *The First New Nation: The United States in Comparative and Historical Perspective* (New York: Basic Books, 1963), 72.

1 Edmund Burke, *Reflections on the Revolution in France*, ed. J. G. A. Pocock (Indianapolis: Hatchett, 1987), 96.

2 A superb discussion of the rise of capitalism can be found in the works of the great French historian Fernand Braudel: *The Mediterranean* (2 vols., first published in France in 1949; English translation, New York: Harper and Row, 1972); and *Civilization and Capitalism* (3 vols., first published in France in 1979; English translation, New York: Harper and Row, 1981). A neo-Marxist perspective is offered by Immanuel Maurice Wallerstein, in *The Capitalist World Economy* (New York: Cambridge University Press, 1990). The view of capitalism as an economic system directed to the creation of wealth—not of subsistence or additional goods but to produce more wealth ad infinitum—originated with Karl Marx and is still generally accepted.

3 Adam Smith, *An Inquiry into the Nature and Causes of the Wealth of Nations*, ed. Edwin Cannan (1776; New York: Modern Library, 1994), bk. 1, chap. 2, 14.

4 Charles P. Kindleberger, *World Economic Primacy, 1550–1990* (New York: Oxford University Press, 1995), 35–105.

5 Kenneth Pomeranz suggests, contrary to the conventional view, that at least until the eighteenth century Japan and China were not far behind the West in economic development and that only with nineteenth-century industrialization did a "European-centered world system" emerge. Kenneth Pomeranz, *The Great Divergence: China, Europe, and the Making of the Modern World Economy* (Princeton, N.J.: Princeton University Press, 2000), 4–5.

6 C. B. Macpherson, *The Political Theory of Possessive Individualism: Hobbes to Locke* (Oxford: Oxford University Press, 1964), 15.

7 James D. Tracy, ed., *The Political Economy of Merchant Empires: State Power and World Trade, 1350–1750* (Cambridge: Cambridge University Press, 1991).

8 Eric Hobsbawm, *Industry and Empire: From 1750 to the Present Day* (London: Penguin, 1969), 40.

9 Karl Polanyi, *The Livelihood of Man* (New York: Academic Press, 1977), 46. See also his classic *The Great Transformation* (Boston: Beacon Hill, 1957), an important work on the emergence of the marketplace economy and its effect on nineteenth-century European thought, first published in 1944; and John Dryzak, *Democracy in Capitalist Times: Ideals, Limits, and Struggles* (New York: Oxford University Press, 1996). An excellent Marxist critique of Polanyi's ideas is Michael Hechter, "Karl Polanyi's Social Theory: A Critique," *Politics and Society* 10, no. 4 (1981): 398–423. See also Michael Novak, *The Catholic Ethic and the Spirit of Capitalism* (New York: Free Press, 1993); and David W. Haslett, *Capitalism with Morality* (New York: Oxford University Press, 1994). For a good critique of rational choice economics, see David Landes, "Introduction: On

Technology and Growth," in *Favorites of Fortune: Technology, Growth, and Economic Development since the Industrial Revolution*, ed. Patrice Higonner, David S. Landes, and Henry Rosovsky (Cambridge, Mass.: Harvard University Press, 1991), 9–17.

10 Robert D. Putnam, *Bowling Alone: The Collapse and Revival of American Community* (New York: Simon and Schuster, 2000), 18–23.

11 Wilson's appeal can be found in "Awakened Nation," *New York Times*, August 8, 1912, 6.

12 Jeffrey Sachs, "Notes on a New Sociology of Economic Development," in *Culture Matters: How Values Shape Human Progress*, ed. Lawrence E. Harrison and Samuel P. Huntington (New York: Basic Books, 2000), 28–41, and especially 35–36.

13 M. M. Postan, *Cambridge Economic History of Europe: Trade and Industry in the Middle Ages* (Cambridge: Cambridge University Press, 1987), 211.

14 G. V. Scamell, *The First Imperial Age: European Overseas Expansion, 1400–1715* (Boston: Rutledge, 1989), 63–87.

15 Earl J. Hamilton, *American Treasure and the Price Revolution in Spain* (New York: AMS Press, 1995), 46–61.

16 Macpherson, *Political Theory of Possessive Individualism*, 207.

17 Saint Thomas Aquinas, *Summa Theologica*, quoted in David Shi, *The Simple Life: Plain Living and High Thinking in American Life* (New York: Oxford University Press, 1985), 9.

18 Charles Tilly, *Coercion, Capital, and European States, AD 990–1992*, rev. ed. (Oxford: Blackwell, 1992), 76.

19 David Little, *Religion, Order, and Laws: A Study in Pre-Revolutionary England* (Chicago: University of Chicago Press, 1984), 97–103.

20 Economic historian Douglass North has stressed institutional innovations, particularly the development of efficient property rights that channel individual effort into value-adding activities, as a primary factor in economic growth: "Efficient economic organization is the key to growth; the development of an efficient economic organization in Western Europe accounts for the rise of the West." Douglass North and R. P. Thomas, *The Rise of the Western World* (Cambridge: Cambridge University Press, 1973), 1–2.

21 For a reformulation of ideology on non-Marxian lines, see Clifford Geertz, "Ideology as a Cultural System," in *Ideology and Discontent*, ed. David E. Apter (Glencoe, Ill.: Free Press, 1964), 47–76. Ellen Meikins Wood, *The Pristine Culture of Capitalism: A Historical Essay on Old Regimes and Modern States* (New York: Verso, 1991); Little, *Religion, Order, and Laws*, 47–62.

22 Christopher Hill, *The World Turned Upside Down* (New York: Viking, 1973), 34–36.

23 Cited in Louis Hartz, *The Liberal Tradition in America: An Interpretation of American Political Thought since the Revolution* (New York: Harcourt, Brace, 1955), 22.

The Compact Edition of the Oxford English Dictionary (Oxford: Oxford University Press, 1971), 1:1419, notes the year 1626 as the earliest usage of "individual" as meaning "a single human being, as opposed to Society, the Family, etc." See Owen Barfield, History in English Words (London: Macmillan, 1954), 166. For the significance of property to English social thinkers of the seventeenth century, see also Macpherson, Political Theory of Possessive Individualism, whose interpretation I have accepted; and, for a differing view, Michael P. Zuckert, Natural Rights and the New Republicanism (Princeton, N.J.: Princeton University Press, 1994).

24 Francis Hutcheson, On Human Nature, ed. Thomas Mautner (Cambridge: Cambridge University Press, 1993), 34.

25 J. G. A. Pocock, Virtue, Commerce, and History: Essays on Political Thought and History (Cambridge: Cambridge University Press, 1985), 27–42.

26 An insightful analysis of the relationship between culture and character types is to be found in David Potter, People of Plenty: Economic Abundance and the American Character (Chicago: University of Chicago Press, 1954), 76–77.

27 R. H. Tawney, Religion and the Rise of Capitalism: A Historical Study (1926; New York: New American Library, 1947), 176.

28 Max Weber, The Protestant Ethic and the Spirit of Capitalism (1904; Los Angeles: Roxbury, 2002). For a consideration of religious factors in explaining economic behavior, see Stephen Innes, Creating the Commonwealth: The Economic Culture of Puritan New England (New York: Norton, 1994); and David Landes, "Culture Makes All the Difference," in Culture Matters: How Values Shape Human Progress, ed. Lawrence E. Harrison and Samuel P. Huntington (New York: Basic Books, 2000), 2–13.

29 Quoted in Andrew Delblanco, The Puritan Ordeal (Cambridge, Mass.: Harvard University Press, 1989), 117.

30 Louis B. Wright, The Atlantic Frontier: Colonial American Civilization (Ithaca, N.Y.: Cornell University Press, 1959), 178.

31 Ibid.

32 Hartz, Liberal Tradition in America, 18; Herbert Applebaum, The Concept of Work in the Ancient, Medieval, and Modern World (Albany: State University of New York Press, 1992), 328–30. For a description of the Puritan emphasis on order and punctuality in daily life and the horror of wasted time, see Christopher Hill, Society and Puritanism in Pre-Revolutionary England (New York: Schocken Books, 1956), chap. 3, and especially p. 127.

33 Macpherson, Political Theory of Possessive Individualism, 90. An interesting set of essays that explores the relationship between the rise of freedom of contract and economic liberty is to be found in Harry Scheiber, ed., The State and Freedom of Contract (Stanford: Stanford University Press, 1998). Scholars of Third World economic development stress the importance of contract and

property rights in determining how rapidly and effectively nations will develop. Jeff Madrick, "The Charm of Property," *New York Review of Books* 48 (May 31, 2001), 41.

34 John Locke, *Two Treatises on Government*, ed. Peter Laslett (1689; Cambridge: Cambridge University Press, 1960). See especially *Second Treatise*, chap. 8; for the quote, see chap. 9, sec. 124.

35 For a discussion of what property and natural rights meant to Locke, see Macpherson, *Political Theory of Possessive Individualism*, 197–228.

36 John Locke, "Notes on Trade," in *Seventeenth-Century Economic Documents*, ed. Joan Thirsk and J. P. Cooper (Oxford: Clarendon, 1991), 96.

37 Hartz, *Liberal Tradition in America*, 18. For the view that Locke's ideas lacked originality and were based on the earlier works of such writers as John Trenchard, Thomas Gordon, Benjamin Hoadley, and Viscount Bolingbroke, see Bernard Bailyn, *The Ideological Origins of the American Revolution* (Cambridge, Mass.: Belknap Press of Harvard University Press, 1967), 34–35.

CHAPTER TWO

1 An excellent comparison of British and Spanish America is provided by J. H. Elliott, *Empires of the Atlantic World: Britain and Spain in America* (New Haven: Yale University Press, 2006).

2 For an interesting attempt to demonstrate that European trading companies were precursors to modern big business, see Ann M. Carlos and Stephen Nicholas, "Giants of an Earlier Capitalism," *Business History Review* 62 (Autumn 1988): 398–419.

3 Edmund S. Morgan, *American Slavery, American Freedom: The Ordeal of Colonial Virginia* (New York: Norton, 1975). A controversy rages over the origins of slavery. Some historians believe that its root cause was the European view of the African as inferior. Others, such as Morgan, view slavery as happening for economic reasons. A very impressive study by Robin Blackburn, *The Making of New World Slavery: From the Baroque to the Modern, 1442–1800* (New York: Verso, 1997), argues that the reason for the emergence of slavery was the callous recognition that in a labor-intensive plantation economy slavery was more profitable than a free-labor system. From the early sixteenth century to the end of the 1860s, it has been estimated that over 11 million Africans were forcibly brought to the Americas.

4 Morgan, *American Slavery, American Freedom*, 277; Robert Fogel and Stanley Engerman, *Time on the Cross* (Boston: Little, Brown, 1974).

5 An excellent general study of the colonial economy is John J. McCusker and Russell R. Menard, *The Economy of British America, 1607–1789* (Chapel Hill: University of North Carolina Press, 1985).

6 For a provocative reinterpretation of the basis of the New England economy, stressing that its early success was due "as much to its strict Puritan society as market factors," see Stephen Innes, *Creating the Commonwealth: The Economic Culture of Puritan New England* (New York: Norton, 1994), 47. The standard view is in Christine Leigh Heyrman, *Commerce and Culture: The Maritime Communities of Colonial Massachusetts, 1690–1750* (New York: Norton, 1986).

7 James Shepherd and Gary Walton, *Shipping, Maritime Trade, and the Economic Development of Colonial North America* (Cambridge: Cambridge University Press, 1972), 160–63, 217–19.

8 Ibid., 49–53, 156–57.

9 Ibid., 160–62.

10 Bernard Bailyn, *The New England Merchants in the Seventeenth Century* (Cambridge, Mass.: Harvard University Press, 1955), 94.

11 Benjamin Franklin, *The Autobiography and Other Writings*, ed. Kenneth Silverman (New York: Penguin, 1986), 66.

12 Ibid., 214.

13 Cotton Mather, *Bonifacius: An Essay to Do Good*, ed. Josephine Percy (Gainesville, Fla.: Scholars' Facsimiles and Reprints, 1967), 17.

14 A useful synthesis of colonial social history is offered in Jack P. Green, *Pursuits of Happiness: The Social Development of the Early Modern British Colonies and the Formation of American Culture* (Chapel Hill: University of North Carolina Press, 1988); and Jack P. Green and J. R. Pole, eds., *Colonial British America: Essays in the New History of the Early Modern Era* (Baltimore: Johns Hopkins University Press, 1984).

15 Franklin, *Autobiography and Other Writings*, xvi.

16 Alan Houston, ed., *Franklin: The Autobiography and Other Writings on Politics, Economics, and Virtue* (Cambridge: Cambridge University Press, 2004), 325–26.

17 T. H. Breen, *The Market Place of Revolution: How Consumer Politics Shaped American Independence* (New York: Oxford University Press, 2004).

18 Mary Beth Norton, *Founding Mothers and Fathers: Gendered Power and the Forming of American Society* (New York: Alfred A. Knopf, 1996).

19 The depiction of colonial farms as largely self-sufficient and non–market oriented has become the subject of lively debate. For contrasting views, see Winifred Rothenberg, "The Market and Massachusetts Farmers, 1750–1855," *Journal of Economic History* 6 (1981): 283–313; and Betty Hobbes Pruit, "Self-Sufficiency and the Agricultural Economy of Eighteenth-Century Massachusetts," *William and Mary Quarterly*, 3rd ser., 41 (1984): 333–64.

20 Leonard W. Labaree et al., eds., *The Papers of Benjamin Franklin* (New Haven: Yale University Press, 1962), 4:226.

21 David Cressy, *Coming Over: Migration and Communication between England and*

New England in the Seventeenth Century (New York: Cambridge University Press, 1987).

22 J. Hector St. John Crèvecoeur, *Letters from an American Farmer* (New York: E. P. Dutton, 1957).

23 Timothy Breen, "An Empire of Goods: The Anglicization of Colonial America, 1690–1776," *Journal of British Studies* 25 (June 1986): 467–99.

24 Robert Beverly, *The History of Virginia: In Four Parts* (1705; Whitefish, Mont.: Kessinger, 2007), 205; J. Willard Hurst, *Law and the Condition of Freedom in the Nineteenth-Century United States* (Madison: University of Wisconsin Press, 1956); Peter H. Hoffer, *Law and People in Colonial America* (Baltimore: Johns Hopkins University Press, 1992), 82.

25 Elizabeth Mensh, "The Colonial Origins of Liberal Property Rights," *Buffalo Law Review* 31 (1983): 47–62.

26 Gordon S. Wood, *The Radicalism of the American Revolution* (New York: Alfred A. Knopf, 1992); Bernard Bailyn, *The Origins of American Politics* (New York: Alfred A. Knopf, 1968), 1.

27 John Orth has argued that statutory regulation and not individual agreement prevailed in the hiring of labor until the second half of the eighteenth century, when the complexity and needs of a commercial society required its reconceptualization in terms of free labor or independent contract. John Orth, "Contract and the Common Law," in *The State and Freedom of Contract*, ed. Harry N. Scheiber (Stanford: Stanford University Press, 1998), 44–65.

28 Wood, *Radicalism of the American Revolution*, 232.

29 America's strong reliance on voluntary associations, often of a temporary nature, has been much commented on. The historical importance of these attitudes in influencing an economic system is explored in Robert Goodin et al., *The Real World of Welfare Capitalism* (New York: Cambridge University Press, 2000). The authors comment that "corporate" societies have very different sorts of social safety nets, with consequences markedly different for employment and productivity than those of the strongly "individualist and free-market oriented" United States. See also Robert Putnam, *Bowling Alone: The Collapse and Revival of American Community* (New York: Simon and Schuster, 2000).

30 James Otis, "The Rights of the British Colony Asserted and Proved," in *The Founders' Constitution*, ed. Philip N. Kurland and Ralph Lerner (Chicago: University of Chicago Press, 1986), 326–27.

31 Franklin, *Autobiography and Other Writings*, 216.

32 An excellent synthesis of much of the recent scholarship on colonial society and thought is Jon Butler, *Becoming America: The Revolution before 1776* (Cambridge, Mass.: Harvard University Press, 2000). Butler sides with those who see the colonies as developing a new "modern" type of society.

33 Adam Smith, *An Inquiry into the Nature and Causes of the Wealth of Nations*, ed. Edwin Cannan (1776; New York: Modern Library, 1994), bk. 1, chap. 8, 80.

34 Joyce Appleby, *Capitalism and a New Social Order: The Republican Vision of the 1790s* (New York: New York University Press, 1984), 13. One might wonder whether this observation would hold true for colonies with large slave populations.

35 David Potter, *People of Plenty: Economic Abundance and American Character* (Chicago: University of Chicago, 1954), 118.

36 Bernard Bailyn, *The Ideological Origins of the American Revolution* (Cambridge, Mass.: Belknap Press of Harvard University Press, 1967), xx.

CHAPTER THREE

1 Alexander Hamilton, James Madison, and John Jay, *The Federalist Papers*, ed. Clinton Rossiter (New York: Signet Classic, 2001), 27.

2 Quoted in Mark R. Rudd, *One Nation Underprivileged: Why Poverty Affects Us All* (New York: Oxford University Press, 2004), 87.

3 Natural rights thinking as presented in the Declaration of Independence did not originate in America. Some scholars trace it to Roman law; others look to the seventeenth century and such thinkers as Grotius, Hobbes, and Locke. An important discussion of the Declaration of Independence is Pauline Maier, *American Scripture: Making the Declaration of Independence* (New York: Alfred A. Knopf, 1997), who argues persuasively that the document and its treatment of natural rights reflected American colonial experience.

4 Adam Smith, *An Inquiry into the Nature and Causes of the Wealth of Nations*, ed. Edwin Cannan (1776; New York: Modern Library, 1994), bk. 4, chap. 9, 745.

5 Charles L. Griswold Jr., *Adam Smith and the Virtues of Enlightenment* (Cambridge: Cambridge University Press, 1998), 77–82.

6 According to Marx, the passion for accumulation "forc[ed] the capitalist to create the misery of the industrial reserve army," the multitude of unemployed or underemployed needed to cope with the pendulum swings of the market.

7 Joyce Oldham Appleby, *Economic Thought and Ideology in Seventeenth Century England* (Princeton, N.J.: Princeton University Press, 1978), 26–39; Neil McKenrick, John Brewer, and J. H. Plumb, *The Commercialization of Eighteenth-Century England* (Bloomington: University of Indiana Press, 1982), 87–93.

8 Smith, *Wealth of Nations*, bk. 1, chap. 1, 5.

9 Smith believed technological change to be a consequence of specialization. But Joel Mokyr, in *The Levers of Riches: Technological Creativity and Economic Progress* (New York: Oxford University Press, 1990), 245n7, has challenged this view: "Before standardization and interchangeable parts . . . the simplification of work brought about by the division of labor as such was not significant."

10 The novelty of this type of manufacturing required new ways of organizing labor. Efficient machine use dictated the breakdown and differentiation of the productive process. Historians now tend to date the onset of the Industrial Revolution to the 1780s rather than, as previously, the 1760s, in order to emphasize the importance of this later-occurring organizational aspect. More to the point, it is estimated that the productivity of a British spinning worker increased an astonishing three-hundred-fold between 1750 and 1820. A consideration of the historiography of the Industrial Revolution is David S. Landes, "The Fable of the Dead Horse; or, The Industrial Revolution Revisited," in Joel Mokyr, ed., *The British Industrial Revolution: An Economic Perspective* (Boulder, Colo.: Westview Press, 1993), 132–70.

11 Patrick O'Brien and Roland Quinault, *The Industrial Revolution and British Society* (Cambridge: Cambridge University Press, 1993), 13–14; Joan Thirsk, *Economic Policy and Projects: The Development of a Consumer Society in Early Modern England* (Oxford: Oxford University Press, 1978).

12 Adam Smith, *The Theory of Moral Sentiments*, ed. D. D. Raphael and A. L. Macfie (1759; Oxford: Oxford University Press, 1976), bk. 1, chap. 1, 5.

13 Smith, *Wealth of Nations*, bk. 4, chap. 2, 484–85.

14 For Ruskin and Carlyle quotes, see Russell Hardin, *Liberalism, Constitutionalism, and Democracy* (New York: Oxford University Press, 2000), 42. Smith, *Wealth of Nations*, bk. 4, chap. 3, 527.

15 Smith, *Wealth of Nations*, bk. 1, chap. 10, 148.

16 Albert Jeremiah Beveridge, *The Life of John Marshall, 1755–1788*, vol. 1 (Boston: Houghton Mifflin, 1926), 417; Charles Beard, *An Economic Interpretation of the Constitution of the United States* (1913; New York: Macmillan, 1960), 324. Alan Kulikoff, *The Agrarian Origins of American Capitalism* (Charlottesville: University Press of Virginia, 1992), offers a synthesis from a Marxian perspective of the historiography of economic development from colonial times to the Civil War that treats the Constitution as an instrument of capitalist development. On the importance of property to the Founding Fathers, see James W. Ely Jr., *The Guardian of Every Other Right: A Constitutional History of Property Rights*, 2nd ed. (New York: Oxford University Press, 1998), 10–57; and Jennifer Nedelsky, *Private Property and the Limits of American Constitutionalism: The Madisonian Framework and Its Legacy* (Chicago: University of Chicago Press, 1990), which stresses the central importance of private property in the framers' conceptualization of government.

17 The Hamilton quote is in Max Farrand, ed., *The Records of the Federal Convention of 1787*, rev. ed., 4 vols. (New Haven: Yale University Press, 1937), 302; for the Rutledge quote, see ibid., 534.

18 Ely, *Guardian of Every Other Right*, 11; Charles Sellers, *The Market Revolution: Jacksonian America, 1815–1846* (New York: Oxford University Press, 1991), 88–89.

19 For an analysis of the importance of institutional environment—laws and their enforcement, moral and ethical norms—or what he calls the "institutional matrix" of capitalism, see Friedrich von Hayek, *The Constitution of Liberty* (Chicago: University of Chicago Press, 1960), 21–24. See also Douglass C. North, *Institutions, Institutional Change, and Economic Performance* (New York: Cambridge University Press, 1990), 3–33.

20 Joseph Ellis, *American Sphinx: The Character of Thomas Jefferson* (New York: Alfred A. Knopf, 1998), 264.

21 David L. Faigman, *Laboratory of Justice: The Supreme Court's 200-Year Struggle to Integrate Science and the Law* (New York: Macmillan, 2005), 36.

22 *Proprietors of Charles River Bridge v. Proprietors of the Warren Bridge*, 36 U.S. 420 (1837).

23 Sellers, *Market Revolution*, 85; see also Jean Edward Smith, *John Marshall: Defender of a Nation* (New York: Henry Holt, 1996), 417–45.

24 *Marbury v. Madison*, 5 U.S. (1 Cranch), 137 (1803); *Dartmouth College v. Woodward*, 17 U.S. (Wheat), 518 (1819).

25 *Gibbons v. Ogden*, 22 U.S. 1 (1824); Herbert Hovenkamp, *Enterprise and American Law, 1836–1937* (Cambridge, Mass.: Harvard University Press, 1991), 33–38.

26 Morton J. Horwitz, *The Transformation of American Law, 1780–1860* (Cambridge, Mass.: Harvard University Press, 1977), 141; Kent Newmyer, *The Supreme Court under Marshall and Taney* (Arlington Heights, Ill.: Harland Davidson, 1969), 57–61.

27 Joyce Appleby, "Commercial Farming and the 'Agrarian Myth' in the Early Republic," *Journal of American History* 68 (March 1982): 833–49.

28 Richard Hofstadter, *The Idea of a Party System: The Rise of Legitimate Opposition in the United States, 1780–1840* (Berkeley: University of California Press, 1969), 11–73. See also Samuel P. Huntington, *Political Order in Changing Societies* (New Haven: Yale University Press, 1968), especially "Political Order and Political Decay," for a discussion of the institutionalization of political organizations.

29 Stanley Lebergott, *Manpower in Economic Growth: The American Record since 1800* (New York: McGraw-Hill, 1967), 167.

30 Alfred D. Chandler Jr., *The Visible Hand: The Managerial Revolution in American Business* (Cambridge, Mass.: Belknap Press of Harvard University Press, 1977), 204. Only Great Britain resembled the United States in the practice of relying on private development.

31 George Rogers Taylor, *The Transportation Revolution: 1815–1860* (New York: Reinhart, 1951); David Hawke, *Nuts and Bolts of the Past: History of American Technology, 1776–1860* (New York: Harper and Row, 1988).

32 For early uses of the term "businessman," see Daniel J. Boorstin, *The Americans: The National Experience* (New York: Random House, 1965), 115. "Busi-

nesswoman" was in use by the end of the nineteenth century but usually denoted an assistant to a businessman until the 1930s.

33 For Seymour quote, see "Agriculture: Its Past and Present," *New-York Daily Times*, September 11, 1852, 1.

34 Glenn Porter and Harold C. Livesay, *Merchants and Manufacturers: Studies in the Changing Structure of Nineteenth-Century Marketing* (Baltimore: Johns Hopkins University Press, 1971).

35 Barbara Tucker, *Samuel Slater and the Origins of the American Textile Industry, 1790–1860* (Ithaca, N.Y.: Cornell University Press, 1984); Francis (Fanny) Wright, *View of Society and Manners in America: In a Series of Letters to a Friend in England during the Years 1819, 1820* (London, 1821). Excerpts can be found at http://nationalhumanitiescenter.org/pds/livingrev/equality/text6/wright .pdf. Accessed May 30, 2008.

36 Kenneth Sokoloff, "Industrialization and the Growth of the Manufacturing Sector in the Northeast, 1820 to 1850" (Ph.D. diss., Harvard University, 1982), chap. 1.

37 Robert F. Dalzell Jr., *Enterprising Elites: The Boston Associates and the World They Made* (New York: W. W. Norton, 1993), 26–76.

38 The older view of Whitney's contribution is found in Constance M. Green, *Eli Whitney and the Birth of American Technology* (Boston: Little, Brown, 1956). For a revisionist view that sees Whitney as much less important, see David A. Hounshell, *From the American System to Mass Production, 1800–1932: Development of Manufacturing Technology in the United States* (Baltimore: Johns Hopkins University Press, 1985). The quote on the first use of technology is from Leo Marx, *The Machine in the Garden* (New York: Oxford University Press, 1964), 61.

39 Hounshell, *From the American System to Mass Production*, 3–4; Robert S. Woodbury, "The Legend of Eli Whitney and Interchangeable Parts," *Technology and Culture* 1 (1960): 235–55; David S. Landes, "French Business and the Businessman: A Social and Cultural Analysis," in Edward M. Earle, ed., *Modern France* (Princeton, N.J.: Princeton University Press, 1951), 333. According to Hounshell, contemporaries referred to what we call the "American system" as the "armory practice." Although in use since the 1880s, it was not until the very early twentieth century that the term "American system" became generally identified with Whitney's work. Hounshell, *From the American System to Mass Production*, 331–36.

40 This development was anticipated and encouraged by the Founding Fathers, who in the Constitution gave Congress the power "to promote the Progress of Science and useful Arts, by securing for limited Times to Authors and Inventors the exclusive Right to their respective Writings and Discoveries." The practice of issuing patents can be traced to the sixteenth century in En-

gland, although Parliament initially was reluctant to issue them for any labor-saving device.

41 Nathan Rosenberg, *Technology and American Economic Growth* (New York: Harper and Row, 1972), 94.

42 Ibid., 87–116. For Singer's marketing strategy, see Bruce Davies, *Peacefully Working to Conquer the World: Singer Sewing Machines in Foreign Markets, 1854–1920* (New York: Arno Press, 1976); and Chandler, *Visible Hand*, 303–5, 402–5. On Cyrus McCormick, see Hounshell, *From the American System to Mass Production*, 153–83, especially 182–85, which compares the Singer and McCormick companies.

43 David S. Landes, *The Wealth and Poverty of Nations: Why Some Are So Rich and Some So Poor* (New York: Norton, 1998), 301; Landes, "French Business and the Businessman," 333–38.

44 Joyce Appleby, *Inheriting the Revolution: The First Generation of Americans* (Cambridge, Mass.: Belknap Press of Harvard University Press, 2000).

45 Nathan Rosenberg, ed., *The American System of Manufactures: The Report of the Committee on Machinery of the United States, and the Special Report of George Wallis and Joseph Whitworth, 1854* (Edinburgh: Edinburgh University Press, 1969).

CHAPTER FOUR

1 Nathan Rosenberg, ed., *The American System of Manufactures: The Report of the Committee on Machinery of the United States, and the Special Report of George Wallis and Joseph Whitworth, 1854* (Edinburgh: Edinburgh University Press, 1969).

2 Alexis de Tocqueville, *Democracy in America*, ed. J. P. Mayer, trans. George Lawrence (Garden City, N.Y.: Doubleday, 1969), 554.

3 P. T. Barnum, *The Art of Money Getting* (1880; New York: Jungle Book, 2007), 1. *The Art of Money Getting* continues to be remarkably popular. Advertisers often give it away free, and it can be downloaded from the web in various editions.

4 Tocqueville, *Democracy in America*, 340–41.

5 Ibid., 344–45; Charles Sellers, *The Market Revolution: Jacksonian America, 1815–1846* (New York: Oxford University Press, 1991), 126.

6 Clarence H. Danhof, *Change in Agriculture: The Northern United States, 1810–1870* (Cambridge, Mass.: Harvard University Press, 1969).

7 Richard D. Brown, *Modernization: The Transformation of American Life, 1600–1865* (New York: Hill and Wang, 1976); J. J. Murphy, "Entrepreneurship and the Establishment of the American Clock Industry," *Journal of Economic History* 26 (June 1966): 169–86.

8 Tocqueville, *Democracy in America*, 536–37; Philip Hone, *The Diary of Philip Hone, 1828–51*, ed. Allan Nevins, 2 vols. (New York: Dodd, Mead, 1921), 2:722.

9 Thomas Jefferson, *Thomas Jefferson: A Chronology of His Thoughts*, ed. Jerry Holmes (New York: Rowman and Littlefield, 2002), 238.

10 Hone, *Diary*, 2:809.

11 Quoted in Michael J. Sandel, *Democracy's Discontent: America in Search of a Public Policy* (Cambridge, Mass.: Harvard University Press, 1996), 153.

12 Thomas Dublin, *Women at Work: The Transformation of Work and Community in Lowell, Massachusetts, 1826–1860* (New York: Columbia University Press, 1979).

13 E. P. Thompson, "Time, Work-Discipline, and Industrial Capitalism," *Past and Present* 38 (December 1968): 73–97; David Brody, *In Labor's Cause* (New York: Oxford University Press, 1993), 23–35; Thorstein Veblen, *Absentee Ownership and Business Enterprise in Recent Times* (New York: B. W. Huensch, 1923), 234–35.

14 David Roediger, *The Wages of Whiteness: Race and the Making of the American Working Class* (New York: Verso Books, 1991).

15 Judith A. McGaw, *Most Wonderful Machine: Mechanization and Social Change in Berkshire Paper Making, 1801–1885* (Princeton, N.J.: Princeton University Press, 1987), 77–88.

16 On "soldiering," or "pacing" as it was more commonly called, see Merritt Roe Smith, "Industry, Technology, and the Labor Question in 19th-Century America," *Technology and Culture* 32 (July 1991): 558–67.

17 Adam Smith, *An Inquiry into the Nature and Causes of the Wealth of Nations*, ed. Edwin Cannan (1776; New York: Modern Library, 1994), bk. 3, chap. 2, 426–39; Ian Simpson Ross, *The Life of Adam Smith* (Oxford: Clarendon, 1995), 281.

18 William Tudor, "The Baltimore Ohio Railroad," *North American Review* 28 (January 1829): 169.

19 Alfred D. Chandler Jr., *Henry Varnum Poor: Business Editor, Analyst, and Reformer* (Cambridge, Mass.: Harvard University Press, 1956).

20 Michael E. Porter, *The Competitive Advantage of Nations: With a New Introduction* (1990; New York: Free Press, 1998). For nineteenth-century urban demographics, see Adna Ferrin Weber's classic study, *The Growth of Cities in the Nineteenth Century: A Study in Statistics* (1899; Ithaca, N.Y.: Cornell University Press, 1965), especially 15–24. David Ward, *Cities and Immigrants: A Geography of Changes in Nineteenth-Century America* (New York: Oxford University Press, 1971), 94–102.

21 Alfred Marshall, "The Housing of the London Poor: Where to House Them," *Contemporary Review* 44 (February 1884): 227.

22 James Stewart, *Three Years in North America*, 2 vols. (Edinburgh: printed for R. Cadell, 1833), 1:23.

23 William H. Dillistin, *Bank Notes, Reporters, and Counterfeiters, 1826–66* (New York: Harper and Row, 1949), 3–4. The role of banks before 1860 is discussed in Donald R. Adams Jr., "The Role of Banks in the Economic Development of the Old Northwest," in *Essays in Nineteenth Century Economic History*, ed. David C. Klingaman and Richard K. Vedder (Athens: Ohio University Press, 1975), 208–46; see also Richard E. Sylla, *The American Capital Market, 1846–1914* (New York: Arno Press, 1975); and Thomas Abernathy, *The Formative Period in Alabama, 1815–23* (Tuscaloosa: University of Alabama Press, 1965).

24 Edward Pessen, *Riches, Class, and Power in America before the Civil War* (Lexington, Mass.: D. C. Heath, 1973); Jeffrey G. Williamson and Peter Lindert, *American Inequality: A Macroeconomic History* (New York: Academic Books, 1980), 53–92. Economic historians seem to agree that inequality rose from the 1830s to roughly 1910, before leveling off; see ibid., 498n8.

25 Arthur M. Schlesinger Jr., *The Age of Jackson* (Boston: Little, Brown, 1945), 163.

26 Tocqueville, *Democracy in America*, 506; Nancy Cott, *The Bonds of Womanhood: Woman's Sphere in New England, 1780–1850* (New Haven: Yale University Press, 1977), especially 63–100; Mary P. Ryan, *Cradle of the Middle Class: The Family in Oneida, New York, 1790–1865* (Cambridge, Mass.: Harvard University Press, 1977); Stuart M. Blumin, *The Emergence of the Middle Class: Social Experience in the American City, 1760–1900* (New York: Cambridge University Press, 1989), 140–41, 146–53. On the home, see Richard L. Bushman, *The Refinement of America: Persons, Houses, Cities* (New York: Alfred A. Knopf, 1992), 271–78.

27 Hone, *Diary*, 2:773.

28 The wife in charge of family purchasing was a nineteenth-century development: "In colonial America 'husbands as providers' typically were responsible for purchasing household goods, furniture and food staples, if they were to be bought." Cott, *Bonds of Womanhood*, 45. However, Cott does not view the wife's new role in consumption as lessening her subordination to the husband. For the argument that it did give the wife new powers over domestic arrangements, see Blumin, *Emergence of the Middle Class*, 185–88.

29 Blumin, *Emergence of the Middle Class*, 138.

30 Ibid., 141; Tocqueville, *Democracy in America*, 198.

31 Horace Mann, "Tenth Annual Report of the Secretary of the Massachusetts State Board of Education" (1846; Boston: Dutton and Wentworth, State Printers, 1849).

32 Ryan, *Cradle of the Middle Class*, 161, 184–85. Ryan believes that socialization was intended to convey values not of the aggressive entrepreneur but of the "cautious, prudent small business-man" so as to ensure the perpetuation of the family's status; but I remain unconvinced. The American birthrate was more than seven children a family in 1820; this dropped to under four children per family by 1900. However, for the educated, native-born, Protestant middle

class, it was considerably lower. Theodore Roosevelt and others worried about this class being swamped by very large immigrant families.

CHAPTER FIVE

1 Ralph Waldo Emerson, *Emerson's Essays*, ed. Edward Waldo Emerson and Waldo Emerson Forbes, 10 vols. (Cambridge, Mass.: Riverside Press, 1909–14), 5:285–86.

2 Henry Thoreau, *Walden* (1853; New York: Houghton Mifflin, 2004), 36.

3 Adna Ferrin Weber, *The Growth of Cities in the Nineteenth Century: A Study in Statistics* (1899; Ithaca, N.Y.: Cornell University Press, 1965), 6. The Nobel Prize–winning economic historian Robert Fogel challenged this view in *Railroads and American Economic Growth* (Baltimore: Johns Hopkins University Press, 1964), arguing that the nation's waterways alone sufficed for economic development. But for arguments on the critical importance of railroads, see W. W. Rostow, *Stages of Economic Growth: A Non-Communist Manifesto* (1960; New York: Cambridge University Press, 1994); and Alfred D. Chandler Jr., *The Railroads: The Nation's First Big Business* (New York: Harcourt, Brace, and World, 1965).

4 George Rogers Taylor, *The Transportation Revolution: 1815–1860* (New York: Reinhart, 1951); Morton Roe Smith, ed., *Military Enterprise and Technological Change* (Cambridge, Mass.: MIT Press, 1985).

5 Walter Licht, *Working for the Railroad: The Organization of Work in the Nineteenth Century* (Princeton, N.J.: Princeton University Press, 1983).

6 *Bangor Daily Whig and Courier*, March 19, 1838, 6.

7 The standard work on investment banking is Vincent P. Carosso, *Investment Banking in America: A History* (Cambridge, Mass.: Harvard University Press, 1970). Also useful are Richard Sylla, *The American Capital Market, 1846–1914* (New York: Arno Press, 1975); and Ron Chernow, *The House of Morgan* (New York: Grove, 2001).

8 John Previts and Barbara Merino, *A History of Accounting in America: An Historical Interpretation of the Cultural Significance of Accounting* (New York: John Wiley, 1976), 57.

9 Ibid., 55–62, 74–86; Robert S. Kaplan, *Relevance Lost: The Rise and Fall of Management Accounting* (Boston: Harvard Business School Press, 1987), 43–62.

10 Alfred D. Chandler Jr., *The Visible Hand: The Managerial Revolution in American Management* (Cambridge, Mass.: Belknap Press of Harvard University Press, 1977), 101–10. The subject of information flow—and the cost of imperfect information—both within an organization and between organizations has attracted considerable recent attention; for a useful summary, see Naomi R. Lamoreaux, Daniel M. G. Raff, and Peter Temin, "Beyond Markets and Hierarchies: Towards

a New Synthesis of American Business History," *American Historical Review* 108 (April 2003): 404–11.

11 Gerald Brock, *The Second Information Revolution* (Cambridge, Mass.: Harvard University Press, 2003), 24–25.

12 Alfred D. Chandler Jr., *Strategy and Structure: Chapters in the History of the American Industrial Enterprise* (Cambridge, Mass.: MIT Press, 1962).

13 On the exegesis of the corporation as a legal business form, see George L. Beer, *The Old Colonial System, 1660–1754*, 2 vols. (New York: Macmillan, 1912); Oscar Handlin and Mary F. Handlin, "The Origins of the American Business Corporation," *Journal of Economic History* 5 (1966): 777–81; Ronald E. Seavoy, *The Origins of the American Business Corporation, 1784–1855* (Westport, Conn.: Greenwood, 1982); Morton J. Horwitz, *The Transformation of American Law, 1780–1860: The Crisis of Legal Orthodoxy* (New York: Oxford University Press, 1992), 114–37.

14 Ibid., 112.

15 Ibid., 127–28.

16 Edwin Merrick Dodd, *American Business Corporations until 1860: With Special Reference to Massachusetts* (Cambridge, Mass.: Harvard University Press, 1954), 365–437; James Willard Hurst, *The Legitimacy of the Business Corporation in the Law of the United States, 1780–1970* (Charlottesville: University of Virginia Press, 1970); Peter H. Hoffer, *Law and People in Colonial America* (Baltimore: Johns Hopkins University Press, 1992). For an excellent analysis of the literature on the subject, see Gregory A. Mark, "The Role of the State in Corporate Law Formation," *International Corporate Law Annual* 1 (2000): 5–9.

17 Herbert Hovenkamp, *Enterprise and American Law, 1836–1977* (Cambridge, Mass.: Harvard University Press, 1991). For a discussion of the early law on limited liability, see Edwin J. Perkins, *American Public Finance and Financial Services, 1700–1815* (Columbus: University of Ohio Press, 1994), 373–76; James W. Hurst, *The Growth of American Law: The Law Makers* (Boston: Little Brown, 1950), 130–33. Early in the nineteenth century, some banks were reluctant to loan to corporations with limited liability since they wanted the security of personal collateral.

18 Seymour Long, "Andrew Jackson and the National Bank," *English Historical Review* 45 (January 1892): 87.

19 Neil Fligstein, *The Transformation of Corporate Control* (Cambridge, Mass.: Harvard University Press, 1990), 53–57.

20 Alfred F. Havighurst, *Britain in Transition: The Twentieth Century* (Chicago: University of Chicago Press, 1985), 10.

21 The absence of the need to maintain a large and expensive military contributed greatly to keeping the role and size of the federal government limited until

World War II. For an interesting argument that concern for the ability to mobilize resources for foreign policy goals and requisite military power has long been critical in shaping both government and economies, see Niall Ferguson, *The Cash Nexus: Money and Power in the Modern World* (New York: Basic Books, 2001).

22 Kenneth M. Stampp, *America in 1857: A Nation on the Brink* (New York: Oxford University Press, 1990).

CHAPTER SIX

1 Ludwig von Mises, *Human Action: An Economic Treatise* (1949; rev. ed., New Haven: Yale University Press, 1963), 289.

2 For a fascinating account of how the Civil War profoundly changed the way Americans thought about work, family, and religion, see Anne C. Rose, *Victorian America and the Civil War* (New York: Cambridge University Press, 1992). On the Civil War and the pace of industrialization, see William N. Parker, *America and the Wider World*, vol. 2 of *Europe, America, and the Wider World: Essays on the Economic History of Western Capitalism* (New York: Cambridge University Press, 1991), 270–73.

3 Andrew Carnegie, *Triumphant Democracy, or, Fifty Years March of the Republic* (1886; Garden City, N.Y.: Doubleday, 1933), 1; Richard Franklin Bensel, *Yankee Leviathan: The Origins of Central State Authority in America* (New York: Cambridge University Press, 1990), 303–65; Richard Franklin Bensel, *The Political Economy of American Industrialization, 1877–1900* (New York: Cambridge University Press, 2000).

4 *Santa Clara v. Southern Pacific Railroad* stated that a corporation is a person for purposes of the Fourteenth Amendment; see Morton J. Horwitz, *The Transformation of American Law, 1870–1960* (New York: Oxford University Press, 1992), 67–73.

5 C. Vann Woodward, *The Origin of the New South, 1877–1917* (Baton Rouge: Louisiana State University Press, 1951), has long been the standard work; but also valuable is Gavin Wright, *Old South, New South* (New York: Basic Books, 1986).

6 William N. Parker, "The South in the National Economy," *Southern Economic Journal* 46, no. 4 (1980): 1019–98.

7 James K. Medbery, *Men and Mysteries of Wall Street* (Boston: Fields, Osgood, 1870), 34.

8 Mark Twain, "The Revised Catechism," *New York Tribune*, September 27, 1891.

9 Robert H. Bremner, *American Philanthropy* (Chicago: University of Chicago Press, 1988), 103.

10 Matthew Josephson, *The Robber Barons: The Great American Capitalists, 1861–1901* (1934; New York: Harcourt, Brace, and World, 1962), foreword; Irving G. Wylie, *The Self Made Man in America: The Myth of Rags to Riches* (New Brunswick, N.J.: Rutgers University Press, 1954), 46. See also John Cawelti, *Apostles of the Self-Made Man: Changing Concepts of Success in America* (Chicago: University of Chicago Press, 1955); and Moses Rischin, ed., *The American Gospel of Success* (Chicago: Quadrangle Books, 1965).

11 The Tilden quote is in Ian Simpson Ross, *The Life of Adam Smith* (Oxford: Clarendon, 1995), 41.

12 Robert E. Gallman, "Trends in the Size Distribution of Wealth in the Nineteenth Century: Some Speculations," in *Six Papers on the Size Distribution of Wealth and Income*, ed. Lee Soltow, National Bureau of Economic Research, vol. 33 of *Studies in Income and Wealth* (New York: Columbia University Press, 1969), 11, 15; Peter H. Lindert and Jeffrey G. Williamson, "Three Centuries of American Inequality," in *Research in Economic History*, ed. Paul Uselding (Greenwich, Conn.: JAI Press, 1976), 1:99.

13 Clarence D. Long, *Wages and Earnings in the United States, 1860–1890* (Princeton, N.J.: Princeton University Press, 1960), 50–68.

14 Charles Francis Adams Jr. and Henry Adams, *Chapters of Erie: And Other Essays* (Boston: J. R. Osgood, 1871), 344. The quote first appeared in an essay titled "Railroad System," which appeared in *North American Review* (April 1868). The 1912 quote is from Charles Francis Adams Jr., *An Autobiography* (Boston: Houghton Mifflin, 1916), 190.

15 William H. Vanderbilt remark to reporters, *New York Times*, October 9, 1882, 1. See also Vanderbilt's letters to the editor, *New York Times*, October 13, 1882, 5.

16 In that year less than 1 percent of Americans invested in public companies.

17 Richard T. Ely, *Monopolies and Trusts* (London: Macmillan, 1912), 27–36.

18 James Bryce, *The American Commonwealth* (New York: Macmillan, 1888), 2:372.

19 *McGuffey's Readers* (1879; Whitefish, Mont.: Kessinger, 2003), 2:28.

20 Of the many works on Rockefeller, the most useful is Ron Chernow, *Titan: The Life of John D. Rockefeller, Sr.* (New York: Random House, 1998); also of interest is Daniel Yergin's superb history of the oil industry, *The Prize: The Epic Quest for Oil, Money, and Power* (New York: Simon and Schuster, 1991).

21 An excellent account of the creation of the Standard Oil Trust is to be found in Ralph W. Hidy and Muriel E. Hidy, *Pioneeering in Big Business, 1882–1911* (New York: Harper, 1955), 40–46.

22 In 1913, the New Jersey state legislature enacted a bill viewed as unfavorable to corporations. Many major corporations quickly transferred to Delaware—and remained there, even though New Jersey repealed the act in 1917. Jonathan Charkham, *Keeping Good Company: A Study of Corporate Governance in Five*

Countries (Oxford: Clarendon, 1994), 174. More than half of the top 500 U.S. corporations were registered in Delaware in 1992.

23 See F. W. Gregory and I. D. Neu, "The American Industrial Elite in the 1870's," in *Men in Business: Essays in the History of Entrepreneurship*, ed. William Miller (Cambridge, Mass.: Harvard University Press, 1952), especially 204.

24 The standard studies of Carnegie are Joseph Frazier Wall, *Andrew Carnegie*, 2nd ed. (Pittsburgh: University of Pittsburgh Press, 1989); and David Nasaw, *Andrew Carnegie* (New York: Penguin, 2006). Also useful, and considerably briefer, is Harold C. Livesay, *Andrew Carnegie and the Rise of Big Business* (Boston: Little, Brown, 1975).

25 Arthur Pond and Samuel T. Moore, eds., *They Told Barron: Conversations and Revelations of an American Pepys in Wall Street* (New York: Harper, 1930), 85.

26 Nasaw, *Andrew Carnegie*, 168–69.

27 Ibid., 134, 400.

28 David Brody, *Steelworkers in America: The Nonunion Era* (New York: Harper and Row, 1969), 17.

29 Partners in the firm were so concerned about what would happen if Carnegie died that in exchange for a clause in their partnership contract permitting Carnegie's estate to be paid off gradually they agreed to a provision that greatly reduced the value of their holdings should they choose to withdraw from the firm. Limited partnerships were of two types. One followed the model described above; the second consisted of passive partners with no responsibility for running the business and no liability for its debts.

30 John Charles Van Dyke, ed., *Autobiography of Andrew Carnegie* (London: Constable, 1920), 168; Ron Chernow, *The House of Morgan* (New York: Grove, 2001), 84. On the significance of the U.S. Steel deal, see George David Smith and Richard Sylla, *The Transformation of Financial Capitalism: An Essay on the History of Capital Markets, Financial Markets, Institutions, and Instruments* (New York: New York University Salomon Center, 1993), 2–5.

31 Andrew Carnegie, "Wealth," *North American Review* 391 (June 1889): 653–54. An excellent work on the strike, which also offers valuable information on the company and the steel industry in general, is Paul Krause, *The Battle for Homestead, 1880–1892: Politics, Culture, and Steel* (Pittsburgh: University of Pittsburgh Press, 1992).

32 The best single work on Morgan is Chernow, *House of Morgan*; on Morgan as a man, see Jean Strouse, *Morgan: American Financier* (New York: Random House, 1999); and, as a banker, see Vincent Carosso, *The Morgans: Private International Bankers, 1854–1913* (Cambridge, Mass.: Harvard University Press, 1987).

33 Lincoln Steffens, *The Autobiography of Lincoln Steffens* (New York: Harcourt, Brace, and World, 1931), 188–90.

34 Money Trust Investigation, testimony of J. Pierpont Morgan to Pujo Committee, printed from the stenographic transcript taken in Washington, D.C., December 18–19, 1912, Pierpont Morgan Library.

35 Maury Klein, *The Life and Legend of Jay Gould* (Baltimore: Johns Hopkins University Press, 1986).

36 Douglas G. Baird and Robert K. Rasmussen, "Control Rights, Priority Rights,
and the Conceptual Foundations of Corporate Law," *Virginia Law Review* 87, no.
5 (September 2001): 927.

37 William James, "Great Men, Great Thoughts, and the Environment," *Atlantic
Monthly*, October 16, 1880, 449.

CHAPTER SEVEN

1 Thorstein Veblen, *The Theory of Business Enterprise* (1904; New York: C. Scribner, 1927), 180–86.

2 Important sectors of manufacturing, such as furniture making and shipbuilding, that did not take the form of large-scale industry and standardized production have been examined in the important work of Philip Scranton; see
"Diversity in Diversity: Flexible Production and American Industrialization,
1880–1930," *Business History Review* 65 (Spring 1991): 27–90; and *Endless
Novelty: Specialty Production and American Industrialization, 1865–1925* (Princeton, N.J.: Princeton University Press, 1997).

3 William Leach, *Land of Desire: Merchants, Power, and the Rise of a New American
Culture* (New York: Pantheon, 1993), 3.

4 W. D. Howells, "A Sennight at the Centennial," *Atlantic Monthly*, July 1876, 96.

5 Quoted in Bernard Alderson, *Andrew Carnegie: The Man and His Works* (Garden
City, N.Y.: Doubleday, Page, 1902), 204.

6 "Centennial Visitors," *New York Times*, October 4, 1876, 11.

7 Western Union's disinterest in Bell's invention was due to its support of Thomas
Edison's effort to develop and patent a phone superior to Bell's. Alexander
Graham Bell suggested that Americans should answer the phone with the
response "ahoy."

8 Robert Freidel and Paul Israel, *Edison's Electric Light: Biography of an Invention*
(New Brunswick, N.J.: Rutgers University Press, 1986).

9 Thomas P. Hughes, *Networks of Power: Electrification of Western Society, 1880–
1930* (Baltimore: Johns Hopkins University Press, 1971); Thomas P. Hughes,
*American Genesis: A Century of Invention and Technological Enthusiasm, 1870–
1970* (New York: Viking Penguin, 1989).

10 Hughes, *American Genesis*, 39–62; Leonard S. Reich, *The Making of American
Industrial Research: Science and Business at GE and Bell, 1876–1926* (New York:
Cambridge University Press, 1985). Reich argues that industrial research was

concentrated in areas that were technologically complicated and that offered great promise for commercial application.

11 "The Standard Oil Inquiry; John D. Rockefeller Testifies before Ohio Investigators," *New York Times*, October 12, 1898, 5.

12 Reich, *The Making of American Industrial Research*, 24.

13 Arthur T. Hadley, "The Railroad in Its Business Relations," *Scribners*, October 1, 1888, 478.

14 Thomas Navin and Marion Sears, "The Rise of a Market for Industrials, 1887–1902," *Business History Review* 29 (1954): 105–38; Ralph Nelson, *Merger Movements in American History: 1895–1956* (Princeton, N.J.: Princeton University Press, 1959), 47–53.

15 Alfred D. Chandler Jr., *The Visible Hand: The Managerial Revolution in American Business* (Cambridge, Mass.: Harvard University Press, 1977), 287–386. For challenges to Chandler, see Naomi R. Lamoreaux, *The Great Merger Movement in American Business, 1895–1904* (Cambridge: Cambridge University Press, 1985), 87–194; and William G. Roy, *Socializing Capital: The Rise of the Large Industrial Corporation in America* (Princeton, N.J.: Princeton University Press, 1999). Lamoreaux sees a thrust toward market control; Roy emphasizes a political and institutional process at work governed by the dynamics of financial power.

16 Henry Clew, *Fifty Years in Wall Street* (1908; New York: Arno Press), 316.

17 Richard S. Tedlow, *New and Improved: The Story of Mass Marketing* (New York: Basic Books, 1990). This book was reissued in 1997 with a new introduction by the Harvard Business School Press.

18 Daniel Horowitz, *The Morality of Spending: Attitudes towards the Consumer Society in America, 1875–1940* (Baltimore: Johns Hopkins University Press, 1985); Leach, *Land of Desire*. On the department store, see ibid., 20–33; on window displays, see ibid., 55–66.

19 A. T. Stewart, who owned New York City's largest stores in the 1860s and 1870s, is often credited with having brought the one-price system from France to America.

20 Jonathan J. Bean, *Beyond the Broker State: A History of the Federal Government's Policies towards Small Business, 1936–61* (Chapel Hill: University of North Carolina Press, 1996), 19–30.

21 Henry Adams, *The Education of Henry Adams: An Autobiography* (Boston: Houghton Mifflin, 1918), 496.

22 Chandler, *Visible Hand*, 11.

23 Stanley Buder, *Pullman: An Experiment in Industrial Order and Community Planning* (New York: Oxford University Press, 1967), 15.

24 Susan Hirsch, *After the Strike: A Century of Labor Struggle at Pullman* (Urbana: University of Illinois Press, 2002), deals mainly with events after 1894 but contains important information on company operations before the Pullman

strike. On the strike, see Almont Lindsay, *The Pullman Strike* (1942; Chicago: University of Chicago Press, 1964). On the model town, see Buder, *Pullman*.

25 *United States Strike Commission's Report on the Chicago Strike of June–July, 1894,* Senate Executive Document No. 7, 53rd Congress, 3rd sess. (Washington, D.C.: Government Printing Office, 1895), 420–21.

26 Firms like Pullman that made custom-designed products tended to rely on inside contracting arrangements. John K. Brown, *The Baltimore Locomotive Works, 1821–19: A Study in American Industrial Practice* (Baltimore: Johns Hopkins University Press, 1995), 115–19.

27 Daniel Nelson, *Managers and Workers: Origins of the New Factory System in the United States, 1880–1920* (Madison: University of Wisconsin Press, 1975), 34–78.

28 Ernest J. Englander, "The Inside Contract System of Production and Organization: A Neglected Aspect of the History of the Firm," *Labor History* 28 (Fall 1987): 429–46.

29 David A. Wells, *Recent Economic Changes and Their Effect on the Production and Distribution of Wealth and the Well-Being of Society* (New York: D. Appleton, 1890), 63.

30 Ibid., 93.

31 John K. Brown, *The Baldwin Locomotive Works, 1830–1915: A Study in American Industrial Practice* (Baltimore: Johns Hopkins University Press, 1995), 115–33; Nelson, *Managers and Workers*, 34–78.

32 Henry Towne, "The Engineer as Economist," *American Society of Mechanical Engineers Transactions* 7 (May 1886): 428–32.

33 On the factory floor and Taylorism, see Daniel Nelson, *Frederick W. Taylor and the Rise of Scientific Management* (Madison: University of Wisconsin Press, 1980). According to Alfred Chandler, *Visible Hand*, 272: "The weakness of Taylor's system was its failure to pinpoint authority and responsibility for getting the departmental tasks done and for maintaining a steady flow of materials from one stage of the process to the next." For an excellent overall assessment of Taylor the man and his ideas, see Robert Kanigel, *The One Best Way: Frederick Winslow Taylor and the Enigma of Efficiency* (New York: Viking, 1997).

34 Frederick Winslow Taylor, *The Principles of Scientific Management* (1911; New York: Norton, 1967), 66.

35 For changes in the organization of work and its effects, see Roy Rosenzweig, *Eight Hours for What We Will: Workers and Leisure in an Industrial City, 1870–1920* (New York: Cambridge University Press, 1983).

36 For the quote, see Sean Dennis Cashman, *America in the Gilded Age: From the Death of Lincoln to the Rise of Theodore Roosevelt*, 3rd ed. (New York: New York University Press, 1993), 8–9. See also Gunther Barth, *City People: The Rise of*

Modern City Culture in Nineteenth-Century America (New York: Oxford University Press, 1980).

37 Unemployment has been estimated at over 16 percent in the periods 1873–76 and 1893–97 as compared to an estimated 25 percent for 1932–33. See Jeffrey G. Williamson and Peter Lindert, *American Inequality: A Macroeconomic History* (New York: Academic Books, 1980), 53–92.

38 Lawrence M. Friedman and Jack Ladinsky, "Social Change and the Law of Industrial Accidents," in *American Law and the Constitutional Order*, ed. Lawrence M. Friedman and Harry N. Scheiber (Cambridge, Mass.: Harvard University Press), 269–72.

39 Buder, *Pullman*, 140–41.

40 Glenn Porter, "Industrialization and the Rise of Big Business," in *The Gilded Age: Essays on the Origins of Modern America*, ed. Charles W. Calhoun (Wilmington, Del.: Scholarly Resources, 1996), 9, 14–15.

41 Sigmund Diamond, *The Reputation of the American Businessman* (Cambridge, Mass.: Harvard University Press, 1955).

42 Stephen Skowronek, *Building a New American State: The Expansion of National Administrative Capacities, 1877–1920* (New York: Cambridge University Press, 1990), offers insight into the struggle between the new need for federal intervention in the economy and older values and institutions.

CHAPTER EIGHT

1 Henry Adams, *The Education of Henry Adams: A Centennial Version*, ed. Edward Chalfant and Conrad Edick Wright (1907; Boston: Massachusetts Historical Society, 2007), 41.

2 T. J. Jackson Lears, "From Salvation to Self-Realization: Advertising and the Therapeutic Roots of the Consumer Culture," in *The Culture of Consumption: Critical Essays in American History, 1880–1980*, ed. Richard Wrightman Fox and T. J. Jackson Lears (New York: Pantheon, 1983), 3.

3 For Spencer's influence, see Richard Hofstadter, *Social Darwinism in American Thought*, rev. ed. (Boston: Beacon, 1955).

4 Thorstein Veblen, *The Theory of Business Enterprise* (1904; New York: Scribner, 1927), 44.

5 Ambrose Bierce, *The Devil's Dictionary*, www.online-literature.com/bierce/devilsdictionary. Accessed June 2008.

6 Albro Martin, *Enterprise Denied: Origins of the Decline of the American Railroads, 1897–1917* (New York: Columbia University Press, 1971). For a view that is more critical of railroad management, see Richard Saunders, *Merging Lines: American Railroads, 1906–1970* (DeKalb: Northern Illinois University Press, 2001).

7 James Bryce, *The American Commonwealth*, 2nd ed. rev. (London: Macmillan, 1891), 1:43. See also 2:406, 2:721.

8 Cited in Hans Thorelli, *The Federal Antitrust Policy* (Baltimore: Johns Hopkins University Press, 1955), 197.

9 The standard works on the origin of the act are William Letwin, *Law and Economic Policy: The Evolution of the Sherman Antitrust Act* (Chicago: University of Chicago Press, 1981); and Thorelli, *Federal Antitrust Policy*. Also of interest is Steven L. Piott, *The Antimonopoly Persuasion: Popular Resistance to the Rise of Big Business in the Midwest* (Westport, Conn.: Greenwood, 1985), 1–10 passim.

10 Charles W. McCurdy, "The Knight Sugar Decision of 1895 and the Modernization of American Corporate Law," *Business History Review* 53, no. 3 (Autumn 1979): 304–42.

11 Walter LaFeber, *The New Empire: An Interpretation of American Expansionism, 1860–1898* (Ithaca, N.Y.: Cornell University Press, 1967).

12 Alfred D. Chandler Jr., *The Visible Hand: The Managerial Revolution in American Business* (Cambridge, Mass.: Harvard University Press, 1977), 334–44; Naomi R. Lamoreaux, *The Great Merger Movement in American Business, 1895–1904* (New York: Cambridge University Press, 1985), chaps. 5–6. On the importance of the role of investment bankers, see William G. Roy, *Socializing Capital: The Rise of the Large Industrial Corporation in America* (Princeton, N.J.: Princeton University Press, 1999).

13 George Brittling Mayer, "Did Antitrust Policy Cause the Great Merger Wave," in *The Causes and Consequences of Antitrust: The Public-Choice Perspective*, ed. Fred S. McChesney and William F. Shughart (Chicago: University of Chicago Press, 1995), 127–45.

14 "Roosevelt Defends His Panama Action," *New York Times*, October 6, 1911, 12.

15 Morton Keller, *Regulating a New Economy: Public Policy and Economic Change in America, 1900–1933* (Cambridge, Mass.: Harvard University Press, 1990), 24; Lamoreaux, *Great Merger Movement*, 12.

16 Keller, *Regulating a New Economy*, 29–30.

17 Robert H. Wiebe, "The House of Morgan and the Executive, 1905–1913," *American Historical Review* 65, no. 1 (October 1959): 54–55.

18 Theodore Roosevelt, *Theodore Roosevelt: An Autobiography* (1913; Whitefish, Mont.: Kessinger, 2004), 516.

19 "Special Message to the Senate and House of Representatives," January 7, 1910, John T. Wooley and Gerhard Peters, *The American Presidency*, http://www.presidency.uscb.edu/ws?pid=68486. Accessed March 15, 2008.

20 "Harlan Attacks Rule of Reason," *New York Times*, May 26, 1911, 6.

21 Ellis W. Hawley, *The New Deal and the Problem of Monopoly: A Study in Economic Ambivalence* (Princeton, N.J.: Princeton University Press, 1966), 8–13.

22 According to Robert Heilbroner and Alan Singer, *The Economic Transformation*

of America: 1600 to the Present (New York: Harcourt Brace Jovanovich, 1984), 126, "by 1904 one or two giant firms controlled at least half the output in seventy-eight different industries." An excellent account of how oligopolies work can be found in Neil Fligstein, *The Transformation of Corporate Control* (Cambridge, Mass.: Harvard University Press, 1990), 98–105. Fligstein distinguishes between two types of oligopolistic practices. In the first, a dominant firm acts as a price setter; in the second, a small number of firms cooperate to set prices while jockeying for market share.

23 Mark Blaug, *Economic Theory in Retrospect* (Cambridge: Cambridge University Press, 1997), 261.

24 The rapidly growing reliance on the electric dynamo after World War I largely explains the impressive gains in productivity in the 1920s. By 1930, electricity accounted for 78 percent of all industrial power.

25 David A. Hounshell, *From the American System to Mass Production, 1800–1932: The Development of Manufacturing Technology in the United States* (Baltimore: Johns Hopkins University Press, 1984), 217–61.

26 On the assembly line, see ibid. On Henry Ford and his company, see Robert Lacey, *Ford: The Men and the Machine* (Boston: Little, Brown, 1985).

27 Hounshell, *From the American System to Mass Production*, 250–58.

28 Robert Kanigel, *The One Best Way: Frederick Winslow Taylor and the Enigma of Efficiency* (New York: Viking, 1997). No less astute a student of management, Peter F. Drucker, *Post-Capitalist Society* (New York: Harper Business, 1993), 33, has credited Taylor with having "first applied knowledge to the study of work, the analysis of work, and the engineering of work." Drucker believes that Taylor sincerely wanted to make workers more productive so that "they would earn decent money."

29 Hounshell, *From the American System to Mass Production*, 228.

30 See, for example, Peter G. Filene, "An Obituary for the Progressive Movement," *American Quarterly* 22 (1970): 20–24; and Daniel T. Rogers, "In Search of Progressivism," *Reviews in American History* 10 (1982): 113–32.

31 Gabriel Kolko, *The Triumph of Conservatism: A Reinterpretation of American History, 1900–1916* (New York: Free Press, 1963); Martin Sklar, *The Corporate Reconstruction of American Capitalism, 1890–1916: The Market, the Law, and Politics* (Cambridge: Cambridge University Press, 1988).

32 Keller, *Regulating a New Economy*, 3.

33 Joel Brinkley, "Cultivating the Grass Roots to Reap Legislative Benefits," *New York Times*, November 1, 1993, 17.

34 On veterans' pensions, see Theda Skocpol, *Protecting Soldiers and Mothers* (Cambridge, Mass.: Harvard University Press, 1992). In this historical account of government benefit programs, Skocpol argues that those that are most successful in being enacted and funded are directed toward helping groups viewed as

worthy, or at least as nonthreatening. Yet, as she notes, Republican efforts in Congress to grant generous pensions for Civil War veterans also made this group a core constituency of the Republican Party at the end of the nineteenth century.

35 Roosevelt, *Theodore Roosevelt: An Autobiography*, 324.

CHAPTER NINE

1 T. J. Jackson Lears, *Fables of Abundance: A Cultural History of Advertising in America* (New York: Basic Books, 1994), 207.

2 Morton Keller, *Regulating a New Economy: Public Policy and Economic Change in America, 1900–1933* (Cambridge, Mass.: Harvard University Press, 1990), 28.

3 Woodrow Wilson, *Woodrow Wilson: The Essential Political Writings*, ed. Ronald J. Pestritto (Lanham, Md.: Rowman and Littlefield, 2005), 112. On Wilson's approach to reform, see Earl Latham, *The Philosophy and Policies of Woodrow Wilson* (Chicago: University of Chicago Press, 1958), 133–39.

4 Michael J. Sandel, *Democracy's Discontent: America in Search of a Public Policy* (Cambridge, Mass.: Harvard University Press, 1996), 218.

5 Quoted in Robert D. Atkinson, *Supply Side Follies: Why Conservative Economics Fails, Liberal Economics Falters, and Innovative Economics Is the Answer* (Lanham, Md.: Rowman and Littlefield, 2006).

6 Jonathan J. Bean, *Beyond the Broker State: A History of the Federal Government's Policies towards Small Business, 1936–61* (Chapel Hill: University of North Carolina Press, 1996), 10.

7 William James, *The Principles of Psychology* (New York: H. Holt, 1890), 47–54.

8 "La Follette Lashes Morgan in Senate," *New York Times*, April 13, 1910, 3.

9 Subcommittee of the Committee on Banking and Finance (Pujo Committee), *Investigation of Finance and Monetary Conditions in the United States* (Washington, D.C.: Government Printing Office, exhibit 134S, B, 1913).

10 The standard account is Robert Craig West, *Banking Reform and the Federal Reserve System, 1863–1923* (Ithaca, N.Y.: Cornell University Press, 1977). A critical view of the origins of the system is James Livingston, *Origins of the Federal Reserve System: Money, Class, and Corporate Capitalism* (Ithaca, N.Y.: Cornell University Press, 1986). A recent study that asserts that Americans, and especially New York bankers, wanted the Federal Reserve System to challenge Britain's domination of world finance is J. Lawrence Broz, *The International Origins of the Federal Reserve System* (Ithaca, N.Y.: Cornell University Press, 1997).

11 Martin Sklar, *The Corporate Reconstruction of American Capitalism, 1890–1916: The Market, the Law, and Politics* (Cambridge: Cambridge University Press, 1988), 425.

12 Olivier Zunz, *Making America Corporate, 1870–1920* (Chicago: University of Chicago Press, 1990).

13 Efforts by academically trained home economists to systematize housekeeping and domestic life through time and motion studies are described by Ruth Schwartz Cowan in *More Work for Mother: The Ironies of Household Technology from the Open Hearth to the Microwave* (New York: Basic Books, 1983).

14 Daniel M. Fox, *The Discovery of Abundance: Simon N. Patten and the Transformation of Social Theory* (Ithaca, N.Y.: Cornell University Press, 1967).

15 Ted Levitt, in a seminal article, "Marketing Myopia," *Harvard Business Review* 38 (July/August 1960): 45–64, reevaluated Ford's business strategy from a marketing perspective and found it fundamentally flawed: "Mass production industries are impelled by a great drive to produce all they can. . . . The profit possibilities look spectacular. All effort focuses on production. The result is that marketing gets neglected."

16 The quote is cited in David I. Levine, "Can Wage Increases Pay for Themselves?" *Economic Journal* 102, no. 414 (September 1992): 1104.

17 An interesting comparison of the differences between Ford's and Taylor's approaches to industrial production is found in Robert Kanigel, *The One Best Way: Frederick Winslow Taylor and the Enigma of Efficiency* (New York: Viking, 1997), 495–97. "Fordism" and "Taylorism" both became synonymous with the American approach to industrial efficiency in the years between the two world wars and were often used interchangeably.

18 James Weinstein, *Corporate Ideal in the Liberal State, 1900–1918* (Boston: Beacon, 1969), 24–27.

19 David Noble, *Forces of Production: A History of Industrial Automation* (New York: Alfred A. Knopf, 1964), 356.

20 For Elton Mayo's industrial philosophy, see his *Human Problems of an Industrial Civilization* (New York: Macmillan, 1933); the quote is on page 243. Critics note that the very small numbers of workers involved call into question the validity of the Hawthorne study, and they also observe correctly that Mayo still retained a paternalistic attitude toward them. For the field of industrial relations or human resources, see Bruce E. Kaufman, *The Origins and Evolution of the Field of Industrial Relations* (Ithaca, N.Y.: Cornell University Press, 1993). A people-oriented approach to personnel management, by industrial psychologists Walter Benis, Chris Argris, and John McGregor, in the 1940s and 1950s, became known as the Human Relations School.

21 Bernard Baruch, *The Public Years* (New York: Holt, Rinehart, and Winston, 1960), 56.

22 Robert P. Cuff, *The War Industries Board: Business-Government Relations during World War I* (Baltimore: Johns Hopkins University Press, 1973).

23 Arthur Schlesinger Jr., *The Crisis of the Old Order, 1919–1932*, vol. 1 of *The Age of Roosevelt* (Boston: Houghton Mifflin, 1957), 57.

24 Alfred Sloan, *My Years with General Motors* (1963; New York: Anchor, 1972), 57–

61. Sloan's book remained the best-selling business book in the United States for twenty years.

25 Lincoln Steffens, *The Letters of Lincoln Steffens*, ed. Ella Winters and Granville Hicks (1938; Westport, Conn.: Greenwood, 1974), 261.

CHAPTER TEN

1 Roland Marchand, *Advertising the American Dream: Making Way for Modernity, 1920–1940* (Berkeley: University of California Press, 1985).

2 Ibid., 19.

3 Ibid., 1.

4 Martha I. Olney, *Buy Now, Pay Later: Advertising, Credit, and Consumer Durables in the 1920s* (Chapel Hill: University of North Carolina Press, 1991).

5 Committee on Recent Economic Change, *Recent Economic Changes in the United States* (New York: McGraw-Hill, 1929), 419–20.

6 Ibid., 464.

7 Kenneth T. Jackson, *Crabgrass Frontier: The Suburbanization of the United States* (New York: Oxford University Press, 1984), 257–58.

8 Richard W. Longtreth, *City Center to Regional Mall: Architecture, the Automobile, and Retailing in Los Angeles, 1920–1950* (Cambridge, Mass.: MIT Press, 1997).

9 Roland Marchand, "The Inward Thrust of Institutional Advertising: General Electric and General Motors in the 1920s," *Business and Economic History*, Second Series, 18 (1989): 96.

10 "Nothing has spread the socialistic feelings in this country more than the automobile. To the countryman they are a picture of the arrogance of wealth, with its independence and carelessness." "Wilson Blames Speeders," *New York Times*, February 28, 1906, 5.

11 It was not until 1914 that a decision was made to make black cars only. David A. Hounshell, *From the American System to Mass Production, 1800–1932: The Development of Manufacturing Technology* (Baltimore: Johns Hopkins University Press, 1984), 273.

12 Ray Batchelor, *Henry Ford, Mass Production, Modernism, and Design* (Manchester, England: Manchester University Press, 1994).

13 Hounshell, *From the American System to Mass Production*, 263–301.

14 William Pelfrey, *Billy, Alfred, and General Motors: The Story of Two Unique Men, a Legendary Company, and a Remarkable Time in American History* (New York: AMACOM, 2006), 118.

15 David Farber, *Sloan Rules: Alfred P. Sloan and the Triumph of General Motors* (Chicago: University of Chicago Press, 2002), 178–87.

16 Daniel J. Boorstin, *The Americans: The Democratic Experience* (New York: Random House, 1972), 548; Marchand, *Advertising the American Dream*, 156–57.

17 Daniel M. G. Raff, "Making Cars and Making Money in the Interwar Automobile Industry: Economies of Scale and Scope and the Manufacturing behind the Marketing," *Business History Review* 65, no. 4 (Winter 1991): 721–75.

18 Walter Lippmann, *The Society* (New York: Alfred A. Knopf, 1937). Alfred D. Chandler Jr., *Strategy and Structure: Chapters in the History of the American Industrial Enterprise* (Cambridge, Mass.: MIT Press, 1962), demonstrated how Sloan's market-driven strategy contributed to his pioneering of GM's multidivisional organizational structure. Chandler praised Sloan's decentralization highly, and his work played a role in the movement of corporations to multidivisional organization in the 1960s. In 1970, about 80 percent of the Fortune 500 corporations were decentralized, as compared to 20 percent in 1945.

19 A 1919 Standard Oil advertisement celebrated car ownership as providing "the means of satisfying one of [man's] most primitive instincts, a desire to venture forth like a true adventurer." Daniel Horowitz, *The Morality of Spending: Attitudes towards Consumer Spending in America, 1875–1940* (Baltimore: Johns Hopkins University Press, 1985), 62.

20 Peter F. Drucker, *The Concept of the Corporation* (New York: John Day, 1946).

21 Woodlief Thomas, "The Growth of Production and the Rising Standard of Living," *Proceedings of the Academy of Political Science* 12 (1927): 651–61. See also Walter Meakin, *The New Industrial Revolution* (1928; New York: Arno Press, 1974).

22 "The 1920s: A Statistical Portrait," http://bss.sfsu.edu/tygiel/hist427/texts/1920seconomy.htm. Accessed June 27, 2008.

23 Bruce Barton, *The Man Nobody Knows* (1925; New York: Collier Books, 1987), 1–2.

24 Stuart Ewen, *Captains of Consciousness: Advertising and the Social Roots of the Consumer Culture* (New York: McGraw-Hill, 1976). Lendol G. Calder, *Financing the American Dream* (Princeton, N.J.: Princeton University Press, 1999), stresses the role of installment credit in the rise of consumerism. See also Olney, *Buy Now, Pay Later*; and John J. Raskob, "The Development of Installment Purchasing," *Proceedings of the Academy of Political Science* 12 (1927): 619–39.

25 Douglas Gomery, *The Hollywood Studio System* (New York: St. Martin's, 1987); Lary May, *Screening Out the Past: The Birth of Mass Culture and the Movies* (New York: Oxford University Press, 1980).

26 Albro Martin, *Enterprise Denied: Origins of the Decline of the Railroad Industry, 1897–1917* (New York: Columbia University Press, 1971); Ellis W. Hawley, "Secretary Hoover and the Bituminous Coal Problem," *Business History Review* 42 (Autumn 1968): 247–70.

27 Joan Hoff Wilson, "Herbert Hoover's Agricultural Policies, 1921–28," in *Herbert Hoover as Secretary of Commerce*, ed. Ellis W. Hawley (Iowa City: University of Iowa Press, 1982), 315–44.

28 Lynn Dumenil, *Modern Temper: American Culture and Society in the 1920s* (New York: Hill and Wang, 1995), 76–97.

29 Lizabeth Cohen, *Making a New Deal: Industrial Workers in Chicago, 1919–1939* (New York: Cambridge University Press, 1990), 100–158; President's Research Committee on Social Trends in the United States, *Social Trends in the United States*, 2 vols. (1933; Westport, Conn.: Greenwood, 1970), 857–911.

30 Barnet Baskerville, *The People's Voice* (Lexington: University Press of Kentucky, 1979), 137.

31 Adolf A. Berle and Gardiner C. Means, *The Modern Corporation and Private Property* (New York: Macmillan, 1932), 124–25, 352, 356, passim.

32 William Miller, "The Recruitment of the American Business Elite," *Quarterly Journal of Economics* 64 (May 1950): 329–37, reprinted in William Miller, ed., *Men in Business: Essays on the Historical Role of the Entrepreneur* (New York: Harper and Row, 1962). The assumption that social homogeneity was essential to effective management is found in Chester I. Barnard, *The Functions of the Executive* (Cambridge, Mass.: Harvard University Press, 1938), 139–48. Barnard was the president of New Jersey Bell.

33 Edward L. Bernays, *Biography of an Idea: Memoirs of Public Relations Counsel Edward L. Bernays* (New York: Simon and Schuster, 1962), 308–9. Roland Marchand's magisterial *Creating the Corporate Soul: The Rise of Public Relations and Corporate Imagery* (Berkeley: University of California Press, 1998) has been rightly hailed as a classic.

34 Ellis W. Hawley, "Herbert Hoover, the Commerce Secretariat, and the Vision of an Associative State, 1921–1928," *Journal of American History* 61, no. 1 (June 1974): 118, 116–40.

35 Ibid.

36 Louis Galambos and Joseph Pratt, *The Rise of the Corporate Commonwealth: United States Business and Public Policy in the 20th Century* (New York: Basic Books, 1988), 21.

37 For the quote, see Sylvia Naser, "Ideas & Trends: Chaos Theory: Unlearning the Lessons of Eco 101," *New York Times*, May 3, 1998, Week in Review, 1. The unfortunate remark cost Fisher much of his reputation at the time, but it has since recovered. He is perhaps best known for his "debt-deflation" theory: with severe deflation, the value of the outstanding debt rises even as the debt gets repaid.

38 David M. Kennedy, *Freedom from Fear: The American People in Depression and War, 1929–1945* (New York: Oxford University Press, 1999), 40–41.

39 Ralph Nelson, *Merger Movements in American Industry: 1895–1904* (Princeton, N.J.: Princeton University Press, 1959), 144–47.

40 Bernard Baruch would later tell the probably apocryphal story that he decided to

sell on the day that the bootblack in his office building offered him tips on what stocks to buy. The story is still frequently quoted.

41 Hoover obviously overstated. After 1925, economic growth in key sectors of the economy, namely home construction and automobiles, slowed, and by 1929 the value of unsold inventories had quadrupled over the previous year. Maury Klein, *Rainbow's End: The Crash of 1929* (New York: Oxford University Press, 2001).

42 The literature concerning the Great Depression and its causes is enormous. I would recommend the following: Michael Bernstein, *The Great Depression: Delayed Recovery and Economic Change in America* (New York: Cambridge University Press, 1987), 1–17; Lester Chandler, *America's Greatest Depression* (New York: Harper and Row, 1970); and Michael D. Bordo, Claudia Goldin, and Eugene N. White, eds., *The Defining Moment: The Great Depression and the American Economy in the Twentieth Century* (Chicago: University of Chicago Press, 1998).

43 Peter Temin, *Did Monetary Forces Cause the Great Depression?* (New York: Norton, 1976), 75–76.

44 Karl Brunner, ed., *Great Depression Revisited* (Leiden, The Netherlands: Martinus Inhofe, 1981), especially 319–58.

45 Herbert Hoover, *The Memoirs of Herbert Hoover: The Great Depression, 1929–41* (New York: Macmillan, 1952), 30.

46 For the argument that the failure of the Fed to act effectively as a lender of last resort to banks contributed to turning a recession into a depression, see Milton Friedman and Anna J. Schwarz, *Monetary History of the United States, 1897–1960* (Princeton, N.J.: Princeton University Press, 1963), 299–332, 391–99. In defense of the Federal Reserve, it should be noted that it lacked experience in handling a crisis of this nature.

47 On Hoover's personality, see Joan Hoff Wilson, *Herbert Hoover: Forgotten Progressive* (Boston: Little, Brown, 1975), 10.

48 For a discussion of differing views of the impact of the Smoot-Hawley tariff on the Great Depression, see Kennedy, *Freedom from Fear*, 49–50, especially note 12.

CHAPTER ELEVEN

1 Ellis Hawley, *The New Deal and the Problem of Monopoly: A Study in Economic Ambivalence* (Princeton, N.J.: Princeton University Press, 1966), 486–89.

2 Obituary of Walter S. Salant, *New York Times*, May 2, 1999.

3 James Reston, *Deadline: A Memoir* (New York: Random House, 1991), 68.

4 For the view of the New Deal as significantly influenced by business interests,

see Colin Gordon, *New Deals: Business, Labor, and Politics in America, 1920–35* (New York: Cambridge University Press, 1994), 4. A concise and useful overview of the "corporate liberalism" hypothesis is provided by Alan Brinkley, *The End of Reform: New Deal Liberalism in Recession and War* (New York: Alfred A. Knopf, 1995), 291n32.

5 David M. Kennedy, *Freedom from Fear: The American People in Depression and War, 1929–1945* (New York: Oxford University Press, 1999), 135–37.

6 Ibid., 366–77.

7 Vincent P. Carosso, *Investment Banking in America: A History* (Cambridge, Mass.: Harvard University Press, 1970).

8 Kennedy, *Freedom from Fear*, 365–67.

9 William Greider, *Secrets of the Temple* (New York: Simon and Schuster, 1987).

10 Joel Seligman, *The Transformation of Wall Street: The History of the Securities and Exchange Commission and Modern Corporate Finance* (Boston: Houghton Mifflin, 1982). A less technical account is provided in John Brooks, *Once in Golconda: A True Drama of Wall Street, 1920–38* (New York: Harper and Row, 1969).

11 Stephen K. Shaw and William D. Peterson, *Franklin D. Roosevelt and the Transformation of the Supreme Court* (Armonk, N.Y.: M. E. Sharpe, 2003), 83.

12 Bernard Bellush, *The Failure of the NRA* (New York: Norton, 1975).

13 James T. Patterson, *Struggle against Poverty, 1900–1980* (Cambridge, Mass.: Harvard University Press, 1981), 61–75.

14 In 2007, the Social Security system covered over 155 million workers and paid 53 million beneficiaries each month. Serious concerns about the viability of the system, however, had led President George W. Bush to propose major changes, including "privatizing" part of each worker's account; this latter was quickly dropped when it proved politically unpopular.

15 Although section 7(a) of the NIRA gave workers the right to form unions and bargain collectively, it lacked enforcement provisions and was generally ineffective.

16 Kennedy, *Freedom from Fear*, 288–93.

17 On Keynes's ideas and his relationship with Roosevelt and the New Deal, see Robert Skidelsky, *John Maynard Keynes: The Economist as Savior, 1920–1937* (New York: Penguin, 1995), 493, 543, 594–96.

18 Theodore Rosenof, *Economics in the Long Run: New Deal Theorists and Their Legacies* (Chapel Hill: University of North Carolina Press, 1997).

19 Brinkley, *End of Reform*, 10–14.

20 Kenneth Rose, *The Economics of Recession and Revival: An Interpretation of 1937–38* (New Haven: Yale University Press, 1954), 179–82. Michael Bernstein found that capital investment varied greatly according to industry but concluded that inadequate aggregate private investment was the major cause of the Depression persisting until 1941; see Michael Bernstein, *The Great Depression: Delayed Re-*

covery and Economic Change in America (New York: Cambridge University Press, 1987), 103–20.

21 Thurman Arnold, *The Folklore of Capitalism* (New Haven: Yale University Press, 1937), 211, 213–42; Hawley, *New Deal and the Problem of Monopoly*, 439–55. Alan Brinkley, in *The End of Reform*, 107–36, believes that after 1937 reformers moved away from concern with business concentration toward the Keynesian concern with countercyclical policies and demand-side economics.

22 Jonathan J. Bean, *Beyond the Broker State: A History of the Federal Government's Policies toward Small Business, 1936–1961* (Chapel Hill: University of North Carolina Press, 1996), 18–98.

23 Hawley, *New Deal and the Problem of Monopoly*, 488.

24 It has been estimated that the fraction of all personal wealth held by the top 1 percent of adults fell from 31 percent in 1939 to 23 percent in 1945; and the share of income received by the top 5 percent fell from 28 percent to 19 percent; see Jeffrey G. Williamson and Peter H. Lindert, *American Inequality: A Macroeconomic History* (New York: Academic Books, 1980), 53–92.

25 Theodore J. Lowi, *The End of Liberalism: Ideology, Policy, and the Crisis of Public Authority* (New York: Norton, 1969); Jonathan Rauch, *Demosclerosis: The Silent Killer of American Government* (New York: Times Books, 1994).

CHAPTER TWELVE

1 Henry Luce, "American Century," *Life* magazine, February 17, 1941, 61–65; Robert Skidelsky, *John Maynard Keynes: Fighting for Freedom, 1937–1946* (New York: Viking, 2000), 337–72; E. F. Penrose, *Economic Planning for Peace* (Princeton, N.J.: Princeton University Press, 1953).

2 S. Rosenthal and Alvin Hansen, "On Economic Progress and Declining Population Growth," *Population and Development Review* 30, no. 4 (December 2004): 798–99; Alvin H. Hansen, *Economic Policy and Full Employment* (New York: McGraw-Hill, 1947).

3 Joseph Schumpeter, *Capitalism, Socialism, and Democracy* (1942; New York: Harper Colophon, 1976), 143–56.

4 Harold G. Vatter, *The United States Economy in the 1950s* (Chicago: University of Chicago Press, 1993), 22.

5 The first mall appeared in Kansas City's Country Club District in the 1920s, and by 1945 there were eight. The great postwar construction of malls contributed to the decay of central cities and Main Streets throughout America.

6 Kenneth T. Jackson, *Crabgrass Frontier: The Suburbanization of the United States* (New York: Oxford University Press, 1986), 231–45.

7 James Stemble Duesenberry, *Income, Saving, and the Theory of Consumer Behavior* (Cambridge, Mass.: Harvard University Press, 1949).

8 Roger Lotchin, ed., *The Martial Metropolis: American Cities in Peace and War* (New York: Praeger, 1984).

9 Burton R. Fisher and Stephen B. Whithey, *Big Business as the People See It* (Ann Arbor: University of Michigan Institute for Social Research, 1951), xii, 57–58. See also Louis Galambos, *The Public Image of Big Business in America, 1880–1940: A Quantitative Study in Social Change* (Baltimore: Johns Hopkins University Press, 1975).

10 John Kenneth Galbraith, *The Affluent Society* (Boston: Houghton Mifflin, 1958). For a fascinating and disturbing analysis of the impact of the automobile and television on American social life at the end of the twentieth century, see Robert D. Putnam, *Bowling Alone: The Collapse and Revival of American Community* (New York: Simon and Schuster, 2000), 204–23.

11 Employment Act of 1946.

12 Ibid.

13 Agatha and Thomas P. Hughes, eds., *Systems, Experts, and Computers: The Systems Approach in Management and Engineering during World War II and After* (Cambridge, Mass.: MIT Press, 2000).

14 Constantinos C. Markides, *Diversification, Refocusing, and Economic Performance* (Cambridge, Mass.: MIT Press, 1995), 28.

15 General Mills' history can be found in G. Donaldson, *Corporate Restructuring* (Boston: Harvard Business School Press, 1990).

16 Postwar diversification is analyzed in Richard P. Rumelt, *Strategy, Structure, and Economic Performance* (Cambridge, Mass.: Harvard University Press, 1974); and Milton Leontiades, *Managing the Unmanageable: Strategies for Success within the Conglomerate* (Reading, Mass.: Addison Wesley, 1986).

17 C. K. Prahaled and R. A. Bettis, "The Dominant Logic: A New Linkage between Diversity and Performance," *Strategic Management Journal* 7 (1986): 485–501.

18 Harvey H. Segal, "The Urge to Merge," *New York Times Magazine*, October 27, 1968, 33.

19 Michael E. Porter, *The Competitive Advantage of Nations* (New York: Free Press, 1989), 76.

20 Jack N. Behrman, *Conflicting Constraints on the Multinational Enterprise: Potential for Resolution* (New York: Council of the Americas, 1974), 6–9. On the postwar rise of multinational corporations, see Raymond Vernon, *Sovereignty at Bay: The Multinational Spread of U.S. Enterprises* (New York: Basic Books, 1971); and Mira Wilkins, *The Maturing of Multinational Enterprise: American Business Abroad from 1914 to 1917* (Cambridge, Mass.: Harvard University Press, 1974). Sumantra Ghoshal and Christopher Bartlett, *Managing across Borders* (Boston: Harvard Business School Press, 1989), have proposed models of four multinational types. They suggest that global competition is forcing many firms to

become "transnational," the fourth type, a network of specialized or differentiated units with attention paid to managing linkages between local firms and the center.

21 Some American companies interfered in the domestic politics of their host country. ITT had cooperated with Hitler's Germany and Franco's Spain in the 1930s and 1940s and was widely believed to have worked with the CIA to overthrow the left-wing government of Salvador Allende in Chile.

22 "Deciding on a Merger," *Wall Street Journal*, March 27, 1964, 30.

23 The emergence of the conglomerate strategy was paralleled by a portfolio theory of finance that argued that risk could largely be avoided through sufficiently diversified investment holdings. The influential article that redirected the focus of financial economists to the question was Harry M. Markowitz, "Portfolio Selection," *Journal of Finance* 7 (March 1952): 77–89. Markowitz received a Nobel Prize for economics in 1990.

24 Neil H. Jacoby, "Conglomerate Corporation," *Center Magazine* (Center for Study of Democratic Institutions) 2 (July 1969): 40–57. One reason for enthusiasm for conglomerates in the 1960s was that it allowed investors to diversify their portfolios without paying the high brokerage fees then being charged for buying shares in individual companies.

25 Harold Geneen and Alvin Moscow, *Managing* (New York: Doubleday, 1984), 67.

26 Robert Sobel, *I.T.T.: The Management of Opportunity* (New York: Times Books, 1964).

27 It should be noted that the ability to cross-subsidize lines of business is not unique to conglomerates—any diversified firm can do this.

28 On the loss of competitive advantage, see Markides, *Diversification, Refocusing, and Economic Performance*, 12.

29 Peter F. Drucker, *A Functioning Society: Selections from Sixty-five Years of Writing on Community, Society, and Policy* (Piscataway, N.J.: Transaction Publishers, 2003), 137; Elizabeth Fones-Wolf, *Selling Free Enterprise: The Business Assault on Labor and Liberalism, 1945–1960* (Champaign: University of Illinois Press, 1994). American business was hardly without blemish. Even the pro-business Eisenhower administration found it necessary to bring price-fixing charges against nearly every large company in the electrical equipment industry.

30 Hillary D. Rodham, "1969 Student Commencement Speech," http://www.welles ley.edu/publicaffairs/commencement/1969/053169hillary.html. Accessed June 2008.

31 Jim F. Heath, *John F. Kennedy and the Business Community* (Chicago: University of Chicago Press, 1969), 232–37.

32 Riley E. Dunlap and Angela G. Mertig, eds., *American Environmentalism: The U.S. Environmental Movement, 1970–1990* (New York: Taylor and Francis,

1992). For the chemical industry's reaction to Rachel Carson's work, see John H. Cushman Jr., "After 'Silent Spring,'" *New York Times*, March 26, 2001, 14A.

33 Stephen Labaton, "The Nation; Let the Markets Rule, Sometimes," *New York Times*, February 11, 2001, 17.

34 Murray L. Weidenbaum, *The Modern Public Sector* (New York: Basic Books, 1969), 17–19.

35 Nixon's action ushered in the development of a major new financial industry—dealing in financial derivatives. Floating exchange rates fueled a search for new mechanisms to hedge against adverse currency fluctuations. In the early 1970s, the Chicago Mercantile Exchange launched new futures and options for Eurodollars (U.S.-dollar denominated deposits at foreign banks or foreign branches of American banks) and foreign currency and a host of derivative contracts; see Leo Melamed, *Escape to the Futures* (New York: John Wiley, 1996).

36 Milton Friedman, "The Role of Economic Policy," *American Economic Review* 58 (March 1968): 1–17; Milton Friedman and Anna J. Schwarz, *A Monetary History of the United States, 1897–1960* (Princeton, N.J.: Princeton University Press, 1963).

CHAPTER THIRTEEN

1 The reasons for the collapse of the American consumer electronics industry are analyzed in Alfred Chandler, *Inventing the Electronic Century: The Epic Story of the Consumer Electronics and Computer Industries* (New York: Free Press, 2001), 13–49.

2 On Detroit's slide, see David Halberstam, *The Reckoning* (New York: Morrow, 1986); and Maryann Keller, *The Rise, Fall, and Struggle for Recovery of General Motors* (New York: Morrow, 1989). On the steel industry's decline, see Paul Tiffany, *The Decline of American Steel: How Management, Labor, and Government Went Wrong* (New York: Oxford University Press, 1988). An overall analysis is provided in Michael E. Porter, *Competitive Strategy: Techniques for Analyzing Industries and Competitors* (New York: Free Press, 1980), especially 291–98.

3 Not all conglomerates faltered. Three highly successful conglomerates were Time Warner, General Electric, and Berkshire Hathaway. The first two surmounted the inherent limitations of the conglomerate form of organization by establishing a highly diversified entity around a central core and an M-form of business organization.

4 For an analysis of economic thinking in the 1970s and since, including the rise of the neo-Keynesian school, see Paul Krugman, *Peddling Prosperity: Economic Sense and Nonsense in the Age of Diminished Expectations* (New York: W. W. Norton, 1994).

5 For a comparison of the ideas of Friedman and Keynes, see Robert Skidelsky, *John Maynard Keynes: Fighting for Freedom, 1937–1946* (New York: Viking, 2000), 506.

6 On union decline, see Michael Goldfield, *The Decline of Organized Labor in the United States* (Chicago: University of Chicago Press, 1987); and Henry S. Farber, "Extent of Unionization in the United States," in *Challenges and Choices Facing American Labor*, ed. Thomas A. Kochan (Cambridge, Mass.: MIT Press, 1985), 15–43. Robert D. Putnam differs from the others in placing less stress on structural changes in the workforce and emphasizing workers' alienation from their unions, in *Bowling Alone: The Collapse and Revival of American Community* (New York: Simon and Schuster, 2000), 80–82.

7 Richard C. Gerstenberg, "The Profile of a Paycheck," *Engineering Management Review* 6, no. 2 (June 1978): 9–10; "Blue Collar Blues," *New York Times*, October 15, 1971, A12.

8 For the costs of regulation to the economy, see Murray L. Weidenbaum and Robert DeFina, *The Cost of Federal Regulation of Economic Activity* (Washington, D.C.: American Enterprise Institute, 1978).

9 Mark Green and Ralph Nader, "Economic Regulation vs. Competition: Uncle Sam the Monopoly Man," *Yale Law Journal* 82, no. 5 (April 1973): 871–89; Ralph K. Winter Jr., "Economic Regulation vs. Competition: Ralph Nader and Creeping Capitalism," *Yale Law Journal* 82, no. 5 (April 1973): 890–902.

10 To address the problems of welfare rolls and unemployment, the Carter administration pushed the enactment of the Comprehensive Training and Employment Act.

11 John Palmer and Isabel V. Sawhill, *The Reagan Experiment: An Examination of Economic and Social Policies under Reagan* (Washington, D.C.: Urban Institute Press, 1982).

12 Robert Hayes and William Abernathy, "Managing Our Way to Economic Decline," *Harvard Business Review* 58 (July/August 1980): 67–78.

13 Alfred P. Sloan, *My Years with General Motors* (1963; New York: Anchor Books, 1972), xiii.

14 Jimmy Carter, "Energy and National Goals: A Crisis of Confidence," http://americanrhetoric.com/speeches/jimmycartercrisisofconfidence.htm. Accessed June 1, 2008.

15 See, for example, Donella H. Meadows et al., *Limits to Growth: A Report for the Club of Rome* (New York: Universe Books, 1972), which sold millions of copies in the United States.

16 *Global 2000 Report to the President of the United States: Entering the 21st Century* (Washington, D.C.: Government Printing Office, 1981).

17 Elinor Langer, "Auto Safety: New Study Criticizes Manufacturers and Universities," *Science* 150 (November 1965): 1138.

18 Ralph Nader, *Unsafe at Any Speed* (New York: Grossman, 1965). GM hired detectives to find dirt on Ralph Nader. After this became known the company was forced to apologize. Nader's book contributed greatly to the enactment of federal auto safety legislation in 1966.

19 In 1980, Congress gave Chrysler a one-and-a-half-billion-dollar loan guarantee. Less than three years later the company repaid the loan in full.

20 Thomas J. Peters and Robert H. Waterman, *In Search of Excellence* (New York: Harper and Row, 1982); Tom Peters, *Liberation Management* (New York: Alfred A. Knopf, 1992), 62.

21 Peters and Waterman, *In Search of Excellence*; Tom Peters, *Thriving on Chaos* (London: Macmillan, 1988).

CHAPTER FOURTEEN

1 Michael C. Jensen and Kevin C. Murphy, "CEO Incentives: It's Not How Much You Pay, But How," *Harvard Business Review* 68, no. 3 (May–June 1990): 138–49.

2 The basic reference for the initial Reagan economic program is *America's New Beginning: A Program for Economic Recovery* (Washington, D.C.: Government Printing Office, 1981); also useful for the background of Reaganomics is Paul Craig Roberts, *The Supply-Side Revolution* (Cambridge, Mass.: Harvard University Press, 1984).

3 David Stockman, *The Triumph of Politics* (New York: Harper and Row, 1986), provides a lively account of the infighting among advisers on preparing the budget and anticipating revenues in the early 1980s.

4 Diana B. Henriques, "Wall Street; a Blue Chip Name Is Not Enough," *New York Times*, January 14, 1990, C1.

5 Devra L. Golbe and Lawrence J. White, "Mergers and Acquisitions in the U.S. Economy: An Aggregate and Historical Overview," in *Mergers and Acquisitions*, ed. Alan J. Auerbach (Chicago: University of Chicago Press, 1988), 25–47.

6 Frank Levy, *The New Dollars and Dreams* (New York: Russell Sage Foundation, 1998), is excellent on the highly contested subject of family incomes. The Nobel economist Robert Solow estimated median annual family income in 2000 at about $45,000. For the decade of the 1990s, see "Cutting the Cake," *Economist* (September 11, 1999): 26.

7 Juliet Schor, *The Overspent American: Upscaling, Downscaling, and the New Consumer* (New York: Harper, 1999), iv; Robert H. Frank, *Luxury Fever: Why Money Fails to Satisfy in an Era of Excess* (New York: Free Press, 1999); Susan Linn, *Consuming Kids: The Hostile Takeover of Childhood* (New York: New Press, 2004).

8 Raymond Williams, *Television: Technology and Cultural Form* (1974; Oxford: Routledge, 2003), 69.

9   Lizabeth Cohen, *A Consumers' Republic: The Politics of Mass Consumerism in Postwar America* (New York: Vintage Press, 2004), 11. Writing on the "culture of consumption" by historians, sociologists, and anthropologists is becoming voluminous. As an introduction to the subject, I recommend Susan Strasser, Charles McGovern, and Matthias Judt, eds., *Getting and Spending: European and American Consumer Societies in the Twentieth Century* (New York: Cambridge University Press, 1998).

10 David Brooks, *Bobos in Paradise: The New Upper Class and How They Got There* (New York: Simon and Schuster, 2000).

11 Stanley Lebergott, *Pursuing Happiness: American Consumers in the Twentieth Century* (Princeton, N.J.: Princeton University Press, 1996). See also Daniel J. Boorstin, *The Americans: The Democratic Experience* (New York: Random House, 1973), 91–129.

12 Jonathan Charkham, *Keeping Good Company: A Study of Corporate Governance in Five Countries* (Oxford: Clarendon, 1994), 238–39.

13 Roland Marchand, *Creating the Corporate Soul: The Rise of Public Relations and Corporate Imagery in Big Business* (Berkeley: University of California Press, 1998), 48–87.

14 Peter Temin and Louis Galambos, *The Fall of the Bell System: A Study in Prices and Politics* (New York: Cambridge University Press, 1987).

15 Charles W. Calomiris, *U.S. Bank Deregulation in Historical Perspective* (New York: Cambridge University Press, 2000).

16 By the time the Resolution and Trust Company closed its doors in December 1995, Washington's losses in the savings and loan fiasco had reached $145 billion.

17 Quoted in Gretchen Morgenstern and Timothy L. O'Brien, "When Citigroup Met WorldCom," *New York Times*, May 16, 2004, Business Section, 1; Richard H. K. Vietor, *Contrived Competition: Regulation and Deregulation in America* (Cambridge, Mass.: Belknap Press of Harvard University Press, 1994), 167–233.

18 For a favorable view of Reagan's antitrust policies, see Louis Galambos, "The Monopoly Enigma, the Reagan Administration's Antitrust Experiment, and the Global Economy," in *Constructing Corporate America: History, Politics, Culture*, ed. Kenneth Lipartito and David B. Sicilia (Chicago: University of Chicago Press, 2004), 149–67.

19 Robert Bork, *The Antitrust Paradox: A Policy at War with Itself* (New York: Basic Books, 1978), 117–46; Marc Allen Eisner, *Antitrust and the Triumph of Economics: Institutions, Expertise, and Policy Change* (Chapel Hill: University of North Carolina Press, 1991). For an interesting debate on antitrust policies, see Nolan E. Clark, "Antitrust Comes Full Circle: The Return to the Cartelization Standard," *Vanderbilt Law Review* 38 (October 1985): 64–76; and D. T. Ar-

menian, *Antitrust Policy: The Case for Repeal* (Washington, D.C.: Cato Institute, 1986).

20 Gregory Marchildon, ed., *Mergers and Acquisitions* (Cambridge, Mass.: Harvard University Press, 1991); Patrick Gaughan, *Mergers, Acquisitions, and Corporate Restructuring* (New York: John Wiley, 1996).

21 Public companies other than small businesses must submit annual reports on form 10-K of the Securities and Exchange Commission and quarterly reports on form 10-Q.

22 William M. Tsutsui, *Manufacturing Ideology: Scientific Management in Twentieth Century Japan* (Princeton, N.J.: Princeton University Press, 1970), 230–35; W. Edwards Deming, *The New Economics for Industry, Government, Education*, 2nd ed. (Cambridge, Mass.: Massachusetts Institute of Technology, Center for Advanced Engineering, 1994). This book includes his "System of Profound Knowledge" and his fourteen points for management.

23 Paul Osterman, "How Common Is Workplace Transformation and How Can We Explain Who Does It?" *Industrial and Labor Relations Review* 47 (January 1994): 173–88; Michael Novak, *Business as a Calling* (New York: Free Press, 1996); Peter Cappelli, *The New Deal at Work: Managing the Market-Driven Workforce* (Boston: Harvard Business School Press, 1999), 146–51.

24 Edward A. Finn Jr., "General Electric," *Forbes*, March 23, 1987, 75–76.

25 Anne B. Fisher, "Jungle Fever," *Fortune*, 12 March 1987, 13.

26 Bryan Burrough and John Helyar, *Barbarians at the Gate: The Fall of RJR Nabisco* (New York: Harper and Row, 1990); Connie Bruck, *The Predators' Ball: The Junk Bond Raiders and the Men Who Staked Them* (New York: Simon and Schuster, 1988); James B. Stewart, *Den of Thieves* (New York: Simon and Schuster, 1991).

27 Drexel Burnham Lambert specialized in selling junk bonds to federally regulated savings and loan companies, which, under the deregulatory Garn–St. Germaine Depository Institutions Act of 1982, were allowed to diversify their portfolios to include assets other than mortgages. By the end of the decade, rising concerns led to the reenactment of the Financial Reform, Recovery, and Enforcement Act of 1989 (FIRREA), which mandated liquidation of all junk bond portfolios by regulated savings and loan institutions by 1994. The rush to divest these assets contributed to Drexel Burnham Lambert's downfall.

28 Tom Peters and Robert Waterman Jr., *In Search of Excellence* (1982; New York: Collins Business Essentials, 2002), 35.

29 Richard Foster, *Innovation: The Attacker's Advantage* (New York: Summit Books, 1986); Gary Hamel and C. K. Prahalad, *Competing for the Future* (Cambridge, Mass.: Harvard University Press, 1994). Hamel, an academician and business consultant, attracted considerable attention in the late 1980s for his views that companies had to conceive of themselves as a "portfolio of core competencies" in order to radically transform themselves.

30 Thomas Petzenger Jr., *The New Pioneers: The Men and Women Who Are Transforming Workplace and Marketplace* (New York: Touchstone, 2000), 5.

31 There have been numerous books written about Bill Gates and Microsoft. On the early history of the company, see James Wallace and Jim Erickson, *Hard Drive: Bill Gates and the Making of the Microsoft Empire* (New York: Harper Business, 1993).

CHAPTER FIFTEEN

1 Ori Brafman and Rod Beckstrom, in *The Starfish and the Spider: The Unstoppable Power of Leaderless Organizations* (New York: Portfolio, 2006), analyze and compare centralized (spider) organizations and decentralized (starfish) organizations, with particular attention to the role of new technology.

2 Peter Cappelli, *The New Deal at Work: Managing the Market-Driven Workforce* (Boston: Harvard Business School Press, 1999), 14.

3 The ratio of managerial and administrative employees to the total workforce in the United States stood at roughly three times that of either Germany or Japan; see Sumantra Ghoshal and Christopher Bartlett, *The Individualized Corporation* (Boston: Harvard Business School Press, 1997), 267–69; see also Tom Peters, *Liberation Management* (New York: Alfred A. Knopf, 1992).

4 Rakesh Khurana, *Searching for a Corporate Savior: The Irrational Quest for the Charismatic CEO* (Princeton, N.J.: Princeton University Press, 2002). Management students divided roughly into three camps on the question of the importance of the CEO. The "leadership" school believes the CEO plays a critical role in a firm's performance. The "constraint" school sees the CEO's role sharply limited by internal and external restraints. A third school suggests that the pertinent question is "when does leadership matter" not "does it matter" as the leader's impact is "always highly case-sensitive."

5 Michael Hammer and James Champy, *Reengineering the Corporation* (New York: Harper Business, 1993). For the remarkable rise to prominence in the 1980s of "management gurus" and such management consulting firms as Boston Consulting Group and McKinsey and Company, see John Micklethwart and Adrian Woolridge, *The Witch Doctors: Making Sense of Management Gurus* (New York: Times Books/Random House, 1997); and Christopher D. McKenna, *The World's Newest Profession: Management Consulting in the Twentieth Century* (New York: Cambridge University Press, 2006).

6 Michael Hammer, "Is Work Bad for You?" *Atlantic Monthly*, August 1999, 87–93.

7 Gary Hamel and C. K. Prahaled, *Competing for the Future* (Cambridge, Mass.: Harvard University Press, 1994), 266–71.

8 Constantinos C. Markides, *Diversification, Refocusing, and Economic Performance* (Cambridge, Mass.: MIT Press, 1995), 8.

9 In 2005, Delphi filed for Chapter 11 bankruptcy. Its restructuring has been one of the biggest and most complex of any U.S. industrial company, with the outcome undecided as of early 2008.

10 In February 2008, GM offered buyouts to its remaining 74,000 unionized wageworkers in the United States in an effort to shrink its payrolls.

11 Kevin Phillips, *Wealth and Democracy: A Political History of the American Rich* (New York: Broadway Books, 2002), 151–55, 395.

12 In the 1960s, the pay of corporate CEOs was about twenty-five times that of hourly production workers; in the 1970s, the ratio was around thirty to one; in 1990 it was about ninety-six to one; ibid.

13 The Accounting Principles Board (APB) statement 25 (October 1972) handled options as capital adjustment transactions that did not flow through the income statement. The Financial Accounting Standards Board (FASB), the successor to APB, in statement 123, required that options be expensed, beginning in June 2005.

14 Jack Welch, *Winning* (New York: Harper Business, 2005).

15 John A. Byrne, *Chainsaw: The Notorious Career of Al Dunlap in the Era of Profit-at-Any-Price* (New York: Harper Business, 1999).

16 Two Stanford professors, James A. Collins and Jerry I. Porras, challenged the view that long-term planning was obsolete, in *Built to Last: Successful Habits of Visionary Companies* (New York: Harper Business, 1994), a study of eighteen companies from American Express to Walt Disney. It found that great companies were led by "clock builders," far-sighted businesspeople who viewed the company as their life work.

17 MIT Commission on Industrial Recovery, *Made in America: Regaining the Productive Edge* (Cambridge, Mass.: MIT Press, 1989).

18 Richard Foster, *Innovation: The Attacker's Advantage* (New York: Summit Books, 1986).

19 Bush pressured Greenspan to lower interest rates in 1991 and believed the Fed's failure to do so prolonged the recession and cost him his reelection. Bob Woodward, *Maestro: Greenspan and the American Boom* (New York: Simon and Schuster, 2000), 84–92.

20 For the dispute over who deserves credit for the prosperity of the 1990s, see Richard W. Stevenson, "The Battle of the Decades: Reaganomics vs. Clintonomics," *New York Times*, February 8, 2000, C1–2; and John W. Sloan, *The Reagan Effect: Economics and Presidential Leadership* (Lawrence: University Press of Kansas, 1999), which credits Reagan but is not uncritical of him.

21 The issue of the repeal of Glass-Steagall, the creation of all-purpose banks, and the subprime mortgage crisis that surfaced in 2007 all remain to be examined fully.

22 A striking difference between the speculative excesses of the 1990s and the

1980s was that the latter often involved "paper shuffling" (downsizing and LBOs) while the "hot" companies of the 1990s helped build the Internet and its attendant new technology.

23 Alan Greenspan, *The Age of Turbulence: Adventures in a New World* (New York: Penguin, 2007), 167–69.

24 Robert J. Shiller, *Irrational Exuberance* (Princeton, N.J.: Princeton University Press, 2000). Claims of a "New Era" or a "New Economy" have risen several times in prosperous periods throughout the twentieth century; see Martin S. Fridson, *It Was a Very Good Year: Extraordinary Moments in Stock Market History* (New York: John Wiley, 1998).

25 Greenspan, *Age of Turbulence*, 176–77, 201–2.

26 The generally accepted view is that AOL stock had been overvalued. There are those, however, who challenge this, arguing that a new accounting standard for valuing human capital in 2002 (FASB 241) that required the write-down of AOL's goodwill account to market value when it failed to deliver expected earnings had compelled the heavy postmerger write-downs.

27 Paul Krugman, *The Great Unraveling: Losing Our Way in the New Century* (New York: W. W. Norton, 2005), 49–51.

28 Gretchen Morgenstern and Timothy L. O'Brien, "When Citigroup Met World-Com," *New York Times*, May 16, 2004, Business Section, 1.

29 Lawrence E. Mitchell, *Corporate Irresponsibility: America's Newest Export* (New Haven: Yale University Press, 2001).

30 Krugman, *Great Unraveling*, 32.

31 Quoted in Gretchen Morgenstern, "The Financial Frontier's Last Deal," *New York Times*, December 21, 2002, C1.

32 Steve Lohr, "From Japan, Lessons in What Policies to Shun," *New York Times*, February 9, 2008, C1.

CHAPTER SIXTEEN

1 Suzanne Berger, *How We Compete: What Companies around the World Are Doing to Make It in Today's Global Economy* (New York: Currency Doubleday, 2006). This work is based on a five-year study of companies throughout the world by the MIT Industrial Performance Center.

2 For a survey of the literature and historical development of the global economy, see David Held et al., *Global Transformations* (Stanford: Stanford University Press, 1999). Jeffrey A. Frieden, *Global Capitalism: Its Rise and Fall in the Twentieth Century* (New York: W. W. Norton, 2006), provides an excellent overview.

3 On the tripartite theory, see Immanuel Wallerstein, *The Modern World System* (New York: Academic Press, 1974).

4 Cited in Douglas A. Irwin, "GATT Turns 60," *Wall Street Journal*, April 9, 2007, A16.

5 Ernest May, ed., *American Cold War Strategy: Interpreting NSC-68* (New York: St. Martin's, 1993), 40.

6 Paul A. Tiffany, *The Decline of American Steel: How Management, Labor, and Government Went Wrong* (New York: Oxford University Press, 1987), 272.

7 Robert Kuttner, *The End of Laissez-Faire: National Purpose and the Global Economy after the Cold War* (New York: Alfred A. Knopf, 1991), 26–27; Marie Laure Djelic, *Exporting the American Model: The Post-War Transformation of European Business* (New York: Oxford University Press, 1998).

8 According to William Borden, by 1947 the United States recognized that Germany and Japan formed "the key to the balance of power" in the Cold War. Germany was the pivot of the larger Marshall Plan, while "the Japanese recovery program formed the sole large-scale American effort in Asia." William S. Borden, *The Pacific Alliance: United States Foreign Economic Policy and Japanese Trade Recovery, 1947–1955* (Madison: University of Wisconsin Press, 1984), 15.

9 A superb analysis of the issues involved in the Bretton Woods Agreement, and especially differences between the U.S. and U.K. positions, is to be found in Robert Skidelsky, *John Maynard Keynes: Fighting for Freedom, 1937–1946* (New York: Viking, 2000), 319–36.

10 Michael Moore, *A World without Walls: Freedom, Development, Free Trade, and Global Governance* (Cambridge: Cambridge University Press, 2003). The author, the director general of the World Trade Organization, is a strong supporter of its policies.

11 Scholars who believe that central banks can implement long-term policies that have significant impact on exchange rates point to Japan and China, whose central banks have long maintained low interest rates to encourage speculators to borrow their currency with which to buy higher-yielding U.S. securities. This is done to maintain a high U.S. dollar exchange rate against their currencies, thus encouraging exports.

12 "The Transition: Excerpts from a Conference Called by Clinton on the State of the Economy," *New York Times*, December 16, 1992, 13.

13 Fred Bergsten and Marcus Noland, *Reconcilable Differences? United States–Japanese Economic Conflict* (Washington, D.C.: Institute for International Economics, 1993).

14 In 1981, the United States pressured Tokyo to accept a quota on cars sent to the United States. In response, the Japanese adapted their marketing strategy, sending higher-priced, upscale models. The handsome profits realized were used in part to build factories in America to "manufacture" quota-exempt Hondas and Toyotas—known as transplants and often containing extensive numbers of parts produced elsewhere.

15 In a prescient study published in 1989, Karel Van Wolferon noted weaknesses in the system—especially that elected officeholders did not play a decisive role in government and that Japan's political system was marred by widespread corruption. *The Enigma of Japanese Power* (New York: Random House, 1989), 44–49.

16 Robert Ozaki, *Human Capitalism: The Japanese Enterprise System as World Model* (New York: Penguin, 1991).

17 Elizabeth Becker, "U.N. Study Brought Uneven Gains," *New York Times*, February 24, 2004, A12.

18 "Backlash: Behind the Anxiety of Globalization," *Business Week*, April 24, 2000, 61.

19 Paul A. Samuelson, "Where Ricardo and Mill Rebut and Confirm Agreements of Mainstream Economists: Supporting Globalization," *Journal of Economic Perspectives* 18, no. 3 (2004): 135–46.

20 Robert Gilpin, *The Challenge of Global Capitalism: The World Economy in the 21st Century* (Princeton, N.J.: Princeton University Press, 2000).

21 Parag Khanna, "Waving Goodbye to Hegemony," *New York Times Magazine*, January 27, 2008, 34–41.

22 Jeffrey E. Garten, *A Cold Peace: America, Japan, Germany, and the Struggle for Supremacy* (New York: Times Books, 1993).

23 Jeffrey Sachs and Howard J. Schatz, "Globalization and the U.S. Labor Market," *American Economic Review* 86, no. 2 (May 1996): 234–39; Dani Rodrik, *Has Globalization Gone Too Far?* (Washington, D.C.: Institute for International Education, 1997), 37–46.

24 Roger Lowenstein, *When Genius Failed: The Rise and Fall of Long-Term Capital Management* (New York: Random House, 2000).

25 William Grieder, *One World Ready or Not: The Manic Logic of Global Capitalism* (New York: Simon and Schuster, 1997); Saskia Sassen, *Globalization and Its Discontents* (New York: New Press, 1999).

26 *Human Development Report 1999: Globalization with a Human Face* (New York: United Nations Development Program/Oxford University Press, 1999), 236–38.

27 Joseph E. Stiglitz, *Making Globalization Work*, with a new foreword (New York: W. W. Norton, 2007), 169–74.

28 The World Bank has received especially harsh criticism as being ineffectual or worse; see William Easterly, *The Elusive Quest for Growth* (Cambridge, Mass.: MIT Press, 2001). Easterly, a senior economist at the World Bank, argues that the World Bank failed to raise growth rates in the countries it tried to help.

29 Alan Blinder, "Offshoring: The Next Industrial Revolution?" *Foreign Affairs* 85 (March/April 2006): 64.

30 The critical importance of political factors in sustaining a global economy is

emphasized by Robert Gilpin (and Jean Millis Gilpin) in *The Challenge of Global Capitalism*.

CHAPTER SEVENTEEN

1 Richard N. Langlois, "The Vanishing Hand: The Changing Dynamics of Industrial Capitalism," *Industrial and Corporate Change* 12 (April 2003): 351–85.

2 Scholars preoccupied by the rise of big business have devoted comparatively little attention to small and medium-sized firms. One scholar who has sought to redress this imbalance is Philip Scranton, in *Proprietary Capitalism: The Textile Manufacture at Philadelphia, 1800–1865* (New York: Cambridge University Press, 1983); and *Endless Novelty: Specialty Production and American Industrialization, 1865–1925* (Princeton, N.J.: Princeton University Press, 1997).

3 Henry Stimson, "The Small Business as a School of Manhood," *Atlantic Monthly* 93 (1904): 337–40.

4 http://www.sba.gov/services/contractingopportunities/sizestandardtopics/size/index.htr. Accessed June 6, 2008.

5 Mansel G. Blackford, *A History of Small Business in America*, 2nd ed. (Chapel Hill: University of North Carolina Press, 2003), 1, 135–36.

6 "Only in farming did small business dramatically decrease in significance. In most other fields—in the sales and service sectors, especially—small firms, while losing market shares to large concerns, remained important"; ibid., 3. Blackford provides a useful corrective to the view that small business lost its economic importance early in the twentieth century. On small business and manufacturing, see Scranton, *Endless Novelty*, 4–11.

7 Thomas Dicke, "The Small Business Tradition," *OAH Magazine of History* 11 (Fall 1996): 11–16; Robert Averitt, *The Dual Economy* (New York: W. W. Norton, 1971).

8 John Kenneth Galbraith, *The New Industrial State* (Boston: Houghton Mifflin, 1967), 97. Galbraith argued that large firms are the engines of economic change because size gives them the resources to undertake grand projects and large market share provides them with the incentives to do so. See his *American Capitalism: The Concept of Countervailing Power* (Boston: Houghton Mifflin, 1952), 117–22.

9 Jonathan J. Bean, *Beyond the Broker State: A History of the Federal Government's Policies towards Small Business, 1936–61* (Chapel Hill: University of North Carolina Press, 1996), 10–11; Burton R. Fisher and Stephen B. Whithey, *Big Business as the People See It* (Ann Arbor: University of Michigan Institute for Social Research, 1951), 21–22, 34–38. Governmental set-asides for small business often do not work because of big firm–small firm collusion. There is also a

question of the value of set-asides from the standpoint of the efficient allocation of resources.

10 Small business is consistently undercounted because much of it takes place in the so-called underground economy, where no taxes are paid or records are kept.

11 Clayton M. Christensen, *The Innovator's Dilemma: When New Technologies Cause Great Firms to Fail* (Boston: Harvard Business School, 1997); Richard Foster and Sarah Kaplan, *Creative Destruction: When Companies That Are Built to Last Underperform the Market—and How to Successfully Transform Them* (New York: Doubleday, 2001).

12 Ray Oakley, Roy Rothwell, and Sarah Cooper, *Management of Innovation in High Technology Small Firms* (New York: Quorum Books, 1988).

13 Zoltan J. Acs and David B. Audretsch, *Innovation and Small Firms* (Cambridge, Mass.: MIT Press, 1990).

14 David Birch, *Job Creation in America: How Our Smallest Companies Put the Most People to Work* (New York: Free Press, 1987); Charles Brown, James Hamilton, and James Medoff, *Employers Large and Small* (Cambridge, Mass.: Harvard University Press, 1990), 88, 89–91.

15 Bennett Harrison, *Lean and Mean: The Changing Landscape of Corporate Power in the Age of Flexibility* (New York: Free Press, 1994), 20.

16 Ibid. See also Paul Du Gay, *The Values of Bureaucracy* (New York: Oxford University Press, 2005). As the title suggests, Du Gay offers a very different view from Harrison of the importance of bureaucracy.

17 D. Hugh Whittaker and Robert E. Cole, *Recovery from Success: Innovation and Technology Management in Japan* (New York: Oxford University Press, 2006); see also Peter Drucker, *Managing in a Time of Great Change* (New York: Truman Talley Books, 1995).

18 Hamilton, Medoff, and Brown, *Employers Large and Small.*

19 Joseph Schumpeter, *The Theory of Economic Development* (Cambridge, Mass.: Harvard University Press, 1934), 93; see also Thomas K. McCraw, *Prophet of Innovation: Joseph Schumpeter and Creative Destruction* (Cambridge, Mass.: Belknap Press of Harvard University Press, 2007).

20 Jonathan Hughes offers ten biographical sketches in an attempt to link the entrepreneurial activity of individuals to larger economic forces, in his engaging *The Vital Few: The Entrepreneur and American Economic Progress*, expanded ed. (New York: Oxford University Press, 1986).

21 Eric Schlosser, *Fast Food Nation* (2002; New York: Harper Perennial, 2005), 5; Stan Luxenberg, *Roadside Empires: How the Chains Franchised America* (New York: Viking, 1985); Carrie Shook and Robert L. Shook, *Franchising: The Business Strategy That Changed the World* (Englewood Cliffs, N.J.: Prentice Hall, 1993),

especially the introduction and chap. 7. The standard history of franchising is Thomas S. Dicke's excellent *Franchising in America: The Development of a Business Method, 1840–1980* (Chapel Hill: University of North Carolina Press, 1992).

22 Ray Kroc, with Robert Anderson, *Grinding It Out: The Making of McDonald's* (New York: St. Martin's, 1987); John F. Love, *McDonald's: Behind the Arches* (Toronto: Bantam Books, 1987).

23 Timothy Bates, "Survival Patterns among Newcomers to Franchising," *Journal of Business Ventures* 13, no. 2 (1998): 113–30.

24 On agribusiness, see Wayne G. Boehl Jr., *Cargill: Trading the World's Grain* (Hanover, N.H.: University Press of New England, 1992); and Jay Statten, *The Embattled Farmer* (Golden, Colo.: Fulcrum, 1987).

25 Small Business Administration, *Annual Report on Small Business and Competition* (Washington, D.C.: Government Printing Office, 1996), 64–66.

26 Charles Brown, James Hamilton, and James Medoff, *Employers Large and Small* (Cambridge, Mass.: Harvard University Press, 1990).

27 John David Skrentny, *The Minority Rights Revolution* (Cambridge, Mass.: Harvard University Press, 2002), 242–43. Many of the gains in public employment resulted from affirmative action programs; see also Juliet E. K. Walker, *The History of Black Business in America: Capitalism, Race, Entrepreneurship* (New York: Twayne, 1998). An irony of Jim Crow laws and the de facto practice of segregation is that they provided black entrepreneurial opportunities, which were lost when the laws ended.

28 Ivan Light and Carolyn Rosenstein, *Race, Ethnicity, and Entrepreneurship in Urban America* (New York: Aldine De Gruyter, 1995), 17–27. In 1999 female entrepreneurs owned 9.1 million businesses in the United States, or 40 percent of the total, but most of these were tiny enterprises whose owners complained that they were ignored by venture capitalists. Ellen Almer, "What Women Need to Know about Starting Up," *New York Times*, November 27, 2000, C9; Jonathan J. Bean, *Big Government and Affirmative Action: The Scandalous History of the Small Business Administration* (Lexington: University Press of Kentucky, 2001).

29 Kyeyoung Park, *The Korean American Dream: Immigrants and Small Business in New York City* (Ithaca, N.Y.: Cornell University Press, 1997); Robert D. Putnam, *Bowling Alone: The Collapse and Revival of American Community* (New York: Simon and Schuster, 2000), 19–21; Robert W. Fairlie and Bruce D. Meyer, "Does Immigration Hurt American Self-Employment?" *NBER Working Papers* 6265 (Washington, D.C.: National Bureau of Economic Research, 1997).

30 Walter A. Friedman and Richard S. Tedlow, "Statistical Portraits of American Business Elites," *Business History* 45, no. 4 (October 2003): 89–113.

31 Harrison, *Lean and Mean*.

32 Ronald Coase, "The Nature of the Firm," *Economica* 4 (November 1937): 386–405.

33 Oliver Williamson, *The Economic Institutions of Capitalism* (New York: Free Press, 1985), chap. 11, "The Modern Corporation." For an interesting effort to apply and develop Williamson's ideas, see Naomi R. Lamoreaux, Daniel M. G. Raff, and Peter Temin, "Beyond Markets and Hierarchies: Towards a New Synthesis of American Business History," *American Historical Review* 108 (April 2003): 404–33.

CHAPTER EIGHTEEN

1 "Letter to the Workingman's Association of New York," in Abraham Lincoln, *The Complete Works of Abraham Lincoln*, ed. Roy Basler (New Brunswick, N.J.: Rutgers University Press, 1956), 7:304.

2 David Cay Johnston, "Gap between Rich and Poor Substantially Wider," *New York Times*, September 5, 1999, 1.

3 Kevin Phillips, *Wealth and Democracy: A Political History of the American Rich* (New York: Broadway Books, 2002), 103; Robert D. Putnam, *Bowling Alone: The Collapse and Revival of American Community* (New York: Simon and Schuster, 2000), 359.

4 Cited by Albert R. Hunt, "People and Politics," *Wall Street Journal*, April 20, 2000, A27. See also Gary Burtless, "Has U.S. Income Inequality Really Increased?" Brookings Institution Paper, January 11, 2007.

5 Walter Friedman and Richard S. Tedlow, "Statistical Portraits of American Business Elites," *Business History* 45, no. 4 (October 2003): 89–113.

6 The same trend toward occupational decline in manufacturing is occurring at equally rapid rates in other major industrial nations, including West Germany and Japan. On the decline in manufacturing jobs, see *Economist*, April 26, 1997, 78–79.

7 Lawrence Mishel, Jared Bernstein, and John Schmitt, *The State of Working America, 1989–99* (Ithaca, N.Y.: Cornell University Press, 1999).

8 In European nations, such as the Netherlands and Denmark, where strong unions and governments have acted to keep up wages and protect job security, the result has been fewer new jobs and much higher unemployment among the young in percentage terms than in the United States.

9 Aaron Bernstein, "Backlash: Behind the Anxiety over Globalization," *Business Week*, April 24, 2000, 42. In 2000, the U.S. Department of Commerce estimated that in the second half of the 1990s, 25 percent of workers losing their jobs had not found another three years later, and those that did earned an average of 7 percent less in the new job.

10 The literature on the affirmative action controversy is large. Especially good on the subject is Michael Rosenfeld, *Affirmative Action and Justice: A Philosophical and Constitutional Inquiry* (New Haven: Yale University Press, 1991).

11 Milton Friedman, "The Social Responsibility of Business Is to Increase Its Profits," *New York Times Magazine*, September 13, 1970, 33, 122–26; "Milton Friedman Responds," *Business and Society Review* 1 (Spring 1972): 5–10. For a critique of Friedman, see Robert Almeder, "The Ethics of Profit: Reflections on Corporate Responsibility," *Business and Society Review* 8 (Winter 1980): 7–15.

12 Christopher Beem, *The Necessity of Politics: Reclaiming American Public Life* (Chicago: University of Chicago Press, 1999), 116–19.

13 An interesting effort by a philosopher to offer perspective on the intractable issues of corporate integrity and social responsibility is Marvin T. Brown, *Corporate Integrity: Rethinking Organizational Ethics and Leadership* (New York: Cambridge University Press, 2005).

14 Adolf A. Berle Jr., *The 20th Century Capitalist Revolution* (New York: Harcourt, Brace, 1954), 163.

15 Adam Smith, *The Theory of Moral Sentiments*, ed. Knud Haakonssen (Cambridge: Cambridge University Press, 2002). A consideration of several types of capitalism is offered in William J. Baumol, Robert E. Litan, and Carl J. Schramm, *Good Capitalism, Bad Capitalism, and the Economics of Growth and Prosperity* (New Haven: Yale University Press, 2007).

16 Mark J. Roe, *Political Determinants of Corporate Governance* (New York: Oxford University Press, 2003).

17 One economic historian has noted that many of the entrepreneurs, such as Rockefeller or Pullman, were not only totally identified with their companies, "but for a time whole industries came to be identified with the names of the powerful individuals who dominated them." Glenn Porter, "Industrialization and the Rise of Big Business," in *The Gilded Age: Essays on the Origins of Modern America*, ed. Charles W. Calhoun (Wilmington, Del.: Scholarly Resources, 1997), 9, 14–15.

18 Adolf A. Berle and Gardiner C. Means, *The Modern Corporation and Private Property* (New York: Macmillan, 1932); John Kenneth Galbraith, *The New Industrial State* (Boston: Houghton Mifflin, 1967). Thorstein Veblen had earlier sought to draw attention to emerging corporate management problems, in *Absentee Ownership and Business Enterprise in Recent Times* (New York: B. W. Huensch, 1923), but this book received little general notice.

19 Neil Fligstein, *The Transformation of Corporate Control* (Cambridge, Mass.: Harvard University Press, 1990), 86–89; Henry Mintzberg, *The Rise and Fall of Strategic Planning: Preconceiving Roles for Planning, Plans, Planners* (New York: Free Press, 1994), 111.

20 Bryan Burrough and John Helyar, *Barbarians at the Gate: The Fall of RJR Nabisco* (New York: Harper and Row, 1990).

21 E. J. Dionne, "Shareholders and Workers in the Same Camp," *Washington Post*, February 20, 2002, 3.

22 Frank Portnoy, "The Gamble of Short-Term Pain for Long-Term Gain," *Financial Times*, February 4, 2008, 7; Michael Useem, *Investor Capitalism: How Money Managers Are Changing the Face of Corporate Capitalism* (New York: Basic Books, 1996).

23 Bruce Ackerman and Ann Alstott, *The Stakeholder Society* (New Haven: Yale University Press, 1999); Robert Ozaki, *Human Capitalism: The Japanese Enterprise System as World Model* (New York: Penguin, 1991).

24 Edmund L. Andrews, "Germany Weighs Overhaul of 'Consensus' Capitalism," *New York Times*, February 14, 2001, C1; Jonathan Charkham, *Keeping Good Company: A Study of Corporate Governance in Five Countries* (Oxford: Clarendon, 1994), 13–17.

25 John Rawls, *A Theory of Justice* (Cambridge, Mass.: Harvard University Press, 1971), 504–5.

26 Herbert Kitschelt et al., eds., *Continuity and Change in Contemporary Capitalism* (New York: Cambridge University Press, 1999).

27 Putnam, *Bowling Alone*, 21.

28 Alexis de Tocqueville, *Democracy in America*, ed. J. P. Mayer, trans. George Lawrence (Garden City, N.Y.: Doubleday, 1969), 526.

29 The quote from *Theory of Moral Sentiments* is in Ian Simpson Ross, *The Life of Adam Smith* (Oxford: Clarendon, 1995), 419; Rawls, *Theory of Justice*, 17, 504–5.

Index

American Sugar Refining Company, 190

Americans with Disabilities Act, 355

American system of interchangeable parts, 79, 82, 117–18

American Telephone and Telegraph (AT&T), 247, 250, 352–53

American Tobacco Company, 164, 180, 199, 252

America Online. *See* AOL–Time Warner merger

Andersen, Kurt, 350

Antitrust enforcement: Theodore Roosevelt administration and, 197–98, 214–15, 219; Wilson administration and, 219–20; during World War I and World War II, 230, 231, 286; in Great Depression era, 278; FDR administration and, 285–86; Nixon administration and, 289, 312; post–World War II, 299; conglomerates encouraged by, 308; Eisenhower administration and, 308, 504 (n. 29); Reagan administration and, 352–53, 356–57; Carter administration and, 356; Clinton administration and, 376; globalization and, 401

Antitrust legislation, 198, 212–13, 219–20, 232, 288–89, 421. *See also specific laws*

The Antitrust Paradox (Bork), 356

AOL–Time Warner merger, 378, 379, 382

Arms manufacturing, 78–79, 82, 92, 229, 232

Arnold, Thurman, 285–86

Arthur Anderson, 383–84

Artificial-entity theory, 114, 186

"The Art of Money-Getting" (Barnum), 82, 83

Associative state, 252–54, 278

Astor, John Jacob, 99, 105

Autobiography (Franklin), 38

Automobile industry: assembly line system, 204–5, 368–69; World War I, 229; impact, economic and cultural, 234, 238–46, 300–301; historical overview, 240; foreign market growth, 309; unions and, 330; regulation of, 332, 341; global competition in, 341, 368, 401–3; bailouts, 341, 451, 506 (n. 19); small business suppliers to, 435–36. *See also specific automobile companies*

Automobile safety standards, 333

The Ax (Westlake), 366

Babbitt (Lewis), 246

Baby boom generation, 297, 300, 331–32, 423

Bailyn, Bernard, 37, 47, 51

Banking Act of 1862, 218

Banking Act of 1933, 275

Banking Act of 1935, 276

Banking industry, 98, 275–76, 354–55, 384–87, 397–400, 402–4. *See also* Federal Reserve System; *specific banks*

The Bank Note Detector (Thompson), 116

Bank of Augusta v. Earle, 114

Bank of the United States, 69–70, 98, 260

Banks, state-chartered, 97–98, 115, 116

Barnum, P. T., 82, 83

Barton, Bruce, 246, 251

Barton, Durstine and Osborn, 202, 244, 251

Baruch, Bernard, 229–30, 257, 278

Bates, Timothy, 433–34

366; employee relations, 367–68; by owners, 370, 455; institutional owners, power of, 372, 456–58, 459–60; primary responsibility of, 451, 454, 456; decentralized, 497 (n. 18). *See also specific systems*

Corporations: eighteenth century, 112–14; responsibility to community, 113, 114, 115, 214, 232, 246, 316, 450–51, 452; constitutional protections of, 113–14, 186, 187; growth in, 116–17; emergence of, 147–49, 159; rationalization of, 152, 158; modern, rise of, 155–56, 158; capital investment, 157–60, 194, 335–36, 340, 342, 348; integration in, 157–62, 164–65, 194–95, 201, 368, 421–22; power of, economic, 179–80, 200, 250; public image, 186–87, 196, 198, 231, 251–52, 315–16; defined, 187; oligopoly in, 200–201; profitability, 200–201, 203–5, 225, 297, 300, 311–14, 367; M-form organization, 232–33, 242–43, 304, 307; quasi-public, 251; failure of, 258, 382–83; diversification in, 304–8, 368; conglomerate building in, 306, 307–8, 310–14; multinational, 306–10, 312, 397, 400; 1970s inertia in, 341–43; bigness, celebration of, 343; tax cuts for, 346; foreign ownership of, 348; de-integration, 359; 1990–2008 overview, 364–67; criminal activity and scandal in, 383–85, 451; transnational, 400, 503 (n. 20); small business vs., 420–23, 425, 437, 439–41; small business alliances and, 423–24, 435–36; minority recruitment and promotion, 449; twenty-first century, 450–54

Cosmetics industry, 247

Cotton production, 77–78, 84, 122–23, 248

Council of Economic Advisers, 302

Council on Economic Priorities, U.S., 454

Court-packing bill of 1937, 281

Craft manufacturing/craft workers, 75, 79–81, 89–90, 92–93, 169, 171

Creating the Corporate Soul (Marchand), 352

Credit, consumer, 245, 245–46, 292, 317, 386

Crèvecoeur, J. Hector St. John de, 44

Croly, Herbert, 212, 224

The Cultural Contradictions of Capitalism (Bell), 328

Culture, American: of individualism and independence, 43–49, 52, 81, 465; of equality, 46, 48, 49, 51–52; youth in, 222; of optimism, 236; of entitlement, 289; counterculture, 322; of immediate gratification, 328; corporate, of infectious greed, 458. *See also* Consumer culture

Dartmouth College v. Woodward, 67, 113–14

Darwin, Charles, 185–86

Davis, George, 318

Debs, Eugene, 168, 187

Debt-deflation theory, 497 (n. 37)

Declaration of Independence, 55–56, 60, 62

Deere, John, 94

Defense spending, 78–79, 92, 229, 232, 292, 299, 303–4, 312, 461

Deming, W. Edwards, 358

Democratic Party, 298, 340

Democratic Republicans, 68–69

Department of Defense, U.S., 305, 375

Madison, John, 53, 63, 64, 69
Madison Avenue, 203, 235
Mahan, Alfred Thayer, 191–92
Mail-order houses, 163, 203
Maine, Henry, 177
Maloney Act, 277
The Managerial Revolution (Burnham), 287
Managing (Geneen), 312
Mandeville, Bernard, 59–60
The Man in the Gray Flannel Suit (Wilson), 315
The Man Nobody Knows (Barton), 246
Manufactories, 58, 91
Manufacturing: innovation in, 57–58; putting-out system of, 57–58, 74–75, 92; factory system, 58–59, 74–75, 87–94; ethic of production, 60; quality in, 67, 169–70, 359; mass production in, 76–80, 100–102, 149–50, 160–62, 170–71, 223; growth in, 86–87, 117; nonfactory production and, 91; urbanization of, 97; global competition in, 117, 149, 335, 336–37, 340–43, 401–2; consumers, benefits to, 125–26; capital financing, 146–47, 292, 296; mechanized technology and growth in, 151–53; standardization in, 157, 171; assembly line system and, 167–68, 204–6; inside contracting practices of, 169–70; management systems, 169–73, 223, 225–28; sick industries and, 248; market segmentation and profitability, 341. *See also* Industrialization
—productivity: value of goods produced, 149, 175; 1866–80, 170, 171, 204–6, 225–28, 235, 249; working conditions and, 227–28; 1940–45, 284, 291, 296; 1945–80, 295, 313;

327, 332, 335, 342, 362; 1990s–2000s, 365, 376, 377, 379, 405
Marbury v. Madison, 66
Marchand, Roland, 235, 236, 352
Marginal utility theory, 282
Maritime insurance, 37
Market economy, 19, 25
Marketing, 149–50, 160–62, 163, 185, 235, 243–44, 306, 315, 427
Marshall, Alfred, 96, 282
Marshall, John, 62, 65–68, 113–14
Marshall Field's, 162, 348
Marshall Plan, 395
Marx, Karl, 9, 10, 13, 57, 202, 349, 392, 450
Materialism, 466
Mather, Cotton, 28, 39
Mayo, Elton, 227–28
McCormick, Cyrus, 94, 179
McGuffey, William Holmes, 129
McKinley, William, 192, 195, 294
Means, Gardiner C., 250, 256, 456
Medbery, James K., 123
Medicare, 347
Men and Mysteries of Wall Street (Medbery), 123
Mercantile Agency (Dun and Bradstreet), 95
Mercantilism, 26, 34–35, 46, 59–60
Merchant banking, 359
Merchant class, 16–20, 25–26, 37–38
The Merchant of Prato (Origo), 23
The Merchant of Venice (Shakespeare), 20
Merger movement, 194–97, 255–56, 306, 310–14, 348, 351, 356–60, 377–79
Microsoft Corporation, 356, 362, 363, 376, 377, 381–83, 423
Middle class, 17, 28, 100–103, 125, 162–64, 221–23, 235, 437–38

Professional Air Traffic Controllers
Organization (PATCO), 346–47
Progress and Poverty (George), 183
Progressive Era reform movement,
183–86, 211–14, 220–22
Progressive Party, 214
The Promise of American Life (Croly),
212
Property rights, 21, 26, 39, 44–45,
62–64, 66–67
Protestant ethic, 23–25, 39
*The Protestant Ethic and the Spirit of
Capitalism* (Weber), 23
Public good. *See* Society
Public land grants, 108
Public relations industry, 198, 203,
251–52, 315, 318
Public Utility Holding Company Act
of 1935, 277
Pujo Committee, 216
Pullman, George M., 107, 155, 165–
70, 518 (n. 17)
Pure Food and Drug Act, 197
Pursuing Happiness (Lebergott), 351
Putting-out system, 74–75, 92

Radio industry, 238
Railroad industry: capital financing,
106, 108–9, 121, 126–28, 142, 143,
145; consolidation and standardization in, 106–7; mergers in, 107–8,
196–97; management in, 110–12;
1877 labor strike and, 124; steel
industry and, 126, 136–41; consumer culture and, 126, 160;
magnates, 126–28, 142–47, 196;
regulation and deregulation, 128,
145, 188, 352; Morganizing, 144–45;
competition faced by, 144–45, 205,
248; time zones and, 150; innovation in, 166; bailouts, 451

Raskin, Jacob, 279
Rawls, John, 462
Reagan, Ronald, administration of,
272, 300, 343–47, 351–57, 359,
417
Reaganomics, 346
Real estate, speculation and develop-
ment, 98, 106, 236, 292, 355
Reengineering, 351–55, 357–62, 367–
69, 371–73
Reengineering the Corporation (Ham-
mer and Champy), 367
*Regents of the University of California v.
Bakke*, 318
Religion and capitalism, 19–20, 23–
25
Report on Roads and Canals (Gallatin),
71
Republican Party, 118, 120, 214, 216,
494 (n. 34)
Resolution and Trust Corporation,
354–55
Restaurant industry, 237, 248
Retail sales, 162–64, 203, 237–38,
245–46, 301, 422
Ricardo, David, 391, 397, 401
Riesman, David, 315
"The Rights of the British Colony
Asserted and Proved" (Otis), 50
The Rise of Silas Lapham (Howells),
186
"The Road to Business Success: A
Talk to Young Men" (Carnegie), 136
Robber barons, 105, 179
The Robber Barons (Josephson), 124
Robinson-Patman Act, 288
Rockefeller, John D., 120, 129–32,
140, 147, 156, 157, 164, 179, 196,
518 (n. 17)
Rodham, Hillary, 316
Rohatyn, Felix G., 351–55

historically, 125, 146, 165, 419; retail, 160–64, 202, 237, 288–89; advantages to, 279, 417–18, 420, 421, 423, 426–27, 428; legislation affecting, 288–89; new jobs created by, 417, 423, 425–26, 437; significance of, 417–18; diversity in, 418; values symbolized by, 418–19; criteria defining, 419–20, 423–24; big business vs., 420–23, 425, 437, 439–41; big business alliances, 423–24, 435–36; failure of, 426–27, 436–37, 439; political savvy/ influence of, 428–29; franchise operations, 431–34; agricultural sector, 434–35; minorities and, 437–39; future of, 439

Smith, Adam, 10, 14, 44, 51, 56–62, 94, 125, 158, 230, 351, 411, 454, 467

Smithsonian Agreement, 321

Smoot-Hawley Tariff Act, 261

Social Darwinism, 186

Social Gospel movement, 185–86

Social Security system, 280, 346, 347, 500 (n. 14)

Society: individual in, 56–62, 203, 349–51; inventing national community in, 64–65; corporate responsibility to, 113, 114, 115, 126, 232, 246, 450–54; class mobility, 135–36; material success, obsession with, 234–36; idealized, 235–36; family values and, 297–98, 299, 300; conformity in, 298, 300, 315; social movements, 318–20, 322. *See also* Consumer culture

Sombart, Werner, 10, 175, 249

Soviet Union, 347, 396, 399

Spanish-American War, 191–92

Spaur, Charles B., 179–80

Specie Circular Act, 98

Specifications Bureau, U.S. Commerce Department, 254

Spencer, Herbert, 186

Stagflation, 321, 325, 326–27, 328–29, 346

Staggers Rail Act, 352

Standard Oil Company of Ohio, 129–32, 134, 156, 164, 165, 180, 193, 197–98

Standard Oil of New Jersey, 134–35, 199

Standard Oil Trust, 133–34, 186

States: rights, 64–65, 67, 118, 190–91; corporate regulatory powers of, 64–65, 112–15, 121, 134–35, 187–88

Steam power, 72, 151, 170, 174, 266

Steavens, G. W., 125

Steel industry, 126, 136–41, 156, 160, 170, 194–95, 230, 394, 446

Steffens, Lincoln, 143, 233

Stock exchanges, regulation of, 276–77. *See also* New York Stock Exchange

Stock jobbing, 108–10

Stockman, David, 345

Stock market: institutional investors, 159–60, 194, 317, 326, 459–60; investment climates, 200, 236, 308, 381, 383; bear market of 1973–74, 314, 326; primary function of, 357; futures, 361; holding periods, 372; individual investors, 380, 460; 2000–2002 slide, 381–82

Stocks and Stock-Jobbing in Wall Street with Sketches of Brokers and Fancy Stocks (anon.), 109

Stock watering, 127, 144

Suburbs, 238–39, 292, 297–98, 501 (n. 6)

Success, determinants of, 22

Tugwell, Rexford, 278, 285

Turner, Frederick Jackson, 68, 184

Turn of the Century (Andersen), 350

Twain, Mark, 119, 123

The 20th Century Capitalist Revolution (Berle), 453

Two Treatises on Government (Locke), 53

Underwood Tariff Act, 216

Underwriting syndicates, 195

Union membership, 178, 254, 280, 299, 331–32

Unions, 89–91, 177–78, 224, 226–27, 230–31, 254, 280–81, 286–87, 298, 316, 330–31, 346–47, 352, 408–9. *See also specific industries*

United Automobile Workers (UAW), 330, 402

United States: Articles of Confederation, 62, 65; expansionism, 68, 70–71, 86, 105, 191–92; migration trends, 122, 124, 290, 299; foreign policy, post–World War II, 295; isolationism, 302; 1960s, 316–20; 1970s, 320–22, 325–26, 335–43; 1990–2008, 364–65, 375–79; imperialism, 389, 410, 413, 414, 415; twenty-first century, 443, 448, 461–67; inequality in, 444–49; social welfare system, 452–53, 463; September 11, 2001, terrorist attacks, 461; social capital, 464–66

—and global economy: historically, 191–94, 393; post–World War II, 295–96, 299, 393–97; competitiveness, 306–7, 321, 327–28, 335, 336–37, 340–43, 348, 349, 394–95; trade relations, 400–401; industrial adaptation, 405–7. *See also* Economy—global

—government: business influence in, 25–26, 37, 179–80, 186–87, 197, 428–29; two-party system, 68–69; Senate millionaires, 124; regulatory role, 184–87; economic interventionist policies, 294, 302–4, 316, 328; expansion of power, 294–96; defense spending, 299, 303–4, 347; budget deficit and national debt, 317, 321–22, 347, 373–77, 379–80; trade balance, 320–21, 328, 395, 401–5; monetary policies, 329–30; deregulation, 332–33, 351–55; conservatism in, 338–40; bailouts, 341, 451, 506 (n. 19); downsizing in, 345–47, 352; trade relations, 374, 396; foreign aid spending, 395–96

—population: colonies, 32, 33; 1776–1820, 70; 1820–1860, 83, 87, 103, 117; 1900, 185; 1945–73, 296, 297, 299, 300

U.S. Steel Corporation, 140, 160, 194–95, 197–98, 199, 200, 214–15, 455

United States v. Addyston Pipe and Steel Company, 191

United States v. E. C. Knight Company, 190

United States v. United States Steel Corp., 232

United Steel Workers of America, 316, 330, 331

Unsafe at Any Speed (Nader), 341

Urban growth and development, 16–18, 32, 94–97, 117, 122, 124, 162, 176–77, 184–85, 214, 248, 290

Uruguay Pact, 398

Utility Companies Holding Act, 280

Utility holding companies, regulation of, 277, 280

Values, cultural and social: capitalism's replacement of, 19–20, 150; critical to America, 25; family, post–World War II, 297–98, 299, 300; divorce rates and, 336, 364; corporate, 358, 383, 458; small business as signifying, 418–19

Van Buren, Martin, administration of, 89

Vanderbilt, Cornelius, 105, 123, 144, 179

Vanderbilt, William H., 126, 144, 165

Vanderbilt heirs, wealth of, 124

Veblen, Thorstein, 89–90, 149, 156–57, 158, 177, 185, 186

Versailles Treaty, 255–56, 282

Vietnam, 317, 321, 338

Virginia Company, 29–31

The Visible Hand (Chandler), 421

Visible hand theory, 158

Volker, Paul A., 334, 346

Voting trust, 132–33, 135, 145

Wabash v. Illinois, 188

Wage gap, 1990–2008, 369

Wagner Act, 280–81

Walden (Thoreau), 342

Wall Street, 108–10, 127–28, 160, 268, 366

Wall Street (film), 357

Wall Street Journal, 127, 423

Wal-Mart, 418, 422, 427, 447

Waltham System, 76

War Industries Board (WIB), 229–30

Warner, Charles Dudley, 123

War of 1812, 74, 75

War Production Board, 278, 291

Washington, George, 46, 66, 78

"Waste in Industry" (Hoover), 253

Watergate scandal, 321, 338, 451

Waterman, Robert H., 342–43, 362

Watson, Glen, 318

Wealth against Commonwealth (Lloyd), 179

Wealth gap, 177, 501 (n. 24); 1820–1900, 99–100, 123–25, 127, 141, 180; 1920s–40s, 249, 291, 408; 1970s–80s, 337, 343, 348–49, 444; 1990s–2000s, 369, 408, 413–14, 444; global, 407–8; racial and ethic correlations, 448

Wealth of Nations (Smith), 10, 51, 58, 60, 62, 454

Weber, Adna Ferrin, 105

Weber, Max, 10, 23, 39, 430

Welch, Jack "Neutron Jack," 370

Welfare, 226–27, 280, 375, 463

Welfare capitalism, 254, 450

Westinghouse, George, 107

Westlake, Donald E., 366

Whitman, Walt, 183

Whitney, Eli, 76–80, 204

Whittaker, D. Hugh, 426–27

Whyte, William H., 315

Wiebe, Robert, 184

Williamson, Oliver, 440–41

Wilson, Charles, 408

Wilson, Sloan, 315

Wilson, Woodrow, administration of, 15, 209, 212–13, 216, 219, 229–30, 240, 253, 285, 430

Women: in workforce, 41–43, 88, 173–75, 223–24, 265, 290, 298, 301–2, 317, 318, 319, 337–38, 349, 449; urban middle-class, 100–102; marketing to, 162–63, 203, 247–48, 252, 270; African American, 174, 223; managerial and executive, 174, 449; economic independence of, 175; household management by, 222, 223–24, 301; cosmetics industry and, 247; small business and, 437–39

Wood, Gordon S., 47, 49

Work, gospel of, 23–25

Worker protections, 179, 224, 279–82, 286–87, 318–20, 355

Workforce: indentured servants in, 30; specialization, 75, 94; agricultural, 84, 238, 239, 446; employment patterns, 84–85, 92–93, 120, 156, 193, 220–22, 225, 288, 309, 312, 326, 336, 366–68, 372–73, 405–6, 408, 411, 425, 427, 446–48, 452; diversity and discrimination in, 88, 166, 174, 223, 225–26, 267, 268, 317–18, 319, 337, 449; working conditions of, 88–89, 227–28; factory hands, 88–91; resistance to change, 93; education, 103, 221, 447; benefits, 167–68, 176; corporate, 173–75, 220–22; deskilling, 206, 223, 225; white-collar, 222; personal habits, controlling, 225–26; welfare work programs and, 226–27; industrial psychology studies of, 227; motivating, 228, 331–32; Great Depression's long-term impact on, 289; World War II–era, 290; Human Resources approach to, 358–60; loyalty, 368; twenty-first century, 446–47; service sector and, 446–47. *See also under* Women

—wages: piece rate, 172, 226, 493 (n. 28); Ford Motor Company and, 224–26; 1920s, 248–49; minimum hourly, 281; post–World War II, 290–91; for union members, 316, 330; 1960s, 317; 1970s–80s, 326, 338, 346; 1990–2008, 385; small vs. big business, 437; service industry and, 447; in European nations, 517 (n. 8). *See also* Family income

Work for wages, 84–85, 90

Working class, 91, 167–68

Workplace regulation, 317–18, 319, 337, 449

World Bank, 296, 305, 397, 407, 410

World Trade Organization (WTO), 392, 398–99, 401, 408

World War I, 229–30, 237

World War II, 284, 286, 290–93

Wozniak, Stephen, 429

Wright, Frank Lloyd, 206

Wriston, Walter, 331

Youth culture, emergence of, 222

Yuppies, 349, 357